P9-DML-115

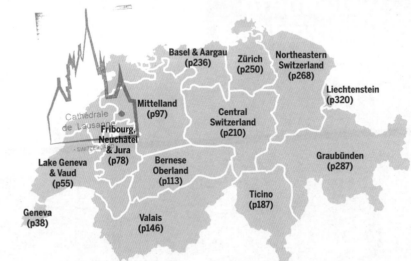

Basel & Aargau (p236)

Zürich (p250)

Northeastern Switzerland (p268)

Liechtenstein (p320)

Mittelland (p97)

Central Switzerland (p210)

Cathédrale de Lausanne

Fribourg, Neuchâtel & Jura (p78)

Graubünden (p287)

Lake Geneva & Vaud (p55)

Bernese Oberland (p113)

Ticino (p187)

Geneva (p38)

Valais (p146)

THIS EDITION WRITTEN AND RESEARCHED BY

Nicola Williams

Kerry Christiani, Sally O'Brien, Damien Simonis

welcome to Switzerland

The Good Life

What giddy romance Zermatt, St Moritz and other legendary names evoke. From the intoxicating chink of Verbier glitterati hobnobbing over Champagne in ice-carved flutes, to the reassuring bell jangle of cows coming home in the Engadine Valley, Switzerland is a harmonious tableau of beautiful images. This small, landlocked country was an essential stop on every Grand Tour – the place where winter tourism was born, where Golden Age mountaineers conquered new heights – and for good reason: no slideshow of such epic proportions is so darn easy to step into, experience and get your hands nice and dirty with. Ride a little red train between peak and pine, soak

in mountain spa water, snowshoe to your igloo, cross medieval bridges and know that life in Switzerland is good.

Action Stations

This country begs outdoor escapade with its larger-than-life canvas of hallucinatory landscapes etched so perfectly one wants to cry – or at least grab boots, leap on board, toot the bike bell and let spirits rip. Skiing and snowboarding in the winter wonderlands of Graubünden, Bernese Oberland and Central Switzerland are obvious choices. But there is plenty to do when pastures are green. Hiking and biking trails abound in both glacier-encrusted mountain areas and lower down along lost valleys, mythical

Look past the silk-smooth chocolate, cuckoo clocks and yodelling – contemporary Switzerland, land of four languages, is all about epic journeys and sublime experiences.

(left) Staubbach Falls in the Lauterbrunnen Valley
(below) Architect Renzo Piano's Zentrum Paul Klee, Bern

lakeshores and pea-green vines. View the natural grandeur from the sky in a balloon basket or parachute, or afloat from a white-water raft. Then there are those must-do-before-death moments like encountering the chiselled north face of the Eiger up close or reaching crevassed ice on Jung-fraujoch (3454m). Most appealing of all, you don't need to be a mountaineer to do it.

Alpine & Urban

Variety is the spice of life in this rich land where Alpine tradition is rooted in the agri-cultural calendar, and soaring mountain backdrops are as common as muck. Travels are mapped by mountain villages with timber storage barns on stilts to keep the rats out and chalet farmsteads brightened with red geraniums and milk churns on a bench waiting to be filled. Ancient markets *(Märit)*, folkloric fairs *(Chilbi)*, flag waving and gastronomic celebrations engrave the passing of seasons in every soul.

The perfect antidote is a surprise set of cities: the capital Bern with its medieval Old Town and world-class modern art, deeply Germanic Basel and its bold architecture, shopping-chic Geneva astraddle Europe's largest lake, tycoon-magnet Zug (play millionaire over a slice of liqueur-soaked cherry cake) and uber-cool Zürich with its rooftop bars and atypical Swiss street grit.

Beard cutting or stone throwing, Paul Klee art or hip club gig: what a euphoric journey indeed.

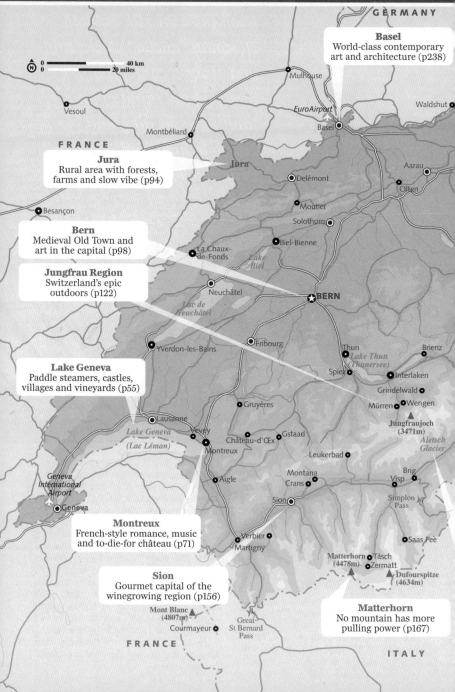

GERMANY

Basel
World-class contemporary
art and architecture (p238)

FRANCE

Jura
Rural area with forests,
farms and slow vibe (p94)

Bern
Medieval Old Town and
art in the capital (p98)

Jungfrau Region
Switzerland's epic
outdoors (p122)

Lake Geneva
Paddle steamers, castles,
villages and vineyards (p55)

Montreux
French-style romance, music
and to-die-for château (p71)

Sion
Gourmet capital of the
winegrowing region (p156)

Matterhorn
No mountain has more
pulling power (p167)

FRANCE

ITALY

Vesoul
Mulhouse
EuroAirport
Waldshut
Basel
Montbéliard
Aarau
Olten
Delémont
Besançon
Moutier
Solothurn
Biel-Bienne
La Chaux-de-Fonds
Lake Biel
Neuchâtel
BERN
Lac de Neuchâtel
Fribourg
Thun
Brienz
Yverdon-les-Bains
Lake Thun (Thunersee)
Spiez
Interlaken
Grindelwald
Gruyères
Mürren
Wengen
Lausanne
Jungfraujoch (3471m)
Vevey
Château-d'Œx
Gstaad
Aletsch Glacier
Montreux
Leukerbad
Lake Geneva (Lac Léman)
Montana
Crans
Brig
Visp
Simplon Pass
Geneva International Airport
Aigle
Sion
Geneva
Saas Fee
Verbier
Martigny
Matterhorn (4478m)
Täsch
Zermatt
Dufourspitze (4634m)
Mont Blanc (4807m)
Courmayeur
Great St Bernard Pass

0 — 40 km
0 — 20 miles

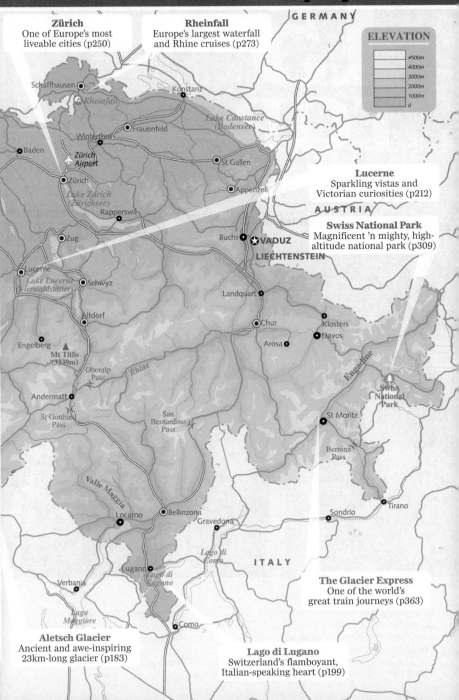

Zürich
One of Europe's most
liveable cities (p250)

Rheinfall
Europe's largest waterfall
and Rhine cruises (p273)

GERMANY

ELEVATION
4500m
4000m
3000m
2000m
1000m
0

Schaffhausen
Rheinfall
Konstanz

*Lake Constance
(Bodensee)*

Winterthur
Frauenfeld

Baden
*Zürich
Airport*

St Gallen

Lucerne
Sparkling vistas and
Victorian curiosities (p212)

Zürich
*Lake Zürich
(Zürichsee)*
Appenzell

Rapperswil

AUSTRIA

Zug

Buchs ★VADUZ

Swiss National Park
Magnificent 'n mighty, high-
altitude national park (p309)

LIECHTENSTEIN

Lucerne
*Lake Lucerne
(Vierwaldstättersee)*
Schwyz

Landquart

Altdorf

Chur
Klosters
Davos

Engelberg ▲
Mt Titlis
(3239m)
Oberalp
Pass
Rhine

Arosa

Engadine

*Swiss
National
Park*

Andermatt

St Gotthard
Pass

San
Bernardino
Pass

St Moritz

Bernina
Pass

Valle Maggia

Locarno
Bellinzona
Gravedona

Sondrio
Tirano

*Lago di
Como*

ITALY

Verbania

Lugano
*Lago di
Lugano*

The Glacier Express
One of the world's
great train journeys (p363)

*Lago
Maggiore*

Como

Aletsch Glacier
Ancient and awe-inspiring
23km-long glacier (p183)

Lago di Lugano
Switzerland's flamboyant,
Italian-speaking heart (p199)

DOUGLAS PEARSON/CORBIS ©

15 TOP
EXPERIENCES

The Glacier Express

1 It's one of the world's most mythical train rides, linking two of Switzerland's glitziest Alpine resorts. Hop aboard the iconic red train with floor-to-ceiling windows in Zermatt, sit back, and savour shot after cinematic shot of green peaks, glistening Alpine lakes, glacial ravines and other hallucinatory natural landscapes. Pulled by steam engine when it first puffed out of the station in 1930, the Glacier Express (p363) traverses 91 tunnels and 291 bridges on its famous journey to St Moritz. The icing on the cake: lunch in the vintage restaurant car.

MARTIN MOOS/LONELY PLANET IMAGES ©

Matterhorn

2 No mountain has more pulling power, more natural magnetism than this charismatic peak – a precocious beauty from birth who demands to be admired, ogled and repeatedly photographed at sunset, sunrise, in different seasons and from every last infuriating angle. And there is no finer place to pander to Matterhorn's every last topographic need than Zermatt (p165), one of Europe's most highly desirable Alpine resorts, in fashion with the skiing, climbing, hiking and hip hobnobbing set since the 19th century. Darling, you'll love it.

ANDY CHRISTIANI/LONELY PLANET IMAGES ©

Hiking in the Swiss National Park

3 No country in Europe is more synonymous with magnificent and mighty hiking than Switzerland, and its high-altitude national park (p309) with eagle-dotted skies is the place to do it. Follow trails through flower-strewn meadows to piercing blue lakes, knife-edge ravines, rocky outcrops and Alpine huts where shepherds make summertime cheese with cows' milk, fresh that morning from the bell-clad herd. Nature gone wild and on the rampage, this is a rare and privileged glimpse of Switzerland before the dawn of tourism.

Europe's Largest Lake

4 The emerald vines marching uphill in perfect unison from the shores of Lake Geneva in Lavaux (p68) are staggering. But the urban viewpoint from which to admire Europe's largest lake is Geneva (p38), French-speaking Switzerland's most cosmopolitan city where canary-yellow mouettes (seagulls) ferry locals across the water and Mont Blanc peeps in on the action. Strolling Old Town streets, savouring a vibrant cafe society and making the odd dash beneath its iconic pencil fountain is what life's about for the 180 nationalities living here.

PHILIPPE ROY/HEMIS/CORBIS ©

Aletsch Glacier

5 One of the world's natural marvels, this mesmerising glacier (p183) of gargantuan proportion in the Upper Valais is tantamount to a 23km long, five-lane highway powering between mountain peaks at altitude. Its ice is glacial-blue and 900m thick at its deepest point. The view of Aletsch from Jungfraujoch will make your heart sing, but for the hardcore adrenalin surge nothing beats getting up close: hike between crevasses with a mountain guide from Riederalp, or ski above it on snowy pistes in Bettmeralp.

JO DAVISON/LONELY PLANET IMAGES ©

MICHEL F FALZONE/JAI/CORBIS ©

Romance in Montreux

6 As if one of the world's most mythical jazz festivals (p72) with open-air concerts on the shore of Lake Geneva is not enough, Montreux has a castle to add to the French-style romance. From the well-known lakeside town with a climate so mild that palm trees grow, a flower-framed footpath follows the water south to Château de Chillon (p72). Historic, sumptuous and among Switzerland's oldest, this magnificent stone château built by the Savoys in the 13th century is everything a castle should be.

CRAIG PERSHOUSE/LONELY PLANET IMAGES ©

Capital Bern

7 Medieval cobbled streets, arcaded boutiques, a dancing clock and folk figures prettily frolicking in fountains since the 16th century: Switzerland's capital city, Bern (p98), just does not fit in with the quintessential 'capital city' image at all. Indeed, few even realise this small town is even the capital, situated in the flat, unassuming, middle bit of the country (hence the region's name, Mittelland) where farms make Emmental cheese. Yet its very unexpectedness, cemented by the new millennium hills of Renzo Piano's Zentrum Paul Klee (p98), is precisely its charm.

GLENN VAN DER KNIJFF/LONELY PLANET IMAGES ©

Lakeside Lucerne

9 Medieval bridge-strolling is the charm of this irresistible Romeo in Central Switzerland. Throw sparkling lake vistas, an alfresco cafe life, candy-coloured architecture and Victorian curiosities into the cooking pot and, yes, lakeside Lucerne (p212) could well be the start of a very beautiful love affair. With the town under your belt, step back to savour the ensemble from a wider perspective: views across the lake of green hillsides, meadows and hidden lake resorts from atop Mt Pilatus, Mt Rigi or Stanserhorn will not disappoint (see p220).

IZZET KERIBAR/LONELY PLANET IMAGES ©

Epic Outdoors

8 No trio are more immortalised in mountaineering legend than Switzerland's 'big three' – Eiger (Ogre), Mönch (Monk) and Jungfrau (Virgin) – peaks that soar to the sky above the traditional 19th-century resort of gorgeous old Grindelwald (p122). And whether you choose to schuss around on skis, shoot down Europe's longest toboggan run on the back of an old-fashioned sledge, bungee-jump in the Gletscherschlucht or ride the train up to Europe's highest station at 3454m, your heart will thump. James Bond, eat your heart out.

MARTIN RUETSCHI/KEYSTONE/CORBIS ©

Splash of the Rheinfall

11 So moved were Goethe and Lord Byron by the wispy waterfalls of Staubbach Falls, fairy-tale threads of spray ensnaring the cliffside in Lauterbrunnen, that they composed poems exalting their ethereal beauty. Yet it is the theatrical, crash-bang-wallop splash of the thunderous Rheinfall (p273), guarded by a twin set of medieval castles, in north-eastern Switzerland that really takes your breath away.

ANDREW BAIN/LONELY PLANET IMAGES ©

Zürich Lifestyle

10 One of Europe's most liveable cities, Zürich (p250) in German-speaking Switzerland is an ode to urban renovation. It's also hip (yes, this is where Google employees shoot down a slide to lunch). With enough of a rough edge to resemble Berlin at times, Zürich means drinking in waterfront bars, dancing until dawn in Züri-West (p259), shopping for recycled fashion accessories in Kreis 5 and boogying with the best of them at Europe's largest street party, the city's wild and wacky, larger-than-life Street Parade in August (p255).

Sion & Valaisian Wine

12 Swiss vintages are hardly plentiful outside Switzerland, making their tasting and discovery in situ a rare and joyous experience. Gentle walking trails tread quietly through steeply terraced vineyards in Valais, producer of the country's most rated wines, and many *vignerons* (winegrowers) open their doors for tasting and buying. For the perfect marriage, pair a vineyard walk with the region's autumnal *brisolée* (p157), the traditional harvest feast built around local chestnuts, cheese, cold meats and *vin nouveau*.

SANDRO VANNINI/CORBIS ©

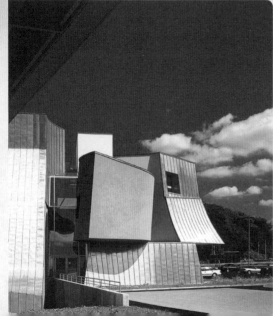

RICHARD BRYANT/ARCAID/CORBIS ©

Art & Architecture in Basel

13 Contemporary architecture of world-class standing is Basel's golden ticket – seven winners of the Pritzker Prize have a living design to ogle in or around this city plump on the Rhine. Kick off with a hop across the German border to the Vitra Design Museum (p239), designed by architect Frank Gehry and devote the rest of the day to Switzerland's best private collection of modern art in a long, light-flooded building by Renzo Piano – aka the dream fusion of art and architecture at Fondation Beyeler (p238).
Vitra Design Museum

Lago di Lugano

14 An intrinsic part of Switzerland's unique charm is its mixed bag of languages and culture. And no spot on Swiss earth exalts the country's Italianate soul with such gusto as Lago di Lugano in Ticino, a shimmering Alpine lake fringed with palm-tree promenades and pretty-girl villages of delicate pastel hues. Lugano (p193), the biggest town on the lake and the country's third-largest affluent banking centre to boot, is vivacious and busy with porticoed alleys, cafe-packed piazzas and boats yo-yoing to other places on the lake.

Rural Jura

15 Tiptoe off the tourist map and into clover-shaped Jura (p94), a fascinating backwater on the French–Swiss border woven from thick dark forests, gentle rolling hills, medieval villages and a go-slow vibe. No piece of scenery is too large, too high or too racy here. Rather, travel in the rural Jura is an exquisite sensory experience laced with inspirational bike rides, cross-country skiing through silent glades, fragrant nights in hay barns, fabulous farm feasts and a cheese cut in flowers.

need to know

Currency
» Swiss franc (official abbreviation CHF, in this book Sfr)

Languages
» German, French, Italian, Romansch

When to Go

Basel
GO Jul & Aug, Dec

Zürich
GO Apr–Aug

Bern
GO Jul & Aug, Nov

Swiss Alps
GO late Dec–early Apr, May–Aug

Geneva
GO Anytime, Jun–Sep

Warm to hot summers, mild winters
Warm to hot summers, cold winters
Mild summers, cold winters
Cold climate
Polar climate, below zero year round

High Season
(Jul & Aug, Dec–Apr)

» In July and August walkers and cyclists hit high-altitude trails.

» Christmas and New Year see lots of activity on the slopes.

» Late December to early April is high season in ski resorts.

Shoulder
(Apr–Jun & Sep)

» Look for accommodation deals in ski resorts and traveller hotspots.

» Spring is idyllic with warm temperatures, flowers and local produce.

» Watch the grape harvest in autumn.

Low Season
(Oct–Mar)

» Mountain resorts go into snooze mode from mid-October to early December.

» Prices are up to 50% less than in high season.

» Sights and restaurants are open fewer days and shorter hours.

Your Daily Budget

Budget up to
Sfr200

» Dorm bed: Sfr30–60

» Free admission to some museums first Saturday or Sunday of every month

» Lunch out (Sfr15–30) and self-cater after dark

Midrange
Sfr200 –300

» Double room in two- or three-star hotel: Sfr150–350

» Dish of the day (tagesteller, plat du jour, piatto del giorno) or fixed two-course menu: Sfr40–70

Top End over
Sfr300

» Double room in four- or five-star hotel: from Sfr350

» Lower rates Friday to Sunday in city business hotels

» Three-course dinner in an upmarket restaurant: from Sfr100

Money

» ATMS at every airport, most train stations and every second street corner in towns and cities. Visa, MasterCard and Amex widely accepted.

Visas

» Not required with passports from the EU, UK, Iceland, Ireland, Norway, USA, Canada, Australia or New Zealand; others need a Schengen visa (p360).

Mobile Phones

» European and Australian phones work. Slip in a Swiss SIM card (p359) to call with a cheaper Swiss number.

Driving

» Drive on the right, the steering wheel is on the left side of the car.

Websites

» **My Switzerland** (www.myswitzerland .com) Swiss tourism

» **SBB CFF FFS** (www .sbb.ch) Swiss railways

» **Switzerland Travel Centre** (www.swiss travelsystems.ch) Transport, including travel passes

» **Swiss Info** (www .swissinfo.ch) Swiss news, current affairs

» **Swiss World** (www .swissworld.org) People, culture, lifestyle, environment

» **Lonely Planet** (www. lonelyplanet .com/switzerland) Information, hotel bookings, traveller forum

Exchange Rates

Australia	A$1	Sfr0.97
Canada	C$1	Sfr0.93
Europe	€1	Sfr1.21
Japan	¥100	Sfr1.24
UK	UK£1	Sfr1.47
US	US$1	Sfr0.95

For current exchange rates see www.xe.com.

Important Numbers

Swiss telephone numbers start with an area code that must be dialled every time, even when making local calls.

Switzerland country code	☎41
International access code	☎00
Police	☎117
Ambulance	☎144
Swiss Mountain Rescue	☎1414

Arriving in Switzerland

» **Zürich Airport**
SBB trains – Up to nine hourly to Hauptbahnhof from 6am to midnight
Taxis – Around Sfr60 to the centre
Coaches – During winter ski season, to Davos and other key resorts

» **Geneva Airport**
SBB trains – At least every 10 minutes to Gare de Cornavin
Taxis – Sfr30–50 to the centre
Coaches & minibuses – In winter to Verbier, Saas Fee, Crans-Montana and ski resorts in neighbouring France

Keeping Costs Down

Switzerland is pricier than ever and compared to other European countries, travellers will feel it keenly. But there are ways to keep costs down. Travel passes (p366) yield savings on trains, boats, buses and cable cars – the Half-Fare Card is an instant 50%-off winner – while summertime camping and sleeping in hay barns (p354) cuts a chunk off accommodation costs. Students and seniors, bring the relevant discount card (p355).

Cash in on visitor or guest cards, usually issued by hotels or hostels at check-in in many towns and cities (Zürich, Geneva, Bern, Basel and Lucerne included) and some regions (Lago di Lugano, Central Switzerland etc). Cards cover free public transport and discounted rates on select sights and activities.

Self-service restaurants in Manor department stores and larger Migros and Coop outlets are excellent value.

what's new

For this new edition of Switzerland, our authors have hunted down the fresh, the revamped, the transformed, the hot and the happening. These are some of our favourites. For up-to-the-minute reviews and recommendations, see lonelyplanet.com/switzerland.

City Beach

1 Zürich is one of Europe's hippest cities and Switzerland's most urban, with a real flair for industrial rejuvenation and artistic innovation. Enter City Beach (p359), a trendy rooftop beach in the Kreis 5 district – 500 tons of golden sand, swimming pools and a bar on the roof of a city car park. Find this summer-only phenomenon – city beach on a car park roof – in Basel and Bern too.

Cow Trekking

2 Riding at cow pace through bucolic countryside is hot in northeastern Switzerland thanks to one farmer's experiential approach to organic dairy farming. Saddle, riding crop and optional picnic provided (p275).

Rigi Kaltbad

3 Ticino architect Mario Botta will knock your socks off with his latest Swiss work, stunning mineral baths and spa with designer views of Lake Lucerne from their Mt Rigi lookout (p223).

Centre PasquArt

4 Switzerland's collection of contemporary art is outstanding and this new gallery in an old hospital in Biel-Bienne has just made it even better (p107).

Lavaux Vinorama

5 Pea-green vines cascading into Lake Geneva are a magnificent sight and Lavaux's latest wine-tasting address, cut out of concrete beneath vineyards, adds a new dimension to visiting the Unesco-listed wine region (p69).

Ice World

6 Why glacial ice is blue, what asexual glacial fleas do, how fast glacial ice moves: the new Eiswelt exhibition above the Aletsch Glacier on Bettmerhorn (2856m) is absolutely riveting (p185).

Urban Tapas

7 It's not a patch on Spanish tapas, but a dozen different 'tapas' is what Geneva bars chalk on the blackboard these days – dining on the cheap in one of Europe's priciest cities (p51).

Mountain-Bike Mastery

8 Waves, vertical curves, high jumps, banked bends and tables: mountain bikers will have a field day at Graubünden's new mountain-bike skill centres in Lenzerheide (p294) and Davos (p307).

Chetzeron

9 This defunct 1960s cable-car station at 2112m in the hip Upper Valais ski resort of Crans-Montana has been restyled as one of Switzerland's hippest mountain hangouts (p162).

Floating Olympic Museum

10 Part of Lausanne's Olympic Museum, the most visited *musée* in Suisse Romande (French-speaking Switzerland), is afloat in a belle époque steamer moored in front of the lakeside mansion (p59).

if you like...

Mountain Vistas

From the Holy Trinity of mountain trio Monk, Ogre and Virgin to the unfathomable trigonometry of the iconic Matterhorn, mountain panoramas in Switzerland are gargantuan, magnificent, soul-soaring. The only requirement to venerate these astonishing vistas: a clear blue sky.

Eiger, Jungfrau & Mönch Hike from Grindelwald/Wengen or ride the cable car to Kleine Scheidegg for dramatic close-ups of Switzerland's big trio (p129)

Aletsch Glacier Shimmering 23km-long glacier, best seen from Bettmerhorn or Eggishorn in the Upper Valais (p183)

Schilthorn 360-degree vista of 200 peaks stretching from Mt Titlis to Mont Blanc in France (p134)

Jungfraujoch Uplifting lookout on 4000m peaks, the Aletsch Glacier and as far as the Black Forest beyond (p129)

Monte Generoso Ogle the Italian lakes, Alps and Apennines atop this 1704m summit (p199)

Männlichen Incredible views of the Grindelwald and Lauterbrunnen valleys reached via Europe's longest cable car (p128)

Art Museums

There is far more to Switzerland than chalet farmsteads with paint-peeling shutters, red geranium blossoms and milk churns on a bench waiting to be filled. Enter its cutting-edge collections of modern and contemporary art.

Fondation Pierre Gianadda, Martigny Picasso, Cézanne et al (p147)

Fondation Beyeler, Basel Switzerland's best collection of contemporary art (p238)

Zentrum Paul Klee, Bern The Swiss answer to the Guggenheim (p98)

Therme Vals This famous spa, a striking quartzite design, is a work of art in itself (p299)

Sammlung Rosengart, Lucerne Blockbuster Picasso collection (p212)

Zürich Clutch of art addresses, including the birthplace of zany Dada movement and a gallery in a rejuvenated brewery (p252)

MAMCO, Geneva Installation art in a 1950s factory (p41)

Stadtlounge, St Gallen Open-air 'living room' installation art (p279)

Sammlung Oskar Reinhart am Römerholz, Winterthur All the modern masters on a country estate (p264)

Hairy Black Runs

Winter snow sports meet Switzerland's hardcore Alpine terrain head-on. Skiers and boarders: get set for the ride of your life with the crème de la crème of white-knuckle pistes.

Mont Fort, Verbier Almost vertical and pummelled with moguls; off-piste, some of Switzerland's best powder (p153)

Swiss Wall, Champéry Heart-stopping, hell-for-leather mogul run famed as one of the world's toughest (p152)

Inferno, Jungfrau Region It just doesn't get better than this 16km black run (p132)

Laax Snowboarding mecca with Europe's smallest and largest half-pipes (p297)

Wengen Aptly named black run 'Oh God' and legendary off-piste White Hare at the foot of the Eiger north face (p131)

Diavolezza, St Moritz Spectacular and jaw-dropping glacier descents at 3000m (p314)

Schlappin & Gotschnawang, Klosters A panoramic gift from heaven for black-run experts (p304)

» Bellinzona's Unesco-listed Castelgrande (p189)

Castles & Abbeys

A decorative smattering of fairy-tale castles and abbeys enhances Switzerland's naturally photogenic looks. Perched high on hills or snuggled low on the water's edge, their settings are picture-perfect.

Chillon Follow the Flower Path from Montreux to this huge stone castle on Lake Geneva's shore (p72)

Thun No *schloss* in Germanic Switzerland is as fairy tale as Thun's red-turreted beauty (p135)

St Gallen This grand abbey safeguards an extraordinary rococo library (p278)

Bellinzona Unesco-listed trio of medieval castles in Italianate Ticino (p189)

Sion Bewitching pair of 13th-century chateaux on rocky outcrops above vines (p156)

Burg Hohenklingen, Stein am Rhein Lap up the vibe of a real McCoy medieval castle over dinner (p275)

Müstair Unesco world treasure: Carolingian and Romanesque frescoes in an abbey (p311)

Aargau *Schloss*-hop in a canton straight out of Arthurian legend. Favourites: Wasserschloss Hallwyl and Lenzburg (p248)

Chocolate

No country is more synonymous with chocolate – and it comes in all shapes and sizes, Matterhorn and Swiss army knife included. More than half of all Swiss chocolate is consumed by the Swiss, making their country the obvious place to savour it.

Interlaken Chocolate-making workshops in a Viennese-style coffee house (p120)

Chocolate Train Ride in a belle époque pullman car from Montreux to a chocolate factory (p363)

St Gallen Hot chocolate, pralines and truffles to die for at Chocolaterie (p280)

Lugano A spin through the history of chocolate and tastings at the Museo del Cioccolato Alprose (p193)

Geneva Soak in a chocolate bath at a city spa (p46)

Broc Watch Swiss chocolate being made at the Cailler chocolate factory (p88)

Fribourg Chocolate at factory prices and creamy hot chocolate with chocolate shavings (p81)

Zürich Café Sprüngli, epicentre of sweet Switzerland, in business since 1836 (p258)

Family Travel

Parents are spoilt for choice in Switzerland's Alpine playground where activities for all ages are squarely covered (p31). But kidding around isn't only about kipping with the cows (p354). Urban Switzerland woos kids with some catchy museums too.

Verkehrshaus, Lucerne Fly a plane or to the moon at the Transport Museum (p213)

Ferme des Moulins, Sembrancher Cheese fondue in a horse-pulled cart (p152)

Zentrum Paul Klee, Bern Interactive art exhibits and workshops (p98)

Musée Suisse du Jeu & Alimentarium, Vevey Games and cookery workshops (p70)

Col du Grand St-Bernard Cuddle and walk St Bernard dogs (p153)

Freilichtmuseum, Ballenberg Age-old crafts on a reconstructed farming hamlet (p139)

Gstaad Loop-the-loop Alpine Coaster, husky rides and guided llama and goat hikes (p143)

Grindelwald Summer scooter trail, gentle walks and ski pistes for every age and ability (p123)

Saas Fee Feed wild marmots and shoot down the mountain on a scooter (p181)

month by month

Top Events

1 **Lucerne Festival,** April

2 **Montreux Jazz,** July

3 **Swiss National Day,** 1 August

4 **Zürich Street Parade,** August

5 **L'Escalade,** December

January

The winter cold empties towns of tourists, but in the Alps the ski season is in full swing. Glitzy celebrity station, lost Alpine village... Switzerland has a resort for every mood.

Cartier Polo World Cup

Upper-crust St Moritz is the chic venue for this four-day event (p315) that sees world-class polo players saddle up and battle it out on a frozen lake. Buy tickets online (www.polomoritz .com), dress up and don't forget your shades.

Harder Potschete

What a devilish day it is on 2 January (p116) in Interlaken when warty ogre-like *Potschen* run around town causing folkloric mischief. The party ends on a high with cockle-warming drinks, upbeat folk music and fiendish merrymaking.

Vogel Gryff

Another old folkloric celebration, this street party (p242) sees a larger-than-life savage, griffin and lion chase away winter in Basel with a drum dance on a city bridge. The savage sails into town on a raft afloat the Rhine.

February

Crisp cold weather in the mountains – lots of china-blue skies now – translates to ski season in top gear. Families mob ski resorts during the February school holidays and accommodation is at its priciest.

Carnival

Never dare call the Swiss goody two-shoes again: pre-Lenten parades, costumes, music and all the fun of the fair sweep through Catholic cantons during *Fasnacht* (carnival). Catch the party – stark raving bonkers – in Lucerne (p217) or Basel (p241).

March

The tail end of the ski season stays busy thanks to temperatures that no longer turn lips blue and, depending on the year, Easter holidays.

Engadine Ski Marathon

Watching 11,000 cross-country skiers warming up to the rousing sound of *Chariots of Fire* is unforgettable – as is, no doubt, the iconic 42km cross-country ski marathon (p315) for the athletes who ski across frozen lakes and through pine forests and picture-perfect snow scenes in the Engadine.

April

Spring with its pretty flower-strewn meadows suddenly pops into that magnificent Alpine vista and the first fair-weather walkers arrive. By the end of the month, most ski resorts have gone into hibernation.

Sechseläuten

Winter's end is celebrated in Zürich (p255) the third Monday of the month with costumed street parades and the burning of a firework-filled 'snowman', aka the terrifying *Böögg*. Be prepared to be scared.

Lucerne Festival

Easter ushers in this world-class music festival

(p215) with chamber orchestras, pianists and other musicians from all corners of the globe performing in Lucerne. True devotees of the festival can return in summer and November.

June

As the weather heats up so Switzerland's festival calendar ups the pace with a bevy of fabulous arts festivals. In the mountains, chalet hotels start to emerge from hibernation to welcome early summer hikers.

☆ St Galler Festspiele

It's apt that Switzerland's 'writing room of Europe', aka St Gallen, should play host to this wonderful two-week opera season (p279). The curtain rises in late June with performances spilling into July.

July

The month of music: days are hot and sun-filled, and lakeshores and Alpine meadows double as perfect summer stages for Swiss yodellers, alpenhorn players and flag throwers.

☆ Montreux Jazz

A fortnight of jazz, pop and rock in early July (p72) is reason enough to slot elegant Montreux into your itinerary. Some concerts are free, some ticketed, and dozens are staged alfresco with lake views from heaven.

☆ Paléo Festival

Another Lake Geneva goodie, this six-day open-air world-music extravaganza (p66) – a 1970s child – is billed as the king of summer music fests. Nyon in late July is the date to put in the diary.

August

It is hot, cloudless and the sun-baked Alps buzz with hikers, bikers and families on holiday – a pedalo on Lake Geneva is a cool spot to watch fireworks on 1 August, Switzerland's national day.

☆ Swiss National Day

Fireworks light up lakes, mountains, towns and cities countrywide on this national holiday celebrating Switzerland's very creation.

☆ Sertig Schwinget

This high-entertainment festival (p307) in Davos sees thickset men with invariably large tummies battle it out in sawdust for the title of *Schwingen* (Swiss Alpine wrestling) champion.

☆ Street Parade

Mid-August brings with it Europe's largest street party in the form of Zürich's famous Street Parade (p255). The techno-parade has been around since 1992 and saw 900,000 revellers converge around seven stages and 29 love mobiles in 2011.

October

As the last sun-plump grapes are harvested and the first bottles of new wine cracked open, sweet chestnuts drop from dew-jewelled trees. It's nippy now, especially at altitude where the first snow closes mountain passes.

☆ Foire du Valais

Cows battle for the title of bovine queen on the last day of the cow-fighting season at this 10-day regional fair (p150) in Martigny in the lower Valais. Everyone rocks up for it, a great excuse to drink and feast.

December

Days are short and it is cold everywhere. But there are Christmas school holidays and festive celebrations around the corner, not to mention the first winter Alpine skiing from mid-December on.

☆ L'Escalade

Torch-lit processions in the Old Town, fires, a run around town for kids and adults alike and some serious chocolate-cauldron smashing and scoffing make Geneva's biggest festival (p46) on 11 December a riot of fun.

itineraries

Whether you've got six days or 60, these itineraries provide a starting point for the trip of a lifetime. Want more inspiration? Head online to lonelyplanet .com/thorntree to chat with other travellers.

Two Weeks
Lost in Graubünden & Ticino

> A circular route that can be picked up at any point. From **Chur**, head north for a detour to pretty **Maienfeld** and its vineyards. Spin east to ski queens **Klosters** and **Davos**, then surge into the Engadine Valley, with pretty towns like **Guarda** and **Scuol** (tempting thermal baths). The road then ribbons southeast to the Austrian border, which you cross to head south through a slice of Austria and Italy, before veering back into Switzerland to contemplate frescos at **Müstair**. Continue southwest through picture-postcard **Zuoz** to chic **St Moritz**. Climb the Julier Pass mountain road and drop down the **Via Mala** gorges to art stop **Zillis**.

The southbound road crosses into Ticino and **Bellinzona**. Steam on past lakeside **Locarno** and up the enchanting **Valle Maggia**. Backtracking to Bellinzona, the main route takes you along the Valle Leventina, with a stop in **Giornico**, before crossing the **St Gotthard Pass** to **Andermatt**. Nip into the monastery of **Disentis/Mustér** before plunging into designer spa waters in highly recommended **Vals**, the last stop before Chur.

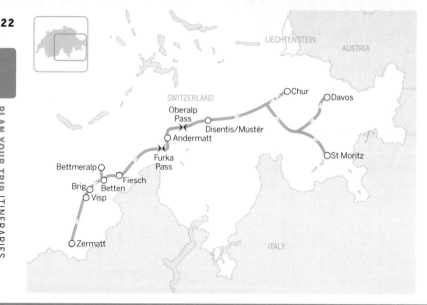

One Day or Week
The Glacier Express

This mythical, 290km train journey has been a traveller-must ever since the birth of winter tourism in the Alps. Do it any time of the year – in one glorious 7½-hour stretch or as several sweet nuggets interspersed with overnights in Switzerland's most glamorous Alpine mountain resorts.

Starting in **Zermatt**, the narrow-gauge railway winds north down the valley to **Visp** and **Brig**. From here it swings northeast along the pretty eastern stretch of the Rhône Valley through the attractive villages of **Betten** and **Fiesch**: hop off in Betten and catch a cable car up to car-free village **Bettmeralp** (and onwards up to Bettmerhorn) or Eggishorn for a peek at the Unesco-listed Aletsch Glacier.

Back in the valley, the Glacier Express trundles towards the **Furka Pass** (which it circumvents by tunnel) and descends on ski resort **Andermatt** before climbing up again to the **Oberalp Pass** (2033m), the literal high point of the journey.

From here it meanders alongside the Vorderrhein River, through **Disentis/Mustér** to **Chur**. The main line continues to **St Moritz**, with a northeast branch to **Davos**.

One Month
Grand Tour

The very best of Switzerland starts in **Geneva** with its vibrant museums and signature pencil fountain, from where a slow road leads east along the southern shore of the lake in France – stop for lunch in **Yvoire** – and a fast road (the A1) shadows the Swiss northern shore (lunch stops **Nyon**, **Vevey** or **Montreux**). The next port of call is art-rich **Martigny** and châteaux-crowned **Sion**, worth lingering in for its wealth of vineyards, wines and memorable Valaisian dining. Continue east along the Rhône Valley, nipping up to **Leukerbad** to drift in thermal waters beneath soaring mountain peaks. In **Visp**, head south to ogle at iconic Matterhorn from the hip streets, slopes and trails of chic, car-free **Zermatt**.

In the second week, get a taste of the Glacier Express with a train trip to **Oberwald**. Stop off in **Betten** for a side trip to **Bettmeralp** with its amazing vistas of the 23km-long Aletsch Glacier from atop Bettmerhorn. From Oberwald, drive north over the Grimsel Pass (2165m) to **Meiringen** (eat meringues!) and west into the magnificent Jungfrau Region with its once-in-a-lifetime train journey up to Europe's highest station; base yourself in **Interlaken** or **Grindelwald**. If you have a head more for Italian passion than hardcore Alpine extremes, stay on the Glacier Express as far as **Andermatt** instead, then motor south into Italianate Ticino for shimmering lake life in the glitzy and gorgeous towns of **Lugano** and **Locarno**.

The third week sees a trip north to **Lucerne** where you can cruise on a boat to lovely Lake Lucerne resorts such as **Weggis** and **Brunnen**. Feast on *Kirschtorte* (cherry cake) in rich old medieval **Zug**, then hit big-city **Zürich** to the north to taste urban Switzerland at its best (five days in all). Should you fancy some border-hopping, **Liechtenstein** is very close by. Unesco-listed **St Gallen** is the next stop from where you can spend a week lapping up Switzerland's north – see the Northern Treasures itinerary.

Ending up in the Jura, it's a quick and easy flit south to Neuchâtel on the northern shore of Lac de Neuchâtel, from where the motorway speeds to Lausanne on Lake Geneva and, eventually, Geneva.

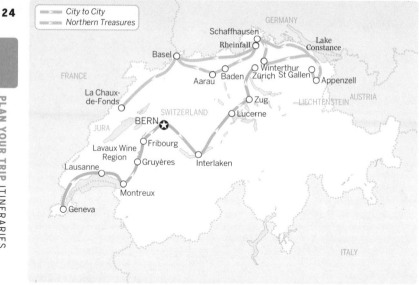

City to City
Northern Treasures

GERMANY

Schaffhausen
Rheinfall
Lake Constance
Basel
Winterthur
Aarau
Baden Zürich St Gallen
Appenzell
La Chaux-de-Fonds
Zug
AUSTRIA
LIECHTENSTEIN
SWITZERLAND
Lucerne
BERN
JURA
Fribourg
Lavaux Wine Region
Gruyères
Interlaken
Lausanne
Montreux
Geneva
FRANCE
ITALY

Two Weeks
City to City

> This Geneva-to-Zürich, 385km trip is for urbanites keen to mix metropolitan fire with small-town charm, eminently doable by car or public transport. Fly into one airport, out the other, or zip back to point A by train in 2¾ hours.

Landing in **Geneva**, explore Switzerland's most cosmopolitan big city then trundle along the shore of Europe's largest Alpine lake to bustling **Lausanne**, a hilly lakeside town with a lively bar and cafe scene and sweet old town. Continue along the same glorious route, aptly dubbed the Swiss Riviera, to the **Lavaux wine region** and beyond to **Montreux**. Then head north to **Gruyères**, land of chateaux, cheese, cream and meringues. Further north, you arrive in **Fribourg** on the French–German language frontier – cross it to pretty Swiss capital **Bern**. Later, drop down to the lakeside towns around **Interlaken** (plenty of top skiing, hiking and other outdoor options around here) then swing north to another bewitching lake lady, **Lucerne**. Rolling onwards to Switzerland's most hip 'n happening city **Zürich**, via tycoon-magnet **Zug**, the atmosphere changes completely.

One Week
Northern Treasures

> In spite of all its natural wonders, Switzerland boasts overwhelming man-made beauty too, and there is no finer spot to appreciate this than in **St Gallen**, the seat of a grand abbey and church complex safeguarding one of the world's oldest libraries (hence its privileged Unesco World Heritage Site status). Say cheese in **Appenzell**, a 50-minute journey from St Gallen on a narrow-gauge railway, then bear west along the southern shore of **Lake Constance** (great summer outdoor action) or to **Winterthur** (art museums and a kid-friendly science centre). Both routes end up in **Schaffhausen**, a quaint medieval town that could easily be German. Don't miss standing in the middle of **Rheinfall**, Europe's largest waterfall.

Next up, continue further west to art-rich **Basel**, either direct or via a pretty southwest detour through **Baden** and **Aarau**, two picture-postcard addresses to get lost in cobbled old-town streets. From Basel, it is an easy drive west again into the deepest depths of Switzerland's unexplored **Jura**. Push west to **La Chaux-de-Fonds** to discover several early works by architect Le Corbusier who was born here.

Outdoor Switzerland

Best Skiing
Verbier Excellent varied terrain, a whopping 412km of pistes, a good snow record and some of the best off-piste powder in Switzerland

Best Hiking
Faulhornweg A classic high-Alpine hike, with photogenic views of the glacier-capped Jungfrau massif and Lakes Thun and Brienz

Best Climbing
Zermatt A holy grail of mountaineering where rock climbers can get to grips with the 4000ers and measure up to Matterhorn

Best Rafting
Ruinaulta Roll along the fast-flowing Vorderrhein and past bizarre limestone formations in the Rhine Gorge

Best Mountain Biking
Klosters & Davos Freeride heaven with 600km of mountain bike tracks, including some challenging descents and single tracks

Planning Your Outdoor Experience

The average 65-year-old calls a four-hour hike over a 2500m mountain pass a *Sonntagsspaziergang* (Sunday stroll), giggly three-year-olds ski rings around you on the slopes and locals bored with 'ordinary' marathons run races backwards and up mountains for fun – to call Switzerland sporty would be an understatement. It's hyperactive.

Why? Just look around you. The landscapes are lyrical: glacial brooks and thundering waterfalls, colossal peaks and dexterously folded valleys. The water is mineral pure, the sky a brighter shade of blue, the air piny fresh. No wonder the Swiss can't keep still with that phenomenal backyard.

When to Go

May–June The crowds are thin and the weather is often fine. Snow patches still linger above 2000m. June is great for hiking with long, warm days and wildflowers carpeting the slopes. Many huts are still closed and mountain transport is limited.

July–August A conga line of high-altitude hikers and cyclists makes its way through the Swiss Alps. All lifts and mountain huts are open (book ahead). The lakes beckon all water-sports fans.

September–early October Pot luck: can be delightful or drab. The larch forests look beautiful in their autumn mantle of gold and temperatures at lower altitudes are still mild. Accommodation prices drop as do the crowds, but many hotels and lifts close.

Mid-October–November Days get shorter and the weather is unpredictable. Expect rain, fog and snow above 1500m. Most resorts go into hibernation.

December–April The slopes buzz with skiers and boarders until Easter, and winter walking trails thread through Alpine resorts. Unless you're tied by school holidays (Christmas, February half-term and Easter), avoid them to get better deals.

Skiing & Snowboarding

In a land where every 10-man, 50-cow hamlet has a ski lift, the question is not *where* you can ski but *how*. Ritzy or remote, party-mad or picture-perfect, virgin or veteran, black run or blue – whatever your taste and ability, Switzerland has a resort to suit.

Ski Run Classifications

Piste maps are available on most tourist office websites and at the valley stations of ski lifts; runs are colour-coded according to difficulty as follows:

Blue Indicates easy, well-groomed runs that are suitable for beginners.

Red Indicates intermediate runs, which are groomed but often steeper and narrower than blue runs. Skiers should have a medium level of ability.

Black For expert skiers with polished technique and skills. They are mostly steep and not always groomed, and may have moguls and steep vertical drops.

Safety on the Slopes

» Avalanche warnings should be heeded and local advice sought before detouring from prepared runs.

» If you're going off-piste or hiking in snowy areas, never go alone and take an avalanche pole, a transceiver or a shovel and, most importantly, a professional guide.

» Before setting foot in the mountains check the day's avalanche bulletin by calling ☎187 or checking online at www.slf.ch.

» The sun is powerful in the Alps and is intensified by snow glare. Wear ski goggles and high-factor sunscreen.

» Layers help you to adapt to the constant change in body temperature. Your head, wrists and knees should be protected.

» Black run look tempting? Make sure you're properly insured first; sky-high mountain rescue and medical costs can add insult to injury.

TOP SLOPES FOR...

Snowboarding Freeriders seeking deep powder, big air and, like, totally *awesome* terrain parks, head to Saas Fee (p180), Laax (p297) and Davos (p305).

Families Picture-book pretty Arosa (p295), Lenzerheide (p293), Bettmeralp (p185) and Klosters (p304) for their fine nursery slopes, kids' clubs and slope-side activities ranging from sledding to skidooing.

Off-piste Explore the virgin powder in the glorious backcountry of Engelberg (p229), Andermatt (p234), Verbier (p154) and Davos (p305).

Glacier skiing For pre- and post-season skiing, schuss across to Glacier 3000 (p143) near Gstaad, glacier-encrusted Mt Titlis in Engelberg (p230) and the snow-sure slopes of Saas Fee (p180).

Scenic skiing Zermatt (p167) for its legendary Matterhorn views and Männlichen (p128) to slalom in the shadow of Eiger, Mönch and Jungfrau.

Scary-as-hell descents Dare to ski the near-vertical Swiss Wall (p152), the mogul-riddled Mont-Fort in Verbier (p154) and the Inferno (p132), a 16km black-run marathon from Schilthorn to Lauterbrunnen.

Cross-country skiing Master your classic or skating technique on the twinkling *Loipen* in Davos (p305), Arosa (p295) and Kandersteg (p142).

Non-skiers Still ski-shy? Try Gstaad (p143) or Grindelwald (p123), where off-piste fun like ice skating, curling, airboarding, horse-drawn sleigh rides, winter hiking and husky sledding keeps non-skiers amused.

Passes, Hire and Tuition

Yes, Switzerland is expensive and no, skiing is not an exception. That said, costs can be cut by avoiding school holiday times and choosing low-key villages over upscale resorts. Ski passes are a hefty chunk out of your budget and will set you back around Sfr70 per day or Sfr350 per week. Factor in around Sfr40 to Sfr70 per day for ski hire and Sfr20 for boot hire, which can be reserved online at www.intersportrent.com. Kids' equipment is roughly half price.

All major resorts have ski schools, with half-day group lessons typically costing Sfr40 to Sfr50 and a full-day off-piste around Sfr100. **Swiss Snowsports** (www.snowsports.ch, in German & French) has a clickable map of 180 ski schools across the country.

Regions

The following ski regions are just a glimpse of what is up in the Alps. Switzerland has scores of fantastic resorts and no attempt has been made to cover them exhaustively. See regional chapters for more.

Graubünden

Rugged Graubünden has some truly legendary slopes. First up is super-chic St Moritz (p314), with 350km of groomed slopes (intermediates are in heaven), fine glacier descents and freeride opportunities. The twin resorts of (pretty) Klosters and (popular) Davos (p304) share 320km of runs; the latter is superb for cross-country and has excellent parks and half-pipes. Boarders also rave about the terrain parks, freeriding and après-ski scene in Laax (p297). Family-oriented Arosa (p295) and Lenzerheide (p293) in the next valley are scenic picks for beginners, intermediates and cross-country fans. Want to give the crowds the slip? Glide across to the uncrowded slopes of Pizol (p303), Scuol (p310), Samnaun (p310) or Pontresina (p318).

Valais & Vaud

One of Switzerland's most enduring images is the perfect pyramid-shaped peak of Matterhorn, soaring 4478m above Zermatt (p167). Snowboarders, intermediates, off-pisters, all are catered for in this car-free resort with 300km of eye-poppingly scenic runs. You can even ski over to Cervinia in Italy. Almost as oops-I-almost-tumbled-over-the-mountain-edge gorgeous is Crans Montana (p162), a great beginners' choice with gentle, sunny slopes and Matterhorn and Mont Blanc puncturing the skyline. Verbier (p154) has a cool 412km of slopes and some terrifically challenging off-piste for experts. Hard-core boarders favour snow-sure, glacier-licked Saas Fee (p180). Snuggling up to France's mammoth Portes du Soleil ski arena, Champéry (p152) has access to 650km of slopes. Queues are few and families are welcome in lesser-known beauties such as Bettmeralp (p185) and Val d'Arolla (p160).

Bernese Oberland

If only all ski resorts were like those in Bernese Oberland. At its winter wonderland heart is the Jungfrau Region (p132), an unspoilt Alpine beauty with its dark timber villages and scenery lovely enough to distract anyone from mastering parallel turns.

The region is criss-crossed with 214km of well-maintained slopes, ranging from easy-peasy to hair-raising, which afford fleeting views of the 'Big Three', Eiger, Mönch and Jungfrau. Grindelwald (p123), Wengen (p131) and Mürren (p133) all offer varied skiing and have a relaxed, family-friendly vibe. For more glitz and Gucci, swing west to Gstaad (p143), which has fine downhill on 250km of slopes and pre- and post-season glacier skiing at nearby Glacier 3000 (p143), framed by 4000m peaks.

ONLINE SKI DEALS

For last-minute ski deals and packages, check out websites like www.igluski.com and www.j2ski.com. Local tourist offices, Snowfinders (www.snowfinders.co.uk) and My Switzerland (www.myswitzerland.com) might also have good-value offers.

Speed to the slopes by prebooking your ski and snowboard hire at Ski Set (www.skiset.co.uk) or Snowbrainer (www.snowbrainer.com), both of which offer discounts of up to 49% on shop rental prices. If you want to skip to the front of the queue, consider ordering your lift pass online, too. Swiss Passes (www.swisspasses.com) gets you a reduction of 5% to 15% on standard lift pass prices.

Central & Northeastern Switzerland

Surprisingly little-known given its snow-sure slopes and staggering mountain backdrop, Engelberg (p229) is dominated by the savage rock and ice walls of glacier-capped Mt Titlis. The real treasures here are off-piste, including Galtiberg, a 2000m vertical descent from the glacier to the valley. Near the St Gotthard Pass, wonderfully wild Andermatt (p234) is another backcountry ski touring and boarder favourite. Families seeking moderate skiing and uncrowded slopes should try Wildhaus (p282) at the foot of the sawtooth Churfirsten range.

Resources

Books

Which Ski Resort – Europe (Pat Sharples and Vanessa Webb) Written by a freestyle champ and a ski coach, this well-researched guide covers the top 50 resorts in Europe.

Where to Ski and Snowboard (Chris Gill and Dave Watts) Bang-up-to-date guide to the slopes, covering all aspects of skiing.

Websites

Bergfex (www.bergfex.com) Comprehensive website with piste maps, snow forecasts of the Alps and details of 111 ski resorts in Switzerland.

On the Snow (www.onthesnow.co.uk) Handy website with reviews of Switzerland's ski resorts, plus snow reports, webcams and lift pass details.

If You Ski (www.ifyouski.com) Resort guides, ski deals and info on ski hire and schools.

MadDogSki (www.maddogski.com) Entertaining ski guides and insider tips on everything from accommodation to après ski.

World Snowboard Guide (www.worldsnowboard guide.com) Snowboarder central. Has the low-down on most Swiss resorts.

Where to Ski and Snowboard (www.wheretoski andsnowboard.com) Resort overviews and reviews, news and weather.

Walking & Hiking

Mighty glaciers and 4000m mountains, remote moors and flower-flecked meadows, limestone ravines and sparkling rivers – Switzerland has an almost indecent amount of natural splendour for its size. More than 60,000km of marked trails criss-cross the country and only by slinging on a backpack and hitting the trail can you begin to appreciate just how *big* this tiny country really is.

Weather

The weather is notoriously fickle in the Alps. Even in August conditions can skip from foggy to sunny, stormy to snowy in the course of a day, so check the forecast on www.meteoschweiz.ch before embarking on long hikes at high altitudes.

Walk Designations

As locals delight in telling you, Switzerland's 62,500km of trails would be enough to stretch around the globe 1.5 times. And with (stereo)typical Swiss precision, the footpaths that criss-cross the country are remarkably well signposted and maintained. That said, a decent topographical map and compass is still recommended for Alpine hikes. Like ski runs, trails are colour-coded according to difficulty:

Yellow Easy. No previous experience necessary.

White-red-white Mountain trails. You should be sure-footed as routes may involve some exposure.

White-blue-white High Alpine routes. Only for the physically fit; some climbing and/or glacier travel may be required.

Pink Prepared winter walking trails.

Walk Descriptions

» The times and distances for walks that appear in this book are provided only as a guide.

» Times are based on the actual walking time and do not include stops for snacks, taking photos, rests or side trips. Be sure to factor these in when planning your walk.

» Distances should be read in conjunction with altitudes – significant elevation can make a greater difference to your walking time than lateral distance.

Safe and Responsible Hiking

To help preserve the ecology and beauty of Switzerland, and to ensure a safe and enjoyable experience, consider the following tips when hiking.

» Pay any fees required and obtain reliable information about environmental conditions along your intended route (eg from park authorities).

BEST HIKES

High-Alpine hike The Faulhornweg (p121) is an unforgettable day hike, with spellbinding views of Lake Thun, Lake Brienz, Eiger, Mönch and Jungfrau.

Mountain view Ogle the rock pyramid of the Matterhorn from Höhenweg Höhbalmen (p177), a long circuit hike taking in wild glaciers, Alpine pastures and 4000m peaks.

Glacier hike Be blown away by the frosty landscape surrounding the Aletsch Glacier (p184) and keep an eye out for black-nosed sheep.

Family hike Skirting the cliff tops, the easygoing Bürgenstock Felsenweg (p216) commands terrific views of Lake Lucerne, Mt Pilatus and Mt Rigi.

Vineyard walk The Bisse de Clavau (p156) walk through the vine-strewn Rhône Valley is especially beautiful on a golden September day.

Off-the-beaten track hike Admire the pristine beauty of the Swiss National Park and Piz Buin views on the challenging Lakes of Macun hike (p312).

Multi-day hike The Zwinglipass (p283) leads through a remote karst wilderness at the foot of the sawtooth Churfirsten.

Summer stroll Amble through rustic hamlets and along old mule trails on the Cima della Trosa (p204) walk, with bird's-eye views of Lago Maggiore.

Cirque walk The high-level Lai da Tuma Circuit (p301) takes in raw granite peaks and highland moors en route to the glittering source of the Rhine.

Eiger close-ups The Kleine Scheidegg (p126) day hike affords mesmerising views of the Eiger north face and other Jungfrau giants with little real effort.

» Walk only in regions, and on trails, within your realm of experience. Increase the length and elevation of your walks gradually.

» Stick to the marked and/or signposted route to prevent erosion and for your own safety.

» Where possible, don't walk in the mountains alone. Two is considered the minimum number for safe walking.

» Take all your rubbish with you, including easily forgotten items such as tinfoil, orange peel, cigarette butts and plastic wrappers.

» Make an effort to use toilets in huts and refuges where provided. Where there is none, bury your waste by digging a small hole 15cm (6in) deep and at least 100m (320ft) from any watercourse.

Regions

Alpine hikers invariably have their sights set high on the trails in the Bernese Oberland, Valais and Graubünden, which offer challenging walking and magnificent scenery. That said, lowland areas such as the vine-strewn Lavaux wine region (p68) and the bucolic dairy country around Appenzell (p281) can be just as atmospheric and are accessible virtually year-round.

In summer, many tourist offices run **guided hikes** – free with a local guest card – including Grindelwald (p123) and Lugano (p195). Other resorts such as Klosters and Davos (p304) and Arosa (p295) give

you a head start with free mountain transport when you stay overnight in summer.

Accommodation

Wanderland (www.wanderland.ch) should be your first port of call for hiker-friendly accommodation, with farmstays, hotels, campsites and Swiss Alpine Club (SAC) huts searchable by route and region.

One of the greatest pleasures of hiking in the Swiss Alps is staying the night at a mountain hut. The **SAC** (www.sac-cas.ch) runs 153 huts and an overnight stay costs between Sfr18 and Sfr28 for members, and between Sfr25 and Sfr35 for non-members. Advance booking is essential. Annual membership costs between Sfr85 and Sfr165 and entitles you to discounts on SAC huts, climbing halls, tours, maps and guides.

Flick to p352 for more details on accommodation. If you are walking in the lowlands and fancy a back-to-nature stay, consider spending the night at a farm or sleeping in a haybarn (p354).

Resources

Books

Walking Easy in the Swiss & Austrian Alps
(Chet Lipton) Covers gentle two- to six-hour hikes in the most popular areas.

100 Hut Walks in the Alps (Kev Reynolds) Gives details of 100 hut-to-hut trails in the Alps for all levels of ability.

Via Ferrata Switzerland (Iris Kürschner) Handy guide with detailed descriptions and maps of 32 *via ferrate* (fixed-rope routes).

Trekking in the Alps (Kev Reynolds) Covers 20 Alpine treks and includes maps and route profiles.

Websites

Get planning with the routes, maps and GPS downloads on the following websites:

My Switzerland (www.myswitzerland.com) Excellent information on walking in Switzerland, from themed day hikes to guided treks and family-friendly walks. An iPhone app covering 32 walks is available for download.

Wanderland (www.wanderland.ch) The definitive website on hiking in Switzerland, with walks and accommodation searchable by region and theme, plus information on events, guides, maps and packages.

Wandern (www.wandern.ch, in German & French) Worth checking out for hiking suggestions and tips, maps and guides (including a limited English-language selection).

Bergfex (www.bergfex.com) Has detailed route descriptions (many in German) and maps, searchable by region, fitness level and length. Free GPS downloads.

Maps

A great overview map of Switzerland is Michelin's 1:400,000 national map No 0729 *Switzerland*. For an interactive walking map, see http://map.wanderland.ch. Alternatively, visit www.myswitzerland.com/map for a zoomable country map.

To purchase high-quality walking maps online, try:

Swiss Hiking Federation (www.swisstopo.ch) Produces large-scale (1:25,000) walking maps that are clear, detailed and accurate.

SOS SIX

The standard Alpine distress signal is six whistles, six calls, six smoke puffs – that is, six of whatever sign or sound you can make – repeated every 10 seconds for one minute. **Mountain rescue** (☑1414) in the Alps is efficient but expensive, so make sure you have adequate insurance.

Kümmerly + Frey (www.swisstravelcenter.com) Has the entire country covered. Most maps are scaled at 1:60,000 and are accurate enough for serious navigation.

Cycling & Mountain Biking

Routes

Switzerland is an efficiently run paradise for the ardent cyclist, laced with 9000km of cycling trails and 4500km of mountain-biking routes.

Andermatt (p234) makes a terrific base if you're keen to test your stamina on the hairpins of mountainous passes such as Furka, Oberalp and St Gotthard. Two striking national routes begin here: a 320km pedal to Geneva via the Rhône glacier and pastoral Goms, and a heart-pounding 430km stretch along the Rhine to Basel. Serious bikers craving back-breaking inclines and arresting views flock to Lenzerheide (p293) and Klosters and Davos (p304).

Mountain and downhill bikers whizz across to Alpine resorts like Arosa (p295) in summer, where cable cars often allow you to take your wheels for free or for a nominal fee. To hone your skills on obstacles, check out the terrain parks in Davos (p307) and Verbier (p154).

Bike Hire

Reliable wheels are available in all major towns and many now offer free bike hire from May to October as part of the eco-friendly initiative **Suisse Roule** (www.suisseroule.ch, in French), including Bern, Thun, Lausanne, Zürich and Geneva.

Available at all major train stations, **Rent a Bike** (www.rent-a-bike.ch, in German & French) has city bikes, mountain bikes, e-bikes and tandems for Sfr33, Sfr50, Sfr50 and Sfr80 per day respectively. For a small additional charge, you can pick your bike up at one station and drop it off at another. Bikes can be reserved online. A one-day bike pass for SBB trains costs Sfr18.

Resources

Veloland (www.veloland.ch) For maps, route descriptions and the low-down on Switzerland's nine national routes, plus details on bike rental and e-bike stations.

KID MAGNETS

» Cow trekking to the Rhine in Hemishofen (p275)

» Zipping above Grindelwald on the First Flyer (p128)

» Llama or goat trekking in Zweisimmen (p144)

» Dashing through the snow on the 15km toboggan run from Faulhorn (p128)

» Having fun above the treetops at the Rheinfall's Adventure Park (p273)

Mountainbikeland (www.mountainbikeland.ch) Useful website for mountain bikers, with details on Switzerland's single-trail and fun tours, and three national routes.

GPS Tour (www.gps-tour.info) Hundreds of GPS cycling and mountain bike tours in Switzerland are available for download on this website.

Adventure & Water Sports

Rock Climbing

Switzerland has been the fabled land for mountaineers ever since Edward Whymper made the first successful ascent of Matterhorn in 1865, albeit a triumph marred with rope-breaking tragedy. Within reach for hard-core Alpinists are some of Europe's most gruelling climbs: Monte Rosa (4634m), Matterhorn (4478m), Mont Blanc (4807m), Eiger (3970m). The names alone of these fearsome giants are redolent of high-altitude adventure.

If you're eager to tackle the biggies, Zermatt's Alpin Center (p167) arranges some first-class climbs to surrounding 4000ers. Wildly scenic Kandersteg (p142) hooks proficient ice climbers with its spectacular frozen waterfalls, while glaciated monoliths like Piz Bernina make Pontresina (p318) a climbing mecca.

The climbing halls in Chur (p291) and Interlaken (p116) are perfect for limbering up.

Read our interview with famous Swiss mountaineer Stephan Siegrist (p118) for more climbing tips. The following websites may also be helpful:

Swiss Alpine Club (SAC; www.sac-cas.ch) Browse for information on countrywide climbing halls, tours and courses.

Schweizer Bergführerverband (Swiss Mountain Guide Association; www.4000plus.ch) Search for a qualified mountain guide or climbing instructor.

Rock Climbing (www.rockclimbing.com) Gives details on hundreds of climbing tours in Switzerland, many with climbing grades and photos.

Verband Bergsportschulen Schweiz (www.bergsportschulen.ch) Find the leading mountain sports schools in Switzerland.

Via Ferrate

For the buzz of mountaineering but with the security of being attached to the rock face, clip onto a *via ferrata* (*Klettersteig* in German). These head-spinning fixed-rope routes are currently all the rage in Switzerland. Some of our favourites include those in Andermatt (p234) and Mürren (p133) for scenery, and Leukerbad (p164) and Kandersteg (p142) for more of a challenge.

Via Ferrata (www.viaferrata.org) provides maps and routes graded according to difficulty.

Paragliding & Hang-gliding

Where there's a beautiful breeze and a mountain, there's tandem paragliding and hang-gliding in Switzerland. Strap into your harness, take a run, jump and be blown away by the rippling mountains, velvety pastures and forests unfolding beneath you.

In the glacial realms of the Unesco-listed Aletsch Glacier, Fiescheralp (p183) is a prime spot to catch thermals, as is First (p123) for spirit-soaring vistas to mighty Jungfrau. If lake scenery is more your style, glide like a bird over glittering Lake Lucerne (p225) and Lago di Lugano (p203).

Bungee Jumping

Regional tourist offices have details of bungee jumping specialists. Great leaps include Grindelwald's glacier-gouged Gletscherschlucht (p123) and the 134m jump from Stockhorn near Interlaken (p115). If you fancy yourself as a bit of a Bond, head to the Verzasca Dam (p208), the world's second-highest bungee jump at 220m, which starred in the opening scene of *GoldenEye*.

EFFORTLESS ALPS

Even if you don't relish the idea of hurling yourself down or hauling yourself up a mountain, there are plenty of ways to appreciate the beauty of the Swiss Alps with no effort or exertion whatsoever. Here are a few of our favourites:

Hot-air ballooning Swoon over phenomenal 360-degree views stretching to Mont Blanc and Eiger in Château-d'Œx (p77). Visit www.ballonfahrt-buchen.ch for more take-off locations.

Horse-drawn sleigh rides Snuggle under a sheepskin, listen to the chime of bells and delight in the views of snow-laden mountains, forests and log chalets on a horse-drawn sleigh ride in Val Fex (p317), Klosters (p304) or Gstaad (p143).

Mountain train rides Survey the glistening Aletsch Glacier from Jungfraujoch (p129), Europe's highest train station at 3454m. Or take the cogwheel train to Gornergrat (p167) for magical views of Matterhorn and the Monte Rosa massif. The nostalgic train ride to Schynige Platte (p120) brings you to an Alpine botanic garden with Eiger, Mönch and Jungfrau views.

Husky sledding Let yelping huskies take the lead on a sled ride in Gstaad (p143).

Scenic cable car journeys The glaciers, waterfalls and cliffs seem close enough to touch on the revolving cable car up to 3020m Mt Titlis (p230). For peerless views of the Swiss Alps and deep into Italy, rise to Matterhorn Glacier Paradise (p167), Europe's highest cable car station at 3883m. James Bond preferred Schilthorn (p134) for its 360-degree panorama reaching all the way to Mont Blanc and the Black Forest on cloudless days.

Skydiving & BASE Jumping

Extreme-sports mecca Interlaken (p115) is the place for heart-stopping skydiving moments. Free fall past the vertical face of Eiger, then, as the pro opens the parachute, drink in the scenery in glorious slow motion.

Even more nerve-wracking is the don't-try-this-at-home pursuit of BASE jumping, the decidedly risky practice of leaping off fixed objects and opening the parachute just before you splat. While this is exhilarating to watch in Lauterbrunnen (p130), this is one sport best left to the experts.

Rafting & Hydrospeeding

In summer, the raging Saane, Rhine, Inn and Rhône rivers create a dramatic backdrop for rafting and hydrospeeding (surfing rapids solo on a glorified bodyboard). Memorable splashes include the thundering Vorderrhein through the limestone Ruinaulta gorge (p298) and rivers near Interlaken (p115). For a full-spin, boulder-loaded challenge, hit the foaming waters of the Inn in Scuol (p310).

Swissraft (www.swissraft.ch, in German & French) has bases all over the country. Expect to pay around Sfr110 for a half-day rafting tour and Sfr140 for hydrospeeding, including transport and equipment.

Kayaking & Canoeing

Lazy summer afternoons are best spent absorbing the slow, natural rhythm of Switzerland's crystal-clear lakes and rivers, for instance Lake Constance (p276) and fjord-like Lake Uri (p224).

See http://kanuland.myswitzerland.com for routes and paddle-friendly accommodation tips. A half-day canoeing tour will set you back between Sfr85 and Sfr120. Tourist offices can provide details on local outfits.

Windsurfing & Waterskiing

Excellent wind sweeps down from the heights in Silvaplana (p316), where you can take kitesurfing and windsurfing lessons or flaunt your skills on two wind-buffeted cobalt lakes.

The rugged mountains rearing up around Lake Thun (p138) make fascinating viewing while windsurfing and wakeboarding. Pretty little Estavayer-le-Lac (p85) also attracts waterskiers and wakeboarders.

Surf www.windsurf.ch (in German) for windsurfing clubs and schools across Switzerland and www.wannakitesurf.com for an interactive map of kitesurfing hotspots.

regions at a glance

No country inspires exploration quite like this tiny country whose four languages and cultural diversity create curiosity and beg discovery. Switzerland's French-speaking wedge – *Suisse Romande* – embraces the country's western fringe from Geneva (no, *not* the capital) and Lake Geneva to the remote Jura in the north and Valais in the east. Moving further east into 'middle ground' Mittelland with Swiss capital Bern as its heart, Germanic Switzerland kicks in – and makes itself heard across the Alps in the country's main outdoor-action playgrounds: the Bernese Oberland, Graubünden and the Engadine Valley. Then there is Ticino, a charismatic pocket of Italian-speaking passion and exuberance in Switzerland.

Geneva

Museums ✓✓
Shopping ✓✓✓
Boats & Lakes ✓✓✓

Close to 150 nationalities jostle for a stool at the bar in this cosmopolitan city of luxury watchmakers and chocolate gods serenaded by Mont Blanc – all this on the western tip of Europe's largest lake. **p38**

Lake Geneva & Vaud

Wine ✓✓✓
Castles ✓✓✓
Pretty Villages ✓✓

Its southern shore belongs to France but the Swiss dress up Lake Geneva's mythical northern shore with emerald terraced vineyards, fairy-tale châteaux, flower paths and dreamy Sunday-best *au-berges* – pure, utter Riviera seduction, *ma chère*. **p55**

Fribourg, Neuchâtel & Jura

Cheese ✓✓✓
Local Wines ✓✓
Rural Life ✓✓✓

Gourmets and fresh-air aficionados swoon over this peaceful, green corner of the country where fruits of the farmland are king – Gruyère cheese, scandalously thick cream, Vully wine and devilish pea-green absinthe. Best sleeps: on farms. **p78**

Mittelland

Art & Architecture ✓✓✓
Old Towns ✓✓✓
The Unexpected ✓✓

Swiss capital Bern with its world-class art museums draws crowds, but its fairy-tale Old Town and counter-culture fun are the real surprises – as are hip sleeps in old-world Solothurn and dashingly sultry lakeshores around Biel-Bienne. **p97**

Bernese Oberland

Adventure Sports ✓✓✓
Stunning Scenery ✓✓✓
Hiking ✓✓✓

It doesn't get more extreme than this. Be it skydiving, ice-climbing or glacial bungee jumping, adrenalin rush here burns. Ritzy film-set resorts, spellbinding glaciers, cinematic peaks: this is the great outdoors on a blockbuster scale. **p113**

Valais

Wine ✓✓
Alpine Action ✓✓✓
Local Tradition ✓✓✓

Eccentric, earthy, as melt-in-your-mouth as Matterhorn's chocolate-box angles: Valais is a rare and traditional breed no one dares mess with. Zermatt, Verbier, the Glacier Express, Switzerland's finest wine – we're talking crème de la crème. **p146**

Ticino

Lakes & Mountains ✓✓✓
Food ✓✓
Hilltop Villages ✓✓✓

Italian weather, Italian style... this Italian-speaking canton is a different side of Switzerland: picture-postcard villages in wild valleys, petrol-blue lakes with palm-fringed shores, alfresco dining beneath chestnut trees. *Buon appetito!* **p187**

Central Switzerland

Views ✓✓✓
Great Outdoors ✓✓✓
Culture ✓✓✓

More Swiss than Swiss, the country's heartland is built from picture-book, William Tell legend: bucket-list sunsets, mythical mountains (off-piste perfection) and shimmering cobalt blue waters. **p210**

Basel & Aargau

Art ✓✓✓
Castles ✓✓
Nightlife ✓✓

The urbanite ticket of northwestern Switzerland, big-city Basel woos with explosive art, avant-garde architecture and a mighty giant of a river that sticks out its tongue east to lick fairy-tale castles and medieval villages. **p236**

Zürich

Nightlife ✓✓✓
Dining Out ✓✓
Culture ✓✓

The party never stops in edgy Züri-West, flipside of the coin to Zürich the banker. Throw nocturnal baths, fine art and international cuisine into the urban mix to get one hell of a potent cocktail. **p250**

Northeastern Switzerland

Back to Nature ✓✓
Culture ✓✓✓
Food ✓✓

Exploring this backwater – a deeply Germanic, rural land of Alpine dairy farms and half-timbered villages – opens the door on a fantastical world of fairy-tale castles, secret libraries, thunderous waterfalls and cows you can ride. **p268**

Graubünden

Winter Sports ✓✓✓
Walking ✓✓✓
Train Journeys ✓✓✓

Skiing mecca of Davos and St Moritz fame, this glamorous region where winter tourism began its dizzying stuff. Dodge paparazzi at a quartzite spa, hike the Swiss National Park and gaze at the mountains aboard the iconic Glacier Express. **p287**

Liechtenstein

Smallness ✓✓✓
Nature ✓
Castle ✓

Thanks to a monarchy that refuses entreaties from neighbours, this pea-sized principality remains staunchly independent. It's got pretty hikes, a royal castle and a booming business in false teeth and passport stamps. **p320**

Look out for these icons:

 Our author's recommendation

A green or sustainable option

FREE No payment required

See the Index for a full list of destinations covered in this book.

On the Road

Geneva

POP 178.600 / AREA 282 SQ KM / LANGUAGE FRENCH

Best Places to Eat

» Auberge Communale de Presinge (p50)

» Le Comptoir (p48)

» L'Adresse (p49)

» L'Entrecôte (p49)

» Omnibus (p50)

Best Places to Stay

» Hôtel Bel'Esperance (p47)

» Edelweiss (p47)

» La Réserve (p47)

» La Cour des Augustins (p47)

» Hôtel Auteuil (p47)

Why Go?

Sleek, slick and cosmopolitan, Geneva is a rare breed of a city: it's one of Europe's priciest, its people chatter in every language under the sun and it's constantly perceived as the Swiss capital (it isn't). Superbly strung around the shores of Europe's largest Alpine lake, this is only Switzerland's third-largest city.

Yet the whole world is here: 200-odd governmental and nongovernmental international organisations fill the city's plush hotels, feast on its incredible choice of international cuisine, and help prop up Geneva's famed overload of banks, luxury jewellers and chocolate shops.

But where's the urban grit? Not in the lakeside's silky-smooth promenades and iconic fountain of record-breaking heights, nor in its pedestrian Old Town. To find the rough cut of the diamond, dig into the Pâquis quarter or walk along the Rhône's industrial shores where local neighbourhood bars hum with attitude. This is the Geneva of the *Genevois*...or as close as you'll get.

When to Go

Geneva is a year-round destination. Winter with its December festivals, toasty lakeside sauna bars and fondue cuisine (not to mention nearby skiing) has a real charm. Then there is spring when many more boats serenade the lake and its quays come alive with city dwellers out for a walk, rollerblade or early evening drink on a waterfront bar terrace. July and August are the months to dip in the lake, dive off jetties, discover the city's alfresco cafe society and picnic in its many pretty parks.

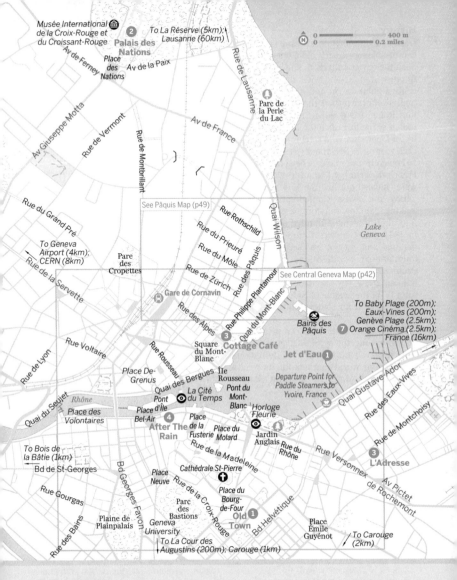

Musée International
de la Croix-Rouge et
du Croissant-Rouge

Palais des
Nations

Place
des
Nations

Av de Ferney

Av de la Paix

To La Réserve (5km);
Lausanne (60km)

Rue de Lausanne

Parc de
la Perle
du Lac

Av de France

Av Giuseppe Motta

Rue de Vermont

Rue de Montbrillant

Lake
Geneva

Rue du Grand Pré

See Pâquis Map (p49)

Rue Rothschild

Quai Wilson

To Geneva
Airport (4km);
CERN (8km)

Rue de la Servette

Parc
des
Cropettes

Rue du Prieuré

Rue du Môle

Rue de Zürich

Rue des Pâquis

Rue Philippe Plantamour

Quai du Mont-Blanc

See Central Geneva Map (p42)

To Baby Plage (200m);
Eaux-Vines (200m);
Genève Plage (2.5km);
Orange Cinéma (2.5km);
France (16km)

Rue de Lyon

Rue Voltaire

Gare de Cornavin

Rue des Alpes

Bains des
Pâquis

Square
du Mont-
Blanc

Cottage Café

Jet d'Eau

Rue Rousseau

Place De-
Grenus

Rhône

Quai des Bergues

Île
Rousseau

Departure Point for
Paddle Steamers to
Yvoire, France

Quai Gustave-Ador

Rue des Eaux-Vives

Quai du Seujet

Place des
Volontaires

Pont
d'Île

La Cité
du Temps

Pont du
Mont-Blanc

Horloge
Fleurie

Rue de Montchoisy

Place
Bel-Air

After The
Rain

Place
de la
Fusterie

Place du
Molard

Jardin
Anglais

Rue du
Rhône

L'Adresse

To Bois de
la Bâtie (1km)

Bd de St-Georges

Rue de la Madeleine

Rue Versonnex

Av Pictet
de Rochemont

Rue Gourgas

Place
Neuve

Cathédrale St-Pierre

Rue de la Croix-Rouge

Place du
Bourg-
de-Four

Parc
des
Bastions

Plaine de
Plainpalais

Geneva
University

Old
Town

Bd Helvétique

Place
Émile
Guyénot

To Carouge
(2km)

Rue des Bains

Bd Georges Favon

To La Cour des
Augustins (200m); Carouge (1km)

N

0   400 m
0   0.2 miles

Geneva Highlights

1 Dash beneath the **Jet d'Eau** (p40) then plunge into the labyrinthine **Old Town** (p40)

2 Learn a worldly thing or two about the Big Bang at **CERN** (p45) and the UN at the **Palais des Nations** (p45)

3 Indulge in a shopping spree in Geneva's Old Town and Pâquis boutiques, lunch at **L'Adresse** (p49) and take afternoon tea at **Cottage Café** (p48)

4 Spoil yourself with a soak in a chocolate bath at **After the Rain** (p46)

5 Sail a belle époque paddle steamer to **Yvoire** (p54) in France

6 Trade in urban chic for lunch at an old-fashioned *auberge* in the Genevan countryside (p50)

7 Watch a box-office hit against the romantic backdrop of twinkling stars, boat lights and the rippling water of Lake Geneva at the **Orange Cinéma** (p52)

History

Occupied by the Romans and later a 5th-century bishopric, rich old Geneva has long been the envy of all. Its medieval fairs drew interest from far and wide, and in the 16th century John Calvin and his zealous Reformation efforts turned the city into 'Protestant Rome'. Savoy duke Charles Emmanuel took a swipe at it in 1602, but was repelled by the Genevans, who celebrate their victory each year on 11 December (p46).

French troops made Geneva capital of the French department Léman in 1798 but they were chucked out in June 1814 and Geneva joined the Swiss Confederation. Watchmaking, banking and commerce prospered. A local businessman founded the Red Cross in 1864 and Geneva's future as an international melting pot was secured as other international organisations adopted the strategically located city and birthplace of humanitarian law as their headquarters. After WWI the League of Nations strived for world peace from Geneva and after WWII the UN arrived.

By the end of the 20th century, Geneva ranked among the world's 10 most expensive cities, relying heavily on international workers and world markets for its wealth. Foreigners (184 different nationalities) make up 45% of Geneva's population.

◎ Sights

Geneva's major sights are split by the Rhône, which flows through the city to create its greatest attraction – the lake – and several distinct neighbourhoods. On the left bank (*rive gauche*), mainstream shopping districts Rive and Eaux-Vives climb uphill from the water to Plainpalais and Vieille Ville (Old

Town), while the right bank *(rive droite)* holds grungy bar- and club-hot Pâquis, the train station area and the international quarter that houses most world organisations.

Many museums are free on the first Sunday of the month. On other days, the Swiss Museum Pass (p355) kicks in. Opening hours are listed for high season (April through October) and are often shorter at other times of year.

VIEILLE VILLE

Geneva's Old Town is a short walk south from the lakeside.

Jardin Anglais   GARDEN
(Map p42; Quai du Général-Guisan) Before tramping up the hill, join the crowds getting snapped in front of the flower clock in the Jardin Anglais, Geneva's flowery waterfront garden landscaped in 1854 on the site of an old lumber-handling port and merchant yard. The Horloge Fleurie, Geneva's most photographed clock, is crafted from 6500 plants and has ticked since 1955 in the garden. Its second hand, 2.5m long, claims to be the world's longest.

Jet d'Eau   FOUNTAIN
(Map p42; Quai Gustave-Ador) Landing by plane, this fountain is the first dramatic glimpse you get of Geneva. The 140m-tall lakeside fountain shoots up water with incredible force – 200km/h, 1360 horsepower – to create the sky-high plume, which is kissed by a rainbow on sunny days. At any one time, 7 tonnes of water is in the air, much of which sprays spectators on the pier beneath. Two or three times a year, it is illuminated pink, blue or some other vivid colour to mark a humanitarian occasion (World Suicide Prevention Day, Breast Cancer Awareness Month, World AIDS Day etc).

The Jet d'Eau is Geneva's third pencil fountain. The first shot in the sky for 15 minutes each Sunday between 1886 and 1890 to release pressure at the city's water station, the second spurted 90m tall from the Jetée des Eaux-Vives on Sundays and public holidays from 1891 onwards, and the third and current was born in 1951.

Cathédrale St-Pierre   CATHEDRAL
(Map p42; Cour St-Pierre; admission free; ◎9.30am-6.30pm Mon-Fri, to 5.30pm Sat, noon-6.30pm Sun) Started in the 11th century, Geneva's lovely cathedral is mainly Gothic with an 18th-century neoclassical facade. Between 1536 and 1564 Protestant John

HAVE YOUR SAY

Found a fantastic restaurant that you're longing to share with the world?
Disagree with our recommendations?
Or just want to talk about your most recent trip?

Whatever your reason, head to lonelyplanet.com, where you can post a review, ask or answer a question on the Thorntree forum, comment on a blog, or share your photos and tips on Groups. Or you can simply spend time chatting with like-minded travellers. So go on, have your say.

Calvin preached both here – see his seat in the north aisle – and in the Gothic **Auditoire de Calvin** (Cour St-Pierre; admission free; ☺10am-noon & 2-4pm Mon-Sat) neighbouring the cathedral. In summer free **organ and carillon concerts** (www .concerts-cathedrale.com; ☺5pm & 6pm Sat Jun-Sep) fill the cathedral with soul.

Don't leave the cathedral without buying a ticket for the **cathedral towers** (adult/child Sfr4/2). Seventy-six steps twist up to the cathedral attic – a fascinating insight into its architectural construction – from where you can hike another 40 steps up the northern or southern towers for a magnificent lake panorama or bell tower and old WWII observation post respectively.

In the cathedral basement, a small **Site Archéologique** (www.site-archeologique .ch; adult/child Sfr8/4; ☺10am-5pm Tue-Sun) displays fine 4th-century mosaics and the tomb of an Allobrogian chieftain.

Musée International de la Réforme
HISTORY MUSEUM

(Map p42; www.musee-reforme.ch; Rue du Cloître 4; adult/child Sfr13/6; ☺10am-5pm Tue-Sun) To the side of the cathedral sits this thoroughly modern museum inside a lovely 18th-century mansion. It focuses on the Reformation, with state-of-the-art exhibits and audiovisuals bringing to life everything from the earliest printed bibles to the emergence of Geneva as 'Protestant Rome' in the 16th century and John Calvin to Protestantism in the 21st century. History buffs will love it. A combined ticket covering museum, cathedral and archaeological site costs Sfr18 for adults and Sfr10 for children.

Musée Barbier-Mueller
ART MUSEUM

(Map p42; www.barbier-mueller.ch; Rue Jean Calvin 10; adult/child Sfr8/5; ☺11am-5pm) Protestant John Calvin lived in the house opposite this refined gallery space, filled with objects from so-called primitive societies – think pre-Columbian South American art treasures, Pacific Island statues, and shields and weapons from Africa.

Musée d'Art et d'Histoire
ART MUSEUM

(Map p42; Rue Charles Galland 2; permanent/temporary collection free/Sfr5; ☺10am-6pm Tue-Sun) Konrad Witz' *La pêche miraculeuse* (c 1440–44), portraying Christ walking on water on Lake Geneva, is a highlight of Geneva's elegant art and history museum, built between 1903 and 1910.

Espace Rousseau
MUSEUM

(Map p42; www.espace-rousseau.ch; Grand-Rue 40; adult/child Sfr10/free; ☺11am-5.30pm Tue-Sun) Small house museum with 25-minute audiovisual display tracing the troubled life of Geneva's greatest thinker, born here in 1712.

PLAINPALAIS

Wedged between the Rhône and Arve rivers, this fairly non-descript district is home to the university and a bevy of museums.

Musée d'Art Moderne et Contemporain
ART MUSEUM

(Map p42; MAMCO; www.mamco.ch, in French; Rue des Vieux Grenadiers 10; adult/child Sfr8/free; ☺noon-6pm Tue-Fri, from 11am Sat & Sun) Set in an industrial 1950s factory, Geneva's museum of modern and contemporary art plays cutting-edge host to young, international and cross-media exhibitions. The museum is free between 6pm and 9pm on the first Wednesday of every month.

Patek Philippe Museum
MUSEUM

(Map p42; www.patekmuseum.com; Rue des Vieux Grenadiers 7; adult/child Sfr10/free; ☺2-6pm Tue-Fri, from 10am Sat) A treasure trove of precision art, this elegant museum by one of Switzerland's leading luxury watchmakers displays exquisite timepieces and enamels from the 16th century to present. The Patek Philippe collection includes pocket watches from the master watchmaker's inception in 1839 to commemorative watches created in the new millennium.

Parc des Bastions
PARK

(Map p42; Place Neuve) It's all statues – not to mention a giant chess board – in this green city park where a laidback stroll uncovers Red Cross cofounder Henri Dufour (who drew the first map of Switzerland in 1865) and the 4.5m-tall figures of Bèze, Calvin, Farel and Knox (in their nightgowns ready for bed no less). Depending on what's on, end with an art-driven exhibition across the square at **Musée Rath** (Place Neuve; adult/child Sfr10/5; ☺10am-6pm Tue & Thu-Sun, to 8pm Wed).

RIGHT BANK

Cross the water aboard a seagull (p54), using Geneva's only road-traffic bridge Pont du Mont-Blanc (notorious for traffic jams) or on foot across pedestrian footbridge Pont de la Machine.

Quai du Mont-Blanc
WATERFRONT

(Map p42) Flowers, statues, outdoor art exhibitions and views of Mont Blanc (on clear

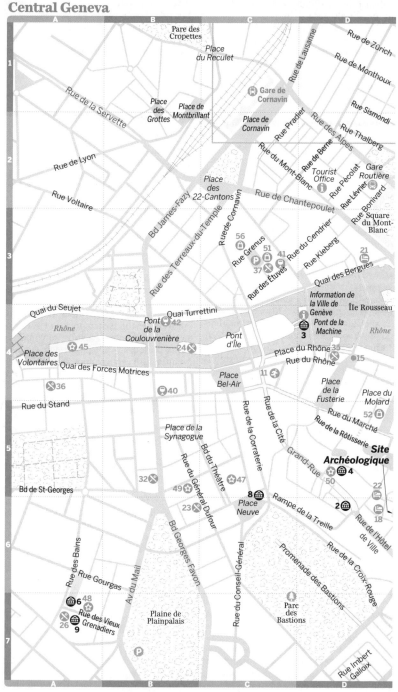

Parc des Cropettes

Place du Reculet

Place des Grottes

Place de Montbrillant

Rue de la Servette

Rue de Lausanne

Rue de Zürich

Rue de Monthoux

Gare de Cornavin

Rue de Sismondi

Place de Cornavin

Rue Pradier

Rue des Alpes

Rue Thalberg

Rue de Lyon

Rue Voltaire

Rue du Mont-Blanc

Rue de Berne

Tourist Office

Rue Pécolat

Gare Routière

Place des 22-Cantons

Rue de Chantepoulet

Rue Lévrier

Rue Bonivard

Square du Mont-Blanc

Bd James-Fazy

Rue de Cornavin

Rue du Cendrier

Rue des Terreaux-du-Temple

Rue Grenus

56

51

41

Rue du Kleberg

21

37

Rue des Étuves

Quai des Bergues

Quai du Seujet

Quai Turrettini

Pont de la Coulouvrenière

42

Information de la Ville de Genève

Île Rousseau

Rhône

45

24

Pont d'Île

Pont de la Machine

3

Rhône

Place des Volontaires

Quai des Forces Motrices

Place du Rhône

35

Rue du Rhône

15

36

Place Bel-Air

11

Place de la Fusterie

Place du Molard

Rue du Stand

40

52

Rue du Marché

Place de la Synagogue

Rue de la Rôtisserie

Site Archéologique

Bd du Théâtre

Rue de la Corraterie

Rue de la Cité

Grand-Rue

50

4

32

49

47

22

Bd de St-Georges

Rue du Général Dufour

23

8

Place Neuve

Rampe de la Treille

2

18

Rue de l'Hôtel de Ville

Bd Georges Favon

Rue des Bains

Rue Gourgas

Av du Mail

Rue du Conseil-Général

Rue de la Croix-Rouge

Promenade des Bastions

6

48

26

9

Rue des Vieux Grenadiers

Plaine de Plainpalais

Parc des Bastions

Rue Imbert Galloix

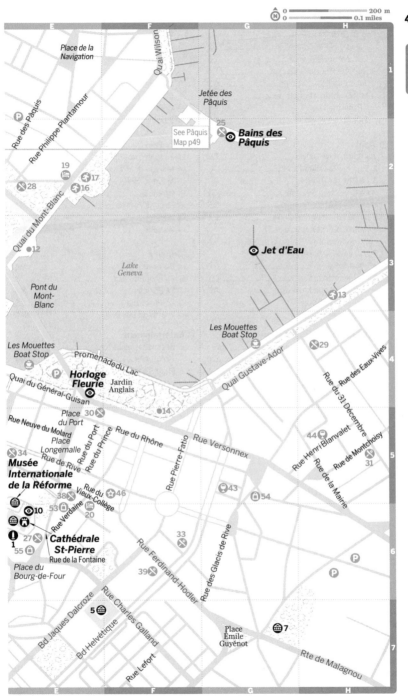

0 — 200 m
0 — 0.1 miles

Place de la
Navigation

Quai Wilson

Jetée des
Pâquis

Rue des Pâquis

Rue Philippe Plantamour

See Pâquis
Map p49

25
◉ **Bains des
Pâquis**

19

17
16

28

Quai du Mont-Blanc

12

Lake
Geneva

◉ **Jet d'Eau**

13

Pont du
Mont-
Blanc

Les Mouettes
Boat Stop

29

Rue des Eaux-Vives

Les Mouettes
Boat Stop

Promenade du Lac

Quai Gustave-Ador

Rue du 31 Décembre

**Horloge
Fleurie**
◉

Jardin
Anglais

Quai du Général-Guisan

14

Rue Henri-Blanvalet

Rue de Montchoisy

Place
du Port

30

Rue Neuve du Molard

Rue du Port

Rue du Prince

Rue du Rhône

Rue Pierre-Fatio

Rue Versonnex

44

Place
Longemalle

Rue de Rive

34

**Musée
Internationale
de la Réforme**

38

Rue du
Vieux-Collège

46

53

20

Rue Verdaine

10

Rue de la Mairie

31

43

54

1

27

**Cathédrale
St-Pierre**

55

Rue de la Fontaine

33

Rue Ferdinand-Hodler

39

Rue des Glacis de Rive

Place du
Bourg-de-Four

Bd Jaques Dalcroze

Rue Charles Galland

5

Bd Helvétique

Place
Émile
Guyénot

7

Rue Lefort

Rte de Malagnou

Central Geneva

days only) abound on this picturesque northern lakeshore promenade which leads past the **Bains des Pâquis** (p46), where Genevans have frolicked in the sun since 1872, to **Parc de la Perle du Lac**, a large park where Romans built ornate thermal baths. Further north, the peacock-studded lawns of **Parc de l'Ariana** ensnare the UN and the pretty **Jardin Botanique**

(Botanical Garden; admission free; ◎8am-7.30pm).

La Cité du Temps   GALLERY
(Map p42; www.citedutemps.com; Pont de la Machine 1; admission free; ◎9am-6pm) This 19th-century industrial building astraddle Lake Geneva was constructed in the 1840s to provide the city's public fountains with water. Today it is a striking exhibition space

with lounge bar, restaurant, some excellent temporary art exhibitions and La Collection Swatch, the world's largest collection of the funky Swiss Swatch watches. Kicking off in 1983, the amusing collection includes everything from *Love Bite,* made in 1998 for Valentine's Day, to the Skin collection, the world's thinnest plastic watches (1997), and the commemorative watches created to mark the 20th anniversary of James Bond. Two computer terminals allow you to design your own Swatch watch and various models are for sale.

Palais des Nations   HISTORIC BUILDING
(Map p39; www.unog.ch; Ave de la Paix 14; adult/child Sfr12/7; ☺10am-noon & 2-4pm Mon-Fri Sep-Mar, 10am-noon & 2-4pm daily Apr-Jun, 10am-5pm daily Jul & Aug) Home to the UN since 1966, the Palais des Nations was built between 1929 and 1936 to house the now-defunct League of Nations. Admission (bring ID card or passport) includes an hour-long tour of the building and entry to the surrounding park where a grey monument sprouts, coated with heat-resistant titanium donated by the USSR to commemorate the conquest of space. Twice-weekly park tours (adult/child Sfr10/5; ☺11am & 2.30pm Tue & Thu) give the complete low-down on the 46-hectare grounds generously peppered with century-old trees and peacocks.

Musée International de la Croix-Rouge et du Croissant-Rouge   MUSEUM
(Map p39; www.micr.org; Ave de la Paix 17; temporary exhibition free, permanent exhibition adult/child Sfr10/free; ☺10am-5pm Wed-Mon) Compelling multimedia exhibits at Geneva's fascinating International Red Cross & Red Crescent Museum trawl through atrocities perpetuated by humanity. The long litany of war and nastiness, documented in films, photos, sculptures and soundtracks, are set against the noble aims of the organisation created by Geneva businessmen and philanthropists Henri Dunant and Henri Dufour in 1864. Take bus 8 from Gare de Cornavin to the 'Appia' stop.

CERN   SCIENCE LABORATORY
(Off Map p39; ☏022 767 76 76; http://outreach.web.cern.ch; admission free; ☺guided tours in English 10.30am Mon-Sat year-round, 3.30pm Mon, Tue, Thu & Fri mid-Jun–mid-Sep) Founded in 1954, the European Organisation for Nuclear Research, 8km west of Geneva near Meyrin, is a laboratory for research into particle physics. It accelerates electrons and positrons

Geneva's bohemian streak strikes in Carouge, where the lack of any real sights – bar fashionable 18th-century houses overlooking courtyard gardens and Musée de Carouge (Place de la Sardaigne 2; admission free; ☺2-6pm Tue-Sun), displaying 19th-century ceramics – is part of the charm.

Carouge was refashioned by Vittorio Amedeo III, king of Sardinia and duke of Savoy, in the 18th century in a bid to rival Geneva as a centre of commerce. In 1816 the Treaty of Turin handed it to Geneva and today its narrow streets are filled with bars, boutiques and artists workshops.

Trams 12 and 13 link central Geneva with Carouge's plane tree-studded central square, Place du Marché, abuzz with market stalls Wednesday and Saturday morning. Horses trot along the streets during April's Fête du Cheval, and horse-drawn carriages line up on Place de l'Octroi in December to take Christmas shoppers for a ride.

down a 27km circular tube (the Large Hadron Collider, the world's biggest machine) and the resulting collisions create new forms of matter.

Two fascinating permanent exhibitions shed light on the ground-breaking work done by the centre: The dazzling Universe of Particles (admission free; ☺10am-5pm Mon-Sat), housed inside a 27m-tall and 40m-diameter globe intended to symbolise planet Earth, is a dazzling interactive voyage into the enigmatic world of particles. Microcosm (admission free; ☺8.30am-5.30pm Mon-Fri, 9am-5pm Sat) likewise uses multimedia to help visitors understand through games, experiments and hands-on workshops just how accelerators recreate the Big Bang among other things.

Those keen to delve deeper can sign up for a two- to three-hour guided tour of the laboratory. Tours start in the Universe of Particles and include a short introduction to CERN's work, a film and a visit to one of the experiments or an accelerator. Book tours at least one month in advance by filling out the form online and bring your ID or passport the day of your visit.

From the train station take tram 18 to its terminus in front of CERN (Sfr3, 40 minutes).

🏃 Activities

After the Rain
SPA

(Map p42; ☑022 819 01 50; www.spa-aftertherain
.ch; Passage des Lions 4; ◷9am-9pm Mon-Sat)
Soothe urban body and soul at this city
spa, a haven of peace and tranquillity in
downtown Geneva, where the icing on
the cake for chocolate fiends is a body
wrap in creamy milk chocolate (Sfr140 for
45 minutes) or – even better – a good old
soak in a milk chocolate bath (Sfr180 for
30 minutes).

👉 Tours

The one-stop shop for boat, bus and elec-
tric-train tours is **Ticket Point** (☑022 781
04 06; www.ticket-point.ch) which has all the
schedules and sells tickets at its waterfront
kiosk on Quai du Mont-Blanc.

CGN
BOAT

(Map p42; ☑0848 811 848; www.cgn.ch; Quai
du Mont-Blanc) Lake cruises, some aboard
beautiful belle époque steamers, by Lake
Geneva's main boat operator.

Swissboat
BOAT

(Map p42; www.swissboat.com; Quai du Mont-Blanc
4; ◷May-Oct) Thematic cruises – castles, nature and so on – around the lake and along
the Rhône River.

STT Train Tours
BOAT

(Map p42; ☑022 781 04 04; www.sttr.ch) Short
city tours along the lake (adult/child Sfr8/5,
45min), into the Old Town (adult/child

Sfr9.90/6.90) and across the border to
Yvoire (adult/child Sfr49/25).

Mini Train Tours
TRAIN

(Map p42; ☑022 735 43 00; Jardin d'Anglais; adult/
child Sfr8/5; ◷10.15am-10.15pm) At least hourly
departures year-round along the left bank
to Parc des Eaux-Vives and back again
aboard a solar-powered red train; count on
45 minutes' journey time.

🎊 Festivals & Events

L'Escalade
EVENT

(www.escalade.ch, in French) Smashing sweet
marzipan-filled *marmites en chocolat*
(chocolate cauldrons) and gorging on the
broken pieces makes Geneva's biggest festival on 11 December loads of fun. Torch-
lit processions enliven the Old Town and
a bonfire is lit in the cathedral square to
celebrate the defeat of Savoy troops in 1602.
A tall tale says the assault was repelled by a
housewife who tipped a pot of boiling soup
over a trooper's head, whacked him with
her cauldron, then raised the alarm.

🛏 Sleeping

Plug into the complete list at www.geneva
-hotel.ch. Rates in Geneva's predominantly
business, midrange and top-end hotels are
substantially higher Monday to Thursday.

When checking in, be sure to get your
free Public Transport Card, which offers
unlimited bus travel for the duration of
your stay.

GENEVA FOR CHILDREN

Predictably, the lake is an endless source of family entertainment: feed the ducks and
swans; rent a pedalo, speedboat or sleek sailing boat from **Les Corsaires** (Map p42;
☑022 735 43 00; www.lescorsaires.ch; Quai Gustave-Ador 33; ◷10.30am-8pm); fly down the
water slide at 1930s lakeside swimming pool complex **Genève Plage** (Off Map p39;
www.geneve-plage.ch; Port Noir; adult/child Sfr7/3.50; ◷10am-8pm mid-May–mid-Sep); or dive
head-first into the pools at historic and hip **Bains des Pâquis** (Map p42; www.bains-des
-paquis.ch, in French; Quai du Mont-Blanc 30; ◷9am-8pm mid-Apr–mid-Sep).

Other amusing options include an electric train tour, the Tarzan-inspired tree park
with rubber tyre swings at lakeside **Baby Plage** (Off Map p39; Quai Gustave-Ador), and the
well-equipped playgrounds for toddlers in lakeside **Parc de la Perle du Lac** (Map p39;
Rue de Lausanne) and **Bois de la Bâtie** (Off Map p39) where peacocks, goats and deer
roam in woods. Kids can wallow in a strawberry milk and candyfloss bath (Sfr120 for
30 minutes) or wrap themselves in a white chocolate body wrap (Sfr90 for 30 minutes)
at the **After the Rain** spa. Every kid adores the stuffed bears, tigers and giraffes,
Swiss fauna and hands-on Wednesday-afternoon workshops at the **Musée d'Histoire
Naturelle** (Map p42; Natural History Museum; Rte de Malagnou 1; admission free; ◷9.30am-
5pm Tue-Sun).

For French or German speakers, www.genevefamille.ch is useful.

TOP CHOICE Hôtel Bel'Esperance   HOTEL $
(Map p42; ☎022 818 37 37; www.hotel-bel
-esperance.ch; Rue de la Vallée 1; s/d/tr/q from
Sfr105/160/195/235; @🛜) This two-star hotel
is a two-second flit to the Old Town and offers extraordinary value for a pricey city like
Geneva. Rooms are quiet and cared for, and
those on the 1st floor share a kitchen. Ride
the lift to the 5th floor to flop in a chair on
its wonderful flower-filled rooftop terrace.

Edelweiss   HOTEL $$
(Map p49; ☎022 544 51 51; www.manotel.com;
Place de la Navigation 2; d/tr from Sfr160/210;
❄@🛜) Plunge yourself into the heart of
the Swiss Alps with this Heidi-style hideout,
very much the Swiss Alps *en ville* with its
fireplace, wildflower-painted pine bedheads
and big, cuddly St Bernard lolling over the
banister. Its chalet-styled restaurant is a key
address among Genevans for traditional
cheese fondue.

La Réserve   HOTEL $$$
(Off Map p39; ☎022 959 59 59; www.lareserve.ch;
Rte de Lausanne 301; d from Sfr435; P❄@🛜≋)
There is absolutely no reason to leave the
premises; the handiwork of Parisian interior-
design god, Jacques Garcia, this mythical
lakeside spa hotel is an extravaganza of
cutting-edge design, embracing everything
from African colonialism to 1960s Barbarella-
style pop and feng shui minimalism. 'Heaven
on Earth' is a fair synopsis.

La Cour des Augustins   BOUTIQUE HOTEL $$
(Off Map p39; ☎022 322 21 00; www.lacourdes
augustins.com; Rue Jean-Violette 15; s/d from
Sfr189/248; P❄@🛜) 'Boutique gallery
design hotel' is how this slick, contemporary
space in Carouge markets itself. Disguised
by a 19th-century facade, its crisp white
interior screams cutting edge. Before leav-
ing, invest in a designer lamp or household
art object from the hotel boutique.

Hôtel Auteuil   DESIGN HOTEL $$
(Map p49; ☎022 544 22 22; www.manotel.com;
Rue de Lausanne 33; d from Sfr320; P❄@🛜) The
star of this crisp, design-driven hotel near
the station is its enviable collection of B&W
photos of 1950s film stars in Geneva. Borrow
the book from reception to find out precisely
who's who and where.

Hôtel Jade   BOUTIQUE HOTEL $$
(Map p49; ☎022 544 38 38; www.manotel.com;
Rue Rothschild 55; d from Sfr160; ❄@🛜) Elegant
ebony and other dark woods contrast with

mellow creams, beige and other natural
hues to create a fashionably understated feel
at this 'feng shui adventure', a stylish bou-
tique hotel designed to soothe, revitalise and
inspire with its ancient Chinese principles
and Zen philosophy.

Hôtel des Bergues   HISTORIC HOTEL $$$
(Map p42; ☎022 908 70 00; www.bergueshotel.
com; Quai des Bergues 33; d from Sfr620; P❄@🛜)
Geneva's oldest hotel continues to live up
to its magnificent heritage. Chandelier-
lit moulded ceilings, grandiose flower
arrangements, original oil paintings in
heavy gold frames and diamonds glittering behind glass is what this lakeside
neoclassical gem from 1834 is all about.
But how can a suite cost Sfr12,500 a
night?

Hôme St-Pierre   HOSTEL $
(Map p42; ☎022 310 37 07; www.homest-pierre.
ch; Cour St-Pierre 4; dm Sfr31, s/d with washba-
sin Sfr48/72; @) In the shade of the cathedral, this boarding house was founded by
the German Lutheran Church in 1874 to
host German women coming to Geneva to
learn French. Women remain the primary
clientele – just six dorm beds are up for
grabs for six lucky guys – and the rooftop
terrace is magical. Book well in advance.

Hôtel Les Armures   HISTORIC HOTEL $$$
(Map p42; ☎022 310 91 72; www.hotel-les-armures.
ch; Rue du Puits St-Pierre 1; s/d from Sfr445/695;
P❄@🛜) This intimate and refined 17th-
century beauty slumbers in the heart of the
Old Town.

Hôtel Beau-Rivage   HISTORIC HOTEL $$$
(Map p42; ☎022 716 66 66; www.beau-rivage.ch;
Quai du Mont-Blanc 13; d from Sfr800; P❄@🛜)
Run by the Mayer family for four generations,
the Beau-Rivage is a 19th-century jewel drip-
ping in opulence.

Auberge de Jeunesse   HOSTEL $
(Map p49; ☎022 732 62 60; www.yh-geneva.ch;
Rue Rothschild 28-30; dm Sfr29, d/q with bathroom
toilet Sfr95/135; @🛜) At this well-equipped,
Hostelling International–affiliated apart-
ment block rates include breakfast and
bunk-bed dorms max out at 12 beds. Non
HI-card holders pay Sfr6 more a night.

City Hostel   HOSTEL $
(Map p49; ☎022 901 15 00; www.cityhostel.ch;
Rue de Ferrier 2; dm Sfr32, s/d Sfr61/88; ⊙recep-
tion 7.30am-noon & 1pm-midnight; P@) Clean,
well-organised hostel near the train station;

it doesn't serve breakfast and parking costs Sfr10 per night.

✖ Eating

Geneva flaunts ethnic cuisines galore. If it's local and traditional you're after, dip into a cheese fondue or platter of pan-fried *filets de perche* (perch fillets). But beware: not all those cooked up are fresh from the lake. Many come frozen from Eastern Europe, so it's imperative to pick the right place to sample this simple Lake Geneva speciality.

PÂQUIS

There's a tasty line-up of more affordable restaurants on Place de la Navigation. For Asian-cuisine lovers without a fortune to blow, try a quick-eat joint on Rue de Fribourg, Rue de Neuchâtel, Rue de Berne or the northern end of Rue des Alpes.

TOP CHOICE Le Comptoir   FUSION $
(Map p49; ☑022 731 32 37; www.lolabar.ch; Rue de Richemont 7-9; mains Sfr15-30; ⊙lunch & dinner Tue-Fri, dinner Sat) To savour the real vibe of this U-shaped space come here at dusk or later when night lights twinkle on sideboards and the Counter's retro decor really comes into its own. We love the faux sheepskins and crystal in the faintly kitsch Lola Bar lounge! The cuisine is a tasty mix of sushi, curries and wok-cooked dishes.

Cottage Café   MEDITERRANEAN $
(Map p42; ☑022 731 60 16; www.cottagecafe .ch; Rue Adhémar-Fabri 7; tapas Sfr9-15; ⊙7.15am-10pm Mon-Sat) Hovering right on the fringe of Pâquis near the waterfront, this quaint little cottage sits plum in a park guarded by two stone lions and a mausoleum (Geneva's Brunswick Monument no less). On clear sunny days, views of Mont Blanc from its garden are swoon-worthy, while lunching or lounging inside is akin to hanging out in your grandma's book-lined living room. From 6pm the wine-bar menu with lots of tapas kicks in.

Buvette des Bains   CAFETERIA $
(Map p42; ☑022 738 16 16; www.bains-des -paquis.ch; Quai du Mont-Blanc 30; mains Sfr15-20; ⊙8am-10pm) Meet Genevans at this earthy beach bar – rough and hip around the edges – at Bains des Pâquis (p46). Grab breakfast, a salad or the *plat du jour* (dish of the day), or dip into a *fondue au crémant* (Champagne fondue). Dining is self-service on trays and alfresco in summer.

Mikado   SUSHI $
(Map p49; Rue de l'Ancien-Port 9; sushi per piece Sfr2.50, mains Sfr6-10; ⊙10am-6.30pm Tue-Fri, to 6pm Sat) If it's authenticity, speed and tasty fast food on a red lacquered tray you want, this quick-eat Japanese delicatessen with tables to sit down at hits the spot a treat.

Les 5 Portes   BISTRO $
(Map p49; ☑022 731 84 38; Rue de Zürich 5; mains Sfr15-20; ⊙6pm-2am Mon, from 9am Tue-Fri, from 5pm Sat, from 11am Sun) The Five Doors – with indeed five doors – is a fashionable Pâquis port of call that successfully embraces the whole gamut of moods and moments – eating and drinking. Its Sunday brunch is a particularly buzzing affair.

Crêperie des Pâquis   CREPERIE $
(Map p49; www.creperie-paquis.com; Rue de Zürich 6; crepes Sfr6-15, brunch Sfr14; ⊙7am-midnight Mon-Fri, from 9am Sat, 9am-11pm Sun) Sweet and savoury, this laidback address with seating both in and out to suit every taste cooks up fabulous crepes with a mindboggling choice of fillings. Don't miss the daily specials chalked on the board.

Le Plantamour   DELI $
(Map p49; www.leplantamour.ch; Rue Philippe Plantamour 37; mains Sfr8-10; ⊙7am-8pm Mon-Sat) No place cooks up a tastier, healthier lunch for a thoroughly affordable Sfr15 than this modern delicatessen with great terrace in a former baker's shop – grab a pre-packaged salad or hot dish at the counter and take a seat outside.

Piment Vert   ASIAN $
(Map p42; www.pimentvert.ch; Place De-Grenus 4; mains Sfr15-20; ⊙lunch & dinner Mon-Fri, lunch Sat) Fast, fresh and trendy sums up Green Chilli Pepper, a hybrid Indian–Sri Lankan bar serving fabulous sushi.

VIEILLE VILLE

Eateries crowd Place du Bourg-de-Four, Geneva's oldest square, in the lovely Old Town. Otherwise, head down the hill towards the river and Place du Molard, packed with tables and chairs for much of the year.

Chez Ma Cousine   CHICKEN $
(Map p42; www.chezmacousine.ch; Place du Bourg-de-Four 6; mains Sfr14.90; ⊙11am-10pm) 'On y mange du poulet' (we eat chicken) is the strapline of this student institution, which appeals for one good reason – generously handsome and homely portions of chicken (half a chicken to be precise),

Pâquis

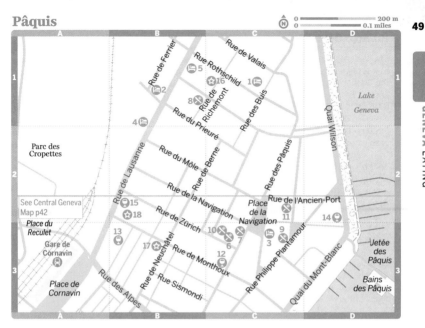

Pâquis

Sleeping
1 Auberge de Jeunesse.............................C1
2 City Hostel B1
3 Edelweiss C3
4 Hôtel Auteuil...B1
5 Hôtel Jade..B1

Eating
6 Crêperie des Pâquis C3
7 Gelatomania C3
8 Le Comptoir..B1
9 Le Plantamour...C3
10 Les 5 Portes..C3

11 Mikado C2

Drinking
12 Café des Arts C3
13 Olé Olé...B3
14 Paillote D2
15 Scandale..B2

Entertainment
16 K-36...C1
17 Le Palais Mascotte.................................B3
18 Milk Klub...B2

potatoes and salad at a price that can't possibly break the bank.

RIVE & EAUX-VIVES

TOP CHOICE **L'Adresse** MODERN **$$**

(Map p42; 022 736 32 32; www.ladresse.ch; Rue du 31 Décembre 32; mains Sfr25-35; lunch & dinner Tue-Sat) Something of an urban loft with a fabulous rooftop terrace, it is all hip at The Address, a hybrid fashion/lifestyle boutique and contemporary bistro at home in renovated artists' workshops. The Genevan address for lunch (great value Sfr18 lunch),

brunch or Saturday slunch, a cross between tea and dinner (ie a casual evening 'meal' of cold and warm nibbles, both sweet and savoury, shared between friends over a drink or three around 5pm).

TOP CHOICE **L'Entrecôte** STEAKHOUSE **$$**

(Map p42; 022 310 60 04; www.relaisentrecote .fr; Rue du Rhône 49; steak & chips Sfr46; lunch & dinner) Key vocabulary to know before entering this timeless classic where everyone eats the same dish is *à point* (medium), *bien cuit* (well done) and *saignant* (rare). Indeed

DON'T MISS

ISLAND DINING

Oh, how the menu lives up to its setting at this unique address on an island in the Rhône. At home in Geneva's old market hall, **Brasserie des Halles de l'Île** (Map p42; ☏022 311 08 88; www.brasserie deshallesdelile.ch; Place de l'Île 1; mains Sfr20-50, brunch Sfr25; ⊙lunch & dinner) is an industrial-style venue that cooks up an entertaining cocktail of after-work aperitifs with music, after-dark DJs and a fabulous seasonal fare of fresh veggies and regional products (look for the Appellation d'Origine Contrôllée products flagged on the menu) cooked 101 ways. In early summer try the *frappé de petits pois glacé à la menthe* (cold pea and mint soup) and spring lamb. Get here early to snag the best seat in the house: a tiny terrace hanging over the water; otherwise go for a seat in the courtyard or cavernous main hall.

the place doesn't bother with menus. Sit down, say how you like your steak cooked and wait for it to arrive – two handsome servings of it (!) pre-empted by a green salad and accompanied by perfectly crisp, skinny fries. Should you have room at the end of it all, the desserts are justly raved about.

Wasabi   JAPANESE $
(www.wasabisushi.ch; sushi per piece Sfr2.50-4; ⊙10am-10pm Mon-Sat) Rue du Vieux Collège (Map p42; Rue du Vieux Collège 4); Bd Helvétique (Map p42; Bd Helvétique 32) Crisp, clean and boldly minimal in design, this quick-eat sushi bar with a handful of outlets around town buzzes with city slickers at lunchtime. Grab a plate of sushi, maki, temaki or other perfectly packaged Japanese bite at the self-service counter, pay and fight for a seat.

PLAINPALAIS

TOP CHOICE **Omnibus**   EUROPEAN $$
(Map p42; ☏022 321 44 45; www.omnibus-cafe .ch; Rue de la Coulouvrenière 23; mains Sfr30-45; ⊙11.30am-midnight Mon-Fri, from 6pm Sat) Don't be fooled or deterred by the graffiti-plastered facade of this Rhône-side, industrial-inspired bar, cafe and restaurant. Inside a maze of retro, romantic and eclectic rooms seduces on first sight. Particularly popular is the back room (reservations essential) with

carpet wall hangings and lots of lace. Its business card is a recycled bus ticket.

Au Grütli   INTERNATIONAL $$
(Map p42; ☏022 328 98 68; www.cafedugrutli .ch; Rue du Général Dufour 16; mains Sfr25-40; ⊙8am-midnight Mon-Thu, to 1am Fri, 4pm-1am Sat, to 11pm Sun) As much cafe as cutting-edge restaurant, this industrial-styled eating space with mezzanine seating is razor sharp. Indonesian lamb, moussaka, scallops pan-fried with ginger and citrus fruits or Provençal-inspired chicken are among its many international flavours.

Café des Bains   MODERN EUROPEAN $$
(Map p42; ☏022 321 57 98; www.cafedesbains.com; Rue des Bains 26; mains Sfr25-50; ⊙lunch Mon-Fri, dinner Tue-Sat) No brand labels, beautiful objects and an eye for design are trademarks of this fusion restaurant opposite the contemporary art museum where Genevan beauties flock. Several dishes woo vegetarians.

Le Pain Quotidien   CAFE $
(tarts & salads Sfr15-30; ⊙7am-6pm Mon-Fri, from 8am Sat & Sun) Bd Helvétique (Map p42; Bd Helvétique 21); Bd Georges-Favon (Map p42; Bd Georges-Favon 32) Choose from a heap of breakfasts (continental, English etc) and brunches (classic, countryside etc) at this twinset of countrified daytime spots.

AROUND GENEVA

Part of the art of dining well in Geneva is to trade in the urban for a good old-fashioned *auberge* (inn) in a surrounding village. 'Country chic' best sums up the experience, which sees well-to-do Genevan families flee the city for Sunday lunch *à la campagne*.

TOP CHOICE **Auberge Communale de Presinge**   ITALIAN $$
(☏022 759 11 35; Rte de La-Louvière, Presinge; mains Sfr25-50; ⊙lunch & dinner Fri-Tue) No village inn could be simpler from the outside nor more staunchly old-world cosy-as-home inside. Around for years, it changed hands a couple of years back – but the 100% authentic and delicious Italian cuisine remains. In season, don't miss its truffles. Take tram 12 from Rive to Graveson then bus C to Presinge (Sfr3, 35 minutes, every half-hour).

Auberge du Cheval Blanc   EUROPEAN $$
(☏022 750 13 43; Rte des Carres 44, Meinier; mains Sfr20-30; ⊙lunch & dinner Tue-Sat) Another flowery address with an idyllic

outside terrace, the White Horse ticks all the right boxes when it comes to 'quintessential country inn'. Its steak tartars and risottos are renowned. Bus A links Rue Pierre Fatio in Rive on the left bank with Meinier (Sfr3, 30 minutes, every half-hour).

Le Lion d'Or   EUROPEAN $$$

(☑022 736 44 32; www.liondor.ch; Place Gautier 5, Cologny; mains Sfr28-90, tasting menu Sfr190; ☺lunch & dinner Mon-Fri) Not so much a village as Geneva's poshest, priciest 'burb where business suits flock for lunch Monday to Friday. Mouth-watering fish and seafood creations honour a fine wine list and the less endowed can dine cheap(er) in the neighbouring bistro with flowery garden. Take bus A from Rue Pierre Fatio to Cologny (Sfr3, 15 minutes, every half-hour).

🍷 Drinking

Summer ushers in dozens of scenic spots around the city where you can lounge in the sun over a mint tea or mojito – Place du Bourg-de-Four in the Old Town and Carouge are strewn with seasonal cafe terraces.

On the water's edge try left-bank kiosk **Paillote** (Map p49; Quai du Mont-Blanc 30; ☺to midnight) or right-bank **Le Paradis** (Map p42; www.terrasse-paradis; Quai Turrettini; ☺9am-9pm) with its Rhône-side striped deck-chairs.

TOP CHOICE ⟩ Yvette de Marseille   BAR

(Map p42; Rue Henri Blanvalet 13; ☺11am-late Tue-Fri, from 5pm Sat) No bar begs the question 'what's in the name?' more than this buzzy drinking hole where you almost forget you're in Geneva. Refreshingly urban and edgy with a choice of tapas chalked on the board, it occupies a mechanic's workshop once owned by Yvette. Note the garage door, the trap door in the floor where cars were repaired and the street number 13 (aka the departmental number of the Bouches-du-Rhône department, home to Marseille).

Scandale   LOUNGE

(Map p49; www.scandale.ch; Rue de Lausanne 24; ☺11am-2am Tue-Fri, from 5pm Sat) Retro '50s furnishings in a cavernous interior bedecked with a fine choice of eclectic seating, including drop-dead-comfy sofas, ensure this lounge bar is never empty. Grub ranges from fully fledged mains (between Sfr24 and Sfr31) to snack-attack salads and bruschetta, and happenings include art exhibitions, Saturday-night DJs and bands.

Boulevard du Vin   WINE BAR

(Map p42; www.boulevard-du-vin.ch; Bd Georges-Favon 3; ☺11am-11pm Mon-Fri; 🛜) Wine sluggers will enjoy this excellent wine shop that doubles as a wine bar with its weekly *dégustation* (tasting) sessions. Food platters add a gastronomic dimension.

Marius   WINE BAR

(Place des Augustins 9; ☺5.30pm-1.30am Mon-Fri) This doll's house–sized *bar à vin* – an old butcher's shop hence the tiles and ceramic – is a great little spot in Plainpalais to discover both regional and natural wines. Pair your chosen vintage with a cold meat, cheese or antipasti platter for the perfect gourmet experience.

Café des Arts   CAFE

(Map p49; Rue des Pâquis 15; ☺11am-2am Mon-Fri, 8am-2am Sat & Sun; 🛜) As much a place to drink as a daytime cafe, this Pâquis hangout lures a local crowd with its Parisian-style terrace and artsy interior. Food-wise, think meal-sized salads, designer sandwiches and a great-value lunchtime *plat du jour* (Sfr19).

Le Cheval Blanc   BAR

(www.lechevalblanc.ch; Place de l'Octroi 15; ☺11.30am-late Tue-Sat, from 10.30am Sun; 🛜)

TOP THREE ICE CREAM SHOPS

Count on paying Sfr3.50 and Sfr6 respectively for a one- and two-ball cornet at these Geneva institutions.

Gelateria Arlecchino (Map p42; Rue du 31 Décembre 1) Left-bank choice a stone's throw from the Jet d'Eau: chocolate and ginger, honey, peanut cream and mango are among the 40 flavours at this lip-licking parlour.

Gelatomania (Map p49; Rue des Pâquis 25) Right-bank choice: a constant queue loiters outside this shop where ice-cream maniacs wrap their tongues around carrot, orange and lemon, cucumber and mint, lime and basil and other exotic flavours.

Mövenpick (Map p42; Place du Rhône) The lux address to sit down riverside and drool over the creamiest of Swiss ice cream topped with whipped cream, hot chocolate sauce and other decadent treats.

TOP FIVE PICNIC SPOTS

With mountains of fine views to pick from, Geneva is prime picnicking terrain for those reluctant to pay too much to eat. Grab a salt-studded pretzel filled with whatever you fancy (between Sfr3.80 and Sfr7) from takeaway kiosk **Maison du Bretzel** (Map p42; Rue de la Croix d'Or 4) and head for one of these favourite picnic spots.

» In the contemplative shade of Henry Moore's voluptuous sculpture *Reclining Figure: Arch Leg* (1973) in the quiet park opposite the Musée d'Art et d'Histoire (p41).

» Behind the cathedral on Terrasse Agrippa d'Aubigné, a tree-shaded park with benches, a sand pit and see-saw for kids, and a fine rooftop and cathedral view.

» On the shingly beach lacing the Pâquis pier, across from the entrance of Les Bains de Pâquis.

» On a bench on Quai du Mont-Blanc with a majestic view of Mont Blanc (sunny days only).

» On the world's longest bench (126m long) on chestnut-tree-lined Promenade de la Treille in Parc des Bastions (p41).

The White Horse is a real Carouge favourite. Quaff cocktails and tapas – some of Geneva's best – at the pink neon-lit bar upstairs, then head downstairs to its club and concert space, **Le Box** (www.lebox.ch).

Le Chat Noir BAR
(www.chatnoir.ch; Rue Vautier 13; ⊙6pm-late Tue-Sat) Another hot address in Carouge packed most nights, the Black Cat is a lovely spot for an after-work aperitif – small selection of tapas to nibble on – and, come dark, live music.

Bar du Nord BAR
(www.bardunord.ch; Rue Ancienne 66; ⊙5pm-2am Thu & Fri, from 9am Sat) One of Carouge's oldest drinking holes, this trendy young bar is stuffed with Bauhaus-inspired furniture, the best whisky selection in town and a small courtyard terrace out back. The best nights are Thursdays and Fridays with good music and DJs, lots of it electro music.

La Bretelle BAR
(Map p42; Rue des Étuves 17; ⊙6pm-2am) Little has changed since the 1970s when this legendary bar opened. The Strap is just the place to tune in to a good old accordion-accompanied French chanson.

Olé Olé BAR
(Map p49; Rue de Fribourg 11; ⊙10am-2am Mon-Fri, from 5pm Sat) Industrial tapas bar with giant street-facing windows and a bar lit by naked bulbs near the train station.

Soleil Rouge WINE BAR
(Map p42; www.soleilrouge.ch; Bd Hélvetique 32; ⊙5-10pm Mon, 10am-11pm Tue & Wed, 10am-midnight Thu-Sat) The address to sip Spanish wine on bar stools outside or in. Watch for flamenco, jazz and other great live sounds from 7pm some evenings.

☆ Entertainment

Buy theatre, concert and gig tickets at **Fnac Billetterie Spectacles** (Map p42; ☐022 816 12 30; Rue de Rive 16), or at box offices inside the Tourist Office and Information de la Ville de Genève.

Le Palais Mascotte CABARET BAR
(Map p49; ☐022 741 33 33; www.palaismascotte.ch; Rue de Berne 43; ⊙6pm-5am Mon-Sat) Closed for years before it reopened as a cabaret bar much-loved by the over 30-somethings, this mythical Pâquis address buzzes with atmosphere. Dine on the top floor, enjoy cabaret on the ground floor and take in concerts followed by '90s dance music in the basement nightclub, **Zazou Club** (⊙11pm-5am Fri & Sat).

Orange Cinéma CINEMA
(Off Map p39; www.orangecinema.ch; Quai Gustave Ador; ⊙Jul & Aug) Glorious summertime open-air cinema with a screen set up on the lakeside.

Bâtiment des Forces Motrices PERFORMING ARTS
(Map p42; www.bfm.ch; Place des Volontaires 4) Geneva's one-time riverside pumping station (1886) is now a striking space for classical music concerts, dance and other performing arts.

Grand Théâtre de Genève OPERA
(Map p42; www.geneveopera.ch; Bd du Théâtre 11) The city's lovely theatre hosts ballet too.

Victoria Hall
MUSIC

(Map p42; ☑022 418 35 00; www.ville-geneve.ch /vh; Rue du Général Dufour 14) Concert hall for the Orchestre de la Suisse Romande and Orchestre de Chambre de Genève; September to April it holds lovely Sunday afternoon concerts starting at 5pm.

Milk Klub
NIGHTCLUB

(Map p49; www.milk-klub.ch; Rue de Monthoux 60; ☺10pm-5am Thu, from 11pm Fri & Sat) The latest club to hit Pâquis pounds out techno, house and loadsa live sets.

SIP
NIGHTCLUB

(Map p42; www.lasip.ch; Rue des Vieux Grenadiers 10; ☺10pm-late Thu-Sat) Find Soul Influenced Product blasting out a wholly mainstream sound in a 1860s Plainpalais factory.

X-S Club
NIGHTCLUB

(Map p42; www.xsclub.ch; Rue de la Pelisserie 19; ☺11.30pm-5am Fri & Sat) Old Town venue for mixed bag of house, pop, R&B, reggae and disco for clubbers aged over 25.

K-36
GAY & LESBIAN

(Map p49; www.k36.ch; Rue de Richemont 9; ☺10pm-5am Thu-Sat) Crazy techno, house, soul and deep techno are the mixed sounds DJs spin at this tiny nocturnal hangout in Pâquis.

🛍 Shopping

Designer shopping is wedged between Rue du Rhône and Rue de Rive. Globus (Map p42; Rue du Rhône 50) and Manor (Map p42; Rue de Cornavin) are the main department stores. Grand-Rue in the Old Town and Carouge (p45) boasts artsy boutiques, or try Geneva's twice-weekly flea market (Plaine de Plainpalais; ☺Wed & Sat).

Maison des Couleurs Fines
ARTS & CRAFTS

(Map p42; www.carandache.ch; Place du Bourg-de-Four 8; ☺2-6.30pm Mon, 10am-6.30pm Tue-Fri, to 5pm Sat) Beautifully designed boutique packed with a rainbow of pencils, pastels, paints and crayons crafted by Swiss colour maker Caran d'Aché in Geneva since 1915.

Le Village
CONCEPT STORE

(Map p42; www.village-geneve.ch; Place des Eaux-Vives 9; ☺9.30am-7pm Mon-Fri, to 6pm Sat) Fashion, design, toys, jewellery, art and homewares cram this hip concept store.

Collection Privée
HOMEWARES

(Map p42; Place De-Grenus 8; ☺11.30am-6.30pm Tue-Fri, to 5pm Sat) Art-deco lamps, furniture and other 20th-century curiosities.

La 3ème Main
HOMEWARES

(Map p42; www.la3main.ch; Rue Verdaine 18) Designer items and accessories for the traveller and at home.

ℹ Information

Medical Services

Hôpital Universitaires de Genève (☑022 372 81 20; www.hug-ge.ch; Rue Micheli du Crest 24; ☺24hr)

SOS Médecins à Domicile (☑022 748 49 50; www.sos-medecins.ch) Home/hotel doctor calls.

Tourist Information

Information de la Ville de Genève (☑022 311 99 70; www.ville-ge.ch; Pont de la Machine; ☺noon-6pm Mon, from 9am Tue-Fri, 10am-5pm Sat) City information point; ticketing desk for cultural events.

Tourist Office (☑022 909 70 00; www.geneve -tourisme.ch; Rue du Mont-Blanc 18; ☺10am-6pm Mon, from 9am Tue-Sat, 10am-4pm Sun)

Websites

City of Geneva (www.ville-ge.ch)

Glocals (www.glocals.com) Globals and locals share their tips.

Lonely Planet (www.lonelyplanet.com /switzerland/geneva)

ℹ Getting There & Away

Air

Aéroport International de Genève (☑0900 571 500; www.gva.ch) 4km from the town centre.

Boat

CGN (Compagnie Générale de Navigation; ☑0848 811 848; www.cgn.ch) runs steamers from Jardin Anglais and Pâquis to other villages on Lake Geneva, including Nyon (adult return Sfr35.40, 1¼ hours) and Lausanne (Sfr60, 3½ hours). Those aged six to 16 pay half-price and kids under six years sail for free. A one-day Carte Journalière CGN pass (Sfr60) allows unlimited boat travel. Eurail and Swiss travel passes (p366) are also valid.

Bus

Bus Station (☑0900 320 320, 022 732 02 30; www.coach-station.com; Place Dorcière) International buses.

Train

Trains to/from Annecy, Chamonix and other destinations in neighbouring France use **Gare des Eaux-Vives** (Av de la Gare des Eaux-Vives). More-or-less-hourly connections run from Geneva's central train station **Gare de Cornavin** (Place de Cornavin) to most Swiss towns:

INTO FRANCE

Day trips from Geneva boil down to a boat trip on the lake, a mountain foray or a meander into neighbouring France.

Oh-so-pretty French **Yvoire** (population 840), a medieval walled village 27km northeast of Geneva on the lake's southern shore, is *the* spot where everybody from diplomats to rubbish collectors dust off the urban cobwebs on weekend afternoons. The postcard village with fishing port and fairy-tale chateau (closed to visitors) has cobbled pedestrian streets to stroll, flowers galore to admire and a restored medieval vegetable garden to visit: **Jardin des Cinq Sens** (Garden of the Five Senses; www.jardin5sens.net; adult/child €10/5.50; ⊙10am-7pm Apr-Sep, 11am-6pm May & Sep, to 5pm Oct). Main street Grande Rue is lined with souvenir shops, touristy boutiques and several restaurants including recommended **Le Bateau Ivre** (☑+33 4 50 72 81 84; www.le-bateau-ivre.fr; Grande Rue; mains €10-20; ⊙lunch & dinner). The **CGN** (p46) boat ride from Geneva's Jardin Anglais or Pâquis (adult return Sfr45.40, 1¾ hours) and the STT Train Tours' (p46) lakeside motor in an old-fashioned bus (adult return Sfr49, daily May to Oct), departing from Place du Rhône, is very much part of the trip. For further information, head to http://shop.lonelyplanet.com to purchase a downloadable PDF of the France chapter from Lonely Planet's *Western Europe* guide.

Quaint Swiss **Hermance**, 16km northeast of Geneva on the French–Swiss border, lures a more discerning crowd with its narrow streets lined with medieval houses, the odd pricey art gallery and the legendary **Auberge d'Hermance** (☑022 751 13 68; www.hotel-hermance.ch; Rue du Midi 12; lunch menu Sfr42, dinner menu Sfr76-120, mains Sfr22-56; ⊙lunch & dinner), one of the region's most prestigious culinary addresses, where chickens are baked whole and served in a magical herbal salt crust. TPG bus E (Sfr4.80, 30 minutes, at least hourly) links Hermance with Rue Pierre Fatio in Rive on Geneva's left bank. Or take a seasonal CGN steamer (one hour).

Geneva Airport (Sfr2.20, six minutes)
Lausanne (Sfr21, 30 minutes)
Bern (Sfr47, 1¾ hours)
Zürich (Sfr82, 2¾ hours)

ⓘ Getting Around

To/From the Airport

The quickest way to and from Geneva Airport is by train. A metered taxi costs between Sfr30 and Sfr50.

Bicycle

Genève Roule (www.geneveroule.ch; 4hr free, then per hr Sfr2) Jetée des Pâquis (Jetée des Pâquis; ⊙9am-7pm May-Oct); Place de Montbrillant (Place de Montbrillant 17; ⊙8am-9pm May-Oct); Place du Rhône (Place du Rhône; ⊙9am-7pm May-Oct) Bike hire requiring proof of ID and Sfr20 cash deposit.

Boat

Yellow shuttle boats called Les Mouettes ('Seagulls') cross the lake every 10 minutes between 7.30am and 6pm. Public-transport tickets from by machines at boat bays are valid.

Car & Motorcycle

Much of the Old Town is off limits to cars and street parking elsewhere can be hard to snag; try public car parks **Parking du Mont Blanc** (Quai du Général-Guisan; per 25 min Sfr1) or **Parking Plaine de Plainpalais** (Av du Mail; per 30 min Sfr1). Before leaving the car park, validate your parking ticket in an orange TPG machine to get one hour's free travel for two people on city buses, trams and boats.

Public Transport

Tickets for buses, trolley buses and trams run by **TPG** (www.tpg.ch) are sold at dispensers at stops and through the **TPG office** (Place de la Gare; ⊙7am-7pm Mon-Fri, 7am-6pm Sat) inside the main train station. A one-hour ticket for multiple rides in the city costs Sfr3 and a ticket valid for three stops in 30 minutes is Sfr2.

Taxi

Pick one up in front of the train station, book online (www.taxi-phone.ch) or call ☑022 331 41 33.

Lake Geneva & Vaud

POP 708,200 / AREA 3212 SQ KM / LANGUAGE FRENCH

Best Places to Eat

» Café St-Pierre (p63)

» Auberge de Dully (p67)

» Hôtel-Restaurant de la Plage (p67)

» Le Chalet (p77)

» Café Romand (p63)

Best Places to Stay

» Hôtel Beau-Rivage Palace (p62)

» Le Léman (p66)

» Auberge de Dully (p67)

» Auberge du Raisin (p68)

» Riviera Lodge (p70)

Why Go?

East of Geneva, Western Europe's biggest lake stretches like a giant liquid mirror between the French-speaking canton of Vaud (north) and France (south). Known to most as Lake Geneva, French speakers call it Lac Léman. Lined by the elegant student city of Lausanne and a phalanx of pretty smaller towns, the Swiss side of the lake presents the marvellous emerald spectacle of tightly ranked vineyards spreading in terraces up the steep hillsides of the Lavaux area – the source of some very fine tipples. Down by the water's edge, the lake is laced by fairy-tale châteaux, luxurious manor houses and modest beaches, often backed by peaceful woodland. In the mild climate around Montreux, palm trees grow.

Then there are the mountains, the magnificent Alpes Vaudoises (Vaud Alps), in the southeast corner of the canton where hikers play in spring and summer, skiers and boarders in winter.

When to Go

Spring and early autumn, with their warm days and riot of beautiful, perfectly manicured flower beds, are perfect seasons to visit. The lakeside flower trail from Montreux to Château de Chillon and Morges' tulip festival make the month of May a must. July ushers in a twinset of world-renowned fests – Montreux' international jazz get-together and Nyon's multifaceted Paléo music fest – while more boats than ever zig-zag around the lake. Swimming in the lake is most pleasant in July and August, while December translates as skiing in the Vaud Alps.

History

As early as 58 BC, Caesar's troops had penetrated what is now southwestern Switzerland. In the following centuries a mix of Celtic tribes and Romans lived a life of peace and prosperity. Aventicum (today Avenches) became the capital, with as many as 20,000 inhabitants, and numerous other towns (such as Lausanne) flourished.

By the 4th century AD, the Romans had largely pulled out of Switzerland and Germanic tribes stepped into the vacuum. Christianised Burgundians arrived in the southwest in the 5th century and picked

Lake Geneva & Vaud Highlights

❶ Meander the **Flower Path** from Montreux to Château de Chillon (p72)

❷ Lap up lovely Lausanne, lingering in its unique **bridge bars** (p65) and the covered staircase linking Old Town to the cathedral and **Musée de l'Art Brut** (p59)

❸ Walk, drink wine and swoon over vines in Unesco-listed **Lavaux** (p68)

❹ Tackle the region's twinset of **high peaks** (p70) for a 360-degree vista of terraced vineyards, quaint villages and Europe's largest lake

❺ Dance to rock, pop and jazz on the lakeshore at world-class music fests **Montreux Jazz** (p72) and **Paléo** (p66) in Nyon

❻ Be hauled up the mountain in a cogwheel railway to **Rochers de Naye** (p74) and drop in on Santa or the marmots

❼ Ski the striking Vaud Alps from **Les Diablerets** (p75)

❽ Discover two thousand years of wine-making in **Aigle** (p76)

SAVVY TRAVEL

The seven-day **Lake Geneva-Alps Regional Pass** (adult/child Sfr119/59) provides free bus and train travel in the Lake Geneva region for three days in seven and half-price travel on the other four days. It also gives 50% off CGN boat services and 25% off some cable cars (including up to Les Diablerets glacier). The five-day version with two days of free travel costs Sfr99 for adults and Sfr49 for children. Holders of one of the various Swiss rail passes (see p367) receive a 20% discount off the Regional Pass.

up the Vulgar Latin tongue that was the precursor to French. Absorbed by the Franks, Vaud became part of the Holy Roman Empire in 1032.

In the 12th and 13th centuries, the dukes of Savoy slowly assumed control of Vaud and embarked on the construction of impressive lakeside castles.

The canton of Bern appreciatively took over those castles when, in 1536, it declared war on Savoy and seized Vaud. Despite the tendency of Bern's bailiffs to siphon off local wealth, by the 18th century Lausanne (the area's capital) was a thriving centre.

The French Revolution in 1789 had heavy consequences for its neighbours. On the urging of Fréderic-César de la Harpe, leader of the Liberal Party, the Directorate in Paris placed Vaud under its protection in December 1797. In 1803, Napoleon imposed the Act of Mediation that created the Swiss Confederation, in which Vaud, with Lausanne as its capital, became one of six separate cantons.

The second half of the 19th century was one of industrial development and comparative prosperity for the canton, later slowed by the turbulence of the two world wars.

LAUSANNE

POP 128,200 / ELEV 495M

This hilly city (pronounced loh-*san*), Switzerland's fifth largest, enjoys a blessed lakeside location. The medieval centre is dominated by a grand Gothic cathedral and, among the museums, its unusual Art Brut collection stands out. Throughout the year Lausanne's citizens are treated to a busy arts calendar, while the lake drums up a plethora of activities on and out the water. Strolling the lakeshore in picturesque Ouchy (once a lakeside village in its own right long since enveloped by the city) is a pure pleasure, as is a meander day or night around Flon, an area of formerly derelict warehouses rejuvenated as a hip urban centre with a cinema complex, art galleries and trendy shops, and restaurants and bars galore.

Dynamic Lausanne is a happening place: contemporary home to Switzerland's highest court (the Federal Tribunal), the International Olympic Committee (IOC), a high-flying international business school (IMD), Tetra Pak and the multinational tobacco conglomerate Philip Morris.

History

The Romans first set up camp on the lake at Vidy, a key halt on the route from Italy to Gaul that came to be known as Lousonna. In the face of an invasion by the Alemanni in the 4th century AD, Lousonna's inhabitants fled to the hilly inland site that became the heart of medieval Lausanne.

In 1529, Guillaume Farel, one of Calvin's followers, arrived in town preaching the Reformation but it wasn't until Bern occupied the city (not a shot was fired) seven years later that the Catholics were obliged to take notice.

From the 18th century, Lausanne exerted a fascination over writers and free-thinkers, attracting such characters as Voltaire, Dickens, Byron and TS Eliot (who wrote *The Waste Land* here).

TEN O'CLOCK AND ALL IS WELL!

Some habits die hard. From the height of the cathedral bell tower, a *guet* (night watchman) still calls out the hours into the night, from 10pm to 2am. Four times after the striking of the hour he calls out: *'C'est le guet! Il a sonné dix, il a sonné dix!'* (Here's the night watchman! It's 10 o'clock, it's 10 o'clock!). In earlier times this was a more serious business, as the *guet* kept a look-out for fires around the town and other dangers. He was also charged with making sure the townsfolk were well behaved and the streets quiet during the solemn moments of church services.

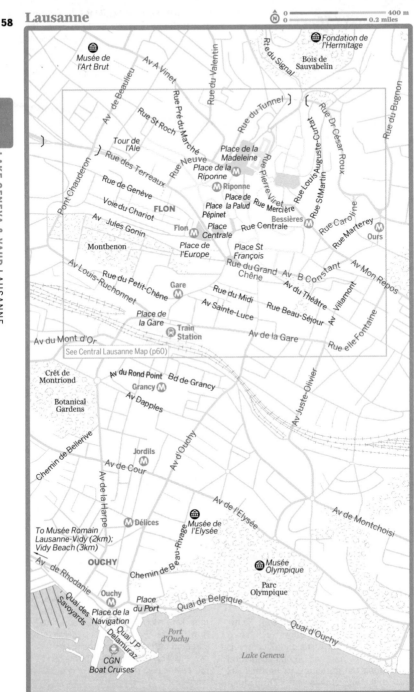

LAKE GENEVA & VAUD LAUSANNE

N   0   400 m
    0   0.2 miles

Fondation de
l'Hermitage

Musée de
l'Art Brut

Av A Vinet

Rue du Valentin

Rte du Signal

Bois de
Sauvabelin

Rue du Bugnon

Av de Beaulieu

Rue St Roch

Rue Pré du Marché

Rue du Tunnel

Rue Louis Auguste-Curtat

Rue Dr César Roux

Tour de
l'Ale

Rue des Terreaux

Rue Neuve

Place de la
Madeleine

Rue Pierre Viret

Rue St Martin

Rue de Genève

Place de la
Riponne

Riponne

Pont Chauderon

Voie du Chariot

FLON

Place de
la Palud

Rue Mercière

Bessières

Rue Caroline

Av Jules Gonin

Flon

Pépinet

Rue Centrale

Rue Marterey

Ours

Montbenon

Place
Centrale

Place de
l'Europe

Place St
François

Av Louis-Ruchonnet

Rue du Petit-Chêne

Gare

Rue du Grand
Chêne

Av B Constant

Av Mon Repos

Av du Théâtre

Av Villamont

Rue du Midi

Rue Beau-Séjour

Av Sainte-Luce

Place de
la Gare

Train
Station

Av de la Gare

Rue elle Fontaine

Av du Mont d'Or

See Central Lausanne Map (p60)

Crêt de
Montriond

Av du Rond Point

Bd de Grancy

Grancy

Botanical
Gardens

Av Dapples

Av Juste-Olivier

Chemin de Bellerive

Jordils

Av d'Ouchy

Av de Cour

Av de la Harpe

Av de Montchoisi

Délices

Av de l'Elysée

To Musée Romain
Lausanne-Vidy (2km);
Vidy Beach (3km)

Musée de
l'Elysée

OUCHY

Av - de Rhodanie

Chemin de Beau-Rivage

Musée
Olympique

Parc
Olympique

Quai des Savoyards

Ouchy

Place de la
Navigation

Place
du Port

Quai de Belgique

Quai d'Ouchy

Quai J P
Delamuraz

Port
d'Ouchy

Lake Geneva

CGN
Boat Cruises

Lausanne, with only 10,000 inhabitants, became the capital of the canton of Vaud in 1803. The city began to take on its present appearance in the latter half of the 19th century when rapid development occurred.

⊙ Sights & Activities

Downhill by the water in Ouchy, Lake Geneva (Lac Léman) is the source of many a sporting opportunity, including sailing, windsurfing, waterskiing and swimming; the tourist office has details. Seasonal stands in front of Château d'Ouchy rent pedalos and kayaks, and cycling and rollerblading are big on the silky-smooth waterfront promenades. West of Ouchy, Vidy Beach, backed by thick woods and parklands, is one of Lake Geneva's few sandy beaches.

Place de la Palud   SQUARE
(Map p60) In the heart of the Vieille Ville (Old Town), this 9th-century medieval market square – pretty as a picture – was originally bogland. For five centuries it has been home to the city government, now housed in the 17th-century Hôtel de Ville (town hall). A fountain pierces one end of the square, presided over by a brightly painted column topped by the allegorical figure of Justice, clutching scales and dressed in blue. What you see is a copy – the 1585 original is in the Musée Historique de Lausanne.

From the eastern end of the square, bear left along Rue Mercière to pick up Escaliers du Marché, a timber-canopied staircase with tiled roof that hikes up the hill to Rue Pierre Viret and beyond to the cathedral.

Cathédrale de Notre Dame   CATHEDRAL
(Map p60; Place de la Cathédrale; ⊙7am-7pm Mon-Fri, 8am-7pm Sat & Sun, to 5.30pm Sep-Mar) Lausanne's Gothic cathedral, Switzerland's finest, stands proudly at the heart of the Old Town. Raised in the 12th and 13th centuries on the site of earlier, humbler churches, it lacks the lightness of French Gothic buildings but is remarkable nonetheless. Pope Gregory X, in the presence of Rudolph of Habsburg (the Holy Roman Emperor) and an impressive following of European cardinals and bishops, consecrated the church in 1275.

Although touched up in parts in following centuries (notably the main facade, which was added to the original to protect the interior against ferocious winds), the cathedral remains largely as it [...] striking element is the elabora[...] on the south flank of the church (w[...] usually for Christian churches, was lo[...] main way in). The painted statuary dep[...] Christ in splendour, the coronation of th[...] Virgin Mary, the Apostles and other Bible scenes. Free 40-minute guided tours run July through September.

MUDAC   ART MUSEUM
(Map p60; www.mudac.ch; Place de la Cathédrale 6; adult/child Sfr10/free, 1st Sat of month free; ⊙11am-6pm, closed Mon Sep-Jun) Otherwise known as the Musée de Design et d'Arts Appliqués Contemporains, this ode to modern design and applied arts hosts some intriguing temporary exhibitions. Find it directly opposite the cathedral entrance.

Musée Historique de
Lausanne   HISTORY MUSEUM
(Map p60; Place de la Cathédrale 4; adult/child Sfr8/free, 1st Sat of month free; ⊙11am-6pm Tue-Thu, to 5pm Fri-Sun) Until the 15th century, the city's bishops resided in this lovely manor across from the cathedral (after which it became a jail, then a court, then a hospital). Since 1918 it has devoted itself to evoking Lausanne's heritage through paintings, drawing, stamps, musical instruments, silverware and so on. Don't miss the film featuring Lausanne in 1638.

Musée Olympique   MUSEUM
(Map p58; Olympic Museum; www.museum.olympic.org; Quai d'Ouchy 1) Lausanne's Musée Olympique is easily the city's most lavish and a real must for sports buffs (and kids). Under renovation until late 2013, its usual home is a gorgeous building atop a tiered landscaped garden in the Parc Olympique. Inside, there is a fabulous rooftop restaurant with champion lake view and a state-of-the-art museum recounting the Olympic story from its inception to present-day through video, archival film and other multimedia. While renovation work is carried out (from April 2012 until late 2013), a fraction of the museum collection can be viewed in a belle époque CGN paddle steamer moored in front of the museum and park.

Musée de l'Art Brut   ART MUSEUM
(Map p58; www.artbrut.ch; Av des Bergières 11-13; adult/child Sfr10/free, 1st Sat of month free; ⊙11am-6pm Tue-Sun) Brut means crude or rough, and that's what you get in this extraordinary gallery, put together by French

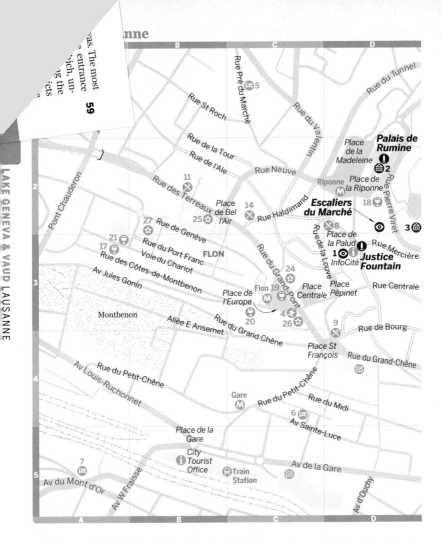

…vas. The most
… entrance
…ich, un-
… the
…cts

59

artist Jean Dubuffet in the 1970s in what was a late 18th-century country mansion. Exhibits offer a striking variety and, at times, surprising technical capacity and an often inspirational view of the world. View sculptures made out of broken plates and discarded rags, faces made out of shells, sculptures in wood, paintings, sketches and much more. Take bus 2 or 3 to the Beaulieu stop.

Musée Cantonal des Beaux Arts ART MUSEUM
(Map p60; www.mcba.ch; Place de la Riponne 6; adult/child Sfr10/free, 1st Sat of month free; ⊙11am-6pm Tue-Thu, to 5pm Fri-Sun) Palais de Rumine,

the neo-Renaissance pile (1904) where the Treaty of Lausanne finalising the break-up of the Ottoman Empire after WWI was signed in 1923, safeguards the city's fine arts museum. Works by Swiss and foreign artists, ranging from Ancient Egyptian art to Cubism, are displayed, but the core of the collection is made up of works by landscape painter Louis Ducros (1748–1810). During temporary exhibitions (many with free admission), the permanent collection is often closed.

The same ticket covers admission to the palace's other smaller museums covering natural history, zoology (with the longest –

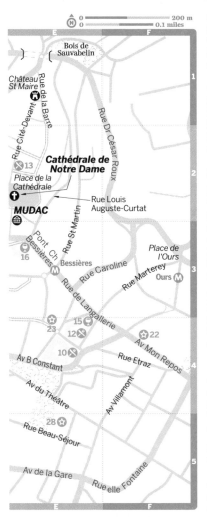

of the Bois de Sauvabelin on Lausanne's northern fringe. A delight to stroll, the wooded park has a lake and contemporary 35m-tall wooden watchtower with spiral staircase to climb (great views).

Prolong the inspiring cultural foray with a guided visit and Sunday brunch (Sfr62) in the foundation's lovely cafe-bistro **L'Esquisse** or, on Friday or Saturday evening, take the guided visit at 6.45pm followed by dinner (Sfr89). Both require advance reservations by telephone .

Bus 16 links Bois de Sauvabelin with Place St François in town.

Musée Romain Lausanne-Vidy   HISTORY MUSEUM
(www.lausanne.ch/mrv; Chemin du Bois de Vaux 24; adult/child Sfr8/free, 1st Sat of month free; ⊙11am-6pm Tue-Sun) Check out the remains of Roman Lousonna and the adjacent museum, housed on the site of a Roman villa, with its modest collection of ancient artefacts.

Musée de l'Elysée   MUSEUM
(Map p58; www.elysee.ch; Av de l'Elysée 18; adult/child Sfr8/free, 1st Sat of month free; ⊙11am-6pm) Excellent temporary photography expositions.

🕝 Tours

CGN   BOAT
(Map p58; ☑0848 811 848; www.cgn.ch; Quai du Mont Blanc) Lake cruises, some aboard beautiful belle époque steamers, by Lake Geneva's main boat operator.

Les Baladeurs   BICYCLE
(www.lesbaladeurs.ch; Place de l'Europe 1b; free; ⊙Jun-Sep) Bring your own bike or borrow one for free from bike-tour organisers Lausanne Roule (p65). Cycling tours are themed and cater to all levels.

Guides d'Accueil MDA   WALKING
(☑021 320 12 61; www.lausanne.ch/visites; adult/child Sfr10/free; ⊙10am & 2.30pm Mon-Sat May-Sep) Walking tours of the Old Town, departing from in front of the Hôtel de Ville (town hall) on Place de la Palud. Themed tours for up to five people on demand.

✹✹ Festivals & Events

Festival de la Cité   CULTURAL
(www.festivalcite.ch) This week-long festival in the first week of July sets the city's streets and squares humming with visual arts and open-air performances of dance, theatre and circus.

almost 6m – stuffed great white shark on show in the world), geology, coins, archaeology and history. The latter gives an overview of the history of the Vaud canton from the Stone Age to modern times.

Fondation de l'Hermitage   ART MUSEUM
(Map p58; ☑021 320 50 01; www.fondation-hermitage.ch; Route du Signal 2; adult/child Sfr18/free; ⊙10am-6pm Tue-Wed & Fri-Sun, to 9pm Thu) Quite extraordinary, high-calibre temporary art expositions – Van Gogh and the like – grace this beautiful 19th-century residence ensnared in the green peace and tranquillity

Central Lausanne

Swiss National Day   EVENT
On 1 August, hire a pedalo early evening and sit back to enjoy fireworks on the lake around 10pm.

🛏 Sleeping

In return for the Sfr2.50 tourist tax added to your hotel bill, you get a Lausanne Transport Card, which gives you unlimited use of public transport for the duration of your stay; pick it up when you check in to your accommodation.

TOP CHOICE **Hôtel Beau-Rivage Palace**   HISTORIC HOTEL **$$$**
(☏021 613 33 33; www.beau-rivage-palace.ch; Place du Port 17-19; d from Sfr550; P❄@🗢🏊) Easily the most stunningly located hotel in town and one of only two five-star options, this luxury lakeside address is suitably sumptuous. A beautifully maintained early 19th-century mansion set in immaculate grounds, it tempts with magnificent lake and Alp views, a spa, two bars and a trio of upmarket terrace restaurants (including a gastronomic temple headed by Anne-Sophie Pic, the only French female chef with three Michelin stars).

Hôtel du Marché   HOTEL **$**
(Map p60; ☏021 647 99 00; www.hoteldumarche-lausanne.ch; Rue Pré du Marché 42; s/d/tr/q Sfr114/133/156/179, s/d with shared bathroom Sfr81/132; P@🗢) For a friendly welcome at a price that won't break the bank, check into this address, a five-minute walk from the Old Town. No-frills rooms are clean and spacious, and the kettle with complimentary tea and coffee in each room is a great touch. On sunny days loll on the tiny tree-shaded terrace out front.

Lausanne GuestHouse   HOSTEL **$**
(Map p60; ☏021 601 80 00; www.lausanne-guesthouse.ch; Chemin des Épinettes 4; dm Sfr38.40, s/d with shared bathroom Sfr88/106, s/d/q with bathroom Sfr97/126/146; P@🗢) An attractive mansion converted into quality backpacking accommodation near the train station. Many rooms have lake views and you can hang out in the garden or terrace. Parking is Sfr10 and there's room to leave your bikes. Some of the building's energy is solar.

Hôtel Elite   BOUTIQUE HOTEL **$$**
(Map p60; ☏021 320 23 61; www.elite-lausanne.ch; Av Sainte Luce 1; s/d/q Sfr155/215/400; P❄@🗢) The same family has run this lovely apricot townhouse of a hotel for three generations. A couple of sun-loungers and tables dot the pretty handkerchief-sized garden and inside at reception it's all fresh flower arrangements and soft background music. Rooms

on the 4th floor look at the lake and the best have a balcony too.

Hôtel du Port
HOTEL $

(☏021 612 04 44; www.hotel-du-port.ch; Place du Port 5; s/d Sfr160/195; ☏) A perfect location in Ouchy, just back from the lake, makes this a good choice. The better doubles look out across the lake (Sfr20 extra) and are spacious (about 20 sq metres). Up on the 3rd floor are some lovely junior suites.

Camping de Vidy
CAMPGROUND $

(☏021 622 50 00; www.campinglausannevidy .ch; Chemin du Camping 3; adult/tent/car Sfr8.50/ 16/3.50; P @ ☏) This camping ground open year-round is just west of the Vidy sports complex, on the lake. Take bus 2 from Place St François and get off at Bois de Vaux then walk underneath the freeway towards the lake. Throw a few francs on top for electricity, rubbish collection and local tourist tax.

✖ Eating

Lausanne's dining scene is laidback. Its best addresses are stylish cafe-bars and bistros that morph, come dusk, into great places for drinks and tapas.

TOP CHOICE Café St-Pierre
MODERN EUROPEAN $

(Map p60; ☏021 326 36 36; www.cafesaintpierre .ch; Place Benjamin Constant 1; mains Sfr20-30, tapas Sfr6-8.50, brunch Sfr10-23; ⏱7.30am-midnight Tue & Wed, to 1am Thu, to 2am Fri, 11am-2am Sat, 11am-6pm Sun; ☏) The very fact that every table is snapped up by noon while waiters buzz between tables and a constantly ringing telephone says it all – this hip cafe-bar rocks! Its interior is retro, trendy and relaxed, and the cuisine is contemporary European – quiches, pasta, salad, fish and so on at lunchtime, creative tapas from 7pm and brunch on weekends. Reserve in advance.

Café Romand
SWISS $

(Map p60; ☏021 312 63 75; Place St François 2; mains Sfr20-30; ⏱11am-11pm Mon-Sat) Hidden in an unpromising looking arcade, this Lausanne legend dating to 1951 is a welcome blast from the past. Everyone from bankers to punks pours into the broad, somewhat sombre dining area littered with timber tables to gorge on fondue, *cervelle au beurre noir* (brains in black butter), tripe, *pied de porc* (pork trotters) and other feisty traditional dishes. Simple omelettes (between Sfr11 and Sfr14), sandwiches (Sfr7) and soups

ensure all tastes are catered for. The kitchen operates all day, rare for this town.

Café de Grancy
MODERN EUROPEAN $

(☏021 616 86 66; www.cafédegrancy.ch; Av du Rond Point 1; mains Sfr20-35, brunch Sfr29; ⏱8am-midnight Mon-Fri, from 10am Sat & Sun; ☏) Something of an iconic address where Lausanne's hip and trendy have long hung out, this place just to the south of the train station has floppy lounges in the front and a tempting restaurant out back. The cuisine is creative – think mozzarella and black tomato salad, smoked clams with peaches and an unbeatable value *pâte du jour* (daily pasta dish) served with salad or soup. Wednesday is fondue day, the first Tuesday of the month is always themed and the weekend ushers in brunch.

Holy Cow
BURGERS $

(Map p60; burgers Sfr20-30) Rue des Terreaux (Rue des Terreaux 10; ⏱11am-11pm Mon-Sat); Rue Marterey (Rue Marterey 1-3; ⏱11.30am-4.30pm Mon-Sat) Its strapline 'Gourmet Burger Company' is no exaggeration: Pick from beef or chicken dressed in dozens of different creative toppings – cranberry and camembert, chorizo with honey and hot chilli. Grab an artisanal beer, sit yourself at a long shared wooden table, give a nod to the B&W photo of Jean-Pierre the farmer and Michel the baker, and wait for your burger to arrive in a straw basket. The smaller branch on Rue Marterey has just one table (otherwise, takeaway).

Café de l'Hôtel de Ville
CAFE $

(Map p60; Place de la Palud 10; salads Sfr13-25; ⏱11.30am-6pm Tue, 9am-11.30pm Wed, from 11.30pm Thu & Fri, 9am-7pm Sat) Old-fashioned salads are the trademark of this retro cafe *à l'ancienne* in the Old Town. Ingredients are locally sourced, often organic, and give a nod to the past in the shape of dried figs and grains. Marie's salad with gooey, oven-baked *tomme* (a type of cheese) is to die for.

L'Éléphant Blanc
MODERN EUROPEAN $$

(Map p60; ☏021 312 64 89; Rue Cité-Devant 4; mains Sfr25-40; ⏱lunch & dinner Tue-Sat) One of just a handful of restaurants behind the cathedral, the White Elephant is one of Lausanne's finest dines. But what's staggeringly good value is its lunchtime *plat du jour* (dish of the day, Sfr18.50) and creative meal-sized salads (between Sfr15 and Sfr25).

Mövenpick ICE CREAM $

(Map p60; Rue Haldimand 20; ice cream Sfr4-10.80; ☺6.30am-8.30pm Mon-Fri, from 8am Sat, from 9am Sun) Pure sweet-toothed decadence is what this design-driven ice-cream gallery by Zürich ice-cream maker Mövenpick is all about.

🍷 Drinking

Eating venues Café St-Pierre and Café de Grancy are stylish drinking addresses too, packed with a hip crowd year-round. If it is sand and a deckchair you're after, head for seasonal **Flon Plage** (Map p60; www .flonplage;ch; Voie du Chariot; ☺May-Sep) – yes, a beach – on the vast central square in the rejuvenated warehouse quarter of Flon.

Bleu Lézard BAR

(Map p60; www.bleu-lezard.ch; Rue Enning 10; ☺7am-late Mon-Fri, from 8am Sat, from 9.30am Sun; ☎) This corner bar and bistro with royal blue paintwork and wicker chairs to match is an old favourite that never loses its appeal – day or night (or at weekends for brunch). Lunch (mains cost between Sfr25 and Sfr30), including some great veggie options, is served until 3pm and when your feet wanna' jive to a live band, there's the basement music club La Cave.

Great Escape PUB

(Map p60; www.the-great.ch; Rue de la Madeleine 18; ☺11.30am-late Mon-Fri, from 10am Sat, from 1.30pm Sun) Everyone knows the Great Escape, a busy student pub with pub grub – great burgers – and an enviable terrace overlooking Place de la Madeleine. From the square, walk up staircase Escaliers de l'Université and turn right at the top.

Pur LOUNGE

(Map p60; www.pur-flon.ch; Port-Franc 17; ☺8am-late Mon-Fri, from 9pm Sat & Sun) Chic, white and overtly hip, this minimalist lounge bar and restaurant with great big terrace is perfect for an aperitif in the evening sun. Find it in Flon.

Luna CAFE

(Map p60; www.cafe-luna.ch; Place de l'Europe 7; ☺7am-late Mon-Fri, from 11am Sat) Modern design bar with weekend DJs and prime real-estate pavement terrace (albeit traffic noisy) on Place de l'Europe.

☆ Entertainment

Lausanne is among Switzerland's busier night-time cities; look for free listings mag *What's Up* (www.whatsupmag.ch) in bars.

Live Music

Hybrid bar-bistro Bleu Lézard is another great live music venue.

Le Romandie LIVE MUSIC

(Map p60; www.leromandie.ch; Place de l'Europe 1a; ☺10pm-4am Tue & Thu-Sat) Lausanne's premier rock club resides in a post-industrial location within the great stone arches of the Grand Pont. Expect live rock, garage and even punk, followed by DJ sounds in a similar vein.

Le Bourg BAR

(Map p60; www.lebourg.ch; Rue de Bourg 51; ☺7pm-late Wed-Sat) What was once an old cinema is now one of central Lausanne's happening drink dens and live music stages. Squeeze upstairs past the bar for a good view down to the stage area. Music can be anything from Afro sounds to local jam sessions.

Les Docks CONCERT VENUE

(www.lesdocks.ch; Av de Sévelin 34; ☺7pm-2am Tue-Sun) Gigs embracing every sound, be it hip-hop, heavy metal or reggae.

Chorus JAZZ

(Map p60; www.chorus.ch; Av Mon Repos 3; ☺8.30pm-2am Thu-Sat) Top jazz venue.

Nightclubs

MAD CLUB

(Map p60; www.mad.ch; Rue de Genève 23; ☺11pm-4am Thu-Sun) With five floors of entertainment, four dance floors and a restaurant called Bedroom, MAD (Moulin á Danse de Lausanne, Lausanne Dance Mill) is a crazy sort of place. Music can be anything, dress code is snappy and 3rd-floor Zapoff Gallery is only for clubbers aged over 28. Sunday (free admission) is gay night.

Le D! Club MUSIC, CLUB

(Map p60; www.dclub.ch; Place Centrale; ☺11pm-5am Wed-Sat) DJs spin house in all its latest sub-forms at this heaving club. Take the stairs down from Rue du Grand Pont and turn right before descending all the way into Place Centrale.

Le Loft CLUB

(Map p60; www.loftclub.ch; Place de Bel-Air 1; ☺10.30pm-5am Thu, from 11pm Fri & Sat) This predominantly red bar and dance space one level down the stairs of the Tour Bel-Air building is a hot late-night option for every urban sound.

DON'T MISS

BRIDGE BARS

When there's a bridge, there's a bar. At least that's how it works in artsy Lausanne where the monumental arches of its bridges shelter the city's most happening summertime bars.

First port of call for that all-essential, after-work drink in the warm evening sun and last port of call before bed is **Les Arches** (Map p60; www.lesarches .ch; Place de L'Europe; ⊙11am-late Mon-Sat, 1pm-midnight Sun), occupying four arches of Lausanne's magnificent Grand Pont (built between 1839 and 1940) above Place de l'Europe. Mid-evening, the crowd moves to **Bourg Plage** (Map p60; www.le-bourg.ch; ⊙2pm-midnight), with pool table, table football, palm trees and deckchairs in one old stone arch of Pont Charles Bessières (built between 1908 and 1910); steps lead up to it from Rue Centrale and down to it from opposite MUDAC on Rue Pierre Veret.

Theatre, Opera & Classical Music

Lausanne has a rich theatre scene; find program listings in local paper *24 Heures*.

Opéra de Lausanne OPERA
(Map p60; www.opera-lausanne.ch; Av du Théâtre 12; ⊙Sep-May) Opera classics alternate with classical and world music concerts.

Théâtre de Beaulieu THEATRE
(www.beaulieu.org; Av des Bergières 10) Venue for opera, ballet, theatre and performances by Lausanne's chamber orchestra and renowned Rudra Béjart Ballet company (www .bejart-rudra.ch).

❶ Information

Canton de Vaud Tourist Office (☎021 613 26 26; www.lake-geneva-region.ch; Av d'Ouchy 60; ⊙8am-5.30pm Mon-Fri)
City Tourist Office (☎021 613 73 73; www .lausanne-tourisme.ch) Train Station (Place de la Gare 9; ⊙9am-7pm); Ouchy (Place de la Navigation 4; ⊙9am-7pm Apr-Sep, to 6pm Oct-Mar)
InfoCité (☎021 315 25 55; www.lausanne.ch /infocite; Place de la Palud 2; ⊙7.45am-noon & 1.15-5pm Mon-Fri)

❶ Getting There & Away

Boat
CGN (☎0848 811 848; www.cgn.ch; Quai JP Delamuraz 17) runs passenger boats (no car ferries) from Ouchy to destinations around Lake Geneva. To hop and off as you please, buy a one-day pass (Sfr60) covering unlimited lake travel. Destinations include the following:
Montreux (Sfr21.10, 1½ hours, up to six daily)
Vevey (Sfr16.50, one hour, up to seven daily)
Nyon (Sfr27.20, 2¼ hours, up to four daily)
Geneva (Sfr60, 3½ to four hours, up to three daily)
Yvoire, France (Sfr28.60, 45 minutes, up to four daily)

Train
You can travel by train to and from the following:
Geneva (Sfr28, 30 to 50 minutes, up to six hourly)
Geneva Airport (Sfr25, 50 minutes, up to four hourly).
Bern (Sfr31, 70 minutes, one or two an hour)

❶ Getting Around

Bicycle
Pick up a bike to pedal around town from **Lausanne Roule** (www.lausanneroule.ch; Place de l'Europe 1b; 4/24hr free/Sfr6; ⊙8am-6pm), under the arches of the Grand Pont. Leave a Sfr20 deposit and ID; reserve in advance online.

Car & Motorcycle
Parking in central Lausanne is a headache. In blue zones you can park for free (one-hour limit) with a time disk. Most white zones are meter parking. Costs vary but max out around Sfr2 an hour with a strict two-hour limit. The lower end of Av des Bains is one of the few streets with free parking.

Public Transport
Buses and trolley buses service most destinations; the m2 Métro line (single trip/day pass Sfr1.90/Sfr8.60) connects the lake (Ouchy) with the train station (Gare) and the Flon district.

AROUND LAUSANNE

Head out of Lausanne, and wine tasting and gastronomy suddenly become key dominators, be it westbound along La Côte (the Coast) or eastbound towards jazz-famed Montreux along a lakeshore pretty enough to be called the Swiss Riviera (p69). For dedicated wine buffs, a tasting pilgrimage to Lavaux's Unesco-protected vineyards is essential.

La Côte

Fantasy castles, imposing palaces and immaculately maintained medieval villages sprinkle the Coast – the luxuriant lakeshore between Lausanne and Geneva where more than half of the Canton de Vaud's wine, mostly white, is produced.

The train line from Geneva follows the course of the lake here, but arriving by a CGN paddle steamer – try to catch one of the beautifully restored belle époque ones – is definitely the more romantic option.

MORGES & AROUND

A pleasant walk west of Lausanne, about 6km from Ouchy, brings you to **St Sulpice**, a semi-suburban settlement whose jewel is the Romanesque church of the same name by the lake. A handful of restaurants are well placed to alleviate hunger. Take bus 2 from Place St François and change to bus 30 at Bourdonette.

Some 12km west of Lausanne, the first town of importance is the wine-growing village of **Morges** (www.morges-tourisme.ch). Dominating its bijou port is the squat, four-turreted 13th-century **Château de Morges** (Place du Port; adult/child Sfr10/3; ☺10am-5pm Jul & Aug, 10am-noon & 1.30-5pm Tue-Fri, 1.30-7pm Sat & Sun Mar-Jun & Sep-Nov), built by Savoy duke Louis in 1286 and home to four military-inspired museums today. Don't miss the 10,000 toy soldiers on parade in the **Musée de la Figurine Historique**.

But the real highlight is the town's **Fête de la Tulipe** (tulip festival), mid-April to mid-May, which turns lakeside Parc de l'Indépendence into a vivid sea of colour as thousands upon thousands of tulips, dahlias and hyacinths burst into bloom. Views across the lake from the park to the snowy hulk of Mont Blanc on the other side of the water are equally impressive.

Continuing towards Nyon is the old village of **St Prex**, which has centuries-old mansions bursting with the colour of creeping ivy and flower boxes; and bijou **Rolle**

MOVING ON?

For tips, recommendations and reviews, head to http://shop.lonelyplanet.com to purchase a downloadable PDF of the France chapter from Lonely Planet's *Western Europe* guide.

with its photogenic 13th-century castle on the shore (closed).

🛏 Sleeping & Eating

Le Léman   B&B **$$**
(☏021 801 33 51; www.lelemangourmand.ch; Rue de Louis-de-Savoie 61, Morges; s/d Sfr180/220) Sleeping *au bord du Lac Léman* (on the shores on Lake Geneva) brings with it a certain inevitable romance and there is no better address to watch bobbing sailing boats from bed than this stylish **restaurant** (mains Sfr30-60; ☺lunch & dinner Tue-Sat, lunch Sun) and *chambre d'hôte* (B&B) on the waterfront in Morges. Rooms would look right at home in the pages of *Elle Décor* and are themed – medieval, nautical, rustic or romantic – and dining – lots of lake fish and seafood – is beneath trees across from Morges' tiny picturesque port on Quai du Mont Blanc. How dreamy is that?

TOP CHOICE Metropolis Café   BISTRO, BAR **$$**
(☏021 803 23 33; Rue de Louis-de-Savoie 20, Morges; mains Sfr20-30; ☺7am-midnight Mon-Wed, to 1am Thu, to 2am Fri & Sat, 9am-midnight Sun; 🛜) Dine beneath turquoise parasols around an age-old stone fountain outside or on vintage flexi-plastic inside at this hybrid eating-drinking space that morphs into a happening bar after dark. Food is fusion and creative – lots of wok dishes, tiger prawns and world spices alongside pasta and risotto. Mains cleverly come in two sizes, the daily special (between Sfr17 and Sfr19) is great value and the Sunday brunch is fabulous.

Café de Balzac   CAFE **$**
(www.balzac.ch; Rue de Louis-de-Savoie 37, Morges; mains Sfr20-25, hot chocolate Sfr6.20-7.20; ☺8.15am-6.30pm Tue-Wed & Fri, to 10pm Thu, 9.15am-5pm Sat, from 11am Sun) Lovers of exotic hot chocolate, teas and salads with an Asian twist should make a pilgrimage to this gorgeous old-fashioned cafe, one block back from the lakeside promenade in the heart of the old centre.

NYON
POP 18,800

Of Roman origin but with a partly Celtic name (the 'on' comes from *dunon,* which means fortified enclosure), Nyon is a pretty lake town pierced at its hilltop-heart by the gleaming white turrets of a fairy-tale château and a tasty lunch address. Somewhat incongruously, the town's six-day **Paléo** (www.paleo.ch) in July, is a key date in Europe's summer festival diary. Switzerland's biggest outdoor international music extravaganza, it lures rock, pop, jazz and folk music lovers from far and wide.

Nyon's castle was started in the 12th century, modified 400 years later and now houses the town's **Musée Historique et des Porcelaines** (History & Porcelain Museum; Place du Château; adult/child Sfr8/free; ☉10am-5pm Tue-Sun) and, in its old stone cellars, the **Caveau des Vignerons** (Place du Château; ☉2-9pm Fri & Sat, 11am-8pm Sun) where you can taste different Nyon wines by local producers. Pay Sfr20 to sample two reds and two whites with a plate of *charcuterie* (cold meats). Don't miss the sweeping view of Lake Geneva from the château terrace. Nearby, in a 1st-century basilica, the **Musée Romain** (Roman Museum; www.mrn.ch; Rue Maupertuis; adult/child Sfr8/free, 1st Sun of month free; ☉10am-5pm Tue-Sun) evokes Nyon's Roman beginnings as Colonia Iulia Equestris.

About 2km north, the 18th-century mansion of **Château de Prangins** (www.chateaudeprangins.ch; château/museum Sfr10/8; ☉10am-5pm Tue-Sun) houses a branch of the **Musée National Suisse** covering Swiss history from 1730 to 1920. Or simply opt for a stroll through the château's perfect French-style gardens with *potager* (vegetable garden) and historical trail.

🛏 Sleeping & Eating

La Barcarolle   HOTEL $$
(☏022 365 78 78; www.labarcarolle.ch; Route de Promenthoux, Prangins; s/d from Sfr270/330; P ❄@ ⬛🏊) If serious lakeside self-pampering is what you're after, this luxury hotel-restaurant is the address. Rooms are four-star, spacious and comfortable, and pander to every need. But it is the magnificent views of the lake, Alps and Mont Blanc – from some room balconies and the bar, restaurant and manicured grounds – that make this place extra special.

TOP CHOICE **L'Auberge du Château**   ITALIAN $$
(☏022 361 00 32; www.aubergeduchateau.ch; Place du Château 8, Nyon; mains Sfr30-50; ☉8am-midnight, closed Sun Oct-Apr) No restaurant and cafe terrace has such a stunning view as this. Filling the pretty pedestrian square in front of Nyon's pretty château, tables look out on the Sleeping Beauty towers and lake beyond. Cuisine is Italian and creative – *taglierini* with figs, simple homemade gnocchi and authentic pizza cooked in a wood-fired oven.

SLEEP EAT WINE COUNTRY

For an authentic taste of viticultural life look no further than **Auberge de Dully** (☏021 824 11 49; www.aubergedully.ch; s/d Sfr130/170; ☉dinner Mon, Thu & Fri, lunch & dinner Sat & Sun, closed mid-Jul–mid-Aug; P🏊), a country inn 8km north of Nyon in the heart of the La Côte vineyards. Cosy, traditional and timeless, it is a real 'Sunday lunch' address. Eight hotel rooms peep on to the village square or the lake and Alps beyond, while downstairs in the kitchen a simple cuisine is lovingly prepared from local produce. Chicken and *gigot d'agneau* (leg of lamb) roasts for hours on a spit inside – a house speciality since 1964 – while hungry diners on the shady terrace outside admire the vegetable patch and vines over a glass of chilled wine. Advance reservations essential.

TOP CHOICE **Hôtel-Restaurant de la Plage**   SWISS $$
(☏022 364 10 35; www.hoteldelaplage.info; Chemin de la Falaise, Gland; s/d with shower Sfr90/130, s/d with shower & toilet Sfr120/150; mains Sfr30; ☉lunch & dinner Tue-Sun Feb–mid-Dec) Approaching from the road, this seemingly insignificant lakeside hotel 7km north of Nyon prompts a double-take to make sure you have the right address. But step one foot inside, note the heaving dining room and crowd waiting on the terrace for a table, and there is no doubting it: this is one of the best places on Lake Geneva for *filets de perche* (perch fillets) pan-fried in an absolutely divine, buttery, herby secret-recipe sauce. Fries and a green salad are included and unless you specify otherwise, you automatically get two (very large!) servings.

COPPET
POP 2759

Midway between Nyon and Geneva, this tightly packed medieval village is a delight to meander through with its lakeside warren of hotels and restaurants bowing at the feet of hilltop, 18th-century **Château de Coppet** (www.coppet.ch; adult/child Sfr8/4; ☉2-6pm Easter-Oct). The rose-coloured stately home belonged to the wily Jacques Necker, Louis XVI's banker and finance minister. The

LAKE LEGEND

Punters pour across the water from France for it... the extraordinary Italian-style ice cream, that is, at Nyon's legendary ice-cream boutique **Gelateria Venezia** (Rue de Rive 44; ice cream Sfr3-7; ⊘11am-7pm) and the frozen yoghurt at **La Yogourterie** (Rue de Rive 48; frozen yoghurt Sfr5-7; ⊘1-7pm) around the corner. Ice-cream flavours tease tastebuds with creative combos such as banana split, After Eight and lots of chocolate variations; while the frozen yoghurt comes *au naturel* from the Moléson cheese dairy near Gruyères (p87) before being flavoured with fruit in Nyon. Daniele Dona of Venetian descent is the culinary force behind the legendary twinset of boutiques. From Nyon's CGN boat jetty on the lakefront, walk one block inland and look for the line outside the door.

pile, sumptuously furnished in Louis XVI style, became home to Necker's daughter, Madame de Staël, after she was exiled from Paris by Napoleon. In her literary salons here she entertained the likes of Edward Gibbon and Lord Byron.

Lavaux Wine Region

East of Lausanne, the mesmerising serried ranks of lush, pea-green vineyards that stagger up the steep terraced slopes above Lake Geneva form the Lavaux wine region – sufficiently magnificent to be a Unesco World Heritage Site. One-fifth of the Canton de Vaud's wine is produced on these steep, gravity-defying slopes.

Walking between vines and wine tasting on weekends in local *caveaux* (wine cellars) are key reasons to explore the string of 14 villages beaded along this fertile and wealthy, 40km stretch of shore. The tourist office in Montreux (p73) is the best place to pick up detailed information and maps.

LUTRY
POP 9300

This captivating medieval village, just 4km east of Lausanne, was founded in the 11th century by French monks. Its central **Église de St Martin et St Clément** was built in

the early 13th century and there's a modest **château** a short way north. Stroll along the pretty waterfront and the slightly twee main street lined with art galleries, antique stores, the occasional cafe and wine cellar **Caveau des Vignerons** (Grand Rue 23; ⊘5-9pm Tue-Fri, 11am-2pm & 5-9pm Sat) where you can taste wine by different local producers. The two main wine types are Calamin and Dézaley, and most of the whites (about three-quarters of all production) are made with the Chasselas grape.

Lutry celebrates its annual wine harvest with parades and tastings during the last weekend in September. The region's oldest wine-producing estate, **Domaine du Daley** (☑021 791 15 94; www.daley.ch; Chemin des Moines, Lutry; ⊘tasting 9am-8pm with appointment, min 4 people), has been a memorable *dégustation* (tasting) address since the 14th century.

The pace quickens after dark thanks to a couple of much-loved live-music venues: jazz club **Caveau du Singe Vert** (Green Monkey Cellar; www.jazzausingevert.ch; Grand Rue 41; admission Sfr30) and **Esprit Frappeur** (www.espritfrappeur.ch; Villa Mégroz, Ave du Grand Pont 20; admission Sfr30), known for *chansons françaises* (French classics).

Bus 9 links Lutry with Place St François in Lausanne. From Lutry a beautiful 5.5km **walking trail** winds east through vines and the tiny hamlets of **Le Châtelard** and **Aran** to the larger wine-making villages of **Grandvaux** and **Riex**. For staggering vine and lake views, hike up to **La Conversion** (3.8km) above Lutry and continue on the high trail to Grandvaux (4km).

CULLY
POP 1800

Lakeside Cully, 5km east of Lutry, is a lovely village for a waterfront meander and early evening mingle with *vignerons* (winegrowers) in its **Caveau des Vignerons** (www.caveau-cully.ch; Place d'Armes 16; ⊘5-9pm Thu-Sun Apr-Oct). Alternatively hike along the well-signposted walking trail uphill to the inland villages of **Riex** and **Epesses**, and have a tipple in a wine cellar there instead before looping back to Cully (4.4km).

Overnight at Cully's **Auberge du Raisin** (☑021 799 21 31; www.aubergeduraisin.ch; Place de l'Hôtel de Ville 1; s/d Sfr180/220; mains Sfr44-68; **P@⊛**), a grand old hotel-restaurant that started taking in weary travellers in the 15th century. Lavaux' finest dining establishment, its rotisserie cooks up a grand meaty meal and a great creative take on fish dishes. Advance reservations are essential.

RIVAZ TO CHARDONNE

TOP CHOICE **Lavaux Vinorama** (021 946 31 31; www.lavaux-vinorama.ch; Route du Lac 2; tasting Sfr13-20; ⊙10.30am-8.30pm Mon-Sat, to 7pm Sun, closed Mon & Tue Nov-Jun), a thoroughly modern tasting and discovery centre 5km east of Cully in Rivaz, is the best place to discover the various appellations of the Lavaux vineyards. Opened in 2010, it sits in a designer bunker at the foot of a terraced vineyard by the lake and is fronted by a shimmering 15m-long bay window decorated with 6000 metallic pixels inspired by the veins of a vine leaf. Inside, a film evokes a year in the life of a wine-growing family and, in the state-of-the-art **Espace Dégustation**, you can sample dozens of different wines. Pick from white and red 'packages' or go the full hog and tuck into a platter of local cheese and cold meats (between Sfr10 and Sfr20) with your own personal pick of eight whites and eight reds.

TOP CHOICE **Villa Le Lac** (www.villalelac.ch; Route de Lavaux 21; adult/child Sfr10/6; ⊙9am-noon Mon, 1.30-5pm Wed Apr-Oct), 4.5km east in Corseaux – and another must for architectural buffs – continues the contrete building theme. Built by Le Corbusier between 1923 and 1924, the little white lakefront house with a functional rooftop sun deck and ribbon windows is the perfect overture to the world-renowned Swiss architect's better-known work. His mother lived here from 1924 until 1960, followed by his brother un-til 1973. Each summer the house now hosts a different exhibition.

From the village of Chardonne, uphill from Corseaux, there are some lovely **walking trails**, including up the kid-easy **Boucle Chardonne** (2.8km) that starts and ends at the funicular station here and swoops in a circle through pea-green vines.

SWISS RIVIERA

Stretching east to Villeneuve, the Swiss Riviera rivals its French counterpart as a magnet for the rich and famous. Magnificent belle époque paddle steamers cruise the lake as they did in 1910, treating passengers to a banquet of gourmet views and paparazzi glimpses of otherwise-hidden lakeside properties, while panoramic trains saunter from the shore to Swiss-perfect mountain scenes. All this barely an hour's drive from Alpine ski spots, in a climate so mild that palm trees and other subtropical flora flourish.

Vevey

POP 18,600

Lakeside Vevey exudes a certain understated swankiness with its tiny but perfect Old Town, lakeside central square and promenades, stylish dining, unusual museums and treasure trove of unusual little boutiques made for post-lunch browsing. Don't miss Charlie Chaplin (p71), signature 'little tramp' cane in hand, posing on the waterfront.

ℹ️ SCENIC TRIPS

The panorama of Lavaux vineyards staggering down to the lake is particularly fine from the back of a boat. CGN's **Fabuleux Vignobles de Lavaux** (Fabulous Lavaux Vineyards) cruise departs from Lausanne twice daily (five times daily between mid-June and mid-September), with stops in Lutry, Cully, Vevey, Chillon and Montreux. A Lausanne–Montreux adult return ticket costs Sfr42.20.

Another fun and easy way to lose yourself in green vines and blue lake views is aboard the **Lavaux Express** (www.lavauxexpress.ch; adult/child Sfr13/5; ⊙Tue-Sun Apr-Oct), a tractor-pulled tourist train that chugs through Lavaux' vineyards and villages. Pick from two routes: Lutry CGN boat pier up to the wine-growing villages of Aran and Grandvaux (one hour return trip), or Cully pier to Riex, Espesses and Dézaley (1¼ hour). In season, the **Train de Caveaux** (adult/child Sfr20/5; ⊙6.30pm Fri-Sun May–mid-Sep) chugs from Lutry to a local *caveau* (cellar bar) where you can taste wine. The **Lavaux Panoramic** (www.lavaux-panoramic.ch; ⊙Sat & Sun Apr-Oct) is another train that runs twice-daily circular vineyard trips from Chexbres to St-Saphorin (adult/child Sfr12/6, one hour) and Chardonne (adult/child Sfr15/7.50, 1½ hours).

DON'T MISS

TWIN PEAKS

Hike up the region's twinset of high peaks for an astonishing, 360-degree bird's-eye vista of Lavaux' unique terraced vineyards tumbling down the hillside into the lake.

Mont Pélerin (1080m) Ride the Golden Pass funicular from Vevey (Sfr14, 11 minutes, every 20 minutes) through vineyards to the village of **Chardonne**, and onwards to the foot of Lavaux' highest mountain. View not yet good enough? From the top funicular station, hike to the satellite-dish-encrusted communication tower near the top of Mont Pélerin and hop in the **Ascenseur Plein Ciel** (www.mob.ch; adult/child Sfr5/3; ◷9am-6pm Apr-Oct), a glass lift on the side of the tower that whisks you another 65m higher to a viewing platform. The panorama of Lavaux, Lake Geneva, the Jura and the Alps is out of this world.

Tour de Gourze (924m) Built in the 12th century as a defence tower, this old stone structure peers out on Lavaux vines, Lake Geneva, the Vaud and the Jura beyond from its hilltop perch. Best of all is the simple wooden chalet-restaurant here, **Café-Restaurant de la Tour de Gourze** (☏021 781 14 74; ◷lunch & dinner Tue-Sat, to 9pm Sun), that cooks up traditional fondues, cheesy *croûtes* (toasted bread smothered in melted cheese) and heavenly sweet meringues with Gruyère double cream. Hike or take the narrow lane that twists up to the tower from **Chexbres**.

◉ Sights

TOP CHOICE **Alimentarium**   MUSEUM

(☏021 924 41 11; www.alimentarium.ch; Quai Perdonnet; adult/child Sfr12/free, audioguide Sfr6; ◷10am-5pm Tue-Fri, to 6pm Sat & Sun) Nestlé's headquarters have been in Vevey since 1814, hence its presence in the form of this museum dedicated to nutrition and all things edible, past and present. Boring it is not. Its displays are clearly meant to entertain as well as inform, starting with the gigantic silver fork that sticks out of the water in front of the lakeside mansion (great picnic spot thanks to the handful of wooden chairs screwed into the rocks here on the lakeshore). Particularly fun are its **cooking workshops** for both adults and kids, **guided tours** (Sfr6 plus museum ticket; ◷11am-noon last Sun of month) for families and **gardening workshops** (Sfr30; ◷9-11am 1st Sun of month). End with a healthy lunch in the **museum restaurant** (lunch Sfr18; ◷noon-1.30pm Tue-Sun mid-Jul–mid-Sep).

Musée Suisse du Jeu   MUSEUM

(www.museedujeu.com; Rue du Château 11, La Tour de Peilz; adult/child Sfr9/3; ◷11am-5.30pm Tue-Sun) Another amusing one for kids, the Swiss Game Museum is, err, just that. Games are arranged by theme – educational, strategic, simulation, skill and chance – and there are several you can play, including outdoor ones in the elegant waterfront grounds. The museum is in a château on

the lakeshore, a 20-minute walk east along lakeside Quai Perdonnet.

Musée Suisse de l'Appareil Photographique   MUSEUM

(www.cameramuseum.ch; Grande Place; adult/child Sfr8/free, workshop Sfr15; ◷11am-5.30pm Tue-Sun) Focus on the instruments rather than the images produced; reserve in advance for photography workshops in the lab at weekends.

🛏 Sleeping

TOP CHOICE **Riviera Lodge**   HOSTEL **$**

(☏021 923 80 40; www.rivieralodge.ch; Place du Marché 5; dm Sfr32, s/d Sfr88/95; 🅿@🛜) Smart in a lovely 19th-century house with salmon-coloured wooden shutters on Vevey's lakeside central square, this hostel could not be better placed. It has a kitchen, laundry, fireplace and – best of all – a fabulous rooftop terrace with a swoon-worthy lake view. Find the reception on the 4th floor.

Hôtel des Trois Couronnes HISTORIC HOTEL **$$$**

(☏021 923 32 00; www.hoteldestroiscouronnes .ch; Rue d'Italie 49; d Sfr450-700, ste Sfr550-6000; 🅿✳@🛜♨) The Three Crowns – an elegant, soft cream and taupe mansion lavishly strung with white flower boxes on the waterfront – is among Lake Geneva's best. Its trio of floors open onto interior galleries, the period decor pays perfect homage to its mid-19th-century origins and its luxury spa is just divine.

Hôtel des Négociants   HOTEL $$

(☎021 922 70 11; www.hotelnegociants.ch; Rue du Conseil 27; s/d Sfr93/143; ❄🗲) Cheerful 1970s hotel with bright rooms and a modern restaurant in the Old-Town heart; breakfast is Sfr15.

✗ Eating & Drinking

Le Littéraire   CAFE $

(www.cafe-litteraire.ch; Quai Perdonnet 33; ⊙9am-9pm; 🗲) Take the local town library, add a trendy cafe with ceiling-to-floor windows facing the lake and an idyllic summertime terrace, and you get this much-loved local favourite. Check the blackboard outside for the good-value *plat du jour* (Sfr19.90).

Le Mazot   SWISS $$

(☎021 921 78 22; Rue du Conseil 7; mains Sfr20-40; ⊙lunch & dinner Mon-Tue & Thu-Sat, dinner Sun) In the heart of the Old Town, this tiny little restaurant with quintessential striped canopy and flower-box pavement terrace is an institution of classic local cooking. Steaks and horse meat fillets in a legendary house sauce (secret recipe) dominates the kitchen.

Le National   CAFE, BAR $$

(www.natio.ch; Rue du Torrent 9; mains Sfr25-30; ⊙11am-late Mon-Sat) There's no missing this canary-yellow hangout just off Grande Place. The cuisine has distinct Asian influences – lots of lemon grass and coconut milk – and on sunny days you can enjoy the shade of an old cedar tree in the backyard. Occasional DJs, VJs and live acts add an after-dark club vibe.

Le Château   SWISS $$$

(☎021 921 12 10; www.denismartin.ch; Rue du Château 2; tasting menu Sfr350; ⊙dinner Tue-Sun, closed 3wks Jul-Aug & 2wks Dec-Jan) Charismatic and engaging, chef Denis Martin is one of the country's biggest names in Swiss contemporary cooking. His tasting menu – think two Michelin stars – is a thrilling succession of 25-odd different bite-sized taste sensations, served in a traditional 17th-century mansion a block from the lake.

🔒 Shopping

Shopaholics, this is heaven! The tiny but perfect maze of boutique-riddled, Old-Town streets that fan out east of central square Grande Place are pure joy to meander. Don't miss the one-off pieces of jewellery, ceramics, bags and frilly parasols – all of which

exude a real old-world elegance – at Ozar, (Rue du Conseil 23), the quirky knick-knacks for the home at **Balthazar** (Rue du Lac 32) and the extraordinary electro-mechanical sculptures by Vevey's resident British goldsmith Charles Morgan at **Galerie d'Art Morgan** (Rue du Théâtre 9).

❶ Information

Tourist Office (☎084 886 84 84; www .montreux-vevey.com; Grande Place; ⊙9am-6pm Mon-Fri, 9am-1pm Sat & Sun May-Sep, 9am-noon & 1-5.30pm Mon-Fri, 9am-noon Sat & Sun Oct-Apr)

❶ Getting There & Around

Vevey is linked by train to Lausanne (Sfr4.90, 15 to 25 minutes) and Montreux (Sfr3.30, five to 10 minutes).

Or indulge in a scenic lakeside cycle from Lausanne (19km) or Montreux (6.5km): **Altmann Sports** (☎021 921 96 77; Rue de la Madeleine 22) in Vevey rents bicycles.

Around Vevey

Celebrities have long loved the Swiss Riviera, Charlie Chaplin (1889–1977) opting for a very large and lovely 14-hectare estate in **Corsier-sur-Vevey** in 1952 after falling out of favour with Hollywood. He stayed in this exclusive little lakeshore hamlet 2km west of Vevey proper for 25 years until his death.

For more than a decade, plans have been afoot to transform Chaplin's former home – the neoclassical **Manoir de Ban** (Route de Fenil 2) dating from 1840 – into a museum dedicated to the life and times of the iconic London-born film star who made everyone laugh. The latest opening date is 2013; check the website www.chaplinmuseum.com for an update.

Montreux

POP 23,000

In the 19th century, writers, artists and musicians (Lord Byron and the Shelleys among them) flocked to this pleasing lakeside resort and it has remained a magnet ever since. Peaceful walks along a lakeshore beaded with 19th-century hotels, a mild microclimate, a hilltop Old Town, the famous jazz fest and a fabulous 13th-century fortress are its main drawcards. Friday morning is market day down by the lake.

GENEVA'S MOST FAMOUS CASTLE

the waterfront in Montreux, the fairy-tale **Chemin Fleuri** (Flower Path) – a silky ooth promenade framed by flowerbeds positively tropical in colour and vivacity – snakes dreamily along the lake for 4km to the magnificent stone hulk of lakeside **Château de Chillon** (www.chillon.ch; Av de Chillon 21; adult/child Sfr12/6; ◷9am-7pm Apr-Sep, 9.30am-6pm Mar & Oct, 10am-5pm Nov-Feb).

Occupying a stunning position on Lake Geneva, this oval-shaped 13th-century fortress is a maze of courtyards, towers and halls filled with arms, period furniture and artwork. The landward side is heavily fortified but lakeside it presents a gentler face. Chillon was largely built by the House of Savoy and taken over by Bern's governors after Vaud fell to Bern. Don't miss the medieval frescos in the **Chapelle St Georges** and the spooky Gothic **dungeons**.

The fortress gained fame in 1816 when Byron wrote *The Prisoner of Chillon,* a poem about François Bonivard, thrown into the dungeon for his seditious ideas and freed by Bernese forces in 1536. Byron carved his name into the pillar to which Bonivard was supposedly chained. Painters William Turner and Gustave Courbet subsequently immortalised the castle's silhouette on canvas, and Jean-Jacques Rousseau, Alexandre Dumas and Mary Shelley all wrote about it.

Count 45 minutes to walk from Montreux to Chillon, or take trolley bus 1. CGN boats and steamers – a wonderful way to arrive – call at Château de Chillon from Lausanne (adult return Sfr33, 1¾ hours), Vevey (adult return Sfr21.60, 50 minutes) and Montreux (adult return Sfr16, 15 minutes).

◉ Sights & Activities

Freddie Mercury Statue MONUMENT
(Place du Marché) Year round, fresh flowers smother the feet of this 3m-tall statue of Freddie Mercury, 'lover of life, singer of songs', in front of Montreux' old covered market on the waterfront. From 1979 until his premature death in 1991, the lead vocalist came to Montreux with rock band Queen to record hit after hit at the Mountain Studios in Montreux Casino – he had an apartment in town and a lakeside chalet in nearby Clarens.

Prince, the Rolling Stones and David Bowie were among others to use the mythical recording studio, owned by Queen from 1979 until 1991 (since relocated to the neighbouring canton of Fribourg). Freddie Mercury fans continue to stream to Montreux each year in September to celebrate the extrovert and often-times outrageous singer with the three-day rock festival Freddie Mercury Memorial.

Related pop trivia: in 1971 British hardrock band Deep Purple was in town to record an album at the casino when a fire broke out (during a Frank Zappa gig no less). The pall of smoke cast over Lake Geneva inspired the band to pen their classic rock number, 'Smoke on the Water'.

Musée de Montreux HISTORY MUSEUM
(www.museemontreux.ch; Rue de la Gare 40; adult/child Sfr6/free; ◷10am-noon & 2-5pm mid-Mar-early Nov) Displays range from Roman finds to period furniture, bathtubs and street signs at Montreux's local history museum inside an old winegrower's house.

✹☽ Festivals & Events

Montreux Jazz MUSIC
(www.montreuxjazz.com) Montreux' best-known fest, established in 1967, lasts two weeks in July. Free concerts take place daily, but tickets cost anything from Sfr75 to Sfr240 for bigger-name gigs. Music is not just jazz; The Strokes, Sting, Arcade Fire, BB King, Paul Simon and Deep Purple (with their big comeback gig in 2011) have all played here.

🛏 Sleeping & Eating

TOP CHOICE **Tralala Hôtel** DESIGN HOTEL **$$**
(✆021 963 49 73; www.tralalahotel.ch; Rue du Temple 2; d Sfr130-280; 🅿❋@🛜) A boutique hotel designed around Montreux' extraordinary musical heritage just had to open – and it has, perched up high from the lake in the old part of Montreux. Rooms come in three sizes – S ('Small & Sexy'), L or XL – and each pays homage to a different artist,

LAKE GENEVA & VAUD MONTREUX

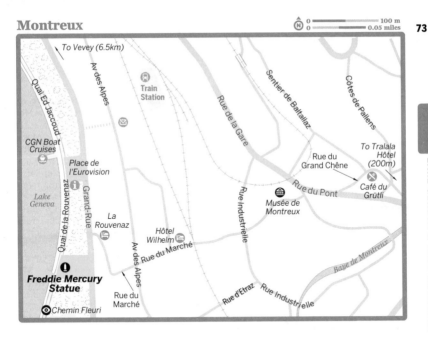

giving guests the chance to sleep with Aretha Franklin, David Bowie and 33 other famous artists.

Hôtel Masson   HISTORIC HOTEL **$$$**
(☑021 966 00 44; www.hotelmasson.ch; Rue Bonivard 5, Montreux-Veytaux; s/d/tr/q Sfr200/270/360/410; Ⓟ🐾) In 1829, this vintner's mansion was converted into a hotel. The old charm has remained intact and the hotel, set in magnificent grounds, is on the Swiss Heritage list of the country's most beautiful hotels. It lies back in the hills southeast of Montreux, best reached by taxi.

La Rouvenaz   HOTEL **$**
(☑021 963 27 36; www.montreux.ch/rouvenaz-hotel; Rue du Marché 1; s/d Sfr130/190; ⓐ) A stylish family-run spot with its own tasty restaurant downstairs and wine bar next door, you cannot get any closer to the lake or the heart of the action. Its six rooms are simple, but pleasant; most have at least a lake glimpse.

Hôtel Wilhelm   HOTEL **$**
(☑021 963 14 31; Rue du Marché 13; d Sfr90-140) Run by the same wine-growing family for four generations, this attractive peppermint-green guesthouse with wrought iron balconies has clearly seen better days. But

if it is as cheap as chips (or almost) you're seeking on the swish Swiss Riviera, then this old stalwart of a hotel stuck in a time warp is just the ticket. No credit cards *(quelle surprise!)*.

Café du Grütli   SWISS **$**
(☑021 963 42 65; Rue du Grand Chêne 8; mains Sfr10-25; ⊙8am-3pm Tue, to midnight Thu-Mon) No Riviera glam at this address, rather a handful of locals who lunch here every day on hearty meat dishes, fondues, omelettes and perfectly crispy rösti. And yes, the hike up the hill to this banana-yellow village cafe around for at least a century definitely warrants dessert. Tummy space allowing, end with banana flambéed in absinthe.

❶ Information

Tourist office (☑084 886 84 84; www.montreux-vevey.com; Rue du Théâtre 5; ⊙9am-6pm Mon-Fri, 9.30am-5pm Sat & Sun)

❶ Getting There & Away

From Lausanne, some three trains an hour (Sfr11.40, 20 to 35 minutes) serve Montreux. Montreux is also on the scenic Golden Pass route (p363) to the Bernese Oberland. For CGN boats, see p53.

WORTH A TRIP

ROCHERS DE NAYE

From Montreux train station a splendid cogwheel train (adult/child return Sfr66.40/33.20, 55 minutes, hourly) hauls itself up the mountain to **Rochers de Naye**, a natural platform at 2042m that has particular appeal for kids with its native marmots, Mongolian-style **yurts** (http://yourtes.goldenpass.ch; adult/child Sfr70/60 incl breakfast, dinner & return train fare) and magical **Santa's Grotto** (Village du Père Noël; www.montreuxnoel .com; adult/child Sfr32/19 incl train; ☉10.15am-5.30pm Wed-Sun late Nov-24 Dec). The train journey is impressive, as are the lake and Alpine views from the top. **Golden Pass Center** (☎0900 245 245; www.goldenpass.ch; ☉8am-6pm), in Montreux train station, handles reservations and ticketing.

NORTHWESTERN VAUD

The Jura mountain chain closes off the northwest of Vaud, running roughly parallel in the north to Lac de Neuchâtel (p89), at whose southern tip sits Yverdon-Les-Bains, a pleasant low-key town where you can take to the waters.

Yverdon-Les-Bains

POP 27.200 / ELEV 437M

The Romans were the first to discover the healthy qualities of Yverdon's hot spa waters and since then the town has made its living from them. It's an enjoyable lakeside resort and Canton de Vaud's second-largest town.

The lake, with its 5km of beaches, boats and water activities, buzzes in summer.

☉ Sights & Activities

Centre Thermal   SPA
(www.cty.ch; 3hr-ticket adult/child Sfr19/11.50, with saunas et al Sfr30; ☉8am-10pm Mon-Sat, to 8pm Sun) You don't need to have aches and pains to languish in the toasty-warm indoor and outdoor pools (temperatures between 28°C and 34°C) at these old baths sourced by water from a 14,000-year-old mineral spring 500m below ground. By the time it hits the surface it has picked up all sorts of salubrious properties from the layers of rock, and

is particularly soothing for rheumatism and respiratory ailments. Pampering perks include saunas, a *hammam* (Turkish bath), a tropical shower, Japanese baths and a giant Jacuzzi.

Maison d'Ailleurs   MUSEUM
(House of Elsewhere; www.ailleurs.ch; Place de Pestalozzi 14; adult/child Sfr9/5; ☉2-6pm Wed-Fri, from 11am Sat & Sun) In the Old Town core, opposite the town's 13th-century château built by one of the Savoy clan, is this thoroughly unique science-fiction museum where you can gawp at a mock-up of a spaceship and while away hours in a room dedicated to HR Giger (of *Alien* fame). Masses of material deals with the science-fiction worlds of figures ranging from Homer to Jules Verne. The latter section is separate and contains models of the fantastical vehicles Verne dreamt up in his novels. The museum only opens when a temporary exhibition is on.

🛏 Sleeping & Eating

Grand Hôtel des Bains   HOTEL $$$
(☎024 424 64 64; www.grandhotelyverdon.ch; Av des Bains 22; d from Sfr240; 🅿❄@🛜🏊) An original belle époque beauty and the big daddy of luxury bath hotels, this four-star address spoils guests with spacious rooms, a romantic white-turreted facade, a gourmet restaurant and its own thermal pool in addition to a direct link with the Centre Thermal.

❶ Information

Tourist Office (☎024 423 61 01; www .yverdon-les-bains.ch/tourisme; Av de la Gare 1; ☉9am-6pm Mon-Fri, 9.30am-3.30pm Sat & Sun)

❶ Getting There & Away

Regular trains run to and from Lausanne (Sfr8.10, 20 to 45 minutes), Neuchâtel (Sfr14.20, 20 minutes) and Estavayer-le-Lac (Sfr4.90, 15 minutes).

SKIING THE VAUD ALPS

Tucked in a captivating Alpine nook, the southeast corner of Vaud is essentially ski country, including in summer when the glacier in Les Diablerets – the flagship resort – comes into its own. Hiking the many well-marked trails in spring and autumn is equally dreamy in this relatively unknown part of the Swiss Alps.

The one exception to this giddy, adrenalin-inducing mountain splendour is small-town Aigle with a fairy-tale château wrapped in vineyards a few kilometres southeast off the shore of Lake Geneva.

Leysin

POP 3800 / ELEV 1350M

Leysin started life as a tuberculosis centre but is now a sprawling ski resort with 60km of runs. Many other sports are on offer, including a *via ferrata* (a vertical 'footpath' negotiated via cables and rungs). The **tourist office** (024 493 33 00; www.leysin.ch; Place Large; 8am-9pm) is based in the New Sporting Centre. Take in the Alpine scenery from the revolving restaurant atop **Mont Berneuse** (2048m); the cable car costs

Sfr22 return (summer) or Sfr47 for the lift/day's skiing (winter).

Hiking Sheep (024 494 35 35; www.hiking sheep.com; dm/d Sfr30/80; P@), a tall, art-deco house two minutes' walk from Grand-Hotel station (Leysin-Aigle train station), gets floods of accolades from happy backpackers. It has a kitchen and good communal facilities.

Les Diablerets

ELEV 1150M

Overshadowed by the mountain of the same name (3209m), Les Diablerets is a key ski resort in the Vaud Alps. Several fairly easy ski runs are open during June and July at **Glacier de Tsanfleuron** (3000m), which gives the Diablerets resort its recent official

WORTH A TRIP

TOP THREE DAY TRIPS

Drifting in thermal waters is all very pleasant but when itchy feet strike, Yverdon cooks up plenty of therapeutic trips.

Charles the Bold & Greta Garbo

There is nothing like a big fat lakeside fortress to set imaginations racing and **Château de Grandson** (www.chateau-grandson.ch; adult/child Sfr12/5; 8.15am-6pm Apr-Oct, to 5pm Nov-Mar), 5km along the lakefront from Yverdon, doesn't disappoint. Its thick stone walls hide a handful of small museums, the history museum evoking the fate of Charles the Bold in early 1476 who, in his battle against Swiss Confederate troops, found some of his routed Burgundian troops strung from apple trees in the castle orchard. The prize exhibit in the château's car museum is Greta Garbo's white Rolls Royce. Regular buses connect Yverdon with Grandson (Sfr3.30, 13 minutes). Or walk.

Music in the Mountains

Music boxes have been made in Sainte Croix, high in the Jura mountains 20km northwest of Yverdon, since the mid-19th century. The town's **Musée du CIMA** (024 454 44 77; Centre International de la Méchanique d'Art, Rue de l'Industrie 2; adult/child Sfr17/8; 1½hr guided tour 3pm Mon, 10.30am, 2pm & 3.30pm Tue-Sun) documents the art of making them. Tours include an enchanting film. Catch a local train from Yverdon to Sainte Croix (Sfr4.90, 35 minutes).

Roman Gods & Romanesque Sundays

Sunday is the day to take a road trip southwest to **Orbe** (where Nescafé was invented in 1938) and its **Musée de Mosaïques Romaines** (adult/child Sfr4/3; 9am-noon & 1.30-5pm Mon-Fri, 1.30-5.30pm Sat & Sun Easter-Oct), a Roman mosaic museum on the site of a 3rd-century Gallo-Roman villa. In the first of several pavilions, a beautiful polychrome depicts Jupiter, Saturn and the other planetary divinities.

Continuing 8km southwest to **Romainmôtier**, cupped wholly in a lush green bowl of vegetation, is the Cluny order's Romanesque **Abbatiale** (www.concerts-romainmotier .ch; admission free; 7am-8pm), a remarkable sandstone church whose origins reach back to the 6th century. The Sunday afternoon concerts held here at 5pm in July and August (4pm selected Sundays spring and autumn) are justly raved about and well worth the trip.

AIGLE

An absolute must for anyone with a passion for wine or turreted castles, Aigle (population 8160), at the southeast end of Lake Geneva, is the capital of the Chablais wine-producing region in southeast Vaud. Grapes grown on the vines carpeting the gentle slopes here make some of Switzerland's best whites.

Two thousand years of wine making is evoked in the compelling **Musée de la Vigne et du Vin** (www.museeduvin.ch; adult/child Sfr11/6; ⊙11am-6pm Jul-Aug, Tue-Sun Apr-Jun & Sep-Oct), a thoroughly modern and interactive wine museum inside Aigle's fairy-tale château. The six hands-on digital experiments – indulge in your own Chasselas grape harvest, make wine etc – in the 'lab' are particularly fun.

Afterwards, cross the castle courtyard to the 13th-century **Maison de la Dîme** and peek at whatever temporary exhibition is on upstairs (entry included in the wine museum ticket price). Then lunch in the lovely **La Pinte du Paradis** (☎024 466 18 44; www.lapinteduparadis.com; Place du Château d'Aigle 2; mains Sfr25-45; ⊙lunch & dinner Tue-Sat Apr-Oct). Its lunchtime Sfr20 menu – eaten between rustic wood and suspended spoons inside or on the terrace with vineyard and Alps view – is great value.

There are several other equally atmospheric places to lunch in the narrow old-world lanes on the approach from Aigle's new town to the old, château-crowned part of Aigle known as the Quartier du Cloître. Nearing the château, the streets smell of red wine as you pass the cellars of local *vignerons* (winegrowers); **Oenothèque du Château** (www.dominico10.com; Chemin du Cloître De Là 2; ⊙9am-5pm Sat & Sun) is a recommended address for tasting and buying biodynamic wine.

Aigle **tourist office** (☎024 466 30 00; Rue de Colomb; ⊙8.30am-noon & 1.30-6pm Mon-Fri, 8.30am-noon Sat Apr-Oct) is in the new town, a 10-minute walk from the château. Regular trains link Lausanne (Sfr7.60, 30 minutes) with Aigle via Montreux. Pick up wheels at **Rent a Bike** (☎051 224 60 04; www.rentabike.ch; per day Sfr33) at Aigle train station.

name, **Glacier 3000** (www.glacier3000.ch). Whether you plan to ski or not, the views are fabulous.

Two cable cars climb up to the glacier from the valley floor, both linked to the village by bus. Starting from Reusch or Col du Pillon you get to Cabane des Diablerets, where another cable car whisks you almost to the summit at Scex Rouge (2971m). Allow time to linger in the striking white cube of glacier restaurant **Botta 3000**, the contemporary handiwork of world-renowned Swiss architect Mario Botta, with gastronomic dining on the top floor and a self-service terrace and picnic area below. From here, the ski back down to Reusch (1350m) is an exhilarating 2000m descent over 14km. A one-day ski pass covering Les Diablerets, Villars, Gryon and the glacier costs Sfr61.

The **tourist office** (☎024 492 33 58; www.diablerets.ch), to the right of the train station, has plenty of information on activities and accommodation.

Hourly trains link Les Diablerets and Aigle (Sfr5.60, 50 minutes).

Villars & Gryon

Villars (www.villars.ch) and nearby Gryon (www.gryon.ch) share a ski pass with Les Diablerets and in winter are linked by a free train for ski-pass holders. Skiing is intermediate with varied runs – ideal for families. In summer, the country is perfect for hiking. One great walk starts at the Col de Bretaye pass (reached by BVB train from Villars), taking you past the pretty **Lac de Chavonnes** and on through verdant mountain country to Les Diablerets. The walk takes about four hours, and you could catch a train from Les Diablerets to Aigle. Views from the Col de Bretaye are magnificent, taking in the Dents du Midi and Mont Blanc.

In Villars, **Hôtel Ecureuil** (☎024 496 37 37; www.hotel-ecureuil.ch; Rue Centrale; s/d Sfr135/230; P🕏) offers pleasant rooms with plenty of timber and a restaurant specialising in grilled meats. Nightlife revolves around entertainment complex **El Gringo** (www.elgringo.ch; Rte des Hôtels; ⊙11pm-4am ski season, Fri & Sat low season).

From Aigle you can reach Villars by an hourly bus (Sfr8.40, 40 minutes). Otherwise, mainline Aigle trains connect in Bex with local trains to Gryon (Sfr5.30, 80 minutes).

To buy ski passes in advance at reduced rates, check out www.easyski.ch.

Pays d'Enhaut

The 'High Country' rises in the northeast corner of Vaud about midway between Aigle and Gruyères. In winter it could almost be considered the Francophone extension of the swank Gstaad ski scene, just over the cantonal frontier.

Château d'Œx is an attractive family resort with a nice selection of moderate ski runs, but the place is best known for all its hot air. Bertrand Piccard and Brian Jones launched their record-breaking, round-the-world, 20-day hot-air balloon ride from here in March 1999 (they landed in Egypt). For one week in the second half of January the place bursts into a frenzy of floating colour as the town hosts the annual Semaine Internationale de Ballons à Air Chaud (www .ballonchateaudoex.ch) involving around 100 hot-air balloons ranging from the standard floater to odd creatures such as a massive Scottish bagpipe player! If you actually want to fly up, up and away yourself, steady your nerves for fiscal turbulence: it costs Sfr390 per adult (Sfr195 for kids aged between 8 and 15 years) for about one hour.

But forget the skiing and hot-air ballooning. The real reason to hang out in Château d'Œx is to see cheese being made and scoff sugary-sweet homemade meringues smothered in far more cream than the doctor ordered at Le Chalet (☑026 924 66 77; www.lechalet-fromagerie.ch; mains Sfr 12-25; ⊙9am-6pm Tue-Sun, to 11pm Fri, cheesemaking 1.30-3.30pm Wed-Sun), a sizeable chalet strung with flower boxes in spring and summer, and surrounded by snow in winter.

Château-d'Œx' tourist office (☑026 924 25 25; www.chateau-doex.ch; La Place) is in the centre, below the hilltop clock tower. There are about 20 places to stay, ranging from chalets to a handful of rather overbearing big hotels. Trains link it with Montreux (Sfr9.30, 65 minutes).

Fribourg, Neuchâtel & Jura

POP 515,000 / AREA 3311 SQ KM / LANGUAGES FRENCH, GERMAN

Best Places to Eat

» Auberge de Mont Cornu (p92)

» Georges Wenger (p95)

» Café Tivoli (p87)

» Café des Arts (p91)

Best Places to Stay

» Auberge aux 4 Vents (p81)

» Eulenhof (p86)

» L'Aubier (p89)

» La Ferme du Bourgoz (p88)

Why Go?

A far cry from the staggering Alpine scenes more readily associated with Switzerland, this gentle corner in the west of the country remains a 'secret'. From the evocative medieval cantonal capitals of Fribourg and Neuchâtel to the mysterious green hills and thick dark Jura forests, from the land of three lakes to gorgeous medieval villages such as Gruyères and St Ursanne, it proffers a wealth of sights and scapes off the tourist track.

Travelling here is a brilliant sensory experience...and that includes the taste buds: savour tradition-rich Appellation d'Origine Contrôllée (AOC) cheeses, let absinthe's green fairy dance on your palate and make sure you try meringues smothered in double cream at least once. And when you need to repent, thousands of kilometres of waistline-saving walking, cycling and cross-country skiing trails – not to mention sailing, skiing and water sports – save the day.

When to Go

Summer is the perfect time to visit these verdant cantons, when the green seems greener and the sunflowers make for a sea of yellow. In autumn, restaurants serving 'la chasse' (game-based dishes) are worth stopping in, while the wine harvest in the Vully region makes for an appealingly tipsy time. Late spring is a good time for outdoor activities, as is early autumn.

⚊ Getting There & Around

Rail connections to/from the main cities, Fribourg and Neuchâtel are straightforward. By road, the A12 freeway linking Bern with Lausanne and Geneva roars down the Canton de Fribourg's central spine.

CANTON DE FRIBOURG

The southernmost of the three cantons, Canton de Fribourg (population 273,200) tots up 1671 sq km on the drawing board. Pre-Alpine foothills rise grandly around its cold craggy feet; Gruyères with its sprinkling of small mountain resorts pierces its heart; and Fribourg heads the canton up

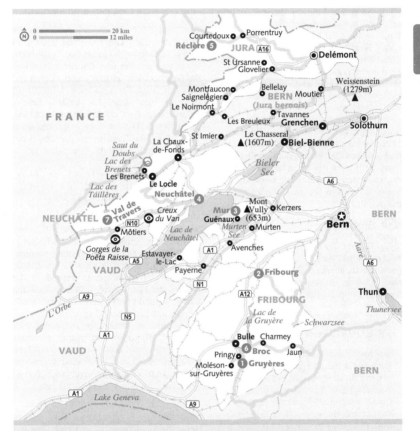

FRIBOURG, NEUCHÂTEL & JURA CANTON DE FRIBOURG

Fribourg, Neuchâtel & Jura Highlights

❶ Enjoy cheese dreams after a day's dairy-fied indulgence in **Gruyères** (p87)

❷ Eyeball the mad-cap creations of **Jean Tinguely** and **Niki de Saint Phalle** (p80) in Fribourg's atmospheric Old Town

❸ Take a big hearty gulp of Vully wine, *saucisson du marc* and old-fashioned fresh air at the **Owl Farm** (p86) in Mur near Lake Murten

❹ Fall under the spell of medieval **Neuchâtel** (p89)

❺ Delve deep into the Jura to discover local life on a **Jurassien farm** (p95) in Réclère

❻ Feed all five senses with a good dose of Swiss chocolate at the **Cailler factory** (p88)

❼ Gambol with the green fairy via a nip (or two!) of absinthe in the **Val de Travers** (p93)

north, where pretty lakeside villages slumber between vineyards and fruit orchards.

What makes this canton most fascinating is its *Röstigraben* (linguistic divide): west speaks French, east speaks German.

Fribourg

POP 34,500 / ELEV 629M

Nowhere is Switzerland's language divide felt more keenly than in Fribourg (Freiburg) or 'Free Town', a medieval city where inhabitants on the west bank of the Sarine River speak French, and those on the east bank of the Sanne speak German. Throw Catholicism and a notable student population into the cultural cocktail and you get a fascinating town with a feisty nightlife and a healthy waft of originality.

Its greatest moment in history saw a messenger sprint from Murten to Fribourg in 1476 to relay the glad tidings that the Swiss had defeated Charles the Bold...only to drop dead with exhaustion on arrival. Onlookers, saddened by this tragic twist, took the linden twig from the messenger's hat and planted it.

◎ Sights

TOP CHOICE **Espace Jean Tinguely –
Niki de Saint Phalle** MUSEUM
(www.mahf.ch, in French; Rue de Morat 2; adult/child Sfr6/free; ☺11am-6pm Wed & Fri-Sun, to 8pm Thu) Jump on the button to watch the

---

FRIBOURG FUNICULAR

Nowhere else in Europe does a funicular lurch up the mountainside with the aid of good old stinky sewage water; indeed on certain days it smells as such too. Constructed in 1899 and managed by the Cardinal Brewery until 1965 (when the municipality took over), the **Funiculaire de Fribourg** (admission Sfr2.40; ☺7-8.15am & 9.30am-7pm Mon-Sat, 9.30am-7pm Sun) links the lower part of the town with the upper every six minutes. The ride in one of two counterbalancing water-powered carriages from the lower Pertuis station (121m; place du Pertuis) to the upper station (618m; Rte des Alpes) takes two minutes and includes bags of great Old Town views.

Retable de l'Abondance Occidentale et du Mercantilisme Totalitaire (1989–90) make its allegorical comment on Western opulence. Created in memory of Fribourg's modern artistic prodigy, Jean Tinguely (1925–91), in a tramway depot dating to 1900, this nifty space showcases his machines alongside the boldly out-there creations of French-American artist Niki de Saint Phalle (1930–2002) who worked with him from the 1950s until his death.

Old Town NEIGHBOURHOOD
The 12th-century Old Town was laid out in simple fashion, with Grand-Rue as the main street and parallel Rue des Chanoines/Rue des Bouchers devoted to markets, church and civic buildings. The settlement later spread downhill into Auge. The bridges here – quaint stone Pont du Milieu and cobbled, roof-covered Pont du Berne – proffer great views. Pont de Zaehringen, Rte des Alpes and Chemin de Lorette are other prime vantage points.

Fribourg's famous Tilleul de Morat (Morat Linden Tree) stands in front of the Renaissance town hall (Grand-Rue).

Musée d'Art et d'Histoire MUSEUM
(www.mahf.ch, in French; Rue de Morat 12; adult/child Sfr8/free; ☺11am-6pm Tue, Wed & Fri-Sun, to 8pm Thu) Fribourg's art and history museum, with an excellent collection of late-Gothic sculpture and painting, is housed in the Renaissance Hôtel Ratzé, with annexes in the former slaughterhouse and armoury. Gothic meets Goth in the underground chamber, where religious statues are juxtaposed with some of Tinguely's sculptural creations combining animal skulls with metal machine components. The bench-clad museum garden, overlooking the river and pierced by a Niki de Saint Phalle sculpture, is a lovely picnic spot.

Cathédrale de St Nicolas de Myre CHURCH
(www.cathedrale-fribourg.ch, in French; Rue des Chanoines 3; ☺9am-6pm Mon-Fri, 9am-4pm Sat, 2-5pm Sun) Before entering this brooding 13th-century Gothic cathedral, contemplate the main portal with its 15th-century sculptured portrayal of the Last Judgment. On your right upon entering, inside the Chapelle du Saint Sépulcre, is a sculptural group (1433) depicting Christ's burial with exceptional lifelikeness and movement.

A 368-step hike up the cathedral's 74m-tall **tower** (adult/child Sfr3.50/1; ☺10am-noon &

2-5pm Mon-Fri, 10am-4pm Sat, 2-5pm Sun Apr-Oct) affords wonderful views.

Église des Cordeliers CHURCH
(Rue de Morat 4; ⊗7.30am-7pm Apr-Sep, to 5.30pm Oct-Mar) Inside this 13th-century church the triptych (1480) above the high altar depicts the Crucifixion. Head through the door on the left as you face the altar to view polychromatic frescos in next-door's convent.

Basilique de Notre-Dame CHURCH
(Rue de Morat 1) Sheltering an 18th-century Crèche Napolitaine featuring 75 figurines re-enacting the nativity, annunciation and scenes from daily life, this church has been recently restored to its former glory.

Industrial Fribourg NEIGHBOURHOOD
Two of Fribourg's more interesting industries include beer and chocolate. Sadly, the Cardinal factory closed down in 2010, but its **Musée de la Bière Cardinal** (⊋084 812 50 00; www.cardinal.ch; Passage du Cardinal; adult/child Sfr10/5; ⊗2-6pm Tue & Thu) is still open for visits.

The burnt red- and caramel-brick **Villars chocolate factory** (Rte de la Fonderie 2; ⊗cafe-shop 8.30am-5.30pm Mon-Fri, 9am-noon Sat), in business since 1901, is the sweetest. Known for its slabs of Swiss chocolate made from Alpine-rich Gruyère milk and kid-loved *têtes au choco* (chocolate-covered marshmallow heads), the factory can't be visited. But its cafe-shop can, much to the joy of locals, who flock here to stock up on chocolate at factory prices (Sfr6 for a 300g bar) and savour hot chocolate topped with whipped cream and chocolate shavings.

Fri Art GALLERY
(www.fri-art.ch; Petites Rames 22; adult/child Sfr6/free; ⊗noon-6pm Wed-Fri, 2-5pm Sat & Sun) A little tricky to track down but worth it if you need a dose of contemporary art. Temporary exhibitions range from the weird to the wonderful, but staff are helpful and the space makes good use of an old seminary.

Musée Gutenberg MUSEUM
(Gutenberg Museum; www.gutenbergmuseum.ch; Place de Notre-Dame 16; adult/child Sfr10/6; ⊗11am-6pm Wed, Fri & Sat, 11am-8pm Thu, 10am-5pm Sun) Duck behind the Basilique de Notre-Dame and embark on a voyage of the printed word in this printing and communication museum, housed in a 16th-century granary. A multimedia show brings the historical exhibition up to 21st-century speed.

Musée Suisse de la Marionnette MUSEUM
(Swiss Puppetry Museum; www.marionnette.ch, in French; Derrière-les-Jardins 2; adult/child Sfr5/4; ⊗10am-5pm Tue-Fri, 2-6pm Sat & Sun; ☎) Puppets prance on the stage for performances and Saturday-afternoon puppetry workshops. There's a nice little cafe onsite too (open 10am to 8pm Wednesday to Sunday).

Planche Supérieure SQUARE
Cross Pont du Milieu and head west towards this broad sloping square, which features the former Commanderie de St Jean, erected by the Knights of the Order of St John in the 13th century.

🛏 Sleeping

🔝 Auberge aux 4 Vents BOUTIQUE HOTEL $$
(⊋026 347 36 00; www.aux4vents.ch; Res Balzli Grandfrey 124; s Sfr130-170, d Sfr180-260, s/d/tr/q with shared bathroom Sfr65/130/170/200; 🅿▩) 'Stylish' scarcely does justice to this imaginative eight-room country inn, 2km north of town, where off-beat design rules. Its four-bedded *dortoir* is surely Switzerland's most luxurious dorm, and the dreamy Blue Room sports a bathtub that rolls out on rails through the window for a soak beneath the stars. To find it, drive north along Rue de Morat and turn right immediately before the train bridge.

Hotel Hine Adon APARTMENT $$
(⊋026 322 37 77; www.hineadon.ch; Rue Pierre-Aeby 11; apt Sfr120-250; @) This nifty newcomer in the heart of the Old Town boasts cleverly configured apartments (from one- to 2½-bedrooms, with full kitchen facilities) that mix old and new design details. Breakfast is served in the handy onsite *boulangerie* and service is sterling. Weekly and monthly rates are very competitive.

Hôtel du Sauvage HISTORIC HOTEL $$
(⊋026 347 30 60; www.hotel-sauvage.ch, in French; Planche Supérieure 12; s/d from Sfr195/280; ☎) Another medieval veteran, this Old-Town house boasts 16 charming rooms above a restaurant in a twinset of 16th-century houses. Find it mere footsteps from the river, flagged with a medieval sign featuring a savage caveman and his club. Free wi-fi.

Hôtel du Faucon HOTEL $
(⊋026 321 37 90; www.hotel-du-faucon.ch, in French; Rue de Lausanne 76; s/d/ste Sfr95/120/200; ⊗reception 7.30am-9pm; ☎) A golden falcon marks the spot: well-placed on Fribourg's main pedestrian street, this

Fribourg

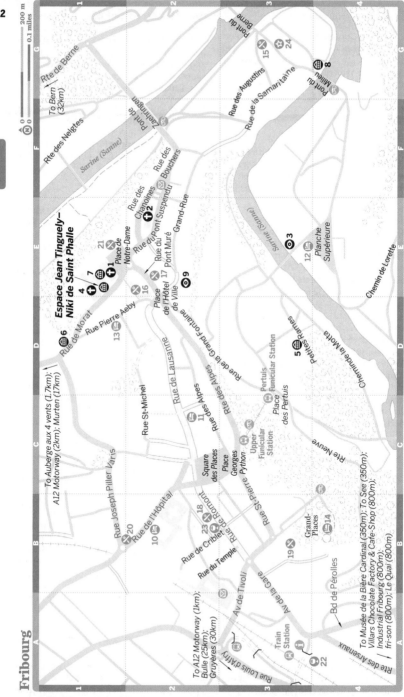

Espace Jean Tinguely–
Niki de Saint Phalle

0 ————— 200 m
0 ————— 0.1 miles

contemporary hideout offers an exceptional price–quality ratio. Furnishings are modern and mod-cons cleverly dotted throughout.

NH Fribourg   BUSINESS HOTEL **$$**
(☎026 351 91 91; www.nh-hotels.com; Grand-Places 14; d incl breakfast Sfr120-230; P❋☎) Notably modern in an outwardly bland apartment block, upmarket NH lures suits with its business facilities, modern decor, restaurant and Jacuzzi-clad suites. Rates fluctuate daily, depending on availability. Wi-fi costs Sfr25 for 24 hours, although it's free in the lobby.

Auberge de Jeunesse Fribourg   HOSTEL **$**
(☎026 323 19 16; Rue de l'Hôpital 2; dm/d/tr/q per person incl breakfast Sfr34/40/45/50; ⊙reception 7.30-10am & 5-10pm Mar–mid-Oct; P☎) The rules are clear at this city hostel in one wing of the 17th-century Hôpital des Bourgeois, opposite Fribourg University. No cooking or eating in rooms, nonmembers pay extra and night owls must ring to enter after 10pm. There's a nice garden attached, with tables for alfresco dining.

🍴 Eating

Auberge de la Cigogne   MODERN EUROPEAN **$$$**
(www.aubergedelacigogne.ch, in French; Rue d'Or 24; mains Sfr35-52, menu du jour/midi Sfr25/52; ⊙lunch & dinner Tue-Sat) This highly revered establishment, housed in a riverside building from the 1770s yet not at all stuffy, has

some brilliant *prix fixe* menus, which feature stellar desserts such as *crème brûlée aux framboises parfumé à lavande* (with raspberries and perfumed with lavender).

Café des Arcades   CAFE **$**
(www.cafedesarcades.ch, in French; Rue des Ormeaux 1; mains Sfr16-25; ⊙7am-11.30pm Mon-Thu, 7am-midnight Fri, 8am-midnight Sat, 10am-10pm Sun) Alive and kicking since 1861, when the light's just so, this place will transport you to another time. An authentic address for breakfast, brunch or lunch.

Café du Gothard   BISTRO **$$**
(Rue du Pont Muré 16; fondue mains Sfr23.50-28; ⊙9am-11.30pm Tue-Fri, 8am-11.30pm Sat & Sun) Tinguely's favourite eating haunt is a kitsch mix of 19th-century furnishings, Niki de Saint Phalle drawings and nostalgia-tinged bric-a-brac. Take your pick from the day's specials chalked on blackboards and revel in this legendary bistro.

Le Mondial   CAFE **$**
(www.cafelemondial.ch; Rue de l'Hôpital 39; mains Sfr14-25; ⊙lunch & dinner Tue-Sun) This airy cafe-bar gets packed at lunchtime and from 5pm (tapas time) and does a nice line in moreish *ballons* (burger-style creations – try the 'anglais', with roast beef, egg, red onion, cornichons and sauce for Sfr17). Service is brisk (sometimes brusque) and the vibe is bustling.

Punkt — ASIAN $$

(www.restaurant-punkt.ch, in French; Place de Notre-Dame 4; rice & noodle mains Sfr20-30; ⊙10am-midnight Tue-Fri, 11am-midnight Sat) A jolt of Pan-Asian modernity in the Old Town, this bamboo-zled eatery has Thai, Korean, Japanese, Singaporean, Indonesian, Chinese and Malaysian offerings, with curries that could use a little more kick.

Gemelli Ristorante & Pizzeria — ITALIAN $$

(www.gemelli-fr.ch; Grand-Places 10; pizza Sfr16-25, mains Sfr27-42; ⊙8am-11.30pm Mon-Thu, to midnight Fri & Sat, 10am-11.30pm Sun) The pizza and Sardinian specialities served inside this glass shoebox may be handsome (and they are), but it's the garden terrace out back that really lures the punters. End your meal with a stroll across the lawn to the Tinguely fountain, created by the Fribourg artist for his mate, Swiss racing driver Jo Siffert, just months before his fatal car accident in 1971.

🍷 Drinking & Entertainment

The buzziest DJ clubs and band venues are in the industrial zone west of the train station. Head to Rte de la Fonderie for a selection of nightspots.

Le Quai — BAR

(www.lequai.ch, in French; Rte de la Fonderie 6; ⊙9am-2pm & 4.30-11.30pm Mon-Thu, 9am-3am Fri, 6pm-3am Sat) This post-industrial lounge-bar seethes with soul and a healthy dose of retro cool. DJs spin sets Friday and Saturday evening.

Café de l'Ancienne Gare — CAFE

(www.cafeanciennegare.ch, in French & German; Gare 3; ⊙9am-11.30pm Mon-Thu, 9am-3am Fri, 1pm-3am Sat, 11am-midnight Sun) In the old train station's 19th-century hall, this hip, easy hang-out also doubles as a nerve centre of sorts for arty happenings involving film, performance and fashion. Decent meals and snacks are available too.

fri-son — MUSIC

(www.fri-son.ch, in French; Rte de la Fonderie 13; ⊙8pm-late Wed-Sun) DJs spin varied sounds inside this graffiti-covered warehouse – one of western Switzerland's biggest stages for live concerts. Buy tickets online.

To See — NIGHTCLUB

(www.toseeclub.com, in French; Passage Cardinal 2c; ⊙10pm-3am Wed, 11pm-3am Thu, 11pm-4am Fri & Sat) Three dance floors, a whole lot of flashing lights and a frenetic crowd flock to this vast clubbing space opposite the old Cardinal brewery.

L'Apart — BAR

(www.lapart.ch; Grand-Places 14; ⊙4pm-3am Mon-Sat; 🛜) Ignore the concrete tower that sits on top and take your pick of all the 1950s seating in this loft-style bar made by Séb and JC. Summer weekends its slick wooden-deck terrace gets packed and DJs fill the place to bursting.

TW — WINE BAR

(www.tmcafe.ch; Level 1, Rue de Romont 29-31; ⊙7am-11.30pm Mon-Wed, to midnight Thu, to 2am Fri, 9am-2am Sat, 2-11.30pm Sun) Trendies drink, dance and do shots as DJs spin electro at Talk Wine, a cafe and lounge bar above a shoe shop. Good for an after-five *apéro*.

La Spirale — LIVE MUSIC

(www.laspirale.ch, in French; Place du Petit St-Jean 39; ⊙Wed-Sun) Jazz, blues, world fusion, Swiss yodelling, Spanish flamenco et al create a potent musical cocktail in this cellar club by the river. Look for the inconspicuous blue door. Buy tickets through www.star ticket.ch or subscribe to a five-entry pass (Sfr90).

ℹ Information

Post

Post office (Av de Tivoli 3; ⊙7.30am-6.30pm Mon-Fri, 8am-4pm Sat)

Tourist Information

Tourist office (📞026 350 11 11; www.fribourg tourism.ch; Av de la Gare 1; ⊙9am-6pm Mon-Fri, to 3pm Sat May-Sep, to 6pm Mon-Fri, to 12.30pm Sat Oct-Apr)

Websites

Pays de Fribourg (www.pays-de-fribourg.ch) Low-down on Fribourg land.

ℹ Getting There & Away

Trains travel hourly to/from Neuchâtel (Sfr20.20, 55 minutes), and more frequently to Geneva (Sfr39, 1½ hours) and Bern (Sfr13.20, 20 minutes). Regular trains run to Yverdon-les-Bains (Sfr18, 55 to 80 minutes) and Lausanne (Sfr23, 45 to 55 minutes).

Buses depart from behind the **bus station**, accessible from the train station, for Avenches (Sfr8.80, 25 minutes), Bulle (Sfr15.40, 55 minutes) and Schwarzsee (Sfr15.40, one hour).

Estavayer-le-Lac

POP 5000 / ELEV 455M

A charming manicured lakeside enclave that has largely preserved its medieval core, Estavayer-le-Lac is a lovely hideout known for frogs – dead or alive.

◉ Sights & Activities

Musée des Grenouilles   MUSEUM
(Frog Museum; www.museedesgrenouilles.ch; Rue du Musée 13; adult/child Sfr5/3; ⊙10am-noon & 2-5pm Tue-Sun Mar-Jun, Sep & Oct, 10am-noon & 2-5pm daily Jul & Aug, 2-5pm Sat & Sun Nov-Feb) Frogs star at the Musée des Grenouilles, caught, stuffed and 'modelled' by François Perrier, a retired Swiss military fellow, in the 1860s. Weapons, Roman coins, 17th-century kitchen utensils et al focus on local history.

Château de Chenaux   CASTLE
Estavayer's castle (1285–90), home to the prefecture and police station, cannot be visited but its ramparts can be strolled. Ask the tourist office for its Circuit des Remparts brochure that maps out a 1½-hour stroll along the original 40m-long and 35m-wide rectangle interspersed with 16 gates and turrets galore. The largest tower, 32m-tall Grand Tour, could only be accessed via a door that stood 9m above ground level and was reached by a drawbridge in medieval times.

Lac de Neuchâtel   LAKE
The lake reins in a buoyant crowd with **Alphasurf's Téléski** (www.alphasurf.ch; 30/60/120 min Sfr22/35/60; ⊙1-7pm May-Sep) that tows waterskiers and wakeboarders around a cableway circuit from the end of a jetty at Nouvelle Plage. You can swim, sail and surf on the gravelly beach here...or listen to a frogs' chorus in the nearby **Grande Cariçaie** (www.grande-caricaei.ch). This chain of marshy reed-fringed lakes strung along the southern edge of Lac de Neuchâtel is a stronghold for common green frogs, pool frogs, tree frogs and common toads. Watchtowers provide a bird's-eye view of the unique frog land.

🍴 Sleeping & Eating

Hôtel du Port   HOTEL $$
(✏️026 664 82 82; www.hotelduport.ch, in French; Rte du Port; s/d/tr/q from Sfr105/164/186/208; 🅿️🛜) The Hôtel du Port sits plump between the lake and Old Town and its rooms have recently undergone a solid renovation and

a visit from Cristiano Ronaldo. Lunch in the garden, kitted out with swings and trampolines for kids, is a pleasant summertime choice.

ℹ️ Information

From the train station walk 400m along Rue de la Gare to town and the **tourist office** (www .estavayer-payerne.ch; Rue de l'Hôtel de Ville 16; ⊙8.30am-noon & 1.30-5.45pm Mon-Fri, 10am-noon & 2-4pm Sat), on the corner of Rte du Port that leads downhill to the lake.

ℹ️ Getting There & Away

Estavayer-le-Lac is on the road/rail route between Fribourg (Sfr13.20, 40 minutes) and Yverdon (Sfr9.80, 17 minutes). Boats call in too (see p92).

Murten

POP 6100 / ELEV 450M

This German-speaking medieval village on the eastern shore of Murten See (Lac de Morat) isn't called Murten (Morat) – derived from the Celtic word *moriduno* meaning 'fortress on the lake' – for nothing. In May 1476 the Burgundy duke Charles the Bold set off from Lausanne to besiege Murten – only to have 8000 of his men butchered or drowned in Murten Lake during the Battle of Murten. The fortifications that thwarted the duke (who escaped) create a quaint little lakeside town well worth a visit.

Canals link Murten See with Lac de Neuchâtel (west) and Bieler See (north) to form the Pays des Trois Lacs (Land of Three Lakes) – a lake district criss-crossed with some 250km of marked roller-skating, cycling and walking paths.

◉ Sights & Activities

Murten is a cobblestone three-street town crammed with arcaded houses. A string of hotel-restaurants culminating in a 13th-century castle (closed to visitors) line **Rathausgasse**; shops and eateries stud parallel **Hauptgasse**, capped by the medieval **Berntor city gate** at its eastern end; while parallel Deutsche Kirchgasse and its western continuation, Schulgasse, hug the city ramparts.

Scale the wooden **Aufstieg auf die Ringmauer** (rampart stairs) behind the **Deutsche Kirche** (German Church; Deutsche Kirchgasse) to reach the covered walkway traversing part of the sturdy medieval walls. It's magical at sunset, but any time is a good time.

FRIBOURG, NEUCHÂTEL & JURA ESTAVAYER-LE-LAC

From late April to mid-October **Navigation Lacs de Neuchâtel et Morat** (see p92 for details) runs tours of Lake Murten (70 minutes, Sfr19). It's worth noting that the lake here is reputed to be the warmest in Switzerland, making it in ideal spot for a summer's dip.

Museum Murten   MUSEUM
(www.museummurten.ch, in French & German; Ryf 4; adult/child Sfr6/2; ⊙2-5pm Tue-Sat, 10am-5pm Sun) In a mill beyond the castle, this museum displays artefacts discovered during the dredging of the Broye Canal in 1829 and cannons used in the Battle of Murten.

🛏 Sleeping & Eating

Hotel Murtenhof & Krone   HOTEL $$
(☏026 672 90 30; www.murten hof.ch; Rathausgasse 1-5; s Sfr120-165, d Sfr160-240; P🖥) The Murtenhof, in a 16th-century patrician's house, mixes old and less-old to create a spacious space to eat and sleep. Its terrace restaurant (mains Sfr21 to Sfr25) cooks up dreamy lake views and fairly traditional cuisine.

Des Bains   MODERN EUROPEAN $$
(www.desbains-murten.ch, in French & German; Ryf 35; mains Sfr30-50; ⊙11am-11.30pm Mon-Thu, 11am-midnight Fri & Sat, 11am-10pm Sun) For lakeside dining, the Baths are prime, with a green lawn tumbling from the tabled terrace down to the water and a menu that features modern flourishes.

Hôtel Le Vieux Manoir   LUXURY HOTEL $$$
(☏026 678 61 61; www.vieuxmanoir.ch; Rue de Lausanne 18, Meyriez; s/d from Sfr300/450; P🖥🐕) This unabashedly luxurious timber Normandy house, built as a whim on the lakeside in the early 1900s, is *the* ultimate splurge. For wooers wanting their loved one to say yes, opt for the solitary table for two at the end of a long jetty, where you can dine at sunset. Find the Old Lake Manor 1km south of Murten in Meyriez.

ℹ Information

Tourist office (www.murten.ch, in German; Französische Kirchgasse 6; ⊙9am-noon & 2-5pm Mon-Fri Oct-Mar, 9am-noon & 1-6pm Mon-Fri, 10am-noon & 1-5pm Sat & Sun Apr-Sep)

ℹ Getting There & Around

From the train station (Bahnhofstrasse), 300m south of the city walls, hourly trains run to/from Fribourg (Sfr11, 30 minutes), Bern (Sfr13.20, 35

minutes) via Kerzers (Sfr4.50, nine minutes) and Neuchâtel (Sfr12.20, 25 minutes). Hourly trains to/from Payerne (Sfr8.80, 20 minutes) stop at Avenches (Sfr4.50, seven minutes).

Murten train station rents **bicycles** (per day Sfr33; ⊙9am-4pm).

Navigation Lacs de Neuchâtel et Morat runs seasonal boats to/from Neuchâtel; see p92. By car, Murten is on the N1 linking Lausanne with Bern.

Around Murten

Overwhelmingly agricultural with bags of green fields and hay barns to roll around in, the countryside around Murten offers a gulp of old-fashioned fresh air. On the western side of the lake, Vully wine is made from grapes grown on the gentle slopes of Mont Vully (653m).

For a real taste of this rural neck of the woods stay at **Eulenhof** (Owl Farm; ☏026 673 18 85; www.fermeduhibou.ch; Rue du Château 24, Mur; sleep on straw incl breakfast adult/child Sfr30/16, dm adult/child Sfr43/26, r per person Sfr65-85; ⊙Jan-Oct; P), a rustic property on the cycling and hiking Sentier du Vins de Vully (Vully wine trail). Farmer Willy and wife Nadja cook up regional cuisine in a terraced garden with a lake view; reserve in advance. To find Eulenhof, 13km north of Murten, follow the lake road north to Guénaux, then head 1km inland to Mur village.

AVENCHES

Roman Aventicum, 8km southwest of Murten, grew on the site of the ancient capital of the Celtic Helvetii tribe and was a major centre in the 2nd century AD, with a population 10 times what it is today. But in the late 3rd century its 5.6km of defensive ramparts failed to withstand attacks by the Alemanni tribe and by the 5th century the town had tumbled into obscurity.

Its Roman glory days are evoked in its amphitheatre, host to a **Musée Romain** (Roman Museum; Av Jomini; adult/child Sfr4/free; ⊙10am-5pm Tue-Sun) and an audience of 12,000 during its July Opera Festival; contact the **tourist office** (www.avenches.ch, in French; Place de l'Église 3) for tickets.

PAYERNE

Payerne, 10km southwest of Avenches (and in Vaud canton), is dominated by the 11th-century, five-apse Romanesque **Abbatiale de Payerne** (Abbey Church; Place du Marché; adult/child Sfr6/3; ⊙10am-noon & 2-6pm Tue-Sun

May-Sep, to 5pm Oct-Apr). The sandstone complex boasts fine sculptural decoration and frescos, hosts exhibitions and concerts. Find details at the neighbouring **tourist office** (www.payerne.ch, in French; Place du Marché 10; ⊙9am-noon & 1.30-6pm Mon-Fri, 10am-3pm Sat).

KERZERS

Tropical butterflies flutter alongside hummingbirds and other exotic birds 11km northeast of Murten at **Papiliorama** (www.papiliorama.ch; adult/child Sfr18/9; ⊙9am-6pm Apr-Oct, 10am-5pm Nov-Mar). Indigenous butterflies flit about in the Swiss Butterfly Garden, tarantulas creep and crawl in **Arthropodarium**, night creatures from Latin America hide in **Nocturama**, and in Jungle Trek – a re-creation of a Belize nature reserve complete with mangroves, tropical dry forest and 7m-high panorama bridge – intrepid explorers do just that.

Papiliorama is 80m from Kerzers train station, linked to Murten by train.

Gruyères

POP 1800 / ELEV 830M

Cheese and featherweight meringues drowned in thick cream are what this dreamy village is all about. Named after the emblematic *gru* (crane) brandished by the medieval Counts of Gruyères, it is a riot of 15th- to 17th-century houses tumbling down a hillock. Its heart is cobbled, a castle is its crowning glory and hard AOC Gruyère (the village is Gruyéres but the 's' is dropped for the cheese) has been made for centuries in its surrounding Alpine pastures.

⊙ Sights & Activities

TOP CHOICE **Château de Gruyères** CASTLE
(www.chateau-gruyeres.ch; adult/child Sfr9.50/3; ⊙9am-6pm Apr-Oct, 10am-4.30pm Nov-Feb) This bewitching turreted castle, home to 19 different Counts of Gruyères who controlled the Sarine Valley from the 11th to 16th centuries, was rebuilt after a fire in 1493. Inside, view period furniture, tapestries and modern 'fantasy art' and watch a short multimedia film. Don't miss the short footpath that weaves its way around the castle.

Sentier des Fromageries WALKING
Cheese is still produced in a couple of traditional mountain chalets along the Sentier des Fromageries, a trail that takes walkers

WORTH A TRIP

CAFÉ TIVOLI

The little town of Châtel-St-Denis has only one thing to warrant a visit but it's something you won't forget in a hurry: truly great fondue *moitié-moitié* (made with Gruyére and Vacherin Fribourgeois). Find it at the much-loved, family-run and very traditional **Café Tivoli** (☑021 948 70 39; www.cafetivoli.ch, in French; Place d'Armes 18; ⊙lunch & dinner Fri-Tue, lunch Wed), where you'll pay about Sfr24 per person for your share of the *caquelon*'s bounty. To get there from Fribourg, take the A12, heading south.

through green Gruyères pastures. Ask at the Maison du Gruyère for the brochure outlining the two-hour walk (7km to 8km).

Museum HR Giger MUSEUM
(www.hrgigermuseum.com; adult/child Sfr12.50/5.50; ⊙10am-6pm May-Oct, 1-5pm Tue-Fri, 10am-6pm Sat & Sun Nov-Apr) Biomechanical art fills this space, dedicated to the man behind the alien in the *Alien* films – Chur-born, Zürich-based Giger (b 1940). The museum bar opposite, **Bar HR Giger** (⊙1-8.30pm Mon, 10am-8.30pm Tue-Sun), is kitted out in the same surrealist style.

A combined museum and château ticket costs Sfr17.

Cheesemaking

La Maison du Gruyère DAIRY
(www.lamaisondugruyere.ch; adult/child Sfr7/3; ⊙9am-7pm Apr-Sep, to 6pm Oct-Mar) The secret behind Gruyère cheese is revealed here in Pringy, 1.5km from Gruyères. Cheesemaking takes place three to four times daily between 9am and 11am and 12.30pm to 2.30pm.

Fromagerie d'Alpage de Moléson DAIRY
(www.fromagerie-alpage.ch, in French; adult/child Sfr5/2; ⊙cheesemaking display 10am, restaurant 9am-7pm early May-end Sep) At this 17th-century Alpine chalet 5km southwest of Gruyères in Moléson-sur-Gruyères (elevation 1100m), cheese is made a couple of times a day in summer using old-fashioned methods. Both dairies sell cheese and serve fondue, *soupe du chalet* (a thick and hearty vegetable and potato soup topped with Gruyère double cream and cheese) and other typical mountain dishes in their dairy restaurants.

DON'T MISS

BROC & BULLE

One of Switzerland's oldest chocolate makers, **Cailler** (www.cailler.ch; Rue Jules Bellet 7, Broc; adult/child Sfr10/free; ◷10am-6pm Apr-Oct, to 5pm Nov-Mar) has been in business since 1825, and the modern facilities here offer anecdotes, samples, demonstrations (on how the famous 'Branch' batons are made) and a sort of sensory overload (no doubt exacerbated by the chance to buy factory seconds a mere 80m up the road). It gets packed on weekends and during holidays – and rightly so. Find the factory 2km north of Gruyères, in Broc, by following the signs to Nestlé.

Bulle, the area's main transport hub 5km northwest of Gruyères, is worth a whistle-stop for a glimpse of its 13th-century **château** (now administrative offices) and **Musée Gruérien** (www.musee-gruerien.ch, in French; Rue de la Condémine 25), which was undergoing a thorough refurbishment when we visited and due to reopen in 2012.

🛏 Sleeping & Eating

Cheese fondue is the natural star of every menu, irrespective of season (locals only eat fondue in winter); *moitié-moitié* is a mix of Gruyère and soft local Vacherin.

La Ferme du Bourgoz   FARMSTAY $
(☎079 252 74 51; www.lafermedubourgoz.ch, in French; Chemin du Bourgoz 14; r per person, incl breakfast Sfr45; P) You'll sleep well thanks to the authentic cheese dreams that a stay at the Murith family's cheesemaking home encourages. Simple, cosy rooms and unbeatable farm-fresh breakfasts, plus chunks of homemade Gruyère for sale.

Chalet de Gruyères   SWISS $$
(www.chalet-gruyeres.ch, in French; Rue du Château 53; fondues & raclettes from Sfr29.50; ◷lunch & dinner daily) A quintessential Gruyères address, this cosy wooden chalet strung with cow bells oozes Alpine charm – and fodder (fondue, raclette, grilled meats). There's a flower-bedecked terrace in the warmer months too.

❶ Information

Tourist office (☎0848 424 424; www.la-gruyere.ch; Rue du Bourg 1; ◷10.30am-noon & 1-4.30pm Sep-Jun, 9.30am-5.30pm Jul & Aug)

❶ Getting There & Around

Gruyères can be reached by hourly bus or train (Sfr15.40, 43 minutes to one hour) from Fribourg to Bulle, where you need to hop on another hourly bus or train (Sfr4.50, 15 to 20 minutes). Gruyères is a 10-minute walk uphill from its train station.

Charmey & the Schwarzsee

From Broc it is a pretty climb into the Pre-Alps of Canton de Fribourg. Charmey (elevation 876m) is the centre of local skiing, with 30km of downhill slopes (1630m). In summer, it's a haven for walkers and mountain bikers. The **tourist office** (☎026 927 55 80; www.charmey.ch; ◷8am-noon & 1.30-6pm Mon-Fri, to 4.30pm Sat, 9am-noon Sun), which is situated just across the car park from its cable car, has trail details, including around Vanil Noir (2389m), the region's highest point.

The thermal baths here, **Les Bains de la Gruyère** (www.les-bains-de-charmey.ch; adult/child 3hr Sfr24/13, half-day Sfr35/25; ◷9am-9pm Mon-Thu, to 10pm Fri & Sat, to 8pm Sun) boast first-class new facilities and provide ample relaxation opportunities, from simple swimming to massages and beauty treatments.

Head east for another 11km and you hit German-speaking territory and the chocolate-box-pretty hamlet of **Jaun** with its twinset of churches. The older one with a wood shingle roof shelters **Cantorama** (www.cantorama.ch, in French & German; concerts Sfr25; ◷2-5pm Sat & Sun mid-Jun–mid-Oct), a music centre with displays on traditional Fribourgeois chants and host to choral concerts. The newer church (1910) has a cemetery with modern wooden crosses that feature carvings of the deceased's former occupation.

Nearby is the mountain lake of **Schwarzsee** (Black Lake; www.schwarzsee.ch), set for winter skiing and summertime hiking. About 2km north of the village is Karl Neuhaus' **Eis Paläste** (Ice Palace; www.eispalaeste.ch; adult/child Sfr8/4; ◷2-9pm Wed-Sun Dec-Mar), a magical construction of turrets, bridges, domes, grottoes and crystal palaces between pine trees – built solely from ice. Illuminated at night, an evening stroll along the sand paths (not to mention a picnic in an igloo) is quite fairy-tale-like.

CANTON DE NEUCHÂTEL

The focus of this heavily forested 800 sq km canton (population 171,700), northwest of its Fribourg counterpart, is Lac de Neuchâtel – the largest lake entirely within Switzerland. Canton capital Neuchâtel sits plumb on its northern shore and the gentle Jura Mountains rise to the north and west. Watchmaking has been a mainstay industry since the 18th century and the canton's two other large towns – La Chaux-de-Fonds and Le Locle – remain firmly on the much-marketed 'Watch Valley' tourist trail.

Together with Biel and Murten lakes, Neuchâtel falls into the Pays de Trois Lacs. With France bang next door, French is *the* language of this rural land.

Neuchâtel

POP 32,800 / ELEV 430M

Its Old Town sandstone elegance, the airy Gallic nonchalance of its cafe life and the gay lakeside air that imbues the shoreline of its lake makes Neuchâtel disarmingly charming. The small university town – complete with spirited *commune libre* (free commune) – is compact enough to discover on foot.

Neuchâtel's town observatory gives the official time-check for all of Switzerland.

◎ Sights

Old Town   NEIGHBOURHOOD
The attractive Old Town streets are lined with fine, shuttered 18th-century mansions and studded with fanciful gold-leaf fountains topped by anything from a banner-wielding knight, **Fontaine du Banneret** (Rue Fleury), to a maiden representing Justice, **Fontaine de la Justice** (Rue de l'Hôpital); see a copy on the street and the original in the Musée d'Art et d'Histoire.

Heading uphill along Rue du Château, walk through the medieval city gate to view the **Tour des Prisons** (Rue Jehanne de Hochberg 5; admission Sfr2; ◎8am-6pm Apr-Sep). Scale it for views over the town below and its lake and Alpine backdrop. Inside the largely Gothic Église Collégiale a mix of Romanesque elements (notably the triple apse) looms large. Facing the main entrance is a statue of Guillaume Farel, who brought the Reformation to town, after which the cathedral was obliged to swap sides.

FREE Château   CASTLE
(☎032 889 40 03; ◎guided tours hourly 10am-noon & 2-4pm Mon-Fri, 2-4pm Sat & Sun Apr-Sep) Behind the church is the 15th-century castle with a pretty courtyard made for meandering. Excellent summertime guided tours (45 minutes) allow you to poke your nose around the castle's innards.

Musée d'Art et d'Histoire   MUSEUM
(Art & History Museum; www.mahn.ch, in French; Esplanade Léopold Robert 1; adult/child Sfr8/free; ◎11am-6pm Tue-Sun) The museum is notable for three clockwork androids made between 1764 and 1774 by watchmaker Jaquet Droz. The Writer can be programed to dip his pen in an inkpot and write up to 40 characters, while the Musician plays up to five tunes on a real organ. The Draughtsman is the simplest, with a repertoire of six drawings. The androids are activated on the first Sunday of the month at 2pm, 3pm and 4pm.

✦ Activities

The port buzzes with summer fun. For a lake cruise contact the Navigation Lacs de Neuchâtel et Morat (see p92).

Marine Service Loisirs   WATER SPORTS
(☎032 724 61 82; www.msloisirs.ch, in French; Port de la Ville; ◎Apr-Oct) You can hire motor boats (Sfr60 to Sfr90 per hour), pedalos (Sfr25 to Sfr35 per hour) and two- or four-seated pedal-powered buggies (Sfr25 to Sfr35 per hour) and bicycles (Sfr25/40 per half-/full day) to cruise along the silky-smooth quays.

FREE Neuchâtel Roule   CYCLING
(☎076 417 50 91; www.neuchatelroule.ch, in French; Esplanade Léopold Robert; ◎7.30am-9.30pm early Apr-late Oct) Pick up a set of wheels for free (for the first four hours) from the seasonal portside kiosk run by Neuchâtel Roule. You'll need to leave a Sfr20 deposit.

✦ Festivals & Events

Jazz, pop and rock set the lakeside jiving during June's open-air Festi'Neuch (www.festineuch.ch, in French). Parades, costumes and drunken revelry ensure fun at the Fête des Vendanges (Grape Harvest Festival), the last weekend in September.

⌦ Sleeping

L'Aubier   HOTEL $$
(☎032 710 18 58; lecafe@aubier.ch; Rue du Château 1; s/d with sink Sfr85/120, with shower &

Neuchâtel

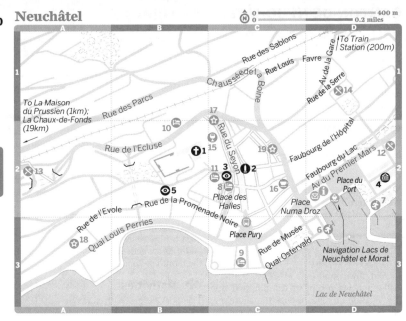

Neuchâtel

toilet Sfr130/180) Soulful sleeping above one of Neuchâtel's greenest eating spaces is what this lovely cafe-hotel is all about. Find it in an old building with diagonal-striped shutters peeping down on a sword-wielding knight.

Auberg'Inn GUESTHOUSE $$
(☏032 721 44 20; www.auberginn.ch; Rue Fleury 1; s/d/tr/q/5-person Sfr100/150/195/240/300; ☎) An atmospheric hostel-style place to stay next

to a chivalrous fountain and above a bar and restaurant, this trend-setting inn flaunts five design-driven rooms on the upper floors (no lift) of a late Renaissance townhouse. Find reception around the back at the Café du Cerf.

Hôtel Beau Rivage LUXURY HOTEL $$$
(☏032 723 15 15; www.beau-rivage-hotel.ch; Esplanade du Mont Blanc 1; s/d from Sfr340/410; ⓟ ❋@⬛) Overlooking the lake and sculpture-

studded gardens, this majestic hotel is all about the five-star magic – as is its spa, verandah bar and the culinary wonders of its restaurant team. Fab packages too.

Hôtel de l'Ecluse   HOTEL $$
(✆032 729 93 10; www.hoteldelecluse.ch; Rue de l'Ecluse 24; s/d incl breakfast Sfr143/196; ☎) Set back off a busy road, this three-star house with blue wooden shutters has modernised rooms with kitchenettes and a cute little stone-clad courtyard out back to lounge in.

✕ Eating

Local specialities include tripe and *tomme neuchâteloise chaude* (baked goat's-cheese starter).

Café des Arts   CAFE $$
(www.cafe-des-arts.ch, in French; Rue Pourtalès 5; mains Sfr28-42; ☺lunch & dinner Mon-Fri, dinner Sat & Sun) Smart and stylish and with a well-deserved reputation among locals, this is a lovely spot for Asian- and Med-influenced modern fare. Sunday nights it's entrecôte night (Sfr35) – definitely one for lovers of steak and Café de Paris butter.

Hôtel DuPeyrou   FRENCH $$$
(✆032 725 11 83; www.dupeyrou.ch, in French; Av Du Peyrou 1; mains Sfr52-56, menus from Sfr95; ☺lunch & dinner Tue-Sat) DuPeyrou presides like a mini-Versailles over manicured gardens. Built between 1765 and 1770, it regales with gastronomic dining in an 18th-century ambience. Come autumn, its game dishes are not to be missed.

L'Aubier   CAFE $
(✆032 710 18 58; Rue du Château 1; snacks from Sfr10;☺noon-7pm Mon, from 7.30am Tue-Fri, 8am-6pm Sat) Perfectly placed in the Old Town shade of Fontaine du Banneret, this green-thinking cafe cooks up a healthy smattering of salads, quiches, tarts and so on – ideal for a spot of lunch.

Famiglia Leccese   ITALIAN $$
(✆032 724 41 10; Rue de l'Ecluse 49; mains Sfr20-30; ☺dinner Tue-Sat, lunch & dinner Sun) Never was there a slice of Italy – Lecce in southern Italy to be precise – outside of Italy so authentic as this earthy, friendly, brilliant and *bellissimo* Italian-run joint. It's tucked out of the way: look for the fairy lights behind Claude Cordey Motos.

La Maison du Prussien   FRENCH $$$
(✆032 730 54 54; www.hotel-prussien.ch; Rue des Tunnels 11; mains Sfr59-80, menus from Sfr120;

☺lunch & dinner Mon-Fri, lunch Sat) This one-time brewery in a grand old house, enclosed by woods and cradled by the impetuous babbling of a nearby brook, is a treat – and it has great rooms too. From Place Pury hop aboard Cormondrèche-bound bus 1, alight at Beauregard and head down the stairs to your right following the signs.

☕ Drinking & Entertainment

Rue des Moulins and nearby Rue des Chavannes in the commune are the places to imbibe.

Chauffage Compris   BAR
(www.chaufaggecompris.ch; Rue des Moulins 37; ☺11am-late Mon-Sat) Despite its name – Heating Included – this retro bar with a decorative tiled entrance is one cool place to loiter, be it for morning coffee, evening aperitif, night-owl drink or easy snacks.

Le Bistrot du Concert   BAR
(www.bistrotduconcert.ch, in French; Rue de l'Hôtel de Ville 4; mains Sfr19-28; ☺8am-late Mon-Sat) A solid all-round address, this industrial-styled bar with busy pavement terrace has a soulful spirit, zinc bar and appealing menu chalked on the blackboard.

La Case à Chocs   CLUB
(www.case-a-chocs.ch, in French; Quai Philippe Godet 20; ☺10pm-2am Fri-Sun) Alternative venue in a converted brewery with live music, DJ sets and a free-spirited vibe when it's cranking.

Bar King   LIVE MUSIC
(www.barking.ch, in French; Rue du Seyon 38; ☺6pm-late Mon-Fri, from 7pm Sat) A good venue for bands, concerts, fringe theatre, jazz and various other gigs.

Paradox   CLUB
(www.paradoxclub.com, in French; Rue des Terreaux 7; ☺10.30pm-4am Thu-Sat, À l'Étage 5pm-late Tue-Sun) Paradox is a trio of funky, steely spaces: À l'Étage (1st-floor bar), Para (club with entrance at Rue des Terreaux 7) and Dox (entrance at Rue de Chavannes 19).

ⓘ Information

Post
Post office (Place du Port; ☺7.30am-6.30pm Mon-Fri, 8.30am-noon Sat)

Tourist Information
Tourist office (www.neuchateltourism.ch; Hôtel des Postes; ☺9am-noon & 1.30-5.30pm Mon-Fri, 9am-noon Sat Sep-Jun, 9am-6.30pm Mon-Fri, 9am-4pm Sat, 10am-2pm Sun Jul & Aug)

ℹ️ Getting There & Away

Boat

Navigation Lacs de Neuchâtel et Morat (☏032 729 96 00; www.navig.ch; Port de la Ville) runs boats late April to mid-October to/from Estavayer-le-Lac (Sfr20.20, 1¾ hours), Yverdon-les-Bains (Sfr35, 2½ hours), Murten (Sfr24, 1¾ hours) and Biel (Bienne; Sfr36, 2½ hours). Buy tickets on board; return fares are double one-way fares quoted.

Train

From the **train station** (Av de la Gare), a 10-minute walk northeast of the Old Town, hourly trains run to/from Geneva (Sfr39, 1¼ to 1½ hours), Bern (Sfr18.60, 30 to 50 minutes), Basel (Sfr36, 1½ hours), Biel (Sfr12.20, 20 minutes) and other destinations. Two per hour serve Yverdon (Sfr14.20, 20 minutes).

ℹ️ Getting Around

Local buses hit transport hub Place Pury and **Transports Public du Littoral Neuchâtelois information & ticket kiosk** (www.tnneuchatel.ch, in French; Place Pury; ☉7am-6pm Mon-Fri, 8.30-11.30am Sat). Bus 6 links the train station and Place Pury.

Around Neuchâtel

INLAND

Soak up views across the three lakes to the Alps in Chaumont (1160m), a ride on bus 7 from Neuchâtel to La Coudre then a 12-minute ride up the mountain on a panoramic funicular (2-zone adult ticket valid 1hr Sfr3.60; ☉7.15am-7pm year-round).

Pushing north along the N20, **Vue-des-Alpes** (1283m) is popular with mountain bikers who fly along two circular 7.3km and 11km trails. The pass also makes an exhilarating stop for kid-clad motorists whose young passengers go bananas over the 700m-long **Toboggan Géant** (www.toboggans.ch; adult/child Sfr4/3; ☉1-6pm Mon-Fri, 10am-6pm Sat & Sun), a luge track that rips down the mountain. In winter, locals sledge, snow-shoe and ski down the gentle slopes (three drag lifts) or along 53km of cross-country trails.

The place to feast on seasonal produce is **Auberge de Mont Cornu** (☏032 968 76 00; Mont Cornu 116; lunch menu Sfr49.50, mains Sfr25-35; ☉lunch & dinner Wed-Sun Apr-Dec), a chalet at 1152m, well-endowed with blossoms and surrounded by cow-spotted fields. The pride and joy of the Lüthi family, the charming inn has a menu built on seasonal and (mostly) local ingredients. Drive 2km north of Vue-des-Alpes along the N20 then turn right to Mont Cornu, following signs for the latter for 3km along a country lane.

Le Corbusier and art-nouveau architecture is the reason to push northwest to **La Chaux-de-Fonds** (pop 37,500), the canton's largest city and Switzerland's highest. In the 18th and 19th centuries the drab grid-plan town was a household name in Europe as the centre of precision

---

CONCRETE KING

Few know that Le Corbusier (1887–1965), often perceived as French, was born in La Chaux-de-Fonds at Rue de la Serre 38. Charles Edouard Jeanneret (the ground-breaking architect's real name) spent his childhood in the clockmaking town whose concrete, Soviet-style grid-plan clearly found its way somewhere into his young psyche.

After stints in the Orient and Berlin, Le Corbusier returned to La Chaux in 1912 to open an architectural office and build Villa Jeanneret for his parents. The architect who, a few years later would become a serious pal of Germany's Walter Gropius and the Bauhaus movement, lived in the house until 1917. Two years later his parents sold up and left town.

The neoclassical house with white facade and shiny roof, now known as **La Maison Blanche** (The White House; www.maisonblanche.ch; Chemin de Pouillerel 12; adult/child Sfr10/free; ☉10am-5pm Fri-Sun), is prized as Le Corbusier's first independent piece of work, and a notable break from the regional art nouveau. Architecturally unrecognisable as Le Corbusier to anyone familiar with his later work, it sat derelict in the leafy hilltop neighbourhood above La Chaux until 2004, when it was renovated, refurnished (with some original furnishings, such as the green canapé in the sitting room) and opened to the public.

The house is one of 11 points on a DIY Corbusier itinerary around several villas designed by the young Le Corbusier in La Chaux, including the Mediterranean-inspired **Villa Turque** (☏032 912 31 23; Rue du Doubs 167; ☉free guided tour 11am-4pm 1st & 3rd Sat of month).

It was in the deepest, darkest depths of the Val de Travers – dubbed the Pays des Fées (Fairyland) – that absinthe was first distilled in 1740 and produced commercially in 1797 (although it was a Frenchman called Pernod who made the bitter green liqueur known with the distillery he opened just a few kilometres across the French–Swiss border in Pontarlier).

Famous drinkers of the *fée verte* (green fairy) in the 19th century included Baudelaire, Rimbaud (whose absinthe- and hashish-fuelled affair with Verlaine scandalised Parisian literary circles), Vincent van Gogh and Oscar Wilde.

From 1910, following Switzerland's prohibition of the wickedly alcoholic aniseed drink, distillers of the so-called 'devil in the bottle' in the Val de Travers went underground. In 1990 the great-grandson of a pre-prohibition distiller in Môtiers came up with Switzerland's first legal aniseed liqueur since 1910 – albeit one which was only 45% proof alcohol (instead of 50% to 75%) and which scarcely contained thujone (the offensive chemical found in wormwood, said to be the root of absinthe's devilish nature). An *extrait d'absinthe* (absinthe extract) quickly followed and in 2005, following Switzerland's lifting of its absinthe ban, the **Blackmint – Distillerie Kübler & Wyss** (www.blackmint .ch) in Môtiers distilled its first true and authentic batch of the mythical brew from valley-grown wormwood. Mix one part crystal-clear liqueur with five parts water to make it green.

watchmaking and still manufactures timepieces today. Get the full story in its **Musée International d'Horlogerie** (International Museum of Watchmaking; www.mih.ch, in French; Rue des Musées 29; adult/child Sfr15/ free; ☺10am-5pm Tue-Sun), a well thought-out museum in a funky concrete bunker, with history and fine arts museums as neighbours.

The **tourist office** (Espacité 1, Place Le Corbusier; ☺9am-noon & 1.30-5.30pm Mon-Fri, 9am-noon Sat Sep-Jun, 9am-6.30pm Mon-Fri, 9am-4pm Sat Jul & Aug) is a five-minute walk north of the train station along Av Léopold Robert.

Hourly trains run from Neuchâtel to/from La Chaux-de-Fonds (Sfr4.90, 30 minutes).

ALONG THE LAKE

Family-scale vineyards have dressed the hilly northwest shore of Lac de Neuchâtel since the 10th century.

At Hauterive, 3km northeast of Neuchâtel, the architecturally arresting museum **Laténium** (www.latenium.ch; adult/child Sfr9/4; ☺10am-5pm Tue-Sun) is a veritable archaeological trip back in time from local prehistory to the Renaissance and has some excellent temporary exhibitions. Take bus 1 from Place Pury to the Musée d'Archéologie stop.

VAL DE TRAVERS

From Noiraigue, plumb in the Travers Valley 22km southwest of Neuchâtel, it is a short walk to the enormous abyss of **Creux du** Van (Rocky Hole – *van* is a word of Celtic origin meaning rock). A product of glacial erosion, the spectacular crescent moon wall interrupts the habitually green rolling countryside hereabouts in startling fashion: imagine an enormous gulf 1km long and 440m deep.

Continuing along the N10 or on the same train from Neuchâtel (Sfr3.50, 35 minutes), you reach **Môtiers** with its pretty castle, absinthe distilleries and cafe-bars with absinthe on the menu (right down to the soufflé). Immediately south from here a 4½-hour to 5½-hour looped walk leads through the Gorges de la Poëta Raisse to high green plains, forest and a 1448m crest.

A spirit-soothing green sleep in this valley is included in the price at **L'Aubier** (✆032 732 22 11; www.aubier.ch; s/d/tr/q incl breakfast from Sfr130/170/290/340), an ecologically sound, small eco-hotel on a biodynamic farm in Montézillon, a hamlet at 750m, 8km southwest of Neuchâtel. Contemporary, light-flooded rooms overlook lush fields of grazing cows. There's also an excellent biodynamic restaurant and shop.

Montagnes Neuchâteloises

The west of the canton is dominated by the low mountain chain of the Jura, which stretches from the canton of the same name to the northeast and into Canton de Vaud in the southwest. Cross-country skiers, hikers and bikers love the locals hills, the Montagnes Neuchâteloises.

LE LOCLE
POP 10,200 / ELEV 950M

Incredibly, the whole lucrative Swiss watch business began ticking in this straggly town when Daniel Jean-Richard (1665–1741) established a cottage industry in the manufacture of timepieces. Drive along the N20 from one town to another past dozens of factories emblazoned with big-name watchmakers Tissot, Tag Heuer, Breitling et al.

Grand 18th-century rooms filled with all manner of clocks make the **Musée de l'Horlogerie du Locle** (Watchmaking Museum; www.mhl-monts.ch, in French; Rte des Monts 65; adult/child Sfr8/free; ⊙10am-5pm Tue-Sun May-Oct, 2-5pm Tue-Sun Nov-Apr) tick. The manor house, Château des Monts, was built for an 18th-century watchmaker atop a hill 3km from the town centre. Bus 1 links the train station with the 'Monts' stop, 150m from the museum.

Le Locle is 8km by train (Sfr2.20, eight minutes, at least hourly) from La Chaux-de-Fonds.

LES BRENETS & SAUT DU DOUBS
Le Doubs River, which springs forth inside France, widens out at the peaceful village of Les Brenets, 6km from Le Locle. For the next 45km on its serpentine northwestern course from here, the river forms the border between the two countries before making a loop inside Switzerland and then returning to French territory.

About a one-hour walk along Lac des Brenets (Lac de Chaillexon on the French side) the river brings you to the **Saut du Doubs**, a splendid crashing waterfall where the river cascades 27m to a natural pool. For non-walkers, **Navigation sur le Lac des Brenets** (NLB; www.nlb.ch) runs regular boats from Les Brenets to the waterfall up to 11 times a day from June to September (adult single/return Sfr9/14), and three daily in April, May and October.

Le Locle–Les Brenets trains (Sfr3.60, seven minutes) are frequent.

CANTON DE JURA

Clover-shaped Canton de Jura (840 sq km, population 70,200) is a rural, mysterious peripheral region that few reach. Its grandest towns are no more than enchanting villages, while deep forests and impossibly green clearings succeed one another across its low mountains. While the Jura mountain range proper extends south through Canton de Neuchâtel and Canton de Vaud into the Haut-Jura in neighbouring France, it is here that its Jurassic heart lies.

Getting around is impossible without your own wheels – two or four – or hiking boots. Travelling between the main towns by pretty red mountain train, look for the set of 13 walking and cycling brochures published by local train company **Chemins de Fer du Jura** (www.cj-transports.ch, in French & German); train schedules and fares are online.

Franches Montagnes

Settlers only began trickling into these untamed 'free mountains' in the 14th century. Heavily forested hill country marking the northern end of the Jura range, the area – undulating at roughly 1000m – is sprinkled with hamlets and is ideal for walking, mountain biking and cross-country skiing. The Doubs River kisses its northern tip.

Saignelégier (population 2530, elevation 1000m), the Jura's main town on the train

---

MONKS' HEADS

For eight centuries, villages around the **Abbaye de Bellelay** (www.domaine -bellelay.ch, in French), 8km north of Tavannes between Moutier and St Imier, have produced a strong, nutty-flavoured cheese now known as monks' cheese. In 1792 revolutionary troops marched in, obliging the monks at the abbey to abandon the cylindrical cheese maturing in their cellars. Troopers, so the story goes, dubbed the cheese Tête de Moine (Monk's Head), perhaps after the curious way tradition demands it be sliced. Shavings are scraped off the top in a circular motion to create a rosette, done since the 1980s with a nifty handled device called a *girolle*.

Tête de Moine is no longer made at the abbey (now a psychiatric hospital) but the semi-hard AOC-protected cheese is found all over the Jura, including at Saignelégier's **Fromagerie de Tête de Moine** (www.tetedemoine.ch; Chemin du Finage 19; adult/child Sfr7/3; ⊙guided visits 3-5pm Fri Mar-Oct).

TOWARDS FRANCE

From Porrentuy one road leads west into France, 16km away. Pick up a mount to canter through the gorgeous green cow-speckled countryside here in Courtedoux, one of just a couple of villages along this gently scenic stretch. Not only do David and Veronique Protti at **Tourisme Équestre** (☎032 466 74 52; www.tourismeequestre.net; La Combatte 79a; ☺Easter-Oct) organise guided horse treks (Sfr30/80/100 per hour/half-/full day), they also rent horse-drawn carriages equipped with barbecue, picnic table and chairs, plates and so on, allowing you to explore the Jura by horse and cart – at a delightfully go-slow speed of 5km/h.

Ferme Montavon (☎032 476 67 23; ferme.montavon@bluewin.ch; Réclère; sleep in straw incl breakfast & shower adult/child Sfr24/13, chambre d'hôte Sfr45/25; ☺Easter-Oct), on the Swiss–French border in Réclère, is a 200-year-old farmhouse with room for guests and a bed of straw in the eaves of a huge hay barn. Four generations live on the farm and it's a wonderfully authentic slice of Swiss life to experience. Advance reservations, including for a hearty dinner of farm produce (Sfr25), are essential.

Nearby **Préhisto Parc** (www.prehisto.ch, in French; adult/child Sfr8/6; ☺10am-noon & 1-5.30pm Easter-Jun & Sep–mid-Nov, 9.30am-6pm Jul & Aug) is a well-put-together dinosaur park with a 2km-long footpath in woods that passes dozens of prehistoric creatures lurking between trees. Underfoot are the **Grottes de Réclère** (admission by 50min French/German guided tour adult/child Sfr9/6), stalagmite-filled caves discovered in 1886. A combined ticket for both costs Sfr15/10 per adult/child. No credit cards. For further information, head to http://shop.lonelyplanet.com to purchase a downloadable PDF of the France chapter from Lonely Planet's *Western Europe* guide.

line between La Chaux-de-Fonds (Sfr14.20, 35 minutes, almost hourly) and Basel (Sfr27, 1½ hours, change at Glovelier), is of little interest in itself but makes for a good base, especially for families, thanks to three-star **Hotel Cristal** (☎032 951 24 74; www.hotel cristal.ch; Chemin des Sports 10; s/d/tr/q from Sfr98/148/179/212; P@🛜), which is modern, well-run and has swimming facilities and an indoor skating rink.

The tourist office, **Jura Tourisme** (www .juratourisme.ch; Rue de la Gruère 1; ☺9am-noon & 2-5.45pm Mon-Fri, 9.30am-1.30pm Sat & Sun), is in the same complex and covers the whole of Jura, and has ample info on farm accommodation.

Cross-country skiers can skate around tiny Montfaucon, 5km northeast, or Les Breuleux, 7km south. **Le Noirmont**, 6km southwest, has the summer bonus of a **Tipi Village** (☎079 449 12 32; www.tipivillage.ch; Le Creux-des-Biches; 2/3/4-6 people Sfr50/70/100; ☺May-Sep) to kip beneath the stars (firewood costs Sfr20 extra).

One of Switzerland's best chefs, Georges Wenger conjures extraordinary Michelin-starred creations from seasonal local produce at his restaurant and boutique hotel, **Georges Wenger** (☎032 957 66 33; www .georges-wenger.ch; Rue de la Gare 2; mains Sfr72-

85, tasting menus Sfr89-235, d from Sfr330; P@) opposite the hamlet's tiny train station.

Northern Jura

Three towns within easy reach of one another are strung out across northern Jura, never far from the French frontier.

DELÉMONT

POP 11,600 / ELEV 413M

Canton de Jura's capital moored alongside the Scheulte River is modest. Its Old Town preserves a whiff of years gone by, with uneven houses topped by improbably tall tiled roofs peeping over 18th-century Église St-Marcel and château (1716–21). The **Musée Jurassien d'Art et d'Histoire** (www.mjah.ch, in French; Rue du 23 Juin 52; adult/child Sfr6/free; ☺2-5pm Tue-Fri, 11am-6pm Sat & Sun) displays a hodgepodge of paintings, religious art and so on but has recently been revamped.

Motorists can follow the signs 3km north out of town to the ruined **Chapelle de Vorbourg**, a dramatically located centre of pilgrimage. Contemporary art and installation lovers will enjoy **La Balade de Séprais** (www.balade-seprais.ch), an open-air sculpture park, 12km northwest.

ST URSANNE
POP 730 / ELEVATION 430M

The Jura's most enchanting village is medieval riverside St Ursanne. As early as the 7th century a centre of worship existed on the site of 12th-century Église Collégiale, a grand Gothic church with a splendid Romanesque portal on its southern flank and intriguing crypt.

Ancient houses, the 16th-century town gates, a lovely stone bridge and a bevy of eating options on miniature central square, Place Roger Schaffter, tumble down towards the Doubs River from the church. The thin crisp apple *tartes flambées* (Sfr12.50) cooked over flames are to die for at the modest 10-room Hôtel-Restaurant de la Demi Lune (032 461 35 31; www.demi-lune.ch; Place Roger Schaffter; s/d from Sfr95/120;), possessed of the only riverside terrace open to the public.

The tourist office (Place Roger Schaffter; 10am-noon & 2-5pm Mon-Fri, 10am-4pm Sat & Sun) has information on river kayaking, canoeing and walking.

Trains link St Ursanne train station, 1km east of the centre, and Porrentruy (Sfr5, 12 minutes).

PORRENTRUY
POP 6660 / ELEV 425M

From Col de la Croix, the road dips through forest and into a plain to the last Jura town of importance before heading into France – pretty Porrentruy. Fine old buildings, now shops, line the main street, Grand Rue, against a backdrop of bulky Château de Porrentuy, now occupied by the cantonal tribunal and various government offices. Scale 44m-tall Tour de Réfous (1270; admission free; 7.15-12.15am & 1.15-6pm), the oldest part of the 13th- to 18th-century hilltop complex, for a fine rooftop view. The walls at its sturdy base are 4.5m thick.

Everything from books and clocks to pharmaceutical objects are displayed in the well-put-together Musée de l'Hôtel Dieu (www.museehoteldieu.ch, in French; Grand Rue 5; adult/child Sfr5/free; 2-5pm Tue-Sun Easter–mid-Nov), Porrentuy's former hospital, worth a meander for its gorgeous baroque building with cobbled courtyard, home to the tourist office (www.porrentruy.ch, in French; Grand Rue 5; 9am-noon & 2-5.30pm Mon-Fri, 9am-noon Sat).

Mittelland

POP 1.2 MILLION / AREA 842 SQ KM / LANGUAGES GERMAN, FRENCH

Includes »

Best Places to Eat

» Altes Tramdepot (p104)

» Restaurant Coopérative St Gervais (p108)

» Gasthaus Bäregghöhe (p110)

» Cantinetta Bindella (p112)

» Pittaria (p112)

Best Places to Stay

» Hotel Schweizerhof (p103)

» Hotel Kreuz Ligerz (p109)

» Hotel Landhaus (p103)

» Villa Lindenegg (p107)

» Möschberg (p110)

Why Go?

It's funny that this flat, unassuming 'middle ground', as its straight-talking name states, should have Switzerland's capital at its heart. In fact, few even realise that riverside Bern is the Swiss capital, because the city is so delightfully languid, laid-back and – dare one say – the essence of 'soft power'.

Yet Bern's middling is precisely what makes it so politically savvy. When politicians had to pick a capital for the troubled Swiss Confederation it leapt out as the un-threatening choice: Geneva was too French, Zürich too German. Bern was just right.

Easily one of the most charming capitals on the planet, its 15th-century Old Town is fairy-tale-like with its terraced stone buildings, covered arcades, clock towers and cobbled streets. The surrounding countryside is as benignly beautiful, with traditional villages and farms speckling the rolling green hills, some of which produce Emmental – the cheese that could not be more Swiss if it tried.

When to Go

Summer is the time to visit for the best chance of warm days, blue skies and miles of lush green meadows dotted with cows, but you will be accompanied by a lot of tour buses. In autumn, the changing foliage on St Peter's Island is particularly dazzling, while Bern parties hearty during the *Zibelemärit* (Onion Market), which takes place on the fourth Monday in November and sees the city celebrating with a giant market selling all things onion-related. See p104 for more details. In the middle of winter, try to feast on *Treberwurst* (p109), a local sausage with a definite alcoholic kick.

ⓘ Information

Schweizer Mittelland Tourismus (☎ 031 328 12 12; www.smit.ch, in German; Bahnhofplatz 10a, Bern) The regional tourist office.

Bern

POP 123,500 / ELEV 540M

Wandering its picture-postcard Old Town, with arcaded stone streets and a provincial, laid-back air, it is hard to believe that Bern (Berne in English and French) is the capital of Switzerland – but it is, plus a Unesco World Heritage Site to boot.

Indeed, on the city's long, cobbled streets, lined with 15th-century terraced buildings and fantastical folk figures frolicking on fountains since the 16th century, you feel as if you're in some kind of dizzying architectural canyon. From the surrounding hills, you're presented with an equally captivating picture of red roofs crammed on a spit of land within a bend of the Aare River.

In a nutshell, Bern captivates. Its drinking scene is dynamic, its alternative arts scene happening and its locals happy to switch

DON'T MISS

BÄRENPARK

A popular folk etymology is that Bern got its name from the bear (*Bär* in German), when the city's founder, Berthold V, duke of Zähringen, snagged one here on a hunting spree. To the dismay of some, there was still a 3.5m-deep cramped bear pit in the city until 2009, when it was (thankfully) replaced by a spacious 6000-sq-metre open-air riverside park dotted with trees and terraces, in which a number of bears roam (although they still have access to the old pit).

You'll find the bear park (www .baerenpark-bern.ch) at the eastern end of the Nydeggbrücke. And with any luck, you'll catch sight of Finn, Björk, Mischa, Mascha, Ursina or Berna as they frolic, swim, eat and poop in the woods, as nature (almost) intended. Watching them play, it's hard to believe that Mischa and Mascha were 10kg orphans when they arrived in Bern from Ussuria. Obviously, there's not much to see in the winter months, when hibernation is the name of the game.

from their famously lilting and slow local dialect to English – which all goes to show that there's more to Bern than bureaucracy.

⊙ Sights

TOP CHOICE Zentrum Paul Klee ART MUSEUM
(www.zpk.org; Monument in Fruchtland 3; adult/child Sfr22/10, audioguides Sfr5; ☉10am-5pm Tue-Sun) Bern's answer to the Guggenheim, the architecturally bold Paul Klee Centre is an eye-catching 150m-long building filled with popular modern art. Renzo Piano's curvaceous building swoops up and down like waves to create a trio of 'hills' in the agricultural landscape east of town.

The middle hill houses the main exhibition space, showcasing 4000 rotating works from Paul Klee's prodigious and often-playful career. Interactive computer displays built into the seating mean you can get the low-down on all the Swiss-born artist's major pieces, while music-driven audio-guides take you on a one-hour DIY musical tour of his work. In the basement of one 'hill' is the fun-packed **Kindermuseum Creaviva** (☉10am-5pm Tue-Sun), an inspired children's museum, where kids can experiment with hands-on art exhibits (included in admission price) or participate in the weekend **Five Franc Studio** (www.creaviva-zpk.org; ☉10am-4.30pm Sat & Sun), where young artists (and older ones too!) pay Sfr5 to work with the atelier's materials and space and get to take their creations home with them.

In the museum grounds, a walk through fields takes visitors past a stream of modern and contemporary sculptures, including works by Yoko Ono and Sol Lewitt.

Take bus 12 from Bubenbergplatz to Zentrum Paul Klee (Sfr4). By car the museum is right next to the Bern-Ostring exit of the A6.

TOP CHOICE Berner Münster CHURCH
(www.bernermuenster.ch; audioguide Sfr5, tower admission adult/child Sfr5/2; ☉10am-5pm Tue-Sat, 11.30am-5pm Sun Easter-Nov, noon-4pm Tue-Fri, to 5pm Sat, 11.30am-4pm Sun rest of year, tower closes 30 min earlier) The high point of the 15th-century Gothic cathedral is its lofty spire. At 100m, it's Switzerland's tallest, and those with enough energy to climb the dizzying 344-step spiral staircase are rewarded with vertiginous views of the Bernese Alps on a clear day. Coming down, take a breather by the **Upper Bells** (1356), rung at 11am, noon and 3pm daily, and the three **Lower Bells**,

Mittelland Highlights

1 Fountain- and bar-hop through the fairy-tale, heritage-listed **Old Town** (p102) of Bern

2 Grin and Bear it at the much-improved **Bärenpark** in Bern

3 Surf the architectural delights of the wave-shaped **Zentrum Paul Klee**

4 Drink in the views to St Peter's Island and Lake Biel from lovely **Ligerz** (p109), with a local wine in hand

5 Meander lazily around Old Town **Solothurn** (p110), allowing time for its baroque cathedral and creative dining and drinking spaces by the water

6 Check out one of Switzerland's newest art spaces, the **Centre Pasqu-Art** (p107) in Biel-Bienne

7 Be cheesy in **Emmental**: eat it, watch it being made at the show dairy, then take your pick of local farms and inns for cheese dreams (p110)

each weighing 10 tonnes, making them Switzerland's largest bells.

Back on terra firma, look at the decorative **main portal** depicting the Last Judgement. The mayor of Bern is shown going to heaven, while his Zürich counterpart is being shown into hell.

Afterwards, wander behind the cathedral to the **Münster Plattform**, a bijou park of boxed hedges and benches, which drops away into a steep cliff. Enjoy a coffee in the sunshine at the pavilion cafe in the park, then ride the **public lift** (admission Sfr1.20) down to the quarter of **Matte** on the river plain. A medieval district of craftsmen, dockworkers and creatives, it had its own distinctive variety of Bernese German.

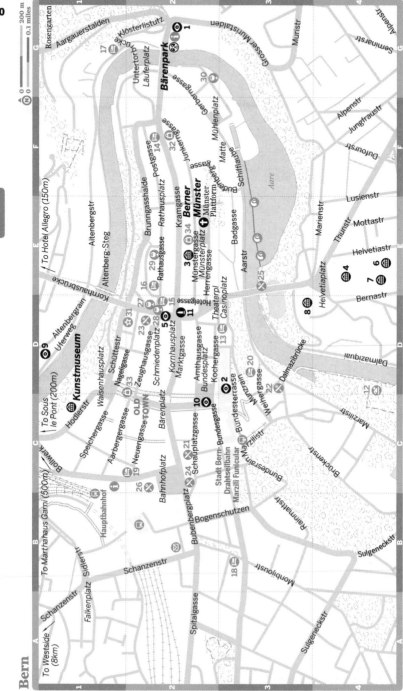

Bern

Bern

Kunstmuseum ART MUSEUM
(www.kunstmuseumbern.ch; Hodlerstrasse 8-12; adult/child permanent collection Sfr7/5, temporary exhibitions from Sfr18; ⊙10am-9pm Tue, 10am-5pm Wed-Sun) The thousands of works at the Museum of Fine Arts represent Switzerland's oldest permanent collection and include examples by Italian artists such as Fra Angelico, Swiss artists like Ferdinand Hodler and Giovanni Giacometti and heavy hitters like Picasso and Cézanne.

Einstein Haus MUSEUM
(www.einstein-bern.ch; Kramgasse 49; adult/child Sfr6/free; ⊙10am-5pm daily Apr-Dec, closed Sun Feb & Mar, closed Jan) The world's most famous scientist developed his special theory of relativity in Bern in 1905. Find out more at the small museum inside the humble apartment where Einstein lived with his young family between 1903 and 1905 while working in the Bern patent office. Upstairs, a 20-minute biographical film tells his life story, while displays elsewhere flesh out the story of the subsequent general equation – $E=mc^2$, or energy equals mass times the speed of light squared – which fundamentally changed our understanding of space, time and the universe. The heartbreaking story of his wife Mileva's life provides a poignant contrast to his fabled scientific success.

FREE **Bundeshäuser** HISTORIC BUILDING
(Houses of Parliament; www.parliament.ch; Bundesplatz) Home of the Swiss Federal Assembly, the Bundeshäuser, built in Florentine style in 1902, contain statues of the nation's founding fathers, a stained-glass dome adorned with cantonal emblems and a 214-bulb chandelier. When the parliament is in recess, there are 45-minute **tours** (admission free; ⊙hourly 9am-4pm Mon-Sat). During parliamentary sessions, watch from the public gallery. Bring official ID to get in.

MITTELLAND BERN

On the vast square in front of parliament spout 26 illuminated **water jets**, representing every Swiss canton. The perfect playground for kids in warmer weather, the square gently hums with city dwellers hanging out – plop yourself down on the pavement and do the same.

Helvetiaplatz Museums MUSEUM
The area called Helvetiaplatz is home to a number of museums, the pick of which is probably the **Historisches Museum Bern** (Bern Historical Museum; www.bhm.ch; Helvetiaplatz 5; adult/child Sfr13/4, Einstein Museum only Sfr18/8; ⌚10am-5pm Tue-Sun). Tapestries, diptychs and other world treasures vividly illustrate Bernese history from the Stone Age to the 20th century in a building that resembles a fairy-tale castle from a distance. Part of the history museum is devoted to a superb permanent exhibition on Einstein.
The **Schweizerisches Alpines Museum** (Swiss Alpine Museum; www.alpinesmuseum.ch; Helvetiaplatz 4; adult/child Sfr12/3; ⌚2-5.30pm Mon, 10am-5.30pm Tue-Sun) outlines the history of Alpine mountaineering and cartography with the help of impressive relief maps, while the **Naturhistorisches Museum** (Natural History Museum; www.nmbe.unibe.ch, in German; Bernastrasse 15; adult/child Sfr8/free; ⌚2-5pm Mon, 9am-5pm Tue, Thu & Fri, 9am-6pm Wed, 10am-5pm Sat & Sun) features the famous moth-eaten and taxidermied remains of Barry, a St Bernard rescue dog. Also in the neighbourhood is the **Museum für Kom-**munikation (www.mfk.ch; Helvetiastrasse 16; adult/child Sfr12/3; ⌚10am-5pm Tue-Sun), housing items from antique phones and stamps to electronic communication devices.

FREE **Gardens** GARDENS
Uphill from the bear pit is the fragrant **Rosengarten** (rose garden), probably known more for its stupendous view over town than its sweet-smelling blooms, although both are worth the climb. The **University Botanical Garden** (www.boga .unibe.ch, in German; ⌚8am-5pm daily) is found via a flight of steps leading from the northern end of Lorrainebrücke. It's a riverside garden with plenty of green specimens to admire and a couple of greenhouses.

Bern Show MULTIMEDIA
(Tourist Center Bärenpark; adult/child Sfr3/1; ⌚9am-6pm Jun-Sep, 10am-4pm Mar-May & Oct, 11am-4pm Nov-Feb) Behind the bears, in the tourist office, is this 20-minute multimedia show on Bern's history in English, French, Spanish, Italian or German.

🏃 **Activities**

FREE **Gurten Hill** WALKING
(www.gurtenpark.ch, in German) Some 3km south of town is Gurten Hill, whose peak boasts a couple of restaurants, a miniature railway, fun trails for bikers, a summer circus, winter sledge runs, an adventure playground and all sorts of other seasonal

---

DON'T MISS

OLD TOWN

Bern's flag-festooned medieval centre is an attraction in its own right, with 6km of covered arcades and cellar shops and bars descending from the streets. After a devastating fire in 1405, the wooden city was rebuilt in today's distinctive grey-green sandstone.

A focal point is Bern's **Zytglogge** (clock tower), once part of the city's western gate (1191–1256). It's reminiscent of the Astronomical Clock in Prague's old town square in that crowds congregate to watch its revolving figures twirl at four minutes before the hour, after which the actual chimes begin. Tours enter the tower to see the clock mechanism from May to October; contact the tourist office.

The clock tower supposedly helped Albert Einstein hone his theory of relativity, developed while working as a patent clerk in Bern.

The great scientist surmised, while travelling on a tram away from the tower, that if the tram were going at the speed of light, the clock tower would remain on the same time, while his own watch would continue to tick – proving time was relative.

Other Bern landmarks are its 11 decorative **fountains** (1545), which depict historic and folkloric characters. Most are along Marktgasse as it becomes Kramgasse and Gerechtigkeitsgasse, but the most famous lies in Kornhausplatz: the **Kindlifresserbrunnen** (Ogre Fountain) of a giant snacking on children!

outdoor fun. Enjoy fine views as you hike down the mountain (about one hour), following the clearly marked paths. To get there, take tram 9 towards Wabern, alight at Gurtenbahn and change to the **Gurten funicular** (www.gurtenbahn.ch, in German; adult one way/return Sfr6/10.50, child Sfr3/5.50; ⊙7am-11.30pm), which goes to the top.

FREE Marzili Pools   SWIMMING
(www.aaremarzili.ch, in German; ⊙May-Sep) In summer, this open-air swimming pool, beside the Aare River, is the perfect place to get a tan and kick back with the locals. The pool is a simple 25m affair, but the expansive lawns, foosball tables and sunbathing racks are often where the action is. Only strong swimmers should dip in the river itself.

Hammam & Spa   HAMMAM
(www.hamman-bern.ch; Weihergasse 3; admission Sfr42, treatments extra; ⊙9am-9.30pm Mon, Tue, Thu & Fri, 1-9.30pm Wed, 10am-8pm Sat & Sun) Housed in an eye-catching octagonal building, Bern's hammam is a lovely place to decompress in a 1001-nights atmosphere. Ladies-only on Tuesday.

Bernrollt   CYCLING
Scenic bike paths on the riverside and in the Bernese hills are plentiful; for free bike hire see p107.

🎎 Festivals & Events

Berchtoldstag   PUBLIC HOLIDAY
(2 Jan) A canton-wide public holiday.

Jazz Festival Bern   MUSIC
(www.jazzfestivalbern.ch) In May. Local and international acts, including Blues.

Gurten Rock Festival   MUSIC
(www.gurtenfestival.ch) Mid-July. A solid indie line-up which has included acts such as Kasabian and The Streets in past years. Buy tickets ASAP.

🛏 Sleeping

The tourist office makes hotel reservations (free) and has information on 'three nights for the price of two' deals, in which many hotels in town participate.

TOP CHOICE Hotel Landhaus   HOTEL $
(☎031 348 03 05; www.landhausbern.ch, in German; Altenbergstrasse 4; dm without/with pillow & quilt Sfr33/38, d without/with bathroom from Sfr120/160, breakfast Sfr8; P@🛜) In a pretty part of town, fronted by the river

and Old Town spires, this boho hotel is well run and has character in spades. Its buzzing ground-floor cafe and terrace attracts a cheery crowd and rooms are both spruce and stylish.

TOP CHOICE Hotel Schweizerhof   LUXURY HOTEL $$$
(☎031 326 80 80; www.schweizerhof-bern.ch; Bahnhofplatz 11; s/d from Sfr450/550; P✳@🛜) The latest player on the remodelled five-star circuit, the Schweizerhof boasts a lavish refurbishment and excellent amenities and service. A hop, skip and a jump from the train station, it's geared for both business and pleasure.

Hotel Goldener Schlüssel   HOTEL $$
(☎031 311 02 16; www.goldener-schluessel.ch; Rathausgasse 72; s/d/tr from Sfr140/180/240; 🛜) Going strong for 500 years, this hotel had a facelift in 2008 and boasts comfy updated rooms and an atmospheric restaurant with great sausage dishes. Splurge on the junior suite (from Sfr300) if you want the loveliest balcony in town.

Marthahaus Garni   GUESTHOUSE $$
(☎031 332 41 35; www.marthahaus.ch; Wyttenbachstrasse 22a; s/d/tr/q without bathroom Sfr70/110/150/200, s/d/tr with bathroom Sfr115/145/180; P@🛜) Plum in a leafy residential location, this five-storey building feels like a friendly boarding house. Clean, simple rooms have lots of white and a smattering of modern art, plus there's a kitchen. Parking costs Sfr10 per day.

SYHA Hostel   HOSTEL $
(☎031 326 11 11; www.youthhostel.ch/bern; Weihergasse 4; dm incl breakfast from Sfr34.90; @🛜) Prettily set just across from the river, this well-organised hostel sports spotless dorms and a leafy terrace, plus a good-value eatery. To get there, follow the paths downhill from the parliament building or ride the funicular (p107).

Hotel Allegro   BUSINESS HOTEL $$
(☎031 339 55 00; www.allegro-hotel.ch; Kornhausstrasse 3; s/d from Sfr250/310; ✳@🛜) Cool and modern, this curved sliver of a building across the river offers excellent views from its front rooms. Complete with very good dining (make a beeline for Mediterraneo), and cigar-smoking and drinking spaces, it's perfect for business travellers. The best room in the house – the 7th-floor penthouse suite – is an ode to Paul Klee. Wi-fi costs Sfr25 per 24 hours.

HAMMER TIME

Market traders take over Bern on the fourth Monday in November during the legendary **onion market** (*Zibelemärit*), a riot of 600-odd market stalls selling delicately woven onion plaits, wreaths, ropes, pies, sculptures and so on alongside other tasty regional produce. Folklore says the market dates back to the great fire of 1405 when farmers from the canton of Fribourg helped the Bernese recover and were allowed to sell their produce in Bern as a reward. In reality, the market probably began as part of Martinmas, the medieval festival celebrating winter's start. Whatever the tale, the onion market is a fabulous excuse for pure, often crazy revelry as street performers surge forth in the carnival atmosphere and people walk around throwing confetti and hitting each other on the head with – bizarrely – squeaky plastic hammers.

Hotel Belle Epoque　　　BOUTIQUE HOTEL **$$**
(☏031 311 43 36; www.belle-epoque.ch; Gerechtigkeitsgasse 18; s/d from Sfr170/240; 🛜) A romantic Old Town hotel with opulent art nouveau furnishings, the Belle Epoque's design ethos sees TVs tucked away into steamer-trunk-style cupboards so as not to spoil the look. It's a small operation, with a popular cafe, so don't be surprised by a few minutes' wait at reception, watched over by a rather disconcerting mannequin. Wi-fi costs Sfr12 per day.

Hotel Glocke Backpackers Bern　　HOSTEL **$**
(☏031 311 37 71; www.bernbackpackers.com; Rathausgasse 75; dm incl breakfast Sfr35-47, s/d without bathroom Sfr74/110, d with bathroom Sfr142; @🛜) Modern bedrooms with maximum six beds, clean bathrooms, a kitchen and a sociable lounge – all in the Old Town – make this many backpackers' first choice, although street noise might irritate light sleepers.

Hotel National　　　　　　　HOTEL **$**
(☏031 381 19 88; www.nationalbern.ch, in German; Hirschengraben 24; s/d without bathroom from Sfr65/130, s/d with bathroom Sfr100/150; 🛜) A quaint, endearing hotel, the National charms with its wrought-iron lift and

Persian rugs over wooden floors. Its good honest restaurant is also appealing.

Hotel Innere Enge　　　　　BOUTIQUE HOTEL **$$**
(☏031 309 61 11; www.innere-enge.ch; Engestrasse 54; d from Sfr315; P🛜) A little out of the city centre, this 26-room jazz hotel is unique. Owned and run with passion the place packs panache. Don't miss its cellar jazz bar.

Bellevue Palace　　　　　　LUXURY HOTEL **$$$**
(☏031 320 45 45; www.bellevue-palace.ch; Kochergasse 3-5; s/d from Sfr389/510; P🛜) For many years this was Bern's only five-star hotel and the guest list has included bigwigs from Nelson Mandela down. It's gilded, polished, sashed and swathed, and suitably discreet. Wi-fi costs Sfr25 per 24 hours.

🍴 Eating

For a munch between meals, nothing beats the *brezels* (pretzels) smothered in salt crystals or sunflower, pumpkin or sesame seeds from kiosks at the train station, or a bag of piping-hot chestnuts.

TOP CHOICE **Altes Tramdepot**　　INTERNATIONAL **$$**
(Bärenpark; mains Sfr19.50-42; ⊙10am-12.30am daily, from 11am winter) You might think that its location, right by the Bear Park, would make this place a tourist trap, but even locals recommend this cavernous microbrewery out the back of the attractive tourist-office building. Swiss specialities compete against wok-cooked stir-fries for your affection and the microbrews go down a treat.

Verdi　　　　　　　　　　　ITALIAN **$$**
(☏031 312 63 68; Gerechtigkeitsgasse 7; pasta & risotto Sfr23-35, mains Sfr32-49) Verdi goes all-out to make an impression and it pays off. With a menu full of dishes from Emilia-Romagna, a solid all-Italian wine list and the kind of attention to decor detail that makes you feel as though you're in an opera, you'll be swept off your feet.

Fugu Nydegg　　　　　　　　ASIAN **$$**
(www.fugu-nydegg.ch; Gerechtigkeitsgasse 16; mains Sfr19-27; ⊙lunch & dinner Mon-Fri, all day Sat & Sun; 🛜) If it's Bangkok-style pad thai, Japanese noodles or Thai fish you're craving, then crisp, cool Fugu hits the spot, although the wok dishes could be done a little faster and a little hotter. The dining area is done up in lime-green, stainless steel and raw concrete inside, or shaded by bamboo outside.

Terrasse & Casa INTERNATIONAL $$

(☑031 350 50 01; www.schwellenmaetteli.ch; Dalmaziquai 11; mains Sfr24.50-44.50; ☺Terrasse 9am-midnight Mon-Sat, 9am-11pm Sun, Casa lunch & dinner Tue-Fri & Sun, dinner Sat) Dubbed 'Bern's Riviera', this twinset of classy hangouts on the Aare is an experience. Terrasse is a glass shoebox with wooden decking over the water, sun loungers overlooking a weir (illuminated at night) and comfy sofa seating – perfect for Sunday brunch or a drink. Casa, by contrast, cooks up Italian food in a cosy, country-style timber-framed house.

Kornhauskeller MEDITERRANEAN $$$

(☑031 327 72 72; Kornhausplatz 18; mains Sfr28-48; ☺lunch & dinner Mon-Sat, dinner Sun, bar 6pm-1am Mon-Wed, to 2am Thu-Sat, to 12.30am Sun) Fine dining takes place beneath vaulted frescoed arches at Bern's surprisingly ornate former granary, now a stunning cellar restaurant serving Mediterranean cuisine. Beautiful people sip cocktails alongside historic stained-glass windows on the mezzanine, and in its neighbouring cafe, punters lunch in the sun on the busy pavement terrace.

Du Nord INTERNATIONAL $$

(www.dunord-bern.ch; Lorrainestrasse 2; mains Sfr22.50-42.50; ☺8am-11.30pm Mon-Thu, to 12.30am Fri) A short walk across the bridge from the Old Town, this gay-friendly space, with an international kitchen and a bar that buzzes with Bern's hippest, is one of the city's neatest addresses. Find it crowned by a pale pink, fairy-tale turret in the leafy Lorraine quarter.

Gartenrestaurant
Marzilibrücke MEDITERRANEAN $$

(Gasstrasse 8; mains Sfr22.50-39.50) Italian meets Indian and gets along surprisingly well at this relaxed spot. And as the name suggests, there's a good garden.

Tibits VEGETARIAN $

(Bahnhofplatz 10; ☺6.30am-11.30pm Mon-Wed, 6.30am-midnight Thu-Sat, 8am-11pm Sun; ✒) This vegetarian buffet restaurant inside the train station is just the ticket for a quick healthy meal, any time of day. Serve yourself, weigh and pay (between Sfr3.30 and Sfr4.20 per 100g).

Markthalle FAST FOOD $

(Bubenbergplatz 9; ☺breakfast, lunch & dinner Mon-Sat) Buzzing with quick-snack action, this covered market arcade is packed with global cheap eats: curries, vegetarian, wok stir-fries, noodles, pizza, southern Indian, Middle Eastern. To be eaten standing at bars or around plastic tables, till around midnight.

Casa Della SWISS $$

(Schauplatzgasse 16; mains Sfr21.50-42.50; ☺10.30am-11.30pm Mon-Fri, 9am-3pm Sat) Paul Klee was here in 1890; expect wholly traditional fare and a local vibe.

Drinking

Bern has a healthy drinking scene. Several spaces, such as Kornhauskeller and Altes Tramdepot, are as much drinking as dining spots. A few bright and busy after-work aperitif bars stud Gurtengasse near the Bundeshäuser and Rathäustrasse.

Café des Pyrénées CAFE

(Kornhausplatz 17; ☺Mon-Sat) With its mix of wine-quaffing lefties, generation-of-68ers and beer-loving students, this lovely Bohemian joint feels like a Parisian cafe-bar. It serves toasted snacks. Service can be hit and miss, but the atmosphere makes up for it.

Dampfzentrale CULTURAL CENTRE

(www.dampfzentrale.ch, in German; Marzilistrasse 47; ☺variable) Host to far more than its action-packed Saturday-night club (from around 11pm), this industrial brick riverside building stages concerts, festivals and contemporary dance, and has a great riverside restaurant terrace (open for lunch and dinner Monday to Friday, and dinner Saturday).

Sous le Pont CULTURAL CENTRE

(www.souslepont.ch; Neubrückstrasse 8; ☺Tue-Sat) Delve into the grungy underground scene around the station, with this bar in the vibrant alternative-arts centre, the Reitschule, an old stone, graffiti-covered building – a former riding school built in 1897 – by the railway bridge.

Volver BAR

(Rathausplatz 8; ☺Tue-Sat) With cool decor and a small selection of tapas, Volver is a hip spot for cocktails and coffees, from morning to midnight.

Cesary CAFE

(Kornhausplatz 11; ☺7am-12.30am Mon-Sat) A slice of Milan's slick, jet-black apero scene has arrived in Bern thanks to Cesary, where you'll find great coffee, even better cocktails and lip-smacking Italian snacks such as piadina and pasta salads.

Wasserwerk
CLUB
(www.wasserwerkclub.ch; Wasserwerkgasse 5; ☺10pm-late Thu-Sat) Bern's main techno venue with bar, club and occasional live music.

Bierhübeli
LOUNGE
(www.bierhuebeli.ch; Neubrückstrasse 43; ☺5pm-11pm Tue-Sat) This old hall with a balcony hosts mainstream international bands and club nights (think over-25s and various '80s and '90s nights). Its chic black, red and grey DJ lounge has a humming beer garden come summer. Take bus 11 to Bierhübeli from the train station.

☆ Entertainment

Cinématte
CINEMA
(www.cinematte.ch; Wasserwerkgasse 7; ☺6pm-11.30pm Mon, Thu & Sun, 6pm-12.30am Fri & Sat) This place has a riverside address with a bamboo-ensnared wooden-decking restaurant terrace (mains Sfr28 to Sfr43) and a hip line-up of art-house/cult films, from 9pm or 9.30pm.

Stadttheater Bern
PERFORMING ARTS
(www.stadttheaterbern.ch, in German; Kornhausplatz 20) Opera, dance, classical music and plays (in German).

Bern Ticket
PERFORMING ARTS
(☎031 329 52 52; www.bernbillett.ch, in German; Nageligasse 1a; ☺noon-6.30pm Mon-Fri, 10am-2pm Sat) Buy theatre and music-concert tickets here, near the theatre.

Stade de Suisse
STADIUM
(www.stadedesuisse.ch, in German; tours adult/child Sfr20/15) Bern's 32,000-seat stadium was built over the demolished Wankdorf Stadium (host to the 1954 World Cup final). Situated northeast of the Old Town, it is home to the local Young Boys team and hosts international matches.

🛍 Shopping

There's a lively atmosphere at Bern's open-air **vegetable, fruit and flower markets** (Bärenplatz, Bundesplatz, Schauplatz & Münstergasse; ☺6am-noon Tue & Sat) and the **general market** (Waisenhausplatz; ☺8am-6pm Tue, 8am-4pm Sat Jan-Nov).

Mooching around the Old Town boutiques, many tucked below the street in bunker-style cellars or above in covered arcades, is delightful. Allow extra time for quaint Gerechtigkeitsgasse and Postgasse with their myriad galleries, antiquarian bookshops, small shops specialising in funky homewares and nifty boutiques, such as **Alpin** (Gerechtigkeitsgasse 19), which specialises in Swiss wine and has an attached cafe, making it perfect for a try-before-you-buy session. Nearby **Holz Art** (Münstergasse 36) sells exquisite hand-carved wooden toys, ornamental chalets and Christmas decorations that will draw gasps from young and old.

Westside
MALL
(www.westside.ch; Riedbachstrasse 100; ☺shops 9am-8pm Mon-Thu, 9am-10pm Fri, 8am-5pm Sat) Bern's snappiest dresser, this state-of-the-art leisure and shopping centre, with dozens of shops, a cinema, restaurants, a water park and spa, was designed by internationally renowned architect Daniel Libeskind. Take tram 8 from Bahnhofplatz to Brünnen Westside Bahnhof stop (Sfr4).

ℹ Information

Post
Post office (Schanzenstrasse 4; ☺7.30am-9pm Mon-Fri, 8am-4pm Sat, 9am-4pm Sun)

Tourist Information
Bern Tourismus (www.berninfo.com) train station (☎031 328 12 12; Bahnhofplatz; ☺9am-8.30pm Jun-Sep, to 6.30pm Mon-Sat, 10am-5pm Sun Oct-May); bear park (☺9am-6pm Jun-Sep, 10am-4pm Mar-May & Oct, 11am-4pm Nov-Feb) Located on the street-level floor of the train station and by the bear park. City tours, free hotel bookings, internet access, multilingual staff.

Websites
Lonely Planet (www.lonelyplanet.com /switzerland/bern)

ℹ Getting There & Away

Air
Bern-Belp airport (☎031 960 21 21; www.alpar .ch) is a small airport with direct flights to/from Munich, Berlin, Hamburg, Barcelona and London City with Lufthansa and various budget airlines.

Bus & Train
Postal buses depart from the western side of the **train station** (Bahnhoftplatz). By rail, there are services at least hourly to most major Swiss destinations, including Geneva (Sfr47, two hours), Basel (Sfr38, one hour), Interlaken Ost (Sfr13, one hour) and Zürich (Sfr47, one hour).

ℹ Getting Around

To/From the Airport

Airport Bus Bern No 334 (www.bernmobil .ch; adult/child Sfr5.80/3.20) links Bern-Belp airport with the train station and vice versa, plus they guarantee you'll make your flight! Buy tickets at the usual machines or on board.

A **taxi** (☑031 371 11 11 or 031 331 33 13) costs about Sfr50.

Bicycle & Scooter

Borrow a bike from one of the three kiosks of **Bernrollt** (www.bernrollt.ch; 1st 4hr free, then Sfr1 per hr; ☺7.30am-9.30pm May-Oct), located at the train station, on Zeughausgasse and just off Bubenbergplatz on Hirschengraben. You'll need ID and Sfr20 as a deposit.

Bus, Tram & Funicular

Get around on foot or hop on a bus or tram run by **Bern Mobil** (www.bernmobil.ch, in German; Bubenbergplatz 17; ☺8am-6pm Mon-Fri). Tickets, available from the Bern Mobil office or ticket machines at stops, cost Sfr2.20 for journeys up to six stops (valid 30 minutes) or Sfr4 for a single journey within zones 1 and 2 (valid one hour).

Moonliner (www.moonliner.ch, in German) night buses transport night owls from Bahnhofplatz two or three times between midnight and 3.30am on Friday and Saturday nights. Fares start at Sfr5; discount passes are invalid.

The **Stadt Bern-Drahtseilbahn Marzili funicular** (one way Sfr1.20; ☺6.15am-9pm) runs from behind the parliament building downhill to the riverside Marzili quarter.

Biel-Bienne

POP 50,500 / ELEV 429M

Slap bang on the *Röstigraben,* Switzerland's French–German divide, double-barrelled Biel-Bienne is the country's most bilingual town. Locals are prone to switching language mid-conversation; indeed much of the time it is a tad tricky to know which one to use.

Biel-Bienne is far from being Switzerland's most picturesque town, and for many Swiss it's often a place to change trains, but to ignore it completely is to miss out on a small but nicely preserved historic centre, the new Centre PasquArt and also the lake that lap's Biel-Bienne's shores and the vineyards that stagger steeply up from it.

◉ Sights & Activities

Old Town   NEIGHBOURHOOD

Delve into the minute Old Town, huddled around the so-called **Ring**, a plaza whose name harks back to bygone days when justice was dispensed here as community bigwigs sat in a semicircle passing judgement on unfortunate miscreants brought before them.

Leading from the Ring, past its colourful 16th-century fountain, is **Burggasse**, home to the stepped-gabled town hall and theatre, Fountain of Justice (1744) and several shuttered houses. The Old Town also features an assortment of gilded fountains, including the seemingly ubiquitous blindfolded **Justice**.

Centre PasquArt   ART MUSEUM

(www.pasquart.ch; Seevorstadt 71-73; adult/ reduced Sfr11/9) With a determinedly modern annexe bolted on to an imposing 1886 edifice that was the city's first hospital, this place is a good sign that Biel is still breathing. Inside you'll find intriguing contemporary art exhibitions with a strong focus on photography and film (right down to an open-air film festival in summer) and works from the permanent collection.

Magglingen Funicular   FUNICULAR

(Seilbahn Magglingen, Funiculaire Macolin; www .funic.ch, in German & French; Seevorstadt; adult/ child Sfr5.40/2.50) Outside town, the funicular scales Magglingen hill, riddled with hiking trails and photogenic views. The tourist office has leaflets outlining short walks.

FREE **Museum Schwab**   MUSEUM

(www.muschwab.ch; Seevorstadt 50; ☺2-6pm Tue-Sat, 11am-6pm Sun) A modest archaeological museum in a bijou villa with what seems like a giant rusty cupboard tacked on to the side.

FREE **Omega Museum**   MUSEUM

(www.omegamuseum.com; Stämpflistrasse 96; ☺9am-5pm Mon-Fri) For watch buffs: this well-done museum also has English-language tours on demand.

🛏 Sleeping

Villa Lindenegg   GUESTHOUSE **$$**

(☑032 322 94 66; www.lindenegg.ch; Lindenegg 5; s Sfr90-220, d Sfr150-280; P🖙) Languishing in a gorgeous park minutes from the centre, this lovely 19th-century country villa with garden offers elegance and personal service at a very affordable price. Its eight rooms mix modern with historic, some have balconies and there is a friendly bistro to dine in or enjoy an early-evening aperitif.

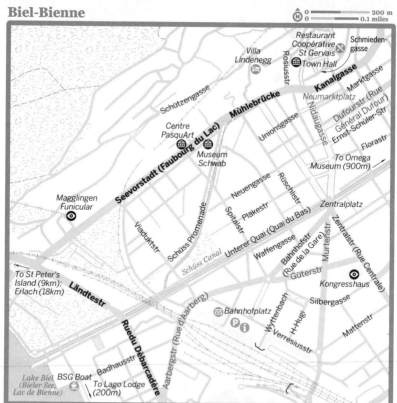

Lago Lodge HOSTEL $

(☑032 331 37 32; www.lagolodge.ch; Uferweg 5; dm Sfr30-36, d with bathroom Sfr84, lunch/dinner Sfr19/23; ☺reception 7-11.30am & 2-10pm; @) Between the train station and the lake, this Swiss Backpackers hostel resembles an American motel with its small dorms – just three to six beds in each. Reception is in the bistro bar, which cooks food and brews wonderful organic beer.

✕ Eating

Biel's Old Town has some pleasant spots to dine, especially in and around the Ring.

TOP CHOICE Restaurant Coopérative
St Gervais BRASSERIE $

(☑032 322 48 22; www.stgervais.ch; Untergasse/Rue Basse 21; mains Sfr15-20; ☺9.30am-12.30am Mon & Wed-Sat, 9.30am-3pm Tue, 11am-11.30pm Sun) Beneath vaulted arches or at its charming, always-packed tables beneath trees, this hip and alternative restaurant, bar and gallery cooks up wholesome, often organic dishes and has a fabulous range of cultural events – concerts, gigs and so forth. Find its programme online.

❶ Information

Post office (Bahnhofplatz 2; ☺7.30am-6.30pm Mon-Fri, 8am-4pm Sat)
Tourist office (☑032 329 84 84; www.biel -seeland.net; Bahnhofplatz 12; ☺8am-12.30pm & 1.30-6pm Mon-Wed & Fri, to 8pm Thu, 9am-3pm Sat) Very helpful kiosk in front of the train station; Old Town tours (Sfr10), public-transport tickets and info.

❶ Getting There & Away

Biel-Bienne is served by train from Bern (Sfr15.20, 35 minutes), Solothurn (Sfr11.20, 15 to 30 minutes) and Neuchâtel (Sfr12.20, 15 to 30 minutes).

A more enjoyable summer connection is by daily **BSG boat** (www.bielersee.ch, in

German & French) to/from Murten (single/ return Sfr54/108, four hours) and Neuchâtel (Sfr36/72, 2½ hours).

Solothurn (single/return Sfr52/104, 2½ hours, three daily Tuesday to Sunday summer, less in spring and autumn) can be reached along the Aare River.

Around Biel-Bienne

Winegrowing villages line the western shore of Lake Biel, and the nature reserve of St Peter's Island (St Petersinsel/Île de St Pierre) sits in the middle. Actually, falling water levels mean this is no longer an island proper but a long, thin promontory jutting out into the lake from the southwest shore near Erlach. It is possible to take a 1¼-hour stroll along this causeway from Erlach, but because of the difficulties in reaching Erlach from Biel-Bienne (you need to catch a train to La Neuveville and an infrequent

bus to Erlach), it's easiest to catch a boat from Biel-Bienne (single/return Sfr22/44, 50 minutes).

Political theorist Jean-Jacques Rousseau spent, he said, the happiest time of his life on St Petersinsel. The 11th-century monastery where he resided is now the renowned Restaurant-Hotel St Petersinsel (☑032 338 11 14; www.st-petersinsel.ch, in German & French; d from Sfr230).

Visiting the island makes a relaxing day trip, and you can hop off and on the BSG boat as you like, including at the drop-dead gorgeous winegrowing villages of Twann (Douanne in French) and Ligerz (Gléresse in French), for memorably scenic wine sipping in both villages. If you're more interested in swimming, take a dip from Erlach, St Peter's Island or La Neuveville, or between Twann and Ligerz.

Neighbouring Lac de Neuchâtel and Lac de Morat (Lake Murten) are connected to

WORTH A TRIP

LIGERZ

The lush green vines that stagger down the steep hillside in strictly regimented lines towards the northern shore of Lake Biel are spectacular.

And there is no better spot to savour this viticultural magnificence, heavy with grapes prior to the autumnal harvest, than Ligerz (Gléresse in French), a quaint lakeside hamlet with a small wine museum (☑032 315 21 32; Le Fornel; adult/child Sfr6/free; ⊙1-5pm Sat & Sun) and an old-fashioned funicular (www.vinifuni.ch, in German & French; adult one way Sfr5.80) that climbs through vines to hilltop Prêles. On clear days views across the vines and beyond to the snowcapped Bernese Alps are breathtaking.

Just up the hill from Ligerz (a 15-minute walk) is Restaurant Aux Trois Amis (☑032 315 11 44; Untergasse 17; ⊙closed Wed), a quintessential village bistro with a tree-shaded terrace that heaves with punters come summertime, purring contentedly as they eat, drink and gaze at the tumbling vines, just centimetres away, and the slate-blue water rippling towards St Peter's below.

Try overnighting at Ligerz' lakefront and the charmingly low-key Hotel Kreuz Ligerz (☑032 315 11 15; www.kreuz-ligerz.ch; Hauptstrasse 17; s/d from Sfr110/185; P☎), an old patrician's house (in the same family for four generations) with painted shutters, terracotta floors and a garden by the water's edge, from where you can take a dip. Its garden bistro serves wine produced from its own vines that march uphill in lines behind. In January and February, don't miss *Treberwurst (saucisse du marc* in French), a sausage traditionally made by winegrowers as they distilled leftover grape skins and pulp to make *Marc* (a fiery type of brandy), hence the sausage's distinct kick. The rest of the year, try the local fish.

Hands down the most idyllic way of getting to Ligerz is on foot along the Sentier du Viticole, a trail that follows the northern shore of Lake Biel from Vingelz (in the east) to Twann and beyond to La Neuveville (in the west). Walking to Twann will take about 25 minutes, and you'll pass charming gardens filled with flowers and fruit trees, numerous places to swim and 'I wish' plots of real estate, all with heavenly views. In Twann taste and buy 300-odd vintages by Lake Biel winegrowers at the custard-yellow Vinethek Viniterra Bielersee (www.vinothek-viniterra-bielersee.ch; Im Moos 4; ⊙5-9pm Tue-Fri, 2-8pm Sat & Sun), just next to the new annexe of the Hotel Fontana.

Lake Biel (Bieler See) by canal, and day-long cruises of all three (Sfr78 with a day ticket) are run year-round by Biel-based **BSG** (www .bielersee.ch, in German & French) and **Navigation Lacs de Neuchâtel et Morat** (www .navig.ch; 🛱) in Neuchâtel.

Emmental Region

One of Switzerland's most famous dairy products – holey Emmental cheese – is what this rural idyll east of Bern is all about. Think a mellow patchwork of quiet villages, grazing cows and fabulous farm chalets with vast barns and overhanging roofs, strung out along the banks of the River Emme.

◉ Sights & Activities

Burgdorf (literally 'castle village') itself is split into two: the Upper Town and the Lower Town. The natural highlight of the quaint old *Oberstadt* (Upper Town), its 12th-century **Schloss** (castle), is straight out of a book with its drawbridge, thick stone walls and trio of museums focusing on castle history, Swiss gold and ethnology. By contrast, in the new Lower Town, the works of Switzerland's foremost photo-realist painter steal the show at the **Franz Gertsch Museum** (www.museum-franzgertsch .ch, Platanenstrasse 3; adult/child Sfr12/8; ☺10am-6pm Wed-Fri, 10am-5pm Sat & Sun).

The road from Burgdorf to **Affoltern**, 6km to the east, is a scenic drive past lumbering old farmsteads, with farmhouses proudly bedecked with flower boxes, winter wood neatly stacked and kitchen gardens perfectly tended.

FREE **Emmentaler Schaukäserei**   DAIRY
(www.showdairy.ch; Schaukäsereistrasse 6, Affoltern; ☺9am-6.30pm Apr-Oct, 9am-5pm Nov-Mar) Watch Emmental cheese being made into 95kg wheels and taste it at the Emmental Show Dairy in Affoltern. Short videos explain the modern production process and how Emmental gets its famous holes, while cheesemaking as it was done in the 18th century happens once a day over an open fire in the 18th-century herdsman's cottage.

🛏 Sleeping & Eating

Our picks for sleeping are outside Burgdorf: Langnau has a handful of traditional chalet-style hotels, window boxes bursting with red geraniums; its tourist office covers the entire Emmental region.

Möschberg   FARMSTAY $
(☎031 710 22 22; www.hotelmoeschberg.ch, in German; Grosshöchstetten; s/d without bathroom Sfr95/130, half-pension Sfr30) This green hotel and cultural centre, 100% organic, situated between fields of cows and gentle walking trails, is a quintessential slice of the Emmental. Rooms are simple but stylish; dinner is a vibrant vegetarian homemade affair with organic wine. Find this friendly house, an agricultural school for women in the 1930s, 14km west of Langnau above dairy-farming hamlet Grosshöchstetten.

Gasthaus Bäregghöhe   GUESTHOUSE $
(☎034 495 70 00; www.baeregghoehe.ch; Trubschachen; s/d Sfr90/150; ☺Wed-Sun Mar-Jan) This five-room family-run inn sits atop a green hill overlooking a lush valley contrasted against a magnificent backdrop of snow-covered peaks. The view from the south-facing terrace is divine; the style art nouveau and stylishly hip; and the cuisine (mains Sfr27 to Sfr41) raved about for miles around. Find it signposted 2.8km uphill along a wiggly country lane from the eastern end of Langnau.

SYHA Hostel   HOSTEL $
(☎034 402 45 26; www.youthhostel.ch/langnau; Mooseggstrasse 32, Langnau; dm incl breakfast from Sfr29.30, d from Sfr72.60, packed lunch Sfr9; ☺closed 24 Dec-10 Jan & late Sep-Nov) This Langnau hostel, a 10-minute walk from Langnau station but well off the beaten track, is a farmhouse-style chalet built in 1768 with a huge overhanging roof, basic rooms and a notably cheery, convivial atmosphere.

❶ Getting There & Around

Hourly trains run by **BLS** (www.bls.ch) link Bern and Burgdorf (Sfr5, 15 minutes). Langnau can be reached by train from Bern (Sfr9), via Burgdorf.

Solothurn

POP 16,200 / ELEV 440M

Solothurn (Soleure in French) is an enchanting little town with a mellow stone-cobbled soul and one very big cathedral: the imposing, 66m-tall facade of St Ursus looms up out of the pavement at one end of the main street. Without it, this could almost be a French village – an impression that makes more sense when you learn of Catholic Solothurn's long-standing links to France. The cathedral standing majestically alongside fountains, churches and city gates gives weight to Solothurn's claim to be Switzerland's most beautiful baroque town.

◉ Sights

Kathedrale St Ursen   CHURCH
(Kronenplatz) Architect Gaetano Matteo Pisoni restrained himself with the classical Italianate facade of Solothurn's monolithic 18th-century cathedral but went wild inside with a white-and-gilt trip of wedding-cake baroque. At the time of research it was being restored after a fire: it should be open by autumn 2012.

Justice Fountain   FOUNTAIN
This fountain (1561) on Hauptgasse – a blindfolded representation of Justice, holding aloft a sword, while the four most important contemporary figures in Europe sit at her feet – may produce a wry smile. The Holy Roman Emperor, in red and white robes, is by Justice's right foot, then proceeding anticlockwise, you'll see the Pope, the Turkish Sultan and...the mayor of Solothurn!

Kunstmuseum   ART MUSEUM
(www.kunstmuseum-so.ch, in German; Werkhofstrasse 30; admission by donation; ⊙11am-5pm Tue-Fri, from 10am Sat & Sun) The centrepiece at the Museum of Fine Arts is Ferdinand Hodler's famous portrait of William Tell. Before arriving in Switzerland, you might never have imagined the national hero as a red-haired, bearded goliath in a white hippy top and short trousers, but you'll see this personification repeated many times. The *Madonna of Solothurn* (1522), by Holbein the Younger, is one of only a small number of other major works, but the museum hosts interesting temporary exhibitions.

Museum Altes Zeughaus   MUSEUM
(www.museum-alteszeughaus.ch, in German; Zeughausplatz 1; adult/child Sfr6/free; ⊙1-5pm Tue-Sat, from 10am Sun) The early 17th-century rust-coloured facade of this vast, multi-windowed arsenal museum is a reminder that Solothurn was once a centre for mercenaries, many of whom fought for French kings.

Baseltor   GATE
Two minutes east of the cathedral, this is the most attractive city gate and the one most enter through. You'll find it close to the city's former bastion, which makes for a decent picnic spot.

Jesuit Church   CHURCH
A stone's throw west of Baseltor down Hauptgasse, this church's (1680-89) unprepossessing facade disguises an interior of baroque embellishments and stucco work. All the 'marble' in here is fake – mere spruced-up wood and plaster.

Zeitglockenturm   LANDMARK
A little further west of the Jesuit church ticks the 12th-century Zeitglockenturm, an astronomical clock where a knight, a king and a grim reaper jig on the hour. Its clock hands are reversed so the smaller one shows the minutes. It sits on Marktplatz, which comes to life on Wednesday mornings when the markets are on.

🛏 Sleeping

For a tiny town, Solothurn surprises with cool sleeping spaces.

Baseltor   BOUTIQUE HOTEL $$
(☏032 622 34 22; www.baseltor.ch, in German; Hauptgasse 79; s/d from Sfr115/190; 🛜) Charmingly set in the shade of the cathedral, this atmospheric inn with steel-grey wooden shutters and an attractive minimalist interior is as much a slow-food, bio-delicious dining spot (mains Sfr29 to Sfr42) as a bed to rest one's weary head. Three of its nine simple but handsome rooms slumber in a separate annexe.

Gasthaus Kreuz & Café
Landhaus   GUESTHOUSE $
(☏032 622 20 20; www.kreuz-solothurn.ch, in German; Kreuzgasse 4; s/d/tr/q without bathroom Sfr55/95/140/160) A riverside choice, this guesthouse/cultural centre exudes a hipster ethos with its cherry-red shared shower block and big rooms with creaky wooden floors and Spartan furnishings. Simple dining and drinking with friends is the lure of its street-level cafe-bar, host to bands, concerts, cultural happenings and Solothurn's biggest dance party of the year on 1 January.

SYHA Hostel   HOSTEL $
(☏032 623 17 06; www.youthhostel.ch/solothurn; Landhausquai 23; dm incl breakfast from Sfr32, d with shower & toilet Sfr99, lunch or dinner Sfr15; ⊙closed Dec-Feb; @🛜) One of Switzerland's most contemporary hostels, this centuries-old building by the river is a striking mix of glass, stainless steel and raw concrete. Dorms sport three to 10 beds, and are

sometimes mixed gender, and the place is equipped for travellers in wheelchairs.

✖ Eating & Drinking

Cantinetta Bindella   ITALIAN $$
(Ritterquai 3; mains Sfr20-49; ⊘lunch & dinner Mon-Sat) Across the road from Sol Heure is this refined Italian with a candlelit interior and white tablecloths beneath trees in its leafy walled garden. The menu embraces all things Tuscan and attracts a devoted crowd.

Pittaria   MIDDLE EASTERN $
(Theatergasse 12; pita mains Sfr11-13, on plate Sfr15-17; ⊘lunch & dinner Tue-Fri, 11am-6pm Sat) The attractions of Palestinian cuisine are on full display, thanks to the heavenly mint tea, homemade mango chutney, creamy hummus and crunchy falafel served up by Pittaria. Expect excellent food (that's also a bargain), a laid-back atmosphere, bench seating covered with Persian rugs and a lot of plush camels.

Sol Heure   BAR
(www.solheure.ch; Ritterquai 10; ☎) Old stone walls, kitsch-meets-cool chairs and a sun-flooded terrace facing the water ensures that half of Solothurn can be found at this cool riverside bar in a former warehouse.

ℹ Information

Tourist office (☎032 626 46 46; www .solothurn-city.ch; Hauptgasse 69; ⊘9am-6pm Mon-Fri, 9am-1pm Sat) By the cathedral.

ℹ Getting There & Away

Solothurn has two trains per hour to Bern on the private RBS line (www.rbs.ch, in German; Sfr12, 45 minutes, rail passes valid). Regular trains also run to Basel (Sfr26 via Olten, one hour) and Biel (Sfr11.20, 15 to 30 minutes).

Boats also connect Solothurn to Biel-Bienne.

Bernese Oberland

POP 856,300 / AREA 5907 SQ KM / LANGUAGE GERMAN

Best Places to Eat

» Benacus (p119)

» Michel's Stallbeizli (p144)

» Restaurant Schönegg (p132)

» Fluss (p137)

Best Places to Stay

» The Hayloft (p142)

» Gletschergarten (p125)

» Hotel Rugenpark (p117)

» Hotel Victoria (p141)

Why Go?

Go for the epic outdoors. Whether you're hiking in the fearsome north face of Eiger with a china-blue sky overhead, carving virgin powder on a crisp winter's morning in Gstaad, or gazing up at the mist-enshrouded Staubbach Falls – the Swiss Alps don't get more beautiful than this. And we're talking big, in-your-face, stop-dead-in-your-tracks beauty. Nowhere are the resorts more chocolate box, the peaks higher, the glaciers grander. Fittingly watched over by Mönch (Monk) and Jungfrau (Virgin), the Bernese Oberland sends spirits soaring to heaven.

Mark Twain wrote that no opiate compared to walking here (and he should know), Arthur Conan Doyle thought Meiringen on the banks of turquoise Brienzersee a pretty spot for a Sherlock Holmes whodunnit, while 007 brought the icy wilderness of Schilthorn to cinema screens. Such masters captured the region's allure, but most photographers fail to do so. Listen for the tutting of tourists at postcard carousels trying – and failing – to find something to match their memories.

When to Go

From ritzy Gstaad to picture-postcard Mürren, the slopes hum with skiers and boarders in winter. Come in January to ring in the New Year ogre-style at Harder Potschete in Interlaken and catch the hell-for-leather Lauberhorn and Inferno ski races. Summer is the time for Alpine hiking and open-air folk festivals galore in the Jungfrau Region. Room rates plunge in autumn, when the crowds are few and the weather often fine. At *Almabtriebe* in September, cows wreathed in flower garlands are brought down from the mountains for another winter of dung-shovelling.

Bernese Oberland Highlights

1 Get dizzy on the zip-wires, hanging bridges and Eiger views on the *via ferrata* in **Mürren** (p133)

2 Hike the classically Alpine **Faulhornweg** (p121), from Schynige Platte to Grindelwald-First

3 Be spellbound by 4000m peaks and the glinting Aletsch Glacier at **Jungfraujoch** (p129)

4 Do some Sherlock Holmes–style detective work for glorious waterfalls and meringues in **Meiringen** (p140)

5 Test your limits canyoning, skydiving, ice climbing and glacier bungee jumping in adventure-sports mecca **Interlaken** (p115)

6 Marvel at the 72 waterfalls cascading down the cliffs in the **Lauterbrunnen Valley** (p130)

7 Slalom like a celebrity on the glitzy slopes of **Gstaad** (p143)

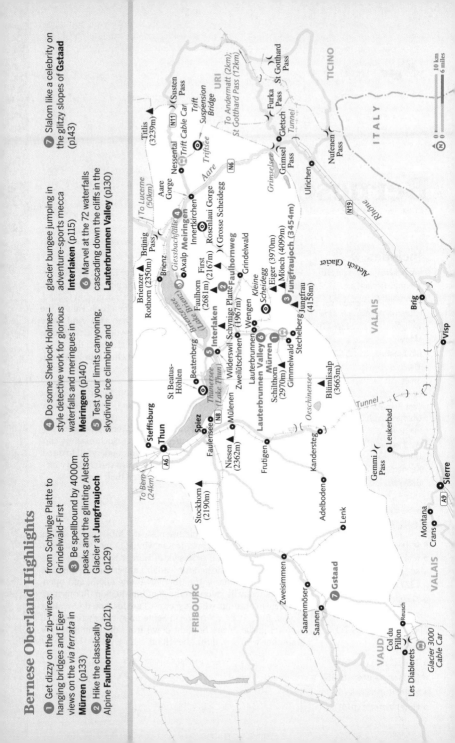

FRIBOURG

VAUD

Les Diablerets

Col du Pillon
Glacier 3000 Cable Car

Reusch

Saanen
Saanenmöser

7 Gstaad

Zweisimmen

Lenk

Adelboden

Kandersteg

Frutigen

Niesen (2362m)

Stockhorn (2190m)

To Bern (24km)

A6

Steffisburg
Thun

Spiez

Faulensee

Thunersee (Lake Thun)

N8

Mülenen

St Beatus-Höhlen

Beatenberg

Interlaken **5**

Wilderswil Schynige Platte (1967m)

Lauterbrunnen
Zweilütschinen

6 Mürren
Schilthorn (2970m)
Gimmelwald

Blümlisalp (3663m)

Oeschinensee

Gemmi Pass

Leukerbad

Lenk

Montana Crans

Tunnel

VALAIS

Sierre

A9

1 Lauterbrunnen Valley
Stechelberg Jungfrau (4158m)

14

Wengen
Kleine Scheidegg

Eiger (3970m)
Mönch (4099m)
3 Jungfraujoch (3454m)

Grindelwald

Faulhorn (2681m) First (2167m) **10** Faulhornweg **2**

Grosse Scheidegg

Rosenlaui Gorge

Axalp **4** Meiringen
Innertkirchen

Giessbachfälle

Brienzer Rothorn (2350m)

Brienzersee (Lake Brienz)

Brienz

Brünig Pass

To Lucerne (50km)

Aare Gorge

N6

Aare

Titlis (3239m)

Susten Pass

14 Trift Cable Car

Nessental Trift Suspension Bridge

Triftsee

To Andermatt (2km); St Gotthard Pass (12km)

Furka Pass St Gotthard Pass

Gletsch *Tunnel*

Grimsel Pass
Grimselsee

Grimsel

Ulrichen

Nufenen Pass

URI

TICINO

ITALY

Aletsch Glacier

Brig

Visp

VALAIS

Rhône

N19

Rhône

N

0   10 km
0   6 miles

The Bernese Oberland is easily accessible by road and train from major Swiss airports, including Basel, Bern, Geneva and Zürich, as well as from Lucerne.

Note that a Swiss or Eurail Pass alone will take you only so far into the Jungfrau Region. See p122 for more information.

INTERLAKEN

POP 5400 / ELEV 570M

Once Interlaken made the Victorians swoon with mountain vistas from the chandelier-lit confines of grand hotels; today it makes daredevils scream with adrenalin-loaded adventures. Straddling the glittering Lakes Thun and Brienz and dazzled by the pearly whites of Eiger, Mönch and Jungfrau, the scenery here is mind-blowing. Particularly, some say, if you're abseiling waterfalls, thrashing white water or gliding soundlessly above 4000m peaks.

Though the streets are filled with enough yodelling kitsch to make Heidi cringe, Interlaken still makes a terrific base for exploring the Bernese Oberland. Its adventure capital status has spawned a breed of funky bars, party-mad hostels and restaurants serving flavours more imaginative than fondue.

◉ Sights

Cross the turquoise Aare River for a mooch around Interlaken's compact and quiet old quarter, Unterseen.

Tourist Museum   MUSEUM
(Obere Gasse 26; adult/child Sfr5/2; ⊘2-5pm Tue-Sun May-Oct) This low-key museum sits on a cobbled, fountain-dotted square in Unterseen. The permanent exhibition presents a romp through tourism in the region with costumes, carriages and other curios.

Heimwehfluh   MOUNTAIN
(www.heimwehfluh.ch, in German; funicular adult/child return Sfr14/7, toboggan Sfr6; ⊘10am-5pm mid-Apr–late Oct) When the sun's out, take the nostalgic funicular up to family-friendly Heimwehfluh for long views across Interlaken. Kids love the bob run down the hill – lay off the brakes to pick up speed.

Harder Kulm   MOUNTAIN
(www.harderkulm.ch, in German; adult/child return Sfr27/13.50; ⊘8.10am-6.25pm late Apr-Oct) For far-reaching vistas to the 4000m giants, ride the funicular to 1322m Harder Kulm.

Many hiking paths begin here if you want to stretch your legs. The wildlife park near the valley station is home to furry Alpine critters, including marmots and ibex.

乔 Activities

Tempted to hurl yourself off a bridge, down a cliff or along a raging river? You're in the right place. Switzerland is the world's second-biggest adventure-sports centre and Interlaken is its busiest hub.

Almost every heart-stopping pursuit you can think of is offered here. You can white-water raft on the Lütschine, Simme and Saane Rivers, go canyoning in the Saxetet, Grimsel or Chli Schliere gorges, and canyon jump at the Gletscherschlucht near Grindelwald. If that doesn't grab you, there's paragliding, glacier bungee jumping, skydiving, ice climbing, hydrospeeding and, phew, much more.

Sample prices are around Sfr110 for rafting or canyoning, Sfr120 for hydrospeeding, Sfr130 for bungee or canyon jumping, Sfr160 for tandem paragliding, Sfr180 for ice climbing, Sfr225 for hang-gliding, and Sfr430 for skydiving. A half-day mountain-bike tour will set you back around Sfr25.

Most excursions are without incident, but there's always a small risk and it's wise to ask about safety records and procedures.

The major operators able to arrange most sports from May to September include the following. Advance bookings are essential.

Alpinraft   ADVENTURE SPORTS
(✆033 823 41 00; www.alpinraft.com; Hauptstrasse 7; ⊘8am-6.30pm)

Outdoor Interlaken   ADVENTURE SPORTS
(✆033 826 77 19; www.outdoor-interlaken.ch; Hauptstrasse 15; ⊘8am-6pm)

Swissraft   ADVENTURE SPORTS
(✆081 911 52 50; www.swissraft.ch; Obere Jungfraustrasse 72)

Scenic Air   SCENIC FLIGHTS
(✆033 821 00 11; www.scenicair.ch, www.skydive switzerland.com) Arranges scenic flights, skydiving and other activities.

Hang Gliding Interlaken   SCENIC FLIGHTS
(✆079 770 0704; www.hangglidinginterlaken.com) Organises hang-gliding above Interlaken. The meeting point is Hotel Splendid.

Bohag   SCENIC FLIGHTS
(✆033 822 90 00; www.bohag.ch, in German; Gsteigwiler) Scenic flight specialist.

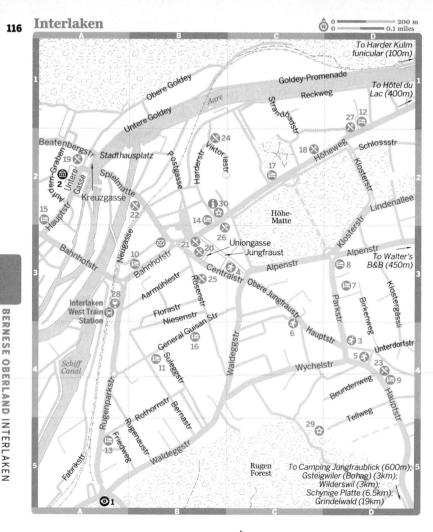

BERNESE OBERLAND INTERLAKEN

K44   ROCK CLIMBING

(www.k44.ch; Jungfraustrasse 44; adult/child Sfr21/14; ⏰4-10pm Mon, 9am-10pm Tue-Fri, to 8pm Sat, to 6pm Sun Oct-Apr, 9am-6pm Tue-Fri & 9am-4pm Sat, closed Sun & Mon May-Sep) Not ready to climb Eiger just yet? Squeeze in some practice at this climbing hall.

Vertical Sport   ROCK CLIMBING

(http://verticalsport.ch; Jungfraustrasse 44; ⏰9-noon & 1.30-6pm Mon-Fri, 9am-4pm Sat) At the same address as K44, this store sells and rents top-quality climbing gear and is run by expert mountaineers who can give sound advice.

✦ Festivals & Events

Cackling, clanging bells and causing mischief, the ogre-like *Potschen* dash through Interlaken on 2 January or Harder Pot-schete (www.harderpotschete.ch, in German). The revelry spills into the night with upbeat folk music and fiendish merrymaking.

Established and emerging brass bands and orchestras take centre stage at the Jungfrau Music Festival (www.jungfrau -music-festival.ch) in early July.

Eiger, Mönch and Jungfrau are always breathtaking but never more so than for runners competing in September's Jungfrau

Interlaken

Marathon (www.jungfrau-marathon.ch) from Lauterbrunnen to Kleine Scheidegg.

An Alpine Olympics of sorts, the **Unspunnenfest** (www.unspunnen-schwinget.ch) features yodelling, alpenhorn playing, *Schwingen* wrestling and stone-throwing, preferably of the historic Unspunnen Stone. The next Interlaken games are planned for 2017.

🛏 Sleeping

Ask your hotel for the useful Guest Card for free bus transport plus discounts on attractions and sports facilities. Call ahead during the low season, as some places close.

TOP CHOICE Hotel Rugenpark
B&B **$$**

(☎033 822 36 61; www.rugenpark.ch; Rugenparkstrasse 19; s/d/q Sfr62/105/175, with bathroom Sfr87/130/200; P@⌘) Chris and Ursula have worked magic to transform this into an incredibly sweet B&B. Rooms remain humble, but the place is spotless and has been enlivened with colourful butterflies, beads and travel trinkets. You'll feel right at home in the shared kitchen and garden, and your knowledgeable hosts are always ready to help with local tips.

Victoria-Jungfrau Grand Hotel & Spa
HISTORIC HOTEL **$$$**

(☎033 828 28 28; www.victoria-jungfrau.ch; Höheweg 41; s/d from Sfr560/680, d with Jungfrau views from Sfr780; P@⌘) The reverent hush and impeccable service here (as well as the prices) evoke an era when only royalty and the seriously wealthy travelled. A perfect melding of well-preserved Victorian features and modern luxury make this Interlaken's answer to Raffles – with plum views of Jungfrau to boot.

Backpackers Villa Sonnenhof
HOSTEL **$**

(☎033 826 71 71; www.villa.ch; Alpenstrasse 16; dm Sfr39-45, s Sfr69-79, tw Sfr118-138; P@⌘⛶) Sonnenhof is a slick combination of ultramodern chalet and elegant art nouveau villa. Dorms are immaculate, and some have balconies with Jungfrau views. There's also a relaxed lounge, a well-equipped kitchen and a leafy garden for kicking back and enjoying the Jungfrau views. Kids are amused in the playroom and special family rates are available.

Hôtel du Lac
HISTORIC HOTEL **$$**

(☎033 822 29 22; www.dulac-interlaken.ch; Höheweg 225; s/d Sfr160/280; @) Smiley oldfashioned service and a riverfront location near Interlaken Ost make this 19th-century hotel a solid choice. It has been in the same family for generations and, despite the mishmash of styles, has kept enough belle époque glory to remain charming.

Walter's B&B
B&B **$**

(☎033 822 76 88; www.walters.ch; Oelestrasse 35; s/d/tr/q Sfr50/66/99/112; P⌘) Walter is a real star with his quick smile, culinary skills and invaluable tips. Sure, the rooms are a blast from the 1970s, but they are super-clean and you'd be hard pushed to find better value in Interlaken. Breakfast (Sfr7) is copious and the fondue dinner, which includes wine and dessert, a bargain at Sfr19 per person.

Swiss Inn
B&B **$$**
(☎033 822 36 26; www.swiss-inn.ch; General Guisanstrasse 23; d Sfr140-160, apt Sfr180-200; P@🛜🚲) A tranquil retreat set in rose-strewn gardens, this handsome villa is run by dream duo Veronica and JP. Opt for a bright, spacious double or a family-sized apartment complete with kitchenette and balcony. Breakfast will set you back an extra Sfr12.

Hotel Krebs
BOUTIQUE HOTEL **$$**
(☎033 826 03 30; www.krebshotel.ch; Bahnhofstrasse 4; s/d/ste 185/290/490; P❄@🛜) This revamped boutique hotel sports rooms in earthy tones with bold splashes of scarlet, black-and-white photos of mountains, and designer flourishes a-plenty. All feature glam bathrooms, flat-screen TVs and wi-fi. Downstairs there's a self-consciously trendy bar and an Asian-French restaurant (mains Sfr34 to Sfr52).

Balmer's Herberge
HOSTEL **$**
(☎033 822 19 61; www.balmers.ch; Hauptstrasse 23; dm Sfr28.50, s/d/tr/q Sfr44.50/77/101/134; P🛜) Adrenalin junkies hail Balmer's for its fun frat-house vibe. These party-mad digs offer beer-garden happy hours, wrap lunches, a pumping bar with DJs, and chill-out hammocks for nursing your hangover. But some travellers think Balmer's should invest backpacker dosh in longer, thicker mattresses and ditch the theme-park feel.

Post Hardermannli
HOTEL **$$**
(☎033 822 89 19; www.post-hardermannli.ch; Hauptstrasse 18; s Sfr90-105, d 135-175; P) An affable Swiss-Kiwi couple, Andreas and Kim, run this ornate, flower-bedecked chalet. Rooms are simple yet comfy, decorated with pine and pastels. Cheaper rooms forgo balconies and Jungfrau views. Home-grown farm produce is served at breakfast.

Hotel Royal St Georges
HISTORIC HOTEL **$$**
(☎033 822 75 75; www.royal-stgeorges.ch; Höheweg 139; s Sfr130-200, d Sfr190-300) High-ceilinged spaces decorated with wrought iron, marble and chandeliers transport you back to the more graceful era of art

LOCAL KNOWLEDGE

STEPHAN SIEGRIST

Professional alpinist, mountain guide and BASE jumper, Stephan Siegrist (www.stephan-siegrist.ch) has travelled all over the world in pursuit of adventure, from Antarctica to the Indian Himalaya. He has opened up some of the most difficult climbing routes on Eiger and lives near Interlaken.

The Bernese Alps

We have some of the most beautiful mountains right here in the Swiss Alps. Eiger, Mönch and Jungfrau are the gems of the Bernese Oberland and I am privileged enough to live on their doorstep. Lauterbrunnen is known for its spectacular waterfalls, cliffs and BASE jumpers. The sport has a very strong presence in the valley.

Favourite Climbs

Jungfrau Region, Haslital and Kanderthal all have an incredible amount of good climbing spots. In Interlaken we are really spoilt! Lehn is one of the more popular climbing spots. The crag is better suited for intermediate to advanced climbers. The rock is very special in the region and the routes are diverse and challenging. It's a great place to go train. The Eiger is a very important place for me and over the years we've been through a lot together; I have shared a lot of intense moments on that mountain! Kanderthal is a great place for ice climbing and hosts the Annual Ice Climbing Festival in Kandersteg.

Getting Started

It's best is to grab a local guidebook or visit one of the climbing shops like Vertical Sport in Interlaken where you can get all the info and gear you need. We also have a few climbing halls in the Bernese Oberland that offer courses to beginners.

BERNESE OBERLAND INTERLAKEN

118

nouveau. Choose between antique-strewn historic rooms and clean-lined, contemporary rooms. There's a small spa and a first-rate restaurant (mains Sfr36 to Sfr46) serving Med-infused Swiss cuisine.

Gasthof Hirschen   HOTEL $$
(033 822 15 45; www.hirschen-interlaken.ch, in German; Hauptstrasse 11; s/d Sfr110/180; P 🛜) With its dark wood, geranium-clad facade and low ceilings, this heritage-listed, 17th-century chalet has plenty of old-world charm. Rooms are 'rustic modern', with parquet floors, downy duvets, bathroom pods and wi-fi. The restaurant (mains Sfr20 to Sfr35) rustles up local favourites.

Hotel Lötschberg/Susi's B&B   HOTEL $$
(033 822 25 45; www.lotschberg.ch; General Guisan Strasse 31; B&B s/d Sfr119/151, hotel s/d Sfr135/178; P @ 🛜) The picture of faded grandeur, this hotel and B&B offer reasonable value. The old-style rooms are bright and clean, though bathrooms are microscopic. Cheery Fritz serves breakfast and feeds guests tips on the area. Other pluses include a kitchen and free wi-fi.

Arnold's B&B   B&B $
(033 823 64 21; www.arnolds.ch; Parkstrasse 3; s Sfr50-60, d Sfr90-120; P) Frills are few but the welcome from Beatrice and Armin is warm at this family-run B&B. The light, home-style rooms are housed in a converted 1930s villa.

Camping Jungfraublick   CAMPGROUND $
(033 822 44 14; www.jungfraublick.ch; Gsteigstrasse 80, Matten; sites per adult Sfr9, tent Sfr10-30; ☺May-Sep; ♿🐕) An attractive campground just 2km south of town, with plenty of tree shade, mountain views and a solar-heated outdoor pool.

Hotel Splendid   HOTEL $$
(033 822 76 12; www.splendid.ch; Höheweg 33; s/d/tr/q Sfr145/240/270/300; 🛜) Right on the main drag, this 100-year-old family-run hotel shelters large, sunny rooms with parquet floors and lots of pine. Light sleepers might have problems nodding off, though.

✕ Eating

Benacus   FUSION $$
(033 821 20 20; www.benacus.ch; Stadthausplatz; mains Sfr26-50; ☺lunch & dinner Tue-Fri, dinner Sat) Super-cool Benacus is a breath of urban air with its glass walls, wine-red sofas, lounge music and street-facing terrace. The TV show *Funky Kitchen Club* is filmed here.

The menu stars creative flavours like perch filets with guacamole and Simmentaler veal with creamy basil mash.

Blueberry's   CAFE $
(Centralstrasse 7; snacks Sfr5-10; ☺9am-9pm Mon-Fri, 10am-9pm Sat, noon-8pm Sun) Every bit as zingy as its name suggests, this lime-walled cafe churns out fresh-pressed juices (try watermelon or apple-mint), appetising wraps and bagels, and spot-on blueberry smoothies.

Little Thai   THAI $
(033 821 10 17; Hauptstrasse 19; mains Sfr16.50-24.50, lunch menus Sfr14.50-20.50; ☺Wed-Mon) Next to Balmer's, this hole-in-the-wall den is authentically Thai, festooned with pics of the King of Thailand, kitschy fairy lights and lucky cats. Snag a table to chomp on Eddie's freshly prepared spring rolls, homemade curries and spicy papaya salads.

La Terrasse   FUSION $$$
(033 828 28 28; Höheweg 41; mains Sfr54-68, tasting menus Sfr115-145; ☺dinner Tue-Sat) La Terrasse is a high-class vision of marble, chandeliers and gleaming silverware. Thanks to chef Lukas Stalder, the food is as exquisite as the setting. The sommelier will help you choose fine wines to go with innovative dishes like roasted scallops with lemon verbena kefir, cherries and liquorice salt.

Goldener Anker   INTERNATIONAL $$
(033 822 16 72; www.anker.ch, in German; Marktgasse 57; mains Sfr25-48; ☺dinner) Even fussy eaters will find dishes that please at this beamed restaurant. The globetrotting menu tempts with everything from sizzling fajitas to red snapper and ostrich steaks. It also has a roster of live bands.

Sandwich Bar   CAFE $
(Rosenstrasse 5; snacks Sfr4-9.50; ☺7.30am-7pm Mon-Fri, 8am-5pm Sat) This crimson-walled, zebra-striped cafe is a great snack spot. Choose your bread and get creative with fillings like air-dried ham with sun-dried tomatoes and brie with walnuts. Or try the soups, salads, toasties and locally made ice cream.

Pizzeria Horn   PIZZERIA $$
(033 822 92 92; Hardererstrasse 35; pizzas Sfr14-22, mains Sfr23.50-42; ☺dinner Wed-Sun) Exposed brick, chunky tables and photos of Don Camillo set the scene at this inviting pizzeria. Find a cosy nook to feast on antipasti and delicious wood-oven pizza. There's alfresco dining on the garden terrace in summer.

Schuh CAFE $
(☎033 822 94 41; Höheweg 56; lunch menu Sfr19.50; ☺9am-midnight) A Viennese-style coffee house famous for its pastries, pralines and park-facing terrace. The menu covers all the bases, from rösti to yellow curry. The chocolate-making workshops at 5pm on Wednesdays and Saturdays (Sfr14.80) are touristy but fun.

Belvédère Brasserie BRASSERIE $$
(☎033 828 91 00; Höheweg 95; mains Sfr18-36) Though attached to the boring-look Hapimag, this brasserie has upbeat modern decor and a terrace with appetising Jungfrau views. Try the veal in merlot sauce or Swiss stalwarts like fondue and rösti.

Swiss Mountain Market SELF-CATERING $
(Höheweg 133; ☺10am-8pm) Fill your picnic basket with regional goodies like buffalo salami, goat sausage, Alpine cheese, preserves, liqueurs and ice cream here.

Coop Pronto SUPERMARKET $
(Höheweg 11; ☺6am-10.30pm) Handy supermarket for stocking up on essentials.

🍷 Drinking

Metro Bar BAR, CLUB
(www.metrobar-interlaken.com; Hauptstrasse 23; ☺9pm-2.30am) With its crazy themed parties and cheap booze, the bar/club at Balmer's is the liveliest haunt for revved-up 20-something travellers. DJs pump out house tunes as the night wears on.

Buddy's Pub PUB
(☎033 822 76 12; Höheweg 33) Pull up a stool, order a draft Rugenbräu or a 'sex on the mountain' (for want of a beach) cocktail and enjoy a natter with the locals. Switzerland's first pub is loud, smoky and convivial.

Per Bacco BAR
(☎033 822 97 92; Rugenparkstrasse 2; ☺9am-midnight Mon-Sat) A slightly more sophisticated and well-dressed clientele props up the horseshoe bar at Per Bacco, which serves Italian wines by the glass.

☆ Entertainment

There are twice-weekly performances of Schiller's *Wilhelm Tell* (William Tell) between mid-June and early September, staged in the open-air theatre in Rugen Forest. The play is in German but an English synopsis is available. Tickets are available from Tellspielbüro (☎033 822 37 22; www .tellspiele.ch; Höheweg 37; tickets Sfr35-58) in the tourist office.

❶ Information

Daniel's Fun Rental (Hauptstrasse 19; per hr Sfr6; ☺9am-10pm Wed-Mon, to 7pm Tue) Speedy internet as well as Skype, printing and scanning facilities.

Hospital (☎033 826 25 00; Weissenaustrasse 27) West of the centre.

Post office (Marktgasse 1; ☺8am-noon & 1.45-6pm Mon-Fri, 8.30-11am Sat) Telephones and stamp machines outside.

Tourist office (☎033 826 53 00; www.interlaken tourism.ch; Höheweg 37; ☺8am-7pm Mon-Fri, 8am-5pm Sat, 10am-noon & 5-7pm Sun Jul-Aug, 8am-noon & 1.30-6pm Mon-Fri, 9am-noon Sat rest of year) Halfway between the stations. There's a hotel booking board outside.

❶ Getting There & Away

Interlaken has two train stations: Interlaken West and Interlaken Ost; each has bike rental, money-changing facilities and a landing stage for boats on Lake Thun and Lake Brienz.

Trains to Lucerne (Sfr56, two hours), Brig via Spiez (Sfr42, one hour) and Montreux via Bern or Visp (Sfr58 to Sfr67, 2½ to three hours) depart frequently from Interlaken Ost train station.

The A8 freeway heads northeast to Lucerne and the A6 northwest to Bern, but the only way south for vehicles without a big detour round the mountains is to take the car-carrying train from Kandersteg, south of Spiez.

Should you wish to hire a car in Interlaken for trips further into Switzerland, big-name rental companies, including **Hertz** (☎033 822 61 72; Harderstrasse 25), are reasonably central.

❶ Getting Around

You can easily get around Interlaken on foot, but taxis, buses and even horse-drawn carriages (around Sfr40) are found at each train station. Alternatively, pick up bikes, scooters, cars and quads for zipping around town at **Daniel's Fun Rental** (www.daniels-fun-rental-interlaken.ch; Hauptstrasse 19), among others.

AROUND INTERLAKEN

Schynige Platte

The must-do day trip from Interlaken is Schynige Platte, a 1967m plateau where the **Alpengarten** (admission free; ☺8.30am-6.30pm) nurtures 600 types of Alpine blooms, including snowbells, arnica, gentian and

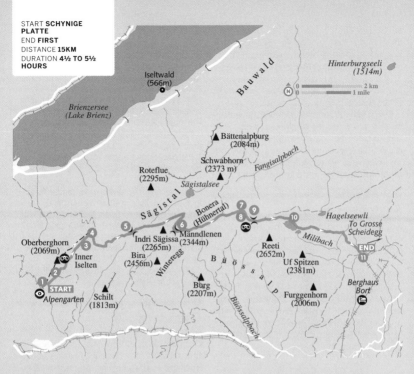

Walking Tour
Faulhornweg

> This high-level route is one of Switzerland's finest, with long views to Thunersee, Brienzersee and the Wetterhorn, Eiger, Mönch and Jungfrau. A recommended map is the SAW 1:50,000 Interlaken (Sfr22.50).

From ① **Schynige Platte** (1967m) you get the first views of Eiger, Mönch and Jungfrau. Walk northeast over rolling pastures past the Alpine hut of ② **Oberberg**, heading gently upward to reach ③ **Louchera** at 2020m.

Head around scree slopes on the western flank of canyon-like ④ **Loucherhorn** (2230m) to cross a low grassy crest. The way dips and rises before coming to ⑤ **Egg**, a boulder-strewn pass at 2067m, 1¼ to 1½ hours from Schynige Platte.

Egg opens out northeastward into the Sägistal, a moorlike valley completely enclosed by ridges. Filling the lowest point, the aquamarine Sägistalsee (1937m) seeps away subterraneously. Skirt the Sägistal's southern side below Indri Sägissa before swinging around the talus-choked gully of Bonera (or Hühnertal). The route picks through rough karst slabs to the wood-shingled mountain hut of ⑥ **Berghaus**

Männdlenen on the saddle of Männdlenen (2344m), one to 1½ hours on.

Make a steeply rising traverse along a broad ledge between stratified cliffs to the ridge of Winteregg. Shortly after a minor turn-off at 2546m, head left to the summit of 2681m ⑦ **Faulhorn**, one to 1¼ hours from Männdlenen. These lofty heights afford a spellbinding 360-degree panorama stretching from Eiger, Mönch and Jungfrau to shimmering Brienzersee and Thunersee and, on clear days, the Black Forest in Germany and Vosges in France. Just below the summit sits 19th-century ⑧ **Berghotel Faulhorn**, the oldest and highest mountain hotel in the Alps.

Look out for marmots as you descend to ⑨ **Gassenboden** (2553m), then drop eastward into the grassy basin of the ⑩ **Bachsee** (2265m). The petrol-blue lake contrasts starkly with the ice-shrouded peaks of Wetterhorn (3701m), Schreckhorn (4078m) and Finsteraarhorn (4274m). A well-trodden path descends through cow-grazed pastures to the gondola-lift station at ⑪ **First**, (2167m), 1½ to two hours from Berghotel Faulhorn.

edelweiss. The biggest draw up here, however, is the hiking. The **Panoramaweg** is an easy two-hour circuit, while the high-level 15km **Faulhornweg** trail is one of Switzerland's star treks. If you're here in July or August, don't miss the **moonlight hikes** that follow the same route.

You reach the plateau on a late 19th-century **cog-wheel train** (www.schynigeplatte.ch, www .jungfraubahn.ch; one way/return Sfr35/60; ◉ closed late Oct-late May) from Wilderswil. Trains run up to Schynige Platte at approximately 40- to 50-minute intervals until around 5pm.

St Beatus-Höhlen

Sculpted over millennia, the **St Beatus Caves** (www.beatushoehlen.ch, in German; adult/child Sfr18/10; ◉ 9.30am-5pm late Mar-late Oct) are great for a wander through caverns of dramatically lit stalagmites, stalactites and underground lakes. Lore has it that in the 6th century they sheltered St Beatus, monk, hermit and first apostle of Switzerland, who apparently did battle with a dragon here. They are a 1½-hour walk or a short Sfr12.80 boat ride from Interlaken.

JUNGFRAU REGION

If the Bernese Oberland is Switzerland's Alpine heart, the Jungfrau Region is where yours will skip a beat. Presided over by glacier-encrusted monoliths Eiger, Mönch and Jungfrau (Ogre, Monk and Virgin), the scenery is positively uplifting. Hundreds of kilometres of walking trails allow you to capture the landscape from many angles, but it never looks less than astonishing.

The 'big three' peaks have an enduring place in mountaineering legend, particularly the 3970m Eiger, whose fearsome north wall has claimed many lives and remained unconquered until 1938. Reaching great heights is easier today; it takes just hours to whizz up by train to Jungfraujoch (3454m), the highest station in Europe.

Summit journeys are only really worth making on clear days, so it's worth checking webcams – such as the ones on www .jungfraubahn.ch and www.swisspanorama .com – before you leave.

Staying in resorts entitles you to a Gästekarte (Guest Card), good for discounts throughout the entire region. Ask your hotel for the card if one isn't forthcoming.

ℹ Getting There & Around

Hourly trains depart for the region from Interlaken Ost station. Sit in the front half of the train for Lauterbrunnen or the back half for Grindelwald. The two sections of the train split up where the two valleys diverge at Zweilütschinen. The rail tracks loop around and meet up again at Kleine Scheidegg at the base of the Eiger, from where the route goes up and back to Jungfraujoch.

The Swiss Half-Fare Card is valid within the entire region. See p129 for details on good-value travel passes such as the Berner Oberland Regional Pass and the six-day Jungfraubahnen Pass.

Without a money-saving pass, sample fares include the following: Interlaken Ost to Grindelwald Sfr10.40; Grindelwald to Kleine Scheidegg Sfr32; Kleine Scheidegg to Jungfraujoch Sfr112 (return); Kleine Scheidegg to Wengen Sfr24; Wengen to Lauterbrunnen Sfr6.40; and Lauterbrunnen to Interlaken Ost Sfr7.20.

Many of the cable cars close for servicing in late April and late October.

Grindelwald

POP 3900 / ELEV 1034M

Grindelwald's sublime natural assets are film-set stuff – the chiselled features of Eiger north face, the glinting tongues of Oberer and Unterer Glaciers and the crown-like peak of Wetterhorn will make you stare, swoon and lunge for your camera. Skiers and hikers cottoned onto its charms in the late 19th century, which makes it one of Switzerland's oldest resorts. And it has lost none of its appeal over the decades, with geranium-studded Alpine chalets and verdant pastures set against an Oscar-worthy backdrop.

◉ Sights

Oberer Gletscher VIEWPOINT
(adult/child Sfr6/3; ◉ 9am-6pm mid-May–Oct) The shimmering, slowly melting Oberer Gletscher is a 1½-hour hike east from the village, or catch a bus to Hotel-Restaurant Wetterhorn. Walk 10 minutes from the bus stop, then clamber up 890 wooden steps to reach a terrace offering dramatic views. A vertiginous hanging bridge spans the gorge.

Gletscherschlucht GORGE
(www.gletscherschlucht.ch; adult/child Sfr7/3.50; ◉ 10am-5pm May–mid-Oct, to 6pm Jul & Aug) Turbulent waters carve a path through this craggy glacier gorge, a 30-minute walk south of the centre. A footpath weaves through tunnels hacked into cliffs veined with pink and

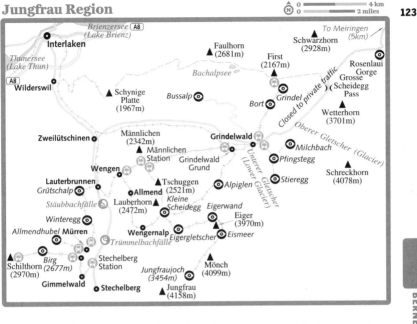

green marble. It's justifiably a popular spot for canyon and bungee jumping expeditions.

🏃 Activities

Summer Activities

Grindelwald is outstanding hiking territory, veined with trails that command arresting views to massive north faces, crevassed glaciers and snow-capped peaks. One of the most stunning day hikes is the 15km Kleine Scheidegg walk from Grindelwald to Wengen.

Other good high-altitude walks – around Männlichen, First and Pfingstegg – can be reached by taking cable cars up from the village. Anyone craving a challenge can tackle the Schwarzhorn *via ferrata,* a giddying 5½-hour scramble from First to Grosse Scheidegg.

Midway between First and Grindelwald is Bort, where you can rent scooters to zoom back down to the valley on a 4.5km marked trail. Rental including the cable car to Bort costs Sfr30 for adults and Sfr22 for children. Kids can enjoy free play at Bort's Alpine playground.

Grindelwald Sports   ADVENTURE SPORTS
(📞033 854 12 80; www.grindelwaldsports.ch; Dorf-strasse 110; ⏰8am-noon & 1.30-6pm, closed Sat & Sun in low season) In the tourist office, this outfit arranges mountain climbing, ski and snowboard instruction, canyon jumping and glacier bungee jumping at the Gletscher-schlucht.

Paragliding Jungfrau   PARAGLIDING
(📞079 779 90 00; www.paragliding-jungfrau.ch) Call ahead to organise your jump from First at a height of 2150m (from Sfr170) or above the Staubbach Falls (Sfr160).

Sportzentrum Grindelwald   SPORT CENTRE
(www.sportzentrum-grindelwald.ch, in German; Dorf-strasse 110) If the weather turns gloomy, Grindelwald's sport centre shelters a swimming pool, mini spa, boulder and climbing halls, an ice rink and an indoor rope park. See the website for opening times and prices.

Winter Activities

Stretching from Oberjoch at 2486m right down to the village, the region of First presents a fine mix of cruisy red and challenging black ski runs. From Kleine Scheidegg or Männlichen there are long, easy runs back to Grindelwald, with Eiger demanding all the attention. For a crowd-free swoosh, check out the 15.5km of well-groomed cross-country skiing trails in the area. Or slip on snowshoes to pad through the winter wonderland in quiet exhilaration on six different trails.

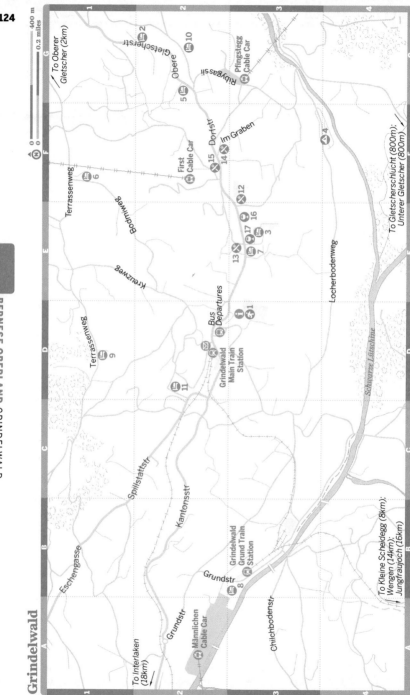

✹ Festivals & Events

In late January, artists get chipping at the World Snow Festival to create extraordinary ice sculptures. SnowpenAir (www .snowpenair.ch) rocks Kleine Scheidegg in late March with a star-studded concert line-up. *Schwingen* (Swiss Sumo-style wrestling), stone-throwing and other Alpine endeavours enliven Grosse Scheidegg in July, while the 90km Eiger Bike Challenge (www.eiger bike.ch) races over hill and dale in August.

🛏 Sleeping

Grindelwald brims with characterful B&Bs and holiday chalets. Pick up a list at the tourist office, or log onto www.wir-grindelwalder .ch for a wide selection of holiday apartments.

Nearly everywhere closes in April and from mid-October to mid-December. Local buses, tourist office guided walks and entry to the sports centre are free with the Guest Card.

TOP CHOICE Gletschergarten   HOTEL $$
(☏033 853 17 21; www.hotel-gletschergarten.ch; Dorfstrasse; s Sfr120-150, d Sfr230-300; P@) The sweet Breitenstein family make you feel at home in their rustic timber chalet, brimming with heirlooms from landscape paintings to snapshots of Elsbeth's grandfather who had 12 children (those were the days...). Decked out in pine and flowery fabrics, the rooms have balconies facing Unterer Gletscher at the front and Wetterhorn (best for sunset) at the back.

Hotel Bodmi   HOTEL $$
(☏033 853 12 20; www.bodmi.ch; Terrassenweg; s/d/apt Sfr200/294/392; P@) Wake up to memorable Eiger views and creamy goat's cheese – courtesy of the resident herd – at this postcard-perfect chalet. Surrounded by meadows, the hotel sits above First cable car station and is a great base for summer hiking and winter skiing. Unwind in the spa or in the restaurant (mains Sfr25 to Sfr45) dishing up market-fresh Alpine fare.

Hotel Tschuggen   HOTEL $$
(☏033 853 17 81; www.tschuggen-grindelwald.ch; Dorfstrasse 134; s Sfr70-95, d Sfr160-190; P🛜) Monika and Robert extend a warm welcome at this dark-wood chalet in the centre of town. The light, simple rooms are spotlessly clean; opt for a south-facing double for terrific Eiger views.

Naturfreundehaus   HOSTEL $
(☏033 853 13 33; www.naturfreundehaeuser.ch; Terrassenweg 18; dm Sfr32-37, d Sfr74-84, breakfast Sfr10; P@🛜🍴) Vreni and Heinz are your welcoming hosts at this wood chalet, picturesquely perched above the village. Creaking floors lead up to cute pine-panelled rooms with check curtains, including a shoebox single that's apparently Switzerland's smallest. Try an Eiger coffee with amaretto or a homemade mint cordial in the old curiosity shop of a cafe downstairs. The garden has wonderful views to Eiger and Wetterhorn.

Gletscherdorf   CAMPGROUND $
(☏033 853 14 29; www.gletscherdorf.ch; sites per adult/child Sfr8/4, tent Sfr8-12; 🛜) Open from May to October, this riverfront campsite near Pfingstegg cable car is among Switzerland's most stunning, with awesome views of Eiger, Wetterhorn and the glinting Unterer Gletscher. Be aware that the closer you get to the river, the colder it gets. The excellent facilities include a common room, laundry and free wi-fi.

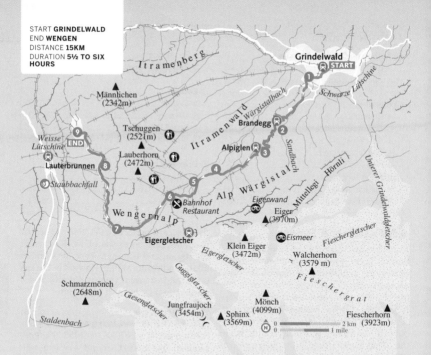

Walking Tour
Kleine Scheidegg

❯ One of the most memorable walks in the
Bernese Oberland, this hike forms the
seventh leg of the Alpine Pass Route. The best
map is the SAW 1:50,000 *Interlaken* (Sfr22.50).

Cross the railway tracks at ❶ **Grindelwald
Grund** and head left for Kleine Scheidegg.
The views southeast to the limestone crown
of Wetterhorn (3701m) and the Unterer
Grindelwaldgletscher are breathtaking. Eiger's
fearsome north face draws ever closer as you
follow the often-steep track shadowing the
Sandbach stream, then dipping in and out
of forest. Pass under an arched rail bridge to
reach ❷ **Restaurant Brandegg**, about one
hour from Grindelwald.

At the road, take the second left
signposted to Alpiglen and head up a gravel
path, which passes through the forest, then
follows the Wengernalpbahn railway tracks.
The trail weaves through meadows flecked
with gentians and thistles in summer, then
ducks under a small rail tunnel before
reaching the delightfully rustic ❸ **Berghotel
Alpiglen**, two to 2½ hours from Grindelwald
Grund.

The trail climbs gently now, skirting below
Eiger's north face, and leading through rolling
pastures. Head past clusters of mountain
pines and farmhouses in the hollow of
❹ **Mettla** (1809m).

Make your way to the ❺ **Arvengarten** ski
lifts to contour the mountainsides at roughly
2000m. This minor pass provides a close-
range vantage point of Eiger (3970m), Mönch
(4099m) and Jungfrau (4158m). Sidling up
around the slopes below the rail line you arrive
at ❻ **Kleine Scheidegg** (2061m), 1¼ to 1¾
hours from Berghotel Alpiglen.

From Kleine Scheidegg train station, the
descent rewards with more dazzling views of
the 'Big Three' and the pearly fin of Silberhorn
(3695m) before reaching ❼ **Wengernalp**
at 1874m. Wonderful views include the
Gspaltenhorn and Schilthorn beyond where
the land plunges into the deep glacial trough of
the Lauterbrunnental. A trail leads northward
through pockets of Alpine forest to cross the
railway lines again, whereafter a well-formed
track skirts the slopes via ❽ **Allmend** to reach
car-free ❾ **Wengen** after 1½ to two hours.

Romantik Hotel
Schweizerhof   HISTORIC HOTEL $$$
(☑033 854 58 58; www.hotel-schweizerhof.com;
Dorfstrasse; s/d/ste with half-board Sfr295/510/640;
P@⌨) The grand dame of Grindelwald, this
plush new art nouveau hotel has stylish rooms
with gleaming slate-floored bathrooms. The
spa is a big draw, with massage jets, treatment rooms, a teeth-chattering ice grotto
and a pool with wide-screen mountain vistas.
The restaurant (mains Sfr26 to Sfr44) uses
home-grown vegetables and herbs.

Alpenblick   HOTEL $$
(☑033 853 11 05; www.alpenblick.info; Obere
Gletscherstrasse; dm Sfr40-45, d Sfr140-180; P⌂)
In a quiet corner of town, 10 minutes' stroll
from the centre, Alpenblick is a great budget
find, with squeaky-clean, pine-filled rooms.
Basement dorms are jazzed up with bright
duvets. There's an American-style diner
(mains Sfr15 to Sfr19) and a terrace with
glacier views.

Residence   HOTEL $$
(☑033 854 55 55; www.residence-grindelwald.ch;
Dorfstrasse; s Sfr100-110, d Sfr170-190; P) This
homey chalet is tucked away in a serene
part of the village with brilliant views to
Wetterhorn. Decorated in neutral hues with
'70s-style trappings, rooms aren't special
but they are spotless. The best rooms have
geranium-smothered balconies.

Mountain Hostel   HOSTEL $
(☑033 854 38 38; www.mountainhostel.ch; Grund-
strasse; dm Sfr37-44, d Sfr94-108; P@⌂) Near
Männlichen cable-car station, this is an
ideal base for sports junkies, with well-kept
dorms and a helpful crew. There's a beer
garden, ski and bike room and TV lounge.
E-bike rental costs Sfr50 per day.

Downtown Lodge   HOSTEL $
(☑033 828 77 30; www.downtown-lodge.ch; Dorfstrasse; dm/s/d Sfr38/50/90; @⌂) Central,
clean and welcoming digs. Dorm buildings
resemble military barracks, but the facilities are comfortably above par with a bistro,
shared kitchen, TV lounge, games room
and free internet.

✗ Eating

Bars, restaurants, bakeries and supermarkets line central Dorfstrasse.

Onkel Tom's Hütte   PIZZERIA $$
(☑033 853 52 39; Im Graben 4; pizzas Sfr13-33;
⌂6pm-midnight Thu, noon-midnight Fri-Tue) Tables

are at a premium in this incredibly cosy
barn-style chalet. Yummy pizzas are prepared fresh in three sizes to suit any appetite.
The encyclopaedic wine list flicks from
Switzerland to South Africa.

Memory   SWISS $$
(☑033 854 31 31; mains Sfr21-30; Dorfstrasse;
⌂11.30am-10.30pm) Always packed, the
Eiger Hotel's unpretentious restaurant
rolls out tasty Swiss grub like rösti,
raclette and fondue. Try to bag a table on
the street-facing terrace.

C & M   FUSION $$
(☑033 853 07 10; mains Sfr23-36; ⌂8.30am-
11pm Wed-Mon) Just as appetising as the
menu are the stupendous views to Unterer
Gletscher from this gallery-style cafe's sunny terrace. Enjoy a salad, coffee and cake,
or seasonally inspired dishes like venison
stew with dumplings and bilberry-stuffed
apple.

Pizzeria da Salvi   PIZZERIA $
(☑033 853 89 89; Dorfstrasse 189; pizza Sfr17-23;)
This cheerful Italian in Hotel Steinbock rolls
out delicious wood-fired pizza. There are 110
different kinds of grappa on the menu.

☕ Drinking

Espresso Bar   BAR
(Dorfstrasse 136; ⌂2pm-1am) Full to the gills
in winter, the misleadingly named Espresso
Bar in the Hotel Spinne draws a boisterous beer-guzzling crowd. It also harbours
kitschy Mexican-themed Mescalero (⌂Mon-
Sat winter, Wed, Fri & Sat summer) with a DJ and
occasional live music.

Avocado Bar   BAR
(Dorfstrasse 158; ⌂3-10pm Mon-Fri, 2-10pm Sat &
Sun; ⌂) This is a young 'n' fun place to kick
back on a leather pouffe with a post-ski
schnapps or people-watch on the terrace
in summer.

ℹ Information

The **tourist office** (☑033 854 12 12; www
.grindelwald.ch; Dorfstrasse 110; ⌂8am-noon &
1.30-6pm Mon-Fri, 9am-noon & 1.30-5pm Sat &
Sun) in the Sportzentrum hands out brochures
and maps. There's an accommodation board with a
phone and a coin-operated internet terminal outside. The post office is next to the main train station.

ℹ Getting There & Around

See p122 for train fares. Grindelwald is off the
A8 from Interlaken. A smaller road continues

from the village over the Grosse Scheidegg Pass (1960m). It's closed to private traffic, but from mid-June to early October postal buses (one way/return Sfr48/96, 1¾ hours) travel this scenic route to Meiringen roughly hourly from 8.15am to 4.15pm.

Around Grindelwald

FIRST

A cable car zooms up to First (www.jungfrau .ch; one way/return Sfr32/54; ☺8.30am-6.30pm, to 4.15pm in winter), the trailhead for 100km of paths, half of which stay open in winter. From here, you can trudge up to Faulhorn (2681m; 2½ hours) via the cobalt Bachalp-see (Lake Bachalp). As you march along the ridge, the unfolding views of the Jungfrau massif are entrancing. Stop for lunch and 360-degree views at Faulhorn. From here, you can either continue on to Schynige Platte (another three hours) and return by train, or you can hike to Bussalp (1800m; 1½ hours) and return by bus to Grindelwald (Sfr22, 32 minutes).

Other great walks head to Schwarzhorn (three hours), Grosse Scheidegg (1½ hours), Unterer Gletscher (1½ hours) and Grindelwald (2½ hours). Early birds can catch a spectacular sunrise by overnighting in a

DON'T MISS

SLIDE & SWING

Not only skiers love the deep powder at First. You can also stomp through the snow on the No 50 trail to Faulhorn in winter. The 2½-hour walk takes in the frozen Bachalpsee and the Jungfrau range in all its wintry glory. Faulhorn is also the starting point for Europe's longest toboggan run (admission free; ☺Dec-Apr), accessible only on foot. Bring your sled to bump and glide 15km over icy pastures and through glittering woodlands all the way back down to Grindelwald via Bussalp. Nicknamed 'Big Pintenfritz', the track lasts around 1½ hours, depending on how fast you race.

Year-round, you can get your pulse racing on the First Flyer (adult/child Sfr25/18, incl cable car Sfr75/43), a staggeringly fast zip-line from First to Schreckfeld. The mountains are but a blur as, secure in your harness, you pick up speeds of around 84km/h.

rustic dorm at Berggasthaus First (☎033 828 77 88; www.berggasthausfirst.ch; dm with half-board Sfr89) by the First cable-car summit station.

First has 60km of well-groomed pistes, which are mostly wide, meandering reds suited to intermediates. The south-facing slopes make for interesting skiing through meadows and forests. Freestylers should check out the kickers and rails at Bärgelegg or have a go on the superpipe at Schreckfeld station.

MÄNNLICHEN

On the ridge dividing the Grindelwald and Lauterbrunnen Valleys, Männlichen (2230m) is one of the region's top viewpoints. Europe's longest cable car (www.maennlichen .ch; one way/return Sfr32/54; ☺8.15am-5.30pm, to 4pm in winter) connects Grindelwald Grund to Männlichen. Another cable car comes up the other side of the ridge, from Wengen (one way/return Sfr24/41).

From Männlichen top station, walk 10 minutes up to the crown of the hill to enjoy the view. At the southern end of the ridge are Tschuggen (2520m) and Lauber-horn (2472m), with the 'big three' looming behind. From here, you notice the differ-ence between the two valleys – the broad expanse of the Grindelwald Valley to the left, and the glacier-carved, U-shaped Lauterbrunnen Valley to the right. To the north you can see a stretch of Thunersee.

If you wish to stay overnight, try cosy Berggasthaus Männlichen (☎033 853 10 68; www.berghaus-maennlichen.ch; s Sfr80-95, d Sfr150-180) in summer. A snow bar lures skiers here in winter. Affording long views across the frosted peaks, the sunny terrace is the perfect spot to kick back with a glühwein.

Männlichen's broad cruising terrain is perfect for skiing in the shadow of Eiger, Mönch and Jungfrau. An alternative for non-skiers is the speedy 45-minute sled run down to Holenstein, negotiating steep bumps and hairpin bends.

If you only have time for one hike from Männlichen, make it the spirit-soaring Panoramaweg to Kleine Scheidegg, tak-ing in wildflower-cloaked pastures, a veri-table orchestra of chiming cowbells, and peerless views of Eiger, Mönch, Jungfrau and the pearl-white pyramid of Silberhorn (3695m). The easygoing trail skirts the base of Tschuggen and knife-edge Lauberhorn to reach Rotstöckli and Kleine Scheidegg in 1½ hours.

Little ones in tow? Keep them amused on the 90-minute Felixweg (www.felix-weg.ch) from Männlichen to Holenstein. Kids can get the low-down on Alpine flora and fauna, spot marmots from the watchtower and ride the flying fox. There are two scenic barbecue areas en route. The trail is not (yet) suitable for buggies.

PFINGSTEGG

Another cable car rises up to Pfingstegg (www.pfingstegg.ch; one way/return Sfr12.60/18.80; ☉8-7pm, to 5.30pm in low season, closed Nov-Apr), where short hiking trails lead to Stieregg, near the deeply crevassed Unterer Gletscher. Check to see whether the trail to Hotel Wetterhorn (☎033 853 12 18; www.grosse-scheidegg.ch) at the base of the Oberer Gletscher (1½ hours) via the Restaurant Milchbach (one hour) is open. Along this, you pass the Breitlouwina, a geologically fascinating rock terrace scarred with potholes caused by moving ice. The website has details on full-moon and sunset hikes.

Kids (and big ones) love to whizz downhill on the summer bobsled (adult/child Sfr5/3; ☉11am-6pm).

Kleine Scheidegg

Eiger, Mönch and Jungfrau soar almost 2000m above you at Kleine Scheidegg (2061m), where restaurants huddle around the train station. Most people only stay for a few minutes while changing trains for Jungfraujoch, but it's worth lingering to appreciate the dazzling views, including those to the fang-shaped peak of Silberhorn.

Kleine Scheidegg is a terrific base for hiking. There are short, undemanding trails, one hour apiece, to Eigergletscher, down to Wengernalp, and up the Lauberhorn behind the village. These areas become intermediate ski runs from December to April. Alternatively, you can walk the spectacular 6km Eiger Trail from Eigergletscher to Alpiglen (two hours) for close-ups of the mountain's fearsome north face.

Basic digs can be found in Restaurant Bahnhof Röstizzeria (☎033 828 78 28; www.bahnhof-scheidegg.ch; dm/d Sfr52.50/135, half-board extra Sfr20) and the more recently renovated Restaurant Grindelwaldblick (☎033 855 13 74; dm Sfr40, half-board extra Sfr25; ☉closed Nov & May), eight minutes' walk towards Grindelwald.

Rambling, creaky and atmospheric, Hotel Bellevue des Alpes (☎033 855 12 12; www.scheidegg-hotels.ch; s Sfr230-250, d Sfr380-430) is a formerly grand Victorian hotel. It has a world-beating location and a rather macabre history of people using its telescopes to observe mountaineering accidents on the Eiger.

Jungfraujoch

Sure, everyone else wants to see Jungfraujoch (3454m) and yes, tickets are expensive, but don't let that stop you. It's a once-in-a-lifetime trip that you need to experience first-hand. And there's a reason why two million people a year visit Europe's highest train station. The icy wilderness of swirling glaciers and 4000m turrets that unfolds at the top is staggeringly beautiful.

The last stage of the train journey from Kleine Scheidegg burrows through the heart of Eiger before arriving at the sci-fi Sphinx meteorological station. Opened in 1912, the tunnel took 3000 men 16 years to drill. Along the way, you stop at Eigerwand and Eismeer, where panoramic windows offer tantalising glimpses across rivers of crevassed ice.

Good weather is essential for this journey; check on www.jungfrau.ch or call ☎033 828 79 31. Don't forget to take warm clothing, sunglasses and sunscreen, as there's snow and glare up here all year. Within the Sphinx

---

ℹ DISCOUNT TRAVEL PASSES

If you intend on spending most of your holiday in the Bernese Oberland, you can save francs with Berner Oberland Regional Pass (www.regiopass-berner oberland.ch; ☉May-Oct). The seven-day pass (Sfr233) gives you three days' unlimited free travel and four days' discounted travel in the region, while the 15-day pass (Sfr290) offers five days unlimited free travel and 10 days discounted travel. Children pay half price.

A good alternative is the Jungfraubahnen Pass (www.jungfrau.ch; ☉May-Oct), which provides six days of unlimited travel throughout the region for Sfr210 (Sfr160 with Swiss Pass, Swiss Card or Half-Fare Card), though you still have to pay Sfr55 from Eigergletscher (just past Kleine Scheidegg) to Jungfraujoch.

weather station, where trains disgorge passengers, there's an Ice Palace gallery of otherworldly ice sculptures, restaurants, indoor viewpoints and a souvenir shop, where you can purchase your very own chunk of Eiger to grace the mantelpiece.

Outside there are views of the moraine-streaked 23km tongue of the Aletsch Glacier, the longest glacier in the European Alps and a Unesco World Heritage Site. The views across rippling peaks stretch as far as the Black Forest in Germany on cloudless days.

When you tire (as if!) of the view, you can zip across the frozen plateau on a flying fox (adult/child Sfr20/15), dash downhill on a sled or snow disc (adult/child Sfr15/10), or enjoy a bit of tame skiing or boarding (adult/child Sfr35/25) at the Snow Fun Park. A day pass covering all activities costs Sfr45 for adults and Sfr25 for children.

If you cross the glacier along the prepared path, in around an hour you reach the Mönchsjochhütte (☎033 971 34 72; dm/incl half-board Sfr28/64; ☺late Mar–mid-Oct) at 3650m. Here you'll share your dinner table and dorm with hardcore rock climbers, psyching themselves up to tackle Eiger or Mönch.

From Interlaken Ost, the journey time is 2½ hours each way and the return fare is Sfr186.20. The last train backs off at 5.45pm in summer and 4.45pm in winter. However, from May through to October there's a cheaper Good Morning Ticket costing Sfr140 if you take the first train (which departs at 6.35am from Interlaken Ost) and leave the summit by noon.

Getting these early trains is easier if your starting place is deeper in the region. Stay overnight at Kleine Scheidegg to take advantage of the excursion-fare train at 8am. From here, a return Good Morning Ticket is Sfr90. The furthest you can walk is up to Eigergletscher (2320m), which saves you Sfr7.80 on a one-way ticket and Sfr13.40 on a return ticket from Kleine Scheidegg.

Even the ordinary return ticket to Jungfraujoch is valid for one month, so you can use that ticket to form the backbone of your trip, venturing as far as Grindelwald and stopping for a few days' hiking, before moving on to Kleine Scheidegg, Jungfraujoch, Wengen and Lauterbrunnen.

Lauterbrunnen

POP 2500 / ELEV 796M

Lauterbrunnen's wispy Staubbach Falls inspired both Goethe and Lord Byron to pen poems to their ethereal beauty. Today the postcard-perfect village, nestled deep in the valley of 72 waterfalls, attracts a less highfalutin crowd. Laid-back and full of chalet-style lodgings, Lauterbrunnen is a great base for nature-lovers wishing to hike or climb, and a magnet to thrill-seeking BASE jumpers.

⦿ Sights & Activities

Hikes heading up into the mountains from the waterfall-laced valley include a 2½-hour uphill trudge to Mürren and a more gentle 1¾-hour walk to Stechelberg. In winter, you can glide past frozen waterfalls on a well-prepared 12km cross-country trail.

For a chance to see BASE jumpers in hair-raising action, head to the base station of Schilthorn – you'll probably hear the almighty whoosh of their descent before you see them.

FREE Staubbach Falls   WATERFALL
(☺8am-8pm Jun-Oct) Especially in the early-morning light, it's easy to see how the vaporous, 297m-high Staubbach Falls captivated prominent writers with its threads of spray floating down the cliffside. What appears to be ultra-fine mist from a distance, however, becomes a torrent when you walk behind the falls. Be prepared to get wet.

Trümmelbachfälle   WATERFALL
(www.truemmelbachfaelle.ch; adult/child Sfr11/4; ☺9am-5pm Apr-Jun, Sep-Nov, 8.30am-6pm Jul & Aug) These glacier falls are more of a bang-crash spectacle. Inside the mountain, up to 20,000L of water per second corkscrews through ravines and potholes shaped by the swirling waters. The 10 falls drain from 24 sq km of Alpine glaciers and snow deposits. A 10-minute bus ride (Sfr3.40) from the train station takes you to the falls.

Doris Hike   HIKING
(☎033 855 42 40; www.doris-hike.ch) Doris' informative guided hikes include glacier, waterfall and high-alpine options. Call ahead for times and prices.

🛏 Sleeping

Hotel Staubbach   HOTEL **$$**
(☑033 855 54 54; www.staubbach.com; s Sfr130-
150, d Sfr150-170, tr Sfr210-240, s/d without bath-
room Sfr100/120; @🛜) The bright rooms with
downy duvets are immaculately kept at this
grand old hotel; the best have balconies with
Staubbach Falls views. There's a sociable
vibe in the lounge with free coffee and a
kids' play area.

Valley Hostel   HOSTEL **$**
(☑033 855 20 08; www.valleyhostel.ch; dm/s/
tw/d/tr/q Sfr28/43/66/76/99/120; 🅿🛜) This
relaxed, family-run hostel has an open-plan
kitchen, a garden with tremendous views of
the Staubbach Falls, a laundry, free wi-fi and
a cat, Tiggy. Most of the spacious, pine-clad
dorms have balconies. The friendly team can
help organise activities from paragliding to
canyoning.

Camping Jungfrau   CAMPGROUND **$**
(☑033 856 20 10; www.camping-jungfrau.ch; sites
per adult/tent/car Sfr9.80/11/3.50, dm Sfr29-32;
@🛜) This Rolls Royce of a campsite also
offers cosy dorms and huts for those craving
more comfort. The top-notch facilities in-
clude a kitchen, kiosk, bike rental and wi-fi.
There's even a dog shower for messy pups!

Gästehaus im Rohr   GUESTHOUSE **$**
(☑033 855 21 82; www.chaletimrohr.ch; r per
person Sfr28; 🛜) Ablaze with scarlet gera-
niums in summer, this 400-year-old chalet
is a bargain. Creaky floorboards and small
windows add to its cosy, old-world charm.
The '70s-style rooms are humble but spot-
less, and there's a huge communal balcony
overlooking the falls.

🍴 Eating & Drinking

TOP CHOICE Airtime   CAFE **$**
(www.airtime.ch; snacks & light meals Sfr6-15;
☺9am-7pm; 🛜) Inspired by their travels in
New Zealand, Daniela and Beni have set
up this funky cafe, book exchange, laundry
and extreme sports agency. Munch wraps,
sandwiches and homemade cakes (try the
chocolate-nut special) as you use the free
wi-fi to check your email. You can book
adrenalin-fuelled pursuits like ice climbing,
canyoning and bungee jumping here.

Flavours   CAFE **$**
(www.flavours.ch; snacks & light meals Sfr6-14;
☺7.30am-6.30pm) Whether you fancy a slap-
up egg-and-bacon breakfast, homemade

cakes with locally roasted coffee or a
smoothie, Flavours is the go-to place. Housed
in the former bakery, it's a grocery store
on one side and a sleek cafe on the other.
Warm up over hearty soups and savoury
quiches. Choc-Rock truffles make a sweet
gift.

Hotel Oberland   SWISS **$$**
(☑033 855 12 41; mains Sfr18-36; ☺11am-9pm)
The street-facing terrace at this traditional
haunt is always humming. On the menu
are Swiss and international favourites from
fondue to pizza, vegetable curry and hybrid
dishes like Indian-style rösti.

Hotel Horner   BAR
(☑033 855 16 73; ☺9.30am-2.30am; 🛜) BASE
jumpers tell hair-raising parachute tales at
this buzzy pub, as they come back down to
earth over a pint or four. The vibe gets club-
bier as the night wears on. Internet access or
wi-fi is free when you buy a drink.

ℹ Information

The **tourist office** (☑033 856 85 68; www.my
lauterbrunnen.com; ☺8.30am-noon & 1.30-
6pm Jun-Sep, 9am-noon & 1.30-5pm Mon-Fri
rest of year) is opposite the train station.

If you're travelling to the car-free resorts of
Wengen and Mürren, there's a multistorey **car
park** (☑033 828 71 11; www.jungfraubahn.ch;
per day/week Sfr13.50/82) by the station, but
it's advisable to book ahead. There is also an
open-air car park by the Stechelberg cable-car
station, charging Sfr5 for a day.

Wengen

POP 1300 / ELEV 1274M

Photogenically poised on a mountain
ledge, Wengen's 'celestial views' have lured
Brits here since Edwardian times. The fact
you can only reach this chocolate-box village by train gives it romantic appeal. From
the bench in front of the church at dusk,
the vista takes on watercolour dreaminess, peering over to the misty Staubbach
Falls, down to the Lauterbrunnen Valley
and up to glacier-capped giants of the
Jungfrau massif. In winter, Wengen
morphs into a ski resort with a low-key,
family-friendly feel.

The highlight in Wengen's calendar is
the world-famous **Lauberhorn downhill
ski race** in mid-January, where pros reach
speeds of up to 160km/h. Mere mortals can
pound powder by taking the cable car to

Männlichen or train to Allmend, Wengernalp or Kleine Scheidegg. Skiing is mostly cruisy blues and reds, though experts can brave exhilarating black runs at Lauberhorn and the aptly named 'Oh God'.

The same areas are excellent for hiking in the summer. Some 20km of paths stay open in winter too. The hour-long forest trail down to Lauterbrunnen is a sylvan beauty.

🛏 Sleeping

Expect summer rates to be roughly 30% cheaper than those quoted below.

Hotel Caprice   BOUTIQUE HOTEL $$$

(☎033 856 06 06; www.caprice-wengen.ch; s Sfr380-540; 🛜) If you're looking for design-oriented luxury in the Jungfrau mountains, this boutique gem delivers with discreet service and authentically French cuisine. Don't be fooled by its cute Alpine trappings; inside it exudes Scandinavian-style simplicity with chocolate-cream colours, slick rooms and a lounge with an open fire.

Hotel Berghaus   HOTEL $$

(☎033 855 21 51; www.berghaus-wengen.ch; s/d from Sfr135/270) Sidling up to the forest, this family-run chalet is a five-minute toddle from the village centre. Rooms are light, spacious and pin-drop peaceful – ask for a south-facing one for dreamy Jungfrau views. Call ahead and they'll pick you up from the train station.

DON'T MISS

SKIING THE JUNGFRAU REGION

Whether you want to slalom wide, sunny slopes at the foot of Eiger or ski the breathtakingly sheer 16km Inferno run from Schilthorn to Lauterbrunnen, there's a piste that suits in the Jungfrau Region. Grindelwald, Männlichen, Mürren and Wengen have access to some 214km of prepared runs and 44 ski lifts. A one-day ski pass for either Grindelwald-Wengen or Mürren-Schilthorn costs Sfr62 for adults and Sfr31 for children, while a seven-day ski pass for these regions will set you back Sfr291/146. Ski passes for the whole Jungfrau ski region cost Sfr129 for adults and Sfr65 for children for a minimum two days, but switching between ski areas by train can be slow and crowded.

Hotel Bären   HOTEL $$

(☎033 855 14 19; www.baeren-wengen.ch; s Sfr90-150, d 190-280; @🛜) Loop back under the rail track and head down the hill to this snug log chalet with bright, if compact, rooms. The affable Brunner family serves a hearty breakfast and the extra Sfr20 for half-board is incredible value.

🍴 Eating & Drinking

Restaurant Schönegg   SWISS $$$

(☎033 855 34 22; mains Sfr39-52; ⊗lunch & dinner Mon-Sun, dinner only winter) Chef Hubert Mayer serves seasonally inspired dishes like home-smoked salmon with apple horseradish and saddle of venison in port wine jus. The pine-clad, candlelit dining room is wonderfully cosy in winter and the mountain-facing terrace perfect for summertime dining.

Santos   CAFE $

(☎078 67 97 445; snacks Sfr6-9; ⊗10am-midnight, closed Mon in summer) Popular with ravenous skiers coming down from the slopes, this Portuguese TV-and-tiles place is the real deal. Mrs Santos whips up burgers, calamari, sandwiches and divine *pastéis de nata* (custard tarts).

Café Gruebi   CAFE $

(☎033 855 58 55; snacks & mains Sfr7-16; ⊗8.30am-6pm Mon-Sat, 1-8pm Sun) Run by a husband-and-wife team, Gruebi offers cheap eats like rösti and goulash. The yummy homemade cakes are baked almost daily by the...husband.

Pickel   ITALIAN $$

(☎033 855 77 77; Am Bahnhof; mains Sfr24-38; ⊗4pm-1am) Exposed brick, log tables and banquettes set the scene at this little restaurant-bar behind the station. It's a relaxed spot for a coffee, homemade schnapps, or well-executed Italian mains like porcini ravioli.

Rocks Bar   BAR

(Dorfstrasse; ⊗4.30pm-12.30am Wed-Mon) The chipper staff, comfy leather sofas, Sky sports and internet (Sfr5 for 30 minutes) make this a good place to unwind. There's two for one at the daily happy hour from 9pm to 10pm.

Crystal Bar   BAR

(Haus Crystal; ⊗8am-midnight) Pumping tunes and occasionally hosting gigs, this relaxed bar draws fun-loving après-ski types. It's opposite Männlichen cable car.

❶ Information

Next to the Männlichen cable car, the **tourist office** (📞033 855 14 14; www.mywengen.ch; ⊘9am-6pm Mon-Sat, 9am-noon & 1-6pm Sun, closed Sat & Sun Nov & Mar-Apr) is minutes from the train station, taking a left at Hotel Silberhorn and continuing 100m further on. Next door is the **post office**.

Stechelberg

POP 260 / ELEV 922M

To witness the drama of the waterfall-gone-mad Lauterbrunnen Valley, where a staggering 72 falls cascade over perpendicular walls of rock, make for Stechelberg. The valley takes its name from *lauter* (clear) and *Brunnen* (spring). To see the cataracts at their thundering best, visit in spring when the snow thaws or after heavy rain. Though long a bolthole for hikers, this tiny, silent village still feels like a well-kept secret.

Blissfully rural **Alpenhof Stechelberg** (📞033 855 12 02; www.alpenhof-stechelberg.ch; r per person Sfr28; ⊘closed Nov) harbours light-filled, neat-and-tidy rooms that offer fantastic value for your franc. A hearty breakfast with local dairy products is served for Sfr12.

Mürren

POP 430 / ELEV 1650M

Arriving on a clear evening, as the train from Grütschalp floats along the horizontal ridge towards Mürren, the peaks across the valley feel so close that you could reach out and touch them. And that's when you'll think you've died and gone to Heidi heaven. With its low-slung wooden chalets and spellbinding views of Eiger, Mönch and Jungfrau, car-free Mürren is storybook Switzerland.

In summer, the **Allmendhubel funicular** (one way/return Sfr12/7.40) takes you above Mürren to a panoramic restaurant. From here, you can set out on many walks, including the famous **Northface Trail** (1½ hours), via Schiltalp to the west, leading through wildflower-strewn meadows with views to the glaciers and waterfalls of the Lauterbrunnen Valley and the monstrous Eiger north face – bring binoculars to spy intrepid climbers. There's also a kid-friendly **Adventure Trail** (one hour).

In winter, there are 53km of prepared ski runs nearby, mostly suited to intermediates, and a **ski school** (📞033 855 12 47;

DON'T MISS

CLIFFHANGER

Feel like an adventure? Little beats Mürren's vertigo-inducing **Klettersteig** (📞033 856 86 86; www.klettersteig-muerren.ch; ⊘mid-Jun–Oct). This high-altitude 2.2km *via ferrata* is one of Switzerland's most astonishing, wriggling across breathtakingly steep limestone cliffs to Gimmelwald. Equipped with harness, helmet and karabiner, you can flirt with mountaineering on ladders that snake across the precipices and bring you to a zip-line – whoa there goes Eiger! – and an 80m-long suspension bridge. Equipment can be rented for Sfr20 per day from Intersport opposite the tourist office. Or you can go with a guide for Sfr95 by contacting **Bergsteigen für Jedermann** (📞033 821 61 00; www.be-je.ch).

www.muerren.ch/skischule) charging Sfr50 for a two-hour group lesson. Mürren is famous for its hell-for-leather **Inferno Run** (www.inferno-muerren.ch) down from Schilthorn in late January. Daredevils have been competing in the 16km race since 1928 and today the course attracts 1800 intrepid amateur skiers. It's also the reason for all the devilish souvenirs.

🛏 Sleeping & Eating

In summer, rates are up to 30% cheaper than the high-season winter prices given below.

Eiger Guesthouse　　　　GUESTHOUSE **$$**
(📞033 856 54 60; www.eigerguesthouse.com; d Sfr140-190, q Sfr240; @🖥) Run by a fun-loving, on-the-ball team, this central pick offers great value. Besides clean, spruced-up rooms (the best have Eiger views), there is a downstairs pub serving tasty grub and a good selection of draught beers.

Hotel Jungfrau　　　　HISTORIC HOTEL **$$**
(📞033 856 64 64; www.hoteljungfrau.ch; s Sfr80-140, d Sfr160-280; 🖥) Set above Mürren and overlooking the nursery slopes, this welcoming family-run hotel dates to 1894. Despite '70s traces, rooms are tastefully decorated in warm hues; south-facing ones have Jungfrau views. Downstairs there's a beamed lounge with an open fire.

Hotel Alpenruh HOTEL **$$**
(☑033 856 88 00; www.alpenruh-muerren.ch; s Sfr140-180, d Sfr200-280; ☎) Lots of loving detail has gone into this much-lauded chalet. Grimacing masks to ward off evil spirits and assorted knick-knacks enliven the place, while the light-flooded rooms feature lots of chunky pine. Guests praise the service, food and unbeatable views to Jungfrau massif.

Hotel Eiger HOTEL **$$**
(☑033 856 54 54; www.hoteleiger.com; s Sfr178-270, d Sfr285-460; ☎▨) This huge wooden chalet harbours sleek and contemporary rooms. The service is first-rate, as are the views from the swimming pool, with picture-windows perfectly framing Eiger, Mönch and Jungfrau.

Tham's ASIAN **$**
(☑033 856 01 10; mains Sfr15-28; ☺dinner) Tham's serves Chinese, Thai and other Asian dishes cooked by a former five-star chef who's literally taken to the hills to escape the rat race. The Sichuan beef and Singapore fried noodles are authentically spicy.

Restaurant La Grotte SWISS **$$**
(☑033 855 18 26; mains Sfr21-35; ☺11am-2pm & 5-9pm) Brimming with cowbells, cauldrons and Alpine props, this kitsch-meets-rustic mock cave of a restaurant is touristy but fun. Fondues and flambées are good bets.

🛈 Information

The **tourist office** (☑033 856 86 86; www .mymuerren.ch; ☺8.30am-7pm Mon-Sat, to 8pm Thu, 8.30am-6pm Sun, reduced hours in low season) is in the sports centre.

Gimmelwald

POP 110 / ELEV 1370M
If you think Mürren is cute, wait until you see Gimmelwald. This pipsqueak of a village has long been a hideaway for hikers and adventurers tiptoeing away from the crowds. The secret is out, though, and this mountainside village is swiftly becoming known for its drop-dead-gorgeous scenery, rural authenticity and sense of calm.

The surrounding hiking trails include one down from Mürren (30 to 40 minutes) and one up from Stechelberg (1¼ hours). Cable cars are also an option (Mürren or Stechelberg Sfr5.80).

🛏 Sleeping & Eating

ᴛᴏᴘ ᴄʜᴏɪᴄᴇ Esther's Guest House GUESTHOUSE **$$**
(☑033 855 54 88; www.esthersguesthouse.ch; s/d/tr/q Sfr55/130/150/180, apt Sfr160-230; ☎📶) Esther runs this charming B&B with love. Drenched with piny light, the rooms are spotless, while the apartments are ideal for families. The attic room is a favourite with its slanted roof and star-gazing window. For an extra Sfr15, you'll be served a delicious breakfast of homemade bread, cheese and yoghurt.

Hotel Mittaghorn GUESTHOUSE **$**
(☑033 855 16 58; d/tr Sfr86/129, half-board per person Sfr15; Poeschenried 39; ◉) Staring in wonder at the mountains is the main pursuit at this stunningly situated wooden chalet, run by the irrepressible Walter and his sidekick, Tom. Creaking floors and doors lead to simple, cosy rooms. Dinners are hearty, jovial affairs. It's a 10-minute uphill walk from the cable-car station.

Mountain Hostel HOSTEL **$**
(☑033 855 17 04; www.mountainhostel.com; dm Sfr28; ☎) A backpacking legend, this basic, low-ceilinged hostel has a sociable vibe. After a sweaty day's hiking, you can kick back in a hammock in the mountain-facing garden, play pool or grab a pizza.

Schilthorn

There's a tremendous 360-degree panorama from the 2970m Schilthorn (www.schilthorn .ch). On a clear day, you can see from Titlis around to Mont Blanc, and across to the German Black Forest. Yet some visitors seem more preoccupied with practising their delivery of the line, 'The name's Bond, James Bond', than taking in the 200 or so peaks. That's because a few scenes from *On Her Majesty's Secret Service* were shot here in 1968–69 – as the fairly tacky Touristorama below the Piz Gloria revolving restaurant will remind you.

From Interlaken, take a Sfr120.80 excursion trip (Half-Fare Card and Swiss Card 50% off, Swiss Pass 65% off) going to Lauterbrunnen, Grütschalp, Mürren, Schilthorn and returning through Stechelberg to Interlaken. A return from Lauterbrunnen (via Grütschalp) and Mürren costs Sfr94.80 as does the return journey via the Stechelberg cable car. A return from Mürren is Sfr74. Ask about discounts for early-morning trips.

En route from Mürren, the cable car goes through the Birg station (2677m), where you can stop to take in marvellous views.

THE LAKES

Anyone who travels to Interlaken for the first time from Bern will never forget the moment they clap eyes on Thunersee (Lake Thun). As the train loops past pastures and tidy villages on the low southern shore, some people literally gasp at the sight of the Alps rearing above the startlingly turquoise waters.

Bordering Interlaken to the east, Brienzersee (Lake Brienz) has just as many cameras snapping with its unbelievably aquamarine waters and rugged mountain backdrop.

Steamers ply both lakes from late May to mid-September. There are no winter services on Brienzersee, whereas special cruises continue on Thunersee. For more information contact BLS ($\boxed{\mathcal{I}}$033 334 52 11; www.bls.ch). A day pass valid for both lakes costs Sfr64 from Tuesday to Sunday, Sfr29 on Monday; children pay half-price. Eurail Passes, the Regional Pass and the Swiss Pass are valid on all boats, and InterRail and the Swiss Half-Fare Card get 50% off.

Thun

POP 43,400 / ELEV 559M

Ringed by mountains, hugging the banks of the aquamarine Aare River and topped by a turreted castle, medieval Thun is every inch your storybook Swiss town. History aside, the town is infused with a young spirit, with lively crowds sunning themselves at riverside cafes and one-of-a-kind boutiques filling the unusual arcades.

◉ Sights & Activities

The tourist office's one-and-a-half-hour guided tours (Sfr15 per person), every Wednesday and Saturday from May to October, take in the Altstadt and castle.

For a magical 360-degree view of Thun, the lake and the glaciated Jungfrau mountains, walk 20 minutes south of the centre to Jakobshübeli viewpoint.

Schloss Thun | TOP CHOICE | CASTLE
(www.schlossthun.ch; adult/child Sfr8/2; ◉10am-5pm) Sitting on a hilltop and looking proudly

> ## ⓘ FREE WHEELING 135
>
> Should you wish to pedal along the river and lake, free city bikes are available for hire from **Thun Rollt** (Aarefeldstrasse; passport & deposit of Sfr20; ◉7.30am-9.30pm May-Oct) close to the station.

back on 900 years of history, Schloss Thun is the castle of your wildest fairy-tale dreams, crowned by a riot of turrets and affording tremendous views of the lake and Alps. It once belonged to Duke Berchtold V of the powerful Zähringen family. Today it houses a **museum**, showcasing prehistoric and Roman relics, tapestries, majolica and plenty of shining armour.

Altstadt NEIGHBOURHOOD
It's a pleasure simply to wander Thun's attractive riverfront Old Town, where plazas and lanes are punctuated by 15th- and 16th-century townhouses. A stroll takes in the 300-year-old Untere Schleusenbrücke, a covered wooden bridge that is a mass of pink and purple flowers in summer. Nearby is the split-level, flag-bedecked Obere Hauptgasse, whose arcades hide boutiques and galleries selling everything from handmade jewellery to chocolate and Moroccan babouches (slippers). At the street's northern tip is cobblestone Rathausplatz, centred on a fountain and framed by arcaded buildings.

FREE Schadau Park GARDENS
Dating to the mid-19th century, candyfloss-pink Schloss Schadau now shelters gourmet restaurant Arts, but it's free to explore its botanical gardens on the banks of Lake Thun. The grounds bristle with tulips and crocuses in spring, rhododendrons in summer, and golden beech trees in autumn. In the park you'll find the 1000-year-old **Kirche Scherzlingen** (◉10am-6pm Apr-Oct), with its beautifully restored Carolingian tower, and the early 19th-century **Thun Panorama** (adult/child Sfr6/5; ◉11am-5pm Tue-Sun May-Oct), which boasts being the world's oldest panoramic painting.

Flussbad Schwäbis SWIMMING
(Grabenstrasse 40; adult/child Sfr4.50/2.50; ◉9am-7pm May-Aug, to 6pm Sep) Cool off in the turquoise Aare River at this open-air pool, with a splash area, slides and sandpit for kids.

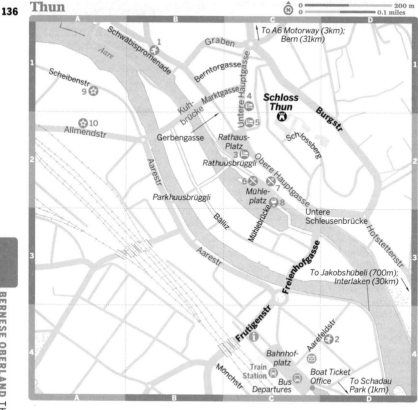

Thun

✷ Festivals & Events

Thun's headliners include the **Bollywood Festival** (www.bollywood-festival.ch, in German) in June, and lakeside musicals at the **Thuner Seespiele** (www.thunerseespiele.ch, in German) and medieval fisherman's jousting at the **Fischerstechen** (www.fischerstechen.ch, in German) in August. On Thursday evenings in July there are free folklore performances on Rathausplatz.

🛏 Sleeping

🌿 **Zunfthaus zu Metzgern** HISTORIC HOTEL **$**
(📞033 222 21 41; www.zumetzgern.ch; Untere Hauptgasse 2; s/d/tr without bathroom Sfr55/110/165) Sitting on Thun's prettiest square is this 700-year-old guild house. Bold artworks glam up the well-kept, parquet-floored rooms. Downstairs the chef uses local organic ingredients to prepare dishes like lamb with caramelised apricots and poached

rainbow trout with fig-vanilla sauce (mains Sfr24 to Sfr44).

Schwert   HISTORIC HOTEL $$
(☑033 221 55 88; www.schwert-thun.ch; Untere Hauptgasse 8; s Sfr75-100, d Sfr145-230; 🐾) Nestled at the foot of the castle is this graceful 18th-century hotel, with an inviting wood-panelled restaurant (mains Sfr28 to Sfr43). Hardwood floors, high ceilings and the occasional antique lend the individually decorated rooms old-world flair.

Hotel Krone   HISTORIC HOTEL $$
(☑033 227 88 88; www.krone-thun.ch; Obere Hauptgasse 2; s Sfr140-210, d Sfr220-330; 🐾) Housed in a 14th-century bakers' guild house on Rathausplatz, the Krone seamlessly combines historic charm with contemporary design. The rooms are bright and spacious, and the homely restaurant (mains Sfr30 to Sfr50) serves Swiss–French cuisine.

✗ Eating & Drinking

TOP CHOICE Fluss   FUSION $$
(☑033 222 01 10; Mühleplatz 9; mains Sfr27-58; ⊘11am-12.30am, closed Sun winter) Right on the banks of the Aare River, this contemporary glass-walled lounge restaurant attracts a young crowd who come for the beautifully prepared sushi, sashimi and herb-infused grill specialities. The olive tree-dotted waterfront deck is perfect for sundowners and people-watching.

Kaffee und Kuchen   CAFE $
(Obere Hauptgasse 34; snacks & light meals Sfr6.50-21; ⊘closed Sun evening & Mon winter) This vaulted cellar has an arty vibe and invites lazy days spent reading, guzzling coffee and lingering over brunch. The homemade food – from breakfast rösti to rich chocolate-chilli cake – is delicious.

Arts   INTERNATIONAL $$
(☑033 222 25 00; www.schloss-schadau.ch; Seestrasse 45; mains Sfr29-56; ⊘closed Mon; 🖉🖼) Ornate stucco and chandeliers create a regal backdrop at this restaurant in the perkily turreted Schloss Schadau. The views of the Jungfrau mountains are as appealing as the seasonal cuisine – think sautéed filet of charr with pea-mint ravioli. Vegetarians and kids are well catered for.

Kaffeebar Mühleplatz   CAFE $
(Mühleplatz 1; snacks Sfr6-15; ⊘10am-12.30am Sun-Thu, 10am-1.30am Fri & Sat, shorter hours

in winter) This is a cool riverside spot for a baguette or coffee.

☆ Entertainment

Mokka   CLUB
(www.mokka.ch, in German; Allmendstrasse 14; ⊘Wed-Sun) Has a top-drawer line-up of DJs, gigs and festivals. Music skips from funk to ska and electro punk.

Konzepthalle6   ARTS CENTRE
(www.konzepthalle6.ch, in German; Scheibenstrasse 6) Cutting-edge design space and cultural centre, hosting events from concerts to poetry slams in a converted factory.

Arena Thun   SPECTATOR SPORT
(☑033 225 18 00; www.arenathun.ch; Weststrasse 12) This new arena is home base to Swiss Super League football giants FC Thun. Take bus 3 from the train station.

ⓘ Information

Post office (Panoramastrasse 1A; ⊘7.30am-7pm Mon-Fri, 8am-noon Sat) Opposite the train station.

Tourist office (☑033 225 90 00; www.thun.ch; Bahnhofplatz; ⊘9am-6.30pm Mon-Fri, to 4pm Sat, plus to 1pm Sun Jul & Aug)

ⓘ Getting There & Away

Thun is on the main north–south train route from Frankfurt to Milan and beyond. Frequent trains run to Interlaken West (Sfr15.20, 30 minutes). Boats glide across the lake to Interlaken Ost (Sfr39) and Spiez (Sfr19). Thun is on the A6 motorway, which runs from Spiez north to Bern.

Spiez

POP 12,500 / ELEV 628M

Hunched around a horseshoe-shaped bay, with a medieval castle rising above emerald vineyards, the oft-overlooked town of Spiez makes a great escape. The vibe is low-key but the setting magical, with views to conical Niesen (2362m) and a fjord-like slither of the lake. Its vines yield crisp, lemony riesling and Sylvaner white wines.

◎ Sights & Activities

Schloss Spiez   CASTLE
(www.schloss-spiez.ch; Schlossstrasse 16; adult/child Sfr10/2; ⊘2-5pm Mon, 10am-5pm Tue-Sun Easter-Jun, mid-Sep–mid-Oct, 10am-6pm Jul–mid-Sep) This turreted medieval castle is smothered in oil paintings of its former masters, the influential von Bubenburg and von Erlach

DON'T MISS

BUNKER MENTALITY

Ever wondered why the radio plays on deep in the heart of a tunnel? Riddled with more holes than an Emmental cheese, Switzerland is full of subterranean surprises, including the formerly top-secret WWII bunkers at **Faulensee** (☎033 654 25 07; www .artilleriewerk-faulensee.ch, in German; adult/child Sfr10/5; ⊙2-5pm 1st Sat of month Apr-Oct) built to house troops defending Thun, Spiez and the Lötschberg railway. During summer, they're open to the public once a month. Cleverly disguised as farmhouses, the entrances to the bunkers are guarded by cannons and connected by underground tunnels in which you'll find offices, laboratories, kitchens and cramped sleeping quarters. Tours last 1½ to two hours, and you'll need to be wearing warm clothing and sturdy shoes. To ask about English explanations, call or email ahead.

Faulensee can be reached by bus from Spiez train station and from Interlaken West by boat (Sfr22/37 one way/return).

families. But it's the view that will grab you, whether from the lofty tower (which also sports 13th-century graffiti) or the banqueting hall.

FREE **Heimat und Rebbaumuseum** MUSEUM (Spiezbergstrasse 48; ⊙2-5pm Wed, Sat & Sun May-Oct) This attractive 18th-century wooden chalet showcases exhibits on wine cultivation. The best time to actually taste local tipples is at the **Läset-Sunntig** (www.laese -t-spiez.ch) wine festival in late September.

Freibad Spiez SWIMMING (www.freibadspiez.ch; adult/child Sfr6/3; ⊙7.30am-8pm mid-May–Aug, 8am-7pm Sep) Spiez' lido attracts sun-worshipping locals and families who come to frolic in the lake or swim laps in the Olympic-sized swimming pool. It has volleyball and tennis courts, minigolf and – wait for it – the longest waterslide in the Bernese Oberland.

🛏 Sleeping & Eating

You'll find many, rather ordinary, pizza and pasta places located around the boat station.

Strandhotel Belvédère HISTORIC HOTEL $$ (☎033 655 66 66; www.belvedere-spiez.ch; Schachenstrasse; s Sfr125-155, d Sfr290-370; ℗@☎) Whisking you back 100 years, the chandelier-lit public areas at this genteel hotel exude art nouveau flair. Some rooms overdo the Laura Ashley–style pastels and florals but they are comfy, especially those with lake-facing balconies. There's a spa and a Gault Millau–rated restaurant (mains Sfr39 to Sfr55).

Seegarten Marina HOTEL $$ (☎033 655 67 67; www.seegarten-marina.ch; Schachenstrasse 3; s Sfr110-130, d Sfr170-220; ℗☎) Sitting prettily on the banks of Lake Thun, this hotel has simple but large and spotless rooms. Friendly service adds to the appeal, as does the waterfront restaurant (mains Sfr18 to Sfr44), dishing up Swiss classics like veal sausage with rösti and perch filets.

ℹ Information

The **tourist office** (☎033 655 90 90; www .thunersee.ch; ⊙8am-6.30pm Mon-Fri, 9am-noon Sat) is outside the train station. It is open shorter hours in the shoulder seasons. Seestrasse, the main street, is down to the left, and leads to the castle (15 minutes).

ℹ Getting There & Away

From Interlaken West, trains run very frequently to Spiez (Sfr9.80, 20 minutes). By boat it's Sfr19 from Thun and Sfr25 from Interlaken West.

Around Lake Thun

For a right royal day out, the grand castles and palaces dotted around Lake Thun can easily be reached by boat.

Scenically perched on the lake, turreted **Schloss Oberhofen** (www.schlossoberhofen .ch; adult/child Sfr10/2; ⊙2-5pm Mon, 11am-5pm Tue-Sun mid-May–mid-Oct) was wrested from Habsburg control after the Battle of Sempach (1386) and now traces Bernese life from the 16th to the 19th centuries. A spin takes in the frescoed chapel, ornate Napoleonic drawing room and Turkish smoking room. The manicured English landscaped **gardens** (admission free; ⊙10am-dusk Apr-Oct) command arresting views of the Bernese Alps.

Oberhofen is 25 minutes by boat from Thun (one way/return Sfr4.60/7.80), or you can take a bus (Sfr3, 20 minutes).

The plaything of a wealthy Prussian baron, silver-turreted **Schloss Hünegg** (www.schloss

huenegg.ch, in German; Staastrasse 52, Hilterfingen; adult/child Sfr9/3; ☺2-5pm Mon-Sat & 11am-5pm Sun mid-May–mid-Oct) is a feast of art nouveau and neo-Renaissance styles, featuring fabulous 19th-century stuccoed salons.

In summer, you can cool off on and around the lake with activities ranging from swimming and messing around in boats to scuba-diving, windsurfing, waterskiing, wakeboarding and sailing. Thun tourist office has a complete list of centres and schools in its *Thunersee* brochure, or see www.thunersee.ch.

Brienz

POP 3000 / ELEV 566M

Quaint and calm, Brienz peers across the exquisitely turquoise waters of its namesake lake to rugged mountains and thick forests beyond. The deeply traditional village has a stuck-in-time feel with its tooting steam train and woodcarving workshops. In town, mosey down postcardperfect Brunngasse, a curving lane dotted with stout wooden chalets, each seemingly trying to outdo its neighbour with window displays of vines, kitsch gnomes and billowing geraniums.

◉ Sights & Activities

Kids can splash around in the water playground on the tree-fringed lake promenade.

Rothorn Bahn   RAILWAY
(www.brienz-rothorn-bahn.ch; one way/return Sfr51/80; ☺hourly 7.30am-4.30pm Jun-late Oct) This is the only steam-powered cogwheel train still operating in Switzerland, climbing 2350m, from where you can set out on hikes or enjoy the long views over Brienzersee to snow-dusted 4000m peaks. Walking up from Brienz takes around five hours.

Schweizer Holzbildhauerei Museum   MUSEUM
(Hauptstrasse 111; adult/child Sfr5/free; ☺9am-6pm May-Sep, 1.30-5.30pm Tue-Sat rest of year, closed Jan & Nov) Several woodcarvers open their attached workshops, including Jobin, which has been in business since 1835. You can see its intricately carved sculptures, reliefs and music boxes in this museum.

🛏 Sleeping & Eating

Pick up a list of holiday apartments and B&Bs at the tourist office.

Hotel Steinbock   HISTORIC HOTEL $$
(☑033 951 40 55; www.steinbock-brienz.ch; Hauptstrasse 123; s Sfr130-160, d Sfr180-220; 🅿🛜) Guarded by a namesake *Steinbock* (ibex), this beautiful pine chalet dates to 1787. Decorated in warm terracotta hues, the plush rooms have organic mattresses, flat-screen TVs and slick bathrooms with pebble-floored showers for a spot of DIY reflexology. There's a cosy restaurant (mains Sfr27 to Sfr46) and wine cellar downstairs.

Camping Aaregg   CAMPGROUND $
(☑033 951 18 43; www.aaregg.ch; Seestrasse 22; sites per adult/car & tent Sfr12/20; ☺Apr-Oct) Set on a little peninsula, this is a peaceful lakeside campsite with excellent facilities including a restaurant and playground. It's a 10-minute walk east of the train station.

Tea-Room Hotel Walz   CAFE $$
(Hauptstrasse 102; mains Sfr29-35; ☺7.30am-10pm, 7.30am-6.30pm Thu-Tue winter) Dirndl-clad waitresses bring hearty meals and cakes to the table at this old-fashioned tea room. Try the unfortunate-sounding but tasty speciality Brienzer Krapfen, pastries filled with dried pears.

Seerestaurant Löwen   SWISS $$
(☑033 951 12 41; Hauptstrasse 8; mains Sfr24-46; ☺11.30am-9.30pm) Sit on the lakeside terrace to choose from a vast array of fish dishes, including beer-battered perch, catfish in wholegrain mustard, and monkfish in green curry. Meat-lovers, children and vegetarians are also catered for.

❶ Information

The train station, boat station, Rothorn Bahn and post office all huddle in the compact centre. The **tourist office** (☑033 952 80 80; Hauptstrasse 148; www.brienz-tourismus.ch; ☺8am-6pm mid-Jun–Oct, closed Sat & Sun in winter) is in the train station.

❶ Getting There & Away

From Interlaken Ost, Brienz is accessible by train (Sfr7.80, 20 minutes) or boat (Sfr28, Apr–mid-Oct). The scenic Brünig Pass (1008m) is the road route to Lucerne.

Around Brienz

FREILICHTMUSEUM BALLENBERG

For a fascinating insight into the rural Switzerland of yore, visit **Ballenberg Open-Air Museum** (www.ballenberg.ch; adult/

child Sfr20/10; ⊙10am-5pm mid-Apr–end Oct), set in 80-hectare grounds east of Brienz. Authentically reconstructed farming hamlets take you on an architectural stroll around Switzerland, with 100 century-old buildings from humble wooden huts in Valais to hip-roofed farmhouses in the Bernese Oberland. Demonstrations from bobbin lace-making to cow herding showcase Swiss crafts and traditions. Picnickers can buy wood-oven bread, homemade cheese and sausage at the shop.

There are two entrances and car parks at each. A bus runs at least hourly from Brienz train station to Ballenberg (Sfr4.20, 20 minutes).

GIESSBACHFÄLLE

Illuminating the fir forests like a spotlight in the dark, the misty Giessbachfälle (Giessbach Falls) plummet 500m over 14 rocky ridges. Europe's oldest funicular, dating to 1879, creaks up from the boat station (one way/return Sfr7/9), but it's only a 15-minute walk up to the most striking section of the falls. Giessbach is easily reached by boat (return from Brienz Sfr16.80, from Interlaken Ost Sfr37).

Overlooking Brienzersee and the thundering falls from its hilltop perch, the lavish 19th-century Grand Hotel Giessbach (⊠033 952 25 25; www.giessbach.ch; s Sfr150-190, d Sfr240-410; ⊙late Apr–mid-Oct) is a romantic retreat with antique-filled rooms, polished service and a restaurant with far-reaching views from its terrace.

EAST BERNESE OBERLAND

Grab your walking boots, do a little Sherlock Holmes-style detective work and you'll unearth natural wonders in the Hasli Valley (Haslital), east of the Jungfrau Region, from slot-like gorges to Europe's highest hanging bridge over the Trift glacier. Base yourself here if you want to embark on tours across the Grimsel and Susten passes.

Meiringen

POP 4600 / ELEV 595M

When the writer Arthur Conan Doyle left his fictional detective Sherlock Holmes for dead at the base of the Reichenbach Falls near Meiringen, he ensured that a corner of Switzerland would forever remain English

eccentric. Every 4 May, fans in tweed deerstalker hats and capes gather here for the anniversary of Holmes' 'death'.

Espionage aside, Meiringen's claim to fame is as the birthplace of those airy eggwhite marvels that grace sweet trolleys from Boston to Brighton – meringues.

◎ Sights & Activities

The Haslital is an outdoorsy wonderland, laced with 300km of marked hiking and cycling trails that lead to wild valleys, waterfalls and high-alpine moors. The 2.7km marmot trail is a kid favourite. The tourist office has E-bike rental for Sfr30/50 for a half-/full day.

When the flakes fall, beginners and intermediates whizz down the region's 60km of slopes; a day ski pass costs Sfr55. Families can stomp along glittering winter walking trails and race on sled runs like the 5.5km one to Grosse Scheidegg (day pass adult/child Sfr37/24).

TOP CHOICE / Reichenbachfälle   WATERFALL
Gazing over the mighty Reichenbach Falls, where the cataract plunges 250m to the ground with a deafening roar, you can see how Arthur Conan Doyle thought them perfect for dispatching his increasingly burdensome hero, Sherlock Holmes. In 1891, in *The Final Problem,* Conan Doyle acted like one of his own villains and pushed both Holmes and Dr Moriarty over the precipice here. Fans have flocked to the site ever since.

To reach the falls, take the funicular (www.reichenbachfall.ch; one way/return adult Sfr7/10, child Sfr6/8; ⊙9am-6pm Jul & Aug, 9-11.45am & 1.15-5.45pm May, Jun, Sep & Oct) which rises from Willigen, south of the Aare River, to the top. It takes an hour to wander back down to Meiringen. Alternatively, take the steep path up the side of the falls to the village of Zwirgi. At Gasthaus Zwirgi, you can rent trotti-bikes (adult/child Sfr20/16) to scoot back down to Meiringen.

Aareschlucht   GORGE
(www.aareschlucht.ch; adult/child Sfr7.50/4; ⊙8am-6pm Jul & Aug, 9am-5pm Apr-Jun & Sep-Oct) Less than 2km from the town is the narrow, 1.4km-long Aare Gorge, where tunnels and galleries lead past milky-blue torrents and limestone overhangs. The canyon is spectacularly illuminated on Thursday evenings in summer.

To make your way here, take the Meiringen-Innertkirchen-Bahn (one way/

return Sfr3.40/6.80; ☻6am-7pm) train running half-hourly on weekdays, less frequently at weekends, from Meiringen to Aareschlucht East, near the eastern entrance.

Gletscherschlucht Rosenlaui   GORGE
(www.rosenlauischlucht.ch; adult/child Sfr7/3.50; ☻9am-6pm Jun-Sep, 10am-5pm May & Oct) Zwirgi is the start of the mountainous Reichenbach Valley, which runs towards Grindelwald. A path leads to Rosenlaui and this dramatic glacier gorge, where a round trail takes in waterfalls and 80m-high cliffs. The walk back to Meiringen takes at least two hours, but hourly buses also ply the route from June to September.

Sherlock Holmes Museum   MUSEUM
(www.sherlockholmes.ch; Bahnhofstrasse 26; adult/child Sfr4/3, combined with Reichenbachfall funicular Sfr11/8; ☻1.30-6pm Tue-Sun May-Sep, 4.30-6pm Wed-Sun rest of year) Real fans won't want to miss this museum in the basement of the English church back in Meiringen. The highlight is a recreated sitting room of 221b Baker Street. Multilingual audioguides are available.

Triftbrücke   BRIDGE
(Trift Bridge; www.trift.ch, in German) The Hasli Valley is laced with 300km of signposted walking trails. A huge hit with outdoorsy types is this 170m-long, 100m-high suspension bridge, Europe's longest and highest. Hikers come to balance above the majestic Trift glacier, as it becomes meltwater more swiftly than it once did. To reach the glacier from Meiringen, take a train to Innertkirchen, then a bus to Nessental, Triftbahn (Sfr9.20, 30 minutes). Here a cable car (www.grimselwelt.ch; one way/return Sfr14/22; ☻9am-4pm Jun-Oct, to 5pm Jul & Aug) takes you up to 1022m, from where it's a 1½- to two-hour walk to the bridge (1870m).

🛏 Sleeping & Eating

TOP CHOICE **Hotel Victoria**   BOUTIQUE HOTEL $$
(☎033 972 10 40; www.victoria-meiringen.ch; Bahnhofplatz 9; s Sfr150, d Sfr190-250, tr Sfr280; 🅿 @) It's the little touches that count at this boutique-chic hotel: from the fresh flowers and designer furnishings in your room to the mountain views and free room service. Simon puts an imaginative spin on French–Asian cuisine in the Gault Millau-rated restaurant (mains Sfr29 to Sfr52), serving delicacies like Thai-style ravioli and beef in red wine sauce with truffle-potato mousse.

Park Hotel du Sauvage   HISTORIC HOTEL $$
(☎033 971 41 41; www.sauvage.ch; Bahnhofstrasse 30; s/d Sfr125/210) Arthur Conan Doyle once stayed in this art nouveau classic, but today it's pensioners on whodunnit weekends who spy on the breakfast buffet. After the old-fashioned grandeur in the lobby, the rooms are something of an anticlimax. Real detectives, however, will find its merits: friendly staff, superb views and perhaps a tweed hat in the wardrobe…

Hotel Alpbach   SWISS $$
(☎033 971 18 31; www.alpbach.ch; Kirchgasse 17; s Sfr95-130, d Sfr180-230) Friendly service is something of a lucky dip, but we can't fault the charming pine-clad quarters at this central hotel. Up the romance by opting for a four-poster bed. There's a small sauna and steam room, as well as a rustic restaurant (mains Sfr24 to Sfr52) festooned with cowbells and accordions.

Frutal   CAFE $
(Bahnhofstrasse 18; cakes Sfr3-6; ☻7am-6.30pm) A kitsch plastic meringue licks its lips in the window of this old-fashioned tea room. You'll do likewise when you taste the feather-light meringues here. Try them with whipped cream (Sfr9.50).

Molki Meiringen   DAIRY $
(Lenggasse; ☻8am-12.15pm & 2-6.30pm Mon-Fri, 7.30am-5pm Sat) Stop by this local dairy for tangy Haslital cheeses and homemade ice cream.

❶ Information

As you exit the train station (bike rental available), you'll see the post office and bus station opposite.

Haslital Pass (3/6 days Sfr100/160; ☻Apr-Oct) Offers unlimited use of local buses, Brienz–Meiringen–Brünig trains, BLS boats and Meiringen–Hasliberg lifts. Children receive free passes when accompanied by their parents.

Tourist office (☎033 972 50 50; www.haslital .ch; Bahnhofplatz; ☻8am-6pm Jul-Aug, Dec-Apr, 8am-noon & 2-6pm btwn seasons) Has info on hiking in the region and E-bike rental for Sfr30/50 per half-/full day.

❶ Getting There & Away

Frequent trains go to Lucerne (Sfr22, 80 minutes, with a scenic ride over the Brünig Pass) and Interlaken Ost (Sfr12.20, 40 minutes, via Brienz). In summer, buses and cars can take the pass southeast (to Andermatt), but the road southwest over Grosse Scheidegg (to Grindelwald) is closed to private vehicles.

WEST BERNESE OBERLAND

At the western side of the Jungfrau are Simmental and Frutigland, dominated by two wildly beautiful river valleys, the Simme and the Kander. Further west is Saanenland, famous for the ritzy ski resort of Gstaad.

Kandersteg

POP 1200 / ELEV 1176M

Turn up in Kandersteg wearing anything but muddy boots and you'll attract a few odd looks. Hiking is this town's raison d'être, with 550km of surrounding trails. An amphitheatre of spiky peaks studded with glaciers and jewel-coloured lakes creates a sublime natural backdrop to the rustic village of dark-timber chalets.

Jagged mountains frame the impossibly turquoise Oeschinensee (www.oeschinensee .ch). A cable car (one way/return Sfr16/23) takes you to within 20 minutes of the lake by foot. Once there, it takes an hour to hike back down to Kandersteg.

Kandersteg has some first-rate hiking in its wild backyard on the cantonal border with Valais. A superb trek is the high-level Gemmi Pass (2314m) to Leukerbad, involving a steep descent. Alternatively, you could walk through flower-strewn pastures in the wildlife-rich Üschenetäli, or trudge 5km up to Blausee (adult/child Sfr5/2) and its nature park to eat fresh organic trout by the shore. For more of a challenge, test the 3½-hour *via ferrata* at Allmenalp. Equipment can be hired at the valley station for Sfr20.

In winter there are more than 50km of cross-country ski trails, including the iced-over Oeschinensee. The limited 15km of downhill skiing is suited to beginners, and day passes cost Sfr39. Kandersteg's frozen waterfalls attract ice climbers and the village hosts the spectacular Ice Climbing Festival in January. Bergsteigen Kandersteg (☎033 675 01 01; www.bergsteigen -kandersteg.ch) offers guided *via ferrata* tours in summer and ice climbing in winter; visit the website for times and prices.

🛏 Sleeping & Eating

Kandersteg's popularity with hikers means there's lots of cheaper accommodation, but many places close between seasons. Ask for the Guest Card for reductions on activities.

TOP CHOICE The Hayloft   B&B $

(☎033 675 03 50; www.thehayloft.ch; Altes Bütschels Hus; s/d/tr Sfr50/96/117) Picture a dark-wood, 500-year-old chalet snuggled against the hillside, flower-strewn meadows where cows graze placidly, views of waterfalls and glaciers – ahhh... this place sure is idyllic! The farm-turned-B&B is in the capable hands of Peter and Kerry, who welcome guests like members of the family and serve delicious breakfasts and dinners (Sfr20). Anchor the dog and Snorkel the cat are a throwback to the pair's round-the-world sailing venture in 1993. See the website for directions.

Hotel zur Post   HOTEL $

(☎033 675 12 58; www.hotel-zur-post.ch, s Sfr55-70, d Sfr100-120) Cheery and central, these good-value digs offer simple rooms with balconies. Downstairs the restaurant has a menu packed with Swiss staples like fondue and rösti (mains Sfr18 to Sfr35). Sit on the terrace when the sun's out.

Hotel Victoria Ritter   HISTORIC HOTEL $$

(☎033 675 80 00; www.hotel-victoria.ch; s Sfr130-180, d Sfr220-330; P🛉🐾) This one-time coach tavern is now an elegant hotel, run by the Platzer family. The Victoria side has traditional 19th-century decor, while the snug wood-panelled rooms in the Ritter are more rustic. There's a fine restaurant, an indoor pool and sauna, a children's club and playground.

Ruedihus   HISTORIC HOTEL $$

(☎033 675 81 81; www.doldenhorn-ruedihus.ch; s/d from Sfr140/270; P) Oozing 250 years of history from every creaking beam, this archetypal Alpine chalet is a stunner. Romantic and warm, the cottage-style rooms feature low ceilings, antique painted furniture and four-poster beds. Home-grown herbs are used to flavour dishes served in the cosy restaurant (mains Sfr34 to Sfr40).

Camping Rendez-Vous   CAMPGROUND $

(☎033 675 15 34; www.camping-kandersteg .ch; sites per adult/child/car Sfr7.50/4.20/3, tent Sfr8-16) At the foot of Oeschinen, this green and pleasant site, open year-round, has a barbecue hut, shop and restaurant.

Hari SUPERMARKET $
(Bahnhofstrasse; ⊘8am-noon & 2-6.30pm Mon-Sat) Stock up on picnic goodies at this tiny grocery store selling fresh bread, home-made yoghurt, and local cheese, honey and wine.

❶ Information

The **tourist office** (✆033 675 80 80; www .kandersteg.ch; ⊘8am-noon & 1.30-6pm Mon-Fri, 8.30am-noon & 3-6pm Sat Jun-Sep, 8am-noon & 2-6pm Mon-Fri, 8.30am-noon & 3-6pm Sat Dec-Mar, 8am-noon & 2-5pm Mon-Fri rest of year) can suggest hiking routes and other activities in the area.

❶ Getting There & Away

Kandersteg is at the northern end of the Lötschberg Tunnel, through which trains trundle to Goppenstein (30km from Brig) and onwards to Iselle in Italy. See www.bls.ch/autoverlad for more details. The traditional way to head south is to hike; it takes a little over five hours to get to the Gemmi Pass and a further 1¾ hours to reach Leukerbad.

Gstaad

POP 3600 / ELEV 1100M

Synonymous with the glitterati and fit-tingly twinned with Cannes, Gstaad appears smaller than its reputation – too little for its designer ski boots, as it were. Michael Jackson, Roger Moore, Paris Hilton and even Marga-ret Thatcher have flexed platinum cards to let their hair down here. While the principal competitive sports are celebrity-spotting and gazing wistfully into Gucci-filled boutiques, others might enjoy the fine hiking and skiing.

🏃 Activities

Winter Activities

Gstaad Mountain Rides' 250km of ski slopes cover a good mix of blues, reds and blacks, and include neighbouring resorts like Saa-nen, Saanenmöser, St Stephan and Zweisim-men. Beginners can test out the snow on gentle, tree-lined runs at Wispile and Eggli, while more proficient skiers can cruise chal-lenging reds at Les Diablerets. A day ski pass costs Sfr62 for an adult and Sfr31 for a child, and under nine-year-olds ski free. Snow-boarders tackle the curves, bowls and jumps at the ski-cross slope at Riedenberg.

Non skiers and families are in their ele-ment in Gstaad, with off-piste fun includ-ing ice skating, curling, horse-drawn trap rides, winter hiking on 30 trails, snowshoe-ing, airboarding at Saanenmöser and snow golf at Wispile. See www.gstaad.ch for the low-down.

Summer Activities

Hiking is the main summer pursuit and the opportunities are boundless, with 300km of marked trails threading through the region. A scenic three-hour hike takes you from Wispile to Launensee, a crystalline Alpine lake, with views of the craggy Wildhorn massif en route. Stop by the tourist office for details on *via ferrate* and mountaineering in the surrounding limestone peaks. Wispile is the best bet for families, with a dairy trail, a petting zoo and a downhill scooter trail (adult/child Sfr15/8) from its middle station.

BERNESE OBERLAND GSTAAD

WORTH A TRIP

GLACIER 3000

One of Switzerland's biggest year-round outdoor playgrounds is **Glacier 3000** (www .glacier3000.ch), situated high above the pass road between Gstaad and Les Diablerets and affording sensational views of 24 4000m peaks. The glacier has the longest skiing season in the Bernese Alps, running from late October through early May. A day ski pass, covering 30km of runs between 1350m and 3000m, costs Sfr61 for adults and Sfr40 for children. Boarders can practise on the rails and boxes at the snow park. If you fancy more of a thrill, visit http://bumpjump.ch (in German) for details on snow kiting.

In summer, hikers can negotiate the dazzling glacier trail from Scex Rouge to Sanetsch Pass, the high-altitude hike to the arrow-shaped Oldenhorn peak at 3123m, and the Gemskopf *via ferrata*. There's plenty up here to entertain the little ones, too, from a loop-the-loop **Alpine Coaster** (Sfr9) to short and scenic **husky rides** (Sfr15); call ✆078 856 83 62 or ✆033 783 01 28 to book ahead for the latter.

To reach the glacier from Gstaad, take one of the frequent buses from the station to Col du Pillon (Sfr10.40, 32 minutes). A cable car rises from Col du Pillon to Glacier 3000 (return adult/child Sfr77/39) from early November to late September.

Cyclists and mountain bikers are in their element with 500km of marked trails in the region. The tourist office website has details on bike rental, hotels and routes. For special packages, see www.velovetobike.ch (in German) and for GPS downloads www.gps-tracks.com. Bikes can be transported for free on seven lifts including Wispile and Eggli. Advance bookings are required for the following activities.

H2O Experience
WATER SPORTS

(☏079 438 74 51; www.h2oexperience.ch) Arranges rafting (Sfr98), canyoning (Sfr90 to Sfr180) and hydrospeeding (Sfr110) on the Saane and Simme Rivers.

Swiss Adventures
ADVENTURE SPORTS

(☏033 748 41 64; www.swissadventures.ch; Alpinzentrum) Organises guided climbs (Sfr99) and *via ferrate* (Sfr125), rafting (Sfr99), canyoning (Sfr125) and, in winter, igloo building (Sfr98) and snowshoe trekking (Sfr98).

Paragliding School Gstaad
PARAGLIDING

(☏079 22 44 270; www.paragstaad.com) Reputable outfit offering tandem flights (from Sfr190) at Wispile, Videmanette and Glacier 3000.

Llama & Co
HIKING

(☏078 718 90 43; www.lama-und-co.ch; Schindelweg 2, Zweisimmen) A sure-fire hit with the kids are these guided llama and goat hikes, from two-hour walks (Sfr35) to full-day treks (Sfr75).

☆ Festivals & Events

Suisse Open
SPORT

(www.allianzsuisseopengstaad.com) Gstaad hosts this famous tennis tournament in late July.

Menuhin Festival
MUSIC

(www.menuhinfestivalgstaad.ch) Top-drawer classic music festival with 50 concerts over seven weeks from July to September.

Freeride Days
SPORT

(www.freeridedays.ch, in German) Freeride events for powder freaks, with ski and snowboard testing and partying at Glacier 3000 in April.

🛏 Sleeping

The following rates are for winter high season; expect discounts of 30% to 50% in summer. The tourist office has a list of self-catering chalets. Many places close from mid-October to mid-December and from April to mid-June.

Hotel Alphorn
HOTEL $$

(☏033 748 45 45; www.gstaad-alphorn.ch; Gsteigstrasse; s/d Sfr137/252; P🅿🛜) A traditional Swiss chalet with a 21st-century twist, the Alphorn has smart rooms with plenty of warm pine, chunky beds and balconies with country views. Downstairs there's a cosy restaurant (mains Sfr27 to Sfr38), a sauna and a whirlpool big enough for two.

Hotel Christiania
GUESTHOUSE $$

(☏033 744 51 21; www.christiania.ch; Untergstaad 26; s/d Sfr205/355; 🛜) This super-centrally located, family-run chalet stands out for its bright, well-kept rooms and five-star welcome. The Egyptian owner cooks delicious Middle Eastern fare from mezze to couscous in the restaurant (mains Sfr16 to Sfr28).

Gstaad Palace
LUXURY HOTEL $$$

(☏033 748 50 00; www.palace.ch; Palacestrasse 28; s Sfr470-620, d Sfr720-1020; P❄@🛜) Opulent, exclusive and – in case you happen to be wondering – accessible by helicopter, this hilltop fairy-tale palace has attracted celebrity royalty like Michael Jackson, Robbie Williams and Liza Minnelli. Lavish quarters, a luxurious spa, several gourmet restaurants and an Olympic pool justify the price tag. Retro disco Green Go is also up here.

Iglu-Dorf
IGLOO $$

(☏041 612 27 28; www.iglu-dorf.com; per person Sfr149-189; late Dec-Easter) Fondue and mulled wine pave the way to subzero slumber land at this 'igloo village', affording magical views to 3000m peaks. Night-time snowshoeing is part of the fun. Up the price for a little Eskimo-style romance in an igloo complete with its own whirlpool.

SYHA Hostel
HOSTEL $

(☏033 744 13 43; www.youthhostel.ch/saanen; dm Sfr38.80-48.80; 🛜) Situated in Saanen, just four minutes away by train, this is a peaceful chalet hostel with bright, clean dorms, a games room and kiosk.

🍴 Eating & Drinking

If Gstaad's ritzy restaurants aren't for you, head for the mountain chalet restaurants at the summit stations of the cable cars.

🅃🄾🄿 Michel's Stallbeizli
SWISS $

(☏033 744 43 37; www.stallbeizli.ch; Gsteigstrasse 38; mains Sfr20-29; ⏰9.30am-6pm mid-Dec–Mar; 🍴) Dining doesn't get more back-to-nature than at this converted barn. In winter, you can feast away on fondue, drink Alpine herbal tea, or munch home-cured meat and cheese, with truly moo-ving views (pardon the pun) to the cud-chewing cows and goats in the adjacent stable. Kids love it.

Wasserngrat
SWISS $$

(☎033 744 96 22; mains Sfr20-50; ⊙9.30am-4.30pm Thu-Sun Aug & mid-Dec–Mar) Marvel at views of Les Diablerets glacier and Gstaad from the slope-side perch of Wasserngrat, where a fire crackles in the rustic-chic restaurant and skiers warm up over fondue on the sunny terrace. Top ingredients like truffles and foie gras flavour classic Alpine dishes.

Apple Pie
CAFE $

(Promenade; light meals Sfr10-22; ⊙9am-10pm) Just as nice as its name suggests, Apple Pie has given Gstaad an injection of cool with bubbly young staff and a Boho vibe. The saliva-inducing French menu skips from crêpes to thick onion soup and crisp apple tart.

Chesery
FRENCH $$$

(☎033 744 24 51; Alte Lauenenstrasse 9; tasting menus Sfr165-178; ⊙Tue-Sun, closed May & Nov) Founded by the Aga Khan in the 1960s, this dairy-turned-Michelin-starred-restaurant is the pinnacle of fine dining in Gstaad. Signature dishes such as wild sea bass with aubergine caviar are served with full-bodied wines and French finesse.

Blun Chi
ASIAN $$

(☎033 748 88 44; Hotel Bernerhof; mains Sfr31-45; ⊙closed Apr; 🖫) This convivial spot rustles up authentic Asian food from spicy Ma-

EASYACCESS CARD   145

From May to October, the three-day easyaccess card (adult/child Sfr36/21) gives you free access to most public transport and mountain railways, entry to the swimming pool, climbing hall, bowling alley and the high-rope park in Zweisimmen, plus discounts on other sights and activities. It's available at the tourist office and most hotels, and can be extended daily at a cost of Sfr12/7 per adult/child.

laysian beef to Sichuan-style chicken, dim sum to tom yum. There's a bamboo-flanked terrace for sunny days.

ℹ Information

The **tourist office** (☎033 748 81 81; www.gstaad.ch; Promenade 41; ⊙8.30am-6.30pm Mon-Fri, 9am-noon & 1.30-5pm Sat & Sun Jul-Aug & Dec-Mar, 8.30am-noon & 1.30-6.30pm Mon-Fri, 10am-noon & 1.30-5pm Sat rest of year) has stacks of info on the area.

ℹ Getting There & Away

Gstaad is on the Golden Pass route between Montreux (Sfr24, 1½ hours) and Spiez (Sfr25, 1½ hours; change at Zweisimmen). There is an hourly service to Geneva airport (Sfr52, three hours) via Montreux. A postal bus goes to Les Diablerets (Sfr13.20, 50 minutes) about five times daily. N11 is the principal road connecting Aigle and Spiez, and it passes close to Gstaad at Saanen.

BERNESE OBERLAND GSTAAD

Valais

POP 312,700 / AREA 5224.5 SQ KM / LANGUAGES FRENCH, GERMAN

Includes »

Best Places to Eat

» Chez Vrony (p178)
» Walliserkanne (p165)
» Le Cube (p156)
» Château de Villa (p161)
» Le Namasté (p155)

Best Places to Stay

» Hôtel Beau Site (p151)
» La Grande Maison (p157)
» Vernissage Berghaus Plattjen (p181)
» Hotel Bahnhof (p168)
» Hotel Arkanum (p161)

Why Go?

Valais is a salacious natural beauty. Her tale is of rags to riches, of changing seasons and celebrities, of an outdoors so great it never goes out of fashion. Wedged in a remote corner of southern Switzerland, this is where farmers were so poor they didn't have two francs to rub together a century ago, where today luminaries sip Sfr10,000 champagne cocktails at Coco Club in Verbier.

Landscapes here leave you dumbstruck: from the unfathomable Matterhorn (4478m) that defies trigonometry, photography and many a karabiner to the Rhône valley's tapestry of vineyards and shimmering 23km Aletsch Glacier. With such backdrops how can any hike, bike or ski tour be anything but great?

As earthy as a vintner's boots in September and as clean as the aesthetic in Zermatt's lounge bars, this canton can be fickle. The west speaks French, the east German, united in matters of cantonal pride by fine wine and glorious cheese.

When to Go

There are two obvious seasons: December to early April when the region bustles with excited ski and snowboard enthusiasts out to enjoy the area's world-class winter sports. Then there are the China-blue sky days of July and August when hikers, bikers and adventure-sport lovers hit the Alps for a summer dose of adrenalin. Late September and October is the secret season to go: leaves turn gold on vines, grapes and chestnuts are harvested, and the autumnal feast of La Brisolée (p346) is laid out on the Valaisian table for all to celebrate.

History

As in neighbouring Vaud, Julius Caesar was an early 'tourist' in these parts. The Roman leader brought an army to conquer the Celtic community living in the valley, penetrating as far as Sierre. Once under Roman domination, the four Celtic tribes of Valais were peaceably integrated into the Roman system. Archaeological remains attest to the passage of the rambling general and his boys from Rome.

Sion became a key centre in the valley when the Bishop of Valais settled there from AD 580. By 1000, the bishop's power stretched from Martigny to the Furka Pass. That authority did not go uncontested. A succession of Dukes of Savoy encroached on the bishop's territory and a Savoyard army besieged Sion in 1475. With the help of the Swiss Confederation, the city was freed at the battle of Planta. Internal opposition was equally weighty and Valais' independently minded communes stripped the bishops of their secular power in the 1630s, shifting control to the Diet, a regional parliament.

The Valais was not invaded again until Napoleon Bonaparte stopped by in 1798, determined to dominate the routes into Italy. Valais joined the Swiss Confederation in 1815.

ⓘ Getting Around

Travelling around the Valais is a grandiose experience thanks to the astonishing road links – high mountain passes, snowbound in winter, and masterfully engineered tunnels – it shares with neighbouring Italy (via the Great St Bernard Pass and Tunnel to Martigny, and the Simplon Pass and Tunnel to Brig) and France (from Chamonix over the Col de la Forclaz, also to Martigny). The N19 enters the far eastern end of the canton via the vertiginous Furka Pass (closed in winter, when cars chug through the mountain on a train instead) and passes through Brig, a key stop on the Glacier Express rail route and train line between Italy (Milan via Domosossola) and Geneva.

LOWER VALAIS

Stone-walled vineyards, tumbledown castle ruins and brooding mountains create an arresting backdrop to the meandering Rhône valley in western Valais. Running west to east, the A9 motorway links towns such as Roman-rooted Martigny and vine-strewn Sion and Sierre, where the French influence shows not only in the lingo but also in the locals' passion for art, wine and pavement cafes.

Glitzy resorts like Verbier and Crans-Montana have carved out reputations for sunny cruising, big panoramas and celebrity style, but there's more. Narrow lanes wriggle up to forgotten valleys such as Val d'Anniviers and Val d'Arolla, packed with rural charm and crowd-free skiing in the shadow of ice-capped mountains.

Martigny

POP 15,900 / ELEV 476M

Once the stomping ground of Romans in search of wine and sunshine en route to Italy, small-town Martigny is Valais' oldest town. Look beyond its concrete high-rises to enjoy a world-class art gallery, Roman amphitheatre and a posse of droopy St Bernard dogs to romp up the surrounding mountains with.

◉ Sights & Activities

The tourist office has details of vineyard walks and cycling trails.

TOP CHOICE Fondation Pierre Gianadda   GALLERY
(www.gianadda.ch; Rue du Forum; adult/10-25yr Sfr20/12; ⊙9am-7pm) Set in a spacey concrete edifice, this renowned gallery harbours a star-studded art collection. A copy of Rodin's *The Kiss* sculpture by the entrance promises great things and the gallery delivers with works by Picasso, Cézanne and van Gogh, occasionally shifted to make space for blockbuster exhibitions. A highlight is the garden where Henry Moore's organic sculptures and Niki de Saint Phalle's buxom *Bathers* peek above the foliage.

Admission also covers the permanent exhibition of Roman milestones, vessels and so on in the upstairs **Musée Archéologique Gallo-Romain** and the classic cars from vintage Fords to Swiss Martinis (the kind you drive, not drink) parked in the downstairs **Musée de l'Auto.**

Musée et Chiens du Saint-Bernard   MUSEUM
(☑027 720 49 20; www.museesaintbernard.ch; Route du Levant 34; museum adult/child Sfr12/7, dog walking & museum adult/child Sfr45/9, audio-guide Sfr3; ⊙10am-6pm) A tribute to the lovably dopey St Bernard, this museum across from the Roman amphitheatre includes real-life fluff bundles in the kennels.

Valais Highlights

① Visit Martigny for fine art at **Fondation Pierre Gianadda** (p147) and **cheese fondue** (p151) with a difference

② Walk a St Bernard dog on the soul-stirring **Col du Grand St Bernard** (p153) – hop to Italy afterwards

③ Lounge alfresco on a chaise lounge in a bubbly whirlpool as snow falls on surrounding peaks at high-altitude thermal spa **Leukerbad** (p163)

④ Board the Glacier Express in **Zermatt** (p165) for one of the world's most spectacular train rides

BERN

Eiger
(3970m) ▲

Mönch
(4107m) ▲

Jungfrau
(4158m) ▲

Aletschhorn
(4195m) ▲

Fafleralp
Blatten
Lötschental

Goppenstein

Rhône Vallée

Riederalp

Mörel

Bettmeralp

Aletsch
Glacier 8

Fiescheralp

Eggishorn
(2927m) ▲

Fiesch

Rhône

Brig

Visp

Simplon
Pass

Simplon
Tunnel

N9

Mattertal

Saastal

Saas Fee

Täsch

4 Zermatt

Gornergrat
(3089m) ▲

Furka
Pass

Grimsel
Pass

Gletsch

URI

St Gotthard
Pass

To Andermatt
(2km)

Airolo

Ulrichen

Münster

Brigerbad

Nufenen
Pass

N19

To St Moritz
(172km)

TICINO

Bignasco

Bosco
Gurin

Cevio

Cimalmotto

ITALY

To Locarno
(13km)

Camedo

Domodossola

To Milan
(71km)

5 Stride, climb or schuss
around the pyramid-perfect
Matterhorn (p167)

6 Feast on a traditional
autumnal banquet and Pinot
noir in gourmet **Sion** (p157)

7 Walk **vineyard trails**
(p156) along 13th-century
irrigation channels in Sion
or between tasting cellars in
Sierre and **Salgesch** (p161)

8 Melt over views of 4000m
peaks soaring above the
never-ending **Aletsch Glacier**
(p183)

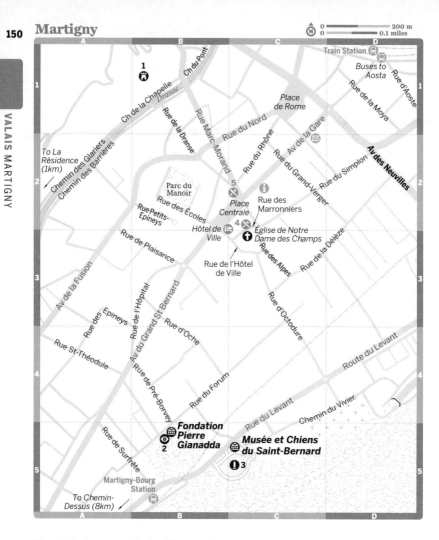

If you're lucky, you might be able to stroke them, and from early August to late September you can join the dogs in Martigny for a 1½-hour weekend walk around town or in nearby woods (reserve in advance). Upstairs an exhibition traces the role of St Bernards in hospice life, on canvas, in advertising and on film.

FREE Château de la Bâtiaz   CASTLE
(◷2-6pm Fri-Sun May-Oct) Clinging to a crag above town, Bâtiaz Castle is worth the 15-minute uphill pant for its far-reaching views over the surrounding vineyards and Rhône valley. Less appealing is the gruesome collection of medieval torture instruments inside. Listed opening hours tend to be irregular; to save yourself a wasted journey check the blue flag is flying before hiking up.

★☆ Festivals & Events

Foire du Valais   TRADITIONAL
Pigs don't fly in Martigny but cows fight: this 10-day regional fair in October climaxes with a bovine bash-about of epic proportions (see p161).

Martigny

Top Sights

	Fondation Pierre Gianadda	B5
	Musée et Chiens du Saint-Bernard	C5

Sights

1	Château de la Bâtiaz	B1
2	Musée Archéologique Gallo-Romain	B5
	Musée de l'Auto	(see 2)
3	Roman Amphitheatre	C5

Eating

4	Café du Midi	C2
5	La Vache Qui Vole	C2

Foire du Lard FOOD

If the idea of watching crunch-tackle cows doesn't appeal, there's sizzling action at Martigny's Bacon Fair in December. Local residents have been picking on the prize porkers since the Middle Ages.

Sleeping

TOP CHOICE **Hôtel Beau Site** HOTEL $

(027 722 81 64; www.chemin.ch; Chemin-Dessus; s/d/q Sfr80/110/200; Jun-Aug, rest of year advance reservation only;) Perched high above town on wooded slopes at 1211m, this eco-friendly art nouveau house dating to 1912 begs guests to sit back, relax and lap up the silent green surrounds crossed with gentle walking trails. Its 13 rooms are simple with shared bathroom and quirky art on the walls, and vegetarian evening meals (Sfr30) are sourced from the hotel veggie patch. There is a sunlit music room with a piano to tinkle on while walkers pour over maps and trail brochures in the library. From Martigny, follow signs for 'Col des Planches and Chemin-sur-Martigny', driving uphill for 7km through Le Bourg and Chemin-Dessous to the hamlet of Chemin-Dessus. Local bus 5 heads up here hourly (25 minutes).

L'Érable Rouge B&B $

(027 746 16 08; erablerouge@mycable.ch; Rue St-Ours 49, Fully; dm/s/d Sfr40/50/100) Dreamily set amid terraced vines, this old winemaker's house with all the right rustic fixtures and fittings is an oasis of peace and tranquillity. Find it 9.5km north of Martigny, in the viticultural hamlet of Branson, near Fully.

La Résidence GUESTHOUSE $

(027 723 16 00; www.residence-martigny.ch; Les Creusats, Martigny-Croix; s/d Sfr70/140;) Sitting pretty in its vineyard setting, this rosy guesthouse has big sunny rooms with garden-facing terraces. The rooms are all named after local Valais vines and wines, and breakfasts of homemade jam, local cheese and ham are a delight.

Eating & Drinking

Everything happens on plane tree-flanked Place Centrale, framed with pavement cafes, bistros and bars.

TOP CHOICE **Café du Midi** CAFE $

(027 722 00 03; www.cafedumidi.ch; Rue des Marronniers 4; fondue Sfr21-29; noon-11pm Wed-Mon) This shabby-chic cafe run by Brigida and Steve across from the church is a great address. Guzzle Trappist brews and gorge on as much raclette as you can handle or dip into one of 10 different fondues, including with tomato, mushrooms or *à la bière* (beer fondue). Even more unusual is its fondue made from melted *chèvre* (goat's cheese). Love or hate it.

La Vache Qui Vole GALLERY, BISTRO $$

(027 722 38 33; Place Centrale 2b; mains Sfr25-45; 10.30am-1am Mon-Sat) Martigny's 'Flying Cow' is a theatrical gallery-style bistro and bar with Boho ambience and cult cow kitsch: from the angelic bovine beauty suspended from the ceiling to snazzy cowbell lights. Check out the quirky Virgin Mary collection upstairs. Salads, pasta, risotto, Sri Lankan curries, local wines by small Valais producers – it's all uniformly delicious.

Information

Tourist office (027 720 49 49; www.martignytourism.ch; Ave de la Gare; 9am-6pm Mon-Fri, to 7pm Sat, 10am-12.30pm & 3-5pm Sun)

Getting There & Away

Martigny is on the main train line running from Lausanne (Sfr23, 50 minutes) to Brig (Sfr25, 55 minutes).

From Martigny the panoramic **Mont Blanc Express** (027 783 11 43; www.tmrsa.ch) goes to Chamonix (1½ hours) in France, and the **St Bernard Express** (027 783 11 43) to Le Châble (26 minutes; ski lift or bus connection for Verbier) and Orsières (26 minutes) via Sembrancher.

Around Martigny

Winter skiing, summer hiking, walking St Bernard dogs over mountain passes and relaxing in thermal waters: exploring Martigny's alpine surrounds is not dull.

CHAMPÉRY

Stuck between the pointy jaws of Dents du Midi and Dents Blanches, this small but beautiful ski resort (1055m) exudes authenticity with its cosy log chalets and friendly locals. At the heart of the ski area is **Les Portes du Soleil** (www.portesdusoleil .com), straddling the Franco–Swiss border, where intermediate, backcountry skiers and snowboarders have 650km of downhill runs to play on. Morzine and Avoriaz in France are just a lift ride away and for speed demons, skiing in Champéry means one thing: the Swiss Wall at Chavanette, a heart-stopping, hell-for-leather mogul run, famed as one of the world's toughest. Pay Sfr57 for a one-day pass or Sfr270 for a six-day ski pass (www .telechampery.ch) covering the entire Portes du Soleil area.

In summer proficient hikers tackle the 40km, multi-day trail around the **Dents du Midi**. Easier but equally as scenic is the amble along **Galerie Défago**, hewn out of the implausibly sheer rock face. The **tourist office** (☎024 479 20 20; www.champery.ch) has more details on walking, biking and climbing in the area.

To sleep and eat well in Champéry swaddle yourself in a sheepskin by the open fire at family-run chalet **Hôtel des Alpes** (☎024 479 12 22; www.hotel-desalpes.ch; Rue du Village 9; s/d 117/234; ☏), or swoon over mountain vistas at art-boutique hotel **Beau-Séjour** (☎024 479 58 58; www.bo-sejour.com; Rue du Village 114; s/d Sfr155/230; ☏).

From Martigny change trains in Aigle to get to Champéry (Sfr25.60, 70 minutes).

VAL FERRET & VAL D'ENTREMONT

Emblazoned with its canine mascot, the St Bernard Express train from Martigny to Orsières branches south at **Sembrancher**, chugging south along the Val d'Entremont through classic Alpine scenery to the Italian border.

Orsières, just off the main Italy-bound N21, marks the beginning of pine-brushed **Val Ferret**. Nip into the **tourist office** (☎027 783 32 48; orisieres@v-sb.ch; Place de la Gare; ◷8.30am-noon & 1.30-5.30pm Mon-Sat) inside the tiny train station to pick up info on the valley and pause for a long lunch at **Les Alpes** (☎027 783 11 01; Place Centrale; menus Sfr115 & Sfr138; ◷lunch & dinner Thu-Mon), a gastronomic brasserie on the central village square, where Samuel and Laëtitia Destaing cook up a stylish mix of modern creativity and tradition.

From Orsières it's a 1¾-hour walk or a short drive to Champex (1471m), a mountain village with a beautiful glassy lake – perfect for a summer dip or fishing spree from the back of a rowing boat. Learn about 4000 different varieties of flowers at the lovely **Jardin Alpin Flore-Alpe** (adult/family Sfr5/ 10; www.flore-alpe.ch; ◷10am-6pm May-Oct, to 8pm Fri Jul & Aug), an alpine garden arranged around a painted 1930s wooden chalet (with dorm beds for Sfr25 – bring your own sleeping bag) that hosts wonderful classical concerts and sculpture exhibitions in summer. From the top of the **Téléchampex chair lift** (www.telechampex.ch; adult single/ return Sfr12/8) at La Breya (2194m), view are truly fabulous, reaching as far as Grand Combin (4314m).

An alternative way to explore the Val d'Entremont or neighbouring Val de Bagnes is by horse and cart over a cheesy fondue. To organise your meal on wheels head for **La Ferme des Moulins** (☎079 402 93 44; Route de Contô, Sembrancher; per person without/with wine Sfr50/66), a working farm with horses and cows, immediately south of Sembrancher along a narrow lane (first left after the Verbier turn-off on the N21) towards Chamoille.

Back on the N21, wildlife spotters with their own wheels could follow the road further south towards **Dranse**, then turn off

ⓘ PASS VALAIS CENTRAL

Travelling between Martigny and Gestelnburg, near Visp, by bus or train? Invest in a Pass Valais Central travel pass (adult/child Sfr48/38) covering three days of unlimited travel within a one-week span. Holders are also privy to various discounts including 20% off the admission price at Martigny's Fondation Pierre Gianadda, Leukerbad's thermal baths, St Léonard's underground lake and so on. The pass is available at tourist offices in Martigny, Sion and Sierre.

Big softie or not, everyone loves a St Bernard, so **Fondation Barry** (☎027 722 65 42; www.fondation-barry.ch) has come up with a clever plan. From July to September, you can accompany the doe-eyed woofers on a 1½-hour walk on the **Col du Grand St Bernard** – a one-off chance to lap up the incredible Alpine scenery and stroke the dogs. Walks (1½ hours) depart Tuesday to Sunday at 10am (brisk, not for little kids) and 2pm (gentle, kid-friendly) and cost Sfr45/9 per adult/child; the same ticket gets you into the breeding centre museum and kennels on the *col*.

In winter the dog-walking action moves to the foundation's kennels in **Martigny** (☎reservations 027 722 65 42; adult/child Sfr45/9; ☺1.30pm Wed, Fri & Sat Jan-Apr), where you can take the St Bernards for a 1½-hour walk along the vineyard-clad **Chemin du Vignoble**.

In **Champex** (☎reservations 027 783 12 27; adult/child Sfr45/9; ☺9.50am & 1.50pm Sun Jan, Sat & Sun Feb) children aged under 10 years can go for a trek in the snow on a sledge pulled by a St Bernard. How absolutely magical!

---

for **Vichères**. A couple of kilometres before reaching the hamlet a footpath leads into the **La Combe de l'A nature reserve**, beautiful on golden autumn days when you can see stags rut at dawn and dusk.

COL DU GRAND ST BERNARD

The N21 climaxes up high on the Great St Bernard Pass (2473m) with Switzerland's border into Italy and a stunning petrol-blue lake. Snowed in and shut to vehicles for up to six months of the year, the only way up or down in winter is on foot (wearing either snowshoes or skis) from the entrance to the road tunnel, **Tunnel du Grand St Bernard**, 6km downhill from the top of the mountain pass. On 20 May 1800 Napoleon famously crossed the pass on foot accompanied by an army of 46,000 men.

So perilous and terrifying was this transalpine crossing that monks established a hospice on the pass in the 11th century to provide spiritual succour and rescue travellers lost in the snow (often after being attacked and robbed by brigands). And so the legend of the great St Bernard dog was born, as they frequently uncovered and rescued lost souls buried in the snow (until the 1950s when helicopters – too small to carry such an enormous 70 to 100kg dog – were used instead). No nose was finer tuned than that of doggie legend Barry (1800–1814), who saved 40 lives, as the interesting exhibition at the **Hospice Breeding Centre** (adult/child Sfr10/6; ☺9am-7pm Jun-early Oct) – a museum and kennels with some 30 dogs to see – explains.

To stay there overnight, providing you have arrived on foot or by bicycle, you can check into the original **Hospice du Grand St Bernard** (☎027 787 12 36; www.gsbernard. net; dm with half-board Sfr48; ☺Jun–mid-Oct with advance reservations) with a beautiful 11th-century chapel and treasury (admission free). Otherwise, **Hôtel de l'Hospice** (☎027 565 11 53; www.hotelhospice.ch; dm Sfr26.80, s/d/ tr/q Sfr69.80/99.60/134.40/159.20; ☺Jun-15 Oct) opposite opens its friendly doors to anyone irrespective of energy level, as does lakeside **Albergo Italia** (☎+39 0165 780 908; www.gransanbernardo.it; d €70-90, breakfast €8; ☺Jun–mid-Oct), spitting distance away in Italy, grandly set across the road from the mountain-pass lake since 1933.

To get to the pass from Martigny in summer, take the St Bernard Express train to Orsières (see p151) then a connecting bus (45 minutes) operated by **TMR** (☎027 721 68 40; www.tmrsa.ch).

Verbier

POP 3000 / ELEV 1500M

Ritzy Verbier is the diamond of the Valaisian Alps: small, stratospherically expensive and cut at all the right angles to make it sparkle in the eyes of accomplished skiers and piste-bashing stars. Yet despite its ritzy packaging, Verbier is that rare beast of a resort – all things to all people. It swings from schnapps-fuelled debauchery to VIP lounges, bunker hostels to design-oriented hotels, burgers to Michelin stars. Here ski bums and celebs slalom in harmony on powder that is legendary.

Unlike smaller resorts, Verbier shuts down between seasons.

⚡ Activities

Something of a recreation mecca, there is an activity to suit every outdoor urge. For an overview and on-the-ground guidance hook up with a local mountain guide at **Les Guides de Verbier** (📞027 775 33 70; www.guideverbier.com; Place de Médran). For a one-stop shop online go to www.verbier booking.com.

Skiing

Verbier's skiing is justifiably billed as some of Europe's finest. The resort sits at the heart of the Quatre Vallées (Four Valleys), comprising a cool 412km of runs and 94 ski lifts. A regional ski pass costs Sfr65 per day. Cheaper passes excluding Mont Fort are also available. The terrain is exciting and varied, with beginners on gentle slopes at **Le Rouge** and intermediates carving long slopes at **La Chaux**. Boarders make for the latter to catch big air on kickers and rails. Experts can tackle short blacks like Savoleyres Nord and the heart-stoppingly steep, mogul-speckled Mont-Fort run. The broad, well-groomed runs from Les Attelas to Verbier are ideal for cruising. Real challenges lie off-piste in the virgin powder for accomplished skiers. It's wise to hire a guide.

Hiking

The walking here is naturally superb. From Les Ruinettes, it takes 1½ hours to ascend to the ridge at Creblet, and down into the crater to Lac des Vaux. Other worthwhile walks include the seven-hour trek to Corbassière glacier, which snakes down from 4314m Grand Combin, and the five-hour **Sentier des Chamois**, a trail popular with wildlife lovers keen to spot chamois, marmots and eagles.

Adventure Sports

Kona Bike Park   MOUNTAIN BIKING
(📞027 775 25 11; www.verbierbikepark.ch; adult/child day pass Sfr30/15; ⊙8am-5 or 5.30pm Jul-Sep, 9am-4.30pm Sat & Sun Jun & Oct) Downhill freaks can flaunt their expertise on routes from Les Ruinettes and Médran or hone their skills in this edgy bike park between trees. It also runs mountain-bike courses.

Centre de Parapente   PARAGLIDING
(📞027 771 68 18; www.flyverbier.ch) If being on the top of a mountain isn't high enough, take to the air hang-gliding or paragliding; 30-minute tandem flights from Sfr190.

★ Festivals & Events

Verbier Festival & Academy   MUSIC
(www.verbierfestival.com) Summer's high-profile classical music festival; July.

🛏 Sleeping

Verbier is doable for ski bums on a budget with pre-planning. If money isn't an issue, there are posh digs galore. Rates nosedive by 30% to 50% in July and August.

TOP CHOICE **Cabane du Mont-Fort**   HUT $
(📞027 778 13 84; www.cabanemontfort.ch; dm winter/summer Sfr52/32, half board Sfr92/72; ⊙Dec–mid-May & Jul–mid-Sep) Above the clouds with mesmerising vistas to the Massif des Combins, this 2457m-high Alpine hut is brilliant for walkers in summer and skiers in winter, with direct access to La Chaux. Expect cosy slumber in pine- panelled

---

SAVVY SKIING: BEST QUEUE-FREE RESORTS

Valais enjoys the luxury of having it all when it comes to ski resorts: from star-studded high-flyers firmly on the paparazzi map like Zermatt (p165) and Verbier (p153) to tiny villages down lost valleys where you can dress as you want and don't have to queue. Oh, and ski passes don't cost the earth.

The perfect mix of big skiing and storybook charm, Bettmeralp (p185) is a pearl of Swiss mountain charm where cars are banned, kids are towed about on wooden Davos sledges and high-altitude slopes cruise breathlessly above the Aletsch Glacier. Car-free Saas Fee (p180) is posher, pricier, bigger and better known but has that same 'go slow, real village' vibe.

In the Lower Valais, the polished teeth of Dents du Midi and Dents Blanches rise majestically above Champéry (p152), which is already on the local radar but less well known internationally, despite being in the Portes du Soleil ski area (together with Avoriaz and Morzine in France). Not far away, the quiet thermal spa of Ovronnaz (p164) is perfect for families with young kids, as are St Luc and Chandolin in the fairy-tale-lost Val d'Anniviers (p162).

dorms, panoramas that will motivate you to rise at dawn and a skier-busy restaurant serving tasty mountain grub.

Le Stop
HOSTEL $

(☎079 549 72 23; www.le-stop.ch; Le Châble; dm Sfr34, breakfast/dinner Sfr11/15) This former bunker has a new raison d'être with no-frills dorms. What you'll get is four walls, a queue for the loo and a rickety bunk, but with Verbier just a cable-car ride away, frankly it's a gift. Important: bring your own sleeping bag.

Les Touristes
HOTEL $

(☎027 771 21 47; www.hoteltouristes-verbier.ch; s/d Sfr75/150, d with shower Sfr180; P) If you think *le chic c'est freak,* try this rustic chalet next to a *fromagerie* (cheese dairy) – the *only* Verbier hotel with less than three stars and to be open year-round. Rooms are modest but comfy with pine trappings, floral bedding and washbasins. Find it a 15-minute walk downhill from Verbier Station, at the bottom end of Verbier village.

Nevaï
HOTEL $$$

(☎027 775 40 00; www.nevai.ch; s/d from Sfr300/500; P@🛜) There's not a whiff of Alpine kitsch in Nevaï's minimalist-chic rooms – think earthy hues, beds dressed in Egyptian cotton, boudoir-style bar with 4m-long fireplace, penthouses with log fires and outdoor whirlpools.

✖ Eating & Drinking

The best addresses to dine (bar one) are piste-side, while Verbier's full-throttle après-ski scene kicks off on the slopes before sliding down to Place Centrale. Out of season (mid-December to April, July and August), pretty much everything is shut.

TOP CHOICE
Le Namasté
SWISS $$

(☎027 771 57 73; www.namaste-verbier.ch; Les Planards; mains Sfr20-35; ☺daily in season, Thu-Sun mid-May–Jun, Sep & Oct) With a name that means 'Welcome' in Tibetan it is no wonder that this cosy mountain cabin is always packed. Jean-Louis – a metal sculptor who creates fantastical beasts from old tools (see them dotted around the chalet) – and his wife Annick are the creative energy behind the place and cuisine is 100% traditional – think fondue, raclette and a wonderful *croûte Namasté.* Ski to it from Savoleyres or be really cool come nightfall and skidoo up, sledge down.

TOP CHOICE
Le Fer à Cheval
PIZZERIA $

(☎027 771 26 69; Rue de Médran; mains Sfr20-30; ☺11.30am-11.30pm) Thank goodness for the Horseshoe, a wholly affordable, down-to-earth and tasty pizzeria with buzzing sunny terrace, electric atmosphere and fabulous pizza any hour. Ask anyone in the know where to eat and this is where they'll send you. Find it footsteps from Place Centrale towards the Médran cable car.

Chez Dany
SWISS $$$

(☎027 771 25 24; Clambin; mains Sfr25-60; ☺lunch daily, dinner with advance reservation) On a sunny plateau between Les Ruinettes and Médran, this buzzy chalet is Prince William's favourite place to tuck into a juicy steak. The terrace affords sweeping views to the Massif des Combins. Revive snow-sore eyes over hot chocolate or cheesy *croûte au fromage.* Again, skidoo or ski up, sledge down.

La Marmotte
SWISS $

(☎027 771 68 34; www.lamarmotte-verbier.com; Les Planards; fondues Sfr30, croûtes Sfr20-25) The other hot piste address for cheesy fondue or *croûte* lunch; next to Le Namasté.

Milk Bar
CAFE $

(Rue de Médran) This mellow hut is famous for its *grands crus de cacao* (hot chocolate), homemade tarts, pancakes and toasty atmosphere.

Pub Mont Fort
PUB

(Chemin de la Tinte 10; ☺3pm-1.30am) In winter, this après-ski heavyweight sells the most beer in Switzerland. Enough said.

☆ Entertainment

Farm Club
NIGHTCLUB

(www.kingsverbier.ch; Route de Verbier Station 55; ☺Dec–mid-Apr) A legend in its own right, this swanky club beneath the Nevaï hotel has rocked since 1971. Look gorgeous to slip past the velvet rope and mingle with socialites out spending daddy's (or sugar daddy's) pension on Moët magnums.

Coco Club
NIGHTCLUB

(Place Centrale; ☺Dec–mid-Apr) Squared smartly at all those celebs and rich folk who love Verbier so much, this uber-cool VIP club is pure unadulterated decadence (ever seen white fur curtains?). Just off the main square beneath 1960s Hotel Bristol, it's famed for Europe's most expensive cocktail – the champagne-based 'Coco

Chalet' cocktail served in a carved ice glass for a cool Sfr10,000. Go on, spoil yourself!

ℹ Information

Tourist office (☑027 775 38 88; www.verbier .ch; Place Centrale; ⊙8.30am-12.30pm & 1.30-6pm Mon-Sat)

ℹ Getting There & Away

Trains from Martigny run hourly year-round to Le Châble (30 minutes) from where you can board a Verbier-bound bus (30 minutes) or, when it's running, the Le Châble–Verbier cable car.

Sion

POP 29,700 / ELEV 490M

French-speaking Sion is bewitching. Deceptively modern and industrial from afar, this town that rises abruptly out of the built-up floor of the Rhône valley is, in fact, enviably gourmet with memorable dining addresses and a surrounding ring of vine-terraced hills. The serpentine Rhône River bisects Sion and a twinset of 13th-century hilltop châteaux play guard atop a pair of craggy rock hills.

Sion moves to a relaxed beat, with winemaking (and tasting) playing an essential role in the town's mantra and pavement cafes lining the helter-skelter of quaint lanes that thread sharply downhill from its castles to medieval Old Town. Market day – a must – is Friday.

◉ Sights

FREE **Château de Tourbillon**   CASTLE
(Rue des Châteaux; ⊙10am-6pm May-Sep, 11am-5pm mid-Mar–Apr & Oct–mid-Nov) Lording it over the fertile Rhône valley from its hilltop perch above Sion, the crumbling remains of this medieval stronghold, destroyed by fire in 1788, are well worth the stiff trudge for the postcard views alone – wear solid shoes as the rocky path is decidedly hairy in places.

Château de Valère   CASTLE
(Rue des Châteaux; guided tour adult/child Sfr4/2; ⊙11am, noon, 2pm & 4pm Mon-Sat, 2pm & 4pm Sun Jun-Sep, 2pm & 4pm Sun Oct-May) Slung on a hillock across from Château de Tourbillon is this 11th- to 13th-century château that grew up around a fortified basilica. The church interior reveals beautifully carved choir stalls and a brightly frescoed apse. But the real highlight is the world's oldest playable organ that juts out from the wall opposite

the apse like the stern of some medieval caravel – the summertime concerts held on Saturday afternoons (from 4pm) are magical.

The château also houses the town's local **Musée d'Histoire** (History Museum; adult/child Sfr8/4; ⊙11am-6pm Jun-Sep, to 5pm Tue-Sun Oct-May).

Musée d'Art   ART MUSEUM
(Place de la Marjorie 19; adult/child Sfr5/2.50, free 1st Sun of month; ⊙11am-5pm Tue-Sun) Lodged in another château midway up the hill linking the Old Town with Sion's hilltop châteaux, this well-curated fine arts museum showcases works by Swiss artists including Ernest Bieler and Caspar Wolf, alongside star pieces by Austrian expressionist Oskar Kokoschka.

🏃 Activities

There is far more to hiking around Sion than seductive strolling between grape-heavy vines. What makes trails in this part of the Rhône Valley so unique are the *bisses* – miniature canals built from the 13th century to irrigate the steeply terraced vineyards and fields.

Best known is the Bisse de Clavau, a 550-year-old irrigation channel that carries water to the thirsty, sun-drenched vineyards between Sion and St Léonard. Vines, planted on narrow terraces supported by drystone retaining walls, are devoted to the production of highly quaffable Valaisian dôle (red) and Fendant (white) wines. Taste them alone or with lunch at Le Cube (☑079 566 95 63; www.verone.ch; mains without/with wine Sfr25/29, tasting menu incl wine Sfr69; ⊙5-9pm Fri, 11am-9pm Sat, 11am-6pm Sun May-Oct), an old winegrower's hut once used to store tools and now transformed into a fabulously stylish address in the vines to wine and dine. Every dish on the tempting menu is paired with an appropriate wine and the natural vista is heady, punchy and out of this world.

The Cube sits on the Bisse de Clavau footpath (7.5km, 2½ hours), part of the Chemin du Vignoble. As you amble look out for brightly coloured butterflies, lizards and dragonflies, fig trees and wildflowers such as yellow dyer's woad. During autumn's grape harvest, keep an eye out for the ingenious lifts vintners use to transport their crop up the vertiginous slopes.

From Sion there are plenty more waterside trails to follow, including along 19th-century Bisse de Montorge (two hours) and Bisse de Lentine (two hours). Ask at the tourist office for the brochure *Randonées le long des bisses*, which maps out and details 22 *bisse* walks in the Valais, or view it online at www.valrando.ch. Those who find themselves hopelessly hooked can visit the **Musée des Bisses** (www.musee-des-bisses.ch) when it opens in 2012, high above Sion in a 17th-century house in Botyre Ayent, 8km northeast.

Sion is also a terrific base for white-water rafting, hydrospeeding and canyoning (Sfr160) with **Swiftraft Activity** (☑027 475 35 10; www.swissraft-activity.ch; Rue du Scex 28).

treks, and sell homemade jam, juice, syrups and fruity liqueurs in their farm shop. Find the farm high above Sion, 5km from town, on the road to Evolène.

Hôtel Elite HOTEL **$$**
(☑027 322 03 27; www.hotelelite-sion.ch; Ave du Midi 6; s/d/tr/q Sfr111/150/220/240; ☑) Aptly named, this bright, modern two-star address just off the main street is the best place to stay in town. Rooms, painted soft apricot hues, are not quite as bold as the pillar-box-red reception.

★★ Festivals & Events

Festival de Sion MUSIC
(www.sion-festival.ch) This month-long international music festival stages some extraordinary classical concerts (piano, violin), a violin competition and accompanying fringe Festival Off with free concerts; mid-August to mid-September.

🛏 Sleeping

In-town options are few and disappointingly cookie-cutter, making it better to stay in Sion's vine-clad surrounds.

Ranch des Maragnènes FARMSTAY **$**
(☑027 203 13 13; www.ranch.ch; dm incl breakfast Sfr30; ☺May-Oct) Snooze in a straw-filled barn, breakfast on bacon and eggs, and canter off into the countryside at this family-run farm with 30 horses to ride. The friendly owners arrange horse-riding lessons and

✕ Eating & Drinking

Food and wine are big reasons to linger. Rue du Grand-Pont, so-called because of the river that runs beneath its entire length, is peppered with tasty places to eat well and drink fine Valais wine.

For a simple coffee or beer try a cafe terrace on the northern side of vast Place du Midi, or beneath several leafy steel pergolas on pedestrian Rue des Ramparts.

TOP
CHOICE **Au Cheval Blanc** SWISS **$$**
(☑027 322 18 67; www.au-cheval-blanc.ch; Rue du Grand-Pont 23; beef Sfr26-59, mains Sfr30-40; ☺10am-midnight Tue-Fri, 11am-midnight Sat) An institution among locals for its great food and convivial vibe, this old-style bistro with the biggest pavement terrace on Rue du Grand-Pont only uses the best local produce. The icing on the cake is its Val d'Hérens beef prepared just as you like it – as tartare,

---

DON'T MISS

LA BRISOLÉE: A TRADITIONAL AUTUMN FEAST

Come the gold-leaf days and smoky dusks of autumn, the last of the grape harvests ushers in the first of the season's sweet chestnuts. And so begins La Brisolée (p346), a fabulous autumnal supper of local produce traditionally shared among family and close friends. Ordering it out is not quite the same, but to savour what is as close as you'll get to the real McCoy try one of these two addresses, highly recommended year-round:

La Cave de Tous-Vents (☑027 322 46 84; www.cave-tous-vents.ch; Rue des Châteaux 16, Sion; mains Sfr25-45; ☺5pm-midnight) Flickering candles illuminate the brick vaults of this medieval wine bar and cellar where loved-up couples dine in cosy nooks. Just as gooey is the fondue, including varieties with saffron or chanterelles. Late September to October, its *brisolée royale* (Sfr32) is a magnificent, help-yourself-to-as-much-as-you-can-eat feast of six different Valais cheeses, hot roast chestnuts, apples, pears and dried meats. Indulge.

La Grande Maison (☑079 830 76 07; www.lagrandemaison.ch; Route du Santesch, Chandolin-près-Savièse; s/d Sfr130/160; mains Sfr18-35, menus Sfr58 & Sfr78; ☺5-11pm Mon-Fri, 11am-midnight Sat & Sun) Up in the hills 6.5km from Sion is this wonderful old house with atmospheric, wood-beamed rooms and a top-notch restaurant where you can feast on autumnal game and fruits of the local forest – a rare and real treat.

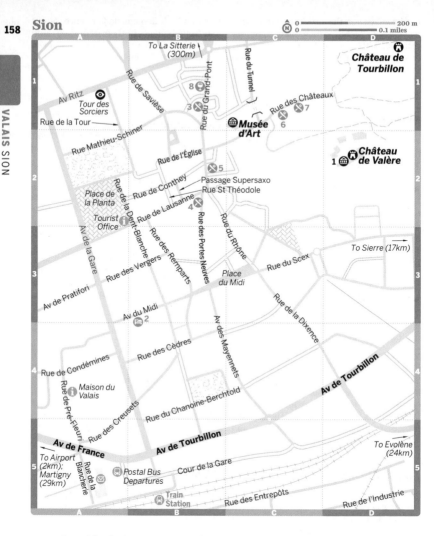

carpaccio, with vinaigrette, as a tagliata filet or 'en rossini'.

TOP CHOICE La Sitterie
SWISS **$$**

(☑027 203 22 12; www.lasitterie.ch; Rue du Rawil 41; menus Sfr65 & Sfr85; ☺lunch & dinner Tue-Sun) A 10-minute uphill walk from the Old Town is this salmon-pink townhouse with red-wine wooden shutters – Sion's most exciting gastronomic address. Young chef Jacques Bovier works with strictly seasonal and local products to create a dining experience that thrills every time (ever had Chasselas grape sorbet?). Lime green and slate-grey dominate the thoroughly contemporary interior and summer dining is in a dreamy flowery garden with terraced vineyard view. Advance reservations essential.

Bagdad Café
BISTRO **$$**

(☑027 322 55 00; Rue de Lausanne 3; tartare Sfr27-37, lunch menu Sfr18, mains Sfr23-28; ☺11am-midnight Mon-Sat, 10am-midnight Sun) If finely chopped raw beef turns you on, this stylish address has your name on it. The house speciality is tartare, perfectly prepared in various ways – exotic, classic, gastronome and even, somewhat incongruously,

Sion

VALAIS AROUND SION

vegetarian (finely chopped veg scented with herbs and cream). Seating is in a lovely minimalist interior with scrubbed wood tables or beneath trees street-side.

Brasserie du Grand-Pont　　INTERNATIONAL **$$**
(☏027 322 20 96; Rue du Grand-Pont 6; mains Sfr25, lunch menu Sfr42; ⊙lunch & dinner Mon-Sat) On sunny days every table, wood or brightly coloured, is pretty much snagged by noon at this buzzing bistro with art-slung walls and bubbly staff. The 'please-everyone' menu travels tastebuds around the Valais and the globe; it even includes breakfast. Note the fabulous Titanic of an old building with rust-coloured shutters and rusty wrought-iron balconies.

L'Enclos de Valère　　SWISS **$$**
(☏027 323 32 30; Rue des Châteaux 18; mains Sfr34-52, lunch/dinner menus Sfr49/85-102; ⊙lunch & dinner Tue-Sat) Midway up the steep cobbled lane to Sion's château twinset is this cottagey restaurant with a beautiful garden bristling with vines and fruit trees (spot the kiwis). The Assiette Valaisanne (Sfr27) – a slate platter of cold meats and cheese – is the perfect light lunch. Game (goat, chamois, venison) dominates autumn's *ardoise* (blackboard menu).

Le Verre à Pied　　WINE BAR
(Rue du Grand-Pont 29; ⊙10.30am-1pm & 4.30-8.30pm Mon-Sat, 10.30am-2pm & 5-8pm Sun) To get under the skin of Sion you have to taste its wine and this no-frills wine bar is the place to do it. Sit in the faintly industrial interior of this hybrid *oenothèque* (wine shop) *caveau* (wine cellar), or outside at an oak barrel, and sip one of five selected Valaisian wines by the glass (Sfr6) – the list is the pick of 150 wines and changes every week. Simple cheese and cold meat platters, oysters and so on prepared by neighbouring

restaurants (what an innovative idea!) quell hunger pangs.

ℹ️ **Information**

Tourist office (☏027 327 77 27; www.sion tourism.ch; Place de la Planta; ⊙9am-12.30pm & 1.30-6pm Mon-Fri, 9am-12.30pm Sat)
Maison du Valais (☏027 327 35 70; www.valais .ch; Rue de Pré-Fleuri 6; ⊙8am-noon & 1.30-5.30pm Mon-Fri)

ℹ️ **Getting There & Around**

Air

Sion airport (www.sionairport.ch; Rte de l'Aéroport), 2km west of the train station, has seasonal scheduled flights to/from London (www.snowjet.co.uk) and Corsica (www.air -glaciers.ch).

Bicycle

Sion Roule (www.sionroule.ch; Place du Scex; ⊙9am-7pm mid-May–mid-Sep) Pick up a free bike and explore Sion's riverbanks and vineyards.

Train

All trains on the express route between Lausanne (Sfr29, 50 to 80 minutes) and Brig (Sfr18.60, 25 to 35 minutes) stop in Sion.

Around Sion

VAL D'HÉRÉMENCE
Out of earshot of tourist footsteps, this valley remains mystifyingly unknown, despite harbouring one of the world's greatest hydraulic marvels, the 285m-high **Grande Dixence dam**. From Sion, follow the signs for this valley and the Val d'Hérens, which share the same road as far as Vex, where you branch right and follow a twisting road 30km to the dam.

From the dam base, it's a 45-minute hike or a speedy **cable car** (www.grande-dixence .ch; adult/child return Sfr10/5; ⊙9.30am-12.20pm

VALAIS SIERRE

WORTH A TRIP

SUBTERRANEAN SAILING

Tiny St Léonard, 5.5km northeast of Sion, hides Europe's biggest underground lake, **Lac Souterrain St Léonard** (www.lac-souterrain.com; adult/child Sfr10/6; ☉9am-5pm mid-Mar–Oct, to 5.30pm Jun-Aug), discovered in 1941. To see the emerald waters shimmer, join a 30-minute guided tour by boat.

Lunch afterwards at **Buffet de la Gare de St Léonard** (☎027 203 43 43; www.buffetdelagare-st-leonard.ch; Ave de la Gare 35; mains Sfr39-42; ☉lunch & dinner Wed-Sun), great-value dining in the village courtesy of the same family since 1918.

Trains link Sion and St Léonard (Sfr2.20, five minutes, hourly).

& 1.15-6.20pm) ride to the top. Framed by snow-dusted crags, the milky-green waters abruptly vanish like a giant infinity pool. Collecting the meltwater of 35 glaciers, weighing 15 million tonnes and supplying a fifth of Switzerland's energy, the dam impresses with both its scale and statistics. Its sheer magnitude prompts little gasps and comments along the lines of 'what if it burst?' Fear not, this is Switzerland.

VAL D'HÉRENS & VAL D'AROLLA

Just like neighbouring Val d'Hérémence, these thickly wooded valleys hide many peculiarities and pastures mown by silky black Hérens cattle. The road wriggles up from Sion through Vex and then **Euseigne**. Before reaching the latter, the road ducks under the wondrous Gaudí-esque rock pinnacles **Pyramides d'Euseigne**. Nicknamed the *cheminées des fées* (fairy chimneys), these needle-thin, boulder-topped spires have been eroded by glaciers into their idiosyncratic forms over millennia.

Edging 8km further south is the valley's main town, **Evolène** (1371m) where you'll find a smattering of hotels and restaurants, including **La Montanara** (☎027 283 1226; www.lamontanara-evolene.ch. Route Cantonale; s/d incl half-board Sfr90/180; P🖙), a mustard-yellow restaurant with sturdy wooden chalet furniture made to look old in cosy attic rooms. Room keys are so big they're locked in ski-boot cupboards allowing guests to leave with a regular key in their pocket.

Don't leave Evolène without sampling the famed local beef at **Au Vieux Mazot** (☎027 283 11 25; www.auvieuxmazot.ch; mains Sfr20-46; ☉10am-midnight), a legendary cafe and restaurant, also known as Chez Raymonde, in the heart of the village. Meat lovers will melt over the Val d'Hérens beef cooked in a traditional wood-fuelled oven. Otherwise, there's typical raclettes, röstis and so on.

Another 5km and you reach the deeply traditional hamlet of **Les Haudères**. Here the road forks. To the left, the road leads 7km up to another pretty mountain settlement, **Ferpècle**, the end of the road and the start of some mountain hiking in the shadow of the pearly white tooth of Dent Blanche (4356m).

The other road veers right, rising steeply onto a wooded ridge before dropping down into another remote valley, the **Val d'Arolla**. After 11km you roll into a modest ski resort. To the east you can decipher Dent Blanche and to the southwest the glaciated Pigne d'Arolla (3796m), one of half a dozen 3600m-plus peaks that encircle Arolla. The village is a stop on the classic multi-day Haute Route from Chamonix to Zermatt. A seasonal dump of snow makes for crowd-free downhill and cross-country skiing in winter.

Sierre

POP 15.600 / ELEV 533M

One of Switzerland's sunniest towns, Sierre is where French-speaking residents say *bonjour* to their German-speaking neighbours. Indeed there's nothing like a glass of the local Pinot noir to loosen linguistic boundaries in the château-dotted vines rising above the town centre.

Sierre's **Marché des Cépages** (http://marchedescepages.ch) held each year in early September is not to be missed. Glass in hand, it is a wonderful walk through vineyards with music, 40 or so local wine-growers to mingle with and much wine to taste and be merry on.

⊙ Sights & Activities

Musée Valaisan de la Vigne et du Vin MUSEUM
(www.museevalaisanduvin.ch; Rue Ste Catherine 4; adult/child Sfr6/free, free with Salgesch wine museum ticket; ☉2-5pm Tue-Fri Mar-Nov) Sierre's big draw is Château de Villa, a 17th-century turreted manor 20 minutes uphill walk from the train station along Ave du Marché. Inside is the region's wine museum, with

old presses and other wine-related curios, as well as an Oenothèque (⊙10.30am-1pm & 4.30-8.30pm) with bulging cellar and 630 different Valais wines to taste and buy. Keep your museum ticket to get into the sister wine museum in Salgesch (see next section) for free.

🛏 Sleeping & Eating

**⌐TOP⌐
CHOICE Château de Villa** SWISS $$
(☎027 455 18 96; www.chateaudevilla.ch; Rue Ste Catherine 4; raclette Sfr31, fondue Sfr23-26) All turreted towers and centuries-old beams, Sierre's showpiece château rolls out a royal banquet of a Raclette – taste five different types of Raclette cheese from the Valais, washed down with perfectly matched local wines. Come the golden-leafed days of late September, chefs roll out that fabulous old Valaisian chestnut, La Brisolée (p157). In summer dining is stylish and outside on fuschia-pink chairs.

Didier de Courten SWISS $$
(☎027 455 13 51; www.hotel-terminus.ch; Rue du Bourg 1; s/d Sfr120/190, mains Sfr79-85, tasting menus Sfr160-235; ⊙Tue-Sat) One of the region's top addresses, this is a gourmet mecca with snazzy digs above – think pared-down chic. Wholly inspired and driven by *produits du terroir* (local produce), Didier de Courten cooks up a strictly seasonal Michelin-starred cuisine in which the natural freshness and flavour of each ingredient shines through. Notably more affordable fare is served in the adjoining brasserie, L'Atelier Gourmand (mains Sfr26, menus Sfr55 to Sfr86).

ℹ Information

Tourist office (☎027 455 85 35; www.sierre -salgesch.ch; Place de la Gare 10; ⊙8.30am-6pm Mon-Fri, 9am-5pm Sat, 9am-1pm Sun)

ℹ Getting There & Away

Around two trains an hour stop at Sierre on the Geneva–Brig line. The town is the leaping-off point for Crans-Montana; a free *navette* (shuttle bus) links the station with the nearby funicular station for Montana (Sfr12.20, 18 minutes).

Salgesch

POP 1400 / ELEV 540M
As dreamy as a Turner watercolour in the golden autumn light, the winegrowing hamlet of Salgesch produced the first-ever Swiss grand cru in 1988. Blessed with chalky soil and sunshine, Salgesch yields spicy Pinot noirs, fruity dôles and mineral Fendants. Many cellars open their doors for tastings. If your passion for wine goes beyond drinking it, you can even help a local winegrower tend vines for the day between April and October; see the website www .salgesch.ch for details.

A real must for wine buffs is the scenic Sentier Viticole (wine trail; 6km) that leads through vineyards from the wine museum inside Sierre's Château de Villa to the gabled Weinmuseum (Wine Museum; adult/child Sfr6/ free, free with Sierre wine museum ticket; ⊙2-5pm Tue-Sun Apr-Nov) in Salgesch – allow 2½ hours for the walk, which takes in 80 explanatory panels about the vines, local winegrowing techniques, the harvest and so on. Complete the theme with dinner and overnight at one of the region's funkiest boutique hotels. Sleep in a wine barrel or press at Hotel Arkanum (☎027 451 21 00; www.hotelarkanum .ch, s/d/q from Sfr98/178/198; P⊙), where each of the lovely beamed rooms has a different wine-related theme. The restaurant (mains Sfr18 to Sfr38) serves delicious Valaisian specialities and Salgesch wines.

Hourly trains link Salgesch and Sierre (Sfr3, three minutes).

COW FIGHTING

It might sound like a load of bull, but cow fights known as the Combats de Reines (*Kuhkämpfe* in German) are serious stuff in Val d'Hérens, organised to decide which beast is most suited to lead the herd to summer pastures. These Moo-Hammad Ali wannabes charge, lock horns then try to force each other backwards. The winner, or herd's 'queen', can be worth Sfr20,000. Genetic selection and embryo freezing are used to get effective contenders to the field of combat. Once selected, they are fed oats concentrate (believed to act as a stimulant) and sometimes wine. Contests take place on selected Sundays from late March to May and from August to September. Combatants rarely get hurt so visitors shouldn't find the competition distressing. There is a grand final in Aproz (a 10-minute postal bus ride west of Sion) in May on Ascension Day, and the last meeting of the season is held at Martigny's Foire du Valais in early October.

MOVING ON?

For tips, recommendations and reviews, head to http://shop.lonelyplanet.com to purchase a downloadable PDF of the Italy or France chapters from Lonely Planet's *Western Europe* guide.

VALAIS CRANS-MONTANA

Crans-Montana

POP 7000 / ELEV 1500M

Crans-Montana has been on the map ever since Dr Théodore Stéphani took a lungful of crisp Alpine air in 1896 and declared it splendid for his tuberculosis patients. Full of sparkling cheer in winter, the modern sprawling resort strung along a string of lakes is now the much-loved haunt of luminaries like Roger Moore and nouveaux-riches Russians.

Skiing is intermediate paradise, with cruising on sunny, almost exclusively south-facing slopes and 360-degree vistas reaching from Matterhorn to Mont Blanc. Downhill runs tot up to 160km, boarders play daredevils in the Aminona terrain park and there's 50km of cross-country trails.

Hiking and mountain biking are naturally big in summer, downhill speed freaks being well-catered for with marked trails and 16 obstacles graded according to difficulty at the Kona Bike Park at the base station of the Crans Cry d'Er cable car.

Sleeping & Eating

Hostellerie du Pas de l'Ours CHALET $$$
(☑027 485 93 33; www.pasdelours.ch; Rue du Pas de l'Ours; ste Sfr600-1650; P@🛜🐾) Complete spoil-yourself-rotten, fairy-tale stuff, this character-filled timber-and-stone mountain hideaway has a roaring fire, suites with whirlpools and fireplaces, outdoor pool framed by manicured lawns, spa and fine-dine restaurant (called The Bear) headed by Michelin-starred chef Franck Reynaud.

TOP CHOICE Chetzeron SWISS $$
(☑027 488 08 09; www.chetzeron.ch; mains Sfr22-42; ☺lunch) Laze in a chic black hammock or sheepskin-cushioned chaise lounge on a sun terrace at 2112m, drool at Christmas-card snow scenes and congratulate yourself on snagging a spot at what has to be one of the hippest mountain hang-outs in the Swiss Alps – a restyled 1960s cable-car

station. Grilled meats, homemade sausages and a choice of vegetarian plates are cooked up in the kitchen, and it should have three double rooms by 2012. Walk in summer, ski/board in winter from the top of Cry d'Er or call for a snowmobile ride.

Le Pavillon SWISS $$
(☑027 481 24 69; Rte de Rawyl; mains Sfr25-50; ☺lunch & dinner high season, Wed-Mon low season) With a sunny terrace overlooking Lac Grenon, this old-world restaurant halfway between Crans and Montana (bus stop Pavillon) attracts in-the-know locals.

ⓘ Information

Tourist office (☑027 485 04 04; www.crans-montana.ch; ☺8.30am-6.30pm Mon-Sat, 10am-12.30pm & 2-5pm Sun, shorter hours low season) Rue Centrale in Crans and Ave de la Gare in Montana.

ⓘ Getting There & Away

See p161 for information on getting to Crans-Montana.

Val d'Anniviers

Brushed with pine and larch, scattered with dark-timber chalets and postcard villages and set against glistening 4000m peaks, this strikingly beautiful, little-explored valley beckons skiers eager to slalom away from the crowds for fresh powder and hikers seeking big nature.

The road south from Sierre corkscrews precipitously past postage-stamp orchards and vineyards, arriving after 13km in the medieval village of Vissoie (www.sierre-anniviers.ch), a valley crossroads for five ski stations. About 11km along a narrow road winding back north towards Sierre is Vercorin (www.vercorin.ch), geared up for families with gentle skiing on 35km of pistes and a handful of places to stay and eat.

Closer and more enticing for skiers are the combined villages of St Luc (www.saint-luc.ch) and Chandolin (www.chandolin.ch), with 75km of broad, sunny runs, a half-pipe for boarders and fairy-tale panoramas. St Luc is 4km east of Vissoie, up a series of switchbacks, and Chandolin another 4km north. The latter is the more attractive of the two, a huddle of timber houses hanging on for dear life to steep slopes at around 2000m. While here, visit Espace Ella Maillart (www.ellamaillart.ch; admission free; ☺10.30am-6pm

Wed-Sun), dedicated to the remarkable Swiss adventurer who lived in Chandolin when she wasn't exploring remote Afghanistan and Tibet, or winning ski races and regattas. Solar system models punctuate the Chemin des Planètes (Planets Trail), an uphill amble from Tignousa (above St Luc) to the **Weisshorn Hotel** (☑027 475 11 06; www.weisshorn.ch; s/d with half-board Sfr150/280; ☺Jun–mid-Oct & late-Dec–mid-Apr). Sitting at 2337m, the grand 19th-century hotel is accessible on foot or by mountain bike only (or on skis in winter, when luggage is transported for you from St Luc).

Back down in Vissoies you could continue to bucolic **Zinal** (www.zinal.ch), via the hamlet of Ayer, for 70km of fine skiing in the shadow of 4000m giants like Weisshorn, Zinal Rothorn and tooth-like Dent Blanche.

Prettier still is storybook **Grimentz** (www.grimentz.ch), where Valaisian granaries built on stilts (originally to keep thieving mice out!) and burnt-timber, geranium-bedecked chalets huddle over narrow lanes. The village makes a charming base for walking or skiing. **Hotel de Moiry** (☑027 475 11 44; www.hoteldemoiry.ch; s/d with half-board Sfr129/258) has comfy digs with all the trappings of a warm mountain chalet. Eat heartily in the restaurant downstairs. Central **Le Mélèze** (☑027 475 12 87; www.lemeleze.ch; d with half-board Sfr136) shelters nine humble pine-panelled rooms and a barn-style restaurant.

The 8km road south along La Gougra stream to cobalt **Lac de Moiry** (2249m) is open only in summer. Another 3km brings you to a smaller dam, where the road peters out. Before you, the Glacier de Moiry sticks out its dirty white tongue, a 1½-hour hike away.

Up to eight postal buses a day run from Sierre to Vissoie for connections to Chandolin (Sfr15.20, 65 minutes) via St Luc, Zinal (Sfr16.20, 65 minutes) and Grimentz (Sfr14.20, one hour). In summer three buses link Grimentz with Lac de Moiry (20 minutes).

UPPER VALAIS

In a xylophone-to-gong transition, the soothing loveliness of vineyards in the west gives way to austere beauty in the east of Valais. Bijou villages of woodsy chalets stand in collective awe of the drum-roll setting of vertiginous ravines, spiky 4000m pinnacles and monstrous glaciers. The effervescent thermal waters of Leukerbad, the dazzling 23km Aletsch Glacier and the soaring pyramid of Matterhorn are natural icons that invite spontaneous applause.

Leuk
POP 350 / ELEV 750M

Most people overlook Leuk in their hurry to reach Leukerbad and, oops, miss this clifftop hamlet stuck in a medieval time warp. Celts, Romans and Burgundians wore the cobbles smooth on narrow lanes that twist past gurgling fountains, timber granaries and vine-clad manors to the Romanesque **Schloss Leuk** (closed), a castle which has been a bishop's residence, torture chamber and the scene of witch trials over the centuries. Most recently, architect Mario Botta got his hands on it, hence the contemporary space-rocket-like addition that soars out of its crenellated tower.

Escapist fantasy **Hotel Schloss** (☑027 473 12 13; www.schlosshotel-leuk.ch; Leukerstrasse 14; s/d Sfr60/100) is humbler and more affordable than its stately exterior suggests, with simple and spotless wood-panelled rooms.

Leuk is on the main rail route from Lausanne to Brig, with half-hourly trains to Sierre (Sfr4.20, seven minutes) and Brig (Sfr11.20, 25 minutes).

Leukerbad
POP 1600 / ELEV 1411M

The road that zigzags 14km up from Leuk past breathtakingly sheer chasms and wooded crags is a spectacular build-up to Leukerbad. Gazing up to an amphitheatre

---

ℹ **UPPER VALAIS ADVENTURE CARD**

Depending on your movements, the Erlebnis Card Oberwallis-Uri-Graubünden (Upper Valais Adventure Card) can save you a good few francs. Valid for two, three or five days, the card costs Sfr99, Sfr129 and Sfr179 respectively and gets you free travel on postal buses in the Upper Valais and the Glacier Express between Zermatt and Disentis; 50% reduction on regional trains, boats and cable cars; and a host of other worthwhile savings. Buy it at any train station.

of towering rock turrets and canyon-like spires, Europe's largest thermal spa resort is pure drama. Beauty-conscious Romans once took Leukerbad's steamy thermal waters, where today visitors soak after clambering up the Gemmi Pass, braving Switzerland's longest *via ferrata* or carving powder on Torrenthorn.

◎ Sights & Activities

Skiing at Torrenthorn (2998m) is mostly easy and intermediate aside from one demanding run descending 1400m.

TOP CHOICE Lindner Alpentherme   SPA
(☑027 472 10 10; www.alpentherme.ch; Dorfplatz; thermal baths 3hr/day Sfr23/28, with sauna village Sfr39/53, Roman-Irish bath with/without soap-brush massage Sfr74/54; ⊙pools 8am-8pm, sauna village & Roman-Irish baths 10am-8pm) The luxury and most intimate choice, these baths proffer a twinset of pools – one in, one out, both 36°C – with whirlpools, jets, Jacuzzi and mountain view you just can't get enough of. To lounge in the traditional Valais Sauna Village – all wood and rustic cartwheels, with several saunas, mill, ice-cold stream and herbal steam rooms – you must be in the nod (no sneaking in with bi-

kini or trunks on – you'll be told to strip off or leave). Equally invigorating is the Roman-Irish bath, a two-hour nude bathing ritual with aromatic soap-brush massage (optional) and 11 different air, steam and thermal baths to drift between. Then, of course, there are all the other delicious treatments like alpine-flower wraps and Valais grape-seed scrubs you can book yourself.

Burgerbad   SWIMMING
(☑027 472 20 20; www.burgerbad.ch; Rathausstrasse; adult/child day ticket Sfr27/14.50, 3hr-ticket Sfr21/12; ⊙8am-8pm) At the bottom of the village near the town hall, this large brash complex sports 10 different indoor and outdoor pools with water ranging in temperature from 28° to 43°C. Throw in whirlpools, massage jets, steam grottoes and a bright orange waterslide and the crowds love it. Kids aged under eight years swim for free.

Klettersteig Gemmi-Daubenhorn   VIA FERRATA
(⊙Jul-Sep) Classified ED (extremely difficult – get the hint), Switzerland's longest *via ferrata* is really only for the truly skilled and surefooted, best tackled with a guide. The complete trail up to the Dauberhorn (2941m)

WORTH A TRIP

TOP THREE THERMAL SPAS

Somehow it feels downright decadent to float alfresco in toasty-warm 35°C thermal water when the Alpine air is so cold and crisp. Throw in a China-blue sky, a chaise longue in a whirlpool and a snowy-mountain vista and you're pretty close to heaven on earth. Leukerbad in Upper Valais is a hot choice in addition to:

Ovronnaz (www.ovronnaz.ch) Combine ski slopes with bath time at this petite but attractive, family-friendly ski resort a 10km north zigzag uphill from Martigny. A combined one-day ski pass and admission to the three pools at thermal baths Les Bains d'Ovronnaz (www.thermalp.ch; adult/child Sfr19/12; ⊙8am-8.30pm or 9pm) costs Sfr58.

Lavey-les-Bains The thermal water at tiny spa Les Bains de Lavey (www.lavey-les-bains .ch; adult 3/4hr Sfr25/32; ⊙9am-9pm Sun-Thu, to 10pm Fri & Sat), just inside the cantonal frontier of neighbouring Vaud and an easy exit off the motorway (follow signs for 'Lavey'), flows from Switzerland's hottest source. Admission includes the lovely modern Nordic Pavilion with traditional sauna, an Espace Oriental with hammam and Turkish baths, and a wonderful Serenity Pavilion where you can chill to music or indulge in an energising chromotherapy séance. Upmarket Grand Hôtel des Bains (☑024 486 15 15; s/d Sfr165/290; ℙ), with a lovely garden and restaurant, adjoins the pool complex; rates include the spa.

Brigerbad (www.brigerbad.ch) In the Upper Valais, seasonal, open-air Thermalbad Brigerbad (www.thermalbad-wallis.ch; adult morning/afternoon/day Sfr12/14/17, grotto Sfr14; ⊙9.30am-7pm Jul & Aug, to 6pm Jun & Sep, 11am-7pm Apr, May & Oct), halfway between Visp and Brig, tempts with six curative pools including one in a grotto with air-con. Children love the curly-wurly water slide down the mountain and there's a campground next door.

is a dizzying eight-hour scramble up rock face along 2.1km of steel cables and 16 steel ladders; the shorter five-hour route traverses 1.3km of cable and four ladders. Views from the top are deservedly extraordinary. Ask about equipment rental and a guide at the Alpincenter (www.alpincenter-leukabad.ch).

Gemmibahn CABLE CAR
(Gemmibahnen; single/return Sfr20/30; ⊙every 30 min 8.30am-noon & 1-5.30pm or 6pm Jun-Sep, 9am-noon & 1-5pm or 5.30pm Oct) This wonderful old red-and-white cable car has transported walkers and outdoor enthusiasts up the sheer mountain ridge to the Gemmi Pass (2322m) and alpine Lake Dauben since the 1950s. A fantastic area for hiking, it is riddled with well-marked trails; grab a map from the tourist office before heading up, and before striding out from the top station make a beeline for the steely panoramic platform to ogle at the incredible panorama of Valais at your feet.

🛏 Sleeping & Eating

Hotel Escher HOTEL $
(☑027 470 14 31; www.hotel-escher.ch; Tuftstrasse 7; s Sfr80-115, d Str130-200; @🔊) The perfect mix of value-for-money and comfort, the Escher is a gorgeous little alpine guesthouse with great views of the village church and towering snow-topped mountains behind. Rooms are cosy modern with feather duvets, TV and crisp white bathrooms. But the real thrill is the spectacular view from the breakfast room – no snoozing over your muesli here! Wi-fi only works in the downstairs lounge.

Maison Blanche HOTEL $$
(☑027 472 10 00; www.lindnerhotels.ch; Dorfplatz; s/d from Sfr109/219; P@🔊🏊) Practically filling the central square, the elegant White House is the flagship of the local Lindner hotel group. Guests want for nothing, including fluffy white bathrobes and matching slippers to stylishly slip into the neighbouring thermal baths run by the hotel. Grab your gown and go girl.

Hôtel de la Croix Fédérale HOTEL $
(☑027 472 79 79; www.croix-federale.ch; Kirchstrasse 43; s/d Sfr85/160) The welcome is heartfelt at this flowery doll-sized chalet wedged between boutiques on main street Leukerbad. Snug rooms are all-pine and the downstairs restaurant serves one of the best feasts in town.

Wildstubel MOUNTAIN HOTEL $
(☑027 470 12 01; www.gemmi.ch; Gemmi Pass; d/q Sfr140/236, dm Sfr51-56) Ride the Gemmi cable car to this functional high-altitude hotel with a mix of bunk-beds and regular doubles, all pine-clad. Given the lack of anything else or anyone around, half-board (between Sfr75 and Sfr86 per person) is a sensible option.

TOP CHOICE⟩ Walliserkanne VALAISIAN $$
(☑027 472 79 79; Kirchstrasse 43; mains Sfr20-50) The dozens of different fondues, perfectly crisp wood-fired rösti (the one with pumpkin is potato perfection) and game dishes make this cosy address a real Valais feast. But the real treat is the house speciality – gargantuan steaks (beef, pork, chicken, venison) sizzling on a hot slate that arrives at the table on a hefty wooden platter with fries or rösti, dipping sauces and a big paper bib so you can really tuck in. Seating is outside or in between wood panelling and tin pots, and service is swift and smiling.

ℹ Information

Tourist office (☑027 472 71 71; www.leukerbad .ch; Ratplatz; ⊙9am-noon & 1.15-6pm Mon-Fri, 9am-6pm Sat, 9am-noon Sun)

ℹ Getting There & Away

Hourly postal buses link Leukerbad with Leuk (Sfr11.20, 30 to 35 minutes).

Visp
POP 6670 / ELEV 650M
All most visitors see of Visp is the station as they board a train to Zermatt or Saas Fee, yet the Old Town is attractive with its cobbled streets and shuttered windows. Wine lovers can work up a thirst on a 2½-hour uphill hike to Visperterminen, famously home to Europe's highest vineyard at 1150m.

Should you get stuck here, there is a cluster of hotels near the train station. Trains run hourly or so to Zermatt (Sfr34, 65 minutes). An hourly postal bus runs to Saas Fee (Sfr16.20, 55 minutes).

Zermatt
POP 5830 / ELEV 1605M
You can almost sense the anticipation on the train from Täsch: couples gaze wistfully out of the window, kids fidget and stuff in Toblerone, folk rummage for their cameras. And then, as they arrive in Zermatt, all give

Zermatt

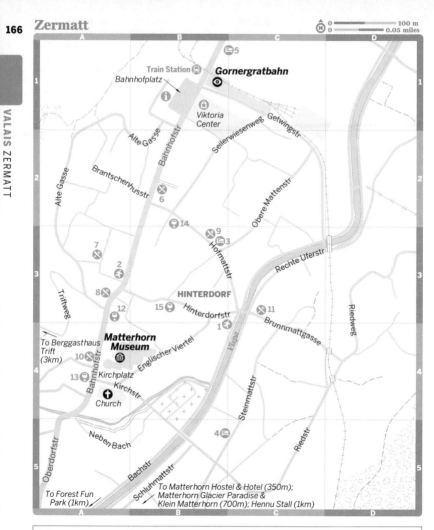

Zermatt

little whoops of joy at the pop-up book effect of one-of-a-kind Matterhorn (4478m). Trigonometry at its finest, topographic perfection, a bloody beautiful mountain – call it what you will, Matterhorn is hypnotic. Like a shark's fin it rises above the town, like an egotistical celebrity it squeezes into every snapshot, like a diva it has moods swinging from pretty and pink to dark and mysterious.

Since the mid-19th century, Zermatt has starred among Switzerland's glitziest resorts. Today it attracts intrepid mountaineers and hikers, skiers who cruise at snail's pace spellbound by the scenery, and style-conscious darlings flashing designer togs in the lounge bars. But all are smitten with the Matterhorn, an unfathomable monolith you can't quite stop looking at.

◉ Sights

It pays to meander away from main strip Bahnhofstrasse with its flashy boutiques and stream of horse-drawn sleds or carriages and electric taxis. Head towards the river along side streets in Hinterdorf, crammed with archetypal Valaisian timber storage barns propped up on stone discs and stilts to keep out the rats.

TOP CHOICE Matterhorn Glacier
Paradise   CABLE CAR
(www.matterhornparadise.ch; adult/child one way Sfr63/31.50, afternoon-return available from 1.30pm Sfr78.50/39; ⊙7am-4.20pm Jul & Aug, 8.30am-3.35pm mid-Oct–Dec, 8.30am-4.20pm rest of year) Views from Zermatt's cable cars and gondolas are all pretty remarkable, but the Matterhorn Glacier Paradise is the icing on the cake. Ride Europe's highest-altitude cable car up to 3883m and gawp at a top-of-the-beanstalk panorama of 14 glaciers and 38 mountain peaks over 4000m from the Panoramic Platform. Don't miss the Glacier Palace, an ice palace complete with glittering ice sculptures, a glacier crevasse to walk through and – one for the kids – an ice slide to swoosh down bum first.

Gornergratbahn   RAILWAY
(www.gornergrat.ch; Bahnhofplatz 7; adult/child one way Sfr39/19.50; journey time 35 to 45 min; ⊙2 or 3 departures hourly 7am-6pm May & mid-Oct–Nov, 7am-10pm Jun-Sep, every 20 min 7am-5.15pm Dec-Apr) This splendid cogwheel railway – Europe's highest – climbs through picture-postcard scenery to Gornergrat (3089m). Sit on the right-hand side of the little red

train to gawp at Matterhorn. Tickets allow you to get on and off en route – there are restaurants at Riffelalp (2211m) and Riffelberg (2582m). In summer an extra train runs once a week at sunrise and sunset – an even more spectacular trip.

Matterhorn Museum   MUSEUM
(www.matterhornmuseum.ch; Kirchplatz; adult/child Sfr10/5, audioguide Sfr5; ⊙11am-6pm, closed Nov) This crystalline, state-of-the-art museum provides a fascinating insight into Valaisian village life, mountaineering, the dawn of tourism in Zermatt and the lives Matterhorn has claimed. Must-sees include Raymond Lambert's reindeer-skin boots (made to measure after his toes were amputated), Roosevelt's letters and the infamous rope that broke in 1865 and turned the first ascent of Matterhorn into a tragedy.

⚐ Activities

An essential stop in activity planning is Zermatt Alpin Center (☑027 966 24 60; www.alpincenter-zermatt.ch; Bahnhofstrasse 58; ⊙9am-noon & 3-7pm mid-Nov–Apr & Jul-Sep), home to Zermatt's ski school and mountain guides. In winter you can buy lift passes here (Sfr75/371 for a one/six-day pass excluding Cervinia, Sfr86/423 including Cervinia).

Skiing
Zermatt is cruising heaven, with mostly long, scenic red runs, plus a smattering of blues for ski virgins and knuckle-whitening blacks for experts. The main skiing areas in winter are Rothorn, Stockhorn and Klein Matterhorn – 350km of ski runs in all with a link from Klein Matterhorn to the Italian resort of Cervinia and a freestyle park with half-pipe for snowboarders.

Summer skiing (20km of runs) and boarding (gravity park at Plateau Rosa on the Theodul glacier) is Europe's most extensive. May to mid-October, lifts operate from 9am to 2pm (7.40am to 1pm July and August) with the last ride up for skiers and boarders from Zermatt at 11.20am (12.20pm September, 1pm May and June). Count Sfr80/120 for a one/two-day summer ski pass.

September to late November, budget skiers can save on weekend packages that involve testing the latest skis on a limited number of runs around Klein Matterhorn Glacier.

Hiking
Zermatt is a hiker's paradise in summer with 400km of trails through some of the most incredible scenery in the Alps – the tourist

CLIMBING MATTERHORN

Some 3000 alpinists summit Europe's most photographed, 4478m-high peak each year. You don't need to be super-human to do it, but you do need to be a skilled climber, in tip-top physical shape and have a week in hand to acclimatise beforehand to make the iconic ascent up sheer rock and ice.

No one attempts Matterhorn without local know-how: mountain guides at Zermatt Alpin Center charge Sfr1380 per person for the 10-hour return climb, including cable car from Zermatt to Schwarzee and half-board accommodation in a mountain hut. Oh, and don't be surprised if you're required to do a training climb first, just to prove you really are 100% up to it. Matterhorn claims some 12 lives each year.

office has trail maps. For Matterhorn close-ups, the ultimate day trek is Höhenweg Höhbalmen.

For those doing lots of walking, a three-day hiking pass is worth the Sfr141 investment. Mid-June to mid-September the Panoramic Pass, costing Sfr125 for one day or Sfr144 for two consecutive days, is also available.

Biking, Climbing & Paragliding

Dorsaz Sport   DIRT BIKING
(www.dorsaz-sport.ch; Schluhmattstrasse; scooter Sfr20/hour; ☺8am-6.30pm) This sports shop next to the Matterhorn Paradise cable car rents chunky off-road scooters (with helmet) to race down the mountain. Ride the Schwarzee cable car as far as Furi (1867m) then scoot down on a semi-paved track.

Forest Fun Park   TREE CLIMBING
(www.zermatt-fun.ch;adult/childSfr32/16; ☺9am-6.30pm Mar-Nov) Let rip Tarzan-style in the forest with zip-lines, river traverses, bridges and platforms all graded according to difficulty.

Paragliding Zermatt   PARAGLIDING
(☎027 967 67 44; www.paragliding-zermatt.ch; Bachstrasse 8) All year round you can ride warm thermals alone or in tandem for above-mountain views guaranteed to make you swoon.

🛏 Sleeping

Book well ahead in winter, and bear in mind that nearly everywhere closes from May to mid- or late June and October to November or early December.

TOP CHOICE **Hotel Bahnhof**   HOTEL **$**
(☎027 967 24 06; www.hotelbahnhof.com; Bahnhofstrasse; dm Sfr40-55, s/d/q Sfr80/110/210; ☎) Opposite the train station, these five-star budget digs have proper beds and spotless bathrooms that are a godsend after scaling or schussing down mountains all day. Rooms for four are fabulous for families. There's a stylish lounge with armchairs to flop in and books to read; and a snazzy open-plan kitchen for preparing your own breakfast.

TOP CHOICE **Firefly Hotel**   BOUTIQUE HOTEL **$$$**
(☎027 967 76 76; www.firefly-zermatt.com; Schluhmattstrasse 55; d/q from Sfr770/1250) Oh to have oodles of cash to while away a few dreamy weeks in this glorious hotel named after a bar on a paradise island where the owners spent many a happy moment one holiday! Rooms, all with kitchenette, sleep two to eight and their cutting-edge design bows to the elements – each is themed fire, water, earth or air. At the very least, sink into a cow-print armchair and enjoy a sundowner in style at its ground-floor Bar 55.

Backstage Hotel   DESIGN HOTEL **$$$**
(☎027 966 69 70; www.backstagehotel.ch; Hofmattstrasse 4; d Sfr450-580; @) Crafted from wood, glass and the trademark creativity of local artist Heinz Julen (the guy behind the Vernissage cultural centre and bar), this place is effortlessly cool – the type of place where bathtubs have legs and practically every bit of furniture is a unique piece. Cube loft rooms are just that – a loft room with a giant glass cube in their centre encasing bathroom, toilet and kitchenette. Fabulous.

Matterhorn Hostel   HOSTEL **$**
(☎027 968 19 19; www.matterhornhostel.com; Schluhmattstrasse 32; dm/d/tr/q Sfr36/92/138/164, breakfast Sfr8; ☺reception 7.30-10am or 11am & 4-9pm or 10pm; @☎) Tucked in a 1960s wooden chalet a two-minute walk from the lifts, this hostel is first-rate. Rooms are modern and its busy ground-floor bar cooks up a great vibe and food. Rates are higher the last fortnight in December and at Easter.

continued on p178

Swiss Dream

Winter Wonderland »
Summer Playground »
Alpine Villages »
Swiss Lakes »

ROBERTO GEROMETTA/LONELY PLANET IMAGES ©

Breathtaking views in the Engadine (p308)

Winter Wonderland

Switzerland never looks better than on a crisp, cold winter's day, when the Alpine heights and forests are blanketed in snow. Shaking up this snow-globe scene are the skiers, snowboarders, sledders, skaters, off-pisters and snowshoers that harness this natural beauty. And what beauty! Nowhere else in Europe are the peaks higher – from the pyramidal Matterhorn (4478m) to Mont Blanc (4807m) – the views more uplifting, the villages more postcard-perfect, the lifts more efficient. One trip and you're hooked.

Whether you want to master parallel turns in Grindelwald with Eiger on the horizon, schuss down black runs in Davos or go off-piste in Engelberg, there's a slope ready and waiting.

Can't ski, won't-in-a-million-years ski? Well, there's plenty to entertain non-skiers in the Swiss Alps. Nearly every resort has winter footpaths and sledding tracks where you can stomp, snowshoe or slide through frozen woodlands and past snowcapped mountains in quiet exhilaration.

SNOW FUN

» Ski in the shadow of mighty Matterhorn in **Zermatt** (p167) and pop over the mountain for lunch in Cervinia, Italy.

» Dash across the frozen plains on a husky-drawn sleigh at **Glacier 3000** (p143) near Gstaad.

» Carve up virgin snow in the backcountry of **Verbier** (p154).

» Snowboard with the pros on the slopes of **Laax** (p297) and **Saas Fee** (p180).

» Say your snowy prayers on the do-or-die Swiss Wall in **Champéry** (p152).

Clockwise from top left
1. Winter scenery at Grindelwald 2. Playing in the snow
3. Sledding in Graubünden

Summer Playground

It's summer in the Alps: the meadows are lush with herbs, the lakes glitter in the valley like jewels. Elsewhere rivers are running deep and swift, and fields of wheat and grapevines are ripening under a china-blue sky. Being a spectator isn't enough. You're itching to engage with the landscape: to climb those mountains, to splash in those lakes, to raft those waters, to cycle over hill and glorious dale. You're in the right place.

Isn't it marvellous that the Swiss are so darned efficient, you muse, as you hike on well-marked trails leading past Eiger's north face to Kleine Scheidegg, up to the remote heights of the Swiss National Park and along the frozen wilderness of the Aletsch Glacier.

For water-loaded adventure, you can raft the foaming waters of the Vorderrhein and kitesurf on Silvaplana. Not enough of a buzz? Get your intrepid self to Interlaken to skydive, paraglide, ice climb, canyon, hydrospeed and (phew!) more.

SUMMER HIGHS

» Bounce upside-down from the 220m **Verzasca Dam** (p208), one of the world's highest bungee jumps.

» Blaze down single tracks in mountain-bike mecca **Davos** (p307).

» Do a tightrope act on Mürren's **via ferrata** (p133), with big-top views of Eiger, Mönch and Jungfrau.

» Hike to the source of the Rhine on the **Lai da Tuma Circuit** (p301).

» Get an eagle's-eye view of the Jungfrau massif paragliding from **First** (p123).

Clockwise from top left
1. Mountain biking in the Val de Bagnes **2.** Paragliding down Mt Rigi to Lake Lucerne **3.** Edelweiss in the Alps **4.** The view over the Aletsch Glacier from Eggishorn

GFC COLLECTION/ALAMY ©

Alpine Villages

Heidi may be fictional, but her Alpine village lifestyle isn't. Switzerland will meet all your storybook fantasies: from hilltop hamlets in the Bernese Oberland with cowbells as your wake-up call, to icicle-hung log chalets in Valais where you can snuggle by a crackling fire as the flakes gently fall. Sound idyllic? You bet.

Val Fex

1 Lost in time and space, Val Fex (p317) nestles amid glacier-encrusted mountains, larch forests and meadows. Romantically reached on foot or by horse-drawn carriage, the tiny hamlets of Fex-Platta and Fex-Cresta are like the Alps before the dawn of tourism.

Village Architecture

2 Pretty villages come thick and fast in Appenzell's bucolic backcountry, but none matches Werdenberg (p282), with its perky medieval castle, geranium-studded timber chalets and pristine Alpine setting.

Mürren & Gimmelwald

3 Mürren (p133) has scenery, skiing and hiking to make your heart sing. Pick a log chalet for dress-circle views of Eiger, Mönch and Jungfrau. To be at one with nature, tiptoe away from the crowds to cute-as-a-button Gimmelwald (p134) nearby.

Corippo

4 With a population of 15, Switzerland's smallest hamlet, Corippo (p209), is more of a family than a village. Tumbling down a wooded hill in the Val Verzasca, its granite houses and mountain backdrop are photogenic stuff.

Aletsch Glacier

5 If you're looking for postcard Switzerland, car-free Riederalp and Bettmeralp are it (p185), with their dreamy Matterhorn views and snuggly timber chalets perched on the edge of the Aletsch Glacier's icy wilderness.

Clockwise from top left
1. The remote village of Val Fex **2.** Swiss village farmhouse
3. Strolling through snow-topped Mürren

ERIC AND DAVID HOSKING/CORBIS ©

GÜNTER GRÄFENHAIN/HUBER/4CORNERS ©

GÜNTER GRÄFENHAIN/HUBER/4CORNERS ©

Swiss Lakes

Glacially cold and deliciously warm, palm-fringed and mountain-rimmed, Alpine and inner-city, green, blue and aquamarine – this little land has a lake for every style and season. Pedal around Lake Constance, sip sundowners by Lake Zurich, or watch the Alps' reflection in a crystal-clear tarn.

Lago Maggiore

1 Switzerland spills over into Italy on Lago Maggiore (p201), which offers the best of two worlds: the grandeur of the Alps and the palm trees, pasta and sunshine of the south. Soak up the lake's unique style in Locarno (p201) and Ascona (p205).

Lakes Thun & Brienz

2 These startlingly turquoise twin lakes (p135) at the foot of the Bernese Alps buzz with sightseers and water-sports enthusiasts in summer. Castle-topped Thun (p135), vine-strewn Spiez (p137) and woodcarving Brienz (p139) are standouts.

Lake Geneva

3 Glide across Lake Geneva (p61) by boat as the soft dusk light paints Mont Blanc pink. Europe's biggest Alpine lake sparkles in cosmopolitan Geneva (p38), by fairy-tale Château de Chillon (p72) and below the steep Lavaux (p68) vine terraces.

Lake Uri

4 Enigmatic in the morning mist and silhouettes of sunset, Lake Uri (p224) is a fitting backdrop for tales of Switzerland's greatest hero, William Tell. Turner liked to paint the lake from Brunnen (p224).

Walensee

5 The Churfirsten mountains rise like an iron curtain behind Walensee (p284). Weesen (p284) makes a fine base for windsurfing, wakeboarding or lolling around the lake in summer. For breathtaking views, head to Seerenbachfälle (p284), Switzerland's highest waterfall.

Right
1. Santuario della Madonna del Sasso, overlooking Locarno **2.** Lake Thun from Schloss Spiez

WALTER BIBIKOW/GETTY IMAGES ©

GLENN VAN DER KNIJFF/LONELY PLANET IMAGES ©

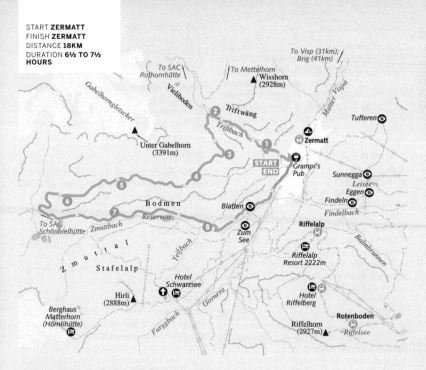

START **ZERMATT**
FINISH **ZERMATT**
DISTANCE **18KM**
DURATION **6½ TO 7½ HOURS**

Walking Tour
Höhenweg Höhbalmen

This circular hike embodies all that is unique about the Swiss Alps, leading you into another world of glittering streams, crevassed glaciers and the entrancing angles of Matterhorn and two dozen other 4000er peaks. Depending on the weather, this route can normally be done June to October.

From Zermatt train station walk along Bahnhofstrasse and turn right at Grampi's Pub onto a cobbled footpath that climbs above town. Cross the Triftbach and climb through larch forest to **1 Pension Edelweiss** (1961m). The path rises gently to recross the stream near a hydroelectricity diversion tunnel, then makes several broad switchbacks above the Triftbach Gorge. Continue uphill to **2 Berggasthaus Trift** (2337m), a great base if you want to split the hike into two days.

Cross the Triftbach a final time, cutting southward over the tiny Alpine meadow, and begin a zigzagging ascent up the grassy slopes. As you climb onto the high balcony of the **3 Höhbalmenstaffel**, a sensational panorama unfolds. The trail contours the rolling fields of **4 Höhbalmen**, where the rare purple-yellow Haller's pasque flower grows, to reach a signpost at 2665m, 40 to 50 minutes from Berggasthaus Trift. Head west: the route traverses narrowing ledges opposite the fearsome north face of Matterhorn, reaching **5 Schwarzläger** (2741m), the highest point of the walk, after 40 to 50 minutes.

Make a steady, sidling descent over the sparse mountainsides of **6 Arben**. The path snakes down to meet a more prominent walking track alongside the high lateral moraine wall left by the receding Zmutt-gletscher. Follow this down left in zigzags through glacial rubble and continue along gentler terraces above the icy cold Zmuttbach, past a waterfall, to **7 Kalbermatten** (2105m), one to 1¼ hours from Schwarzläger.

Head on down above a reservoir, bearing right at a junction by the dam wall, to **8 Zmutt** (1936m), a photogenic hamlet with a whitewashed chapel. From here a footpath descends through hay fields to intersect with a gravelled lane. After the Schwarzsee cable-car station turn left to Zermatt, 1¼ to 1½ hours from Kalbermatten.

continued from p168

Chesa Valese
CHALET **$$**

(☎027 966 80 80; www.chesa-valese.ch; Steinmatt-strasse 2; s/d Sfr165/260) A dreamy address the other side of the river, this traditional burnt-red wood chalet with traditional slate-roof conservatory and flowery garden is romantic, charming and ablaze with red geraniums in summer. Rooms are cosy country style and the very best stare brazenly at Matterhorn.

✗ Eating

For first-rate Italian pizza in the sun with a Matterhorn view **Klein Matterhorn** (☎027 967 01 42; www.kleinmatterhorn-zermatt.com; pizza Sfr17-24), opposite the Matterhorn Glacier Express cable car station, is *the* address. Dozens of places line Bahnhofstrasse, including the busy **Brown Cow Pub** (Bahnhofstrasse 41; burgers Sfr12-14; ☺9-2am), which serves pub grub all day.

TOP CHOICE ⟩ Chez Vrony
SWISS **$$**

(☎027 967 25 52; www.chezvrony.ch; mains Sfr25-60) Ride the Sunnegga Express to 2288m then ski halfway down blue piste 6 to what must be Zermatt's cosiest, toasti-est, tastiest address on the slopes (Robbie

---

MAN OR MATTERHORN

On 13 July 1865 Edward Whymper led the first successful ascent of Matterhorn via Hörnli ridge, but the descent was marred by tragedy when four team members crashed to their deaths in a 1200m fall down the North Wall.

Yet the tragedy put Zermatt on the map, and soon other plucky souls came to climb Matterhorn and the surrounding giants, including a 20-year-old Winston Churchill, who scaled Monte Rosa (4634m) in 1894, and Franklin D Roosevelt, who climbed Matterhorn in 1881.

As you wander Hinterdorfstrasse, look out for the fountain commemorating Ulrich Inderbinen (1900–2004), a Zermatt-born mountaineer who climbed Matterhorn 370 times, the last time at age 90. Nicknamed the King of the Alps, he was the oldest active mountain guide in the world when he retired at the ripe old age of 95.

Williams loves the place). Cuddle up in a fleecy blanket or lounge on a chaise longue so low it really would be better by a pool and revel in the effortless romance of this century-old farmhouse. Its dried meat, homemade cheese and sausage – all organic – come from their own cows that graze away the summer on the high alpine pastures (2100m) surrounding it. Advance reservations essential in winter.

TOP CHOICE ⟩ Whymper Stube
VALAISIAN **$$**

(☎027 967 22 96; www.whymper-stube.ch; Bahnhofstrasse 80; fondue Sfr25-27, mains Sfr22-43) An advance reservation is essential at this legendary address, known for its excellent raclette and fondues, both cheese and meat. Service is relaxed and friendly, tables are packed tightly together, and the place has a real buzz. End on a high with a decadent meringue and cream, giant enough to challenge the Matterhorn.

Bayard Metzgerei
STREET FOOD **$**

(Bahnhofstrasse 9; hot dog Sfr6; ☺noon-6.30pm Jul-Sep, 4-6.30pm Dec-Mar) Join the line in the street for a sausage (pork, veal or beef) and chunk of bread to down with a beer on the hop – or at a bar stool with the sparrows in the alley by this butcher's shop.

Myoko
JAPANESE **$$**

(Bahnhofstrasse; sushi Sfr29-39, menus Sfr64-148) This stylish address is as much about loung-ing alfresco in its flowery green summer garden as it is feasting on sushi, sashimi and teppanyaki cooked before your very eyes.

Z'art
MODERN EUROPEAN **$$**

(☎027 967 45 25; www.zermattart.ch; Zum Steg 3; mains Sfr26-33; ☺4pm-late Tue-Sun) Sit on the terrace and enjoy the hypnotic gush of the nearby river or savour contemporary art strung in a smart, minimalist interior. In the kitchen the chef gives a gourmet kick to classics such as club sandwiches, veal tartare and fillet of beef. Great pasta too.

The Pipe
FUSION, BISTRO **$**

(☎079 758 53 24; www.chakralounge.com; Hof-mattstrasse 7; mains Sfr25; ☺10.30am-10.30pm Jun-Sep, to midnight Dec-Apr, closed Mon & Tue May, Oct & Nov) This jammin' Afro-Asian den is as chilled and laid-back as its 'surfer cantina' tag playfully suggests. Let tastebuds do somersaults over hot and fruity spring-bok curry, apricot-glazed Karoo lamb with a liquoricey Shiraz and other hot fusion dishes.

TOP THREE SKY-HIGH SLEEPS

Zermatt is all about big views and there's no better way to the heart of its trademark mountain panorama than to check into a hotel above the clouds.

For those who fancy the atmosphere and views of an Alpine mountain hut but shiver at the thought of thin mattresses, icy water or – heaven forbid – hiking several hours to reach the place, Switzerland's highest hotel at 3000m is the No 1 address. **Kulmhotel Gornergrat** (027 966 64 00; www.gornergrat-kulm.ch; d incl half-board from Sfr195), at the top of Gornergrat, cocoons skiers, walkers and hedonist mountain-admirers in sleek rooms with downy duvets and picture-perfect views of Monte Rosa, Matterhorn and other 4000m peaks. When the crowds leave at sunset, the century-old hotel is magical.

Precisely for those who love a long trudge up to bed – to 2337m to be exact – is **Berggasthaus Trift** (079 408 70 20; dm/d with half-board Sfr65/154; late Jun-Sep), run by Hugo (a whizz on the alpenhorn) and Fabienne at the foot of the Triftgletscher. A stiff two-hour hike from Zermatt, it has simple rooms, mesmeric views of its glacial 4000m surrounds and a great terrace to kick back on over home-cured beef and oven-warm apple tart. Call in advance to ensure a bed.

Then there is the ground-breaking **Monte Rose Hütte** (027 967 21 15; www.section-monte-rosa.ch; dm Sfr45, incl half-board Sfr83), dramatically perched on the edge of the Monte Rose glacier at 2883m and accessible only on foot via a tough five-hour glacial trail (only for serious mountaineers with a guide). Nicknamed the 'Mountain Crystal', the completely isolated, crystalline hut is a wooden construction clad in silver aluminium; it's solar powered, recycles its water, and is deemed the last word in state-of-the-art Alpine self-sufficiency.

Stefanie's Crêperie　　　　CREPERIE $

(Bahnhofstrasse 60; snacks Sfr5-16; 11am-midnight) Perfectly thin, light crêpes served to go on the main street.

🍷 Drinking

Still fizzing with energy after schussing down the slopes? Zermatt pulses in party-mad après-ski huts, suave lounge bars and Brit-style pubs. Most close (and some melt) in low season.

TOP CHOICE Vernissage Bar　　　　LOUNGE BAR

(www.vernissage-zermatt.ch; Hofmattstrasse 4; 5pm-2am) The ultimate après-ski anti-thesis, Vernissage exudes grown-up sophistication. Local artist Heinz Julen has created a theatrical space with flowing velvet drapes, film-reel chandeliers and candlelit booths. Catch an exhibition, watch a Bond movie in the decadent cinema, then practise your 007 martini pose in the lounge bar.

Hennu Stall　　　　BAR

(www.hennustall.ch; Klein Matterhorn; 2-7pm) Last one down to this snowbound 'chicken run' is a rotten egg. Hennu is the wildest après-ski shack on Klein Matterhorn. Order a caramel vodka and take your ski boots grooving to live music on the terrace. A metre-long 'ski' of shots will make you cluck all the way down to Zermatt.

Z'alt Hischi　　　　BAR

(www.hischibar.ch; Hinterdorfstrasse 44; 9.30pm-2am) Hidden on what must be Zermatt's most charming street, this busy watering hole comes packaged in an ancient, 'I've-seen-it-all' wooden chalet.

Elsie Bar　　　　WINE BAR

(www.elsiebar.ch; Kirchplatz 16; 4pm-midnight) Copper pots are strung from the ceiling at this bijou wine bar – old-world and English-style – across from the church.

ℹ Information

Tourist office (027 966 81 00; www.zermatt.ch; Bahnhofplatz 5; 8.30am-6pm mid-Jun–Sep, 8.30am-noon & 1-6pm Mon-Fri, 8.30am-6pm Sat, 9.30am-noon & 4-6pm Sun rest of year)

ℹ Getting There & Away

Car

Zermatt is car-free. Motorists have to park in Täsch (www.matterhornterminal.ch; Sfr14.50/day), load luggage onto a trolley (Sfr5) and ride the Zermatt Shuttle (adult/child Sfr7.80/3.90, 12 minutes, every 20 minutes from 6am to 9.40pm) train the last 5km to Zermatt.

Taxi

Dinky electro-taxis zip around town transporting goods and the weary (and taking pedestrians perilously by surprise – watch out!). Pick one up at the main rank in front of the train station on Bahnhofstrasse.

Train

Trains to Täsch depart roughly every 20 minutes from Brig (Sfr31, 1½ hours), stopping at Visp en route. Zermatt is also the starting point of the Glacier Express to Graubünden, one of the most spectacular train rides in the world.

Saas Fee

POP 1700 / ELEV 1800M

Hemmed in by a magnificent amphitheatre of 13 implacable peaks over 4000m and backed by the threatening tongues of nine glaciers, this village looks positively feeble in the revealing light of summer. Until 1951, only a mule trail led to this isolated outpost and locals scraped a living from farming.

Today Saas Fee is a chic, car-free resort where every well-to-do skier and hiker wants to be. Modern chalets surround the village but its commercial heart, well-endowed with old timber chalets and barns on stilts (once used to store hams and grain), retains a definite old-world, Heidi-style charm.

◉ Sights

Allalin   GLACIER

Year-round, an underground funicular steadily climbs up to an icy 3500m, where the world's highest revolving restaurant on the Allalin glacier basks in glorious 360-degree views of Saas Fee's 4000m glacial giants. Whatever the season, wrap up warm to visit the subzero **Eispavillion** (Ice cave; adult/child Sfr5/3 or free for non-skiers with return cable-car ticket), hollowed out 10m below the ice surface, or soar down Feegletscher's 20km of summer ski slopes that bask in the sun above 2700m. A two-/five-day summer ski pass (July and August) costs Sfr129/301. To reach the glacier, take the cable car up to Felskinn (3000m) then the Mittelallalin funicular to the top; a Saas Fee–Allalin return costs Sfr106.

Saaser Museum   MUSEUM

(Dorfstrasse 6; admission Sfr4; ☺10-11.30am & 1.30-5.30pm) Meander along the main street, past the church, to this old wooden Valaisian house where village life in the 19th century is evoked through traditional embroidered costumes, household items and other ethnographic exhibits. The exhibition on

glacial history is particularly fascinating, as is the original study of German writer Carl Zuckmayer (1896–1977), who called Saas Fee home.

Feeblitz   LUGE

(Panoramastrasse; 1/6/10 descents adult Sfr6.50/36.50/59, child Sfr4/22.50/36; ☺10am-6pm Jul & Aug, noon-5.30pm Sep, 1-6pm Nov school hols & mid-Dec–Apr) Cross the bridge across the river and turn left along Mischistrasse to reach Saas Fee's speed-fiend luge track, next to the Alpin Express cable car. Kids under eight ride for free with a parent.

🏃 Activities

Skiing & Snowboarding

Saas Fee's slopes are snow-sure, with most skiing taking place above 2500m and the glacier acting like a deep freeze. The 145km of groomed, scenic pistes are more suited to beginners and intermediates, though experts willing to take a guide to go off-piste will find bottomless powder. Ski-mountaineering is possible along the famous Haute Route to Chamonix. The resort is a snowboarding mecca and regularly hosts world championships. Boarders gravitate towards the kickers, half-pipe and chill-out zone at the glacial **freestyle park** on Allalin in summer and lower down the slopes at Morenia (2550m) in winter. A one-day ski lift pass costs Sfr68 and a six-day ski lift pass costs Sfr346; kids aged under nine ride for free.

Swiss Ski & Snowboard School   SKIING

(☎027 957 23 48; www.skischule-saas-fee.ch; Dorfplatz 1) Book lessons with the main ski school on the central church square.

Mountain Guide Office   SNOW SPORTS

(☎027 957 44 64; www.saasfeeguides.ch; Obere Dorfstrasse 75) Around the corner from the ski school – the experts to contact for guided off-piste skiing, ski touring, snowshoeing, glacier trekking, ice climbing and gorge walking.

Hiking

The tourist office has bags of information (including hiking maps and booklets outlining short themed walks) on 350km of summer trails ranging from kid-easy to jaw-droppingly challenging. Several easy walks, such as the stroll to the village from Hannig (see Mountain Scootering) or Spielboden involve taking a cable car up and ambling down. Gentler strolls follow

They may spend nine-tenths of their lives underground (sleeping, hiding from predators and in hibernation), but come the warm sunny days of July, marmots pop out of their painstakingly-dug tunnels and burrows beneath the slopes to stretch their legs, take in the air and unwittingly entertain walkers.

The rocky southern-facing slopes above the tree line in Spielboden (2443m) shelter colonies of the small alpine mammal known for its shrill whistle. Atypically unfearful of humans, these Valaisian marmots happily eat carrots, peanuts and bread from your hand – the boldest will even let you pet and cuddle them.

To see marmots close-up, ride the Längfluh cable car to Spielboden (single/return Sfr27/19) and buy some *marmeltierfutter* (marmot food, aka small plastic bags of chopped carrot, bread chunks and peanuts in shells which the marmots shell themselves) for Sfr3.50 from the restaurant across from the cable car station. Then amble downhill along the steep path keeping your eyes peeled. It takes 2½ hours to walk down to Saas Fee village – break en route for lunch or a drink at Gletscher Grotte.

the fast-flowing Vispa and meander through forest to Saas-Almagell. Summer walkers can buy individual one-way tickets for cable cars or a seven-day Hiking Pass (adult/family Sfr138/279).

Mountain Scootering

In summer whisk yourself up to Hannig (2350m) to indulge in a stunning glacial panorama while kids run riot on a wood-crafted playground with a 14m tube slide outside the one restaurant here. Hire a mountain scooter and helmet from the top station (☑027 957 26 15; Hannigbahn top station; one descent Sfr9, half-/full day incl helmet Sfr20/30; ☺8.45am-4.45pm) and fly down the mountain on a bone-rattling, 5.5km-long dirt track. The less adventurous can walk (1½ hours). A one-way ticket to Hannig costs Sfr19, a return ticket Sfr27 and a one-day pass good for unlimited scooter or sledge descents Sfr33.

December to April, the same path becomes a sledge run (one descent Sfr18, sledge rental Sfr6), particularly magical after dark when you can sledge down by torchlight (6pm to 9pm Tuesday and Thursday).

🛏 Sleeping

In season (December to April, July and August) hotels only offer half-board. Most close completely in May and November. Watch for special summer deals which often throw unlimited use of cable cars in for free. Irrespective of season, hotel guests and those staying in self-catering chalets get a free Visitor's Card which yields a bonanza of savings, including on car parking fees, cable cars and so on.

TOP CHOICE Vernissage Berghaus Plattjen   MOUNTAIN HOTEL **$$**
(☑027 957 12 05; www.vernissage-berghaus.ch; Plattjen; dm/tr incl half-board Sfr100/360) 'Where dreams have no end' is the apt strapline of this stylish, design-driven address half-way up the mountain at 2418m, near the Plattjen cable car station (2567m). Sheepskins dress lounge chairs on the terrace and rooms fuse cosy alpine with clean-cut contemporary. Its terrace restaurant is one of the top addresses to lunch on the slopes.

Hotel Waldesruh   CHALET **$$**
(☑027 958 64 64; www.hotelwaldesruh.ch; Gletscherstrasse 14; s/d incl half-board Sfr169/338) This three-star chalet is an ecstatic I'll-be-first-in-the-queue hop from the ski lifts. The family that runs it is affable and old-style hotel rooms are comfy with balconies overlooking the glacial slopes. Oh, and there are regular alpenhorn and glockenspiel performances.

Romantik Hotel Beau-Site   CHALET **$$**
(☑027 958 15 60; www.beausite.org; s/d Sfr195/350; @🛜🏊) Right in the village heart on the main drag, Beau-Site is as beautiful as its name suggests. Service is polished, rooms are classically elegant with antique furnishings and on winter days nothing beats the fireplace bar or the spa's steam baths, grotto-like pool and saunas.

Hotel GletscherGarten   CHALET **$$**
(☑027 957 21 75; www.hotelgletschergarten .ch; Obere Dorfstrasse 51; s/d incl half-board Sfr113/226; @🛜) This large wooden chalet tempts with four tiers of simply gorgeous

ON THE SLOPES

Follow the hip crowd to stylish **Vernissage Berghaus Plattjen** (p181) or historic wooden chalet **Gletscher Grotte** (☑027 957 21 60; www.gletschergrotte.ch; mains Sfr15-30; ☺10am-4pm Dec-Apr), where you can snuggle up in sheepskin and feast on raclette, rösti and other heart-warming winter fodder. Ski to either in winter (December to April) and ride the cable car up/walk in summer (mid-June to mid-October).

cream-and-chocolate coloured balconies and a riot of summertime geraniums.

Hotel Britannia HOTEL $$
(☑027 958 60 00; www.hotel-britannia.ch; Obere Dorfstrasse 46; s/d incl half-board Sfr120/240; @☺) With its summer garden, kids, play area and downstairs pizzeria, the Britannia is a real family address.

✖ Eating

Fletschhorn GASTRONOMIC $$$
(☑027 957 21 31; www.fletschhorn.ch; mains Sfr65-70, lunch menu Sfr90, 6-/9-course dinner menu Sfr175/205) Nestled 8km from town in a forest glade with dramatic mountain views, this Michelin-starred restaurant is one of Switzerland's top addresses. Chef Markus Neff interprets French cuisine with finesse, with signatures such as crispy, rosemary-infused suckling pig and roast pigeon with black truffles. The sommelier will help you choose a bottle of wine from the 30,000 on the list. Call ahead and staff will pick you up.

Zur Mühle SWISS $$
(☑027 957 26 76; Dorfstrasse 61; mains Sfr15-30) From the village church follow Dorfstrasse downhill to this snug riverside address bedecked with sheepskins, cow-print curtains and copper pans. Rösti is the mainstay and comes in various creative guises – with venison cutlets in mushroom and thyme sauce or calf liver pan-fried in Porto.

La Ferme VALAISIAN $$
(☑027 958 15 69; Obere Dorfstrasse 32; mains Sfr20-59) Dirndl-clad maidens bring traditional Valaisian specialities to the table at this barn-style restaurant, decked out with hops, cowbells and farming implements. Try tender lamb loin cooked in Alpine hay or fresh river trout.

La Gorge SWISS $$
(☑027 958 16 80; www.lagorge.ch; Blomattenweg 1; mains Sfr38) Head to the Gorge to feast on incredulous aerial views of glacial white water racing in the gorge far below; a second terrace stares at the Allalin glacier. Two stone knight-in-shining-armour turrets complete the unusual setting.

🍷 Drinking

TOP CHOICE **CofFee** CAFE
(www.coffeebar.ch; Obere Dorfstrasse 38) Sit in the late afternoon sun and slurp an ice-cold shake or smoothie at this chilled 'bar & smooth music' address halfway up the main drag. Chocoholics note, the rockslide brownies are heavenly (as are the aperitifs with tasty antipasti and cheese platters to graze on at sundown).

Popcorn! BAR
(www.popcorn.ch; Obere Dorfstrasse 47; ☺9pm-4am) A hip, long-standing favourite that never seems to lose its street-cred, this bar has a new location – and has been reshaped as a 'Popcorn deluxe' model in the process. Find it inside the five-star Ferienart hotel on the main street.

Black Bull Snow Bar BAR
(Dorfstrasse 17; ☺3.30pm-2am) Near the river, this wooden hut with bar stools to squat on outside (no inside seating) is high-energy people-watching terrain.

Nesti's Ski Bar BAR
(Dorfstrasse 53; ☺3.30pm-2am) Always packed, this busy bar beneath Hotel Christiania is a buzzy après-ski favourite. Nip in for a spiced glühwein or three.

ℹ Information

Tourist office (☑027 958 18 58; www.saas-fee.ch; Obere Dorfstrasse 2; ☺8.30am-noon & 2-6pm Mon-Fri, 8am-6pm Sat, 9am-noon & 3-6pm Sun, shorter hours low & mid-season) Opposite the post office and bus station.

ℹ Getting There & Away

Buses depart half-hourly from Brig (Sfr18.60, 1¼ hours) and Visp (Sfr16.20, 45 minutes). From Brig it's marginally faster to get the train and change at Visp. You can transfer to/from Zermatt at Stalden Saas.

Saas Fee is car-free; park at the village entrance (Sfr17/12.50 per day winter/summer) and walk or pay around Sfr23 for an **electric taxi** (☑079 220 21 37) to take you to your hotel.

Brig

POP 11,900 / ELEV 688M

Close to the Italian border and bisected by the Rhône and Saltina Rivers, Brig has been an important crossroads since Roman times. Though often overlooked en route to Mont Blanc or Milan, it's worth lingering to see the cobbled Stadtplatz, framed by alfresco cafes and candy-hued townhouses, as well as the fantastical baroque palace.

◉ Sights

Stockalperschloss CASTLE
(Alte Simplonstrasse 28; adult/child Sfr8/free; ☺hourly 50-min guided visit 9.30-4.30pm Jun-Sep, to 3.30pm May & Oct) Kaspar von Stockalper (1609–91), a shrewd businessman who dominated the Simplon Pass trade routes, built this whimsical palace and dubbed himself the 'Great Stockalper'. Locals didn't think he was so great and sent him packing to Italy. His palace remains with its baublelike onion domes and arcaded inner courtyard. Wander for free the main court and beautiful baroque gardens with quintessential parterres, fountains and clipped hedges.

⊨ Sleeping & Eating

Cafe terraces and restaurants abound on central square Hauptplatz and Alte Simplonstrasse, the pedestrian street leading from square to castle.

Hotel du Pont HOTEL **$$**
(☑027 923 15 02; www.hoteldupont.ch; Marktplatz 1; d Sfr150-180, mains Sfr26-30, menu Sfr55; ☺Feb-Dec) This traditional inn is pretty as a picture with its alpine melody of gushing river, wooden shutters painted aubergine and potted flowers. Dining is a tasty mix of meaty Valaisian and pasta-driven Italian.

Schlosshotel HOTEL **$**
(☑027 922 95 95; Am Schlosspark; www.schloss hotel.ch; s/d from Sfr80/138; P@🖙) Upmarket and so close to the palace you can almost polish the domes.

❶ Information

Tourist office (☑027 921 60 30; www.brig -tourismus.ch; Bahnhofplatz 1; ☺8.30am-noon & 1.30-6pm Mon-Fri)

Brig is on the Glacier Express line from Zermatt to St Moritz and the main line between Italy (Milan via Domodossola) and Geneva (Sfr58, 2½ hours).

Aletsch Glacier

Bidding Brig farewell, you enter another world. As you approach the source of the mighty Rhône and gain altitude, the deep valley narrows and the verdure of pine-clad mountainsides and south-facing vineyards that defines the west of the canton switches to rugged wilderness. Along the way is a string of bucolic villages of geranium-bedecked timber chalets and onion-domed churches, waiting to be counted off like rosary beads.

Out of view from the valley floor lies the longest and most voluminous glacier in the European Alps. The Aletsch Glacier (Aletschgletscher) is a seemingly never-ending, 23km-long swirl of deeply crevassed ice that slices past thundering falls, jagged spires of rock and pine forest. It stretches from Jungfrau in the Bernese Oberland to a plateau above the Rhône and is, justly so, a Unesco World Heritage Site.

FIESCH & EGGISHORN

Most people get their first tantalising glimpse of Aletsch Glacier from Jungfraujoch, but picture-postcard riverside Fiesch on the valley floor is the best place to access it. From the village ride the cable car (www .eggishorn.ch; adult/child return Sfr42.80/21.40) up to Fiescheralp – a hot spot for paragliding – and continue up to Eggishorn (2927m). Nothing can prepare you for what awaits on exiting the gondola.

Streaming down in a broad curve around the Aletschhorn (4195m), the glacier is just like a frozen six-lane superhighway. In the distance, to the north, rise the glistening summits of Jungfrau (4158m), Mönch (4107m), Eiger (3970m) and Finsteraarhorn (4274m). To the west of the cable-car exit, spy Mont Blanc and Matterhorn.

A humble stroll around the loose and rocky rise – barren bar the Horli-Hitta mountain hut where you can savour one of Switzerland's most amazing sights over a cherry-liqueur coffee and rösti (Sfr23 to Sfr27) – commands peerless views of the glacier and the frosted peaks that razor their way above it. Look across the vast glacial stream and note the distinct line,

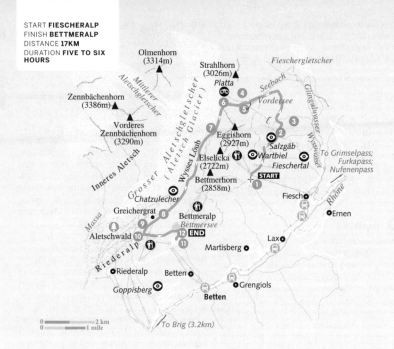

Olmenhorn (3314m)

Strahlhorn (3026m)

Platta

Fieschergletscher

Zennbächenhorn (3386m)

Mittlerer Aletschgletscher

Vordersee

Seebach

Vorderes Zennbächenhorn (3290m)

Grosser (Aletschgletscher
Aletsch Glacier)

Eggishorn (2927m)

Salzgäb

Wartbiel

Fieschertal

To Grimselpass; Furkapass; Nufenenpass

Inneres Aletsch

Elselicka (2722m)

Wysses Läub

Bettmerhorn (2858m)

START

Glinguwasser

Wyswasser

Fiesch

Rhone

Ernen

Chatzulecher

Grosser (

Greichergrat

Bettmeralp

Bettmersee

END

Massa

Aletschwald

Martisberg

Lax

Riederalp

Riederalp

Betten

Goppisberg

Betten

Grengiols

To Brig (3.2km)

0 ——— 2 km
0 ——— 1 mile

Walking Tour
Aletsch Glacier

〉 This high-Alpine walk is a nature-gone-wild spectacle of moors, jagged mountains and deeply crevassed glaciers. From ❶ **Fiescheralp cable-car station** (2212m), views are immediately spectacular as you walk northeast along the flat dirt trail. Bear right past the path going up to Eggishorn and the turn-off to Märjela via the small ❷ **Tälli tunnel** – to shorten the route by an hour walk through the tunnel (bring a torch).

The route soon becomes a broad well-graded foot track, lined with bilberry bushes and tantalising glimpses of Fieschergletscher's icy tongue. Wind your way around the slopes high above the Fieschertal, up through the grassy, rock-strewn gully of ❸ **Unners Tälli**. Begin a steeper climb in several switchbacks to a small wooden cross erected on a rock platform.

Follow white-red-white markings westward across rocky ledges to the tiny valley of the ❹ **Märjela**; a signpost marks the junction of trails coming from the Fieschertal and the Tälligrat. Around two hours from Fiescheralp, you reach the ❺ **Gletscherstube mountain**

hut (2363m), a cosy wooden hut where you can lunch or overnight.

Head down past several little tarns, crossing the stream at a cairn before making your way down to the ❻ **Märjelensee** (2300m) after 30 to 35 minutes. Bordered by the icy edge of the Aletsch Glacier, this lake presents a dramatic picture. Climb southward around a rocky ridge and sidle up to a signposted path fork at ❼ **Roti Chumma** (2369m). Take the lower right-hand way along a magnificent route high above what seems like an endless sweep of ice. After ❽ **Biel**, a saddle on the Greichergrat at 2292m where a path turns down right to the Aletschwald, head southwest along a tarn-speckled ridge. Continue along the grassy slopes to ❾ **Moosfluh** (2333m).

The route continues along the ridge on a short section of marked foot track (not on some walking maps), cutting down leftward to the inky blue ❿ **Blausee** (2204m). Duck under the chairlift and drop eastward to ⓫ **Bettmersee** for a refreshing dip. From here a dirt road leads to ⓬ **Bettmeralp**.

several metres higher than today's ice, where the shrinking glacier reached a century ago: in 1856 it covered 163 sq km, 128 sq km in 1973, and a disconcerting 117 sq km today. At its deepest point the ice is 900m thick.

For a substantially hairier experience, tackle Eggishorn's dizzying *Klettersteig (via ferrata)* with a mountain guide; Fiesch tourist office (☏027 970 60 70; www.fiesch .ch; Furkastrasse 44; ⏱8.30am-noon & 1.30-5pm Mon-Fri, plus 9am-4pm Sat high season) can hook you up.

BETTMERALP & RIEDERALP

This twinset of family-friendly car-free hamlets, accessible only by cable car, is the stuff of Swiss Alpine dreams. Paved with snow December to March, kids are pulled around on traditional wooden Davos sledges and skis are the best way to get to the local supermarket. With the run at the top of the Bettmerhorn cable car (2647m) skirting the edge of the Aletsch Glacier, skiing here is a sensationally picturesque and dramatic affair – 104km of intermediate or easy ski runs in all the so-called **Aletsch Arena** (www .aletscharena.ch) ski area, with a one-day ski pass costing Sfr53 (Sfr58 including cable car up from the valley).

Hiking in the summer is equally as mindblowing. From Bettmeralp (1950m) take the cable car to Bettmerhorn (adult/child return Sfr20/15) for a dramatic bird's-eye glacier view. Exit the station and follow the wooden walkway through cinematically oversized boulders to the so-called *Eis Terrasse* (Ice

DON'T MISS

ULTIMATE GLACIER VIEW

Let's get this straight: views of the Aletsch Glacier from Eggishorn (2927m) and Bettmerhorn (2647m) are mindblowing, thrilling, enthralling. But, if you've got the guts and head for heights, the ultimate panoramic platform is the 124m-long Aletschji-Grünsee suspension bridge across the terrifyingly untamed, 80m-deep Massa Gorge at the foot of the Aletsch Glacier. You need nerves of steel to cross it but glacial views are unparalleled. Pick up the trail, accessible June to October, behind the Mountain Resort Riederfurka hotel (count five hours for the complete trail from Belalp to Riederalp).

Terrace) where information panels tell you about the glacier and several marked footpaths start. Afterwards learn why glacial ice is blue, see what asexual glacial fleas do and stand on a treadmill to feel how fast glacial ice moves at Eiswelt (Ice World; admission free; ⏱9am-4pm Jun–mid-Oct & Dec-Apr), a fascinating exhibition inside the cable-car station exploring glacial research at Aletsch in the 19th century.

As much a summer-must in neighbouring Riederfurka (2065m), a chairlift ride or 20-minute walk uphill from Riederalp (1925m), are the exhibitions on local flora and fauna and Alpine garden at Pro Natura Zentrum Aletsch (www.pronatura.ch/aletsch; adult/child Sfr8/5; ⏱9am-6pm mid-Jun–mid-Oct) inside Villa Cassel, an exquisite, half-timbered villa built as a summer residence on the slopes for a rich Englishman in 1902. The tea room here serves delicious organic cakes and light meals and hosts some great alfresco events in summer – nature workshops and walks, the occasional cinema screening, brunch on the grass etc.

Bettmeralp tourist office (☏027 928 60 60; www.bettmeralp.ch), on the main street in the village, has information on guided walks on the glacier, as does its counterpart in Riederalp (☏027 928 60 50; www.riederalp.ch).

It's an easy 20-minute amble between trees from Bettmeralp to Riederalp; electric shuttle buses (summer) and snowmobiles (winter) also link the two.

🛏 Sleeping & Eating

TOP CHOICE Villa Cassel   HISTORIC HOTEL $$
(☏027 928 62 20; d with breakfast/half-board Sfr160/210, dm with breakfast/half-board Sfr50/70; ⏱mid-Jun–mid-Oct) Short but sweet is the season at this fabulous mountain-side villa, the stunning summer pad of wealthy Englishman Ernest Cassel who – so the story goes – had to pay local farmers to stuff the bells of their cows with hay after their incessant ringing upset one of his house guests – a young Winston Churchill no less. Rooms today are simple pine with shared bathrooms.

TOP CHOICE Mountain Resort
Riederfurka   MOUNTAIN HOTEL $
(☏027 929 21 31; www.artfurrer.ch; Riederfurka; dm incl breakfast Sfr60, d Sfr80) Planted firmly on the *alpages* (pasture) up high in Riederfurka, this oasis of peace, tranquillity and Alpine tradition has been around with the

PULVERISING COW PATS

The smart folk of Riederalp have put their own twist on a centuries-old tradition. In days of old, farmers leading cattle down from the high Alpine plains at the end of summer would smash up the dried dung (to prevent it smothering the grass beneath) and spread it out as fertiliser. Inspired by this rural (and very necessary) ritual, locals hold their very own Chüefladefäscht (cow pat festival) each year at the end of August. The aim of the game: to strike as many cow pats as possible with your choice of instrument, be it golf club, pitch fork or good old Wellington boot (aka cow-pat football). The fun part is the miniscule rolls of paper stuck in certain cow pats – pluck it out with your bare hands if you dare and discover what tombola-style prize you have won!

cows since the mid-19th century. Rooms are cosy, with lots of wood, and the restaurant – hearty mountain fare – is one of the best on the slopes.

Kik's Lodge   HOSTEL $

(☏079 311 37 15; www.kiks-lodge.ch; Bettmeralp; dm without/with breakfast Sfr40/55) This simple but cosy chalet happily sits next to Albi's Mountain Rock, Bettmeralp's best après-ski bar midway along its main street. The lodge operates as a hostel in July and August, but is usually rented out during the ski season.

La Cabane   CHALET $$

(☏027 927 47 27; www.lacabane.ch; d Sfr275-325; @ 🛜) Dreamy four-star chalet on main street Bettmeralp.

Chüestall   SWISS $$

(☏027 927 15 91; www.chuestall-blausee.ch; mains Sfr20-40; ⊙lunch Jun-Oct & Dec-Apr) 'Cowshed' is what its name means and that is exactly what this thoroughly modern address on the slopes at 2207m was until 1962. In summer look out for flyers advertising raclette evenings, Sunday brunches and the like Walk or

ski to it from the top of the Moosfluh cable car in Riederalp or Bettmeralp's Blausee (Blue Lake – yes, it's by a lake) chairlift.

ⓘ Getting There & Away

The base stations for these resorts – Mörel (for Riederalp), Betten (Bettmeralp) and Fiesch – are on the train route between Brig and Andermatt. Cable-car departures (Sfr9.20) are linked to train arrivals.

FIESCH TO THE FURKA PASS

The trail out of Valais weaves northeast from Fiesch, with more postcard-cute villages along the way, including Niederwald, where Cäsar Ritz (1850–1918), founder of the luxury hotel chain, was born and is now buried. Of them all Münster, with its babbling brook and tightly packed chalets dropping down the hill from its bright white church, is the most charming.

At Ulrichen you must make a decision. You can turn southeast down a narrow road that twists its way south out of the Valais and into the mountains that separate the canton from Ticino. Impressively barren country that at times recalls the stark beauty of the Scottish Highlands and Spanish Pyrenees leads you to the Nufenen Pass (Passo di Novena) at 2478m, probably the most remote gateway into Switzerland's Italian canton. Dropping down the other side, the first major town is Airolo, 24km east of the pass along the quiet, almost gloomy Val Bedretto.

Should you decide to push on east of Ulrichen, you will head slowly upwards towards Gletsch. From here the mighty Grimsel Pass, with its spectacular views west over several lakes in Bern Canton and eastern Valais, lies a short, steep drive north, but it is often closed, even in summer.

Marking the cantonal frontier with Uri is the vertiginous Furka Pass (2431m), the run up to which offers superlative views over the fissured Rhône glacier to the north. Open in summer only, it is the gateway into southeast Switzerland. Car trains in Oberwald negotiate the trip underground when the pass is shut. The train surfaces at Realp near Andermatt.

Ticino

POP 333,750 / AREA 2813 SQ KM / LANGUAGE ITALIAN

Best Places to Eat

» Ristorante Castelgrande (p192)

» Grotto Ca' Rossa (p208)

» Ecco (p206)

» Ristorante Santabbondio (p197)

» Osteria del Centenario (p205)

Best Places to Stay

» Hotel & Hostel Montarina (p196)

» Caffè dell'Arte (p203)

» Albergo Antica Posta (p206)

» Al Pentolino (p206)

» Hotel Internazionale (p192)

Why Go?

The summer air is rich and hot. Vespas scoot along palm-fringed promenades. A baroque campanile chimes. Kids play in piazzas flanked by pastel-coloured mansions. Italian weather. Italian style. And that's not to mention the Italian gelato, Italian pasta, Italian architecture, Italian language. But this isn't Rome, Florence or Naples. Ticino is the Switzerland that *Heidi* never mentioned.

The Alps are every bit as magnificent as elsewhere in Switzerland, but here you can admire them while sipping a full-bodied merlot at a pavement cafe, enjoying a hearty lunch at a chestnut-shaded *grotto* (rustic Ticino-style inn or restaurant), or floating in the mirror-like lakes of Lugano and Locarno. Ticino tempers its classic Alpine looks with Italian good-living.

To the north, the stunning medieval fortress town of Bellinzona keeps watch over valleys speckled with homely hamlets and Romanesque chapels. Rearing above them are wild, forested peaks with endless hiking options past lakes and roaring mountain streams.

When to Go

Get into the carnival swing with feasting, parading and merrymaking at the pre-Lenten Rabadan in Bellinzona. Spring brings hikers to the wildflower-cloaked Alps and classical music fans to the Lugano Festival. Lugano stages open-air concerts in July, while Locarno zooms in on cinematic talent at its much-lauded film festival in August. Vintners in Mendrisio and Bellinzona toast the wine harvest in September. On a golden autumn day, nothing beats slow-cooked game and new wine in one of Ticino's rustic *grotti*.

History

Ticino, long a poor, rural buffer between the Swiss-German cantons north of the Alps and Italy to the south, was absorbed by the Swiss in the late 15th century after centuries of changing hands between the lords of Como and the dukes of Milan.

The founding cantons of the Swiss Confederation – Uri, Scwhyz and Unterwalden – defeated a superior Milanese force at Giornico in the Valle Levantina in 1478 and took Bellinzona in 1503, thus securing the confederation's vulnerable underbelly. In 1803, Ticino entered the new Swiss Confederation,

Ticino Highlights

① Roam the trio of medieval castles in **Bellinzona** (p189) for spirit-soaring views of the Old Town and the Alps

② Be spellbound by lake and mountain views from **Monte Brè** and **Monte San Salvatore** (p199) above Lugano

③ Indulge in Alpine cheese, merlot wines and gorgeous scenery in **Mendrisio** (p201)

④ Live a heart-stopping moment bungee jumping, rafting, paragliding and bouldering in the rugged **Val Verzasca** (p209)

⑤ Hike and cycle to wispy waterfalls, granite villages

and authentic *grotti* in the **Valle Maggia** (p207)

⑥ Soak up the Mediterranean flair of **Locarno** (p201) in the postcard-pretty Old Town, lakefront gardens and lido

⑦ Catch the spectacular **Centovalli Railway** (p207) over hill and dale to Domodossola in Italy

concocted by Napoleon, as a free and equal canton.

With such a small percentage of the Swiss population, the canton counts for little in big national decisions. Wages are lower (as much as 25%) than in most of the rest of Switzerland and unemployment (at more than 4%) is above the national average (2.9%). Ticinesi are attracted by big brother Italy, but often suffer a sense of indifference, if not inferiority (not aided by the parading Prada brigade from Milan), next to their southern cousins.

Big news currently is the Gotthard Base Tunnel, the world's longest at 57km, set to open in 2017. When it does, the train time from Zurich to Milan will be cut by one-and-a-half hours.

❶ Information

The website www.ticino.ch gives the low-down on regional events, activities, itineraries, transport, accommodation and food. Numerous brochures can be downloaded online, as can a free iPhone app of Lugano.

Ask about the 31 mountain huts run by the **Federazione Alpinistica Ticinese** (www.fat-ti .ch, in Italian) along hiking trails. They and other huts (often unstaffed) are listed at www .capanneti.ch (in Italian and German).

Wine is a big part of the Ticino experience. Get *Le Strade del Vino* map-guide, which details wineries around the canton, or log onto www .ticinowine.ch (in Italian and German).

❶ Getting There & Around

Ticino's closest international airport is **Milan Malpensa** (www.airportmalpensa.com), 85km south of Lugano. The airport is served by airlines including British Airways, KLM, American Airlines and easyJet. Frequent airport buses make the run to Lugano (€23) and Bellinzona (€26).

The A2 motorway links Como in the south of the canton to the St Gotthard Tunnel in the north; the latter is notorious for traffic jams, so check www.gotthard-strassentunnel.ch before heading out. Helter-skelter pass roads link Ticino to the rest of Switzerland, including the San Bernardino Pass to Graubünden, the St Gotthard Pass to Central Switzerland and the Nufenenpass to Valais.

The canton is crisscrossed with well-marked cycling trails. Bikes can be hired from major train stations, including those in Airolo, Bellinzona, Locarno and Lugano. One-day bike hire costs Sfr50 for an e-bike and Sfr33 for a country/mountain bike. For details, see www .e-bike-park.ch (in German).

BELLINZONA

POP 17,300 / ELEV 230M

Placed at the convergence point of several Alpine valleys, Bellinzona is visually unique. Inhabited since Neolithic times, it is dominated by three grey-stone medieval castles that have attracted everyone from Swiss invaders to painters like William Turner. Turner may have liked the place, but Bellinzona keeps a surprisingly low profile, in spite of its castles forming one of only 11 Unesco World Heritage sites in Switzerland.

The main castle, Castelgrande, stands upon a rocky central hill, which was a Roman frontier post and Lombard defensive tower, and was later developed as a heavily fortified town controlled by Milan. The three castles and valley walls could not stop the Swiss-German confederate troops from overwhelming the city in 1503, thus deciding Ticino's fate for the following three centuries.

◉ Sights & Activities

The city's three imposing castles are the main draw. Read up on them at www .bellinzonaunesco.ch. To visit all three, get a general ticket (adult/concession Sfr10/4), valid indefinitely.

TOP CHOICE Castelgrande
CASTLE

(Monte San Michele; admission to grounds free; ⊗9am-midnight Tue-Sun, to 6pm Mon) Rising dramatically above the Old Town, this medieval stronghold is Bellinzona's most visible icon. Head up Scalinata San Michele from Piazza della Collegiata, or take the lift, buried deep in the rocky hill in an extraordinary concrete bunker-style construction, from Piazza del Sole.

The castle's **Museo Archeologico** (Archaeological Museum; adult/concession Sfr5/2; ⊗10am-6pm Mon-Sun) has a modest collection of finds from the hill dating to prehistoric times. More engaging is the display of 15th-century decorations taken from the ceiling of a former noble house in central Bellinzona. The pictures range from weird animals (late medieval ideas on what a camel looked like were curious) to a humorous series on the 'world upside down'. Examples of the latter include an ox driving a man-pulled plough and a sex-crazed woman chasing a chaste man!

After wandering the grounds and the museum, stroll west along the **Murata** (admission free; ⊗10am-7pm), the castle's snaking ramparts, with photogenic views of vine-streaked mountains and castle-studded hills.

Castello di Montebello　　　　　CASTLE
(Salita ai Castelli; admission to castle free, museum adult/child Sfr5/2; ☺castle 8am-8pm mid-Mar–Oct, museum 10am-6pm mid-Mar–Oct) On cloudless days, you can see Lago Maggiore from this 13th-century hilltop fortification. The fortress is one of Bellinzona's most impressive with its drawbridges, ramparts

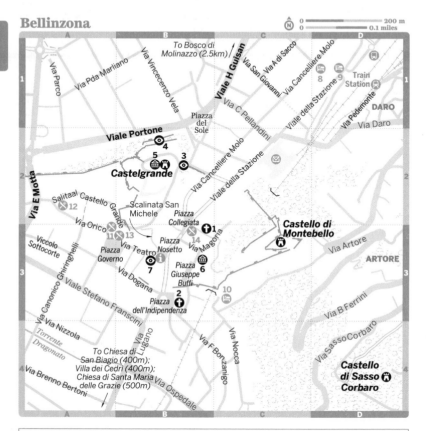

Bellinzona

⊙ Top Sights

⊙ Sights

⊜ Sleeping

⊗ Eating

and small museum catapulting you back to medieval times.

Castello di Sasso Corbaro CASTLE
(adult/child Sfr5/2; ⊘10am-6pm mid-Mar–Oct) From Castello di Montebello, it's a 3.5km climb to the last in Bellinzona's castle trilogy. Perched high on a wooded hillside, the castle is an austere beauty with its impenetrable walls and sturdy towers.

Villa dei Cedri GALLERY
(www.villacedri.ch, in Italian; Piazza San Biagio 9; adult/child Sfr8/5; ⊘2-6pm Tue-Fri, from 11am Sat & Sun) Housed in a handsome 19th-century villa, this gallery presents mostly local and northern Italian works of the 19th and 20th centuries. Just as appealing are the palm-studded gardens (admission free; ⊘7am-8pm Apr-Sep, to 6pm Oct-Mar).

Chiesa di Santa Maria delle Grazie CHURCH
(Via Convento; ⊘7am-6pm) This 15th-century church has an extraordinary fresco cycle (recently restored after being damaged by fire in 1996) of the life and death of Christ. The centrepiece is a panel depicting Christ's crucifixion.

Chiesa Collegiata dei SS Pietro e Stefano CHURCH
(Piazza Collegiata; ⊘8am-1pm & 4-6pm) Light streams through the rose window above the portal in this Renaissance church, lavishly adorned with frescos and baroque stucco. It sits on Piazza Collegiata, a cobblestone

TICINO BELLINZONA

WORTH A TRIP

TICINO'S NORTHERN VALLEYS

North of Bellinzona, two wild and remote valleys spread out at the foot of piebald peaks forming a natural barrier with Central Switzerland and Graubünden. With their grey-stone villages nestling in chestnut woods and centuries-old *grotti* (simple eateries housed in original stone buildings once used as storage), the Valle di Blenio and Valle Leventina are an authentic taste of Ticino mountain life.

Trains run twice hourly from Bellinzona to Biasca (Sfr7.80, 16 minutes), the gateway to the Valle di Blenio. Here the 13th-century Chiesa di SS Pietro e Paolo stands proud and *grotti* serve up hearty home cooking on the aptly named Via ai Grotti. From Biasca, the barren-looking valley extends north to majestic, brooding peaks and the Lukmanier Pass (Passo di Lucomagno). Footpaths thread through the entire valley and there is some modest skiing near the pass. If you're keen to hit the trail, a great base is Olivone at the base of dagger-shaped Sosto (2221m). Fine hikes take you up to shimmering Lago di Luzzone and the pristine Greina plateu. The website www.blenioturismo.ch (in Italian and German) has accommodation listings.

From Biasca, the freeway powers on northwest to Airolo in the Valle Leventina and then on to the mighty St Gotthard Pass. High above it is strung a series of mountain hamlets offering superlative views, great walking and the occasional fine feed. Shadowing the railway line, a walking route (www.gottardo-wanderweg.ch, in German and Italian) runs from the Reuss valley in Uri (starting at Erstfeld) down the Valle Leventina. At traditional Grotto Val d'Ambra (☑091 864 18 29; mains Sfr15-28; ⊘Tue-Sun Easter-Sep) in Personico, try *brasato* (braised beef) with home-produced wine in the chestnut-shaded garden. Giornico is worth a stop for its two Romanesque bridges, the finest example of a Romanesque church in Ticino (Chiesa di San Nicolao) and the picturesque old centre. At Rodi-Fiesso, the broad valley floor narrows to a claustrophobic gorge and, slightly beyond, you reach the sleepy valley town of Piotta. Here Europe's steepest funicular (return adult/child Sfr22/10; ⊘May-Oct) heads up above the Strada Alta to Lago Ritom, a high dam from where walkers can head into the mountains.

The 2114m St Gotthard Pass (Passo di San Gottardo) lies 7km north of Airolo. You can opt for the 17km tunnel or, when snow doesn't close it, the mountain road, which climbs in sweeping curves through the bald Alpine terrain. Hikers and mountain bikers love Ospizio San Gottardo (☑091 869 12 35; www.gotthard-hospiz.ch; s/d Sfr120/190), a 13th-century guesthouse recently given a contemporary makeover. The hourly train to Airolo from Bellinzona (Sfr22, 55 minutes) continues as far as Zürich and passes through the valley towns.

square framed by graceful 18th-century patrician houses, many with decorative wrought-iron balconies.

Palazzo del Comune
HISTORIC BUILDING

(Piazza Nosetto) Bellinzona's restored Renaissance town hall is worth a peek for its beautiful three-storey inner courtyard of loggias and frescos showing historic scenes of Bellinzona.

Chiesa di San Biagio
CHURCH

(Piazza San Biagio; ☉7am-noon & 2-5pm) This 14th-century church is one of Bellinzona's most evocative with its original frescos of the medieval Lombard-Siena school.

Museo in Erba
MUSEUM

(www.museoinerba.com; Piazza Giuseppe Buffi; admission Sfr5; ☉8.30-11.30am & 1.30-4.30pm Mon-Fri, 2-5pm Sat & Sun) This kid-focused museum stimulates an interest in art through games. Usually two exhibitions are put on each year.

Chiesa di San Rocco
CHURCH

(Piazza dell'Indipendenza; ☉7-11am & 2-5pm Mon-Sat) This ochre-hued church is noteworthy for its huge fresco of St Christopher and a smaller one of the Virgin Mary and Christ.

🎎 Festivals & Events

Rabadan
CARNIVAL

(www.rabadan.ch, in Italian) Costumed parades, street theatre, jangling jesters and marching bands infuse Bellinzona with carnival fever seven-and-a-half weeks before Easter Sunday.

La Bacchica
TRADITIONAL

(www.bacchica.ch, in Italian) A traditional vintners' festival in September, with wine-tasting, folk processions, plays and music aplenty.

🛏 Sleeping

Charming digs are few and far between. Many functional hotels are strung out along Viale della Stazione.

Hotel Internazionale
HOTEL $$

(☏091 825 43 33; www.hotel-internazionale.ch; Viale della Stazione 35; s Sfr135-150, d Sfr200-260, tr Sfr285-315; ❀❀) Sitting opposite the train station, this candyfloss-pink hotel seamlessly blends turn-of-the-20th-century features like wrought iron and stained glass with streamlined 21st-century design. Many of the light, contemporary rooms have castle views.

Ostello della Gioventù
HOSTEL $

(☏091 825 15 22; www.youthhostel.ch/bellinzona; Via Nocca 4; dm Sfr38-41, s Sfr63-73, d Sfr94-100; ❀) Housed in Villa Montebello, at the foot of the eponymous castle, the youth hostel occupies what for 100 years was a high-class girls' school.

Casa Jolanda
APARTMENT $$

(☏091 825 75 03; www.casajolanda.com; Via Visconti 1; apt Sfr120-200; ❀❀) There's plenty of room to spread out at these simple, spacious apartments opposite the station, with home comforts such as well-equipped kitchens, flat-screen TVs and DVD players.

Bosco di Molinazzo
CAMPGROUND $

(☏091 829 11 18; www.campingtcs.ch; Via San Gottardo 131; sites per adult/child/tent/car Sfr9/5/11/3; ❀) Situated 2.5km north of town, this leafy site is well equipped with a laundry, shop, playground and children's activities.

🍴 Eating

Fresh produce from Alpine cheeses to crusty bread and fruit is sold at the Saturday morning market on Piazza Nosetto.

TOP CHOICE Ristorante Castelgrande
ITALIAN $$

(☏091 814 87 87; www.ristorantecastelgrande.ch; Castelgrande; mains Sfr35-60; ☉lunch & dinner Tue-Sun) It's not often you get the chance to eat inside a Unesco World Heritage site. The medieval castle setting alone is enough to bewitch. Seasonal Ticino specialities like guinea fowl in a chestnut-beer sauce with white polenta are married with top-notch wines.

Locanda Orico
ITALIAN $$

(☏091 825 15 18; Via Orico 13; pasta Sfr30-40, mains Sfr45-62; ☉lunch & dinner Tue-Sat) Chef Lorenzo allows each flavour to shine with his imaginative, unfussy recipes at this Michelin-starred temple to good food. Creations such as pumpkin gnocchi in jugged chamois meat and glazed suckling pig with mustard-grain salsa are presented and served with finesse.

Grotto Castelgrande
ITALIAN $$

(☏091 814 87 87; Salita al Castelgrande; mains Sfr27-32; ☉lunch & dinner Tue-Sun) For the best view of Bellinzona's castles illuminated, book a table on the vine-strewn terrace of this atmospheric vaulted cellar. Dishes like potato gnocchi with Ticino sausage and wild fennel strike perfect balance.

Osteria Zoccolino
OSTERIA $
(Piazza Governo 5; mains Sfr14-20; ⊘lunch & dinner Mon-Sat) A photographer runs this arty osteria that fills at lunchtime, with crowds digging into salads, pasta and risotto.

Giardino Pizzeria
PIZZERIA $
(☑091 835 54 24; Via Orico 1; pizza Sfr12-26; ⊘lunch & dinner Tue-Mon) Giardino attracts a faithful local following for its pizza – thin, crisp and delicious.

Peverelli
CAFE $
(Piazza Collegiata; light meals & snacks Sfr6-16; ⊘lunch & dinner Mon-Sat) Facing the church on Piazza Collegiata, this is a lively spot for people-watching over an ice cream, sandwich or coffee and torte.

ⓘ Information
Bisi (Via Magoria 10; per hr Sfr5; ⊘10am-6m Mon-Fri) Intercultural library with internet access.

Post office (Viale della Stazione 18; ⊘7.30am-6.30pm Mon-Fri, 9am-noon Sat)

Tourist office (☑091 825 21 31; www.bellinzonaturismo.ch; Piazza Nosetto; ⊘9am-6.30pm Mon-Fri, to noon Sat) In the restored Renaissance Palazzo del Comune (town hall). Has city audioguides (Sfr7).

ⓘ Getting There & Away
Bellinzona is on the train route connecting Locarno (Sfr8.40, 27 minutes) and Lugano (Sfr12.20, 30 minutes). It is also on the Zürich–Milan route. Up to six postal buses head northeast to Chur (Sfr49, 2¼ hours), departing from beside the train station.

LUGANO
POP 55,100 / ELEV 270M

Ticino's lush, mountain-rimmed lake isn't its only liquid asset. The largest city in the canton is also the country's third most important banking centre. Suits aside, Lugano is a vivacious city, with chic boutiques, bars and pavement cafes huddling in the spaghetti maze of steep cobblestone streets that untangle at the edge of the lake and along the flowery promenade.

⊙ Sights
Take the stairs or the funicular (Sfr1.10, open 5.20am to 11.50pm) down to the centre, a patchwork of interlocking *piazze*. Porticoed lanes weave around the busy main square, Piazza della Riforma,

MARIO BOTTA IN THE PINK

Lugano's Mario Botta (born 1943 in nearby Mendrisio) has made a name for himself as a leading light in contemporary architecture and has left an indelible mark on and around Lugano. Botta seems to have a thing for right angles and the colour pink. In the centre of town, his landmarks include the **BSI** (Via San Franscini 12), a series of interconnected monoliths formerly known as the Banca del Gottardo; the pink brick office block at Via Pretorio 9 known to locals as the **Cherry Building** because of the cherry tree planted on the roof; and the roof of the TPL local bus terminus on Corso Pestalozzi. At night it is illuminated...in light pink.

which is presided over by the 1844 neoclassical Municipio (town hall) and even more lively when the Tuesday and Friday morning markets are held.

Chiesa di Santa Maria degli Angioli
CHURCH
(St Mary of the Angels; Piazza Luini; ⊘7am-6pm) This simple Romanesque church contains two frescos by Bernardino Luini dating from 1529. Covering the entire wall that divides the church in two is a grand didactic illustration of the crucifixion of Christ. The closer you look, the more scenes of Christ's Passion are revealed. The power and vivacity of the colours are astounding.

Museo d'Arte Moderna
GALLERY
(www.mdam.ch; Riva Antonio Caccia 5; adult/child Sfr12/free; ⊘10am-6pm Tue-Sun, to 9pm Fri) There's more cutting edge creativity at this contemporary art space, housed in Villa Malpensata. Recent exhibitions have zoomed in on the work of Man Ray and Italian comic-strip artist Hugo Pratt.

Museo del Cioccolato Alprose
MUSEUM
(www.alprose.ch; Via Rompada 36, Caslano; adult/child Sfr3/1; ⊘9am-5.30pm Mon-Fri, to 4.30pm Sat & Sun) Chomp into some cocoa culture at this choc-crazy museum – a sure-fire hit with kids. Whiz through chocolate history, watch the sugary substance being made and enjoy a free tasting. The shop, cunningly, stays open half an hour longer. Take the Ferrovia Ponte Tresa train (Sfr7).

TICINO LUGANO

Lugano

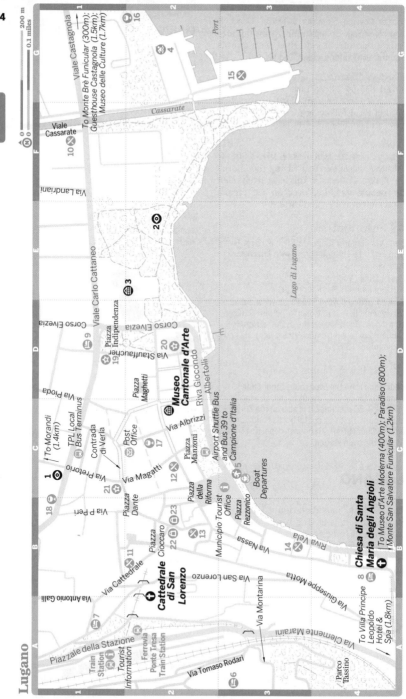

To Monte Brè Funicular (300m);
Guesthouse Castagnola (1.5km);
Museo delle Culture (1.7km)

Viale Castagnola

16

4

Port

15

Cassarate

Viale
Cassarate

10

Via Landriani

2

Lago di Lugano

3

Corso Elvezia

Viale Carlo Cattaneo

Corso Elvezia

Piazza
Indipendenza

20

Via Stauffacher

6

Via Pioda

Piazza
Maghetti

Museo
Cantonale d'Arte

Riva Giocondo
Albertolli

TPL Local
Bus Terminus

Post
Office

17

Via Albrizzi

To Morandi
(1.4km)

Contrada
di Verla

Via Magatti

Piazza
Manzoni

Airport Shuttle Bus
and Bus 39 to
Campione d'Italia

Via Pretorio

1

18

21

Via Peri

Piazza
Dante

12

Piazza
della
Riforma

Municipio Tourist
Office

5

Piazza
Rezzonico

Boat
Departures

To Museo d'Arte Moderna (400m); Paradiso (800m);
Monte San Salvatore Funicular (1.2km)

22

23

13

Piazza
Cioccaro

11

Via Cattedrale

Cattedrale
di San
Lorenzo

Via San Lorenzo

Piazza
Nassa

14

Riva Vela

Chiesa di Santa
Maria degli Angioli

8

Via Giuseppe Motta

Via Antonio Galli

7

Piazzale della Stazione

Train
Station

Tourist
Information

Ferrovia
Ponte Tresa
Train Station

Via Montarina

Via Clemente Maraini

To Villa Principe
Leopoldo
Hotel &
Spa (1.8km)

Parco
Tassino

Via Tomaso Rodari

6

200 m
0.1 miles

Lugano

Cattedrale di San Lorenzo   CATHEDRAL
(St Lawrence Cathedral; Via San Lorenzo; ⊙6.30am-6pm) Lugano's early 16th-century cathedral boasts a Renaissance facade and contains some fine frescos and ornate baroque statues. Out front there are far-reaching views over the Old Town's jumble of terracotta rooftops to the lake and mountains.

Museo delle Culture   ART MUSEUM
(www.mcl.lugano.ch; Via Cortivo 26; adult/child Sfr12/free; ⊙10am-6pm Tue-Sun) Neo-classical Villa Heleneum houses this ethnic art museum, about 1.7km from central Lugano. The brew of tribal relics from far-off countries includes a collection of masks and statues soaked in sexuality. The glorious Mediterranean **gardens** (admission free; ⊙6am-11pm) nurture lemon trees, camellias and wisteria. Take bus 1 from the train station.

Museo Cantonale d'Arte   GALLERY
(www.museo-cantonale-arte.ch; Via Canova 10; adult/child Sfr7/free, special exhibitions Sfr12/free; ⊙2-5pm Tue, from 10am Wed-Sun) This regional art gallery celebrates the work of modern artists (mostly 19th- and 20th-century masters) from the region.

Lungolago   GARDENS
This lakefront promenade necklaces the shore of glassy Lago di Lugano, set against a backdrop of rugged mountains. Linden and chestnut trees provide welcome shade in summer, while tulips, camellias and magnolias bloom in spring. The flower-strewn centrepiece is **Parco Civico** (⊙6am-11pm; admission free), where peach-hued **Villa Ciani** (⊙10am-6pm Tue-Sun) hosts regular art exhibitions.

🏃 Activities

Swimming, sailing, wakeboarding and rowing on the lake, as well as hiking in the surrounding mountains and valleys, are popular summer pursuits – the tourist office has details. Lugano makes a great base for exploring the region's 300km of mountain bike trails; see www.lugano-tourism.ch for route maps and GPS downloads.

You can hire pedalos (Sfr18 per hour) by the boat landing.

Lido   SWIMMING
(Viale Castagnola; per day Sfr10; ⊙9am-7pm May & Sep, to 7.30pm Jun-Aug) East of the Cassarate stream is the lido, with beaches and a swimming pool.

Società Navigazione del Lago di Lugano   BOAT TOUR
(Viale Castagnola 12; www.lakelugano.ch; ⊙Apr-late Oct) A relaxed way to see the lake's highlights is on one of these cruises, including one-hour bay tours (Sfr24.20) and three-hour morning cruises. Visit the website for timetables.

FREE Lugano Tours   GUIDED TOUR

Departing from the tourist office, Lugano's brilliant free guided tours include a spin of the city centre on Mondays (9.30am to noon), of the city's parks and gardens on Sundays (10am to noon) and, best of all, to the peak of Monte Brè on Fridays (2.20pm to 6.30pm) – even the funicular ride up there is free!

Festivals & Events

This classy town takes in some classical tunes during the Lugano Festival (www.luganofestival.ch) from April to May. Free open-air music festivals include Estival Jazz (www.estivaljazz.ch) for three days in early July and the Blues to Bop Festival (www.bluestobop.ch) in late August. The lake explodes in a display of pyrotechnical wizardry around midnight on 1 August, Switzerland's National Day.

Sleeping

Many hotels close for at least part of the winter.

TOP CHOICE Hotel & Hostel

Montarina   HOTEL, HOSTEL $

(☎091 966 72 72; www.montarina.ch; Via Montarina 1; dm Sfr27, s Sfr80-90, d Sfr110-130; P🅿🛜🏊♿) Occupying a bubblegum-pink villa dating to 1860, this hotel and hostel duo extends a heartfelt welcome. Mosaic floors, high ceil-

ings and wrought-iron balustrades are lingering traces of old-world grandeur. Choose between the dorms in the vaulted basement, wood-floored antique rooms and contemporary rooms with private bathrooms. There's a shared kitchen-lounge, toys to amuse the kids, a swimming pool set in palm-dotted gardens and even a tiny vineyard. Breakfast costs an extra Sfr12.

Villa Principe Leopoldo

Hotel & Spa   HISTORIC HOTEL $$$

(☎091 985 88 55; www.leopoldohotel.com; Via Montalbano 5; s Sfr510-670, d Sfr600-790; P🅿✳🛜🏊) This red-tiled residence set in sculptured gardens was built in 1926 for Prince Leopold von Hohenzollern, of the exiled German royal family. It oozes a regal, nostalgic atmosphere. The gardens and many of the splendid rooms offer lake views. Prices reach for the stars but so does the luxury – gourmet restaurants, tennis courts, a spa, heated pools, personal trainers, you name it.

Guesthouse Castagnola   GUESTHOUSE $

(☎078 632 67 47; www.gh-castagnola.com; Salita degli Olivi 2; apt Sfr80-200; P🅿🛜) Kristina and Mauro bend over backwards to please at their B&B, housed in a beautifully restored 16th-century townhouse. Exposed stone, natural fabrics and earthy colours dominate in apartments kitted out with Nespresso coffee machines and flat-screen TVs. A generous breakfast is served in the courtyard.

DON'T MISS

WHAT'S COOKING IN TICINO?

Switzerland meets Italy in Ticino's kitchen and some of your most satisfying eating experiences in Ticino will happen in *grotti* – rustic, out-of-the-way restaurants, with granite tables set up under the cool chestnut trees in summer. The trilingual *Guida a Grotti e Osterie* gives a great overview.

Alongside the Ticinese specialities below, perch, whitefish and *salmerino* (a cross between salmon and trout, only smaller) are popular around lakes Lugano and Maggiore. The region's bounty of new wine, chestnuts, game and mushrooms make autumn a tasty season to visit.

Polenta Creamy, savoury maize cornmeal dish

Brasato Beef braised in red wine

Capretto in umido alla Mesolcinese Tangy kid meat stew with a touch of cinnamon and cooked in red wine

Cazzöla A hearty meat casserole served with cabbage and potatoes

Mazza casalinga A mixed selection of delicatessen cuts

Cicitt Long, thin sausages made from goat's meat and often grilled

Robiola Soft and creamy cow's milk cheese that comes in small discs

The guesthouse is in Castagnola, 2km east of the centre; bus 1 stops close by.

Hotel International au Lac   HISTORIC HOTEL $$
(☎091 922 75 41; www.hotel-international.ch; Via Nassa 68; s Sfr120-185, d Sfr195-330; ☺Apr-Oct; P❄️🐾📶🏊) Choose a front room to gaze out across Lago di Lugano at this century-old hotel on the lakefront. Rooms are comfortable, with a smattering of antique furniture, and the garden-fringed pool invites relaxation. The restaurant (mains Sfr29 to Sfr39) serves wonderfully fresh fish.

SYHA Hostel   HOSTEL $
(☎091 966 27 28; www.luganoyouthhostel.ch; Via Cantonale 13, Savosa; dm/s/d Sfr42/73/106; 📶🏊♿) Housed in the Villa Savosa, this is one of the more enticing youth hostels in the country with bright well-kept dorms, a barbecue area, a swimming pool and lush gardens. Take bus 5 to Crocifisso.

Hotel Pestalozzi   HOTEL $$
(☎091 921 46 46; www.pestalozzi-lugano.ch; Piazza Independenza 9; s/d Sfr104/176, s/d without bathroom Sfr68/116; ❄️) A renovated art-nouveau building shelters this hotel, with rooms decorated in reds, blues and creams. Cheaper ones have a shared bathroom in the corridor.

Hotel Federale   HOTEL $$
(☎091 910 08 08; www.hotel-federale.ch; Via Paolo Regazzoni 8; s/d Sfr165/230; P📶) If you can afford the grand top floor doubles with lake views, this curiously shaped pink place beats many multi-stellar places hands down. It's in a quiet spot with immaculately kept rooms, a restaurant with alfresco seating and a little fitness room.

✖ Eating

For pizza or pasta, any of the places around Piazza della Riforma are lively enough.

Ristorante Santabbondio   ITALIAN $$$
(☎091 993 23 88; www.ristorante-santabbondio.ch; Via Fomelino 10, Sorengo; mains Sfr72-75, tasting menus Sfr84-158; ☺lunch & dinner Wed-Mon) Michelin-starred Santabbondio is Lugano's culinary star. Olive trees hint at chef Martin Dalsass' olive-oil obsession. Specialities like zucchini flowers with buffalo-milk ricotta and Breton red mullet with squid and pistachio sauce are exquisitely cooked and presented. Dine in the elegant beamed restaurant or on the chestnut-shaded terrace. It's a seven-minute

train ride from Lugano; take the S S60 to Sorengo Laghetto.

Al Portone   ITALIAN $$
(☎091 923 55 11; www.ristorantealportone.ch; Viale Cassarate 3; mains Sfr30-50; ☺lunch & dinner Tue-Sat) Bold artworks grace this contemporary gourmet haunt. Here Silvio and Sabrina ply you with such creative delights as John Dory with beetroot pannacotta, and butter-soft veal shanks infused with pepper and grappa. It has a three-course set lunch (Sfr58) and a tasting feast menu at night (Sfr120).

Grand Café Al Porto   CAFE $
(Via Pessina 3; light meals Sfr14-24, cakes Sfr4-6; ☺8am-6.30pm Mon-Sat) Going strong since 1803, this cafe is the vision of old-world grandeur with its polished wood panelling and pineapple-shaped chandeliers. The tortes, pastries and fruit cakes are irresistible. Upstairs is the frescoed Cenacolo Fiorentino, once a monastery refectory.

L'Antica Osteria del Porto   ITALIAN $$
(☎091 971 42 00; Via Foce 9; mains Sfr29-35; ☺lunch & dinner Wed-Mon) Set back from Lugano's sailing club, this is the place for local fish and Ticinese dishes like polenta crostini with porcini. The terrace overlooking the Cassarate stream is pleasant, as are the lake views.

Bottegone del Vino   ITALIAN $$
(☎091 922 76 89; Via Magatti 3; mains Sfr28-42; ☺lunch & dinner Mon-Sat) Favoured by the lunchtime banking brigade, this is a great place to taste fine local wines over a well-prepared meal. The menu changes daily and might include steamed turbot fillet or ravioli stuffed with fine Tuscan Chianina beef. Knowledgeable waiters fuss around the tables and are only too happy to suggest the perfect Ticino tipple.

Bottega dei Sapori   CAFE $
(Via Cattedrale 6; snacks & light meals Sfr6.50-18; ☺7.30am-7.30pm Mon-Wed, to 9pm Thu-Fri, 9am-7.30pm Sat) This high-ceilinged cafe-bar does great salads, panini (for instance air-dried beef, goat's cheese and rocket) and coffee. The pocket-sized terrace is always packed.

La Cucina di Alice   ITALIAN $
(☎091 922 01 03; Riva Vela 4; mains Sfr36-55; ☺lunch & dinner) Bird houses and cute ducks hang from the walls at this girly pretty restaurant, serving fresh fish and inventive concoctions such as green-tea pasta.

🍷 Drinking

Soho Café
LOUNGE

(Corso Pestalozzi 3; ⊙7am-8pm Mon, to 1am Tue-Fri, 7pm-1am Sat) All those good-looking Lugano townies crowd in to this long, orange-lit bar for cocktails. Chilled DJ music creates a pleasant buzz.

Café Time
BAR

(Via Canova 9; ⊙8am-1am Mon-Sat) Buried inside an unlikely shopping arcade, this bar attracts the local movers and shakers. Relax against the high-backed burgundy leather benches over a fine wine or cocktail with tasty bar snacks.

Al Lido
LOUNGE

(Viale Castagnola 6; ⊙6pm-1am Thu-Sat Jun-Sep) Partygoers flock to this cool summertime beach lounge for DJ beats, drinks and flirting by the lakefront.

☆ Entertainment

NYX Club & Lounge
LOUNGE, CLUB

(www.nyxlugano.ch; Via Staffaucher 1; ⊙lounge 5pm-1am Tue-Sat, club 11.30pm-4am Thu-Sat) This hipper-than-thou lounge and club on the casino's second floor attracts a young, fashion-conscious crowd. Its lake views, DJs, creative cocktails and finger food have made it Lugano's latest party pen.

Privilege
CLUB

(www.privilegelugano.ch; Piazza Dante 8; ⊙11pm-5am Fri & Sat) Downstairs from street level, this central club attracts a pretty mixed crowd with go-go girls and guys, and the occasional spurt of live music.

New Orleans Club
CLUB

(www.neworleansclublugano.com; Piazza Indipendenza 1; ⊙5pm-1am Mon-Sat) This is another lively spot with Latin, hip-hop and disco nights.

🛍 Shopping

Pedestrian-friendly Via Nassa is a catwalk for designers like Bulgari, Louis Vuitton and Versace. Its graceful arcades also harbour jewellery stores, cafes and galleries. For one-off gifts, explore steep, curving Via Cattedrale, where boutiques and galleries sell antiques, vintage clothing, crafts and handcrafted jewellery.

Gabbani
FOOD & DRINK

(www.gabbani.com; Via Pessina 12) Look for the giant sausages hanging in front of this irresistible delicatessen. The same people operate a tempting cheese shop, the **Bottega del Formaggio**, across the road at No 13.

ℹ Information

There are several free wi-fi hotspots dotted across town, including central Piazza Manzoni. ATMs are widely available.

Hospital (☎091 811 61 11; Via Tesserete 46) Hospital north of the city centre.

Main post office (Via Della Posta 7; ⊙7.30am-6.15pm Mon-Fri, 8am-4pm Sat) In the centre of the Old Town.

Tourist office (www.lugano-tourism.ch) Municipio (☎091 913 32 32; Riva Giocondo Albertolli; ⊙9am-7pm Mon-Fri, 9am-6pm Sat, 10am-6pm Sun); Train Station (⊙2-7pm Mon-Fri, 11am-7pm Sat) Reduced hours November through March.

ℹ Getting There & Away

Air

Lugano airport (☎091 610 11 11; www.lugano-airport.ch) is served by a handful of Swiss-Italian carriers including **Darwin Airline** (www.darwinairline.com) and **Swiss** (www.swiss.com).

Bus

To St Moritz, postal buses runs direct via Italy (Sfr69, four hours, daily late June to mid-October and late December to early January). All postal buses leave from the main bus depot at Via Serafino Balestra, but you can pick up the St Moritz and some other buses outside the train station 15 minutes later.

Car & Motorcycle

You can hire cars at **Hertz** (☎091 923 46 75; Via San Gottardo 13) and **Avis** (☎091 913 41 51; Via Clemente Maraini 14).

ℹ LUGANO REGIONAL PASS

The money-saving Lugano Regional Pass (Sfr94 for three days or Sfr111 for seven days) covers travel on Lago di Lugano and regional public transport (including the funiculars up Monte Brè and Monte San Salvatore). It also gives half-price transport to and around Locarno and Lago Maggiore. The pass is available at train stations, tourist offices and some hotels.

WORTH A TRIP

LAKE ESCAPES

For a bird's-eye view of Lugano and the lake, head for the hills. The **funicular** (www
.montebre.ch; one-way/return Sfr15/23) from Cassarate (walk or take bus 1 from central
Lugano) scales Monte Brè (925m) from March to December. From Cassarate a first
funicular takes you to Suvigliana to connect with the main funicular. Or take bus 12 from
the main post office to Brè village and walk about 15 minutes.

From Paradiso, the **funicular** (www.montesansalvatore.ch; one-way/return Sfr21/28) to
Monte San Salvatore operates from mid-March to mid-November. Aside from the views,
the walk down to Paradiso or Melide is an hour well spent.

A lovely place to stay is the **Locanda del Giglio** (☑091 930 09 33; www.locandadel
giglio.ch; dm/d Sfr55/160) in Roveredo, Capriasca, 12km north of Lugano. It is a warm
timber building powered by solar energy. Rooms have balconies offering mountain views
and even lake glimpses. Take a bus from Lugano to Tesserete (30 minutes) and change
there for another to Roveredo (about 10 minutes).

❶ Getting Around

A shuttle bus runs to the airport from Piazza Manzoni (one-way/return Sfr10/18) and the train station (one-way/return Sfr8/15). See timetables on www.shuttle-bus.com. A **taxi** (☑091 605 25 10) to the airport costs around Sfr30.

Bus 1 runs from Castagnola in the east through the centre to Paradiso, while bus 2 runs from central Lugano to Paradiso via the train station. A single trip costs Sfr1.60 to Sfr2 (ticket dispensers at stops indicate the appropriate rate) or it's Sfr5 for a one-day pass. The main local bus terminus is on Corso Pestalozzi.

LAGO DI LUGANO

Much can be seen in one day if you don't fancy a longer excursion. Boats are operated by the **Società Navigazione del Lago di Lugano** (www.lakelugano.ch). Examples of return fares from Lugano are Melide (Sfr24.20), Morcote (Sfr33) and Ponte Tresa (Sfr40.60). If you want to visit several places, buy a pass: one, three or seven days cost Sfr40, Sfr60 or Sfr71 respectively. There are reduced fares for children.

The departure point from Lugano is by Piazza della Riforma. Boats sail year-round, but the service is more frequent from late March to late October. During this time some boats go as far as Ponte Tresa, so you could go one-way by boat and return to Lugano on the Ponte Tresa train.

Gandria

Gandria is an attractive, compact village almost dipping into the water. A popular trip is to take the boat from Lugano and walk back along the shore to Castagnola (around 40 minutes), where you can visit Villa Heleneum and Villa Favorita, or simply continue back to Lugano by foot or bus 1.

Across the lake from Gandria is the **Museo delle Dogane Svizzere** (Swiss Customs Museum; admission free; ⏰1.30-5.30pm late Mar-early Oct), accessible by boat. It tells the history of customs (and more interestingly smuggling) in this border area. On display are confiscated smugglers' boats that once operated on the lake.

Campione d'Italia

It's hard to tell, but this really is a part of Italy surrounded by Switzerland. There are no border formalities (but take your passport anyway), many cars in the village have Swiss number plates, and they use Swiss telephones and Swiss francs. Euros (and any other hard currency), however, are equally welcome in Campione d'Italia.

The 12-storey **casino** (www.casinocampione it; admission free; ⏰10.30am-5am Sun-Thu, to 6am Fri & Sat), converted by Lugano's favourite architect, Mario Botta, into Europe's biggest in 2005, does a brisk business. Smart dress is required. From noon to midnight you can take bus 39 from Lugano's Piazza Manzoni (one-way/return Sfr6.80/13.60) to Campione d'Italia.

Monte Generoso

From this summit (1701m) you can survey lakes, Alps and the Apennines on a clear day. Monte Generoso can be reached by boat (except in winter). You can also drive

Lago Di Lugano

to Capolago, then take the rack and pinion **train** (www.montegeneroso.ch; return adult/child Sfr39/19.50; ☺Apr-Oct & early Dec-early Jan).

Ceresio Peninsula

South of Lugano, this peninsula is created by the looping shoreline of Lago di Lugano. Walking trails dissect the interior and small villages dot the lakeside. The postal bus from Lugano to Morcote goes via either Melide or Figino, and departs approximately hourly. Year-round boats also connect Morcote and Melide to Lugano.

MONTAGNOLA

German novelist Hermann Hesse (1877-1962) chose to live in this small town in 1919 after the horrors of WWI had separated him from his family. As crisis followed crisis in Germany, topped by the rise of the Nazis, he saw little reason to return home. He wrote

some of his greatest works here, at first in an apartment in Casa Camuzzi. Nearby, in Torre Camuzzi, is the **Museo Hermann Hesse** (www.hessemontagnola.ch; Torre Camuzzi; adult/reduced Sfr7.50/6; ☺10am-6.30pm Mon-Sun Mar-Oct, to 5.30pm Sat & Sun Nov-Feb). Personal objects, some of the thousands of watercolours he painted in Ticino, books and other odds and ends help re-create something of Hesse's life. From Lugano, get the Ferrovia Ponte Tresa train to Sorengo and change for a postal bus (Sfr3.40, 18 minutes).

MELIDE

Melide is a bulge of shore from which the A2 freeway slices across the lake. The main attraction is **Swissminiatur** (www.swiss miniatur.ch; Via Cantonale; adult/child Sfr19/12; ☺9am-6pm mid-Mar–Oct), where you'll find 1:25 scale models of more than 120 national attractions. It's the quick way to see Switzerland in a day.

Trains run to Lugano (Sfr3.40, six minutes).

MORCOTE

With its narrow cobbled lanes and endless nooks and crannies, this peaceful former fishing village (population 746) clusters at the foot of Monte Abostora. Narrow steps lead 15 minutes uphill to **Chiesa di Santa Maria del Sasso**, peeking above slender cypress trees and commanding dazzling lake views. The church is embellished with 16th-century frescos. From there continue another 15 minutes to the high-altitude hamlet of **Vico di Morcote**. About 5km further is Carona, worth a visit for the **Parco Botanico San Grato** (admission free), hilltop botanical gardens with sensational lake and mountain views.

Set in subtropical parkland, **Parco Scherrer** (adult/child Sfr7/2; ☺10am-5pm mid-Mar–Oct, to 6pm Jul-Aug), 400m west of the boat stop, offers a bustling range of architectural styles, including copies of famous buildings and generic types (eg Temple of Nefertiti, Siamese teahouse).

There are several lakeside sleeping options. **Albergo della Posta** (☎091 996 11 27; www.hotelmorcote.com, in Italian & German; Piazza Grande; s Sfr95-135, d Sfr120-160), open March through November, has charming little rooms with wooden floors; most also have views across the lake. It has its own restaurant.

The walk along the shore to Melide takes around 50 minutes.

Mendrisio & Around

POP 11,600 / ELEV 354M

Sidling up to Italy, this southern corner of Ticino – easily explored by bicycle – is sprinkled with vineyards and quaint villages crowned by Italianate baroque churches. Mendrisio is the district capital and has a useful tourist office (☑091 641 30 50; www.mendrisiotourism.ch; Via Lavizzari 2; ☺9am-noon & 2-6pm Mon-Fri, 9am-noon Sat), near the central Piazza alla Valle. The town springs to life for the Maundy Thursday Procession and the Wine Harvest in September, where you can sample the region's best merlots.

Housed in a restored 17th-century palazzo, Atenaeo del Vino (☑091 630 06 36; www.atenaeodelvino.ch; Via Pontico Virunio 1; mains Sfr36-42; ☺lunch & dinner Tue-Sat) matches seasonal fare (think asparagus, mushrooms, seafood, game) with top regional wines drawn from its cavernous cellar. The ambience is relaxed and homely.

Trains run to Mendrisio from Lugano (Sfr7.20, 20 minutes).

Exiting southeast from Mendrisio, a side road leads about 15km uphill and north along the Valle di Muggio. The valley is famous for its *Zincarlin,* a pungent soft cheese made from raw cow or goat's milk, which is rolled by hand and aged with salt and white wine. This pretty drive ends abruptly in the hamlet of Roncapiano, where a 2½-hour hike to Monte Generoso begins.

Meride

POP 330 / ELEV 583M

The Museo dei Fossili (www.montesangiorgio.ch; admission free; ☺8am-6pm) in Meride, northwest of Mendrisio, displays vestiges of the first creatures to inhabit the region – reptiles and fish dating back more than 200 million years. It may sound dry but the finds are important enough to warrant Unesco recognition of the area around Monte San Giorgio (where they were uncovered) as a World Heritage Site.

Near the town is a circular nature trail. Postal buses run frequently between Meride and Mendrisio (Sfr4.20, 25 minutes), with onward train connections to Lugano.

LAGO MAGGIORE

Only the northeast corner of Lago Maggiore is in Switzerland; the rest slices into Italy's Lombardy region. Navigazione Lago Maggiore (www.navigazionelaghi.it) operates boats across the entire lake. Limited day passes cost Sfr17.40, but the Sfr28 version is valid for the entire Swiss basin. There are various options for visiting the Italian side.

Locarno

POP 15,200 / ELEV 205M

With its palm trees and much-vaunted 2300 hours of sunshine a year, Locarno has attracted pasty northerners to its warm, Mediterranean-style setting since the late 19th century. The lowest town in Switzerland, it seemed like a soothing spot to host the 1925 peace conference intended to bring stability to Europe after WWI. Long before, the Romans appreciated its strategic position on the lake and Maggia river.

◎ Sights

Città Vecchia   NEIGHBOURHOOD

Locarno's Italianate Old Town fans out from Piazza Grande, a photogenic ensemble of arcades and Lombard-style houses. A craft and fresh produce market takes over the square every Thursday. From here, narrow lanes thread north to the baroque-gone-mad Chiesa Nuova (Via Cittadella), guarded by a giant bas-relief St Christopher and with cherubs and stucco smothering its pastel-painted interior. Standing proud on fountain-dotted Piazza Sant'Antonio, the Chiesa di Sant'Antonio is best known for its altar to the *Cristo Morto* (Dead Christ).

Castello Visconteo   CASTLE

(Piazza Castello; adult/child Sfr7/5; ☺10am-noon & 2-5pm Tue-Fri, 10am-5pm Sat & Sun Apr–mid-Nov)

ℹ️ LAGO MAGGIORE CARD

Save with the Lago Maggiore Card (Sfr66 for adults, Sfr33 for children), which includes a return cable-car ride from Orselina to Cimetta, entry to the lido, a day ticket for boat trips on the Swiss side of Lago Maggiore and entry to the botanical gardens on Isole di Brissago. It's available at tourist offices in Locarno and Ascona from April to mid-October.

Named after the Visconti clan that long ruled Milan, this stout 15th-century castle's nucleus was raised around the 10th century. It now houses a museum with Roman and Bronze Age exhibits and also hosts a small display (in Italian) on the Locarno Treaty.

Santuario della Madonna del Sasso
RELIGIOUS

Overlooking the town, this sanctuary was built after the Virgin Mary supposedly appeared in a vision to a monk, Bartolomeo d'Ivrea, in 1480. There's a highly adorned

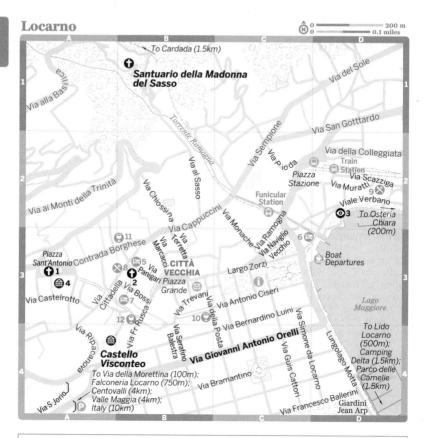

Locarno

church (⊙8am-6.45pm) and several rather rough, near-life-size statue groups (including one of the Last Supper) in niches on the stairway. The best-known painting in the church is *La Fuga in Egitto* (Flight to Egypt), painted in 1522 by Bramantino.

A **funicular** (one-way/return Sfr4.50/6.60) runs every 15 to 30 minutes from the town centre past the sanctuary to Orselina, but the 20-minute walk up a chapel-lined path known as the Via Crucis is fairly easygoing (take Via al Sasso off Via Cappuccini).

FREE **Giardini Pubblici** GARDENS
(Lungolago Motta) Locarno's climate is perfect for lolling about the lake. Bristling with palms and banana trees, these botanical gardens are a scenic spot for a picnic or swim, and tots can let off steam in the adventure playground.

Pinacoteca Casa Rusca GALLERY
(Piazza Sant'Antonio; adult/child Sfr8/5; ⊙10am-noon & 2-5pm Tue-Sun) This gallery occupies a beautifully restored 18th-century townhouse, Casa Rusca. Recent exhibitions include one dedicated to the voluptuous figurative art of Fernando Botero.

Falconeria Locarno WILDLIFE RESERVE
(www.falconeria.ch; Via delle Scuole 12; adult/child Sfr20/15; ⊙10am-noon & 2-4.30pm Tue-Sun mid-Mar–Oct) Kids will love the displays of falconry here.

FREE **Parco delle Camelie** GARDENS
(Via Respini; ⊙9am-5pm) Wander among fragrant camellia blooms and ponds at these pretty lakefront gardens.

🏃 Activities

The lakefront is made for aimless ambles, or rent an e-bike (Sfr29 per day) from the tourist office to explore further.

From the Orselina funicular stop, a cable car rises to 1332m **Cardada** (⊙8am-8pm daily Jun-Aug, to 6pm or 7pm Mon-Fri Sep-May), and then a chair lift soars to **Cimetta** (www.cardada.ch; return adult/child Sfr25/9, incl ski lift Sfr36/22; ⊙9.15am-12.30pm & 1.30-4.50pm Mon-Sun Mar-Nov) at 1672m. From either stop there are fine views and walking trails. Paragliding is possible at Cimetta, as is skiing in winter.

🏊 **Lido Locarno** SWIMMING
(www.lidolocarno.ch, in Italian; Via Respini 11; adult/child Sfr12/6.50, incl waterslides Sfr17/10.50; ⊙8.30am-9pm) Locarno's shiny new lido has several pools, including an Olympic-sized one, children's splash areas and waterslides, and fabulous lake and mountain views. The huge complex uses solar and hydropower.

✨ Festivals & Events

Christmas markets twinkle in December and Locarno goes carnival crazy in March.

Moon and Stars MUSIC
(www.moonandstarslocarno.ch) The stars shine at this open-air music festival in July. Big names like Sting, Santana, Jack Johnson and Joe Cocker graced the stage in 2011.

Festival Internazionale di Film FILM
(☎091 756 21 21; www.pardo.ch) Locarno has hosted this two-week film festival in August since 1948. At night, films are screened on a giant screen in Piazza Grande.

🛏 Sleeping

During the film festival in August, room prices soar by 50% to 100%.

TOP CHOICE **Caffè dell'Arte** B&B $$
(☎091 751 93 33; www.caffedellarte.ch; Via Cittadella 9; d Sfr149-189; 🛜) Sublime details like gilded Venetian mirrors, chandeliers, frescos and zebra-stripe fabrics lend character to the wood-floored rooms at this B&B. Nespresso machines offer home-style comfort, and breakfast is a work of edible art. Downstairs is a gallery-cafe, serving excellent coffee and focaccia (Sfr10), and a small boutique.

Vecchia Locarno GUESTHOUSE $
(☎091 751 65 02; www.vecchia-locarno.ch; Via della Motta 10; s Sfr55-90, d Sfr100-140; @🛜) A sunny inner courtyard forms the centrepiece of this laid-back guesthouse. Rooms are bright and simple, the best with views over the Old Town and hills. Breakfast (Sfr5) is served at the vegetarian Indian restaurant next door. Rates drop by 50% on the third night.

Hotel Garni Millenium B&B $$
(☎091 759 67 67; www.millennium-hotel.ch; Via Dogana Nuova 2; s Sfr160-200; d Sfr190-200; ✳🛜) Housed in the 19th-century old customs house, this baby-blue B&B has friendly service, dreamy lake views and jazz-themed rooms.

Camping Delta CAMPGROUND $
(☎091 751 60 81; www.campingdelta.com; Via Respini 7; campsites Sfr47-57, plus per adult/

Walking Tour
Cima della Trosa

❯ This high-level route traverses the rounded mountaintops, affording eagle's-eye perspectives of Lago Maggiore and Alpine peaks, and passing centuries-old hamlets and villages only accessible on foot. The most detailed map is Orell Füssli's 1:25,000 *Locarno/Ascona* (Sfr30).

From the upper cable-car station at ❶ **Cardada**, head right, climbing around the open slopes to reach the rustic stone hut of ❷ **Capanna Lo Stallone** in the grassy hollow of Alpe Cardada (1486m), after 30 to 40 minutes. The track cuts back left over the bracken-covered mountainsides, then swings right to skirt the forest and arrive at 1671m ❸ **Capanna Cimetta**.

Below the upper chairlift station, the left-hand path descends quickly to a saddle (1610m) with a springwater fountain. Make a rising traverse of the southwestern slopes of ❹ **Cima della Trosa**. A short side trail brings you to the cross mounted on the windswept 1869m summit after a further 35 to 45 minutes.

The path soon winds down Cima della Trosa's northeastern flank to a minor col (1657m). From here a side trip to the often-snow-dusted peak of ❺ **Madone** (2039m) takes 1½ to two hours; the straightforward route follows the ridge, with some harmless rock-scrambling higher up and arresting views.

Descend in broad zigzags to ❻ **Alpe di Bietri** (1499m), stopping for creamy goat's cheese made at the dairy, then continuing on an old mule trail tracing the northern slopes of Valle di Mergoscia. The route descends gently past dilapidated houses and rustic hamlets to reach ❼ **Bresciadiga** (1128m), 1¼ to 1¾ hours from Cima della Trosa.

Bear right at a junction, leading past small shrines before coming into a car park. Stroll 600m downhill to intersect with the main road, then follow the sealed road left up steep, vine-clad hillsides to arrive at the square beside the large baroque church of postcard-pretty ❽ **Mergoscia**, sitting high above the Val Verzasca, after a final one to 1¼ hours. From Mergoscia, buses run every two hours back to Locarno (Sfr7.20, 36 minutes).

child Sfr20/6) Although pricey, this camping ground has great facilities and is brilliantly located between the shores of Lago Maggiore and the Maggia river. Open March through October.

✖ Eating

Osteria del Centenario   OSTERIA $$$
(☑091 743 82 22; Viale Verbano 17; mains Sfr41-62; ☺lunch & dinner Mon-Sat) Down by the lake, this is a top culinary address, turning out such clever dishes as suckling pig in peanut-curry crust and passionfruit crème brûlée with rose ice cream. Service is attentive and the ambience discreetly elegant.

Cittadella   SEAFOOD $$
(☑091 751 58 85; Via Cittadella 18; mains Sfr25-44; ☺lunch & dinner Tue-Sun) Fish is as fresh as it comes at this popular trattoria, whether you go for whole sea bass or spaghetti with clams. Choose between the beamed dining room and the vine-clad terrace.

Osteria Chiara   OSTERIA $$
(☑091 743 32 96; Vicolo della Chiara 1; mains Sfr19-42; ☺lunch & dinner Tue-Sat) Tucked away on a cobbled lane, this has all the cosy feel of a *grotto*. Sit at granite tables beneath the pergola or at timber tables by the fireplace for homemade ravioli and hearty meat dishes like veal with porcini mushrooms. From the lake follow the signs up Vicolo dei Nessi.

☕ Drinking

Barca Locarno   LOUNGE
(www.barcalocarno.ch, in Italian; Via Borghese 14; ☺5pm-1am Mon-Sun) For atmosphere, you can't beat this slinky lounge bar, with white sofas gathered around the cobblestone, vine-draped courtyard of a 15th-century palazzo. Hosts occasional live music.

Pardo Bar   PUB
(www.pardobar.com; Via della Motta 3; ☺4pm-1am Mon-Sun; 🛜) Ticinese beers, pub grub (snacks Sfr5 to Sfr9.50), free wi-fi and a people-watching terrace.

Bar Sport   BAR
(Via della Posta 4; ☺8am-1am Mon-Fri, 10am-1am Sat, 2pm-1am Sun) A laid-back bar with a popular beer garden and a red-walled dance space.

❶ Information

The **tourist office** (☑091 791 00 91; www.ascona-locarno.com; Largo Zorzi 1; ☺9am-6pm Mon-Fri, 10am-6pm Sat, 10am-1.30pm & 2.30-5pm Sun) is nearby. Ask about the Lago Maggiore Guest Card and its discounts. It has shorter hours between November and mid-March.

❶ Getting There & Away

Trains run every one to two hours from Brig (Sfr52, 2¾ to 3¾ hours), passing through Italy (bring your passport). Change trains at Domodossola. There are also runs to and from Lucerne (Sfr54, 2¾ to three hours). Most trains to Zürich (Sfr58, 2¾ to three hours) go via Bellinzona.

Postal buses to the surrounding valleys leave from outside the train station, and boats from near Piazza Grande. There is cheap street parking (Sfr3 for 10 hours) along Via della Morettina.

Ascona

POP 5,500 / ELEV 196M

If ever there was a prize for the 'most perfect lake town', Ascona would surely win hands-down. Palm trees and pristine houses in a fresco painter's palette of pastels line the promenade, overlooking the glassy waters of Lago Maggiore to the rugged green mountains beyond. Michelin-starred restaurants, an 18-hole golf course and the Old Town's boutiques, galleries and antique shops attract a good-living, big-spending crowd.

◉ Sights & Activities

Museo Comunale d'Arte Moderna   GALLERY
(www.museoascona.ch, in Italian; Via Borgo 34; adult/child Sfr10/7; ☺10am-noon & 3-6pm Tue-Sat, 10.30-12.30pm Sun Mar-Dec) Housed in 16th-century Palazzo Pancaldi, this museum showcases paintings by artists connected to the town, among them Paul Klee, Ben Nicholson, Alexej Jawlensky and Hans Arp.

Isole di Brissago   ISLAND
(www.isolebrissago.ch, in Italian; Via Borgo 34; adult/child Sfr8/2.50; ☺9am-6pm Apr-late Oct) Boats glide across Lago Maggiore to this speck of an island, famous for its botanical gardens designed in the 19th century. Magnolias, orchids, yuccas and agaves are among the 1700 species that flourish here.

Lido Ascona   SWIMMING
(Via Lido 81; adult/child Sfr4/3; ☺8.30am-5.30pm Mon-Sun Jun–mid-Sep) If you fancy a swim in the lake, head to this lido with a beach, diving platform, volleyball court and slides for the kids.

AscoNautica WATER SPORTS
(☑091 791 51 85; www.asconautica.ch; Via Cappelle) This reputable outfit arranges water sports including sailing, waterskiing and wakeboarding. See the website for prices.

✦ Festivals & Events

Top-drawer jazz acts perform at the ten-day JazzAscona (www.jazzascona.ch) from late June to early July. Settimane Musicali (www.settimane-musicali.ch), an international classical music festival, runs from late August to mid-October.

🛏 Sleeping & Eating

Ascona brims with hotels and eateries, especially along the lakefront.

Albergo Antica Posta GUESTHOUSE $$
(☑091 791 04 26; www.anticaposta.ch; Via Borgo; s Sfr110-140, d Sfr200-225) Nestled in the heart of town, this attractively converted 17th-century townhouse has nine bright, parquet-floored rooms. The restaurant (mains Sfr32 to Sfr42) serves market-fresh cuisine and opens onto a vine-clad courtyard.

Castello Seeschloss HISTORIC HOTEL $$
(☑091 791 01 61; www.castello-seeschloss.ch; Piazza Motta; s/d Sfr184/348; P❋🌀≋) This is a 13th-century castle turned romantic waterfront hotel in the southeast corner of the Old Town. The most extraordinary rooms, some full of frescos, are in the ivy-covered tower.

Ecco FUSION $$$
(☑091 785 88 88; www.giardino.ch; Via del Segnale; mains Sfr66-74; ⊙lunch & dinner Wed-Sun mid-Mar–mid-Nov) Super-chic Ecco flaunts two Michelin stars. Chef Rolf Fliegauf gives seasonal ingredients a twist in specialities like Norway lobster with smoked tongue and green apple, and meltingly tender Sisteron lamb with black garlic.

Antico Ristorante Borromeo ITALIAN $$
(☑091 791 92 81; Via Collegio 16; mains Sfr29-38; ⊙lunch & dinner Tue-Sun) Whether you sit in the wisteria-draped garden in summer or in the vaulted dining room in winter, this place is big on atmosphere. The food is good, too, with *primi* like homemade lemon pasta with almond pesto, followed by mains like thyme-infused lamb.

ℹ Information

The **tourist office** (☑091 791 00 91; www.ascona-locarno.com; Via B Papio 5; ⊙9am-6pm Mon-Fri, 10am-6pm Sat, to 2pm Sun) has plenty of info on activities and accommodation.

ℹ Getting There & Away

Bus 1 from Locarno's train station and Piazza Grande stops at Ascona's post office with departures every 15 minutes (Sfr3, 20 minutes). Boat services on Lago Maggiore stop at Ascona.

WESTERN VALLEYS

The valleys that reach north and west of Locarno paint an idyllic rustic picture with their little clusters of stone houses with heavy slate roofs, burbling mountain streams and inviting *grotti*.

Centovalli

The 'hundred valleys' is the westward valley route to Domodossola in Italy, known on the Italian side as Val Vigezzo. As you head west of Ponte Brolla, 4km west of Locarno, the road winds out in a string of tight curves, high on the north flank of the Melezzo stream, which is largely held in check by a dam.

Grey stone villages clinging to the hillsides such as Verdasio, Rasa and Bordei make serene bases for mountain hikes. Al Pentolino (☑091 780 81 00; apt Sfr150-180), in the heart of Verdasio, has converted a beautiful 450-year-old manor house into bright apartments complete with well-equipped kitchens. Freshly caught trout and organic local beef are served at the granite tables beneath the pergola in the restaurant (mains Sfr30-35; ⊙lunch & dinner Wed-Sun).

At Re, on the Italian side, there is a procession of pilgrims on 30 April each year, a tradition that originated when a painting of the Madonna was reported to have started bleeding when struck by a ball in 1480. The bulbous basilica was built in the name of the Madonna del Sangue (Madonna of the Blood) between 1922 and 1950.

MOVING ON?

For tips, recommendations and reviews, head to http://shop.lonelyplanet.com to purchase a downloadable PDF of the Italy chapter from Lonely Planet's *Western Europe* guide.

VALLE ONSERNONE

For total peace and big wilderness, make a detour to Valle Onsernone, just north of Centovalli. Once known for its granite mines, this silent, little-known valley is dotted with clusters of stone houses, forming attractive hamlets.

Spruga is a popular starting point for high-alpine hikes and walks. The main road curves further north to **Vergeletto**, quiet except for the roar of the mountain stream past its houses and church. About 2km further west is the delightful **Locanda Zott** (☎091 780 60 87; s Sfr70, d Sfr120-130), with its busy restaurant downstairs and humble, spick-and-span rooms upstairs, some with own shower. The road peters out 6km west and the territory is great for hiking.

Make the excursion to nearby **Gresso**, a close-knit hamlet scenically perched at 999m, where you may find a lone osteria open for lunch.

Up to five daily buses run from Locarno to Spruga (Sfr17.20, 1¼ hours). Change at Russo for Vergeletto and Gresso.

To see the valley in beautiful slow motion, hop aboard the panoramic **Centovalli Railway** (www.centovalli.ch, in Italian & German). Departing from Locarno for Domodossola (one-way adult/child Sfr35/17.50, 1¾ hours, 11 daily), the train trundles across 83 bridges and burrows through 34 tunnels, offering superlative views of waterfalls, vineyards, craggy mountains and chestnut forests.

Valle Maggia

Nature has certainly worked its *maggia* (magic) in this broad, sunny valley, where 3000m peaks tower above cascading waterfalls, and granite villages cling to steep hillsides. The Maggia river twists through the valley until it splits at the main town, Cevio, the first of several divisions into smaller valleys.

⊙ Sights & Activities

Some 700km of hiking trails crisscross the valley, and there's abundant craggy terrain for mountain and downhill bikers; see www.vallemaggia.ch for routes and maps. Imposing crags attract experienced climbers in Ponte Brolla, Val Bavona and Bosco Gurin.

Bosco Gurin   VILLAGE
A road of seemingly endless hairpin bends snakes up to Bosco Gurin, a minor ski centre (with 30km of pistes) and sun-kissed high-pasture village of slate-roofed, white-washed houses. It is the only village in Ticino where the main language is German, a heritage of Valais immigrants. This heritage is spelled out in artefacts at the stone-and-wood

Walserhaus (www.walserhaus.ch, in Italian & German; adult/child Sfr5/1; ⊙10-11.30am & 1.30-5pm Tue-Sat, 1.30-5pm Sun Apr-Oct).

Cevio   VILLAGE
The centrepiece of Cevio is its vibrant 16th-century **Pretorio** (magistrate's court), covered in the family coats-of-arms of many of the area's rulers, mostly from the 17th century. About 1km away, the core of the Old Town is graced with 16th-century mansions. A short walk away (signposted) are *grotti,* cellars carved out of great blocks of granite that tumbled onto the town here in a landslide.

Fusio   VILLAGE
This pretty village sits surrounded by woods at the head of **Val Lavizzara**. From here the road leads to the dam holding back the emerald **Lago Sambuco**, from where you can hike on to other lakes as well as north over the mountains into Valle Leventina.

Valle di Campo   VALLEY
A winding forest road brings you to this broad, sunny, upland valley. The prettiest of its towns is **Campo**, with its scattered houses and Romanesque belltower. The valley is closed off by **Cimalmotto**, which offers rugged mountain views.

Val Bavona   VALLEY
A smooth road follows a mountain stream through Val Bavona, where narrow meadows are cradled between steep rocky walls. Its series of tightly huddled stone and slate-roofed hamlets is protected by a local foundation, but only inhabited from April to October. For all that, its hamlets are irresistible. The impossibly pretty

grey-stone hamlet of **Foroglio** is dominated by the wispy spray of its 100m waterfall (a 10-minute walk away).

At the end of the valley, just after San Carlo, a **cable car** (adult/child return Sfr20/10; ☺mid-Jun–early Oct) rides up to **Robiei dam** (www.robiei.ch, in Italian) and its startlingly turquoise reservoir, tailor-made for a day's mountain hiking.

Chiesa di San Giovanni Battista CHURCH
The centrepiece of Mogno is this extra-ordinary 1996 cylindrical church designed by Mario Botta. The grey (Maggia granite) and white (marble from Peccia) interior doorway has a strangely neo-Romanesque air to it.

Via Alta WALKING
This challenging 52km, six-day hike is one of the region's showcase walks, leading from Locarno to Fusio (or vice versa) through the Valle Maggia and Val Verzasca. Following old mule and goat trails, the hike takes you to jewel-coloured lakes, mountain refuges and high Alpine peaks, including 3071m Campo Tencia.

Avegno SWIMMING
If you're tempted to take a dip in the glacially cold Maggia river, Avegno's sandy beaches and natural rock pools are the place to do it.

🛏 Sleeping & Eating

Visit www.vallemaggia.ch for a list of the valley's hotels, farmstays, B&Bs and holiday apartments; expect to pay between Sfr35 and Sfr55 per person.

Antica Osteria Dazio GUESTHOUSE $$
(☎091 755 11 62; www.osteriadazio.ch, in German; s Sfr60-80, d Sfr170-190; ℗) This beautifully renovated guesthouse open between March and November has loads of timber, Alpine charm and mountain views. A fire crackles in the beamed restaurant (mains Sfr14 to Sfr20), serving dishes like creamy porcini risotto, local cheese and salami.

Hotel Walser HOTEL $$
(☎091 754 11 81; www.hotel-boscogurin.ch; Bosco Gurin; s/d/tr Sfr120/160/205, half-board per person Sfr32; ℗) This relaxed hotel shelters bright, spacious rooms, a sauna, a small gym and a restaurant dishing up appetising local fare.

📷 **Camping Bella Riva** CAMPGROUND $
(☎091 753 14 44; www.tcs.ch; Gordevio; sites per adult/child/tent Sfr12/6/14; ℗ 🛜 🏊) Attractively situated near the river, this well-kept campground has shady pitches and a solar-powered swimming pool.

Grotto Ca' Rossa SWISS $$
(☎091 753 28 32; www.grottocarossa.ch, in Italian; Località Ronchini; mains Sfr25-40; ☺lunch & dinner Tue-Sun) Spilling out onto a flower-strewn garden, this *grotto* is an atmospheric spot for Tessin specialities, from homemade pasta to butter-soft *brasato* (braised beef) in merlot.

Ristorante La Froda SWISS $$
(☎091 754 11 81; Foroglio; meal Sfr45-50; ☺lunch & dinner Mon-Sun Apr-Oct) Sit at one of five timber tables by the fireside for heaped servings of melt-in-the-mouth *stinco di maiale* (pork shank), served with the best polenta you are likely to taste. Wash down with a glass of merlot.

ℹ Information

The valley's **tourist office** (☎091 753 18 85; www.vallemaggia.ch; ☺9am-noon & 2-5pm Mon-Fri, 9am-noon Sat) is in Maggia.

ℹ Getting There & Away

Regular buses run from Locarno to Cevio and Bignasco (Sfr16.20, 50 minutes), from where you make less regular connections into the side valleys. A bus runs four times a day from

DON'T MISS

A BOND-STYLE BOUNCE

Fancy yourself as a bit of a Pierce Brosnan? The 220m-high Verzasca Dam (Europe's highest) is the striking backdrop for scenes in the Bond movie *GoldenEye,* and nothing could be more 007 than the dizzying bungee jump from the top. The experience is five seconds of pure heart-stopping, mind-bending adrenalin. You can make the big jump on weekends between Easter and October for Sfr255. Local bungee experts include **Trekking Outdoor Team** (☎091 780 78 00; www.trekking.ch) and **Swissraft** (☎081 911 52 50; www.swissraft.ch, in German & French).

If nose-diving off a dam doesn't appeal, both companies arrange other active pursuits, including canyoning, climbing, rafting, canoeing, paragliding and skydiving.

Bignasco to San Carlo (Sfr12.20, 30 minutes), between April and October.

Val Verzasca

About 4km northeast of Locarno, this rugged 26km valley snakes north past the impressive dam, which is fed by the gushing Verzasca river, whose white stones lend the transparent mountain water a scintillating emerald hue.

Just beyond the dam, look to the left and you will see Switzerland's smallest hamlet, Corippo (population 15), a cluster of granite-built, slate-roofed houses seemingly pasted on to the thickly wooded mountain flank. To reach it you cross the Gola Verzasca, a delightful little gorge.

About 5km upstream, Lavertezzo is known for its narrow, double-humped, Romanesque bridge (rebuilt from scratch after the 1951 floods destroyed it) and the natural pools in the icy stream. Be careful, as storms upstream can turn the river into a raging torrent in no time. Stay at riverside Osteria Vittoria (☑091 746 15 81; www.osteriavittoria.ch; s Sfr80-100, d Sfr120-140; ℗), a bustling family lodge with its own restaurant and garden. Most rooms have balconies with views over the Verzasca.

Another 12km takes you to Sonogno, a once abandoned hamlet at the head of the valley, enveloped by chestnut and beech woods.

The two-day, 34km Sentiero Verzasca trail takes in all of the above highlights; visit http://wanderland.myswitzerland.com for route maps and details. Bouldering and climbing pros are in their element in this rocky valley.

Postal buses operate to Sonogno from Locarno as often as once hourly (Sfr18, 1¼ hours).

Central Switzerland

POP 718,400 / AREA 4484 SQ KM / LANGUAGE GERMAN

Best Places to Eat

» Ski Lodge Engelberg (p231)

» Wirtshaus Galliker (p218)

» Takrai (p218)

» River House Boutique Hotel (p234)

» Hess (p231)

Best Places to Stay

» The Hotel (p217)

» Ski Lodge Engelberg (p230)

» The Bed & Breakfast (p218)

» River House Boutique Hotel (p234)

» Rigi Kulm Hotel (p223)

Why Go?

To the Swiss, Central Switzerland – green, mountainous and soothingly beautiful – is the very essence of 'Swissness'. It was here that the pact that kick-started a nation was signed in 1291; here that hero William Tell gave a rebel yell against Habsburg rule. Geographically, politically, spiritually, this is the heartland. Nowhere does the flag fly higher.

You can see why locals swell with pride at Lake Lucerne: enigmatic in the cold mist of morning, molten gold in the dusky half-light.

The dreamy city of Lucerne is small enough for old-world charm yet big enough to harbour designer hotels and a world-class gallery full of Picassos. From here, cruise to resorts like Weggis and Brunnen, or hike Mt Pilatus and Mt Rigi. North-east of Lucerne, Zug has *Kirschtorte* (cherry cake) as rich as its residents and medieval heritage. Come snow-time, head to the Alps for Andermatt's austere mountain-scapes or Engelberg for powdery off-piste perfection.

When to Go

Any time is a good time to visit Lucerne, although it does get packed in the summer months and during the Lucerne Festival. For places such as Andermatt and Engelberg, winter is the obvious time for taking advantage of skiing and snowboarding opportunities, although late spring, summer and early autumn are wonderful for walking and hiking. Zug and Lake Uri are at their best in summer, when swimming in the lakes is heavenly.

Getting There & Around

The nearest major airport is Zürich, and road and rail connections are excellent in all directions. An interesting way to leave the region is aboard the Wilhelm Tell Express (p363).

If you don't have a Swiss or Eurail Pass (both of which are valid on lake journeys), consider purchasing the regional **Tell-Pass** (www.tell-pass .ch; per 7/15 days Sfr180/246), which is valid from 1 April until 31 October. Sold at Lucerne tourist office and all boat stations, the Tell-Pass provides free travel for two or five days, and half-price fares for the remainder.

The handy **Vierwaldstättersee Guest Card**, available when you stay overnight anywhere in the region, offers benefits, including discounts on sporting facilities and 10% to 50% off certain cable cars, as well as reductions on museum admission in Lucerne and elsewhere.

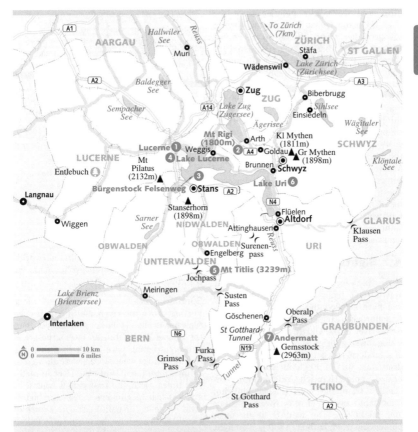

Central Switzerland Highlights

❶ Revel in the melodious atmosphere of **Lucerne** (p212), Switzerland's prettiest city

❷ Witness the awe-inspiring sunrise from the top of **Mt Rigi** (p223) – a time-honoured tradition that never disappoints

❸ Be dazzled by the blues of Lake Lucerne on the vertiginous **Bürgenstock Felsenweg** (p216) clifftop walk

❹ Cruise **Lake Lucerne** (p220) and witness the play of light and shadow, mist and magic

❺ Twirl above the crevassed glacier of **Mt Titlis** (p230) via cable car

❻ Feel the spirit of William Tell by walking the **Swiss Path** (p225) around fjord-like Lake Uri

❼ Hike to the source of the Rhine in summer or cruise snowy backcountry in winter in **Andermatt** (p234)

Lucerne

POP 59,500 / ELEV 435M

Recipe for a gorgeous Swiss city: take a cobalt lake ringed by mountains of myth, add a well-preserved medieval Altstadt (Old Town) and a reputation for making beautiful music, then sprinkle with covered bridges, sunny plazas, candy-coloured houses and waterfront promenades. Lucerne is stunning, and deservedly popular since the likes of Goethe, Queen Victoria and Wagner savoured her views in the 19th century. Legend has it that an angel with a light showed the first settlers where to build a chapel in Lucerne, and today it still has amazing grace.

One minute it's nostalgic (its emotive lion sculpture, its fondness for tradition), the next highbrow, with concerts at acoustic marvel KKL and the Sammlung Rosengart's peerless Picasso collection. Though the shops are still crammed with what Mark Twain so eloquently described as 'gimcrackery of the souvenir sort', Lucerne doesn't only dwell on the past, with a roster of music gigs keeping the vibe upbeat. Carnival capers at Fasnacht, balmy summers, golden autumns – this 'city of lights' shines in every season.

◉ Sights

TOP CHOICE **Kapellbrücke**   BRIDGE

You haven't really been to Lucerne until you have strolled the creaky 14th-century Kapellbrücke (Chapel Bridge), spanning the Reuss river in the Old Town. The octagonal water tower is original, but its gabled roof is a modern reconstruction, rebuilt after a disastrous fire in 1993. As you cross the bridge, note Heinrich Wägmann's 17th-century triangular roof panels, showing important events from Swiss history and mythology. The icon is at its most photogenic when bathed in soft golden light at dusk.

TOP CHOICE **Lion Monument**   MEMORIAL

(Löwendenkmal; Denkmalstrasse) By far the most touching of the 19th-century sights that lured so many British to Lucerne is the Lion Monument. Lukas Ahorn carved this 10m-long sculpture of a dying lion into the rock face in 1820 to commemorate Swiss soldiers who died defending King Louis XVI during the French Revolution. Mark Twain once called it the 'saddest and

CENTRAL SWITZERLAND LUCERNE

DON'T MISS

SAMMLUNG ROSENGART

Lucerne's blockbuster cultural attraction is the **Sammlung Rosengart** (Rosengart Collection; www.rosengart.ch; Pilatusstrasse 10; adult/child Sfr18/10; ◉10am-6pm Apr-Oct, 11am-5pm Nov-Mar), occupying a graceful neoclassical pile. It showcases the outstanding collection of Angela Rosengart, a Swiss art dealer and close friend of Picasso who, in an act of great civic generosity, made some 200-odd works available to the public. Alongside works by the great Spanish master are paintings and sketches by Cézanne, Klee, Kandinsky, Miró, Matisse and Monet, including the first item ever bought by Rosengart, Swiss artist Paul Klee's childlike *X-chen* (1938).

Complementing this collection are some 200 photographs by David Douglas Duncan of the last 17 years of Picasso's life with his family in their home near Cannes in France. It's a uniquely revealing series and principally a portrait of the artist as an impish craftsman, lover, friend and father.

---

most moving piece of rock in the world'. For Narnia fans, it often evokes Aslan at the stone table.

Spreuerbrücke   BRIDGE

Further down the river, the Spreuerbrücke (Spreuer Bridge) is darker and smaller than the Chapel Bridge, but its 1408 structure is entirely original. Lore has it that this was the only bridge where locals were allowed to throw *Spreu* (chaff) into the river in medieval times. Here, the roof panels consist of artist Caspar Meglinger's movie-storyboard-style sequence of paintings, *The Dance of Death*, showing how the plague affected all levels of society.

Museggmauer   VIEWPOINT

(City Wall; ◉8am-7pm Apr-Oct) For a bird's-eye view over Lucerne's rooftops to the glittering lake and mountains beyond, wander the medieval ramparts. A walkway is open between the **Schirmerturm** (tower), where you enter, and the **Wachturm**, from where you have to retrace your steps. You can also ascend and descend the **Zytturm** or **Männliturm** (the latter not connected to the ramparts walkway).

Verkehrshaus   MUSEUM
(www.verkehrshaus.ch; Lidostrasse 5; adult/child Sfr28/14, incl cinema Sfr38/24; ⊙10am-6pm Apr-Oct, to 5pm Nov-Mar) The fascinating interactive Transport Museum is quite deservedly Switzerland's most popular museum, and is a great kid-pleaser. Alongside space rockets, steam locomotives, flying bicycles and dugout canoes are hands-on activities such as flight simulators, broadcasting studios and even bikes to ride.

It shelters a planetarium and a **3D cinema** (www.imax.ch; adult/child Sfr22/19) with hourly screenings between 11am and 8pm. There's also a collection of technology-related paintings, drawings and sculptures by Swiss artist Hans Erni. Should you feel peckish, a large cafeteria and the smart Picard restaurant should do the trick. Take bus 6, 8 or 24 to the Verkehrshaus stop.

Kultur und Kongresszentrum   ARTS CENTRE
(Arts & Congress Centre; www.kkl-luzern.ch; Europaplatz) French architect Jean Nouvel's waterfront Kultur und Kongresszentrum (KKL) is a postmodern jawdropper in an otherwise historic city. But don't think a strikingly handsome face implies a superficial soul: the main concert hall's acoustics are as close to perfect as humankind has ever known, according to many musicians and conductors who have performed here. The trick is that the tall, narrow concert hall, partly built below the lake's surface, is surrounded by a reverberation chamber and has an adjustable suspended ceiling, all creating a bubble of silence. All the accolades showered upon the hall have raised the profile of the tripartite Lucerne Music Festival, increasingly one of the highlights on the global music calendar.

Inside you'll find the **Kunstmuseum** (Museum of Art; www.kunstmuseumluzern.ch; Level K, KKL; adult/child Sfr16/7; ⊙10am-6pm Thu-Sun, to 8pm Tue-Wed). The permanent collection garners mixed reviews, but keep an eye out for great temporary exhibitions.

Bourbaki Panorama   LANDMARK
(www.bourbakipanorama.ch; Löwenplatz 11; adult/child Sfr12/7; ⊙9am-6pm Apr-Oct, 10am-5pm Nov-Mar) Edouard Castres' painstakingly detailed depiction of the Franco–Prussian War of 1870–71, a 1100-sq-metre circular painting of miserable-looking troops and civilians, is brought to life by a moving narrative (also in English). Recent renovations have provided retail space, cinemas, a library and a good-sized cafe-bar.

Gletschergarten   LANDMARK
(Glacier Garden; www.gletschergarten.ch; Denkmalstrasse 4; adult/child Sfr12/7; ⊙9am-6pm Apr-Oct, 10am-5pm Nov-Mar) The Gletshcergarten houses a strip of rock bearing the scars (including huge potholes) inflicted on it by the glacier that slid over it some 20 million years ago. Devotees of kitsch will love getting lost in the *Thousand and One Nights*–style mirror maze inspired by Spain's Alhambra Palace. Combined entry with the Bourbaki Panorama costs Sfr21 for adults and Sfr11 for children.

Historisches Museum   HISTORY MUSEUM
(History Museum; www.hmluzern.ch, in German; Pfistergasse 24; adult/child Sfr10/5; ⊙10am-5pm Tue-Sun) Cleverly organised into a series of attention-grabbing themes, from lust and lasciviousness to government and tourism, and even the humble cervela sausage. Be guided through your chosen story in German or English thanks to a barcode-reading audio guide. A great little cafe is attached.

Natur-Museum   MUSEUM
(Nature Museum; www.naturmuseum.ch; Kasernenplatz 6; adult/child Sfr6/2; ⊙10am-5pm Tue-Sun) Anyone intrigued by stuffed critters and creepy crawlies shouldn't miss this hands-on museum. Highlights feature a woodland trail with real trees and a mushroom computer (don't eat the red spotty ones), plus the fabled *Luzerner Drachenstein* (Luzern Dragon Stone), which, according to legend, fell from a dragon's mouth as it was flying over Mt Pilatus. Modern science suggests that the 15th-century stone was probably a meteorite.

Richard Wagner Museum   MUSEUM
(www.richard-wagner-museum.ch; Richard-Wagner-Weg 27; adult/child Sfr6/free; ⊙10am-noon & 2-5pm Tue-Sun mid-Mar–Nov) Housed in the composer's former residence in Tribschen, on the lake's southern shore, this museum harbours historic musical instruments including rarities such as a regal (portable organ). Take bus 6, 7 or 8 from the train station to Wartegg.

🏃 Activities

There's no better way to appreciate the region's gorgeous scenery than the two-hour Bürgenstock Felsenweg (p216) hike. The tourist office can give details on other walks in the area, such as the gentle amble from Schwanenplatz to Sonnmatt.

Strandbad Lido   SWIMMING
(www.lido-luzern.ch; Lidostrasse 6a; adult/child Sfr7/4; ⊙9am-8pm Jun-Aug, 10am-7pm May &

Sep) Perfect for a splash or sunbathe is the Strandbad Lido, a lakefront beach with a playground, volleyball court and heated outdoor pool near Camping Lido. Or you can swim for free on the other bank of the lake by Seepark, off Alpenquai.

Lucerne

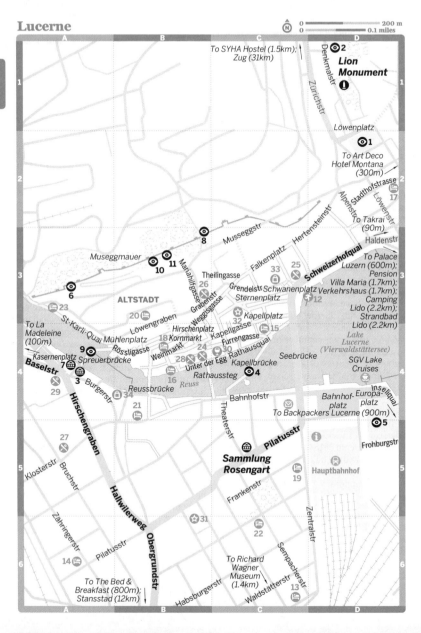

Skyglide PARAGLIDING
(☎041 620 20 22; www.skyglide.ch; paragliding from Sfr160) This well-regarded outfit will collect you, get you nice and high and then throw you from a great height over Lake Lucerne – and won't you just love them for it? Planes depart from Buochs.

SNG BOAT TOUR
(☎041 368 08 08; www.sng.ch, Alpenquai 11) On the northern side of Seebrücke, SNG rents out pedalos (from Sfr30 per hour) and small motor boats (from Sfr57 per hour) and offers cheap 60-minute lake cruises (adult/child Sfr16.50/free).

Next Bike CYCLING
(☎041 50 80 800; bikes per hour/day Sfr2/20) The train station offers bike rental through Next Bike, where you call the number, provide credit card details and receive a numbered code to open a combination lock. Check out the routes circumnavigating the lake. An easygoing, scenic option is the 16km pedal to Winkel via Kastanienbaum, leading mostly along the lakefront.

Festivals & Events

Lucerne Festival MUSIC
(www.lucernefestival.ch) The world-class Lucerne Festival is divided into three separate seasons: Easter, summer and 'at the Piano' (in November). Concerts take place in the KKL and around town.

Sleeping

Most hotels offer winter discounts – sometimes up to one-third off, but you'll be lucky to get a bed (or any kip for that matter) at Fasnacht, so book well ahead. Visit www.luzern-hotels.ch for inspiration.

ALTSTADT

Tourist Hotel HOTEL $
(☎041 410 24 74; www.touristhotel.ch; St-Karli-Quai 12; s/d/tr/q Sfr140/180/220/260; @ 📶) Don't be put off by the uninspired name and institutional-green facade of this central, riverfront cheapie. Dorms are basic,

Lucerne

Top Sights
- Lion Monument ... D1
- Sammlung Rosengart ... C5

Sights
- 1 Bourbaki Panorama ... D2
- 2 Gletschergarten ... D1
- 3 Historisches Museum ... A4
- 4 Kapellbrücke ... C4
- 5 Kultur und Kongresszentrum ... D5
- Kunstmuseum ... (see 5)
- 6 Männliturm ... A3
- 7 Natur-Museum ... A4
- 8 Schirmerturm ... B3
- 9 Spreuerbrücke ... A4
- 10 Wachturm ... B3
- 11 Zytturm ... B3

Activities, Courses & Tours
- 12 SNG ... D3

Sleeping
- 13 Cascada ... C6
- 14 Hotel Alpha ... A6
- 15 Hotel des Alpes ... C4
- 16 Hotel des Balances ... B4
- 17 Hotel Hofgarten ... D2
- 18 Hotel Krone ... B4
- 19 Hotel Waldstätterhof ... C5
- 20 Jailhotel Löwengraben ... B3
- 21 Romantik Hotel Wilden Mann ... B4
- 22 The Hotel ... C6
- 23 Tourist Hotel ... A3

Eating
- Bam Bou ... (see 22)
- 24 Bodu ... B4
- 25 Confiserie Bachmann ... C3
- 26 Jazzkantine ... B3
- KKL World Café ... (see 5)
- 27 Restaurant Drei Könige ... A5
- 28 Restaurant Schiff ... B4
- 29 Wirtshaus Galliker ... A4

Drinking
- 30 Rathaus Bräuerei ... C4

Entertainment
- 31 Penthouse ... B6
- Pravda ... (see 31)
- 32 Stadtkeller ... C3

Shopping
- 33 Casagrande ... C3
- 34 Flea Market ... B4

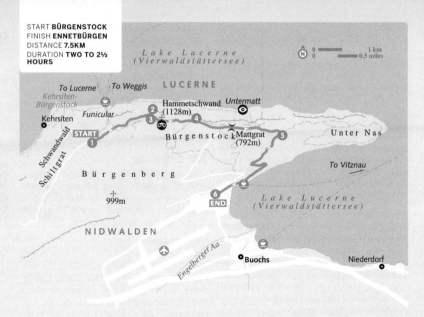

Walking Tour
Bürgenstock Felsenweg

This panoramic half-day walk contours the Bürgenstock, a high limestone ridge which forms a peninsula reaching across Lake Lucerne. Although some walkers may find the clifftop path unnerving, the route is gentle, safe and suitable for families. The best available walking map is Nidwalder Wanderwege's 1:25,000 *Nidwalder Wanderkarte* (around Sfr22.50).

To reach the trail head, take a ferry to Kehrsiten-Bürgenstock. From the upper funicular station at ① **Bürgenstock** (874m), walk east through the Bürgenstock Hotels resort, then turn left onto a broad gravelled walkway. Continue through ferny woodlands, where frequent breaks in the trees offer views across sparkling Lake Lucerne.

After 30 to 35 minutes, you come to the ② **Hammetschwand-Lift**. This skeletal 160m structure, built in 1905, is still the highest free-standing lift in Europe. You can either take the minute-long ride (adult/child Sfr10/5) to Hammetschwand for a full panorama or continue straight to Chänzeli. If you opt for the lift, savour the panorama at

③ **Hammetschwand Restaurant** before walking to the lookout at 1128m, from which a trail leads through pastures and mixed woodlands to Chänzeli.

Alternatively, forgo the lift and take an alternative route through a series of short tunnels blasted into the vertical rock walls. Then follow the white-red-white marked path (signposted *Waldstätterweg*) east along the wooded crest of the ridge via ④ **Chänzeli** (1025m). The trail zigzags down through the forest to reach Mattgrat (792m), 25 to 30 minutes on.

Make your way up past a small private cableway, bearing left at a fork not far before you get to the historic ⑤ **St Jost Kapelle** after 20 to 25 minutes. Then take a signposted path that doubles back briefly left alongside an overgrown fence. After crossing a minor road the route steers right again and sidles along the lightly forested lakeside to meet a sealed street at the edge of ⑥ **Ennetbürgen**. Follow this straight down past the ferry dock to arrive at the village centre, 40 to 50 minutes from St Jost.

but rooms cheerily modern, with flat-screen TVs. There are also cheaper rooms with shared bathrooms. Private parking costs Sfr15 a day.

Hotel des Balances
HOTEL $$$
(☎041 418 28 28; www.balances.ch; Weinmarkt 4; s Sfr290-330, d Sfr390-430, ste Sfr530-630; P🖥) Behind its elaborately frescoed facade, this hotel flaunts a light and airy design ethos, with ice-white rooms, gilt mirrors and inlaid parquet floors. Suites have river-facing balconies. Parking costs Sfr27 per day.

Jailhotel Löwengraben
HOTEL $$
(☎041 410 78 30; www.jailhotel.ch; Löwengraben 18; s/d/tr/q Sfr110/170/240/300) This former prison has novelty value, but you might get a jailhouse shock when you enter your cell to find barred windows, bare floorboards and a prefab bathroom. It's OK for a laugh, but not for quality shut-eye, with thumping music in the downstairs Alcatraz club.

Hotel des Alpes
HOTEL $$
(☎041 417 20 60; www.desalpes-luzern.ch; Furrengasse 3; s/d Sfr160/254; 🖥) Facing the river and Kapellbrücke, the location is this hotel's biggest draw. The rooms are turn-of-the-21st-century comfy, though light sleepers might find them noisy.

Hotel Krone
HOTEL $$
(☎041 419 44 00; www.krone-luzern.ch; Weinmarkt 12; s/d/tr/q Sfr200/320/405/480; 🖥) Smart and central, Krone combines a historic facade with good, pared-down rooms. Its sister hotel, the Magic, stands in riotously decorated contrast but is also a good deal.

CENTRAL LUCERNE

TOP CHOICE The Hotel
DESIGN HOTEL $$$
(☎041 226 86 86; www.the-hotel.ch; Sempacherstrasse 14; ste Sfr430-1000; P❄🖥) This shamelessly hip hotel, bearing the imprint of architect Jean Nouvel, is all streamlined chic, with refined suites featuring stills from movie classics on the ceilings. Downstairs, Bam Bou is one of Lucerne's hippest restaurants and the simple summer terrace across the street is a cool place to idle. Parking costs Sfr35 per day.

Hotel Waldstätterhof
HOTEL $$
(☎041 227 12 71; www.hotel-waldstaetterhof.ch; Zentralstrasse 4; s Sfr170, d Sfr270-315; P🖥) Behind its faux-Gothic, red-brick exterior,

The next time someone grumbles about the Swiss being so irritatingly orderly and well behaved, send them to Lucerne for Fasnacht – they'll *never* use those tired clichés again. More boisterous than Basel or Bern, this six-day pre-Lenten bash is stark raving bonkers. The fun kicks off on 'Dirty Thursday' with the character Fritschi greeting the crowds from the town hall and a canon signalling that hedonistic misrule can begin. Warty witches, leering ogres, jangling jesters, it doesn't matter which costume or mask you choose – dress up, drink and dance, it's tradition! Guggenmusik bands (literally) rock the bridges, acrobats and actors perform, and parades fill the streets with colour, chaos and ear-splitting music in the build up to Mardi Gras (Fat Tuesday).

this hotel has smart, modern rooms with hardwood-style floors and high ceilings, plus excellent service. Each year an entire floor is renovated. Light sleepers might want to book a room in the newer, better-sound-proofed annex. Wi-fi costs Sfr10 for 12 hours (total); parking is Sfr17 a day.

Hotel Alpha
HOTEL $
(☎041 240 42 80; www.hotelalpha.ch; Zähringerstrasse 24; s/d/tr Sfr75/150/185; P🖥) Easy on the eyes and wallet, this hotel is in a quiet residential area 10 minutes' walk from the Old Town. Rooms are simple, light and spotlessly clean, and there are cheaper rooms with shared bathroom. Wi-fi is free for the first hour, then Sfr1 per hour. Parking is Sfr10 per day.

Cascada
HOTEL $$
(☎041 226 80 88; Bundesplatz 18; www.cascada.ch; s Sfr149-279, d Sfr266-356; P@🖥) Popular with business travellers, this is a smart, central option, with a Spanish restaurant/tapas bar on the premises. Murals of Swiss waterfalls in each spacious room soften the somewhat corporate vibe. Courtyard-facing rooms are quieter than the others. Parking costs Sfr20 per day.

Romantik Hotel Wilden Mann
BOUTIQUE HOTEL $$$
(☎041 210 16 66; www.wilden-mann.ch; Bahnhofstrasse 30; s Sfr165-410, d Sfr270-425, ste

Sfr360-525; 🐾) Classically elegant rooms adorned with stucco, ruby-red fabrics and antique dressers attract romantics to this 16th-century stunner near the river. The 1st-floor terrace is heaven for alfresco dining.

Hotel Hofgarten   HOTEL **$$**
(☑041 410 88 88; www.hofgarten.ch; Stadthofstrasse 14; d Sfr219-310; P🐾) In a building dating from 1650, this hotel has striking, individually decorated rooms. The Mies van der Rohe furniture in room 226 sets the tone. It has a sister establishment, the Hotel zum Rebstock, where Kafka once stayed. Both have lovely courtyard dining areas. Parking is Sfr25 per day.

AROUND CENTRAL LUCERNE

TOP CHOICE ⟋ **The Bed & Breakfast**   B&B **$**
(☑041 310 15 14; www.thebandb.ch; Taubenhausstrasse 34; s/d/tr/q with shared bathroom Sfr80/120/165/200; P@🐾) This friendly B&B feels like home – with stylish, contemporary rooms, crisp white bedding and scatter cushions. Unwind in the garden or with a soak in the old-fashioned tub. Take bus 1 to Eichof. It's only open between March and October, and parking is Sfr10 per day.

Backpackers Lucerne   HOSTEL **$**
(☑041 360 04 20; www.backpackerslucerne.ch; Alpenquai 42; dm/d Sfr32/72; @🐾) Could this be backpacker heaven? Right on the lake, this is a soulful place to crash with art-slung walls, bubbly staff, a well-equipped kitchen and immaculate dorms with balconies. It's a 15-minute walk southeast of the station.

Camping Lido   CAMPGROUND **$**
(☑041 370 21 46; www.camping-international.ch; Lidostrasse 19; sites per adult/child Sfr10/5, tent site Srf10-20, dm Sfr25; P🐾) On the lake's northern shore, east of town, this shaded ground also has four- to eight-bed wooden cabins (sleeping bag required). There's a playground, laundry, bike hire and a games room with wi-fi. Take bus 6, 8 or 24 to Verkehrshaus.

Art Deco Hotel Montana   DESIGN HOTEL **$$$**
(☑041 419 00 00; www.hotel-montana.ch; Adligenswilerstrasse 22; s Sfr200-375, d Sfr250-560; 🐾) Perched above the lake, this opulent Art Deco hotel is reached by its own funicular. The handsome rooms reveal attention to detail, from inlaid parquet floors to period lighting. Many have glorious views, as do the terrace and entrance.

SYHA Hostel   HOSTEL **$**
(☑041 420 88 00; www.youthhostel.ch/luzern; Sedelstrasse 12; dm/d from Sfr37.40/94.80; P@🐾) These Hostelling International digs are modern, well run and clean, with facilities such as bike hire, games and a kids' corner. Value-for-money meals are available throughout the day. Take bus 18 from the train station to Jugendherberge.

Pension Villa Maria   PENSION **$**
(☑041 370 21 19; www.villamaria-luzern.ch; Haldenstrasse 36; s Sfr90-150, d Sfr130-160; P@🐾) People feel at home at this comfy, welcoming pension with clean, no-frills rooms, a lovely garden and a sun-filled breakfast room. Open between April and October, it's a 15-minute lakefront stroll from the centre, or take bus 6 or 8 to the Dietschiberg stop.

Palace Luzern   LUXURY HOTEL **$$$**
(☑041 416 16 16; www.palace-luzern.ch; Haldenstrasse 10; r from Sfr400, ste from Sfr550; P@🐾) This luxury belle époque hotel on the lakefront is sure of its place in many a heart. Inside it's all gleaming marble, chandeliers, airy rooms and turn-of-the-20th-century grandeur. Parking is Sfr35 per day; wi-fi an extortionate Sfr45 for 30 hours.

✗ Eating

TOP CHOICE ⟋ **Wirtshaus Galliker**   SWISS **$$**
(☑041 240 10 02; Schützenstrasse 1; mains Sfr24-48; ⊙lunch & dinner Tue-Sat, closed Jul–mid-Aug) Don't eat for a day before visiting this old-style tavern, passionately run by the Galliker family over four generations since 1856. It attracts a lively bunch of regulars. Motherly waitresses dish up Lucerne soul food (rösti, *chögalipaschtetli* and the like) that is batten-the-hatches filling. Book ahead for dinner.

Takrai   THAI **$**
(www.takrai.ch; Haldenstrasse 9; mains Sfr15.50-21.50; lunch Mon, lunch & dinner Tue-Sat) Judging by the anaconda of a queue at lunchtime, this pint-sized Thai joint is the place to be. The emphasis here is on local organic produce and everything – from feisty papaya salads to the generously portioned curries – strikes a perfect balance. If you can't nab a table, order takeaway and chow down lakeside.

Bam Bou   ASIAN **$$$**
(Sempacherstrasse 14; mains Sfr46-56; ⊙lunch & dinner) The Hotel's below-street-level

CENTRAL SWITZERLAND LUCERNE

restaurant resembles a lacquered bento box and thrills with its pan-Asian menu. The Japanese flavours tend to win the most praise and the daily specials are wallet-friendly and more-ish.

Bodu
FRENCH $$

(041 410 01 77; Kornmarkt 5; mains Sfr18-58; lunch & dinner) Banquettes, wood panelling and elbow-to-elbow tables create a warm ambience at this classic French-style bistro. Here locals huddle around bottles of Bordeaux and bowls of *bouillabaisse* (fish stew) or succulent sirloin steaks. Reservations strongly advised.

Restaurant Drei Könige
MODERN EUROPEAN $$

(Klosterstrasse 10; mains Sfr22.80-44.50; lunch & dinner Mon-Sat) A high-ceilinged, retro-fitted bar-restaurant, this place has whopper-sized traditional and fusion meals and cheery service, attracting young hipster types and stalwart locals alike.

Jazzkantine
CAFE $

(www.jsl.ch, in German; Grabenstrasse 8; pasta Sfr16, sandwiches Sfr7-14.50; 7am-12.30am Mon-Sat, from 4pm Sun) With its long bar, sturdy wooden tables and chalkboard menus, this is an arty haunt. Go for tasty Italian dishes and very good coffee. Check the schedule for jazz workshops and gigs, which take place downstairs.

Restaurant Schiff
SWISS $$

(Unter der Egg 8; mains Sfr26.50-44; lunch & dinner) Under the waterfront arcades and lit by tea lights at night, this restaurant has bags of charm and is a great spot to catch some sun. Try fish from Lake Lucerne and *chögalipaschtetli* (vol-au-vents stuffed with meat and mushrooms).

Confiserie Bachmann
SWEETS $

(Schwanenplatz 7; 7am-7pm Mon-Wed & Fri, to 9pm Thu, to 5.30pm Sat, 9.30am-7pm Sun) Swiss milk chocolate flows from a fountain at this sugar-coated temple. You'll find pastries, gelati, salads and sandwiches, plus Switzerland's longest praline counter. There are other branches at the train station and throughout town.

KKL World Café
INTERNATIONAL $

(Europaplatz 1; mains Sfr14.50-24.50; 9am-midnight) This slick bistro-cum-cafeteria stocks salads and sandwiches in its glass counters, but also offers wok dishes at lunch and dinner.

🍷 Drinking & Entertainment

Rathaus Bräuerei
BREWERY

(Unter der Egg 2; 8am-midnight Mon-Sat, to 11pm Sun) Sip home-brewed beer under the vaulted arches of this buzzy tavern that brews its own, or nab a pavement table and watch the river flow.

Schüür
LIVE MUSIC

(www.schuur.ch, in German; Tribschenstrasse 1) Live gigs are the name of the game here: think everything from metal, garage, pop, Cuban and world, plus theme nights with DJ-spun Britpop and '80s classics. All this plus a fantastically beachy outdoors area, complete with bar.

La Madeleine
LIVE MUSIC

(www.lamadeleine.ch; Baselstrasse 15) This is a lovely little spot for a low-key gig, with two performance areas and a cosy-glam bar. Over 25s only.

Penthouse
LOUNGE

(Astoria Hotel, Pilatusstrasse 29) This rooftop bar has all the trappings of a regular five-star joint but a refreshingly 'all types' crowd. Cocktails are more like mocktails though. On the ground floor is the swanky **Pravda** nightclub (Wednesday to Saturday); expect R&B and house anthems.

Stadtkeller
TRADITIONAL MUSIC

(www.stadtkeller.ch; Sternenplatz 3) Alphorns, cowbells, flag throwing, yodelling – name the Swiss cliché and you'll find it at this folksy haunt.

🛍 Shopping

Mosey down Haldenstrasse for art and antiques or Löwenstrasse for vintage threads and souvenirs. Fruit and vegetable stalls spring forth along the river quays every Tuesday and Saturday morning. There's also a flea market on Burgerstrasse each Saturday from May to October.

Rockstore
OUTDOOR EQUIPMENT

(www.rockstore.ch; Hirschmattstrasse 34; noon-6.30pm Mon, from 10am Tue, Wed & Fri, 10am-8pm Thu, 9am-4pm Sat) Helpful staff and a solid range of quality outdoor gear and equipment ensure that you're properly kitted out should you go adventuring in the surrounding wilds.

Casagrande
SOUVENIRS

(Grendelstrasse 6; 8am-10pm Mon-Sat, 10am-7.30pm Sun) Our favourite temple of kitsch might tempt you to spend on Heidi dolls, cuckoo clocks, yodelling marmots and – heaven forbid – his 'n' hers cow mugs.

ⓘ Information

Discount Cards

Guest Card Stamped by your hotel, this entitles you to discounts on museum entry, some sporting facilities and lake cruises.

Lucerne Card (24/48/72hr Sfr19/27/33) Sold at the tourist office and train station, this offers unlimited travel on public transport (excluding SGV boats), 50% discount on museum entry, plus reductions on activities, city tours and car hire.

Post

Post office (cnr Bahnhofstrasse & Bahnhofplatz; ⊙7.30am-6.30pm Mon-Fri, 8am-4pm Sat) By the Hauptbahnhof (main train station).

Tourist Information

Luzern Tourism (⌨041 227 17 17; www.luzern .com; Zentralstrasse 5; ⊙8.30am-7.30pm Mon-Fri, 9am-7.30pm Sat & Sun) Reached from Zentralstrasse or platform 3 of the Hauptbahnhof. Offers city walking tours. Call for hotel reservations.

ⓘ Getting There & Away

Frequent trains connect Lucerne to Interlaken West (Sfr56, two hours) via Zofingen or Olten, Bern (Sfr36, one hour), Lugano (Sfr56, 2½ hours), Geneva (Sfr74, three hours) via Olten or Biel-Bienne and Zürich (Sfr23, one hour).

WORTH A TRIP

ENTLEBUCH

Located southwest of Lucerne, the 39,000-plus sq km **Entlebuch** (www .biosphaere.ch, in German) area (a mixed mountain and highland ecosystem) was declared a Unesco Biosphere Reserve in 2001. Far from being a lonely wilderness outpost, the reserve is home to some 17,000 people keen to preserve their traditional way of life, which, this being Switzerland, involves a good amount of dairy farms. The landscape of karst formations, sprawling moors (some 25% of the area), Alpine pastures and mountain streams, which rises from 600m to some 2350m above sea level, makes for some wonderful hiking opportunities. For details pop into the **park office** (⌨041 485 88 50; Chlosterbüel 28, Schüpfheim).

The A2 freeway connecting Basel and Lugano passes by Lucerne, while the A14/A4 provides the road link to Zürich.

For information on boat transport, see below. The departure points are the quays around Bahnhofplatz and Europaplatz.

ⓘ Getting Around

Should you be going further than the largely pedestrianised Old Town, city buses leave from outside the Hauptbahnhof at Bahnhofplatz. Tickets cost Sfr2.20 for a short journey, Sfr3 for one zone and Sfr4.20 for two. Ticket dispensers indicate the correct fare for each destination. A zone 101 day ticket (Sfr6) covers the city centre and beyond; Swiss Pass holders travel free. There's an underground car park at the train station.

Lake Lucerne

Majestic peaks hunch conspiratorially around Vierwaldstättersee – which twists and turns as much as the tongue does when pronouncing it. Little wonder English speakers use the shorthand Lake Lucerne!

To appreciate the views, ride up to Mt Pilatus, Mt Rigi or Stanserhorn. When the clouds peel away or you break through them, precipitous lookout points reveal a crumpled tapestry of green hillsides and shimmering cobalt waters below, with glaciated peaks beyond. It's especially atmospheric in autumn, when fog rises like dry ice from the lake, and in winter, when the craggy heights are dusted with snow.

Apart from its mountain viewpoints, the lake offers tucked-away resorts, all reachable by boat. The far eastern reach of Lake Lucerne – Lake Uri or Urnersee – is home to the Rütli Meadow, where the country was supposedly born.

ⓘ Getting Around

The **Lake Lucerne Navigation Company SGV** (⌨041 367 67 67; www.lakelucerne.ch) operates boats (sometimes paddle-steamers) daily. This excludes the Lake Uri section of the lake, where services only go past Rütli in winter on Sundays and national holidays.

From Lucerne, destinations include Alpnachstad (one-way/return Sfr25/42, 1¾ hours), Weggis (one-way/return Sfr18.40/35, 50 minutes), Vitznau (one-way/return Sfr25/42, 1¼ hours), Brunnen (one-way/return Sfr37/58, 1¾ hours) and Flüelen (one-way/return Sfr43/66, 3¼ hours). Longer trips are relatively cheaper than short ones, and you can alight as often as you want. An SGV day ticket costs Sfr66 for

Lake Lucerne

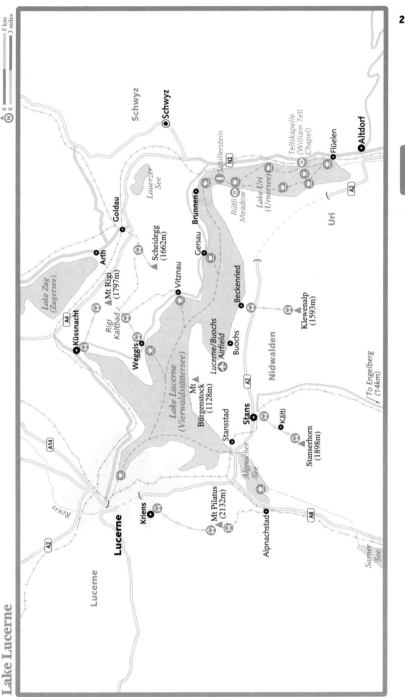

adults and Sfr33 for children. Swiss and Eurail passes (on days selected for travel only) are valid on scheduled boat trips, while InterRail entitles you to half-price tickets. Passes will get you discounts on selected mountain railways and cable cars.

If driving, you'll find that roads run close to the shoreline most of the way around – excluding the stretch from Flüelen to Stansstad. Here, the A2 freeway ploughs a fairly straight line, sometimes underground and usually away from the water.

MT PILATUS

Rearing above Lucerne from the southwest, **Mt Pilatus** (www.pilatus.com) rose to fame in the 19th-century when Wagner waxed lyrical about its Alpine vistas and Queen Victoria trotted up here on horseback. Legend has it that this 2132m peak was named after Pontius Pilate, whose corpse was thrown into a lake on its summit and whose restless ghost has haunted its heights ever since. Poltergeists aside, it's more likely that the moniker derives from the Latin word *pileatus,* meaning cloud covered – as the mountain frequently is.

From May to October, you can reach Mt Pilatus on a classic 'golden round-trip'. Board the lake steamer from Lucerne to Alpnachstad, then rise with the world's steepest cog railway to Mt Pilatus. From the summit, cable cars bring you down to Kriens via Fräkmüntegg and Krienseregg, where bus 1 takes you back to Lucerne. The reverse route (Kriens–Pilatus–Alpnachstad–Lucerne) is also possible. The return trip costs Sfr91 (less with valid Swiss, Eurail or InterRail passes).

For an above-the-treetops adventure in summer, head for **Pilatus Seilpark** (Rope Park; www.pilatus-seilpark.ch; Fräkmüntegg; adult/child Sfr27/20; ⊘10am-5pm May Oct), where 10 head-spinning trails from high-wire bridges to tree climbs are graded according to difficulty. Fräkmüntegg is also the starting point for Switzerland's longest **summer toboggan run** (adult/child Sfr8/6; ⊘10am-5pm May-Oct), a speedy 1.35km downhill ride.

Mt Pilatus is fantastic for **walking**. Hikes include a steep, partially roped 2.8km scramble (June to September) from Fräkmüntegg to the summit, an easy 3.5km walk through forest and moor from Krienseregg to Fräkmüntegg, and the 1.5km trudge from Pilatus-Kulm to Tomlishorn, affording views that stretch as far as the Black Forest on a clear day. Climbers can tackle the dizzying

Galtigentürme rock pillars or Holzwangflue's gullies where ibex often roam.

In winter, try **sledging** 6km through snowy woodlands from Fräkmüntegg to Kriens. A return ticket between Kriens and Fräkmüntegg by cable car costs Sfr38 for adults and Sfr19 for children. Free sledge hire is available at Fräkmüntegg station.

It's more traditional to stay overnight at Mt Rigi, but there are two hotels on Pilatus. The recently renovated 19th-century **Pilatus-Kulm** (☏041 329 12 12; www.pilatus.ch /en/hotel-pilatus-kulm; s Sfr210-250, d Sfr260-300, ste Sfr250-540) offers a very swanky mountain-top sleeping experience, with good discounts in the low season and fine dining.

STANSERHORN

Looming above the lake, 1898m **Stanserhorn** (www.stanserhorn.ch) boasts the region's only revolving restaurant. Rotating once every 43 minutes, the star-shaped **Rondorama** offers 360-degree views looking back to Titlis and peaks which take on a watercolour dreaminess at dusk. Kids love the marmot park at the summit, where whistling critters can be observed in a near natural habitat. In May 2012, the almost completely transparent **CabriO** cable car will start gliding, offering amazing on-the-go views for those ascending the 'horn.

You can journey up by vintage funicular from Stans to Kälti, then take the cable car. Both operate from mid-April to early November. The funicular's base station is a five-minute walk from Stans train station. The single trip from Stans to Stanserhorn costs Sfr32 for adults and Sfr8 for children. If you're driving, you can save an hour by parking at Kälti.

Stans is on the Lucerne–Engelberg railway (one-way from Lucerne Sfr8.40). The **tourist office** (Bahnhofplatz 4; ⊘9am-noon & 2-5pm Mon-Fri) can be found by ascending the external spiral staircase at the train station and will help out with accommodation. Dorfplatz, the hub of the town centre, is located behind the station, overlooked by an early baroque church. Here, too, is the well-regarded **Hotel Engel** (☏041 619 10 10; www.engelstans.ch; Dorfplatz 1; s/d from Sfr100/140; ⓟ@⊚), hiding wonderfully sleek and streamlined rooms behind its historic facade.

BECKENRIED

Beckenried, on the southern shore, is a bus ride from Stans. Just a few minutes' walk from the boat station is a cable car to **Klewenalp** (www.klewenalp.ch; one-way/return Sfr22/35), an underrated skiing destination, with 40km of well-prepared red and blue runs, which become hiking, climbing and mountain biking trails in summer. A map at the top outlines the options. Bike hire is available at the base station for Sfr50 per day, which includes your cable car ticket.

MT RIGI

Blue, no red, no dark... Turner couldn't quite make up his mind about how he preferred 1797m **Rigi** (www.rigi.ch), so in 1842 the genius painted the mountain in three different lights to reflect its changing moods. On a clear day, there are impressive views to a jagged spine of peaks including Mt Titlis and the Jungfrau giants. To the north and west, you overlook Arth-Goldau and Zugersee, which curves around until it almost joins Küssnacht and an arm of Lake Lucerne. The sunrises and sunsets viewed from the summit are the stuff of bucket lists.

At **Mineralbad & Spa Rigi Kaltbad**, the trend for major spachitecture was taking shape during our visit. Expect the Mario Botta–designed temple to relaxation to be opened during 2012.

The 33-room **Rigi Kulm Hotel** (☎041 880 18 88; www.rigikulm.ch; s Sfr148-203, d Sfr228-318; ☎) is the only major establishment at the summit and commands stirring views. The natty streamlined rooms mix old and new furnishings and boast immaculate bathrooms, plus there's a good restaurant and stylishly decorated self-service cafeteria for those not staying the night.

Rigi is a magnet to hikers; for recommended routes, check www.rigi.ch. There are several easy walks (one to two hours) down from Rigi Kulm to Rigi Kaltbad, with wonderful views. Or ask the tourist offices in Lucerne or Weggis for information on the Rigi Lehnenweg, a scenic 17.5km trek around the mountain.

Hiking up the mountain is another story. It's at least a 4½-hour walk from Weggis, but you could take the cable car from Küssnacht to Seeboldenalp (one-way/return Sfr13/22), where a steepish path leads to the summit in just over two hours. While hiking on Rigi, watch out for the *Chlyni Lüüt*, tiny 'wild folk' with supernatural powers who in mythology once inhabited Rigi!

For those of a less energetic bent, two rival railways carry passengers to the top. One runs from Arth-Goldau (one-way/return Sfr40/64), the other from Vitznau (one-way/return Sfr45/72). The Vitznau track gives the option of diverting at Rigi Kaltbad and taking the cable car to or from Weggis instead. Holders of Swiss, Eurail and InterRail passes receive a 50% discount on fares, and children under 16 travel free when accompanied by a parent.

WEGGIS
POP 4200 / ELEV 440M

Sheltered from cold northerlies by Mt Rigi, Weggis enjoys a mild climate, sprouting a few palm and fig trees by the lakefront. It's hard to believe this genteel resort with small-town friendliness was the birthplace of the rebellious 'Moderner Bund' art movement, the forerunner of Dada. A cable car runs from here up to Rigi Kaltbad (one-way/return Sfr29/47).

🛏 Sleeping

Post Hotel Weggis   HOTEL $$
(☎041 392 25 25; www.poho.ch; Seestrasse 8; s Sfr225-285, d Sfr280-340; P❋☎) Like a surrealist casino, this place's decor won't be forgotten in a hurry, but the service is top-notch and dining options great, especially Weggiser Stübli, a snug, wood-panelled traditional eatery. There's also a spa and a 45,000-bottle wine cellar. Parking is Sfr15 a day.

SeeHotel Gotthard   HOTEL $$
(☎041 390 21 14; www.gotthard-weggis.ch; s Sfr90-155, d Sfr150-265; @☎) This friendly waterfront hotel has natty, modern and spotless rooms; the best with lake views. Guests can use the wellness/swimming area at the adjacent hotel. It's closed mid-October to mid-December.

Park Hotel Weggis   LUXURY HOTEL $$$
(☎041 392 05 05; www.phw.ch; Hertensteinstrasse 34; s/d from Sfr413/550; P@☎) A lavish lakefront beauty, with manicured gardens and a great Zen-inspired spa. Understated elegance and smooth service is the order of the day. Revel in the lakefront views, the private beach or the Michelin-starred restaurant, Annex.

Budget-Hotel Weggis   HOTEL $
(☎041 390 11 31; www.budgethotel.ch; Parkstrasse 29; s/d/tr Sfr60/112/128, with shared bathroom Sfr46/187/108) Doing what it says on the label well, this cheapie keeps even pernickety customers happy with clean, simple rooms. It's

up the hill from the boat station. Payment in advance.

✗ Eating & Drinking

Grape   AMERICAN $$

(☎041 392 07 07; Seestrasse 60; pizza Sfr17-25, mains Sfr23-73; ⊗lunch & dinner Thu-Tue) Weggis' California dreamer is this hip haunt with a menu that skips from wood-fired pizza to modern burger combos to desserts like Coca Cola brownies. Takeaway available.

Tiffany's   BAR

(Seestrasse 48; snacks Sfr9.50-18.50; ⊗Wed-Mon; ☎) You can almost picture the waves lapping and bouzouki playing at this Greek-style cafe. The owner has recreated a Paros taverna to a tee – from the blue-white paint job to the plastic fishnets and sunny terrace. Nibble on dolmades and aubergines while sipping cocktails.

ⓘ Information

The **tourist office** (www.the-best-of-lake -lucerne.ch; Seestrasse 5; ⊗8.30am-6pm Mon-Fri, 9am-4pm Sat & Sun) is next to the boat station.

Lake Uri

Scything through rugged mountains, the fjord-like Lake Uri (Urnersee) finger of Lake Lucerne mirrors the country's medieval past in its glassy turquoise waters. Take the ferry from Brunnen towards Flüelen and you'll glimpse a near 30m-high natural obelisk, the **Schillerstein**, protruding from the water. Its gold inscription pays homage to Friedrich Schiller, the author of the play *Wilhelm Tell,* so instrumental in creating the Tell legend.

The next stop is the **Rütli Meadow**, the cradle of Swiss democracy. This is where the Oath of Eternal Alliance was allegedly signed by the three cantons of Uri, Schwyz and Nidwalden in 1291 and later where General Guisan gathered the Swiss army during WWII in a show of force against potential invaders. As such, this is hallowed ground to Swiss patriots and the focus of national day celebrations on 1 August. As well as an almighty flag, there's an obligatory souvenir shop doubling as a cafe.

An important port of call is the serene **Tellskapelle** (William Tell Chapel), covered in murals depicting four episodes in the Tell legend, including the one that's supposed to have occurred on this spot, his escape from Gessler's boat. There's a huge carillon that chimes behind the chapel. Approaching from land instead of water you pass – would you Adam and Eve it – apple orchards, which might make your crossbow twitch if you had one.

After crossing into another founding canton, Uri, the boat finally chugs into Flüelen, which was historically a staging post for the mule trains crossing the St Gotthard Pass. Today it's a stop on the main road and rail route. Near the town is **Altdorf**, where William Tell is reputed to have performed his apple-shooting stunt. A statue of the man himself stands in the main square, and Schiller's play is sometimes performed in Altdorf's Tellspielhaus. In nearby Bürglen (believed to be William Tell's birthplace), you can visit the **Tell Museum** (www.tellmuseum.ch; Postplatz; adult/ child Sfr5.50/1.50; ⊗10am-5pm Jul & Aug, 10am-11.30am & 1.30-5pm May, Jun, Sep & Oct), a collection of Tell-related objects, documents and artistic works.

Brunnen

POP 8500 / ELEV 435M

Tucked into the folds of mountains, where Lake Lucerne and Lake Uri meet at right angles, Brunnen enjoys mesmerising views south and west. A regular guest, Turner was so impressed by the vista that he whipped out his watercolours to paint *The Bay of Uri from Brunnen* (1841). As the local föhn wind rushes down from the mountains, it creates perfect conditions for sailing and paragliding. And don't forget the folkloric hot air of the weekly alphorn concerts in summer.

🏃 Activities

Adventure Point   CANOEING

(☎079 247 74 72; www.adventurepoint.ch, in German) Adventure Point arranges guided canoe and kayak tours (Sfr80), or you can go it alone for around Sfr60 per person. For adrenalin-charged thrills, check out its canyoning (from Sfr125) excursions in the area.

Urmiberg   CABLE CAR

(www.urmiberg.ch, in German; cable car one-way/ return Sfr11/19) Glide over the treetops to Urmiberg for views over the pointy peaks ringing Lake Uri and Lake Lucerne. Kids travel for half-price.

Equipped with a decent pair of walking boots, you can circumnavigate Lake Uri on foot via the **Swiss Path** (Weg der Schweiz; www.weg-der-schweiz.ch, in German & French) from Brunnen to Rütli, inaugurated to commemorate the 700th anniversary of the 1291 pact. As the spectacular views unfold, so too does the symbolism – the trail is divided into 26 sections, each representing a different canton, from the founding trio to Johnny-come-lately Jura (1979). As you stride, bear in mind that 5mm of track represents one Swiss resident, so populous Zürich spans 6.1km and rural Appenzell Innerrhoden a mere 71m.

The 35km, two-day walk over hill and dale takes in some of Central Switzerland's finest scenery, cutting through meadows flecked with orchids and ox-eye daisies, revealing classic Alpine panoramas, shimmying close to the lakeshore and then dipping back into ferny forest. You'll pass historically significant landmarks such as the Tellskapelle and the obelisk commemorating Schiller. To get a true sense of the area, it's worth completing the entire trail, but it can be broken down into shorter chunks. See the website for maps and distances.

Lakeside Beach Hopfräben

Brunnen   SWIMMING
(adult/child Sfr4/2; ☺10am-7pm May-Sep) The best of Brunnen's two lakeside beaches, this one has a giant hammock, sun loungers, a lifeguard, a wading pool and pontoons. Find it west of the town centre, near the campsites. The other beach (closer to the town centre) is free and is slated for an overhaul.

Touch and Go   PARAGLIDING
(☑041 820 54 31; www.paragliding.ch; Parkstrasse 4) If you want to go higher, this outfit offers tandem paragliding flights from Sfr180. It can also organise flights over Lakes Lucerne and Zug, plus flights from Mt Pilatus.

🛏 Sleeping

Hotel Alfa + Schmid   HOTEL **$$**
(☑041 820 18 18; www.schmidalfa.ch; Axenstrasse 5-7; s Sfr75-120, d Sfr130-220; [P][@]) Spread across two lakefront buildings, this hotel has some inviting rooms with citrusy colour splashes, parquet-style floors and wrought-iron balconies. Budget rooms forgo the best views. The plant-filled terrace restaurant is renowned for its fresh lake fish (mains Sfr26 to Sfr36).

Schlaf im Stroh   FARMSTAY **$**
(☑041 820 06 70; www.schlafimstroh-bucheli.ch; Schulstrasse 26a; adult Sfr25, child Sfr14-17; [P]) Who's the scarecrow in the mirror? You, after spending a night in the straw at the Bucheli-Zimmermann family's farmhouse. Kids love the farmyard animals, and a hearty breakfast is included (evening meals on request). Only open May through October.

Waldstätterhof   HOTEL **$$**
(☑041 825 06 06; www.waldstaetterhof.ch; Waldstätterquai 6; s/d from Sfr200/310; [@][☎]) Queen Victoria and Winston Churchill top the list of famous past guests at this grand waterfront hotel. First impressions are good, what with the private swimming area, breakfast included in the price and bustling summer terrace, but the rather corporate rooms are in need of a major update.

Two decent campsites in west Brunnen are open from Easter to September: family-run **Camping Urmiberg** (☑041 820 33 27; sites per adult/child/tent/car Sfr6.30/3.40/7/2.70) and lakefront **Camping Hopfreben** (☑041 820 18 73; www.camping-brunnen.ch, in German; sites per adult/child/tent/car Sfr7.50/3.50/8/5), which is a little better overall.

🍴 Eating & Drinking

Gasthaus Ochsen   EUROPEAN **$$**
(Bahnhofstrasse 18; mains Sfr15.90-33.90; ☺lunch & dinner) Welcome to Brunnen's oldest haunt. It specialises in chicken in a basket, and we're willing to bet that the Swiss celebs whose photos line the walls here didn't veer from the joint's more-ish signature dish. There's also a great little apéro bar under the same ownership just across the way.

Mezcalito   MEXICAN **$$**
(Axenstrasse 9; mains Sfr27.50-47; ☺dinner Mon-Fri, lunch & dinner Sat & Sun) Sombreros, technicolour throws and a lively vibe attract munchers to this Mexican-style joint just across the road from the waterfront. Cheesy nachos, fajitas and burritos are washed down with potent house cocktails.

Quai 2
BAR

(Waldstätterquai 2; ☺8am-late Mon-Fri, 9am-1am Sat; 🛜) Brunnen's coolest bar has friendly service and a decent little list of wine and cocktails. It's a handy spot to wait for boats and even has a first-rate change room for bubs.

Badhüsli
BAR

(www.badhüsli.ch, in German; lakefront; ☺from 2pm Tue-Sun) This cave-like den, with a tree-shaded terrace overlooking the lake, has theatrical red velvet benches and stone walls, making it a charming spot for a drink. Don't miss the fondues in winter.

ℹ Information

The helpful **tourist office** (☏041 825 00 40; www.brunnentourismus.ch; Bahnhofstrasse 15; ☺8.30am-6pm Mon-Fri, 9am-1pm Sat & Sun Jun-Sep, 8.30am-noon & 1.30-5.30pm Mon-Fri Oct-May) has information and internet access. The office is five minutes from the train station (follow the signs). The Vierwaldstättersee Guest Card entitles you to discount bike rental from the City Hotel and free entrance to the town's two lakeside beaches.

ℹ Getting There & Away

By far the most pleasant way to reach Brunnen is to take a boat from Lucerne (Sfr37, 1¾ hours). The train (Sfr16.20, 45 minutes to one hour) is cheaper and quicker, although a change in Arth-Goldau is often necessary. There are also road connections from Lucerne, Zug and Flüelen, and bus 2 connects Brunnen with Schwyz frequently and fast.

Schwyz

POP 14,200 / ELEV 516M

The arrow-shaped Mythen mountains (1898m and 1811m) give Schwyz its edge. And not only the peaks here are jagged. Surrounded by cow-grazed pastures, this unassuming little town is the birthplace of that pocket-sized, multifunctional camping lifesaver – the Swiss army knife. As if that wasn't enough, it's also home to the most important document in Swiss history, the 1291 charter of federation.

◎ Sights

If you're planning on visiting the last three sights on this list, it's worth picking up the Museen in Schwyz pass for Sfr10, which has no expiry date.

Hauptplatz
SQUARE

Most action in Schwyz spirals around the gurgling fountain on cobbled Hauptplatz (main square), dominated by the **Rathaus** (town hall), complete with elaborate 19th-century murals depicting the Battle of Morgarten, and the baroque **St Martin's Church**.

Bundesbriefmuseum
HISTORY MUSEUM

(www.bundesbriefmuseum.ch, in German; Bahnhofstrasse 20; adult/child Sfr4/free; ☺9-11.30am & 1.30-5pm Tue-Fri, 9am-5pm Sat & Sun) The Museum of Federation is worth a visit alone to eyeball the original 1291 charter of federation signed by Nidwalden, Schwyz and Uri cantons. It's accompanied by some academic bickering in German and French about its authenticity, as many historians question the accuracy of Switzerland's founding 'myths'. Pick up an English booklet at the front desk. The museum is closed on Saturday and Sunday mornings November through April.

Forum der Schweizer Geschichte
HISTORY MUSEUM

(www.landesmuseen.ch; Hofmatt; adult/child Sfr8/free; ☺10am-5pm Tue-Sun) The Forum of Swiss History was under wraps when we passed through, but the helpful staff was keen to point out that it will be totally revamped and will have reopened by late October 2011. The cultural hub of the National Museum, it focuses on the foundation of the Swiss Confederation and makes for an engaging experience for young and old alike.

Ital Reding-Hofstatt
HISTORIC BUILDING

(www.irh.ch; Rickenbachstrasse 24; adult/child Sfr5/free; ☺2-5pm Tue-Fri, 10am-noon & 2-5pm Sat & Sun 1 May-31 Oct) Set in baroque gardens, the turreted Ital Reding-Hofstatt was once the home of mercenary soldiers. Roam the 17th-century manor's beautiful wood-panelled rooms and vaulted cellar for a taste of the past. Across the way lies House Bethlehem, a Lilliputian house dating from 1287.

Victorinox
OUTDOOR EQUIPMENT

(www.victorinox.ch; Schmiedgasse 57; ☺7.30am-noon & 1.15-6pm Mon-Fri, 8am-3pm Sat) Handy and brilliantly compact, Swiss army knives can be bought at the source at Victorinox's factory shop. Karl Elsener founded the company in 1884 and, after a shaky start, hit pay dirt with the 'Officer's Knife' in 1897.

🏃 Activities

Hölloch Caves   ADVENTURE SPORTS
(www.hoellgrotten.ch, in German) Venture to the bowels of the earth at the eerie Hölloch caves in Muotatal, some 35 minutes from Schwyz. The 190km labyrinthine caves are the longest in Europe and the fourth-biggest in the world. You'll need a guide, sturdy footwear and warm clothing to explore them. **Trekking Team** (☑041 390 40 40; www.trekking.ch; short tours adult/child Sfr20/10, expeditions from Sfr175/88, bivouac tour from Sfr395/195) arranges everything from short tours to day expeditions penetrating further into the core of the mountain. A claustrophobe's nightmare, a troglodyte's dream, the overnight bivouac tours offer a surreal experience including (it could only happen in Switzerland) a fondue feast in the inky cavern darkness.

Adventure Point   ADVENTURE SPORTS
(☑079 247 74 72; www.adventurepoint.ch, in German) Adventure Point tempts with a range of adrenalin-charged activities, from caving in Hölloch (Sfr95) to canyoning in Muotaschlucht (Sfr125) and snowshoeing tours (from Sfr65).

Stoos   HIKING
(www.stoos.ch) Plenty of hikes begin from nearby Stoos on a plateau above Vierwaldstättersee, affording long views across the Muotatal to Rütli, Rigi and Pilatus.

🛏 Sleeping & Eating

The following Sleeping options have good food available for guests, and Hauptplatz has a number of restaurants to choose from.

Wysses Rössli   HOTEL $$
(☑041 811 19 22; www.wrsz.ch; Am Hauptplatz; s/d from Sfr120/220; 🅿@🛜) Goethe once stayed at this centuries-old hotel, whose spacious rooms have been renovated in generic modern style. The restaurant serves Swiss cuisine with a Mediterranean-style twist.

Hirschen   HOSTEL $
(☑041 811 12 76; www.hirschen-schwyz.ch; Hinterdorfstrasse 14; dm Sfr32, s/d Sfr59/102, with bathroom Sfr70/124; 🅿@🛜) This cheerful pad makes up for fairly basic digs with a friendly vibe and a welcome drink. There's a kitchen, pub, courtyard and tidy social calendar. To get here, follow the signs from Hauptplatz.

My Thing   CAFE $
(☑041 810 30 00; Hauptplatz 7; snacks/mains Sfr7.50/20.80; ⏱6.30am-midnight Mon-Fri, 8am-midnight Sat, 8am-10pm Sun) Retreat to a cosy nook in the cave-like cellar at this local cafe. Scatter cushions and candlelight make it a snug spot to munch baguettes and salads or nurse a glass of merlot. Sit on the postage-stamp terrace when the sun's out.

ℹ Information

The **tourist office** (☑041 810 19 91; www.info-schwyz.ch, in German; Bahnhofstrasse 4; ⏱6.30am-6.30pm Mon-Fri, 7.30am-noon Sat) by the bus station has stacks of info on the area.

ℹ Getting There & Away

Schwyz is 30 minutes away from Zug (Sfr9.20) on the main north–south rail route; Lucerne is 40 minutes away (Sfr14.20). Schwyz train station is in Seewen district, 2km from the centre. To reach the centre, take any bus outside the station marked Schwyz Post, and alight at Postplatz.

Schwyz centre is only a few kilometres' detour off the A4 freeway, which passes through Brunnen. The two towns are connected by regular AAAG services (bus 2).

Einsiedeln

POP 14,200 / ELEV 900M

Pilgrims flock to Einsiedeln, Switzerland's answer to Lourdes. The story goes that in AD 964 the Bishop of Constance tried to consecrate the original monastery but was halted by a heavenly voice, declaring: 'Desist. God Himself has consecrated this building.' A papal order later recognised this as a genuine miracle. Even if you don't believe in miracles, the fabulously over-the-top interior of the abbey church is a must-see.

Einsiedeln is south of Zürichsee (Lake Zürich) and west of Sihlsee (Lake Sihl). The train station and the post office are in the town centre opposite Dorfplatz; head through this square and turn left into Hauptstrasse. The church is at the end of this street, overlooking Klosterplatz (a 10-minute walk).

👁 Sights & Activities

Klosterkirche   CHURCH
(Abbey Church; ☑055 418 61 11; www.kloster-einsiedeln.ch, in German; Benzigerstrasse; ⏱5.30am-8.30pm) All roads lead to the Klosterkirche,

so follow the crowds flowing towards this baroque edifice, the 18th-century handiwork of Caspar Moosbrugger. The interior dances with colourful frescos, stucco and gold swirls. Yet most pilgrims are oblivious to the marbled opulence, directing their prayers to the holiest of holies, the **Black Madonna**, a tiny statue in a chapel by the entrance.

Bethlehem Diorama RELIGIOUS
(www.diorama.ch; Benzigerstrasse 23; adult/child Sfr5.50/2.50; ⊙10am-5pm Easter-Oct, 1-4pm Dec-6th Jan) Continuing the devout theme that dominates this town is this diorama, which claims to be the world's largest nativity scene. You can buy a combined ticket for it and the Panorama Painting for Sfr9 for adults and Sfr5 for children.

Panorama Painting of Calvary RELIGIOUS
(www.panorama-einsiedeln.ch; Benzigerstrasse 36; adult/child Sfr5.50/2.50; ⊙10am-5pm Easter-Oct, 1-4pm Dec-6th Jan) Further down the street from the Bethlehem diorama, this enormous panoramic depicts Christ on the Cross, with explanations in no less than nine languages.

Statue of St Benedikt VIEWPOINT
For a fine view over the abbey complex to the surrounding hills, wander through the monastery stables and continue uphill for 15 minutes to this statue.

Devil's Bridge BRIDGE
A two-hour walk north of Einsiedeln and back will bring you to the narrow, wood-covered Devil's Bridge (Teufelsbrücke), also built by abbey master Caspar Moosbrugger.

❶ Information

The **tourist office** (☏055 418 44 88; www .einsiedeln.ch, in German; Hauptstrasse 85; ⊙9am-noon & 1-5pm Mon-Fri, 9am-noon & 1-4pm Sat, 10am-1pm Sun) is near the church and can help you find a bed in any of the town's numerous hotels.

❶ Getting There & Away

Einsiedeln is in a rail cul-de-sac, so getting there usually involves changing at Biberbrugg. It is also within range of Zürich's S-Bahn trains. Zürich itself (Sfr17.20) is one hour away (via Wädenswil). Some of the trains to Lucerne (Sfr22, one hour) require a change at Goldau. From Einsiedeln to Schwyz, you can take the scenic 'back route' in summer: catch a postal bus to Oberiberg, then private bus (Swiss Pass not valid) from there.

Engelberg

POP 3800 / ELEV 1050M

Engelberg (literally 'Angel Mountain') attracts two kinds of pilgrims: those seeking spiritual enlightenment in its Benedictine monastery and those worshipping the virgin powder on its divine slopes. Framed by the glacial bulk of Mt Titlis and frosted peaks, it's little wonder the scenery here features in many a Bollywood production. It's a miracle that despite its deep snow, impeccable off-piste credentials and proximity to Lucerne, Engelberg remains lesser known than other resorts of its size. A blessing, some say.

⊙ Sights

Engelberg Monastery MONASTERY
(☏041 639 61 19; tours adult/child Sfr8/free; ⊙1hr tour 10am & 4pm Wed-Sat Jun-Oct & Dec-Apr) The Engelberg valley was once ecclesiastically governed and the Benedictine abbey was the seat of power. Now the resident monks teach instead of rule, but their 12th-century home has kept its grandeur. Rebuilt after a devastating fire in 1729, it contains rooms decorated with incredibly detailed wood inlays, and a baroque **monastery church** (admission free).

`FREE` **Show Cheese Dairy** DAIRY
(www.schaukaeserei-engelberg.ch; ⊙9am-6.30pm Mon-Sat, 9am-5pm Sun) On the monastery grounds is a state-of-the-art cheesemaking operation, where you can watch the cheesemakers, savour dairy goodies in the bistro and buy creamy silo-free cheeses and other Swiss-themed souvenirs.

☝ Activities

Hiking

There are some 360km of marked hiking trails in and around Engelberg. For gentle ambles and gorgeous scenery, head for Brunni on the opposite side of the valley. The cable car (one-way/return in summer Sfr18/30) goes up to Ristis at 1600m, where a chairlift takes you to the **Brunni Hütte** (☏041 637 37 32; www.berghuette.ch; adult Sfr62, child Sfr15-38), a refurbished mountain hut. From here you can watch a magnificent sunset before spending the night.

In summer, it's possible to leave Engelberg on foot. The Surenenpass (2291m) is a great day hike to Attinghausen, where you can take a bus to Altdorf and the southern end of Lake

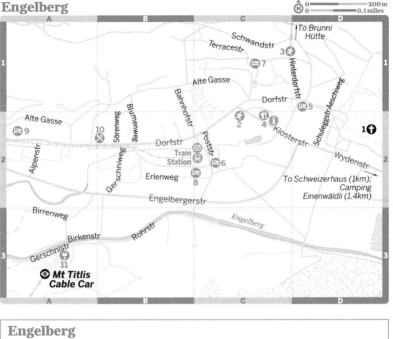

Engelberg

Uri. From Jochpass, a path goes to Meiringen via Engstlenalp and Tannalp. The highest point you reach is 2245m. Pick up a map and check on snow conditions before attempting these more demanding treks.

Skiing & Snowboarding
Snowboarders catch big air on Titlis, Engstlenalp and the half-pipe at Jochpass, while novice and intermediate skiers slide over to family-friendly Brunni and Gerschnialp for baby blues and cruisy reds. The real thrills

for powder hounds, however, lie off-piste. Backcountry legends include Laub (try to ski it in one go like the locals, if you fancy feeling the burn), Steinberg and the biggest leg-burner of all, Galtiberg, running from Klein Titlis to the valley 2000m below. A one-day ski pass costs Sfr60.

There's a **Ski & Snowboard School** (☎041 639 54 54; www.skischule-engelberg.ch; Klosterstrasse 3) inside the tourist office, and places to hire and buy ski/snowboard gear

MT TITLIS

With a name that makes English speakers titter, **Titlis** (www.titlis.ch) is Central Switzerland's tallest mountain, has its only glacier and is reached by the world's first revolving cable car, completed in 1992. However, that's the last leg of a breathtaking four-stage journey. First, you glide up to Gerschnialp (1300m), then Trübsee (1800m). Transferring to a large gondola, you head for Stand (2450m) to board the Rotair for the head-spinning journey over the dazzling **Titlis Glacier**. As you twirl above the deeply crevassed ice, peaks rise like shark fins ahead, while tarn-speckled pastures, cliffs and waterfalls lie behind.

A glacial blast of air hits you at Titlis station (3020m). Inside is a kind of high-altitude theme park, with a marvellously kitsch **ice cave** where you can pick a tune (funk, an upbeat yodelling number, the Indian national anthem…) and watch neon lights make the sculpted ice tunnels sparkle. There's also an overpriced restaurant and a nostalgic **photo studio** on the 4th floor, which specialises in snaps of Bollywood stars in dirndls. Strike a pose with a giant Toblerone or an alphorn against a backdrop of fake snowy mountains from Sfr35.

The genuine oohs and ahs come when you step out onto the **terrace**, where the panorama of glacier-capped peaks stretches to Eiger, Mönch and Jungfrau in the Bernese Oberland. It's a 45-minute hike to the 3239m summit (wear sturdy shoes). Otherwise, enjoy the snowboarding and skiing. The **Ice Flyer chair lift** (adult/child Sfr12/6) will take you down to the glacier park where there are free snow tubes, scooters and sledges to test out. The nearby freestyle park has a half-pipe and good summer snowboarding.

The return trip to Titlis (45 minutes each way) costs Sfr86 from Engelberg. However, in fine weather, you can walk some sections. Between Stand and Trübsee, the Geologischer Wanderweg is open from July to September; it takes about two hours up and 1½ hours down. From Trübsee up to Jochpass (2207m) takes about 1½ hours, and down to Engelberg takes around the same time.

If you're hiking, destinations from Engelberg include Gerschnialp (one-way/return Sfr7/10), Trübsee (Sfr20/28) and Stand (Sfr34/48). Reductions on all fares, including to Titlis, are 50% for Swiss, Eurail and InterRail pass holders.

The cableway is open 8.30am to 5pm daily (last ascent 3.40pm, last descent 4.50pm), but closes for maintenance for two weeks in early November.

throughout town. Shops hire skiing and snowboarding equipment at fairly standard rates from about Sfr50 per day, less if you rent the equipment over a longer period. The staff at Ski Lodge Engelberg is a great source of information too, or stop by Dani's **Okay Ski Shop** (Hotel Bellevue), where hardcore riders hang out and exchange tips.

Engelberg hosts the **FIS Ski Jumping World Cup** (www.weltcup-engelberg.ch), which takes place in December.

Adventure Sports

Outventure   ADVENTURE SPORTS
(☑041 611 14 41; www.outventure.ch, in German; Stans) For an adrenalin rush in summer, this Stans-based outfit offers a lot of fun, including bungee jumping (Sfr170) and paragliding (from Sfr150) and other activities, such as guided *via ferrata* tours and canyoning trips.

Bike 'n' Roll   BICYCLE RENTAL
(☑041 638 02 55; www.bikenroll.ch, in German; Dorfstrasse 31; ☺8.30am-noon & 2-6.30pm Mon-Sat) Get kitted out with a mountain bike from Sfr30 or join a two-wheeled adventure. Rents out climbing gear, should you want to tackle one of Engelberg's five *vie ferrate*.

🛏 Sleeping

The rates quoted are for the high winter season. Expect discounts of 30% to 50% in summer. Many hotels close in the shoulder seasons.

TOP CHOICE **Ski Lodge Engelberg**   HOTEL $$
(☑041 637 35 00; www.skilodgeengelberg.com; Erlenweg 36; s/d/tr Sfr145/250/330; P🛜) This lodge is run by sociable Swedish pro skiers who make the most of their surrounds.

The hotel fuses original art-nouveau flair with 21st-century comforts in smart rooms dotted with black-and-white action shots and old skis. Après-ski here can include a Swedish sauna, gazing up at the snowy peaks from an outdoor hot tub or sharing ski tips over chef Jonas' excellent New Nordic cuisine.

Alpenclub Engelberg BOUTIQUE HOTEL $$
(☑041 637 12 43; www.alpenclub.ch; Dorfstrasse 5; s/d Sfr110/220, s/d ste Sfr240/480; P🔊) A romantic gem in the heart of Engelberg, the Alpenclub's eight rooms echo some 200 years of history – think low wood beams, solid walls and animal-skin rugs. The Steinberg room has stellar Mt Titlis views. Parking costs Sfr8 per day.

Hotel Edelweiss HOTEL $$$
(☑041 639 78 78; www.edelweissengelberg.ch; Terracestrasse 10; s Sfr208, d Sfr376-416; @) Expect a wonderfully warm welcome at this turn-of-the-20th-century hotel. Many of the high-ceilinged, well-maintained but dated rooms afford glacier views. Its communal dining areas retain their grandeur and there are excellent facilities for those travelling with kids, thanks to no fewer than four playrooms and supervised afternoon fun. Prices are almost halved outside absolute peak season (ie winter weekends), making this a great midrange option.

Hotel Bellevue-Terminus HOTEL $$
(☑041 639 68 68; www.bellevue-engelberg.ch; Bahnhofplatz; r Sfr160-320; P@) Once the grand dame of Engelberg, this Victorian-era hotel is slowly but surely getting a facelift. Some of the simpler, slightly tatty rooms may still be on offer when you read this, and will be cheaper than the listed prices. The new rooms are downright natty.

Camping Eienenwäldli CAMPING $
(☑041 637 19 49; www.eienenwaeldli.ch; sites per adult/child/small tent/car from Sfr9/4.50/12/2) Attached to the well-regarded Sporthotel Einenwäldli, this deluxe family-run campsite has access to its restaurant and spa facilities. Ski and shuttle buses will drop you less than a minute from the gate.

SYHA hostel HOSTEL $
(☑041 637 12 92; www.familienherberge.ch, in German; Dorfstrasse 80; dm from Sfr36, d from Sfr92; P@) Ten minutes' walk from the station, this 112-bed chalet-style hostel is clean and modern, with some very large dorms and

facilities such as a luggage and boot room, billiards/foosball room and a big garden.

✖ Eating & Drinking

TOP CHOICE **Ski Lodge Engelberg** MODERN EUROPEAN $$
(☑041 637 35 00; www.skilodgeengelberg.com; Ehrlenweg 36; mains Sfr29-39; 🔊) Chef Jonas Bolling conjures up extraordinarily good New Nordic cuisine, using local (often grown on the premises), in-season produce that's both pretty as a picture and perfect for refuelling after a tough day on the slopes (the three-course skier's menu is a steal at Sfr55). If you're not a guest of the hotel, be sure to reserve a table in the high season.

TOP CHOICE **Hess** MODERN EUROPEAN $$
(☑041 637 09 09; www.hess-restaurant.ch; Dorfstrasse 50; mains Sfr22-44; ☺lunch & dinner Wed-Sun) Crisp linen, hardwood floors and earth tones create a chic backdrop for seasonal/local taste sensations created by Isolde and Ulf Braunert. Its daily menu is great value and service smart. Settle in with a degustation menu (Sfr74 to Sfr125) or get comfy in the Gault Millau–listed cigar lounge.

Yucatan MEXICAN $$
(Bahnhofplatz; mains Sfr27.50-37; ☺from 3pm) Engelberg's après-ski heavyweight is this lively Mexican joint. Mega chilli burgers and caipirinhas fuel parties with DJs, bands and jiving on the bar.

Alpenclub SWISS $$
(☑041 637 12 43; Dorfstrasse 5; pizza Sfr15-26, mains Sfr28.50-47; ☺dinner Mon-Fri, from 11.30am Sat & Sun) This low-ceilinged, candlelit tavern, creaking under the weight of its 200-year history, feels like romance central. Feast away on fondue or Italian staples.

Schweizerhaus SWISS $$
(☑041 637 12 80; Schweizerhausstrasse 41; mains Sfr26-54; ☺9am-11pm, closed Wed May-Nov) Going strong since 1744, this traditional chalet has a light-filled, modern annexe and serves up hearty but refined servings of local produce and Swiss wines.

Chalet BAR
(Titlis base station; ☺3-8pm) For slope-side glühwein imbibing, this log chalet right next to the start of the Titlis cable car is handy.

Spindle CLUB
(Dorfstrasse 5; ☺10pm-4am Wed, Fri & Sat) Revellers spill out of the Yucatan and into Spindle

for after-hours clubbing. It's packed to the gunnels at weekends.

ℹ Information

The **tourist office** (☑041 639 77 77; www .engelberg.ch; Klosterstrasse 3; ☺8am-6.30pm Mon-Sat) is a five-minute walk from the train station and can help with hotel reservations. The standard-issue Guest Card, from all accommodation, is good for various discounts.

ℹ Getting There & Around

Engelberg is at the end of a train line, about an hour from Lucerne (Sfr16.40). If on a day trip, check the Lucerne tourist office's Mt Titlis excursion tickets. A small road off the A2 freeway near Stans leads to Engelberg.

Between early July and mid-October, a free shuttle bus leaves the Engelberg train station roughly every half-hour for all the village's major hotels and attractions. In winter, there are free ski buses to and from the slopes.

Zug

POP 25,700 / ELEV 426M

On the face of it, Zug appears like many other Swiss towns: lapped by a lake and ringed by mountains. However, this is the richest city in one of the world's richest countries. But you probably won't care as you devour *Kirschtorte* (cherry cake), stroll the cobblestoned medieval streets or savour million-dollar sunsets, because Zug's low-key like that.

◎ Sights & Activities

Altstadt   NEIGHBOURHOOD
Zug Old Town is a medieval time capsule. It starts at the town's emblem, the **Zytturm** (Clock Tower; Kolinplatz), whose distinctive roof is tiled in blue-and-white cantonal colours. Walking through the arch, you can veer off into the pedestrian-only lanes of Fischmarkt, Ober Altstadt and Unter Altstadt, punctuated by frescoed 15th-century townhouses and hole-in-the-wall boutiques. Keep an eye out for the fountain depicting **Gret Schell**, an old hag of a Fasnacht character, who lugs her drunken husband home in a basket. The Old Town lies 1km south of the train station; follow the main train station exit into the roundabout at the head of Alpenstrasse and head south for another 700m.

Kunsthaus Zug   ART MUSEUM
(Dorfstrasse 27; www.kunsthauszug.ch; adult Sfr10-15, child free; ☺noon-6pm Tue-Fri, 10am-

5pm Sat & Sun) The local art museum holds a superb collection of Viennese Modernist works by Klimt, Kokoschka and Schiele. There are regular high-profile temporary exhibitions.

Museum in der Burg   HISTORY MUSEUM
(☑041 728 29 70; Kirchenstrasse 11; adult/child Sfr10/free; ☺2-5pm Tue-Sat, from 10am Sun) Uphill from the clock tower is the local museum, an 11th-century castle with paintings, costumes and a 3D model of the town, plus special themed exhibitions. It's an excellent introduction to Zug – and its past tendency to partially sink into the lake.

Landsgemeindeplatz   SQUARE
On the waterfront you'll find this popular square, with an aviary of exotic birds, including kookaburras, hornbills and a family of scarlet ibis.

FREE **Seebad Seeliken**   BEACH
(Artherstrasse 2) Shaded by chestnut trees, this lakefront beach, just south of the Old Town, is perfect for a swim or sunbathe and justifiably popular with locals. Another beach, **Strandbad Zug**, lies west of the Old Town on Chamer Fussweg. It has shaded areas, picnic tables and a kiosk.

Schönegg Funicular   CABLE CAR
This funicular rises to Zugerberg (988m), with impressive views and hiking trails. The Zug day pass (Sfr14) is the best deal, as it covers all bus rides and the funicular. Bus 11 gets you to the lower funicular station.

City bikes   BICYCLE RENTAL
(☑041 761 33 55; Bundesplatz; ☺9am-9pm May-Oct) Bikes are loaned out for free (ID and deposit required).

Marcello's   WATER SPORTS
(www.zuger-see.ch, in German) On the waterfront near Landsgemeindeplatz, pedalos (Sfr22 for 30 minutes, Sfr35 for one hour), rowing boats (Sfr22 for 30 minutes, Sfr35 for one hour) and stand-up paddle boards (Sfr20 for one hour) are for hire. Prices quoted are for weekends, ie slightly more expensive than weekdays.

🛏 Sleeping

With city slickers frequently staying overnight, Zug's hotels often have a corporate feel. Guesthouses offer a homelier vibe – pick up a list from the tourist office.

Once upon a time, Zug was home to struggling farmers. But 1946 marked the start of its rags-to-riches transformation, when the cantonal government decided to implement one of the world's lowest tax rates. Suddenly global multinationals bypassed Zürich to flock here; not because of the Alpine vistas and bucolic charm, but because some bright spark had the idea to create a tax haven in Central Switzerland. Today Zug's 29,000-odd registered companies include Alliance Boots, Biogen, Shell Brands International, the world's richest commodities trader Glencore International and commodities hedge fund Krom River.

With personal income tax hovering between 8% and 12.5%, Zug has become a magnet to tycoons eager to save a bob. Among them is pardoned tax fugitive and aptly named billionaire Marc Rich, famous for his Iran oil dealings in the early 1980s. His Marc Rich Group is based in Zug.

Though Zug might seem unassuming, even a modest apartment can cost at least Sfr1.5 million, so you need to be rich to milk this cash cow.

CENTRAL SWITZERLAND ZUG

Hotel Guggital   HOTEL **$$**
(☑041 728 74 17; www.hotel-guggital.ch; Zugerbergstrasse 46; s Sfr125-177, d Sfr190-225; 🕸) Perched above the lake with fine views to Pilatus and Rigi, this family-run hotel offers quiet and compact rooms, some with balconies. Bus 11 will get you here from the train station.

Hotel Löwen am See   HOTEL **$$$**
(☑041 725 22 22; www.loewen-zug.ch; Landsgemeindeplatz; s/d from Sfr220/290; ❄@) Sitting on a cobbled square in the Old Town and facing the lake, this place has plain, comfy rooms. The Mediterranean restaurant downstairs, Domus, is very popular.

Ochsen Zug   HOTEL **$$$**
(☑041 729 32 32; www.ochsen-zug.ch, in German; Am Kolinplatz; s/d/ste from Sfr190/275/360; P@🕸) It dates from 1480 and once hosted Goethe, but the Ochsen is now a slick business hotel with a historic facade. Suite 503 has wonderful views of the Zytturm and the lake. Parking costs Sfr14.

Camping Zugersee   CAMPGROUND **$**
(☑041 741 84 22; Chamer Fussweg 36; sites per adult/child/tent Sfr9/4.50/11; ⊙8am-11.45am & 2-9pm Apr-Sep; P@🕸) On the shore of the lake, 2km west of the centre. An excellent attractive site, with free swimming in the vicinity.

SYHA hostel   HOSTEL **$**
(☑041 711 53 54; www.youthhostel.ch; Allmendstrasse 8; dm/d from Sfr34.50/102; P@🕸) Modern and clean, Zug's hostel is a 10-minute walk from the station, heading right in the

direction of the Sportanlagen. It's handy for the Strandbad Zug too. Closed early December through mid-March.

✗ Eating & Drinking

Schiff   MODERN EUROPEAN **$$**
(☑041 711 00 55; Graben 2; mains Sfr23.50-59; ⊙lunch & dinner, bar until 12.30am or 2am) Wood panelling and stained glass evoke rustic elegance in the back room of the Schiff. The menu fuses Swiss and world flavours. After dinner, head upstairs to Panorama Bar for dreamy views.

Confiserie Albert Meier   BAKERY **$**
(Alpenstrasse 16; cakes from Sfr4.50; ⊙7am-6.30pm Mon-Fri, 8am-4pm Sat) This old-style cafe is a quaint marriage between an English tea room (with the Pogues as the soundtrack) and an ultra-Swiss bakery selling *Zuger Kirschtorte* (cake made from pastry, biscuit, almond paste and butter cream, infused with cherry liqueur). Many locals say Albert Meier bakes some of the best, so grab an individual slice (Sfr4.50) or the whole cake (Sfr19.50 to Sfr49.50).

Gasthaus Rathauskeller   EUROPEAN **$$$**
(☑041 711 00 58; Ober Altstadt 1; Bistro Sfr26.50-98, Zunftstube Sfr34-135; ⊙11am-midnight Tue-Sat) You can't miss the late-Gothic Rathauskeller's frescoed facade. The downstairs bistro serves marvellous high-end takes on classic local ingredients (such as *cervela*), while the swish upstairs restaurant has creaky floors, gilt Rosenthal crockery and delicacies such as lobster ragout with summer truffles.

ℹ Information

The **tourist office** (☎041 723 68 00; www.zug tourismus.ch; Reisezentrum Zug, inside main train station; ⊙9am-7pm Mon-Fri, to 4pm Sat, to 3pm Sun) has city maps and you can find money-exchange counters at the train station.

ℹ Getting There & Away

Zug is on the main north–south train route from Zürich (Sfr14.20, 25 to 45 minutes) to Lugano, where trains from Zürich also branch off to Lucerne (Sfr11.20, 20 to 30 minutes) and the Bernese Oberland.

By road, the north–south N4 runs from Zürich, sweeps around the western shore of Zugersee and joins the A2, which continues through Lucerne and the St Gotthard Pass and on to Lugano and Italy. The N25 peels off the N4 north of Zug, completes the course around the eastern shore of the lake, then rejoins the A4 at Goldau.

Boats (www.zugersee-schifffahrt.ch, in German) depart from Zug's Schiffsstation, north of Landsgemeindeplatz, and travel south to Arth in the summer among other destinations. Swiss Pass holders go half-price.

Andermatt

POP 1300 / ELEV 1447M

Blessed with austere mountain appeal, Andermatt contrasts low-key village charm with big wilderness, but that's all set to change. The Orascom leisure development group has invested Sfr1 billion into transforming Andermatt's former army barracks into a year-round megaresort (www.ander mattresort.com) complete with six five-star hotels and an 18-hole high-altitude golf course. The creation of 2000-odd jobs is expected to give a much-needed boost to Andermatt's economy, but critics say it will strain the already-fragile Alpine environment, despite eco-friendly measures such as renewable energy policies.

Once an important staging-post on the north–south St Gotthard route, Andermatt is now bypassed by the tunnel, but remains a major crossroads, with the Furka Pass corkscrewing west to Valais and the Oberalp Pass looping east to Graubünden.

◉ Sights & Activities

As Andermatt is situated near four major Alpine passes – Susten, Oberalp, St Gotthard and Furka – it's a terrific base for driving, cycling or bus tours. Check www.postbus.ch for the bus tours offered this year.

Gemsstock   MOUNTAIN

The 2963m mountain attracts hikers in summer and intermediate skiers coming for the snow-sure slopes in winter. The region is also beloved by off-piste skiers seeking fresh powder. The cable car from Andermatt costs Sfr36 for a one-way ticket and Sfr50 for a return ticket. Ski passes cost Sfr56 per day for Gemsstock, Sfr45 for Nätschen/Gütsch and Sfr29 for Realp. Toboggan runs, well-prepared walking trails and sleigh rides appeal to non-skiers in winter.

Oberalp Pass to Lai da Tuma   HIKING

A spectacular hike leads from the nearby Oberalp Pass to sparkly Lai da Tuma (p301), the source of the Rhine. For a vertigo-inducing climb, check out the Diavolo *via ferrata*, three hours of granite scrambling and clambering over grassy ledges. It affords dizzying perspectives over the Devil's Bridge (named after a legend that the devil himself built the bridge after hearing his name called out) traversing a steep ravine.

Steam Trains   RAILWAY

(www.furka-bergstrecke.ch) From Realp, along the flat valley, steam trains run to Furka Fridays through Sundays between late June and early October (daily from mid-July to late August).

🛏 Sleeping & Eating

The tourist office can help find private rooms, but be warned that many places close between seasons.

🗏 River House Boutique Hotel   DESIGN HOTEL $$

(☎041 887 00 25; www.theriverhouse.ch; Gott-hardstrasse 58; d Sfr190-290, ste Sfr300-440; P🗂) This stylish eco-hotel in a 250-year-old building is truly special. The Swiss-American owners have used local materials for the beautiful rooms with inlaid parquet floors and beams, and each room has its own personality. Its restaurant (mains Sfr17 to Sfr45) features local, eco-friendly produce whipped into something special by chef Austen, plus Swiss wines. Reserve in advance if you're not a guest. Parking costs Sfr15 per day.

Hotel Sonne   HOTEL $$

(☎041 887 12 26; www.hotelsonneandermatt.ch; Gotthardstrasse 76; s Sfr85-110, d Sfr150-190; P) An inviting glow beckons you to this dark wood chalet. Rooms are a blast from the '70s but snug with comfy beds and loads of pine.

Downstairs, the beamed restaurant (mains Sfr17 to Sfr39) is as cosy as can be, but the welcome itself could sometimes be warmer.

Toutoune   MEDITERRANEAN **$$**
(Gotthardstrasse 91; mains Sfr23.50-55) This modern restaurant has an appealing menu that highlights sun-drenched flavours. Chow down on just-right falafel or well-executed pasta dishes, washed down with Italian wine.

ℹ Information

The train station is 400m north of the village centre. The **tourist office** (☎041 888 71 00; www.andermatt.ch; Gotthardstrasse 2; ⊙9am-5pm Mon-Fri, 10am-4pm Sat & Sun), 200m to the left of the station, shares the same hut as the postal bus ticket office.

ℹ Getting There & Away

Andermatt is a stop on the Glacier Express from Zermatt to St Moritz. For north–south destinations, change at Göschenen, 15 minutes away. **Matterhorn Gotthard Bahn** (www.mgbahn.ch) can supply details about the car-carrying trains over the Oberalp Pass to Graubünden and through the Furka Tunnel to Valais. Postal buses stop by the train station. The 15km St Gotthard Tunnel is one of the busiest north–south routes across the Alps, running from Göschenen to close to Airolo (Ticino), bypassing Andermatt. The new St Gotthard Base Tunnel, designed for high-speed and freight trains, will be the world's longest rail tunnel and should be operational by 2016.

Basel & Aargau

POP 456,900 / AREA 1958 SQ KM / LANGUAGE GERMAN

Best Places to Eat

» St Alban Stübli (p243)

» Acqua (p243)

» Restaurant Schlüsselzunft (p243)

» Oliv (p243)

» Charon (p243)

Best Places to Stay

» Au Violon (p242)

» Hotel Krafft (p243)

» SYHA Basel St Alban Youth Hostel (p242)

» Les Trois Rois (p243)

» Der Teufelhof (p242)

Why Go?

Tucked up against the French and German borders in the northwest corner of the country, business-like Basel straddles the majestic Rhine. The town is home to top-flight art galleries, museums and avant-garde architecture, and boasts an enchanting old town centre.

The Beyeler Foundation offers one of the most important art collections in Switzerland, there's an absorbing museum devoted to madcap sculptor Jean Tinguely and there are showpieces by some of the world's best contemporary architects in nearby Vitra Design Museum in Weil am Rhein, Germany.

Excursions outside Basel lead the curious visitor to the country's finest Roman ruins at Augusta Raurica, a short train ride east of Basel along the Rhine, and to a gaggle of proud castles and pretty medieval villages scattered across the rolling countryside of Aargau canton. A journey along the Aare takes in the canton's coquettish medieval capital, Aarau, the equally fetching thermal-bath town of Baden and charming castle-topped Lenzburg.

When to Go

Although Basel is famous for its Fasnacht and Vogel Gryff festivals in spring and winter, the best time to visit is in summer. The city shucks off its notorious reserve to bask in some of the hottest weather in Switzerland. As locals bob along in the fast-moving Rhine, whiz by on motor scooters, and dine and drink on overcrowded pavements, you might feel like you're in Italy, rather than on the border with France and Germany. The *Christkindlmarkt* (Christmas market) in the Old Town creates a special magic in the four weeks leading up to Christmas.

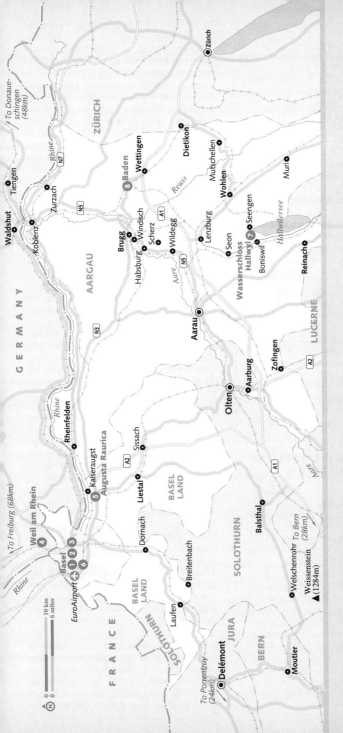

Basel & Aargau Highlights

1 Take in the art at **Fondation Beyeler** (p238)

2 Join in the festivities of **Fasnacht** (p241)

3 Explore the pretty **Old Town** (p238) of Basel

4 Pop across the border to Weil am Rhein's **Vitra Design Museum** (p239)

5 Admire Switzerland's most extensive Roman remains at **Augusta Raurica** (p246)

6 Hit the **bars** (p244) of Kleinbasel for a big night out

7 Visit the pretty moated castle of **Wasserschloss Hallwyl** (p248)

8 Take a thermal soak in **Baden** (p247)

BASEL

POP 166,200 / ELEV 273M

Basel is the closest Switzerland comes to having a seaport; the Rhine is navigable for decent-sized ships from this point until it reaches the North Sea in Holland. It follows a gentle bend through the city, from southeast to north.

Basel's year-round attractions, including the engaging Old Town, are mostly concentrated in Grossbasel (Greater Basel) on the south bank of the Rhine. Over the river, Kleinbasel (Little Basel) is a grittier area, long home to this rich city's working class. The relief bust of *Lällekeenig* ('Tongue King') – there's a copy at the crossroads at the southern end of Mittlere Brücke – sticking his tongue out at the northern end, just about sums up the old attitude between the two sides of town.

History

The Romans founded a colony in Raurica, east of Basel, in Celtic territory in 44 BC. By the time the city (Basileum) was first mentioned in 3rd-century texts, the Romans had established a fort on the heights around what is now the Münster as part of a defence system along the Rhine.

Medieval Basel changed hands several times, passing from the Franks to Burgundy and later to the Habsburgs. In 1501, the city, which had increasingly come to be run by its powerful *Zünfte* (guilds), joined the Swiss Confederation.

By the beginning of the 20th century, Basel was a busy industrial, trade and banking centre. Little has changed since, with the chemical and pharmaceutical industries at the forefront of an economy that contributes 20% of the country's exports. Its importance as a centre of art collections also has a long tradition. In the 1930s, the Kunstmuseum acquired a priceless collection of modern works from Nazi Germany that Hitler and company considered to be 'degenerate art'.

◎ Sights

Opening hours are given for high season (April through October); hours are usually shorter at other times of the year. For more on the city's 30-plus museums and galleries, grab the relevant tourist office booklet or check out www.museenbasel.ch.

Altstadt NEIGHBOURHOOD

The medieval Old Town in the heart of Basel is a delight. Start in Marktplatz, which is dominated by the astonishingly vivid red facade of the 16th century **Rathaus** (town hall). A walk about 400m west of Marktplatz through the former artisans' district along Spalenberg leads uphill to the 600-year-old **Spalentor** city gate, one of only three to survive the walls' demolition in 1866.

The narrow lanes that riddle the hillside between Marktplatz and the Spalentor form the most captivating part of old Basel. Lined by impeccably maintained, centuries-old houses, lanes like Spalenberg, Heuberg and Leonhardsberg are worth a gentle stroll.

About 400m south of Marktplatz is Barfüsserplatz, named after the eponymous church that was deconsecrated in the 18th century and long the seat of the Historisches Museum Basel. The lanes around here are lined with shops and eateries.

Just south of Barfüsserplatz is the zany **Tinguely Fountain** (Theaterplatz), which has all sorts of wacky machines spewing and shooting forth water. It is a foretaste of the madcap moving sculptures in the Museum Jean Tinguely.

[TOP CHOICE] **Fondation Beyeler** ART MUSEUM
(www.fondationbeyeler.ch; Baselstrasse 101, Riehen; adult/child Sfr25/6; ◎10am-6pm Mon-Tue & Thu-Sun, 10am-8pm Wed) Of all the private Swiss collections made public, that of the former art dealers Hildy and Ernst Beyeler is the

---

THE EXPLOSIVE WORLD OF JEAN TINGUELY

Raised in Basel, Jean Tinguely (1925–91) was indefatigable, working on his art, including countless installations, until shortly before his death. Known above all for his 'kinetic art', or sculptural machines, Tinguely spent much of his life in Paris, immersed in the artistic avant-garde. Not all of his machines were designed for posterity; among his more spectacular installations (at a time when installation art was in its infancy) was his self-destructible *Homage to New York*, which failed to completely self-destruct in the gardens of New York's Museum of Modern Art in 1960. A more successful big bang was his *Study for an End of the World No 2* in the desert near Las Vegas in 1962.

most astounding. In the Beyeler Foundation collection, sculptures by Miró and Max Ernst are juxtaposed against tribal figures from Oceania. The walls of this long, low, light-filled, open-plan building designed by Italian architect Renzo Piano are hung with 19th- and 20th-century works by the likes of Picasso and Rothko. The admission price may seem steep, but the breadth of the collection is near overwhelming. Take tram 6 to Riehen from Barfüsserplatz or Marktplatz.

Vitra Design Museum   MUSEUM
(www.design-museum.de; Charles Eames Strasse 1, Weil am Rhein; adult/child €8/free; ☺10am-6pm) Always fancied seeing the amazing Bilbao Guggenheim Museum in Spain and find yourself in Basel? Pop across the German border to this design museum for a small taste of the same. Not only is the main museum building designed by the Guggenheim's architect, Frank Gehry, the surrounding factory complex of famous furniture manufacturer Vitra comprises buildings by other cutting-edge architects, such as Tadao Ando, Zaha Hadid and Álvaro Siza. Exhibitions cover all aspects of interior design, starting in the 19th century and reaching towards contemporary furniture. Catch bus 55 from Claraplatz in Kleinbasel to the Vitra stop (30 minutes). Border checks are possible, so take your passport.

Historisches Museum Basel   HISTORY MUSEUM
(www.hmb.ch; Barfüsserplatz; adult/child Sfr7/free, 1st Sun of month free; ☺10am-5pm Tue-Sun) One of the most wide-ranging collections in the city, the offerings at the Basel History Museum include pre–Christian-era archaeological finds, a trove of religious objects from the cathedral and plenty of material documenting the city's development. Centuries of applied arts, ceramics, weaponry and much more are housed in the former Barfüsserkirche (the Barefooted Ones Church, after the barefoot Franciscan friars who founded it in the 14th century). Highlights include the fine 16th-century choir stall and 15th-century tapestries depicting the dance of death.

Further collections are spread across three other sites. The Musikmuseum (Im Lohnhof 9; ☺2-6pm Wed-Sat, 11am-5pm Sun) contains a veritable orchestra of instruments. The star item of the Haus zum Kirschgarten (Elisabethenstrasse 27-29; ☺10am-5pm Tue-Fri, 1-5pm Sat) is a collection of fine Meissen porcelain. Admission to each is the same as for the main museum, or you can purchase a combined ticket for Sfr14 for all three.

The Kutschenmuseum (Brüglingen, St Jakob im Botanischen Garten; admission free) houses 19th- and 20th- century carriages, sleighs and dog carts.

Münster   CATHEDRAL
(www.muensterbasel.ch; Münsterplatz; 10am-5pm Mon-Fri, to 4pm Sat, 11.30am-5pm Sun) This 13th-century cathedral is a mix of Gothic exteriors and Romanesque interiors and was largely rebuilt after an earthquake in 1356. The tomb of the Renaissance humanist Erasmus of Rotterdam (1466–1536), who lived in Basel, lies in the cathedral's northern aisle. In the crypt are remnants of the cathedral's 9th-century predecessor. You can climb the soaring Gothic towers (Sfr4) in groups of two or more. The two chunky, red-stone, late-Gothic cloisters date mostly to the 15th century but contain Romanesque vestiges.

Kunstmuseum   MUSEUM
(Museum of Fine Arts; www.kunstmuseumbasel .ch; St Alban-Graben 16; adult/childt Sfr15/free; ☺10am-5pm Tue-Sun) The city's principle art museum concentrates on two periods: from 1400 to 1600, and from 1800 to the present day. The smaller contemporary collection features Picassos and Rodins, and has a spread of works that include artists working today. That collection spills over into the nearby Museum für Gegenwartskunst (Museum of Contemporary Art; ☎061 206 62 62; www.kunstmuseumbasel.ch; St Alban-Rheinweg 60; adult/child Sfr12/free; ☺11am-5pm Tue-Sun), which is above all the setting for temporary exhibitions of contemporary art. A combined ticket for the two museums costs Sfr25.

Museum Jean Tinguely   MUSEUM
(www.tinguely.ch; Paul Sacher-Anlage 2; adult/child Sfr15/free; ☺11am-6pm Tue-Sun) Built by leading Ticino architect Mario Botta, this museum dedicated to the often wacky artistic concoctions of Jean Tinguely resonates with playful mischievousness. Unfortunately, you're not allowed to touch most of his 'kinetic' sculptures (see boxed text, opposite), which would rattle, shake or twirl if you did, but with springs, feathers and wheels radiating at every angle, they look appealingly like the work of a mad scientist. The collection includes his Leonardi da Vinci–style sketches for yet

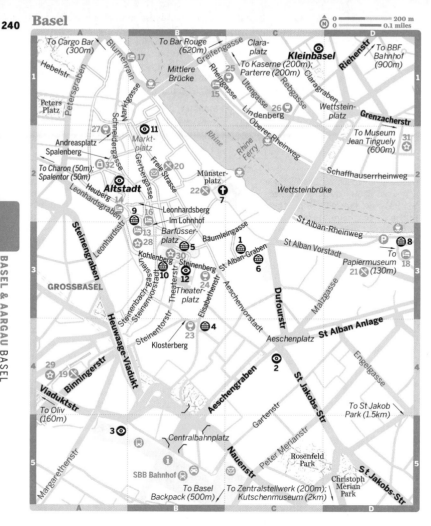

more phantasmagorical thingamajigs and encompasses items spanning the length of his career. Catch bus 31 from Claraplatz.

Antikenmuseum Basel MUSEUM
(www.antikenmuseumbasel.ch, in German & French; St Alban-Graben 5; adult/child Sfr10/free; ⊙10am-5pm Tue-Sun) Across the road from the Kunstmuseum, the Antiquities Museum contains the country's most impressive collection of ancient artefacts, most of which encompass the centuries from the heyday of the Pharaohs in Egypt to Roman times.

Papiermuseum MUSEUM
(www.papiermuseum.ch; St Alban-Tal 37; adult/child Sfr12/free; ⊙2-5pm Tue-Sun) Set in an old paper mill astride a medieval canal and complete with a functioning waterwheel, the Paper Museum evokes centuries past, when a dozen mills operated around here. This one produced paper for centuries and the museum explores that story. Just to the east stands a stretch of the old city wall.

Puppenhausmuseum MUSEUM
(www.puppenhausmuseum.ch; Steinenvorstadt 1; adult/child Sfr7/free; ⊙10am-6pm) Basel's Doll

House Museum attracts teddy-bear fans from all over the place. Indeed, the museum claims to have the world's biggest collection of teddy bears and a total of 6000 objects displayed over four floors. There are doll houses galore too, many extraordinarily detailed and on a scale of 1:12.

Schaulager GALLERY
(www.schaulager.org; Ruchfeldstrasse 19, München-stein; adult/child Sfr10/free; ⏱10am-6pm Tue, Wed & Fri, to 7pm Thu, 1-5pm Sat, 10am-5pm Sun Apr-Sep) A kind of art bunker, the Schau-lager was designed by Herzog & de Meu-ron. The sharply contoured, mostly white gallery is partly rendered in earth dug out from around the foundations. A huge video screen on the front facade gives you a fore-taste of the rolling temporary exhibitions inside. Catch tram 11 from Barfüsserplatz or Marktplatz.

🏃 **Activities**

The tourist office's *Experiencing Basel: Five Walks across the Old Town of Basel* pamphlet lists five walks across town. You can download it from www.basel.com or pick up an audio-visual version, the iGuide, at the tourist office for Sfr15 for four hours or Sfr22 for one day.

Between mid-April and mid-October **Basler Personenschiffahrt** (☎061 639 95 00; www.baslerpersonenschifffahrt.ch) operates city/harbour **boat cruises** (Sfr18; ⏱2pm Tue-Sat), as well as a range of options for long trips to Rheinfelden, or brunch, jazz and dinner jaunts. Cruises depart from Schiff-flände, near Mittlere Brücke.

Swimming in the Rhine river or sunbath-ing on its banks are popular summer pas-times.

⭐ **Festivals & Events**

Fasnacht CARNIVAL
Basel makes much of its huge Fasnacht spring carnival. The festival kicks off at exactly 4am on the Monday after Ash Wednesday with the **Morgestraich**, when streetlights are extinguished and a pro-cession winds its way through the central district. Participants wear elaborate cos-tumes and masks. The main parades are on the Monday and Wednesday afternoons, with Tuesday afternoon reserved for the children's parade. It's also worth visiting Liestal (Sfr5.30, 11-16 minutes by train from

DON'T MISS

EXPLORING ARCHITECTURAL BASEL

Basel and its environs boast buildings designed by seven winners of architecture's Pritzker Prize. Four of those winners – Frank Gehry, Álvaro Siza, Tadao Ando and Zaha Hadid – have works over the German border at the **Vitra Design Museum** (p239).

Some works by Herzog & de Meuron are more central. The Basel-based duo is renowned for designing London's Tate Modern and Beijing's Olympic Stadium. In Basel, as well as the **Schaulager** (p241) and the stadium at **St Jakob Park** (p245), you'll find their wonderful **lace-iron facade** at Schützenmattstrasse 11 and the matt-black **Zentralstellwerk** at Münchensteinerstrasse 115 – surely the only railway goods depot to be an architectural icon! Right by the main train station (SBB Bahnhof) is their surprising glass **Elsässer Tor**.

The renowned Italian architect Renzo Piano is responsible for the **Fondation Beyeler** (p238). Ticino architect Mario Botta hasn't won the Pritzker as yet, but his **Museum Jean Tinguely** (p239) and the offices of the **Bank for International Settlements** at Aeschenplatz 1 are well worth checking out.

Basel) on the Sunday evening before the Morgestraich for the **Chienbäse**, a dramatic fire parade.

Vogel Gryff   TRADITIONAL
This festival is held at the end of January as a symbolic way of chasing away winter from Kleinbasel. The three key figures – *Vogel Gryff* (the griffin), *Wilder Mann* (the savage) and *Leu* (the lion) – dance to the beat of drums on a raft on the Rhine and later in the streets of Kleinbasel.

Leading trade events include the **MUBA** (www.muba.ch, in German & French) Swiss industries fair every spring, the **Herbstmesse** (Autumn Fair; www.messen-maerkte.bs.ch) in October, **Baselworld: The Watch and Jewellery Show** (www.baselworld.ch) in March and **ART Basel** (www.artbasel.ch), the contemporary art fair, in June.

Other events include the **Swiss Indoors** (www.swissindoorsbasel.ch) tennis championship, held in Basel in late October and early November, and one of Switzerland's biggest annual sporting events. Basel-born record-breaker Roger Federer took his eighth home-town title (out of 12 played) there in 2011. Jazz fans should keep an eye on Basel's **Offbeat Jazz Festival** (www.jazzfestivalbasel .ch), held over two weeks in the second half of April.

🛏 Sleeping
Book ahead if coming for a convention or trade fair. There are no trade fairs in July or August, but some Basel hotels annoyingly close then. When you check in, remember to ask for your mobility ticket, which entitles you to free use of public transport.

For a wide range of B&Bs in the area, visit www.bbbasel.ch.

GROSSBASEL

TOP CHOICE ⯌ **Au Violon**   HOTEL **$$**
(☎061 269 87 11; www.au-violon.com; Im Lohnhof 4; s Sfr123-185, d Sfr146-208; ☎) The doors are one of the few hints that quaint, atmospheric Au Violon was a prison from 1835 to 1995. Most of the rooms are two cells rolled into one and either look onto a delightful cobblestone courtyard or have views of the Münster. Sitting on a leafy hilltop, it also has a well-respected restaurant.

Der Teufelhof   HOTEL **$$$**
(☎061 261 10 10; www.teufelhof.com; Leonhardsgraben 49; s/d in Galeriehotel from Sfr151/251, r in Kunsthotel Sfr180-748; 🅿) 'The Devil's Court' fuses two hotels into one. The Kunsthotel's nine rooms have varying colour schemes, parquet floors and crisp white bedding. The larger Galeriehotel annexe, a former convent, is more about stylish everyday design, but the rooms vary considerably in size and atmosphere. An excellent restaurant caps it all off.

SYHA Basel St Alban Youth Hostel   HOSTEL **$**
(☎061 272 05 72; www.youthhostel.ch/basel; St-Alban Kirchrain 10; dm Sfr41.80, s 120, d Sfr133.60; ☎) A swank new youth hostel in a very pleasant part of town in a building that mixes old with contemporary design. It's 15 minutes on foot from the SBB Bahnhof and

a few minutes from the Rhine. Rooms have up to six beds.

Les Trois Rois
LUXURY HOTEL $$$

(☎061 260 50 50; www.lestroisrois.com; Blumenrain 8; r from Sfr405; ☎) Without doubt the top address in town, The Three Kings offers public areas and rooms that combine a dignified elegance of times gone by (anyone for a waltz in the ballroom?) with key indispensable mod cons, such as the state-of-the-art Bang & Olufsen media centre in each room. Rates include access to the sauna amd gym, and a free minibar. Room rates drop around 25% at weekends.

Basel Backpack
HOSTEL $

(☎061 333 00 37; http://baselbackpack.com; Dornacherstrasse 192; dm from Sfr32, s/d Sfr80/100; @) Converted from a factory, this independent hostel has cheerful, colour-coded eight-bed dorms and more sedate doubles and family rooms. It has a crisp feel, and for a little more you can get yourself a king-size bed. They rent out bicycles (Sfr20 a day) and offer internet, breakfast (Sfr8) and laundry services (for a fee).

Hotel Stadthof
HOTEL $

(☎061 261 87 11; www.stadthof.ch; Gerbergasse 84; s/d Sfr80/130) You'll need to book ahead at this spartan but decent central hotel. Set above a pizzeria on an Old Town square, the nine rooms are squeaky clean (with shared loo and shower) and the owners of this centuries-old building are very friendly.

KLEINBASEL
Hotel Krafft
BOUTIQUE HOTEL $$

(☎061 690 91 30; www.hotelkrafft.ch; Rheingasse 12; s/d from Sfr170/270, with river view Sfr200/320) The Krafft appeals to design-savvy urbanites. Sculptural modern chandeliers dangle in the creaky-floored dining room overlooking the Rhine, and minimalist tea bars (all stainless steel, grey and Japanese teapots) adorn each landing of the spiral stairs.

✖ Eating

Basel's culinary culture benefits from the city's location bang up against the French and German borders and its long history of immigration, especially from southern Europe.

GROSSBASEL

TOP CHOICE **St Alban Stübli**
SWISS, EUROPEAN $$$

(☎061 272 54 15; www.st-alban-stuebli.ch; St Alban Vorstadt 74; mains Sfr40-55; ☉lunch & dinner Mon-Fri) Set in a quiet street, it looks like a typical cosy tavern but is an exquisite haven for gourmet cooking, local and French. One of many savoury success stories is the *Perlhuhnbrust mit Speck an Salbeijus mit Saisongemüse und Risotto mit Oliven und Tomaten* (guinea fowl breast with bacon and sage juice, vegetables and an olive and tomato risotto).

Acqua
ITALIAN $$

(☎061 564 66 66; www.acquabasilea.ch; Binningerstrasse 14; mains Sfr18-45; ☉lunch & dinner Tue-Fri, dinner Sat) For a special experience, head to these converted waterworks beside a quiet stream. The atmosphere is glam post-industrial, with brown-leather banquettes, candles and chandeliers inside bare stone and concrete walls and floors. The food is Tuscan, and Basel's beautiful people drink in the attached lounge bar.

Restaurant Schlüsselzunft
INTERNATIONAL $$$

(☎061 261 20 46; www.schluesselzunft.ch; Freie Strasse 25; mains Sfr36-58; ☉lunch & dinner, closed Sun Jun-Aug) Housed in a 15th-century guildhouse that had a neo-Renaissance remake early in the 20th century, this restaurant is an exercise in elegant dining. Tables are arranged over a vast area, including in a kind of internal courtyard with sweeping staircase. How about *Thunfischsteak mit Orangenkruste auf Sesam-Algengemüse und Basmatireis* (orange-crusted tuna steak with a sesame and algae vegetable accompaniment and Basmati rice)?

Oliv
MEDITERRANEAN $$

(☎061 283 03 03; www.restaurantoliv.ch; Bachlettenstrasse 1; mains Sfr30-42; ☉lunch & dinner Tue-Fri, dinner Sat) Trendy Oliv leans towards fresh and varied Mediterranean cooking. You might be tempted by the aubergine ravioli or the *Wolfsbarsch im Ofen gebacken auf Zucchetti-Artischockenragout an Zitronensauce* (oven-baked sea bass with squash-artichoke ragout with lemon sauce). They have a set lunch for between Sfr25 and Sfr32 and in summer they open a pleasing little outdoor dining area.

Charon
SWISS, FRENCH $$

(☎061 261 99 80; Schützengraben 62; mains Sfr40-52; ☉lunch & dinner Mon-Fri May-Sep, Tue-Sun Oct-Apr) In what looks like someone's home, this understated restaurant with art-nouveau decorative touches offers carefully prepared dishes leaning slightly to French tastes. One of the house specialities is the *Seezunge gebraten mit Minikapern* (a whole slab of sole baked with baby capers). Or tuck into a pistacchio sausage from Vaud on a bed of lentils.

Zum Isaak EUROPEAN $$

(☎061 261 47 12; www.zum-isaak.ch; Münsterplatz 16; dishes Sfr22-38; ☺lunch & dinner) With a sober but pleasant interior and a charming, leafy and cobblestone garden dining area out the back, this handy spot for the Münster offers a brief but eclectic menu. You might plump for the *Entenbrust*, strips of duck breast dripping in a honey and balsamic sauce and served with rosemary-speckled oven potatoes.

KLEINBASEL

Parterre VEGETARIAN $$

(☎061 695 89 98; www.parterre.net; Klybeckstrasse 1b; mains Sfr19-35; ☺10am-11pm Mon-Wed, to midnight Thu-Sat) An eclectic mix of dishes, with a hefty vegetarian contingent, stud the menu in this alternative, post-industrial canteen-style place overlooking the Kaserne Park. In summer, grab a table outside!

🍷 Drinking

Steinenvorstadt and Barfüsserplatz teem with teens and 20-somethings on the weekends. A more interesting area is Kleinbasel, around Rheingasse and Utengasse. There is a slight air of grunge, quite a few watering holes and something of a red-light zone to lend it edge.

GROSSBASEL

Zum Roten Engel BAR, CAFE

(☎061 261 20 08; Andreasplatz 15; ☺9am-midnight Mon-Sat, 10am-10pm Sun) This student-filled venue, spilling onto an irresistible, tiny cobblestone square, is great for a latte and snacks by day and a glass of wine or three in the evening. It's a temperate way to start the

ⓘ ONE-STOP, TRI-NATIONAL CULTURE PASS

If you're planning on travelling extensively from Basel through Alsace in France and as far north as Mannheim in Germany, consider investing in a Museumspass, which gives admission to 190 museums over one year. The pass for one adult costs Sfr118 (or €73) and includes up to five children under 18 years of age.

night. They do a relaxed brunch from 11am to 4pm on Sundays (Sfr18.80).

Cargo Bar BAR

(☎061 321 00 72; www.cargobar.ch; St Johanns Rheinweg 46; ☺4pm-late) A nice halfway house between cool and alternative, located in a tucked-away spot on the river. Art installations, live gigs, video shows and DJ performances pepper this art bar's busy calendar. Gigs, ranging from jazz through folk to electro, generally start at 9pm. In summer, they scatter a few tables out along the riverside street.

Campari Bar BAR

(☎061 272 83 83; www.restaurant-kunsthalle.ch; Steinenberg 7; ☺8am-late) A soothing spot for an upscale cocktail moment. Especially in warmer weather, the terrace is perfect for a sip, natter and a listen to the water play of the Tinguely Fountain.

Atlantis BAR

(☎061 228 96 96; www.atlan-tis.ch; Klosterberg 13; ☺5pm-late Tue-Sat) Leather-topped stools are strung behind the long, curving and – on DJ weekend nights – packed bar. Themes change constantly and range from funk to '90s. Maybe this is why it attracts a mostly 30-something crowd. It has a summer rooftop terrace and does lunch Monday to Friday.

KLEINBASEL

TOP CHOICE Consum BAR

(☎061 690 91 35; Rheingasse 19; ☺5pm-midnight) With its chilled music, exquisite tiled floor, timber furniture and breezy feel, this is a marvellous spot to take your wine tastebuds around the world. They will open one of more than 100 bottles for you if you order just three decilitres (about three glasses). Accompany with tasty cheese and cold meat platters.

Bar Rouge BAR

(☎061 361 30 21; www.barrouge.ch; Level 31, Messeplatz 10; ☺5pm-late) This plush red bar, with panoramic views from the 31st floor of the ugly glass *Messeturm* (trade fair tower), is the city's most memorable. Hipsters, and a few suits early on weekday evenings, come to appreciate the regular DJs and events. There's jazz on Mondays, ladies' night on Thursdays and a disco versus salsa duel on Saturdays.

Hirscheneck BAR

(☎061 692 73 33; Lindenberg 23; ☺9am-midnight Sun-Thu, 10am-2am Fri & Sat) A relaxed, grungy,

ACID HOUSE

Home to the Roche and Novartis companies, the Basel region is the epicentre of Switzerland's multibillion-franc pharmaceutical industry.

In 1943 a chemist at the Sandoz company, Albert Hofmann (1906–2008), accidentally absorbed an experimental compound through the skin of his fingertips while searching for a migraine cure and (oops!) took the world's first 'acid trip'.

The lysergic acid diethylamide (LSD) provoked a series of psychedelic hallucinations. Hofmann liked it so much, he tried it again.

Later, LSD was taken up by writers and artists, such as Aldous Huxley, who saw it as a creative force. Its mind-bending properties also made it a favourite with the 'far out' flower-power generation of the 1960s, around which time it was outlawed in most countries.

almost knockabout place with an urban vibe (try to spot someone *without* piercings), this corner bar has tables on the footpath and regular gigs and DJs – it would be right at home in the eastern half of Berlin.

Kaserne BAR
(www.kaserne-basel.ch; Klybeckstrasse 1b) Opening times depend on what's on at this busy location for alternative theatre as well as drinking and dancing.

☆ Entertainment

For a comprehensive rundown on what's happening in town, pick up the monthly *Basel Live* brochure from the tourist office. The Stadtcasino (www.stadtcasino.ch) and other big venues about town like the Messe (trade fair) buildings are often used to host big musical acts.

Live Music

The **Basel Symphony Orchestra** (www .sinfonieorchesterbasel.ch) and **Basel Chamber Orchestra** (www.kammerorchesterbasel.ch) both play at the Stadtcasino.

TOP
CHOICE ⟩ **Bird's Eye Jazz Club** JAZZ
(☑061 263 33 41; www.birdseye.ch; Kohlenberg 20; ☺8-11.30pm Tue-Sat Sep-May, Wed-Sat Jun-Aug) This is among Europe's top jazz dens,

attracting local and headline foreign acts. Concerts start most evenings at 8.30pm. **245**

Sudhaus Warteck MUSIC
(☑061 681 44 10; www.sudhaus.ch; Burgweg 15; ☺Aug-May) Offers a colourful cultural calendar, with anything from African percussion to '50s dance tunes on the menu.

Nightclubs

Die Kuppel CLUB
(☑061 564 66 00; www.kuppel.ch, in German; Binningerstrasse 14; ☺from 9pm Tue, 11pm Thu & 10pm Fri & Sat) This is an atmospheric wooden dome, with a dance floor and cocktail bar, located in a secluded park. Salsa, soul, house and '70s and '80s music are regularly on the bill. The closing time is late and flexible. The place is set to get a major overhaul.

Sport

FC Basel SPECTATOR SPORT
(www.fcb.ch) Basel is home to one of Switzerland's top football teams, which plays at St Jakob Park, 2km east of the main train station (SBB Bahnhof). Take tram 14 from Barfüsserplatz or Marktplatz.

🛍 Shopping

The area around Marktplatz and Barfüsserplatz teems with shops, selling everything from fashion to fine foods.

Long, pedestrian-only Freie Strasse, which runs southeast from Marktplatz, is lined with stores of all persuasions.

Spalenberg, a lovely climbing lane to explore in its own right, is home to a line-up of intriguing boutiques. **Weihnachtshaus Johann Wanner** (☑061 261 48 26; www .johannwanner.ch; Spalenberg 14) is a well-known Christmas store – pick up festive decorations year-round.

If you're in Basel in the run-up to Christmas, you'll sample plenty of the season's cheer at the Christmas markets set up in Barfüsserplatz and Marktplatz. Grab some glühwein and meander.

Marktplatz hosts a food market on the weekends year-round.

ℹ Information

Discount Card

BaselCard (24/48/72hr from Sfr20/27/35) offers entry to nine museums (permanent collections only) and Basel Zoo (www.zoobasel .ch, in German), plus guided tours and ferry rides. If you don't have a mobility ticket (available from your hotel), consider the 24-hour

BASEL & AARGAU BASEL

version for Sfr25, which includes unlimited free public transport.

Medical Services
Universitätsspital (☑061 265 25 25; www .unispital-basel.ch; Petersgraben 4)

Post
Main post office (Rüdengasse 1; ⊘7.30am-6.30pm Mon-Wed, to 7pm Thu-Fri, 8am-5pm Sat)

Tourist Information
Basel Tourismus (☑061 268 68 68; www .basel.com) SBB Bahnhof (Bahnhof; ⊘8.30am-6pm Mon-Fri, 9am-5pm Sat, to 3pm Sun & holidays); Stadtcasino (Steinenberg 14; ⊘9am-6.30pm Mon-Fri, to 5pm Sat, 10am-3pm Sun & holidays) The Stadtcasino branch organises two-hour English-language walking tours of the city centre (adult/child Sfr15/7.50), usually starting at 2.30pm Monday to Saturday May through October, and on Saturdays the rest of the year.

Websites
Lonely Planet (www.lonelyplanet.com /switzerland/basel)

❶ Getting There & Away
Air
EuroAirport (☑061 325 31 11; www.euroairport .com) serves Basel (as well as Mulhouse in France and Freiburg in Germany). Located 5km north in France, it has flights to and from a host of European cities.

Boat
An enjoyable, if slow, way to travel to/from Basel is by boat along the Rhine. The main landing stage is between Johanniterbrücke and Dreirosenbrücke.

Viking River Cruises (www.vikingrivers.com) runs an eight-day trip from Amsterdam starting from around UK£1195.

Car & Motorcycle
The A35 freeway heads down from Strasbourg and passes by EuroAirport, and the A5 hugs the German side of the Rhine.

Train
Basel has two main train stations: the Swiss/French train station SBB Bahnhof, in the city's south, and the German train station BBF (Badischer) Bahnhof, in the north.

Two trains an hour run from SBB Bahnhof via Olten to Geneva (Sfr70, 2¾ hours). As many as seven, mostly direct, leave every hour for Zürich (Sfr31, 55 minutes to 1¼ hours).

❶ Getting Around
Buses run every 20 to 30 minutes from 5am to around 11.30pm between the airport and SBB Bahnhof (Sfr3.80, 20 minutes). The trip by **taxi**

(☑061 325 27 00, 061 444 44 44) costs around Sfr40.

If you're not staying in a hotel in town, tickets for buses and trams cost Sfr2, Sf3.20 and Sfr8.50 for up to four stops, the central zone and a day pass respectively.

Small ferries cross the Rhine at four points (Sfr1.60, day passes not valid) constantly from about 9am to 5pm or dusk, whichever comes sooner.

AROUND BASEL

Augusta Raurica
By the Rhine, these **Roman ruins** (☑061 816 22 22; www.augustaraurica.ch; admission free; ⊘10am-5pm) are Switzerland's largest. They're the last remnants of a colony founded in 43 BC, the population of which grew to 20,000 by the 2nd century AD. Today, restored features include an open-air theatre and several temples.

There's also a **Römermuseum** (Roman Museum; Giebenacherstrasse 17; adult/reduced Sfr7/5; ⊘1-5pm Mon, from 10am Tue-Sun), in the Kaiseraugst, which features an authentic Roman house among its exhibits.

The train from Basel to Kaiseraugst takes 11 minutes (Sfr5.30); it's then a 10-minute walk to the site.

AARGAU CANTON

Stretching between Zürich to the east and the canton of Basel Land to the west, Aargau is the homeland of the Habsburgs, the clan that eventually came to rule over the Austro-Hungarian Empire but lost all its territories here to the independent-minded Swiss. Pretty towns and craggy castles dot its main waterway, the Aare river.

Rheinfelden
POP 11,200 / ELEV 285M

Home to Feldschlösschen beer, Rheinfelden, which is just inside Aargau canton on the south bank of the Rhine, 24km east of Basel, has a pretty, semi-circular **Altstadt** (Old Town). Several medieval city gates, defensive towers and parts of the old walls still stand. They say the triangular **Messerturm** (Knife Tower) is so named because it once contained a shaft lined with knives. Anyone thrown in would be sliced to bits.

The pedestrianised main street, Marktgasse, is lined with shops, eateries and the occasional tavern. At its western end, an early 20th-century bridge leads to the Inseli, a once-fortified island that lies in the middle of the Rhine and forms a part of German Rheinfelden on the north bank. Bring your passport.

The **Feldschlösschen brewery** (☏084 812 50 00; www.feldschloesschen.ch; Theophil-Roniger Strasse; tours Sfr12) is housed in a 19th-century building that could be a rough imitation of Hampton Court, only with its own railway and smelling like, well, a brewery. Its name means 'little castle in the field' – a pretty accurate tag. Two-hour tours (in German) with beer tastings theoretically take place twice a day Monday to Friday and on alternate Saturdays. You are supposed to book but you might get on the list just by wandering by in the morning. The brewery is a 10-minute walk from the train station.

Rheinfelden is a short train ride from Basel (Sfr7.40, 11 to 17 minutes).

Baden

POP 17,500 / ELEV 388M

People have been coming to Baden since Roman times for its mineral baths. Its health-resort hotels, bunched together at a bend in the river, could come straight from Thomas Mann's *The Magic Mountain*.

◎ Sights & Activities

Sulphure Springs BATHS

Baden has 19 mineral-rich springs, which are believed to be helpful in treating rheumatic, respiratory, cardiovascular and even some neurological disorders. Head for the public **ThermalBaden** (☏056 203 91 12; www.thermalbaden.ch; Kurplatz 1; adult/child Sfr16/10; ⊙7.30am-9pm Mon-Fri, to 8pm Sat & Sun), where you can opt for sauna and massage add-ons. A major revamp of the

facility, designed by architect Mario Botta, is planned for the coming years.

Some of the spa hotels allow nonguests into their bathing facilities. Various spas and wellness centres are also available – count on a minimum of around Sfr40 for basic facilities.

Altstadt NEIGHBOURHOOD

The Old Town is adorned by a fetching covered timber bridge, or **Holzbrücke**, cobbled lanes and an assortment of step-gabled houses. Climb the hundreds of stairs near the **Stadtturm** (city tower) for a bird's-eye view from the ruined hilltop castle.

Stiftung Langmatt ART MUSEUM

(☏056 200 86 70; www.langmatt.ch; Römerstrasse 30; adult/child Sfr12/free; ⊙2-5pm Tue-Fri, 11am-5pm Sat & Sun Mar-Nov) West of the spas, the Langmatt Foundation houses a cornucopia of French Impressionist art in a stately home.

🛏 Sleeping & Eating

SYHA Hostel HOSTEL $

(☏056 221 67 36; www.youthhostel.ch/baden; Kanalstrasse 7; dm Sfr40, s/d Sfr92/105; ⊙closed mid-Dec–mid-Mar; P @) One of Switzerland's best-looking hostels, this has grey slate floors, earth-red walls and top-quality materials. Members of Hostelling International pay about 20% less. Walk from the train station to the Old Town, cross the Limmat river at Holzbrücke and take the first right into Kanalstrasse to find it.

Atrium-Hotel Blume HOTEL $$

(☏056 200 02 00; www.blume-baden.ch; Kurplatz 4; s Sfr170-200, d Sfr220-330; ❀) An atmospheric old place featuring a wonderful inner courtyard with a fountain and plants; it also has a small thermal pool. Rooms give on to inner galleries that, on the 1st floor, are crammed with breakfast tables and sometimes rowdy diners. No matter, they usually finish dessert by 8pm!

Roter Turm MODERN EUROPEAN $$

(☏056 222 85 25; www.restaurant-roterturm.ch; Rathausgasse 5; mains Sfr24-39; ⊙9am-midnight Mon-Sat) A hip diner and bar in the heart of the Old Town, this Slow Food member offers a mix of modern European, mainly Italian, cuisine alongside more traditional dishes. Gather in the inner courtyard and look out for temporary art exhibitions.

MOVING ON?

For tips, recommendations and reviews, head to http://shop.lonelyplanet.com to purchase a downloadable PDF of the Germany chapter from Lonely Planet's *Western Europe* guide.

🍷 Drinking

Baden is a quiet town, but a few bars bring some weekend life to the centre.

UnvermeidBAR   BAR

(☎056 200 84 84; Rathausgasse 22; ⊙10am-late Tue-Sat, to 8pm Sun) A relaxing place to sip wine is the Bohemian UnvermeidBAR (a play on words in which BAR is part of the word for inevitable), with its grand piano, chandelier, giant mirrors and disturbing artwork.

ℹ Information

Tourist office (☎056 200 87 87; www.baden.ch; Oberer Bahnhofplatz 1; ⊙noon-6.30pm Mon, 9am-6.30pm Tue-Fri, to 4pm Sat). Just opposite the train station.

ℹ Getting There & Away

Baden is 16 minutes away from Zürich by train (Sfr10.40). It is also within Zürich's S-Bahn network (lines S6 and S12, Sfr4.10, 30 minutes).

Southwest along the Aare

The Aare is the longest river located entirely in Switzerland. This tributary of the Rhine rises in glaciers in the Bernese Alps and numerous captivating spots dot its way through Aargau.

BRUGG & WINDISCH
POP 15,800 / ELEV 351M

Ten minutes west of Baden by train lies the Habsburg settlement of Brugg, created as a toll stop on the Aare. Hauptstrasse (Main St), lined by step-gabled houses and pretty facades, winds down to the one-time toll bridge, still guarded by the 13th-century stone **Schwarzer Turm** (Black Tower). The tower was in use as a prison until 1951.

Attached at the hip to Brugg is Windisch, which started life as Roman Vindonissa. Sparse remnants of the one-time Roman garrison town include the foundations of the east gate, along the road leading out of town towards Baden. The gate stands just in front of what was a Franciscan **monastery**, founded by the Habsburgs in 1311. The pleasant three-sided cloister and adjacent Gothic church are now part of a psychiatric institution, set in fields in which you are at liberty to wander.

You can get to Brugg by regional train or the S12 line of the Zürich S-Bahn network (Sfr4.10).

HABSBURG

A vertical stone fortress that would not be out of place in Arthurian legend or a Monty Python sketch, the Habsburg castle was built in 1020 and gave its name to a house that would one day become one of Europe's greatest ruling dynasties.

As in Monty Python's version of Camelot, however, the Habsburgs soon tired of this particular fortress castle (in spite of the views over broad green fields and nearby villages) and it changed hands many times before winding up property of Aargau canton in 1804. It houses administrative offices, a small display on Habsburg history and a hearty **restaurant** (☎056 441 16 73; www.schlosshabsburg.ch; mains Sfr30-55; ⊙9am-midnight Tue-Sun May-Sep, Wed-Sun Oct-Apr).

Buses run every two hours from Brugg train station to Habsburg village (Sfr4, 11 minutes), from where it's a 10-minute uphill walk to the fortress.

WILDEGG

Another tall beauty of a castle awaits 5.5km south of Habsburg atop a green hill at **Schloss Wildegg** (☎062 887 08 30; adult/child Sfr10/2; ⊙10am-5pm Tue-Sun Apr-Oct). The location is lovely and inside the castle is a display on centuries of Swiss history, as seen through the archives and possessions of the Effinger clan, who took over the castle in 1483.

Trains run from Brugg to Wildegg (Sfr5.80, five to 10 minutes).

LENZBURG
POP 8000 / ELEV 406M

From Lenzburg train station, a 30-minute stroll takes you through the once-medieval village, whose fine houses were rebuilt in a low-key baroque fashion after a fire in the 18th century, and on up a leafy hill path to the Kyburg clan's **Schloss Lenzburg** (☎062 888 48 40; www.schloss-lenzburg.ch; adult/child Sfr12/6, gardens only Sfr4/2; ⊙10am-5pm Tue-Sun Apr-Oct). Inside the castle's main tower and one-time dungeon are several floors of period furniture, ranging from medieval times to the 19th century.

Direct trains from Baden (via Brugg) run hourly to Lenzburg train station (Sfr9.60, 25 minutes), from where there are occasional buses to the village and castle.

WASSERSCHLOSS HALLWYL

About 20km south of Lenzburg is one of the prettiest **castles** (☎062 767 60 10; www.schlosshallwyl.ch; adult/child Sfr12/6; ⊙10am-

---

CASTLE PASS

A single ticket for castle fanatics includes the castles of Hallwyl, Lenzburg and Wildegg and costs Sfr27 for adults and Sfr11 for children.

5pm Tue-Sun Apr-Oct) in northern Switzerland. This 'Water Castle' is so named because it is built in the middle of a river – a natural moat. It is, in fact, two modest castles joined by a bridge.

Walking paths wind out southwards towards Hallwilersee, a peaceful lake that can be criss-crossed by ferry.

A half-hourly S-Bahn (running between Lucerne and Lenzburg) calls in at Boniswil (Sfr5.80, 22 minutes from Lenzburg), from where it's a 1km walk east to the castle on the way to Seengen.

AARAU

POP 15,800 / ELEV 383M

The cantonal capital is the charming result of medieval town planning draped on a rising spur of land overlooking the broad flow of the Aare river. Founded by the Kyburgs, the city passed for a time under Habsburg rule before being overrun by Bern canton in 1415. In March 1798, occupying French revolutionary authorities declared Aarau capital of the Swiss republic. This moment of glory was short-lived, as the republican government moved to Lucerne in September.

◉ Sights

Altstadt NEIGHBOURHOOD

Built on a rising spur that, at its highest end (where the 15th-century church is), juts high above the Aare river, the walled Old Town of Aarau is irresistible. Its grid of streets is lined with gracious, centuries-old buildings, all quite different and diverting. More than 70 buildings have in common grand roofs hanging out well beyond the facades over the streets, their timber undersides gaily decorated.

Aargauer Kunsthaus ART MUSEUM

(☏062 835 23 30; www.aargauerkunsthaus.ch; Aargauerplatz; adult/child Sfr15/free; ☺10am-5pm Tue, Wed & Fri-Sun, to 8pm Thu) For a dose of centuries of Swiss art and the occasional temporary exhibition, call by Aargau's home to the fine arts, about 250m south of the Old Town along Vordere Vorstadt and housed in a striking building that was renovated by Herzog & de Meuron in 2003.

⏢ Sleeping & Eating

You'll find plenty of restaurants and bars in the medieval core, but Aarau's three hotels lie just outside.

Gasthof zum Schützen HOTEL $$

(☏062 823 01 24; www.gasthofschuetzen.ch; Schachenallee 39; s/d Sfr118/184) The cheapest option in town, these friendly and functional digs are modern and aimed in part at the business crowd. Rooms are spotless and mostly spacious.

Restaurant Halde 20 SWISS, ITALIAN $$

(☏062 823 45 65; www.halde20.ch; Halde 20; mains Sfr25-65; ☺lunch Mon, lunch & dinner Tue-Fri, dinner Sat) Down from the main bustle, but still inside the Old Town, is this homey Swiss-Italian mix, where you can try anything from good pasta to a juicy veal steak with chanterelles in a whisky sauce.

ⓘ Information

Aargau Tourismus (☏062 823 00 73; www .aargautourismus.ch; Hintere Vorstadt 5; ☺9am-noon & 1-5pm)

ⓘ Getting There & Away

There are direct trains from Baden (Sfr13.40, 25 to 35 minutes, three or four times an hour) and Basel (Sfr20.20, 35 minutes, hourly).

Zürich

POP 368,700 / AREA 1729 SQ KM / LANGUAGE GERMAN

Best Places to Eat

» Alpenrose (p257)
» Coco (p257)
» les halles (p257)
» Kronenhalle (p258)
» Café Sprüngli (p258)

Best Places to Stay

» Townhouse (p256)
» Hotel Otter (p256)
» Lady's First (p256)
» Hotel Widder (p256)
» Kafi Schnaps (p256)

Why Go?

Zürich is an enigma. A savvy financial centre with possibly the densest public transport system in the world, it also has a gritty, post-industrial edge that at times echoes parts of Berlin.

Switzerland's biggest city is not only efficient, it is also undeniably hip. The locals are hard-working early risers but, come clock-off time, they throw themselves wholeheartedly into a festive vortex – the summer Street Parade is one of Europe's largest public parties.

Much of the ancient centre, with its winding lanes and tall church steeples, has been kept lovingly intact. The city, however, is no stick-in-the-mud stranger to contemporary trends. Nowhere is that clearer than in the edgy Züri-West area, the epicentre of the city's nightlife.

Outside the city, Uetliberg is a magnet for walkers and there are countless pretty spots, such as Rapperswil, along the lake. Winterthur, to the northeast, is a cultural powerhouse, with major art and science museums.

When to Go

Zürich is an attractive city to visit at any time of year, but in spring and summer it becomes particularly lively when summertime cafe life spills on to the streets and locals enjoy lakeside and river bathing. Watch out for the August Street Parade (p255).

Winter sets the chilly backdrop that will see you seeking out cosy moments in the city's fine old restaurants and taverns, or bar-hopping in Züri-West. In the four weeks before Christmas you can also catch the big indoor *Christkindlmarkt* (Christmas market).

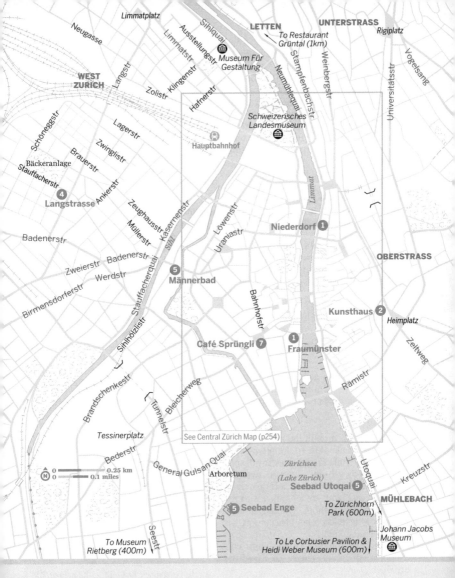

Zürich Highlights

1 Wander the streets of **Niederdorf** and the area around the **Fraumünster** (p252)

2 Admire the extensive art collections in the **Kunsthaus** (p252)

3 Join the throngs for the August **Street Parade** (p255)

4 Lose yourself in a long night out along **Langstrasse** (p259)

5 Hang out with the locals for some summer lake and river **bathing** (p253)

6 Head up the **Uetliberg** (p263) for the view

7 Indulge in pastries and chocolate at **Café Sprüngli** (p258)

8 Allow the kids to be amazed at **Technorama** (p266) in Winterthur

History

Today frequently voted Europe's most liveable city, Zürich started life as a Roman encampment called Turicum. Germanic tribes moved in by AD 400 and, in 1336, the already prosperous town underwent a minor revolution as craftsmen and traders took power, expelling the nobles and creating the 13 *Zünfte* (guilds) that long directed the city's fortunes. Many still exist today and come out to play for the Sechseläuten festival (p255).

In 1351, Zürich joined the Swiss Confederation and, in the early 16th century, became a key player in the Reformation under Huldrych Zwingli. In the following centuries, it grew rich on textiles and banking.

Due to Switzerland's neutrality during both world wars, Zürich attracted all sorts of personalities, from James Joyce to Vladimir Lenin. The counter-cultural Dada art movement was born in Zürich in the wake of the horrors of WWI. It was dead by 1923, but its disturbing spirit lived on in the works of Georg Grosz, Hans Arp and Max Ernst. Dadaist works are on display in Zürich's Kunsthaus.

Since the early 1990s, the city has shed much of its image as a dour town of Protestant bankers and morphed into one of central Europe's hippest hang-outs.

◉ Sights

The city spreads around the northwest end of Zürichsee (Lake Zürich), from where the Limmat river runs further north still, splitting the medieval city centre in two. The narrow streets of the Niederdorf quarter on the river's east bank are crammed with restaurants, bars and shops. The central areas around the lake, especially Niederdorf, are best explored on foot.

To keep in touch with the city's contemporary art scene, check out www.artin zurich.ch.

TOP CHOICE **Kunsthaus** ART MUSEUM
(Museum of Fine Arts; Map p254; ☑044 253 84 84; www.kunsthaus.ch; Heimplatz 1; adult/child Sfr16/free; ☉10am-8pm Wed-Fri, to 6pm Tue, Sat & Sun) Zürich's impressive fine arts gallery boasts a rich collection of largely European art that stretches from the Middle Ages through a mix of Old Masters to Alberto Giacometti stick-figure sculptures, Monet and Van Gogh masterpieces, Rodin sculptures and other

19th- and 20th-century art. The museum is free on Wednesdays.

Fraumünster CATHEDRAL
(Map p254; www.fraumuenster.ch; in German; Münsterhof; ☉10am-6pm Apr-Oct, to 4pm Nov-Mar) The 13th-century cathedral is renowned for its distinctive stained-glass windows, designed by the Russian-Jewish master Marc Chagall (1887–1985). He did a series of five windows in the choir stalls in 1971 and the rose window in the southern transept in 1978. The rose window in the northern transept was created by Augusto Giacometti in 1945.

Schweizerisches Landesmuseum HISTORY MUSEUM
(Swiss National Museum; Map p254; ☑044 218 65 11; www.musee-suisse.ch; Museumstrasse 2; adult/child Sfr10/free; ☉10am-5pm Tue-Sun) Inside a purpose-built cross between a mansion and a castle sprawls an eclectic and imaginatively presented permanent collecion that includes an extesnive tour through Swiss history. Collections range from ancient arms to coins, and traditional crafts to a series of rooms recreating the interiors of everything from a 15th-century convent to contemporary pads crammed with designer furniture.

Museum für Gestaltung MUSEUM
(Design Museum; Map p251; ☑043 446 67 67; www.museum-gestaltung.ch; Ausstellungstrasse 60; adult/concession Sfr9/6; ☉10am-8pm Wed, 10am-5pm Tue & Thu-Sun) Consistently impressive and wide-ranging, the exhibitions at this design museum include anything from works by classic photographers like Henri Cartier-Bresson to advertising for design furniture of yesteryear. Graphic and applied arts dominate the permanent collections, with anything from canned fruit tins to typewriters on display. Take trams 4 or 13.

Museum Rietberg ART MUSEUM
(Off Map p251; ☑044 206 31 31; Gablerstrasse 15; adult/concession permanent collection Sfr12/10, special exhibitions Sfr16/12; ☉10am-5pm Tue & Fri-Sun, to 8pm Wed & Thu) Set in three villas in a leafy park and fronted by a striking emerald glass entrance, the museum houses the country's only assembly of African, Oriental and ancient-American art. This wide-ranging collection is frequently complemented by temporary exhibitions. Take tram 7.

Cabaret Voltaire GALLERY
(Map p254; ☑043 268 57 20; www.cabaret voltaire.ch; Spiegelgasse 1; admission varies;

12.30-6.30pm Tue-Sun) Birthplace of the zany Dada art movement, this bar-cum-artspace came back to life in 2004 as a hotbed of contentious art exhibitions and socially critical artistic ferment. In a sense, it sums up the city's contemporary trick of combining its obvious wealth with a sense of devilish social-artistic trouble-making. Entry to the bar is free and it's open until midnight Tuesday through Saturday.

Migros Museum
MUSEUM

(☑044 277 20 50; www.migrosmuseum.ch; Limmatstrasse 270; adult/child Sfr8/free, combined admission with Kunsthalle Zürich Sfr12/free; ☺noon-6pm Tue & Wed-Fri, to 8pm Thu, 11am-5pm Sat & Sun) Pending renovations at its initial home in the former Löwenbräu brewery, which are due for completion in mid-2012, the Migros Museum, which holds more than 450 works of contemporary art in hand, has moved to temporary premises at Albisriederstrasse 199. The artists represent a rollcall of the past few decades of contemporary creativity. Tram 3 from the Hauptbahnhof runs close by.

Grossmünster
CATHEDRAL

(Map p254; www.grossmuenster.ch; Grossmünsterplatz; ☺10am-6pm Mar-Oct, to 5pm Nov-Feb). More of Augusto Giacometti's work is on show across the river from Fraumünster in the twin-towered landmark cathedral founded by Charlemagne in the 9th century.

The firebrand preacher from the boondocks, Huldrych Zwingli (1484–1531), began speaking out against the Catholic Church here in the 16th century, and thus brought the Reformation to Zürich. You can also climb the southern tower, the **Karlsturm**. **Zwingli's house**, where he lived and worked, is nearby at Kirchgasse 3.

St Peterskirche
CHURCH

(St Peter's Church; Map p254; St Peterhofstatt; ☺8am-6pm Mon-Fri, to 4pm Sat, 11am-5pm Sun) From any position in the city, it's hard to overlook the 13th-century tower of this church. Its prominent clock face, 8.7m in diameter, is the largest in Europe. Inside, the choir stalls date from the 13th century but the rest of the church is largely an 18th-century remake.

Kunsthalle Zürich
GALLERY

(☑044 272 15 15; www.kunsthallezurich.ch; Limmatstrasse 270; adult/child Sfr8/free, combined admission with Migros Museum Sfr12/free; ☺noon-6pm Tue & Wed-Fri, to 8pm Thu, 11am-5pm Sat &

Sun) Like the Migros Museum, the 'Art Hall' features changing exhibitions of contemporary art and has had to move temporarily from the Löwenbräu site to the Museum Bärengasse (Bärengasse 20-22).

FREE Johann Jacobs Museum
MUSEUM

(Map p251; ☑044 388 61 51; www.johann-jacobs -museum.ch; Seefeldquai 17) Coffee is the name of the game and the permanent collection includes everything from coffee pots to paintings of coffee houses. It's about 500m south of Bellevueplatz along the east side of the lake, but is closed until mid-2012.

Beyer Museum
MUSEUM

(Map p254; ☑043 344 63 63; www.beyer -chronometrie.ch; Bahnhofstrasse 31; adult/concession Sfr8/3; ☺2-6pm Mon-Fri) Inside the premises of a purveyor of fine timepieces is this little jewel of a small museum, which chronicles the rise of timekeeping, from striated medieval candles to modern watches.

FREE Le Corbusier Pavilion & Heidi Weber Museum
MUSEUM

(Off Map p251; www.centrelecorbusier.com; Zürichhorn Park; ☺2-5pm Sat & Sun Jul-Sep) Set in quiet parkland, the last item designed by iconoclastic Swiss-born (naturalised French) architect Le Corbusier, looks like a 3D Mondrian painting set. Completed after Le Corbusier's death, it contains many of his architectural drawings, paintings, furniture and books – collected by fan and friend Heidi Weber. It's about 1.2km south of Bellevueplatz along the east side of the lake.

FREE James Joyce Foundation
MUSEUM

(Map p254; ☑044 211 83 01; www.joycefoundation .ch; Augustinergasse 9; ☺10am-5pm Mon-Fri) James Joyce spent much of WWI in Zürich and wrote *Ulysses* here. The foundation hosts regular public readings in English from *Ulysses* (5.30pm to 7pm Tuesday) and *Finnegan's Wake* (7pm to 8.30pm Thursday).

🏊 Activities

Zürich comes into its own in summer, when the parks lining the lake are overrun with bathers, sun seekers, in-line skaters, footballers, lovers, picnickers, party animals and preeners. Police even patrol on rollerblades!

From May to mid-September, official swimming areas known locally as *Badis* open around the lake and up the Limmat river. There are also plenty of free, unofficial places to take a dip. Official swimming

Central Zürich

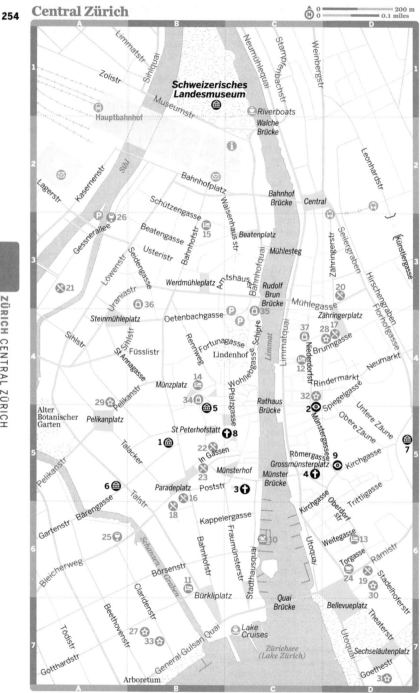

0 200 m
0 0.1 miles

Limmatstr
Sihlquai
Zolistr
Limmatstr
Neumühlequai
Stampfenbachstr
Weinbergstr

Schweizerisches Landesmuseum

Museumstr
Riverboats
Walche Brücke

Hauptbahnhof

Leonhardstr

Lagerstr
Kasernenstr
Sihl
Bahnhofplatz
Bahnhof Brücke
Central

Schützengasse
Waisenhaus str
Beatenplatz

Gessnerallee
26
Beatengasse
Bahnhofstr
15
Mühlesteg

Zähringerstr
Seilergraben
Künstlergasse

Usteristr
Werdmühleplatz
Amtshäus
Rudolf Brun Brücke
Rudolf
Brun
Brücke
35
Hirschengraben
Florhofgasse

Löwenstr
Seidengasse
Mühlegasse
20
Zähringerplatz

21
Uraniastr
Oetenbachgasse
37 28 17
Brunngasse

Steinmühleplatz
36
Rennweg
Fortunagasse
Niederdorfstr
Neumarkt

Sihlstr
St Annagasse
Füsslistr
Lindenhof
12
Rindermarkt

Münzplatz
14
Wohllebgasse
Pfalzgasse
Schipfe
32
Spiegelgasse
Untere Zäune

29
Pelikanstr
34
5
2
Münstergasse
Obere Zäune

Alter Botanischer Garten
Pelikanplatz
St Peterhofstatt
8
Rathaus Brücke
9
Kirchgasse
7

1
22
In Gassen
Römergasse
Grossmünsterplatz
4

Talacker
23
Münsterhof
3
Münster Brücke

6
Paradeplatz
Poststr
Kirchgasse
Oberdorf str
Trittligasse

18
16
Kappelergasse
Weltegasse
13

Gartenstr
Bärengasse
25
Fraumünsterstr
Torgasse
Rämistr

Bleicherweg
Börsenstr
Bahnhofstr
10
24 19
Stadelhoferstr
30

Schanzen Graben
11
Bürkliplatz
Stadthausquai
Bellevueplatz
Theaterstr

Claridenstr
Beethovenstr
27 33
Quai Brücke
Lake Cruises
Sechseläutenplatz

Tödistr
Gotthardstr
General Gulsan Quai
Zürichsee (Lake Zürich)
Utoquai
Goethestr
3

Arboretum

areas are usually wooden piers with a pavilion and most offer massages, yoga, saunas and snacks. Admission is Sfr6, and swimming areas are generally open from 9am to 7pm in May and September and 9am to 8pm from June to August.

Seebad Enge SWIMMING
(Map p251; ☎044 201 38 89; www.seebadenge.ch; Mythenquai 9; Sfr7; ☺mid-May–mid-Sep) At this trendy bath, the bar opens until midnight when the weather is good. It also operates a **sauna** (Sfr27; ☺11am-11pm Sep-Apr, 8-11pm mid-May–mid-Sep, women only Mon), more of a winter attraction but open on summer evenings too. It's about 700m southwest of Bürkliplatz. On the opposite shore, adjacent to the Zürichhorn park and 400m south of Bellevueplatz, is **Seebad Utoquai** (Map p251; ☎044 251 61 51; Utoquai 49; Sfr5; ☺7am-8pm mid-May–mid-September).

FREE **Letten** SWIMMING
(☎044 362 92 00; Lettensteg 10) This bathing area further north up on the east bank of the river near Kornhausbrücke is where Züri-West trendsetters swim, barbecue, skateboard, play volleyball, or just drink at the bars and chat on the grass and concrete.

★ Festivals & Events

The following are just the most important; for a full list of events, see www.zuerich .com.

Sechseläuten PARADE
(www.sechselaeuten.ch, in German) During this spring festival on the third Monday of April, guild members parade down the streets in historical costume and a fireworks-filled 'snowman' (the *Böögg*) is ignited to celebrate the end of winter.

Street Parade PARADE
(www.street-parade.ch) This techno celebration in the middle of August has established itself as one of Europe's largest and wildest street parties since its first festive outing in 1992.

ZÜRICH WITH CHILDREN

In summer, time spent having a dip in the Limmat river or lake is a pleasant investment for the whole family. A walk along the Planetenweg in **Uetliberg** (p263) combines views with exercise and education on the planets.

Parents wanting a one-stop lesson in Swiss history should not fear taking their children to the **Schweizerisches Landesmuseum** (p252), a clever and attractively laid out museum with interactive screens, book corners and even a short slide from the highest part of the history section down to the beginning. With its garden setting, the **Museum Rietberg** (p252) can also be a clever compromise between art and the outdoors.

If you are in town for the **Knabenschiessen**, young ones will doubtless be fascinated by this adolescent shooting fest.

Knabenschiessen   SHOOTING
(www.knabenschiessen.ch, in German) A major shooting competition for 12- to 17-year-olds over a weekend in September.

🛏 Sleeping

Finding a room on the weekend of the Street Parade is tough and prices skyrocket. Prices also sometimes head north for various major trade fairs (including those in Basel).

TOP CHOICE **Townhouse**   BOUTIQUE HOTEL **$$$**
(Map p254; ☑044 200 95 95; www.townhouse.ch; Schützengasse 7; r Sfr195-425; ☎) With luxurious wallpapers, wallhangings, parquet floors and retro furniture, the 21 rooms in these stylish digs come in an assortment of sizes from 15 sq m to 35 sq m. Located close to the main train station, it offers such touches as a DVD selection and iPod docking stations.

Hotel Otter   HOTEL **$$**
(Map p254; ☑044 251 22 07; www.hotelotter .ch; Oberdorfstrasse 7; s Sfr125, d Sfr155-175) The Otter has 17 rooms with a variety of colour schemes ranging from white and blue stripes to olive green. You might get pink satin duvet covers. Studio apartment–style rooms with kitchens are another option.

Lady's First   HOTEL **$$**
(☑044 380 80 10; www.ladysfirst.ch; Mainaustrasse 24; s Sfr230-270, d Sfr290-395; ☎) Immaculate and generally spacious rooms provide a pleasant mixture of traditional parquet flooring and designer furnishings. The hotel spa and its accompanying rooftop terrace are for female guests only.

Hotel Widder   HOTEL **$$$**
(Map p254; ☑044 224 25 26; www.widderhotel .ch; Rennweg 7; s/d from Sfr560/755; P ✳ @ ☎) A stylish hotel in the equally grand district of Augustiner, the Widder is a pleasing fusion of modernity and traditional charm. Rooms and public areas across the eight town houses that make up this place are stuffed with art and designer furniture.

Kafi Schnaps   HOTEL **$**
(www.kafischnaps.ch; Kornhausstrasse 57; r per person Sfr44-59) Set in a onetime butcher's shop, this is a bustling little spot that happens to have a collection of five cheerful little rooms (which you can book online), each named and decorated after a fruit-based liquor. The **bar** (☉8am-midnight Mon-Fri, 9am-midnight Sat & Sun) is grand for a coffee, beer or even, you guessed it, brunch.

SYHA hostel   HOSTEL **$**
(☑043 399 78 00; www.youthhostel.ch; Mutschellenstrasse 114, Wollishofen; dm Sfr48, s/d Sfr123.50/150; @ ☎) A bulbous, purple-red 1960s landmark houses a busy hostel with 24-hour reception and dining hall, flat-screen TVs and sparkling modern bathrooms. Dorms are quite small but prices include sheets and breakfast. Take tram 7 to Morgental, or the S-Bahn to Wollishofen.

Hotel Plattenhof   DESIGN HOTEL **$$**
(☑044 251 19 10; www.plattenhof.ch; Plattenstrasse 26; s Sfr175-275, d Sfr265-405; P ☎) This youthful minimalist design hotel in a quiet residential area has low Japanese-style beds, Molteni furniture and oak parquet floors, plus mood lighting in some rooms. It's cool without being pretentious, and even the 'old' rooms are stylishly minimalist. Downstairs in the same building is a hip cafe.

Hotel Seegarten   HOTEL **$$**
(☑044 388 37 37; www.hotel-seegarten.ch; Seegartenstrasse 14; s Sfr195-295, d Sfr295-405; ☎) Rattan furniture and vintage tourist posters give this place an airy Mediterranean atmosphere, which is reinforced by its proximity to the lake and the on-site Restaurant Latino.

Romantik Hotel Florhof
HOTEL $$$

(☎044 250 26 26; www.florhof.ch; Florhofgasse 4; s Sfr245-330, d Sfr395-570; ☎) Set in a lovely garden, this onetime noble family's mansion contains 35 tastefully appointed rooms and is a stone's throw from the Kunsthaus (p252).

Dakini
B&B $

(☎044 291 42 20; www.dakini.ch; Brauerstrasse 87; s Sfr80-100, d Sfr140; ☎) This relaxed B&B attracts a bohemian crowd of artists and trendy tourists. Four double rooms and two singles, each with its own colour scheme and a couple with balconies, spread across a couple of apartments over two floors, sharing the kitchen and bathroom on each. A scrumptious and filling breakfast in the cool cafe downstairs is thrown in.

Hotel Foyer Hottingen
HOTEL $

(☎044 256 19 19; www.hotelhottingen.ch; Hottingerstrasse 31; dm Sfr45, s Sfr95-130, d Sfr125-180; ☎) This place is a good deal better inside than outside appearances would suggest. The 32 rooms are clinical but good value and some have a balcony. Each floor has showers and a communal kitchen and on the top floor is a dorm for women only with a rooftop terrace.

Baur au Lac
HOTEL $$$

(Map p254; ☎044 220 50 20; www.bauraulac.ch; Talstrasse 1; s/d from Sfr540/870; ☎☎☎) This family-run lakeside jewel is set in a private park and offers all imaginable comforts and a soothing sense of privacy. Rooms are decorated in classic colours, adding to the sense of quiet well-being. Throw in the spa, restaurants and faultless service and you can see why VIPs flock here.

Hotel Rothaus
HOTEL $$

(☎043 322 10 50; www.hotelrothaus.ch; Sihlhallenstrasse 1; s Sfr99-179, d Sfr139-198) Smack in the middle of the Langstrasse action, you'd never guess this cheerful red-brick place was once a brothel. A variety of fresh, airy rooms and suites are complemented by a busy little eatery-bar downstairs.

City Backpacker
HOSTEL $

(Hotel Biber; Map p254; ☎044 251 90 15; www.city-backpacker.ch; Niederdorfstrasse 5; dm Sfr36, s/d Sfr75/114; ☎☎) Friendly and well equipped, if a trifle cramped. In summer, you can always overcome the claustrophobia by hanging out on the rooftop terrace. Be warned, this is a youthful party hostel.

✖ Eating

Denizens of Zürich have the choice of an astounding 2000-plus places to eat and drink. Traditional local cuisine is very rich, as epitomised by the city's signature dish, *Zürcher Geschnetzeltes* (sliced veal in a creamy mushroom sauce).

TOP CHOICE Alpenrose
SWISS $$

(☎044 271 39 19; Fabrikstrasse 12; mains Sfr25-45; ☺lunch & dinner Wed-Sun) With its timber-clad walls, 'No Polka Dancing' warning and fine cuisine from regions all over the country, the Alpenrose makes for an inspired meal out. You could try risotto from Ticino, or *Pizokel* (aka *Bizochel*, a kind of long and especially savoury *Spätzli*) from Graubünden or fresh perch filets.

Coco
EUROPEAN $$

(Map p254; ☎044 211 98 98; www.coco-grill.ch; Bleicherweg 1a am Paradeplatz; mains Sfr25-45; ☺lunch & dinner Mon-Fri, dinner Sat) For straightforward, juicy grilled meats and fish, this is the place to be. Secreted down a short alley just off Paradeplatz, you first encounter a teeny front bar, good for a pre-dinner wine. The almost conspiratorial dining area is out the back.

les halles
FRENCH $

(☎044 273 11 25; www.les-halles.ch; Pfingstweidstrasse 6; mains Sfr20-29; ☺11am-late Mon-Sat) This joyous scrum of timber tables in Kreis

INDUSTRIAL CONVERSION

Symbolic of the renaissance of once-industrial western Zürich is the **Schiffbau** (Schiffbaustrasse). Once a mighty factory churning out lake steamers and, until 1992, turbine-engine parts, this enormous shell has been turned (at considerable cost) into the seat of the **Schauspielhaus** (www.schauspielhaus.ch), a huge theatre with three stages. It is worth just having a look inside. It is also home to stylish restaurant LaSalle (www.lasalle-restaurant.ch), upstairs bar Nietturm (www.nietturm.ch) and jazz den Moods (p262).

Pop around to **Giessereihalle** in **Puls 5** (www.puls5.ch; Technoparkstrasse). This one-time foundry has been converted into a multiuse centre with restaurants, bars and offices.

ZÜRICH EATING

5 is the best place in town to sit down to *Moules mit Frites* (mussels and fries). Hang at the bustling bar and shop at the market. It is one of several chirpy bar-restaurants in formerly derelict factory buildings in the area.

Kronenhalle
SWISS $$$

(Map p254; ☑044 251 66 69; Rämistrasse 4; mains Sfr28-65; ⊙noon-midnight) A haunt of city movers and shakers in suits, the Crown Hall is a brasserie-style establishment with an old-world feel, white tablecloths and lots of dark wood. Impeccably mannered waiters move discreetly below Chagall, Miró, Matisse and Picasso originals. Push the boat out for a Chateaubriand in Béarnaise sauce (Sfr152).

Café Sprüngli
CAFE $$

(Map p254; ☑044 224 47 46; www.spruengli.ch; Bahnhofstrasse 21; ⊙7.30am-5.30pm Mon-Fri, 8am-3pm Sat) Sit down for cakes, chocolate and coffee at this epicentre of sweet Switzerland, in business since 1836. You can have a light lunch too, but whatever you do, don't fail to check out the heavenly chocolate shop around the corner on Paradeplatz.

Restaurant Kreis 6
SWISS, MEDITERRANEAN $$

(☑044 362 80 06; www.restaurantkreis6.ch; Scheuchzerstrasse 65; mains Sfr28-40; ⊙lunch & dinner Mon-Fri, dinner Sat) Whether beneath the high whitewashed vaulting or out in the summer garden (with shady pergola), this makes a charming and romantic spot for a range of Mediterranean dishes in the warmer months and a tendency to Swiss comfort meals, such as *Kalbswienerschnitzel mit Preiselbeeren, dazu Kopfsalat mit Kürbiskernen* (veal schnitzel with cranberries, lettuce and pumpkin seeds), in winter. Tram 15 runs close by.

Restaurant Zum Kropf
SWISS $$

(Map p254; ☑044 221 18 05; www.zumkropf.ch; In Gassen 16; mains Sfr26-46; ⊙11.30am-11.30pm Mon-Sat) Notable for its historic interior, with marble columns, stained glass and ceiling murals, Kropf has been favoured by locals since 1888 for its hearty Swiss staples and fine beers.

Raclette Stube
SWISS $$

(Map p254; ☑044 251 41 30; www.raclette-stube .ch; Zähringerstrasse 16; mains Sfr28-40; ⊙dinner) For the quintessential Swiss cheese experience, raclette, pop by this welcoming *Stube*, which feels like a warm country restaurant. They do fondue too.

Café Zähringer
CAFE $

(Map p254; Zähringerplatz 11; mains Sfr23-28; ⊙6pm-midnight Mon, from 9am Tue-Sun) This very-old-school alternative cafe serves up mostly organic, vegetarian food around communal tables. They have huge vegetarian and carnivores' Sunday brunch menus (Sfr21.50).

Lade
BISTRO $

(☑043 317 14 34; www.nietengasse.ch; Nietengasse 1; mains Sfr20-45; ⊙lunch & dinner Mon-Sat) Set on a leafy back lane of Kreis 4, this is the kind of spot you might find in London's Stoke Newington or Berlin's Prenzlauer Berg. There's a short menu of dishes, ranging from salads to pasta, on offer in this modest former general store with a mellow ambience.

Zeughauskeller
SWISS $$

(Map p254; www.zeughauskeller.ch; Bahnhofstrasse 28a; mains Sfr18.50-34.50; ⊙11.30am-11pm) The menu (in eight languages) at this huge, atmospheric beer hall offers 20 different kinds of sausages, as well as numerous other Swiss specialities, including some of a vegetarian variety. There's no shortage of fine frothy beers either.

Fribourger Fondue-Stübli
SWISS $

(☑044 241 90 76; www.fondue-stuben.ch; Rotwandstrasse 38; mains Sfr23-28; ⊙closed Jun-Aug) One of three branches of this minichain located around town, this is a cosy, warm spot for indulging in your fondue fantasy. Bright gingham adorns the timber tables and matches the steaming red pots of delicious hot melted cheese.

Restaurant Grüntal
SWISS, ITALIAN $$

(Off Map p251; ☑043 960 37 73; www.gruental -restaurant.ch; Breitensteinstrasse 21; mains Sfr28-38; ⊙dinner Tue-Sat) A simple enough place with a limited menu about evenly split between Italian dishes and local fare, the 'Green Valley' has no valley but a nice view of the Limmat river from the balcony.

Restaurant Reithalle
SWISS, INTERNATIONAL $$

(Map p254; ☑044 212 07 66; www.restaurant -reithalle.ch; Gessneralle 8; mains Sfr20-34; ⊙lunch & dinner) Fancy eating in the stables? The walls are still lined with the cavalry horses' feeding and drinking troughs. Straw has been replaced by a menu of Swiss and international dishes, including vegetarian options. Part of a former barracks complex, it's a boisterous, convivial location, but keep in mind that tables are cleared at 11.30pm to turn the place into a dance club.

Giesserei
SWISS $$

(☑044 205 10 10; www.diegiesserei.ch; Birchstrasse 108; mains Sfr26-40; ⊘lunch & dinner Mon-Fri, dinner Sat) This former factory in Oerlikon is a winner with its scuffed post-industrial atmosphere and pared-down menu (three starters, three mains and three desserts). The abundant Sunday brunch (October through May) is renowned across town. Take tram 11 to Regensbergbrücke from the Hauptbahnhof.

Tibits by Hiltl
VEGETARIAN $

(☑044 260 32 22; www.tibits.ch; Seefeldstrasse 2; meals per 100g Sfr3.60-4.10; ⊘lunch & dinner) Tibits is where with-it, health-conscious inhabitants of Zürich head for a light bite. There's a tasty vegetarian buffet, fresh fruit juices, coffee and cakes.

🍷 Drinking

Options abound across town, but the bulk of the more animated drinking dens are in Züri-West, especially along Langstrasse in Kreis 4 and Hardstrasse in Kreis 5.

Café Odeon
CAFE

(Map p254; www.odeon.ch; Am Bellevueplatz; ⊘daily) This one-time haunt of Lenin and the Dadaists is still a prime people-watching spot for gays and straights alike. Come for the art-nouveau interior, the OTT chandeliers and a whiff of another century. It serves food too.

Longstreet Bar
MUSIC BAR

(www.longstreetbar.ch; Langstrasse 92; ⊘8pm-late Tue-Sat) The Longstreet is a music bar with a varied roll call of DJs coming in and out. Try to count the thousands of light bulbs in this purple-felt-lined one-time cabaret. The biggest nights are Tuesday, Wednesday, Friday and Saturday.

City Beach
BAR

(www.city-beach.ch; Förrlibuckstrasse 151; ⊘noon-midnight mid-May-Aug) Head to the car-park roof to discover tropical Zürich – two pools, a sandy 'beach', bars and chilled music – for the perfect start to a long evening that could finish in the Q Zürich (p260) clubbing to the wee hours.

Liquid
LOUNGE

(www.liquid-bar.ch; Zwinglistrasse 12; ⊘5pm-late Mon-Sat) With its striped wallpaper and moulded plastic chairs in the form of boiled

ZÜRI-WEST

The reborn hip part of the city, known as Züri-West and stretching west of the Hauptbahnhof, is primarily made up of two former working-class districts: Kreis 4 and Kreis 5. At night, it becomes a hedonists' playground.

Kreis 4, still a red-light district and centred on Langstrasse, is lined with opportunity shops, eateries, bars and peep shows.

Langstrasse continues north over the railway lines into Kreis 5, where it quietens down a little but still offers plenty of options. The main focus of Kreis 5 action is along what the city fathers have dubbed the Kulturmeile (Culture Mile; www.kulturmeile.ch), Hardstrasse.

eggs broken in half, this is a kitsch kind of setting, with mostly lounge-oriented music nights. A groovy way to get ready for the latter half of the night.

Nordbrücke
BAR

(www.nordbruecke.ch; Dammstrasse 58; ⊘4pm-1am Mon, 7:30am-late Tue-Fri, 9am-late Sat & Sun) This lively local bar by a railway line is simple and authentic. Punters of all descriptions get in here – the ones you come across will depend on the time of day. In summer they get the grill going for some sizzling food. The occasional live gig and DJ sets pepper the programme in random fashion. They even have an apartment for rent upstairs. Across the road you'll find a small Saturday flea market.

Café des Amis
CAFE, BAR

(www.desamis.ch; Nordstrasse 88; ⊘8am-late Tue-Fri, 9am-late Sat, to 6pm Sun) A good weekend brunch stop (until 4pm), this is above all a popular new place to hang out and drink, anything from coffee to cocktails. In summer, spread out in the generous, cobbled terrace area.

Rio Bar
BAR

(Map p254; www.riozurich.ch; Gessnerallee 17; ⊘8am-midnight Mon-Fri, from 9am Sat, 10am-10pm Sun) With its terrace on the Sihl river and an almost cheekily retro look inside, this makes a tempting, if tiny, stop at any time and whatever the weather. They have a limited menu for the peckish.

DON'T MISS

WATERSIDE TIPPLING

The **Frauenbad** (Stadthausquai)and **Männerbad** (Schanzengraben) public baths are open only to women and men respectively during the day, but they open their trendy bars to both sexes at night. At the former, up to 150 men are allowed into the **Barfussbar** (Barefoot Bar; ☎044 251 33 31; www.barfussbar.ch; ☻8pm-midnight Wed-Thu & Sun mid-May–mid-Sep). You leave shoes at the entrance – drink while you dip your feet in the water! Sunday night is open-air disco night. At the Männerbad, women come in the evenings to the **Rimini Bar** (☎044 211 95 94; www.rimini.ch; ☻7.30pm-midnight Sun-Thu, from 6.45pm Fri, from 5pm Sat), open in good weather only.

La Stanza   BAR
(Map p254; www.lastanza.ch; Bleicherweg 10; ☻7am-late Mon-Fri, 10am-1.30am Sat, 10am-10pm Sun) Nicely placed in the upscale area of Enge, this stylish Italian bar attracts business people by day, and media starlets and even students at any time. It's as much about posing as sipping your mixed drinks. They do a nice Sunday brunch.

☆ Entertainment

Züritipp (www.zueritipp.ch) comes out on Thursdays with the *TagesAnzeiger* newspaper, which is jammed with info on what's on. Also look for the quarterly *Zürich Guide*.

Clubs

Generally dress well and expect to pay Sfr15 to Sfr30 admission. Be aware that men can only enter some clubs if they are 21 or older (ID will be requested). Otherwise, the cut-off age in most places is 18 for both sexes.

ZÜRI-WEST

TOP CHOICE **Q Zürich**   CLUB
(www.qzurich.ch; Förrlibuckstrasse 151; ☻11pm-late Fri & Sat, 5-10pm Sun) This car-park club is for those who take their dancing – to house, hip hop, mash up, electro and R&B – more seriously than seeing and being seen. The closing times are less radical than in days of yore, but the crowd remains as enthusiastic as ever. For pre-clubbing drinks and a dip, try the nearby City Beach (p259).

Supermarket   CLUB
(www.supermarket.li; Geroldstrasse 17; ☻11pm-late Thu-Sat) Looking like an innocent little house, Supermarket boasts three cosy lounge bars around the dance floor, a covered back courtyard and an interesting roster of DJs playing house and techno. The crowd tends to be mid-20s. Take a train from Hauptbahnhof to Hardbrücke.

Labor Bar   CLUB
(www.laborbar.ch; Schiffbaustrasse 3; ☻9pm-2am Thu, 10pm-late Fri & Sat) The epitome of retro chic, with lots of Plexiglas and diffused coloured light. Always filled with beautiful people from their late 20s up, music tends to be mainstream and easy to dance to.

Club Komplex 457   CLUB
(www.komplex457.ch; Hohlstrasse 457; ☻8pm-late Wed-Sun) The latest addition to Zürich's busy club circuit is also the scene of occasional live concerts, generally of a powerful rock variety. DJs spin all sorts, with techno taking pride of place. In summer, you can come along early (from 5pm) for a drink on the upstairs terrace (also open lunchtime when the weather is nice). Take bus 31 from Hauptbahnhof.

CENTRAL ZÜRICH

Kaufleuten   CLUB
(Map p254; www.kaufleuten.com; Pelikanstrasse 18; ☻11pm-late Tue-Sun) An opulent art-deco theatre with a stage, mezzanine dance floor and bars arranged around the dance floor, Zürich's 'establishment' club plays house, hip hop and Latin rhythms to a slightly older crowd.

Mascotte   CLUB
(Map p254; www.mascotte.ch; Theaterstrasse 10; ☻9.30pm-late Mon, Wed & Fri-Sun) The old variety hall 'Corso' is now a popular club with huge windows facing Sechseläutenplatz and the lake. The Monday night session, with funk, soul and dancefloor jazz, is a mellow way to start the week.

Adagio   CLUB
(Map p254; www.adagio.ch; Gotthardstrasse 5; ☻8pm-late Tue, 6pm-late Wed, 9pm-4am Thu-Sat) Adagio seems like a scene from a medieval thriller with its vaulted and frescoed ceiling. It plays a broad range of dance music appealing to an older, well-heeled crowd.

Cultural Centres

Rote Fabrik   PERFORMING ARTS
(www.rotefabrik.ch; Seestrasse 395) This once counter-cultural and now largely mainstream

institution stages rock concerts, original-language films, theatre and dance performances. There's also a bar and a restaurant. Take bus 161 or 165 from Bürkliplatz.

Kanzlei PERFORMING ARTS
(www.kanzlei.ch; Kanzleistrasse 56; ☺11pm-late Fri & Sat) Kanzlei is similar to Rote Fabrik. What is a school playground by day morphs into an outdoor bar session by night, especially in summer. Kanzlei's club action happens downstairs, underground.

Kino Xenix CINEMA, BAR
(www.xenix.ch; Kanzleistrasse 52) Located in the same spot as Kanzlei, Kino Xenix is an independent art-house cinema with a bar.

Gay & Lesbian Venues

Zürich has a lively gay scene, which includes Café Odeon (p259).

Barfüsser BAR
(Map p254; http://barfuesser.ch; Spitalgasse 14; ☺11.30am-late Mon-Fri, 2pm-2am Sat, 3.30-11.30pm Sun) One of the first gay bars in the country and still going strong, Barfüsser now incorporates a sushi bar and has mellowed over the years – gays and straights feel equally at home.

Pigalle BAR
(Map p254; www.pigalle-bar.ch; Marktgasse 14; ☺6pm-late) In business since the 1950s, this cupboard of a bar hosts a jukebox with boisterous hits of years gone by and a regular clientele that can get good-naturedly rowdy at times. Some punters tipple on the street but duck inside to soak in the music-hall-style decor.

Daniel H BAR
(☎044 241 41 78; www.danielh.ch; Müllerstrasse 51; ☺5pm-late Mon-Fri, 7pm-2am Sat) An easy-going lounge-bar arrangement (with a tiny courtyard at the side), the 'Dani H' is a cruisy place to start the night. It is hetero-friendly.

Live Music

Aside from the high-brow stuff, Zürich has an effervescent live-music scene. Many of the bars and clubs mentioned earlier in this chapter offer occasional gigs.

LOCAL KNOWLEDGE

THIERRY DÉLÈZE, JOURNALIST

My home town, Lausanne, is a big village, which is part of its charm, but Zürich is Switzerland's most interesting city. This is where the most is going on and, in addition, it's a beautiful city that offers an incredible quality of life. Economically, it is the country's powerhouse, but perhaps it is a little too well organized. The language difference means that I will always feel a little foreign, but above all, I feel Swiss in Zürich and Romand in Lausanne. It's important to understand the local dialect if you decide to live in Zürich and I get by in Züritütsch. The so-called Röstigraben is more than anything a humourous way of describing certain socio-cultural differences between the French- and German-speaking parts of the country, but they hardly constitute a 'ditch' (Graben)! I would miss the city if I had to leave.

Favourite Venue

On Sunday nights, the Helsinki is great for a beer and the country-rock by the Trio from Hell – the best way to get ready for the new working week.

Delicious Dish

The Zürcher Geschnetzeltes, of course! Veal strips Zürich-style, served with rösti and a creamy, white-wine sauce.

Top View

The Uetliberg peak is perfect for an overview of the city and surrounding region. In town, you really get a feel for the old city in Lindenhof.

Summer Time

Bathing and drinking in the Badis (baths) of the Limmat river by day and...having another drink there by night.

TOP CHOICE **Helsinki Hütte** LIVE MUSIC
(www.helsinkiklub.ch; Geroldstrasse 35; ⊘8pm-late Tue-Sun) Little more than a leftover hut from the area's industrial days, the Helsinki attracts people of all tastes and ages for its low-lit, relaxed band scene. Settle in for anything from the regular country nights on Sundays to soul and funk. Take the train one stop from Hauptbahnhof to Hardbrücke.

Moods JAZZ
(www.moods.ch; Schiffbaustrasse 6; ⊘7.30pm-late Mon-Sat, 6-10pm Sun mid-Sep–mid-Jun) One of the city's top jazz spots, although other musical genres such as Latin and world music grab the occasional spot on its busy calendar.

Dynamo LIVE MUSIC
(www.dynamo.ch; Wasserwerkstrasse 21; ⊘8pm or 9pm-4am) Various spaces in this spot on the west bank of the Limmat river lend themselves to concerts with powerful sound, anything from rock or reggae to lashings of heavy metal. There's usually something every night.

Tonhalle MUSIC
(Map p254; www.tonhalle-orchester.ch; Claridenstrasse 7) An opulent venue used by Zürich's orchestra and chamber orchestra.

Opernhaus OPERA
(Map p254; www.opernhaus.ch; Falkenstrasse 1) The city's premier opera house enjoys a worldwide reputation.

Sport

Letzigrund Stadium SPECTATOR SPORT
(cnr Herden & Baslerstrasse) Local football team FC Zürich (www.fcz.ch) is one of the country's best and plays at the Letzigrund Stadium. Take bus 31 to Letzipark.

🛍 Shopping

For high fashion, head for Bahnhofstrasse and surrounding streets. Across the river funkier boutiques are dotted about the lanes of Niederdorf. For grunge, preloved gear and some none-too-serious fun young stuff, have a stroll along Langstrasse in Kreis 4.

The leading markets include the flea market at **Bürkliplatz** (⊘8am-4pm Sat May-Oct), the year-round **Flohmarkt Kanzlei** (www.flohmarktkanzlei.ch; Kanzleistrasse 56; ⊘8am-4pm Sat) and **Rosenhof** (Map p254; www.rosenhof.ch; Rosenhof; ⊘10am-8pm Thu, to 5pm Sat Mar-Dec), but the tourist office has details of more options.

TOP CHOICE **Freitag** ACCESSORIES
(www.freitag.ch; Geroldstrasse 17) The Freitag brothers turn truck tarps into water-resistant carry-all chic in their factory. Everything is recycled and every item is original. Their outlet is equally impressive – a pile of containers. They call it Kreis 5's first skyscraper and shoppers can climb to the top. Take the train from Hauptbahnhof to Hardbrücke.

Fidelio CLOTHING
(Map p254; www.fideliokleider.ch; Münzplatz 1) One of the city's best clothes boutiques, Fidelio sells a wide range of men's and women's wear, from designer labels to street fashions. This is one of four branches around town.

Heimatwerk SOUVENIRS
(Map p254; www.heimatwerk.ch; Uraniastrasse 1) Good-quality, if touristy, souvenirs are found here, including fondue pots, forks, toys and classy handbags.

Jelmoli DEPARTMENT STORE
(Map p254; www.jelmoli.ch; Bahnhofstrasse) The basement food hall is the highlight of this legendary department store, Zürich's first, biggest and best.

ℹ Information

Discount Card

ZürichCard (adult/child per 24hr Sfr20/14, per 72hr Sfr40/28) Available from the tourist office and the airport train station, this provides free public transport, free museum admission and more.

Emergency

Police station (☏044 411 71 17; Bahnhofquai 3)

Internet Access

e-cafe.ch (www.e-cafe.ch; Uraniastrasse 3; per min Sfr0.30; ⊘7am-11pm Mon-Fri, from 8am Sat, 10am-10pm Sun) You can connect your laptop.

Medical Services

Bellevue Apotheke (☏044 266 62 22; www.bellevue-apotheke.com; Theaterstrasse 14) 24-hour chemist.

UniversitätsSpital Zürich (University Hospital; ☏044 255 11 11; www.usz.ch; Rämistrasse 100).

Post

Hauptbahnhof post office (Hauptbahnhof; ⊘7am-9pm)

Tourist information

Zürich Tourism (☏044 215 40 00; www.zuerich.com; Hauptbahnhof; ⊘8am-8.30pm

UETLIBERG

A top half-day trip from Zürich starts off by taking the train (line S10) from Hauptbahnhof to Uetliberg at 870m (20 minutes, half-hourly). A five-minute uphill walk takes you to the top of the mountain, where you have fine views over the city and lake and the chance to climb to a 30m-high viewing deck of the 72m-high, triangular-based **Uetliberg Aussichtsturm** (viewing tower), not to be confused with the nearby TV tower. From here, follow the one-and-a-half-hour **Planetenweg** (Planetary Path) along the at times heavily wooded mountain ridge as it gently dips and rises en route to Felsenegg. You pass scale models of the planets and enjoy lake views along the way. Various other walking and mountain-bike trails also criss-cross the mountain countryside. At Felsenegg, a cable car descends every six to 10 minutes to Adliswil, from where frequent trains return to Zürich (line S4, 16 minutes). Buy the Sfr16.40 Albis-Netzkarte, which gets you to Uetliberg and back with unlimited travel downtown.

Mon-Sat & 8.30am-6.30pm Sun) For hotel reservations through the tourist office, call ☑044 215 40 40.

Websites
Lonely Planet (www.lonelyplanet.com /switzerland/zurich)

ⓘ Getting There & Away

Air
Zürich Airport (☑043 816 22 11; www.zurich -airport.com) is 9km north of the centre, with flights to most European capitals as well as some in Africa, Asia and North America.

Car & Motorcycle
The A3 approaches Zürich from the south along the southern shore of Zürichsee. The A1 is the fastest route from Bern and Basel. It proceeds northeast to Winterthur.

Europcar (☑044 271 56 56; Josefstrasse 53), **Hertz** (☑0848 82 20 20; Morgartenstrasse 5) and **Avis** (☑044 296 87 87; Gartenhofstrasse 17) all also have airport branches.

Train
Direct trains run to Stuttgart (Sfr64), Munich (Sfr95), Innsbruck (Sfr48) and other international destinations. There are regular direct departures to most major Swiss towns, such as Lucerne (Sfr23, 45 to 50 minutes), Bern (Sfr47, 56 minutes) and Basel (Sfr31, 55 minutes).

ⓘ Getting Around

To/From the Airport
Up to nine trains an hour go to/from the Haupt-bahnhof between around 6am and midnight (Sfr6.40, nine to 14 minutes).

Bicycle
City bikes (www.zuerirollt.ch) may be borrowed or rented from a handful of locations, including

Velostation Nord (Museumstrasse; ⊘8am-9.30pm) across the road from the north side of the Hauptbahnhof. ID and Sfr20 must be left as a deposit. Rental is free if you bring the bike back on the same day and Sfr10 a day if you keep it overnight.

Boat
Lake cruises (☑044 487 13 33; www.zsg.ch) run between April and October. They leave from Bürkliplatz. A small circular tour *(kleine Rund-fahrt)* takes 1½ hours (adult/child Sfr8.20/ 4.10) and departs every 30 minutes between 11am to 7.30pm. A longer tour *(grosse Rund-fahrt)* lasts four hours (adult/child Sfr24/12). Pick tickets up at ZVV (local transport) ticket windows.

Riverboats (adult/child Sfr4.10/2.90, every 30 min Easter to mid-October) run by the same company head up the Limmat river and do a small circle around the lake (one hour). Board at the Schweizerisches Landesmuseum stop.

Car & Motorcycle
Parking is tricky. The two most useful **car-parking garages** (www.parkhaeuser.ch; up to Sfr43 a day) are opposite the main post office and at Uraniastrasse 3.

Public Transport
Zürich's **ZVV** (www.zvv.ch) public transport system of buses, S-Bahn suburban trains and trams is completely integrated. Services run from 5.30am to midnight, and tickets must be bought in advance. Every stop has a dispenser. Either type in the four-figure code for your destination or choose your ticket type: a short single-trip *Kurzstrecke* ticket valid for five stops (Sfr2.60), a single ticket for greater Zürich valid for an hour (Sfr4.10) or a 24-hour city pass for the centre, Zone 10 (Sfr8.20).

Taxi

Taxis are expensive and usually unnecessary given the quality of public transport. Pick them up at the Hauptbahnhof or other ranks, or call ☎044 444 44 44.

AROUND ZÜRICH

Rapperswil-Jona

POP 26,000 / ELEVATION 405M

A pleasant excursion is to Rapperswil (part of the Rapperswil-Jona conurbation). It has a quaint old town and a children's zoo. The **tourist office** (☎0848 811500; www .zuerichsee.ch; Hintergasse 16; ⊗8.30am-noon & 1.30-5pm Mon-Fri) is in the heart of the Old Town.

Sights & Activities

Polenmuseum　　　　MUSEUM, CASTLE
(www.muzeum-polskie.org; adult/child Sfr4/2; ⊗1-5pm, closed Mon-Fri Nov-Mar) North of the train station, the Old Town is dominated by a 13th-century castle, which is worth a climb for the views. It is a popular wedding spot and has the unique if old-fashioned Polish Museum inside, which details the story of Poles in Switzerland, Polish immigration, WWII and, more recently, the Solidarność trade union and Pope John Paul II. The museum is closed in January and February.

Circus Knie　　　　ZOO
(www.knie.ch) All the Swiss know this family-run national circus based in Rapperswil, which has been travelling the length and breadth of the country (on tour from March to November) since 1919. The circus employs about 100 animals and the Knie have another 300 at **Knies Kinderzoo** (Children's Zoo; www.knieskinderzoo.ch; Oberseestrasse; adult/child Sfr10/4.50; ⊗9am-6pm early Mar-Oct), southeast of the train station (signposted). Kids can ride ponies, elephants and camels, applaud performing sea lions and learn about a host of creatures, from giraffes and apes to kangaroos and tortoises.

Kunst(zeug)haus　　　　ART MUSEUM
(www.kunstzeughaus.ch; Schönbodenstrasse 1; adult/child Sfr10/free; ⊗2-6pm Wed-Fri, 11am-6pm Sat & Sun) Since mid-2008, this enormous art space, a converted arsenal with a very-21st-century wavy roof, has been devoted to exhibitions of contemporary Swiss art.

Sleeping & Eating

Restaurants line Rapperswil's Fischmarktplatz and Hauptplatz.

Jakob　　　　HOTEL $$
(☎055 220 00 50; www.jakob-hotel.ch; Hauptplatz 11; s Sfr97-127, d Sfr166-189; 🐾) Right in the heart of town, Jakob is the best midrange hotel choice, with chic rooms in neutral tones. It also has a restaurant, bar (often with live music, mainly jazz) and lounge for sampling whiskies.

Getting There & Away

Rapperswil can be reached by S5, S7 or S16 from Zürich's main train station (Sfr15.80, 35 to 45 minutes) or by boat from Bürkliplatz (two hours). Much better value for a day trip is the **9-Uhr Tagespass** (9 O'Clock Day Pass, Sfr24), valid all day from 9am Monday to Friday and all day Saturday, Sunday and holidays.

Winterthur

POP 98,200 / ELEVATION 447M

Switzerland's sixth-largest city gave its name to one of Europe's leading insurance companies and is equally known for its high-quality museums.

The greater Winterthur area counts almost 150,000 inhabitants, many of them young families who have exchanged the exorbitant prices of Zürich for a 25-minute commute.

A Museumsbus minivan shuttle (Sfr5) leaves the train station hourly between 9.45am and 4.45pm for the Sammlung Oskar Reinhart am Römerholz, the Museum Oskar Reinhart am Stadtgarten and the Kunstmuseum.

Sights

Winterthur owes much of its eminence as an art Mecca to collector Oskar Reinhart, a scion of a powerful banking and insurance family. His collection was bequeathed to the nation and entrusted to his hometown when he died in 1965. Consider picking up the Winterthur Museumspass (Sfr20 for one day excluding Technorama and Sfr30 for two days with Technorama).

Sammlung Oskar Reinhart am Römerholz　　　　GALLERY
(www.bundesmuseen.ch/roemerholz; Haldenstrasse 95; adult/student Sfr12/9; ⊗10am-5pm Tue & Thu-Sun, to 8pm Wed) The collection, housed in a charming country estate (equipped with a

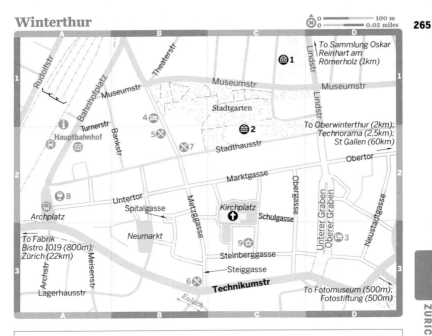

Winterthur

◉ Sights

🛏 Sleeping

✖ Eating

🍷 Drinking

🎭 Entertainment

pleasant cafe), is particularly fascinating in the way it seeks to bridge the gap between traditional and modern art, juxtaposing the likes of Cézanne, Goya, Rembrandt and Rubens with Monet, Picasso, Renoir and Van Gogh. Take bus 3 to Spital or get the Museumsbus.

Museum Oskar Reinhart am Stadtgarten   ART MUSEUM
(http://museumoskarreinhart.ch; Stadthausstrasse 6; adult/student Sfr12/8; ⊙10am-8pm Tue, to 5pm Wed-Sun) Reinhart's 500-strong collection of Swiss, German and Austrian works of art from the 18th and 19th centuries is on show in a museum on the edge of the central city's park.

TOP CHOICE Fotomuseum   MUSEUM
(www.fotomuseum.ch; Grüzenstrasse 44; permanent collection adult/concession Sfr8/6; ⊙11am-6pm Tue & Thu-Sun, to 8pm Wed) Winterthur's outstanding Photography Museum is another highlight. The vast collection includes many great names and styles from the earliest days of this art in the 19th century to the present. There's more in the **Fotostiftung** (Photo Foundation; ☎052 234 10 30; www.fotostiftung.ch; Grüzenstrasse 45; adult/concession Sfr7/5; ⊙11am-6pm Tue & Thu-Sun, to 8pm Wed) over the road. The combined price for these and other related photo exhibitions is Sfr17 for an adult and Sfr13 for a concession ticket.

Kunstmuseum
MUSEUM

(www.kmw.ch, in German; Museumstrasse 52; adult/concession Sfr15/12; ⏲10am-8pm Tue, to 5pm Wed-Sun) For a satisfying stroll through a solid collection of the 19th- and 20th-century classics, the city's main Art Museum is worth some of your time. Many of the standard suspects, from Kandinsky to Klee, are represented, along with an impressive slew of contemporary creators.

Technorama
MUSEUM

(www.technorama.ch; Technoramastrasse 1; adult/child Sfr25/14; ⏲10am-5pm Tue-Sun) Had enough art? What about a science session? Technorama is an extraordinary voyage into the hands-on multiple worlds of science. It offers some 500 interactive experiences (explained in English, French, German and Italian) that can't fail to fascinate kids, and plenty of adults too! Look into Europe's biggest plasma ball or admire the toy trains. Take bus 5 from the Hauptbahnhof.

Schloss Kyburg
CASTLE

(www.schlosskyburg.ch; adult/child Sfr8/3; ⏲10.30am-5.30pm Tue-Sun) Just outside the city, Kyburg weaves interactive fun into the texture of its ancient castle buildings (try on a suit of armour – but not the torture instruments!). The 15th-century murals in the castle's chapel showing Christ as the judge at the Last Judgment are especially vivid. Out the back, a vegetable and herb garden flourishes, much as in past centuries.

Take the S-Bahn to Effretikon, then the bus to Kyburg. Ask the tourist office for the Kyburg leaflet, with transport timetables. The journey takes 30 minutes each way.

🛏 Sleeping

Winterthur is an easy day trip from Zürich.

Albani
HOTEL $

(☎052 212 69 96; www.albani.ch; Steinberggasse 16; s/d/t Sfr77/95/120) Not only a happening bar where live music is the order of the day, this place also has nine simple but cheerful rooms with a gleaming white cleanliness. Showers and a phone are in the corridor. Guests get free entry to concerts and parties in the bar downstairs. Very cool indeed.

Taverne zum Kreuz
HOTEL $$

(☎052 269 07 20; www.taverne-zum-kreuz.ch; Stadthausstrasse 10b; s/d Sfr149/181) A charmingly lopsided half-timbered tavern from the 18th century, which has cosy rooms full of character. Downstairs is an equally warm restaurant and bar. Prices are shaved somewhat at weekends.

Hotel Loge
HOTEL $$

(☎052 268 12 00; www.hotelloge.ch; Oberer Graben 6; s/d Sfr195/250) With its own bar, restaurant and even a cinema, this designer place provides all the comfort and style you will ever need. Some of the 17 spacious rooms behind the Gothic entrance offer nice views across the leafy avenue to the Old Town.

🍴 Eating

Bars and cheap restaurants are clustered along Neumarkt, offering a wide array of different ethnic cuisines.

Gasthaus Rössli
SWISS, GERMAN $$

(☎052 213 66 44; Steiggasse 1; mains Sfr22-34; ⏲lunch & dinner Tue-Sat) For typical Swiss-German fare in a mountain-style, wood-clad eatery, you can't go past the Little Horse. The Wiener schnitzel is a house classic that is prepared at your table and the *Hackbraten* (meatloaf) is famous across town.

Restaurant Strauss
INTERNATIONAL $$

(☎052 212 29 70; www.strauss-winterthur.ch; Stadthausstrasse 8; mains Sfr29-39; ⏲lunch & dinner Mon-Sat) Winterthur's gourmet night out happens in the crimson-toned Strauss, where you will be treated to elegant dining. In summer, try the less formal garden dining area. The food ranges from Thai to creative European, and you can while away some time in the wine bar or smoking area (*fumoir*).

Fabrik Bistro 1019
SWISS $

(www.church.ch/das_fabrikbistro_d.php; Jägerstrasse; mains Sfr15; ⏲11.30am-1.30pm Mon-Fri) Southwest of the Hauptbahnhof in a one-time factory zone that is being revamped to accommodate new businesses, a youth church organization has moved in and created this hip little eatery staffed by enthusiastic unemployed folks who serve up a filling set lunch menu. From Archplatz, cross under the railway line and head south along Bahnmeisterweg, which becomes Zur Kesselschmiede, then turn right on Jägerstrasse to reach the entrance to the complex.

Akazie
MEDITERRANEAN $

(☎052 212 17 17; Stadthausstrasse 10; mains Sfr28-46; ⏲lunch & dinner Mon-Sat) Decked out in timber, this inviting, cosy location serves

MOVING ON?

For tips, recommendations and reviews, head to http://shop.lonelyplanet.com to purchase a downloadable PDF of the Germany chapter from Lonely Planet's *Western Europe* guide.

up creative nouvelle Mediterranean cuisine that comes in old-fashioned portions, washed down with wines from as far off as Sardinia.

Drinking & Entertainment

Gotthard BAR
(Untertor) Winterthur's student population keeps the many bars humming at all hours. Indeed, Gotthard literally keeps the taps flowing 24/7, although you'll have trouble getting in between 1am and 7am (theoretically reserved for regulars).

Albani LIVE MUSIC
(www.albani.ch; Steinberggasse 16) Although not more than a couple of hundred punters can squeeze in, Albani is a magnet for the live gig aficionados, attracting local and international acts. Friday and Saturday nights, DJs take over for club sounds.

ⓘ Information

Discount Card A museums pass costs Sfr20 for one day and Sfr30 for two days and gives you entry to almost all the sights.

Post office (Bahnhofplatz 8; ⊙7.30am-7pm Mon-Fri, 8am-5pm Sat)

Tourist office (☑052 267 67 00; www.winterthur-tourismus.ch; near platform 1, Hauptbahnhof; ⊙8.30am-6.30pm Mon-Fri, to 4pm Sat)

ⓘ Getting There & Around

Four to five trains an hour run to Zürich (Sfr11.80, 21 to 28 minutes). The A1 freeway goes from Zürich, skirts Winterthur and continues to St Gallen and Austria.

As local bus tickets to Oberwinterthur cost Sfr4.10, it's better to get a 24-hour pass for Sfr8.20 instead.

Northeastern Switzerland

POP 902,860 / AREA 4418 SQ KM / LANGUAGE GERMAN

Best Places to Eat

» Bäumli (p280)

» Fischerzunft (p272)

» Schlössli Worth (p273)

» Burg Hohenklingen (p275)

» Segreto (p280)

Best Places to Stay

» Park Villa (p271)

» Lofthotel Murg (p285)

» Märchenhotel Bellevue (p286)

» Schloss Wartegg (p278)

Why Go?

Northeastern Switzerland is the place to tiptoe off the map and back to nature for a few days. Here country lanes unravel like spools of thread, weaving through Appenzell's patchwork meadows, past the fjord-like waters of Walensee and south to remote hamlets engulfed by the glacier-licked peaks of the Glarus Alps. This region calls for slow touring: whether you're cycling through cornfields and apple orchards on a cloudless summer's day, or walking through Klettgau's gold-tinged vineyards in the diffused light of autumn.

From the thunderous Rheinfall to the still waters of Lake Constance, nature is on a grand scale here. Completing the storybook tableau are castle-topped towns like Stein am Rhein and Schaffhausen, their facades festooned with frescos and oriel windows; while in graceful St Gallen, the abbey library literally catches your breath with its rococo splendour.

When to Go

Summer brings folksy festivals galore to the rural hinterland and open-air concerts to St Gallen and Schaffhausen. Fireworks light up the Rheinfall and Kreuzlingen on Lake Constance in August. Make the most of warm-weather cycling around Lake Constance and hiking in the Alps. Autumn is toasted with new wine in Klettgau's vineyards, while winter's arrival brings twinkling Christmas markets to the region's towns and skiers to its slopes.

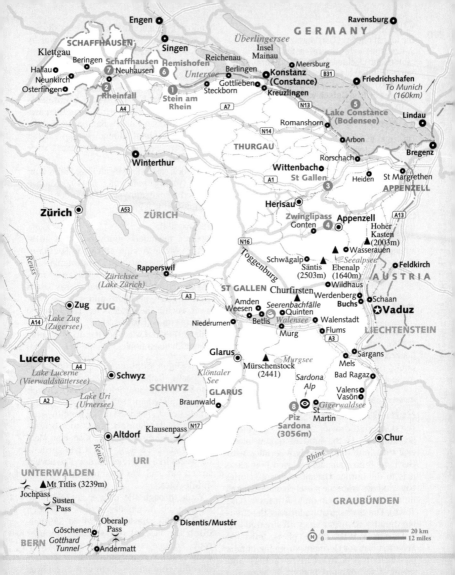

Northeastern Switzerland Highlights

1 Slip back to the Middle Ages exploring the half-timbered heart of **Stein am Rhein** (p274)

2 Feel the spray of the **Rheinfall** (p273), Europe's largest waterfall

3 Enjoy a fascinating romp through literary history at St Gallen's **Stiftsbibliothek** (p278), a rococo masterpiece

4 Hike through the magnificent karst mountains above Appenzell on the **Zwinglipass** (p283)

5 Pedal, walk or canoe over to Germany and Austria on **Lake Constance** (p276)

6 Meet Daisy and co at **Bolderhof** (p275) in Hemishofen, where you can cow trek to the Rhine

7 Admire the **ornate oriel windows** (p270) in Schaffhausen

8 Lose the crowds and find remote Alpine wilderness around **Piz Sardona** (p285)

ⓘ Information

The tourist region of Ostschweiz (Eastern Switzerland) unites several easterly Swiss cantons and Liechtenstein (p320). Information can be found on the pages of **Switzerland Tourism** (www.myswitzerland.com) or the official website of **Ostschweiz Tourismus** (http://ostschweiz.ch).

ⓘ Getting There & Around

This area lies between Zürich and Friedrichshafen (Germany) airports and can be conveniently reached from either by public or private transport. Road and rail link Zürich with Schaffhausen, Stein am Rhein, St Gallen and even Linthal (for Braunwald). Alternatively, a ferry crosses the lake from Friedrichshafen to Romanshorn, which also has good car and train links.

Several areas, such as the Bodensee region around Lake Constance and Appenzell, offer regional passes. For details, see the individual sections.

SCHAFFHAUSEN CANTON

Cyclists love touring this relatively flat region, and lower-end accommodation is booked up swiftly on weekends. Excellent public transport and manageable distances make it an easy day trip from Zürich too.

Schaffhausen

POP 34,600 / ELEV 404M

Schaffhausen is the kind of quaint medieval town one more readily associates with Germany – no coincidence, given how close it is to the border. Ornate frescos and oriel bay windows grace the pastel-coloured houses lining the pedestrian-only Altstadt (Old Town). The city's signature fortress, the circular Munot, lords over a vineyard-streaked hill.

During WWII, Allied pilots 'mistook' Schaffhausen for Germany, dropping bombs on the outskirts twice in April 1944 and giving it the dubious honour of being the only bit of Swiss soil to take a direct hit during the war.

⊙ Sights

Opening hours are given for high season (April through October); many sights have reduced hours at other times.

Vorstadt   NEIGHBOURHOOD

Schaffhausen is often nicknamed the *Erkerstadt* because of its 170 *Erkers* (oriel bay windows), which citizens built as a display of wealth. One of the most noteworthy windows belongs to the 17th-century **Zum Goldenen Ochsen** (Vorstadt 17), whose frescoed facade displays, among other things, an eponymous Golden Ox. The 16th-century **Zum Grossen Käfig** (Vorstadt 45) presents an extraordinarily colourful tale of the parading of Turkish sultan Bajazet in a cage by the triumphant Mongol warrior leader Tamerlane. The centuries-old frescos were freshened up in 1906.

A block east, the eye-catching **Haus zum Ritter** (Vordergasse 65), built in 1492, boasts a detailed Renaissance-style fresco depicting, you guessed it, a knight.

Fronwagplatz   SQUARE

Vorstadt meanders south past the 16th-century **Mohrenbrunnen** (Moor Fountain) into the old market place, Fronwagplatz. At the southern end stands the **Metzgerbrunnen** (Butcher's Fountain) and there's also a William Tell–type figure and a large clock tower. Facing the latter is the late baroque **Herrenstube** (Fronwagplatz 3), which was built in 1748 and was once the drinking hole of Schaffhausen nobles.

Allerheiligen Münster   CATHEDRAL

(All Saints' Cathedral; Münsterplatz; ⊙10am-noon & 2-5pm Tue-Sun) Schaffhausen's church was completed in 1103 and is a rare and largely intact specimen of the Romanesque style in Switzerland. It opens to a beautifully simple **cloister** (⊙7.30am-8pm Mon-Fri, from 9am Sat & Sun), which has gardens that seem like a tangled forest. The herbal garden out back has been tended since the Middle Ages.

Walk through the cloister to reach the **Museum zu Allerheiligen** (www.allerheiligen.ch; Baumgartenstrasse 6; adult/child Sfr9/free; ⊙11am-5pm Tue-Sun), showcasing treasures from antique cameos to Schaffhausen fossils and Etruscan gold jewellery. The art collection contains works by Otto Dix, Lucas Cranach the Elder and contemporary Swiss artists.

FREE Munot   FORTRESS

(⊙8am-8pm May-Sep, 9am-5pm Oct-Apr) East of the Haus zum Ritter, Vordergasse becomes Unterstadt, where you'll find stairs through vineyards to the 16th-century fortress. The unusual circular battlements were built with forced labour following the Reformation. Climb the spiral staircase for views over a patchwork of rooftops and spires to the Rhine and wooded hills fringing the city.

Herrenacker SQUARE
Framed by pastel-coloured houses with steep tiled roofs, this is one of Schaffhausen's prettiest squares. In August, it's an atmospheric backdrop for music fest Das Festival (www.das-festival.ch); Mika and Bryan Ferry were headliners in 2011.

✦ Activities

Rhybadi SWIMMING
(Rheinuferstrasse; adult/child Sfr3/1.50; ☺7am-8pm Mon-Fri, 9am-7pm Sat & Sun May-Sep) If you're itching to leap into the Rhine, you can at this rickety 19th-century wooden bathhouse. There are diving boards and old-fashioned changing rooms reminiscent of an era when 'proper' folk bathed fully clothed.

Altstadt Walks WALKING TOUR
(adult/child Sfr14/7; ☺10am Tue & 2pm Sat May–mid-Oct) These one-hour tours of the Old Town kick off at the tourist office. The well-informed guides speak German, English and French.

Untersee und Rhein BOAT TOUR
(☎052 634 08 88; www.urh.ch, in German; Freier Platz; one-way Sfr46.20; ☺Apr-Oct) The 45km boat trip from Schaffhausen to Konstanz via Stein am Rhein and Reichenau is one of the Rhine's more-beautiful stretches. The journey takes 3¾ hours downstream to Schaffhausen and 4¾ hours the other way. See the website for timetables.

🛏 Sleeping

The tourist office can advise on B&Bs (expect to pay Sfr55 for a single, Sfr95 for a double) and holiday apartments.

Park Villa HOTEL $$
(☎052 635 60 60; www.parkvilla.ch; Parkstrasse 18; s/d from Sfr170/190, without bathroom from Sfr80/130; ℗) The eclectic furniture in this faintly gothic house resembles a private antique collection, with an array of four-poster beds, Persian carpets, chandeliers, patterned wallpaper and fake Ming vases in rooms. Dine in Louis XVI splendour in the banquet room.

Hotel Kronenhof HOTEL $$
(☎052 635 75 75; www.kronenhof.ch; Kirchhof-platz 7; s Sfr125-145, d Sfr175-205, ste Sfr265; ☎)

A guesthouse since 1489, the Kronenhof has welcomed the likes of Goethe and Tsar Alexander. A recent makeover has spruced up the historic interior, with the best rooms now flaunting dark wood floors, crimson walls and bold art. The Ox bistro does a good steak. Rates drop 20% Friday to Sunday.

Fischerzunft BOUTIQUE HOTEL $$
(☎052 632 05 05; www.fischerzunft.ch; Rhein-quai 8; s/d Sfr210/295) The sloping tiled roof and creamy-pink exterior of this low-slung Rhine-side mansion contain this charming boutique hotel, known above all for its gourmet restaurant. Rooms are individually decorated, often with lashings of chintzy floral fabrics.

Hotel Promenade HOTEL $$
(☎052 630 77 77; www.promenade-schaffhausen.ch; Fäsenstaubstrasse 43; s Sfr145-175, d Sfr200-250; ℗☎) The welcome couldn't be warmer at this homely hotel, with large, sunny rooms, a rose garden and a restaurant dishing up seasonal cuisine. It's 600m west of Herrenacker.

ZAK Hotel & Backpackers HOSTEL $
(☎052 625 42 60; www.zaksh.ch; Webergasse 47; dm/s/d Sfr45/70/110; ☎) These no-frills

---

DON'T MISS

FREEWHEELING ALONG THE RHINE

The Rhine flows swiftly through the heart of Schaffhausen and there's no better way to explore further afield than by hiring your own set of wheels. A number of well-marked trails shadow the river and weave through the surrounding countryside. Scenic rides include the 20km Rheinfall-Rheinau route, which leads past the thundering Rheinfall to the Benedictine monastery Kloster Rheinau. Or quaff wine as you peddle through vineyards and past half-timbered houses on the 43km Klettgau Wine Route. Details of these and other routes are given on www .veloland.ch.

At the train station, Rent a Bike (☎051 223 42 17; www.rentabike.ch, in German) rents out Flyer e-bikes, city bikes and tandems for Sfr50, Sfr33 and Sfr80 respectively per day. Book online or by calling ahead.

backpacker digs, with a bar and games room, are handy for exploring the Old Town.

Eating

Stadthausgasse is takeaway street, rolling out quick eats from pizza to Thai. Head to Fronwagplatz for bakeries, delis, gelatarias and alfresco cafes.

Fischerzunft FUSION $$$
(☏052 632 05 05; www.fischerzunft.ch; Rheinquai 8; mains Sfr54-75; ☺lunch & dinner Wed-Sun) André Jaeger and Jana Zwesper entice with

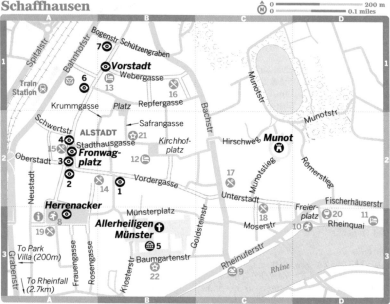

Schaffhausen

European-Asian taste sensations at this Michelin-starred restaurant by the Rhine, with an elegant beamed dining room and riverside terrace. Match perfectly spiced fish dishes and handmade desserts with top wines from the cellar.

Wirtschaft Zum Frieden SWISS $$
(☎052 625 47 67; www.wirtschaft-frieden.ch; Herrenacker 11; mains Sfr39-48; ⊙lunch & dinner Tue-Sat;) Locals have been eating, drinking and making merry at this cosy wood-panelled inn since 1445. Join them today for good, honest regional fare, such as braised veal cheeks with potato-celery puree or lake fish as well as vegetarian specials such as curries and dumplings prepared with market-fresh vegetables.

Gerberstube TRADITIONAL $$
(☎052 625 21 55; www.gerberstube.ch; Bachstrasse 8; mains Sfr45-70; ⊙lunch & dinner Tue-Sat) Behind their 1708 rococo facade, the opulent dining rooms of what in medieval times was a guildhall are a tempting setting for carefully prepared traditional cooking. Tuck into rich oxtail soup with port wine, or less-traditional curry scampi.

Café Vordergasse CAFE $
(Vordergasse 79; snacks & light meals Sfr10-20; ⊙6am-7pm Mon-Fri, 7am-5pm Sat, from 10am Sun) This art nouveau-style tearoom spills out onto an ever-popular pavement terrace. Try sandwiches, salads and quiches with a homemade lemonade or smoothie.

Fass-Beiz CAFE $
(Webergasse 13; mains Sfr17.50-24.50; ⊙lunch & dinner Mon-Sat) This laid-back, alternative cafe does tasty sandwiches and lunch specials. Music gigs, theatre performances and art exhibitions take place in the cellar below.

Schäfli SWISS $$
(☎052 625 11 47; Unterstadt 21; mains Sfr18-35; ⊙lunch & dinner Tue-Sat) Schäfli has been sizzling up *Rindsfilets* (steak filets) with sauces like pepper, cognac or herb since 1970.

Chäs Marili DELI $
(Fronwagplatz 9; ⊙lunch & dinner Mon-Sat) Cheese, glorious cheese is what you'll find here, alongside other goodies for your picnic basket.

🍷 Drinking & Entertainment

Güterhof LOUNGE
(☎052 630 40 40; www.gueterhof.ch; Freierplatz 10, ⊙8am-late) This half-timbered building was once the goods depot for Rhine river transport companies. It's now a super-sleek combination of bar (with outdoor seating), cafe, restaurant and sushi bar.

Cuba Bar CLUB
(Safrangasse 2; ⊙4pm-late Mon-Sun) Shabby-chic Old Town party hotspot where DJs spin house, pop and funk.

Kammgarn LIVE MUSIC
(www.kammgarn.ch, in German; Baumgartens-trasse 19) Tune into the local live music and cultural scene at this textile-factory-turned-arts-centre, which also houses an industrial-cool restaurant (mains Sfr23 to Sfr32).

ℹ Information

Main post office (Bahnhofstrasse 34; ⊙7am-6.30pm Mon-Fri, 8am-5pm Sat) Opposite the train station.

Tourist office (☎052 632 40 20; www.schaff hauserland.ch; Herrenacker 15; ⊙9.30am-6pm Mon-Fri, 9.30am-12pm & 1.30-6pm Sat & Sun).

ℹ Getting There & Away

Direct hourly trains run from Zürich (Sfr18.60, 55 minutes). Local trains head half-hourly to Stein am Rhein (Sfr7.80, 25 minutes). Trains to St Gallen (Sfr28, 1½ to two hours) usually involve a change at Winterthur or Romanshorn. There is plenty of parking (around Sfr1.20 per hour) on the fringes of the Old Town.

Rheinfall

Ensnared in wispy spray, the thunderous Rheinfall (Rhine Falls; www.rheinfall.ch) might not give Niagara much competition in terms of height (23m), width (150m) or even flow of water (700 cu metre per second in summer), but it's a stunning sight nonetheless.

Two medieval castles overlook the falls. The smaller Schlössli Worth on the north bank harbours a lounge-style restaurant (☎052 672 24 21; www.schloessliwoerth.ch, in German; mains Sfr32-44; ⊙11.30am-11.30pm, closed Wed Sep-Mar), with floor-to-ceiling windows affording magical views of the falls, strikingly illuminated after dark. Market-fresh cuisine such as pike perch with lemon-rocket risotto is paired with fine local wines.

The more imposing Schloss Laufen on the south bank boasts 1000 years of history and overlooks the falls at closer quarters. If the sound of the waterfall lulling you to sleep at night appeals, you can stay at its

SYHA hostel (☑052 659 61 52; www.youth hostel.ch/dachsen; dm Sfr28.50-36).

Most views of the falls are free, but to get close up to the rushing waters on the south side of the falls, you pay Sfr5 for an adult and Sfr3.50 for a child at the Schloss Laufen souvenir shop (open daily) to descend the staircase to the Känzeli viewing platform.

During summer, ferries (www.maendli.ch, in German) flit in and out of the water at the bottom of the falls. Some merely cross from Schloss Laufen to Schlössli Worth (adult/child Sfr2/1) but the round trip that stops at the tall rock in the middle of the falls (adult/child Sfr8/4), where you can climb to the top and watch the water rush all around you, is far more fun.

For an above-the-treetops perspective of the falls, visit the new Adventure Park (www.ap-rheinfall.ch, in German; adult/child Sfr40/26; ☑10am-7pm Mon-Sun Apr Oct), one of Switzerland's biggest rope parks, with routes graded according to difficulty.

To get to the Rheinfall, you can catch bus 1 or 6 from Schaffhausen train station to Neuhausen Zentrum (Sfr3, 13 minutes), then follow the yellow footprints to a point where you can go right towards Schlössli Worth or left across the combined train and pedestrian bridge to Schloss Laufen.

If you come by train from Schaffhausen or Winterthur to Schloss Laufen am Rheinfall (April to October only), you'll need to climb the hill to the castle. By car, you'll pull up in the car park behind the castle.

Klettgau

West of Schaffhausen spreads the red-wine-producing territory of Klettgau, which spills over into neighbouring Germany. Like sheets of corduroy, the serried ranks of mostly Pinot Noir vineyards are draped over pea-green fields and gentle rises.

Sprinkled about this soothing countryside are engaging villages. The most striking is the medieval Neunkirch, 13km from Schaffhausen. Others worth passing through include Beringen, Hallau and Osterfingen. Some of these slow-paced hamlets come to life in mid-October for wine festivals. In particular, look out for Osterfingen's Trottenfest (www.trottenfest.ch, in German), when vintners throw open their doors for tastings. If you come at any other time, head for Bad Osterfingen (☑052 681 21 21; Zollstrasse; mains Sfr30-45; ☑lunch & dinner Wed-Sun), where you'll be regaled with hearty local cooking and the best *Spätzli* (egg noddles) around for miles.

Buses from Schaffhausen serve these villages.

Stein am Rhein

POP 3200 / ELEV 407M

Stein am Rhein looks as though it has leaped out of the pages of a Swiss fairy tale, with its miniature steam train, leafy river promenade and gingerbready houses. The effect is most overwhelming in its cobblestone Rathausplatz, where houses of all shapes and sizes, some half-timbered, others covered in frescos line up for a permanent photo op. Why isn't this place on Unesco's World Heritage list?

◉ Sights & Activities

Look out for daredevil kids diving from the bridge into the Rhine as you wander along the leafy river promenade. If you'd rather paddle along it, the SYHA hostel rents out canoes and kayaks for Sfr27 and Sfr36 respectively per day.

Rathausplatz   SQUARE
Often hailed Switzerland's most beautiful town square (no mean feat!), the elongated Rathausplatz is picture book stuff. The fresco-festooned Rathaus (town hall) soars above the 16th-century houses named according to the pictures with which they are adorned, like *Sonne* (Sun) and *Der Weisse Adler* (The White Eagle).

Museum Lindwurm   MUSEUM
(www.museum-lindwurm.ch; Unterstadt 18; admission Sfr5; ☑10am-5pm Mon-Sun Mar-Oct) A four-storey house has been converted into this museum, whose living rooms, servants' quarters and kitchen replicate the conditions enjoyed in the mid-19th century by a bourgeois family.

Klostermuseum St Georgen   MUSEUM
(adult/child Sfr5/3; ☑10am-5pm Tue-Sun Apr-Oct) Also worth a look is this monastery museum between the Rathaus and the Rhine. A Benedictine monastery was built here in 1007, but what you see today, including the cloister and magnificent *Festsaal* (grand dining room), is largely a late-Gothic creation.

🛏 Sleeping

Given the abundance of gorgeous houses, there's a disappointing lack of hotels with

WORTH A TRIP

MILKY WAY

Forget horses, donkeys and llamas; the latest craze to sweep this corner of Switzerland is cow trekking. Yes, *cow* trekking. And it's all thanks to the madcap brainwave of local farmer Heinz Morgenegg, who runs the **Bolderhof** (☑052 742 40 48; www.bolderhof.ch) in Hemishofen, 3km west of Stein am Rhein. Today, cow trekking is part of the Morgenegg family's experiential approach to organic dairy farming, which includes farm Olympics, cheese-making workshops and cow-drawn carriage rides.

Simply pick your brown-eyed beauty – with names like Umbra, La Paloma and Oklahoma – saddle up and ride at cow pace through bucolic countryside to the banks of the Rhine. The cows can sense a soft touch and have been known to suddenly make a sprint for the freedom of a meadow full of luscious grass, so a firm hand (and riding crop) is needed. A 1½-hour jaunt costs Sfr90 per person, a half-day trek including a picnic Sfr150 per person.

character in town. You may be better off finding private lodgings through the tourist office.

SYHA hostel HOSTEL $
(☑052 741 12 55; www.youthhostel.ch/stein; Hemishoferstrasse 87; dm Sfr30-32.50, s/d/q Sfr42/73/146; ☁⚑) On the banks of the Rhine, this neat-and-tidy hostel has attractive gardens, a barbecue area, playground and canoe hire. It's a 15-minute stroll northwest of Rathausplatz.

Hotel Adler HOTEL $$
(☑052 742 61 61; www.adlersteinamrhein.ch; Rathausplatz 2; s/d Sfr130/185; ☁) Behind the frescoed exterior lie simple yet comfortable rooms. The location on Rathausplatz is the big draw. The dining areas have a pleasingly old-fashioned feel about them and the grub, while nothing outlandishly creative, hits the spot. Local fish is a safe bet.

Rheingerbe GUESTHOUSE $$
(☑052 741 29 91; Schiffländi 5; s/d Sfr90/60) The rooms in this pretty four-storey house are a little old-fashioned, with dark timber beds and simple furniture. You need to book to get a room with river views.

🍴 Eating

Half-timbered houses serving Swiss grub line the Rhine, but the quality can be hit or miss.

Burg Hohenklingen SWISS $$
(☑052 741 21 37; www.burghohenklingen.ch; Hohenklingenstrasse 1; mains Sfr39-58 ☁10am-10.30pm Tue-Sat, to 5pm Sun) For medieval atmosphere, you can't beat this 12th-century hilltop fortress, with superb views over

Stein am Rhein. Tuck into Swiss classics in the Rittersaal (Hall of Knights). It's a 30-minute uphill walk from the Old Town.

La P'tite Crêperie CREPERIE $
(Unterstadt 10; crêpes Sfr6.90-12.90; ☁11am-7pm) Mary-Ann is the crêpe queen at this hole-in-the-wall place with a Boho feel. Feast away on her fabulously light crêpes with cheese and *Bündnerfleisch* (air-dried beef), maple syrup or – what could be more Swiss? – Toblerone. It's closed Tuesdays and Wednesdays during low season.

Rhy Lounge INTERNATIONAL $$
(☑052 741 66 70; Öhningerstrasse 10; mains Sfr26.50-46.50; ☁lunch & dinner Tue-Sat; ⚑) A favourite summertime hang-out for its chestnut-shaded terrace, this sleek bistro and lounge bar is a five-minute walk east from Rathausplatz. The food skips from avocado-shrimp salad to Danish meat balls, and there's a kids menu.

ℹ️ Information

The tiny **tourist office** (☑052 742 20 90; www.steinamrhein.ch; Oberstadt 3; ☁9.30am-noon & 1.30-5pm Mon-Fri) lies east of the central Rathausplatz.

MOVING ON?

For tips, recommendations and reviews, head to http://shop.lonelyplanet.com to purchase a downloadable PDF of the Austria chapter from Lonely Planet's *Western Europe* guide.

ⓘ Getting There & Away

Stein am Rhein is on the direct hourly train route that links Schaffhausen (Sfr7.80, 25 minutes) with St Gallen (Sfr29, 1½ hours).

LAKE CONSTANCE

Before package holidays began whisking the locals and their beach towels abroad in the '70s and '80s, Lake Constance (Bodensee) was the German Mediterranean, with its mild climate, flowery gardens and palm trees. The 'Swabian Sea', as it's nicknamed, is Central Europe's third largest lake, straddling Switzerland, Germany and Austria. It's a relaxed place to wind down for a few days, whether cycling through apple orchards and vineyards, heron-spotting in the lake's wetlands, or taking to its glassy waters by canoe.

Come in spring for blossom, summer for lazy beach days and autumn for new wine. Almost everything shuts from November to February.

ⓘ Information

The **Bodensee Erlebniskarte** (www.bodensee-erlebniskarte.de; 3/7/14 days Sfr102/131/181) discount card is sold from mid-April to mid-October. In its most expensive version, it entitles the holder to free unlimited ferry travel, entrance to many museums and attractions, including the Zeppelin Museum in Friedrichshafen and Insel Mainau, and a return journey up the Säntisbahn (p284).

ⓘ Getting There & Away

Good rail services link Zürich to Konstanz (Sfr30, 80 minutes) and Munich (Sfr89, 4¼ hours) in Germany. Trains (Sfr8, 15 minutes) run between Bregenz in Austria and St Margrethen in Switzerland.

WORTH A TRIP

A SPIN OF THE LAKE

Hopping across the Swiss–German border from Kreuzlingen brings you to the high-spirited, sunny university town of **Konstanz** (www.konstanz.de), well worth a visit for its Romanesque cathedral, pretty Old Town and tree-fringed harbour. Edging north of Konstanz, you reach the Unesco-listed Benedictine monastery of **Reichenau** (www.reichenau.de), founded in AD 724. Close by is **Insel Mainau** (www.mainau.de; adult/child €15.90/8.50; ☺dawn-dusk), a pleasantly green islet with 45 hectares of Mediterranean-style gardens, including rhododendron groves, a butterfly house and a waterfall-strewn Italian garden.

Stepping across to the lake's northern flank you arrive in the wine-growing town of **Meersburg** (www.meersburg.de), where cobbled lanes thread past half-timbered houses up to the perkily turreted medieval castle. Just east of here is **Friedrichshafen**, forever associated with the Zeppelin, the early cigar-shaped craft of the skies, which made its inaugural flight in 1900. The **Zeppelin Museum** (www.zeppelin-museum.de; adult/child €7.50/3; ☺9am-5pm Mon-Sun) traces the history of this bombastic, but ill-fated, means of air transport. Still on German turf is the postcard-perfect island town of **Lindau** (www.lindau.de), with its lavishly frescoed houses, palm-speckled promenade and harbour watched over by a lighthouse and Bavarian lion. For further information, head to shop .lonelyplanet.com to purchase a downloadable PDF of the Germany chapter from Lonely Planet's *Western Europe* guide.

Lindau sits just a few kilometres north of Austria and the town of **Bregenz** (www.bregenz.ws), which hosts the highly acclaimed **Bregenzer Festspiele** from mid-July to mid-August, where opera and orchestral concerts are staged on a vast water-borne stage. Rising dramatically above the town is the Pfänder (1064m). A **cable car** (adult/child return €11/5.50; ☺8am-7pm Apr-Oct) glides to the summit, where panoramic views of Lake Constance and the not-so-distant Alps unfold.

Even if you don't have your own car, getting around by bike or boat is a breeze. Well-signposted and largely flat, the 273km **Bodensee-Radweg** (Lake Constance Cycle Route; www.bodensee-radweg.com) encircles the lake, weaving through fields of ripening wheat, vineyards, orchards and shady avenues of chestnut and plane. Most train stations in the region rent out bikes. **La Canoa** (www.lacanoa.com, in German) has canoe rental points in all major towns on the lake; see the website for details.

Getting Around

Various ferry companies, including Switzerland's **SBS Schifffahrt** (www.sbsag.ch, in German), Austria's **Vorarlberg Lines** (www.bodensee schifffahrt.at) and Germany's **BSB** (www.bsb -online.com), travel across, along and around the lake from mid-April to late October, with the more-frequent services starting in late May. A Swiss Pass (p366) is valid only on the Swiss side of the lake.

Trains tend to be the easiest way to get around on the Swiss side, buses on the German bank. The B31 road hugs the north shore, but can get busy. On the south shore, the N13 shadows the train line around the lake.

Kreuzlingen

POP 19,000 / ELEV 404M

Kreuzlingen, in the Swiss canton of Thurgau, is often eclipsed by its prettier, more vivacious sister, Konstanz in Germany. That said, its lakefront location is charming, as is its **SYHA hostel** (☑071 688 26 63; www .youthhostel.ch/kreuzlingen; Promenadenstrasse 7; dm Sfr31.20; ☺Mar-Nov), occupying a former manor house. Otherwise the most sensible option is to change trains at Kreuzlingen station and head straight to Konstanz (Sfr3, three minutes); there is no passport control. Should you need more details, try the **tourist office** (☑071 672 38 40; www.kreuzlingen -tourismus.ch; Sonnenstrasse 4; ☺10am-12.30pm & 1.30-6pm Mon-Fri). Direct trains run every 30 minutes between Kreuzlingen and Schaffhausen (Sfr17.20, 55 minutes).

The lakeside road between Kreuzlingen and Stein am Rhein is dotted with quaint half-timbered Thurgau villages, such as **Gottlieben**, **Steckborn** and **Berlingen**. Near the latter is **Schloss Arenenberg** (www.napoleonmuseum.tg.ch; Salenstein; adult/ child Sfr12/5; ☺1-5pm Mon, from 10am Tue-Sun), the handsome lakefront mansion where France's Napoleon III grew up.

Romanshorn & Arbon

ELEV 400M

Despite its one prominent church spire, Romanshorn (population 9200) is of minimal sightseeing interest – little more than a staging point as you go to or from Friedrichshafen on the ferry.

The medieval town centre of Arbon (population 13,500), 8km southeast, is more appealing, with its half-timbered houses and ancient chapels.

It's about a 1km walk from the train station to the **tourist office** (☑071 440 13 80; www.arbon.ch; Schmiedgasse 5; ☺9-11.30am & 2-6pm Mon-Fri, 9-11.30am Sat) in the historic centre, watched over by its 16th-century castle, **Schloss Arbon**. The castle's **Historisches Museum** (Alemannenstrasse 4; adult/child Sfr4/2; ☺2-5pm May-Sep, Sun only Mar-Apr & Oct-Nov) races you through 5500 years of history, from the Stone Age to the 18th-century linen trade. On one lane, centuries-old houses bear frescos depicting trades of yore.

Set in a pretty partly timbered house, **Gasthof Frohsinn** (☑071 447 84 84; www .frohsinn-arbon.ch; Romanshornerstrasse 15; s/d Sfr122.50/185) has light, airy rooms and its own microbrewery. Venture down to the vaulted cellar (mains Sfr17 to Sfr42.50) for a cold frothy one and hearty fare like veal sausages with onion-beer sauce.

For a down-on-the-farm experience, sleep in the straw and sip home-pressed apple juice at the blissfully tranquil **Frasnacht Strohhotel** (☑071 446 4772; Kratzern 39, Frasnacht; per adult/child Sfr27/19; ⊕). The farm is just off the Bodensee Radweg, 2.5km west of Arbon. If you don't want to schlep your own sleeping bag, you can rent one for Sfr3.

Romanshorn and Arbon are on the train line between Zürich and Rorschach.

Rorschach

POP 8820 / ELEV 398M

Nothing to do with the psychiatric ink-blot tests of the same name, the quiet waterfront resort of Rorschach is backed by a wooded hill. Although something of a faded beauty, the town has some fine 16th- to 18th-century houses with oriel windows.

There are three train stations: Rorschach Stadt, Rorschach Hafen and Rorschach Hauptbahnhof. If coming from St Gallen, alight at Rorschach Stadt station (Sfr4.60, 17 minutes) and walk 500m northeast through the centre to Rorschach Hafen station (on the line from Arbon and Schaffhausen), the nearby **tourist office** (☑071 841 70 34; www .tourist-rorschach.ch; Hauptstrasse 56; ☺8.30-noon & 1.30-6pm Mon-Fri) and the cogwheel train (Bergbahn Rorschach-Heiden) that leaves to the health resort of **Heiden**.

Rorschach Hafen station is handily located on Hauptstrasse, in the heart of the Old Town. Walk left (east) from the station to see some fine oriel windows, particularly at numbers 33 and 31 and the town hall, number 29. There are more on Mariabergstrasse. Out on the lake is the 1920s **Badhütte** (Bathing Hut), attached to land by a little covered bridge, which is a pleasant place for a drink.

Walk right from the train station to find the main hotels or, for an exceptional escape, book into the magnificent fantasy palace **Schloss Wartegg** (☑071 858 62 62; http://wartegg.ch; Rorschacherberg; s Sfr145-155, Sfr220-270; P), a 10-minute drive from central Rorschach on the hillside above town. This 16th-century former royal Austrian castle is set in leafy grounds with towering sequoias and Lake Constance views. Organic regional produce is served at breakfast.

ST GALLEN & APPENZELL CANTONS

The cultural high point of a journey around the extreme northeast of the country is a visit to St Gallen's legendary abbey, with its extraordinary rococo library. To explore the surrounding canton of St Gallen is to dive into a deeply Germanic, rural world.

The Appenzellers are the butt of many a cruel joke by their fellow Swiss, a little like Tasmanians in Australia or Newfoundlanders in Canada. As Swiss Germans say, Appenzellers *hätte ä langi Laitig* (have a very long cable): it takes a while after you tug for them to get the message.

Such devotion to rural tradition has an upside. Locals go to great lengths to preserve their heritage and this green, hilly region is sprinkled with beautiful, timeless villages. Both cantons are criss-crossed by endless hiking, cycling and mountain-biking trails.

St Gallen

POP 72,700 / ELEV 670M

St Gallen's history as the 'writing room of Europe' is evident in its principal attraction today: the sublime rococo library of its huge Catholic abbey, which rises gracefully above a fountain-dotted courtyard.

Local lore has it that St Gallen began with a bush, a bear and an Irish monk who should have watched where he was going. In AD 612, the tale goes, itinerant Gallus fell into a briar and considered the stumble a calling from God. After a fortuitous

encounter with a bear, in which he persuaded it to bring him a log, take some bread in return and leave him in peace, he used the log to begin building the hermitage that would one day morph into St Gallen's cathedral.

◉ Sights

Multilingual guided tours of the Old Town (Sfr20 per person) kick off at the tourist office at 2pm Monday to Saturday from May to October.

Stiftsbibliothek   LIBRARY
(www.stiftsbibliothek.ch; Klosterhof 6d; adult/child Sfr10/7; ◉10am-5pm Mon-Sat, to 4pm Sun) St Gallen's 16th-century library is one of the world's oldest and the finest example of rococo architecture in Switzerland. Along with the rest of the monastery complex surrounding it, the library forms a Unesco World Heritage Site.

Filled with priceless books and manuscripts painstakingly handwritten by monks during the Middle Ages, it's a dimly lit confection of ceiling frescos, stucco, cherubs and parquetry. Only 30,000 of the total 150,000 volumes are in the library at any one time, and only a handful in display cases, arranged into special exhibitions. If there's a tour guide in the library at the time, you might see the monks' filing system, hidden in the wall panels.

Kids are enthralled by the 2700-year-old mummified corpse in the far right corner.

Dom   CATHEDRAL
(Klosterhof; ◉9am-6pm Mon, Tue, Thu & Fri, 10am-6pm Wed, 9am-4pm Sat, noon-5.30pm Sun) The twin-towered cathedral is only slightly less ornate than the library, with dark and stormy frescos and aqua-green stucco embellishments. Oddly, entry is by two modest doors on the north flank – there is no door in the main facade, which is actually the cathedral's apse! Concerts are sometimes held – consult www.kirchenmusik.ch. The cathedral is closed during services.

St Laurenzen-Kirche   CHURCH
(Zeughausgasse; ◉9.30-11.30am & 2-4pm Mon, 9.30am-6pm Tue-Fri, to 4pm Sat) St Gallen's cathedral gets all the attention, but this Protestant neo-Gothic church is also beautiful, with its mosaic-tiled roof, delicate floral frescos and star-studded ceiling resembling a night sky. Climb the **tower** (adult/child Sfr5/2.50; ◉10am & 3pm) for views over the town's terracotta rooftops and spires.

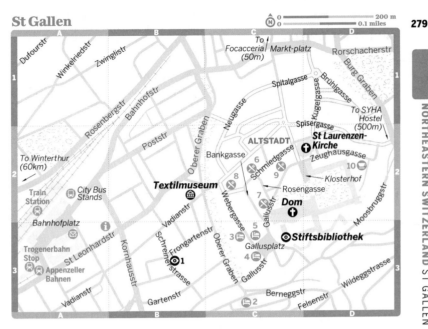

St Gallen

Textilmuseum   MUSEUM
(www.textilmuseum.ch; Vadianstrasse 2; adult/child
Sfr14/free; ⊙10am-5pm Fri-Wed, to 8pm Thu) St
Gallen has long been an important hub
of the Swiss textile industry, and this is
the most interesting of the town's several
museums. Butterflies dance across the
purple walls of the museum's lounge bar, a
fashionable coffee spot.

FREE **Stadtlounge**   LANDMARK
(City Lounge; Schreinerstrasse; ⊙24hr) Quite
astonishingly, part of historic St Gallen is
covered by a rubberised red tennis-court
coating, with in-situ outdoor-furniture-like
chairs, sofas, tables and even a car. This zany
art installation project by Pipilotti Rist and
Carlos Martínez is intended as an 'outdoor
living room'.

✦ Festivals & Events

Open Air St Gallen   MUSIC
(www.openairsg.ch) Music festival hosting
big-name rock and pop acts in early July.

St Galler Festspiele   OPERA
(www.stgaller-festspiele.ch, in German) Two-week
outdoor opera season (from about 20 June
to the end of the first week of July), held in
the square behind the cathedral.

DON'T MISS

ALTSTADT ORIELS

Many houses of Old St Gallen boast elaborate *Erker* (oriel bay windows), especially around Gallusplatz, Spisergasse, Schmiedgasse and Kugelgasse. The city's tourism folk have counted them all up and reckon there are 111 oriel windows! Some bear the most extraordinary timber sculptures – a reflection of the wealth of their one-time owners, mostly textile barons.

🛌 Sleeping

St Gallen is a business town, which can make beds scarce and prices high.

Hotel Dom BOUTIQUE HOTEL **$$**
(☑071 227 71 71; www.hoteldom.ch; Webergasse 22; s/d Sfr175/245; ☐🕸) An almost startlingly modern hotel, plonked in the middle of the Old Town. The room decor is razor-sharp with clean lines, backlit walls and bold colours. Genuinely friendly staff and a generous breakfast buffet sweeten the deal.

Einstein Hotel HISTORIC HOTEL **$$$**
(☑071 227 55 55; www.einstein.ch; Berneggstrasse 2; s Sfr175-225, d Sfr300-450; ☐@🕸) Silk curtains, cherry-wood furnishings and plush lamb-wool rugs grace the spacious rooms at this grand 19th-century pile. Relax with a swim in the strikingly lit atrium pool or a massage in the spa. The panoramic rooftop restaurant (mains Sfr26 to Sfr48) emphasises regional cuisine.

Hotel Vadian HOTEL **$$**
(☑071 228 18 78; www.hotel-vadian.com; Gallusstrasse 36; s Sfr99-150, d Sfr150-240; 🕸) You can't get much closer to the heart of St Gallen at these prices. The hotel was recently given an overhaul and varied modern rooms are in perfect nick. Some have nice touches, like ceiling beams.

Schwanen GUESTHOUSE **$**
(☑071 222 65 62; www.schwanenpizza.ch, in German; Webergasse 23; s/d/tr Sfr95/160/230) Set above a pizzeria, the Schwanen's rooms are clean, compact and simple. The location just steps from the abbey is a boon.

SYHA Hostel HOSTEL **$**
(☑071 245 47 77; www.youthhostel.ch/st.gallen; Jüchstrasse 25; dm Sfr32, s/d/q per person Sfr60/45/37; @) Nestling in leafy grounds, this modern hillside hostel is only a 15-minute walk from the Old Town – or take the Trogenerbähnli (S12) from the train station to Birnbäume.

🍴 Eating & Drinking

St Gallen is noted for its *Erststock-Beizli*, traditional taverns situated on the 1st floor of half-timbered houses.

Bäumli TOP CHOICE SWISS **$$**
(☑071 222 11 74; Schmiedgasse 18; mains Sfr22-47; ☺lunch & dinner Tue-Sat) A late-medieval building houses a timeless eatery that showcases all the typical 1st-floor specialities, from bratwurst with fried onions (Sfr12.80) to lamb cutlets, Wiener schnitzel, *Cordon bleus* (pork schnitzel stuffed with ham and cheese), *Geschnetzeltes* (a sliced pork or veal dish) and *Mostbröggli* (smoked beef jerky).

Segreto ITALIAN **$$**
(☑071 290 11 11; www.segreto.ch; Abacus-Platz 1; mains Sfr42-45; ☺lunch & dinner Tue-Fri, dinner Sat) Clean, bright Mediterranean flavours dominate at this chic Italian. Imaginative starters like veal tartar with black olives, basil and white tomato ice cream are followed by homemade pasta and mains such as poached halibut with raspberry sauce. The wine list is first-rate. It's 4km north of town; take bus 12 to Abacus-Platz.

Wirtschaft zur Alten Post FUSION **$$**
(☑071 222 66 01; Gallusstrasse 4; mains Sfr22-47; ☺lunch & dinner Tue-Sat) Things are a little ritzy at this upmarket but historical *Beizl* (tavern), where St Gallen specialities like fat veal sausages with rösti are complemented by more-original creations such as Pyrenean milk-fed lamb in an olive-herb crust.

Focacceria CAFE **$**
(Metzgergasse 22; foccacia Sfr6.50-16.50; ☺11am-midnight Tue-Sat) Join the midday crowds here for delicious focaccia prepared with homemade antipasti and spreads, speciality teas and coffees.

Metzgerei Gemperli SAUSAGES **$**
(Schmiedgasse 34; sausages from Sfr6.50; ☺8am-6.30pm Mon-Fri, 7am-5pm Sat) Bite into the best OLMA bratwurst, served plain in a *Bürli* (bun), at this butcher–sausage stand combo.

Chocolaterie CAFE **$**
(☑071 222 57 70; Gallusstrasse 20; ☺1-6.30pm Mon, 9am-6.30pm Tue-Fri, to 5pm Sat) For

exquisite chocolate in liquid and solid forms, this half-timbered place opposite the cathedral is surely the devil's work. Try a smooth, cocoa-rich hot or cold chocolate.

Trüffelschnüffler CAFE $
(Zeughausgasse 14; ⊙1.30-6.30pm Wed-Fri, 10am-5pm Sat) 'Truffle sniffer' is the name of this arty cafe-cum-craft-shop. Stop by for drinks and handmade gifts, ranging from groovy printed bags to wood-carved Swiss army knives.

ⓘ Information

Main post office (Bahnhofplatz 5; ⊙7am-7.30pm Mon-Wed & Fri, to 8pm Thu, to 4pm Sat, 3-6pm Sun)
Tourist office (☑071 227 37 37; www.st.gallen -bodensee.ch; Bahnhofplatz 1a; ⊙9am-6pm Mon-Fri, 10am-4pm Sat) There's another self-service information point, where you can pick up brochures, in the Chocolaterie.

ⓘ Getting There & Away

St Gallen is a short train or bus ride from Romanshorn (Sfr9, 25 minutes). There are also regular trains (only four of them direct) to Bregenz in Austria (Sfr18, 35 to 50 minutes), Chur (Sfr33, 1½ hours) and Zürich (Sfr28, 65 minutes via Winterthur).

By car, the main link is the A1 freeway, which runs from Zürich and Winterthur to the Austrian border.

Appenzell

POP 5700 / ELEV 785M

Appenzell is a feast for both the eyes and the stomach. Behind the gaily decorative pastel-coloured facades of its traditional buildings lie cafes, *confiseries* (sweets and cake shops), cheese shops, delicatessens, butchers and restaurants offering local specialities. It's absolutely perfect for a long lunch and a lazy wander along the crystal-clear Sitter river.

FUN FOR FREE

Stay in Appenzell for three nights or more and you'll receive the Appenzeller Ferienkarte, which entitles you to free use of public transport and most cable cars, access to local museums and pools, plus one day's free bike hire and entry to the Natur-Moorbad.

⊙ Sights & Activities

Countless hiking trails thread up into the Alps from Appenzell; see www.appenzell .info for inspiration. A great family walk is the 5km Barfusspfad (barefoot trail), which skips through meadows and over mountain brooks to Gonten.

Trekking bikes and e-bikes can be rented at the train station for Sfr25 and Sfr45 per day respectively.

Opening hours are given for high season; many sights have reduced hours from November to March.

Altstadt NEIGHBOURHOOD
The centrepiece of the Old Town is photogenic Landsgemeindeplatz, with elaborately painted hotels and restaurants around its edges. The open-air parliament takes place on this square on the last Sunday of April, with locals wearing traditional dress and voting (in the case of the men, by raising a short dagger).

The buildings along Hauptgasse are also admirable. The village church has gold and silver figures flanking a baroque altar.

FREE Brauerei Locher BREWERY
(Industriestrasse 12; beer tasting Sfr1.50; ⊙10am-12.15pm & 1-5pm, closed Mon Nov-Mar) Pure local spring water goes into the refreshing Appenzeller Bier brewed here. The hands-on visitor centre whisks you through brewing history and processes. At the front you can taste three mini beers and buy beers like hoppy Vollmond (full moon) and alcohol-free Leermond (empty moon).

Appenzell Museum MUSEUM
(Hauptgasse 4; adult/child Sfr7/3; ⊙10am-noon & 2-5pm Mon-Sun) Beside the tourist office, this museum fills you in on traditional customs with its collection of 15th-century flags and banners, embroidery, folk art and (more grimly) historic torture instruments.

Museum Liner GALLERY
(www.museumliner.ch, in German; Unterrain-strasse 5; adult/child Sfr9/6; ⊙10am-noon & 2-5pm Tue-Fri, 11am-5pm Sat & Sun) Appenzell's contemporary art gallery sits on the other side of town from the train station. The building (whose metallic sheen gives it the appearance, in profile, of a saw) is more interesting than the collection, dedicated to local artists Carl August Liner and his son Carl Walter.

Natur-Moorbad SPA

(☑071 795 31 21; www.naturmoorbad.ch, in German; Gontenbad) At this moor bath, dating to 1740, you can dip in mud-laden water from the moors (Sfr30) to help with stress or skin conditions (adding in nettles, ferns and other plants), or luxuriate in a pampering rose bath (Sfr109 for two).

🛏 Sleeping & Eating

The tourist office can advise on B&Bs, holiday apartments and farmstays in the area. Most restaurants charge roughly Sfr12 to Sfr14 for *Käseschnitte* (cheese on toast) and other snacks, and Sfr20 to Sfr40 for main courses.

Gasthaus Hof GUESTHOUSE $

(☑071 787 40 30; www.gasthaus-hof.ch; Engelgasse 4; s/d/tr/q Sfr85/130/180/220; 🛜) Just off Landsgemeindeplatz, this cheap-sleep option has simple but spacious rooms with timber-clad walls. The old-school restaurant comes with plenty of local bonhomie.

Hotel Appenzell HISTORIC HOTEL $$

(☑071 788 15 15; www.hotel-appenzell.ch; Landsgemeindeplatz; s/d Sfr130/220; 📶) With its broad, brightly decorated facade, this typical Appenzeller building houses generously sized rooms with wooden beds. Decor combines gentle pinks and blues with frilly lace on the picture windows. The restaurant offers a wide-ranging seasonal menu that includes vegetarian dishes.

Marktplatz INTERNATIONAL $$

(☑071 787 12 04; Kronengarten 2; mains Sfr23-43; ☺lunch & dinner Fri-Tue; 🍴) Sit on the terrace on one of Appenzell's prettiest squares or in the cosy wood-carved interior. The food is surprisingly creative for these rural parts – think beef with wild peach salsa or red curry with rabbit. There's also a children's menu.

Gasthaus Linde SWISS $

(071 787 13 76; Hauptgasse 40; mains Sfr18-30; ☺lunch & dinner Fri-Wed) This warm, wood-panelled tavern oozes local character and does excellent Appenzell beer fondue. More adventurous diners can tuck into offal specialities.

ℹ Information

The **tourist office** (☑071 788 96 41; www .appenzell.info, in German; Hauptgasse 4; ☺9am-noon & 1.30-6pm Mon-Fri, 10am-5pm Sat) has details on the Appenzeller Ferienkarte.

ℹ Getting There & Away

From St Gallen, the narrow-gauge train to Appenzell (Sfr13.20, 45 minutes) leaves from the front and to the right of the main train station. Departures from St Gallen are approximately every half-hour, via Gais or Herisau (where you must occasionally change trains).

Around Appenzell

Scattered with Alpine dairy farms and quaint villages, the countryside surrounding Appenzell makes for some highly scenic driving along narrow winding roads.

◉ Sights & Activities

FREE **Appenzeller Schaukäserie** DAIRY

(www.showcheese.ch; Stein; ☺8.30am-6.30pm Mon-Sun) Cheese-lovers could pop into this dairy, which runs through the manufacturing process, explaining how cheeses like the famous Räss get their sweaty-socks smell (a coating of herbs and brine).

Volkskunde Museum MUSEUM

(www.appenzeller-museum-stein.ch; Stein; adult/child Sfr7/3.50; ☺10am-5pm Tue-Sun) This folksy museum provides an overview of Appenzell life, its collection spanning everything from pastoral paintings to cheesemaking traditions.

Werdenberg VILLAGE

Blink and you'll miss this village and that would be a shame! Founded in 1289, it is said to be the oldest settlement of timber houses in Switzerland. This huddle of some 40-odd houses lies between an oversized pond and a grapevine-covered hill topped by the **Schloss Werdenberg** (www.schloss -werdenberg.ch; adult/child Sfr6/5; ☺11.30am-6pm Tue-Fri, 10am-6pm Sat & Sun).

Wildhaus VILLAGE

Sitting pretty between the shark fin–like peaks of the Churfirsten range and Säntis is the family-friendly village of Wildhaus. This is a relaxed base for hiking in summer and skiing on 60km of pistes (a day pass costs Sfr53 for an adult and Sfr30 for a child) in winter at **Toggenburg** (www.toggen burg.ch). Activities like guided donkey walks and llama trekking keep kids amused.

One kilometre short of the small ski resort of Wildhaus, the modest timber house (thought to be one of the oldest in the country) where Huldrych Zwingli was born stands preserved in **Lisighaus** (signposted).

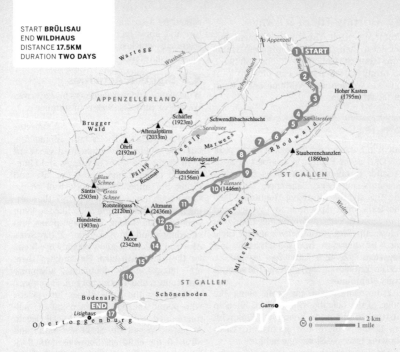

Walking Tour
Zwinglipass

〉 This moderately challenging two-day hike
leads through karst scenery and rural
valleys to cross a pass at the northern foot of
the Churfirsten. The SAW 1:50,000 *Appenzell
227T* (Sfr22.50) is a detailed map. Buses run
frequently from Appenzell to the trailhead in
Brülisau (Sfr4.60, 15 minutes).

From ① **Brülisau**, follow the signposted
road southeast to ② **Pfannenstiel** (940m).
Continue into the ③ **Brüeltobel** gorge, which
rises over a watershed to reach ④ **Gasthaus
Plattenbödeli** after 1¼ hours. Take the
Waldabstieg down left to the ⑤ **Sämtisersee**,
a striking lake. Bear right at ⑥ **Appenzeller
Sämtis**, and head on toward the towering
peaks of the Alpstein. The dirt track peters
out at ⑦ **Rheintaler Sämtis** (1295m), and
a foot track continues up to the grassy
⑧ **Chalberweid** below the canyonlike
Marwees Ridge. Ascend southward via a steep
gully onto a tiny saddle from where the stark,
elongated Fälensee (1446m) slides into view,
1½ hours from the Gasthaus Plattenbödeli.
Perched above Fälensee is ⑨ **Berggasthaus
Bollenwees**, a scenic hut to spend the night.

Skirt the Fälensee's northern flank, sidling
across broad scree fields to reach the
⑩ **Alphütte Fälenalp** dairy farm. Above you,
spectacular needles protrude from the rock
walls of the Hundstein (2156m). Make
a steep ascent along a ridge to the stone
shelters at ⑪ **Häderen**, 1¼ hours from
Bollenwees. The route now rises more gently
through karst fields with views to the bishop's
mitre-shaped peak of Altmann (2436m).
Cross the ⑫ **Zwinglipass** (2011m), a
plateau pitted with depressions and sink-
holes, then descend leftward to arrive at the
⑬ **Zwinglipasshütte**, 50 minutes on. From
the terrace, there are views of the Churfirst-
en's seven sawtooth peaks. Drop down
the mountainside to pass ⑭ **Chreialp**
(1817m). Steep switchbacks zigzag down to
⑮ **Teselalp** (1433m) at the end of a farm
track, after one hour. Follow the dirt road for
1.25km, bear left onto a foot track, then head
400m down via ⑯ **Flürentobel** chasm,
before branching right through clearings in
the spruce forest. Continue down to
⑰ **Wildhaus**, 50 to 60 minutes from Teselalp.

❶ Getting There & Away

From Appenzell, there is a frequent bus service to Stein (Sfr6.80, 12 minutes). Trains run from St Gallen to Buchs (Sfr19.80, 55 minutes), where you can pick up local buses to Werdenberg, Wildhaus and Schaan in Liechtenstein.

Säntis

Small in Swiss terms, the jagged Säntis peak (2503m) is the highest in this part of Switzerland. It offers a marvellous panorama encompassing Lake Constance, Zürichsee, the Alps and the Vorarlberg Mountains. Take the train from Appenzell to Urnäsch and transfer to the bus (approximately hourly) to Schwägalp (Sfr9). From Schwägalp, the cable car, **Säntisbahn** (www.saentisbahn.ch; one-way/return Sfr29/41; ☺7.30am-6pm Jun–mid-Oct, 8.30am-5pm mid-Oct–May) glides to the summit every 30 minutes.

From Säntis, you can walk along the ridge to the neighbouring peak of Ebenalp (1640m) in about 3½ hours. At Wildkirchli on Ebenalp there are prehistoric caves showing traces of Stone Age habitation.

The descent to the jewel-coloured **Seealpsee** on foot takes 1½ hours. Alternatively, a **cable car** (www.ebenalp.ch, in German; one-way/return in May-Nov Sfr19/27, half-/full day in Dec-Apr Sfr28/33) runs between the summit and Wasserauen approximately every 30 minutes. Wasserauen and Appenzell are connected by rail (Sfr4.60, 11 minutes). By the lake, family-run dairy **Seealpkäse** (☎079 441 22 73; www.seealpchaes.ch, in German; ☺Jun-Aug) sells delicious cheese specialities, including varieties made with wild garlic and chilli. For a glowing complexion, you can bathe in whey in a wooden bathtub (Sfr45) and gaze up at the mountains.

Back in Schwägalp, you can hire Nordic walking poles, snowshoes and sledges for Sfr7, Sfr19 and Sfr10 per day respectively at **Berghotel Schwägalp** (☎071 365 66 00; www.saentisbahn.ch; dm/s/d/tr Sfr50/95/160/240), a rustic mountain hotel with cosy pine-clad rooms and a show dairy.

Walensee

Walensee is a long finger of a lake along the A3 freeway (and railway line) that connects Zürich with Graubünden. The limestone Churfirsten mountains rise spectacularly above its north flank, occasionally interrupted by a coastal hamlet or upland pasture and, about halfway along the lakefront, seemingly cracked open by Switzerland's highest waterfall.

◎ Sights & Activities

Windsurfers and wakeboarders breeze across Walensee's turquoise waters in summer.

Flumserberg   MOUNTAIN
(www.flumserberg.ch) For a little Alpine fun, take the winding mountain road westward from Flums to a series of villages and Flumserberg, perched high above the lake and facing the impenetrable rock wall of the Churfirsten range. The mountain is the starting point for high-alpine hikes like the 13km 7-Gipfel Tour, taking in seven peaks and affording mind-blowing views of the Swiss Alps and Walensee. Allow roughly 6½ hours for the round trip hike. For families, there are buggy-friendly footpaths, adventure playgrounds and a toboggan run, Floomzer.

In winter the same slopes lure skiers, who pound the powder on 65km of well-maintained pistes catering to all levels. A day ski pass costs Sfr53 for adults and Sfr26.50 for children. Snowboarders flock here for the terrain parks, half-pipe and excellent freeriding opportunities.

Seerenbachfälle   WATERFALL
This series of three colossal waterfalls, thundering down 585m from top to bottom, is fuelled by a complex network of underground rivers running through the mountain rock from as far away as the peak of Säntis. The middle waterfall, a 305m drop, is considered Switzerland's highest. The closest you can reach by car is Betlis, a 30-minute hike away.

Weesen   WALKING
Petite and pretty, Weesen is the perfect base for exploring the lake, with a Geneva-style fountain shooting high into the air. A path along Walensee's north shore links Weesen to Walenstadt (about 6½ hours) or vice versa. The walk takes you along the lake shore, through dense forest and meadows and past a smattering of houses.

Murgsee   WALKING
A challenging, classic Alpine trail leads from Maschgenkamm top station to the inky blue Murgsee lakes. You'll hike through silent pastures cloaked in wildflowers, and forests of chestnuts and pines. The round trek takes around seven hours (not including stops).

SARDONA

A wild and wonderful area of glaciated mountains rises up around Piz Sardona (3056m), the highest peak in St Gallen. Few have the pleasure of exploring this Alpine area, spread out along the boundary with Graubünden. The 32,000-hectare Swiss Tectonic Arena Sardona was designated a Unesco World Natural Heritage site in 2008 for its unique geology. It's one of the best places in the world to observe mountain creation and plate tectonics.

To get there, take one of two minor roads southwest from Bad Ragaz. Both climb rapidly, one passing via Pfäfers and the other via Valens and Vasön. Where they join, you enter the Taminatal, a spectacular valley, mixing high pastureland with dense forest (the autumn colours are nearly as vivid as in Maine in the USA).

After 20km you reach the foot of the jewel-coloured Gigerwaldsee reservoir. The road climbs to skirt its southern shore and reach St Martin, a stuck-in-time Walser-speaking hamlet. You can stay at the dark-wood **chalet** ([⬚]081 306 12 34; www.sankt-martin.ch, in German; dm/s/d Sfr36/70/120; ⊙May–mid-Oct), the perfect base for a couple of days' majestic walking.

An easy trail heads two hours west to the scenic lookout at Sardona Alp. Another hour is needed to reach the mountain refuge **Sardona Hütte** ([⬚]081 306 13 88; dm adult/child Sfr31/16 ⊙Jul-Sep) at 2158m.

Amden
WALKING

A 6km drive northeast of Weesen leads to the high pasture plateau of Amden, with arresting lake and mountain views. It seems like Zeus himself scattered the houses and barns here. There is some nice walking amid the green fields and a bit of snow activity in winter.

Schiffsbetrieb Walensee
BOAT TOUR

(www.walenseeschiff.ch) Boats regularly cross Murg and Quinten. From April to mid-October there are also regular boats between Weesen and Walenstadt, calling in at various spots along the way (including Betlis and Quinten).

🛏 Sleeping & Eating

There are a few cheaper places further away from the lake, outside Weesen.

Lofthotel Murg
BOUTIQUE HOTEL $$

([⬚]081 720 35 75; www.lofthotel.ch; Murg; s Sfr120-180, d Sfr180-240; 🛜) A 19th-century cotton mill has been reincarnated as the Lofthotel, affording fine views of the Churfirsten mountains and Walensee. Clean lines, polished concrete and bold artworks define the industrial-chic rooms, which sport flat-screen TVs and iPod docks. Farm-fresh produce and homemade preserves are served at breakfast (Sfr20).

Parkhotel Schwert
HISTORIC HOTEL $$

([⬚]055 616 14 74; www.parkhotelschwert.ch; Hauptstrasse 23, Weesen; s/d Sfr129/190; 🛜) Looking back on 600 years of history, this elegantly restored hotel has individually decorated rooms with parquet floors. Market-fresh fish, meat and French classics are on the menu in the brasserie and on the lake-facing terrace.

Landgasthof Paradiesli
GUESTHOUSE $$

([⬚]055 611 11 79; s/d with bathroom Sfr135/170, without bathroom Sfr75/140; 🛏) The silence is interrupted only by the distant roar of the waterfalls, birdsong and cowbells at this beautiful spot in upper Betlis. The lodge has rustic rooms, a fine garden (not to mention the pet llamas) and views south to the shore and mountains beyond.

Hotel Siesta
HOTEL $

([⬚]081 733 00 13; www.hotel-siesta.ch, in German; Tannenboden, Flumserberg; s/d Sfr190/260; 🛏) A warm and friendly family-run sleeping option near the slopes. Prices drop considerably in summer.

Fischerstube
SWISS $$

([⬚]055 616 16 08; Marktgasse 9, Weesen; mains Sfr30-50; ⊙lunch & dinner Thu-Tue) Snowy white linen and bottle-green wood panelling create a refined backdrop for well-executed fish dishes here. Pair fine wines with local whitefish and perch.

Hotel Walensee Trattoria
ITALIAN $$

([⬚]055 616 16 04; Hauptstrasse 27, Weesen; mains Sfr26-38; ⊙lunch & dinner Mon-Sun; 🛏) The pasta, fish and wood-fired pizza are spot-on

WORTH A TRIP

KLÖNTAL

Reaching west of Glarus, the 12km Klöntal is one of the country's least touched valleys (and back-door route into Schwyz canton). Klöntaler See is a mirror-still lake backed on its south side by the sheer walls of the Glärnisch mountains. A couple of majestic waterfalls open up clefts in this massif. At the lake's west end you'll find a camping ground and a couple of hotels. Hotel Vorauen (☎055 640 13 83; www.vorauen.ch; dm/s/d Sfr52/90/120) has a handful of timber-lined rooms and primary-coloured dorms.

at this convivial trattoria, which has a leafy terrace for summer dining. There's a kids' menu for the little ones.

❶ Getting There & Away

Both Walenstadt and Weesen are handily located on the A3 freeway from Zürich. By train from Zürich, get off at Ziegelbrücke (Sfr21, 45 minutes), which is a 15-minute walk from central Weesen, or change for trains on to Walenstadt.

GLARUS CANTON

The spiky, glacier-capped peaks of the Glarus Alps rise above stout wooden farmhouses and lush pastures in this little-explored canton, linked to the centre of the country by the vertiginous Klausenpass. Its northern boundary touches Walensee and provides much of the Alpine beauty that can be observed from the lake's north shore. For more information, contact Glarner Tourismus (☎055 610 21 25; www.glarus.ch; in German; Niederurnen).

Glarus

POP 12,200 / ELEV 472M

Nestling at the foot of the austerely beautiful Glarus Alps, Glarus is the capital of the eponymous canton. Two-thirds destroyed by fire in 1861, the town is a graceful 19th-century creation with some fine residential buildings and the occasional typical old timber rural house that survived the flames. A

couple of hotels overlook the park in front of the main train station. Hotel Stadthof (☎055 640 63 66; www.hotelstadthof.ch, in German; Kirchstrasse 2; s/d/tr Sfr90/140/150; ❷) has 12 rather plain but clean brightly whitewashed rooms with parquet flooring, some of which look over the park.

Some trains from Zürich (Sfr24, 60 minutes) require a change at Rapperswil or Ziegelbrücke. From St Gallen (Sfr26, 1¼ hours) the trip is longer.

Braunwald

POP 300 / ELEV 1256M

The attractive car-free mountain resort of Braunwald basks in sunshine on the side of a steep hill, gazing at the snowcapped Tödi Mountain (3614m) and overlooking valley pastures and fir forests below.

The Braunwaldbahn (one-way/return Sfr7.80/15.60) climbs the hill from the Linthal Braunwaldbahn station. Braunwald Tourism (☎055 653 65 65; www.braunwald.ch; ☷8am-noon & 1.30-5pm Mon-Fri) is on the top floor of the funicular station.

Braunwald is a terrific base for hiking in summer, and you'll find pamphlets at the funicular station outlining several routes, including to the Oberblegisee, a green-tinted Alpine lake. If you're up for a challenge, tackle the five-hour *via ferrata* at Eggstock. In winter the resort has family appeal, with moderate skiing and off-piste fun from sledding to snow-tubing.

A converted grand Victorian fairy-tale hotel, the Märchenhotel Bellevue (☎055 653 71 71; www.maerchenhotel.ch; r per person from Sfr175; ❷❸❹) combines elegant modern rooms with saunas and bars for adults and all manner of playthings for children. Parents can relax in the rooftop spa area while kids are looked after in the play area.

Less than two minutes from the funicular station, Hostel Adrenalin (☎079 347 29 05; www.adrenalin.gl; Braunwald; r per person Sfr35) is the hub of the young snowboarding and adventure-sports community in winter, with video games and lots of parties. There is a Sfr20 surcharge for a one-night stay and breakfast costs an extra Sfr8.

Trains run roughly hourly from Linthal Braunwaldbahn to Zürich (Sfr28, 1½ hours) via Ziegelbrücke (Sfr10.40, 40 minutes). It's a 1¼-hour drive from Zürich along the A3.

Graubünden

POP 192,621 / AREA 7106 SQ KM / LANGUAGES GERMAN, ROMANSCH, ITALIAN

Why Go?

Ask locals what it is that makes their canton special and they'll wax lyrical about how, well, wild it is. In a country blessed with supermodel looks, Graubünden is all about raw natural beauty. Whether it's wind-battered plateaux in Engadine where clouds roll over big-shouldered mountains, the Rhine gouging out knife-edge ravines near Flims, or the brooding Alpine grandeur of the Swiss National Park, this wonderfully remote region begs outdoor escapades.

While you've probably heard about Davos' sensational downhill skiing, St Moritz' glamour and the tales of Heidi (fictionally born here), vast swathes of Graubünden remain little known and ripe for the exploring. Strike into Alps on foot or follow the lonesome passes that corkscrew high into the mountains and chances are you will be alone in exhilarating landscapes, where only the odd marmot or chamois and your own little gasps of wonder break the silence.

Best Places to Eat

» Bündner Stube (p291)

» Burestübli (p296)

» Schloss Brandis (p303)

» Chesa Veglia (p316)

» Kaffee Klatsch (p308)

Best Places to Stay

» Gasthaus Bargis (p304)

» Hotel Kurhaus (p294)

» Posta Veglia (p298)

» Hotel Engiadina (p310)

» Vetter (p296)

When to Go

Graubünden's slopes buzz with skiers from mid-December to Easter. Cross-country pros swish across to Davos for the FIS Nordic in December, while upper-crust St Moritz attracts a discerning crowd at January's Polo World Cup on Snow. Summer cranks up the craziness: see men do battle with their beards in Chur and with their bulk *Schwingen* (Alpine wrestling) in Davos in August. Many resorts hibernate from May to mid-June and October to November. If you do rock up then, you might bag a good deal and some surprisingly nice weather.

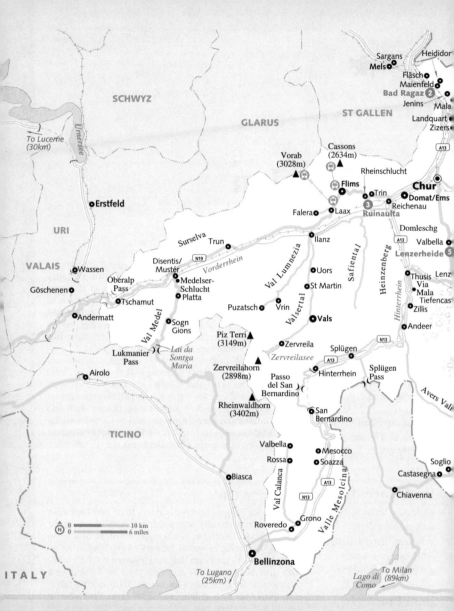

Graubünden Highlights

1 Be elevated by high-altitude hiking and evocative Alpine scenery in the **Swiss National Park** (p309)

2 Cure your Heidi headache in the soothing thermal waters of **Tamina Therme** (p303), Bad Ragaz

3 Raft or hike past bizarre limestone formations in the **Ruinaulta** (p298), or Rhine Gorge

4 Take a horse-drawn carriage to the silent and sublimely pretty **Val Fex** (p317)

5 Get on your bike and ride heart-pulsing single tracks

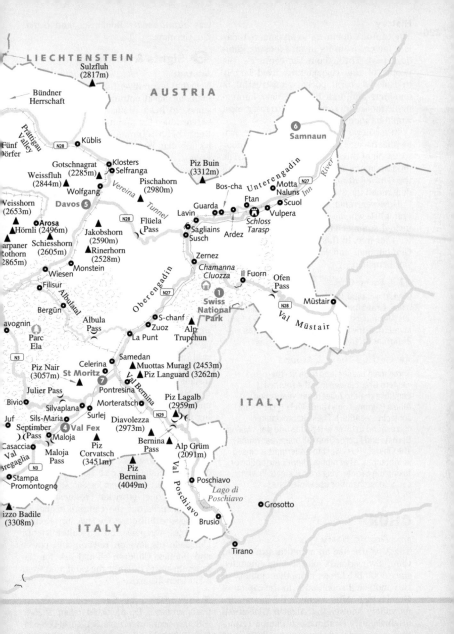

LIECHTENSTEIN

Sulzfluh
(2817m)

Bündner
Herrschaft

AUSTRIA

Prättigau
Valley

Fünf
Dörfer

N28   Küblis

Gotschnagrat
(2285m)

Klosters
Selfranga

Weissfluh
(2844m)

Wolfgang

Vereina
Tunnel

Pischahorn
(2980m)

Piz Buin
(3312m)

Samnaun   6

Unterengadin

Bos-cha

Motta
Naluns   N27

Davos   5

Weisshorn
(2653m)

Arosa

Hörnli
(2496m)

Schiesshorn
(2605m)

arpaner
othorn
2865m)

Jakobshorn
(2590m)

Rinerhorn
(2528m)

Flüela
Pass

Lavin

Guarda

Ardez

Sagliains
Susch

Ftan

Scuol

Vulpera

Schloss
Tarasp

Inn River

Monstein

Wiesen

Filisur

Bergün

Oberengadin

N27

Zernez

Chamanna
Cluozza

Il Fuorn

Ofen
Pass

Müstair

avognin

Parc
Ela

N3

Albula
Pass

S-chanf
Zuoz
La Punt

Alp
Trupchun

Swiss
National
Park   1

Val   Müstair

Piz Nair
(3057m)

St Moritz   7

Celerina

Samedan

Muottas Muragl (2453m)

Piz Languard (3262m)

Julier Pass

Pontresina

Bivio

Silvaplana

Morteratsch

Surlej

Piz Lagalb
(2959m)

ITALY

Juf

Sils-Maria

Diavolezza
(2973m)

N29

Septimber
Pass   4 Val Fex

Maloja

Maloja
Pass

Piz
Corvatsch
(3451m)

Bernina
Pass

Alp Grüm
(2091m)

Casaccia
Val
regaglia

N3

Piz
Bernina
(4049m)

Val Poschiavo

Poschiavo

Lago di
Poschiavo

Grosotto

Stampa
Promontogno

izzo Badile
(3308m)

ITALY

Brusio

Tirano

History

The canton's openness to all comers today is a far cry from its inward-looking, diffident past. Throughout the centuries, the people of this rugged area lived largely in isolated, rural pockets, mistrustful of outsiders and, aided by the near impregnable mountain terrain, able to resist most would-be conquerors.

In medieval times the region was known as Rhaetia, and was loosely bound by an association of three leagues (*Drei Bünde*). The modern name for the canton derives from the *Grauer Bund* (Grey League). Graubünden joined the Swiss Confederation in 1803.

However, much more important was the year 1864, when a hotel owner in St Moritz invited summer guests to stay for the winter – for free. In this way, winter tourism in Graubünden, and later all of Switzerland, was launched.

ℹ Information

Chur, the capital, houses the cantonal tourist office, **Graubünden Ferien** (www.graubuenden.ch; Alexanderstrasse 24; ⊘8am-noon & 1-5pm Mon-Fri), in the building marked 'Publicitas', 200m east of the train station.

ℹ Getting There & Around

Three main passes lead from northern and western Graubünden into the southeast Engadine region: Julier (open year-round), Albula (summer only) and Flüela (year-round subject to weather). These approximately correspond to three exit points into Italy: Maloja, Bernina and Fuorn/Ofen (all open year-round). The Oberalp Pass west to Andermatt is closed in winter but, as at Albula, there's the option of taking the car-carrying train instead. In winter, carry snow chains or use winter tyres.

CHUR

POP 33,400 / ELEV 585M

The Alps rise like an amphitheatre around Chur, Switzerland's oldest city, inhabited since 3000 BC. Linger more than an hour or two and you'll soon warm to the capital of Graubünden. After a stint in the mountains, its gallery showcasing Alberto Giacometti originals, arty boutiques, authentic restaurants and relaxed bars are a refreshing cultural tonic.

When the city was almost destroyed by fire in 1464, German-speaking artisans arrived to rebuild and, in the process, inadvertently suppressed the local lingo. So it was *abunansvair* Romansch and *Guten Tag* German.

◎ Sights & Activities

Altstadt   NEIGHBOURHOOD

Near the Plessur River, the **Obertor** marks the main medieval entrance to Chur's cobblestone Old Town. Alongside the stout **Maltesertor** (once the munitions tower), and the **Sennhofturm** (nowadays the city's prison), it's all that remains of the old defensive walls.

The city's most iconic landmark is **St Martinskirche** (Kirchgasse 12) with its distinctive spire and clock face. The 8th-century church was rebuilt in the late-Gothic style in 1491 and is dramatically lit by a trio of Augusto Giacometti stained-glass windows. St Martin presides over a burbling stone fountain in front of the church.

Follow Kirchgasse uphill to reach **Kathedrale St Maria Himmelfahrt** (Hof; ⊘6am-7pm Mon-Sat, 7am-7pm Sun), a 12th-century cathedral with a late 1400s Jakob Russ high altar containing a splendid triptych.

Bündner Kunstmuseum   ART MUSEUM

(www.buendner-kunstmuseum.ch; Postplatz; adult/child Sfr12/free; ⊘10am-5pm Tue-Sun) This gallery in the neoclassical Villa Planta gives an insight into the artistic legacy of Graubünden-born Alberto Giacometti (1877–1947) and his talented contemporaries, including Giovanni Segantini and Ernst Ludwig Kirchner. Chur-born Angelika Kaufmann's enigmatic *Self Portrait* (1780) is a standout.

Rätisches Museum   HISTORY MUSEUM

(www.raetischesmuseum.gr.ch; Hofstrasse 1; adult/child Sfr6/free; ⊘10am-5pm Tue-Sun; ⛟) Housed in a baroque patrician residence, this museum spells out the canton's history in artefacts, with Bronze Age jewellery, Roman statuettes, weapons and agricultural tools, alongside displays on religion and power and politics. Children should ask for the museum key to discover the exhibition from a kid-friendly angle.

Brambrüesch Cable Car   CABLE CAR

(Kasernenstrasse 15; adult/child return Sfr25/5; ⊘8.30am-5pm mid-Jun–late Oct & mid-Dec–mid-Mar) This cable car whisks you to Brambrüesch at 1600m for a summer hike through wildflower-strewn heights. It's in action again in winter, together with a couple of lifts, allowing locals to warm up for more-serious downhill skiing elsewhere in Graubünden.

Kletterhalle Ap'n Daun
ROCK CLIMBING

(www.kletterhallechur.ch; Pulvermühlestrasse 20; climbing adult/child Sfr20/9, bouldering Sfr10/6; ⊙9am-10.30pm Mon-Fri, 10am-7pm Sat & Sun) Limber up on the bouldering and climbing walls here. Instruction (including children's courses) and equipment rental are available.

City Tours
GUIDED TOUR

(adult/child Sfr12/6) Two-hour guided city tours depart from the tourist office at 2.30pm every Wednesday from April to October, or download MP3 tours from www .churtourismus.ch.

✯✯ Festivals & Events

Churer Fest
CULTURAL

(www.churerfest.org, in German) Chur's big summer bash in mid-August involves three days of concerts, feasting, cow-milking marathons and kiddie fun.

Internationales Alpenbarttreffen
CULTURAL

Careless whiskers make barbers' razor blades twitch at the International Alpine Beard Festival in August, where the hairiest men of the mountain do battle.

🛏 Sleeping

Romantik Hotel Stern
HISTORIC HOTEL $$

(☎081 258 57 57; www.stern-chur.ch; Reichsgasse 11; s/d Sfr150/290; P@🛜) Part of Switzerland's romantic clan, this centuries-old hotel has kept its flair, with vaulted corridors and low-ceilinged, pine-filled rooms. Call ahead and they'll pick you up from the station in a 1933 Buick.

Zunfthaus zur Rebleuten
HISTORIC HOTEL $

(☎081 255 11 44; www.rebleuten.ch; Pfisterplatz 1; s Sfr70-85, d Sfr128-148) Housed in an imposing frescoed building on a pretty square, the Zunfthaus zur Rebleuten looks proudly back on 500 years of history. The 12 rooms are fresh and inviting. Especially romantic (watch your head) are those in the loft.

JBN
HOSTEL $

(☎081 284 10 10; www.justbenice.ch; Welschdörfli 19; dm Sfr35-43, s Sfr65-99, d Sfr110-158, tr Sfr147; @🛜) JBN is a backpacker's dream, offering spacious dorms decorated with original photography and quirky touches like dog's-backside coat hangers. The sports bar pumps up the volume at weekends, so choose a mountain-facing room if decibels affect your slumber.

Hotel Freieck
HOTEL $$

(☎081 255 15 15; www.freieck.ch; Reichsgasse 44; s Sfr90-150, d Sfr150-220, tr Sfr180-240; P) Occupying a beautiful 16th-century building, Freieck is a seamless blend of history and modernity. Exposed stone, beams and vaults lend character, while rooms are bright and contemporary.

✗ Eating

TOP CHOICE Bündner Stube
SWISS $$

(☎081 258 57 57; Reichsgasse 11; mains Sfr25-42; ⊙lunch & dinner Mon-Sun) Candlelight and wood panelling create a warm atmosphere in Romantik Hotel Stern's highly regarded restaurant. The chef keeps it fresh and seasonal, serving asparagus in spring, game in autumn. Bündner specialities like *Capuns, Maluns* and *Gerstensuppe* are beautifully cooked and presented.

Zunfthaus zur Rebleuten
SWISS $$

(☎081 255 11 44; Pfisterplatz 1; mains Sfr26-43; ⊙lunch & dinner Mon-Sun) This hotel's first-floor restaurant is delightfully cosy with its dark-wood panelling and heart-carved chairs. Sit inside or on the terrace for well-executed regional dishes like braised veal cheeks with polenta and *Pizokel* with morels.

Hofkellerei
SWISS $$

(☎081 252 32 30; Hof 1; mains Sfr19-39; ⊙lunch & dinner Tue-Sun) Wooden floorboards creak as you enter this vaulted Gothic restaurant. Take a pew to feast on regional flavours like *Pizokel* with plums and *Capuns* under the wrought-iron chandeliers.

Evviva
CAFE $

(Kornplatz 9; snacks & mains Sfr13-18.50; ⊙10am-8pm Mon-Wed, 10am-10pm Thu-Fri, 9am-10pm Sat) An inviting cafe, with a sunny terrace, on the square, delicious Italian gelato and authentic pasta, gnocchi and risotto on the menu.

🍸 Drinking & Entertainment

A buoyant student population keeps the bars and clubs pumping, especially over the weekends around Untere Gasse and Welschdörfli.

Tom's Beer Box
PUB

(Untere Gasse 11; ⊙5pm-midnight Mon-Thu, 3pm-1am Fri & Sat) The bottle-top window is a shrine to beer at this chilled haunt, where locals spill outside to socialise and guzzle one of 140 brews.

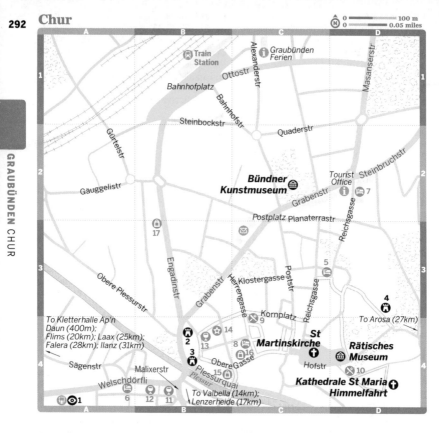

Giger Bar

THEME BAR

(www.hrgiger.com; Kalchbühl Center, Comercial-strasse 23; ⊙8am-8pm Mon-Fri, 8am-5pm Sat) For sheer novelty factor, it's worth taking bus 1 to this sci-fi bar, with its ribcage-shaped chairs and tendril-like mirrors. It's the handiwork of Chur-born surrealist HR Giger, the brains behind Ridley Scott's 1979 film *Alien*.

Felsenbar

BAR

(Welschdörfli 1; ⊙8pm-2am Tue-Thu, 8pm-3am Fri & Sat) Themed parties from DJ battles to beer pong attract a vivacious bunch to this all-black haunt, set around a horseshoe bar.

Schall und Rauch

BAR

(Welschdörfli; ⊙5pm-2am Mon-Thu & Sun, 5pm-3am Fri & Sat) Grungy haunt with a loop fireplace sequence to give you a warm feeling even without imbibing.

Werkstatt Chur

ARTS CENTRE

(Untere Gasse 9; www.mellowdie.com, in German; ⊙5pm-midnight Tue-Thu & Sun, 5pm-1am Fri &

Sat) A coppersmith factory turned dynamic cultural centre, hosting gigs, jam sessions, art-house film screenings, plays and parties. See the website for details.

🛍 Shopping

Keramik Ruth

HANDICRAFTS

(Obere Gasse 31; ⊙1.30-5.30pm Tue & Thu, 11am-4pm Sat) Ruth displays her sweet-shop-bright pottery at this hobbit-sized shop – from hand-thrown pots to polka-dotty teapots.

Rätische Gerberei

HANDICRAFTS

(Engadinstrasse 30; ⊙1.30-6.30pm Mon, 8am-noon & 1.30-6pm Tue-Fri) Upstairs are mountains of fluffy sheepskins, downstairs are genuine cowbells for a fraction of the price you'd pay elsewhere.

Metzgerei Mark

FOOD & DRINK

(Obere Gasse 22) Impressed by local meat specialities? Head to this butcher, where there is *Bündnerfleisch, Rohschinken*

◎ Top Sights

Bündner Kunstmuseum C2
Kathedrale St Maria Himmelfahrt D4
Rätisches Museum D4
St Martinskirche C4

◎ Sights

1 Brambrüesch Cable Car A4
2 Maltesertor B4
3 Obertor B4
4 Sennhofturm D3

◎ Sleeping

5 Hotel Freieck C3
6 JBN A4
7 Romantik Hotel Stern D2
8 Zunfthaus zur Rebleuten C4

◎ Eating

Bündner Stube .... (see 7)
9 Evviva C4
10 Hofkellerei D4
Zunfthaus zur Rebleuten .... (see 8)

◎ Drinking

11 Felsenbar B4
12 Schall und Rauch B4
13 Tom's Beer Box B4

◎ Entertainment

14 Werkstatt Chur B4

◎ Shopping

15 Keramik Ruth B4
16 Metzgerei Mark C4
17 Rätische Gerberei B3

(cured ham) and all sorts of *Salsiz* (sausage) to salivate over.

❶ Information

You can change money (from 7am to 8pm) at the train station. The UBS bank has a handy central branch with ATMs on Poststrasse.

Post office (Postplatz; ⊙7.30am-6.30pm Mon-Fri, 8am-noon Sat) Just outside the Old Town.

Tourist office (☑081 252 18 18; www.chur tourismus.ch; Bahnhofplatz 3; ⊙7.30am-8pm Mon-Fri, 8am-6pm Sat & Sun) Has stacks of info and maps on the region and can arrange city tours.

❶ Getting There & Away

There are rail connections to Klosters (Sfr21, 1¼ hours) and Davos (Sfr27, 1½ hours), and fast trains to Sargans (Sfr10.40, 20 minutes), with onward connections to Liechtenstein and Zürich (Sfr38, 1¼ to 1½ hours). Postal buses leave from the terminus above the train station. The A13 freeway runs north from Chur to Zürich and Lake Constance.

Chur is the departure point for one of Switzerland's most memorable rail journeys, the **Bernina Express** (www.rhb.ch) to Lugano. The four-hour route takes in 55 tunnels and 196 bridges. A one-way ticket costs Sfr82; seat reservation is an additional Sfr12/9 in summer/winter.

❶ Getting Around

Bahnhofplatz is the hub for all local buses, which cost Sfr2.60 per journey (valid for changes for 30 minutes). Services become less frequent after 8pm.

The Old Town is mostly pedestrians only. Look for signs to several parking garages on the edge of the Old Town (eg on Gäuggelistrasse), charging around Sfr2 per hour.

Car Rental

If you plan to hire a car, try **Avis** (☑081 300 33 77; Kasernenstrasse 37), in the Carrosserie Claus car body shop, or **Hertz** (☑081 252 32 22; Triststrasse 15).

AROUND CHUR

Lenzerheide & Valbella

ELEV 1500M

Straddling the petrol-blue Heidsee, these twin resorts bombard you with mountainous wooded splendour and appeal to families with their low-key atmosphere.

🏃 Activities

Among the area's 170km of hiking trails, the five- to seven-hour trek to 2865m **Parpaner Rothorn** stands out as one of the best. Kids can let off excess energy on the **Globi Trail**, with activities from pine-cone throwing to splashy water games. In high season, kid-friendly activities range from circus days to llama trekking and igloo building – ask the tourist office for details.

Little Lenzerheide is one of the top mountain-biking and freeriding centres in the country, with 305km of marked routes, 1000km of self-guided GPS tours and

Graubünden's rugged, high-alpine terrain is harnessed by some of Switzerland's greatest railways. The panoramic **Rhätische Bahn** (Rhaetian Railway; www.rhb.ch) is a staggering feat of early 20th-century engineering, traversing viaducts and tunnels and commanding wide-screen views of forested slopes, jewel-coloured lakes and snowcapped peaks. See the website for advance bookings, seat reservations and special deals. The Half Fare, Swiss Card and Swiss Pass give substantial discounts; see www.swisstravelsystem.ch for details.

The Rhaetian Railway's two flagship routes are the Glacier Express (p316) and the Bernina Express (p293). The Glacier Express from St Moritz to Zermatt is a once-in-a-lifetime journey, scaling the Furka, Oberalp and Bernina passes, and taking in highlights such as the canyon-like Rhine Gorge and the six-arched, 65m-high Landwasser Viaduct. The Bernina Express from Chur to Lugano climbs high into the glaciated realms of the Alps and skirts Ticino's palm-fringed lakes. The stretch from Thusis to Tirano is a Unesco World Heritage site.

several knuckle-whitening downhill tracks. To master dirt jumping and other tricks, head to the new **Skill Center** (⊙11am-4pm) at the Rothorn base station. **Activ Sport Baselgia** (www.activ-sport.ch; Voa Sporz 19; ⊙8.30am-noon & 2-6.30pm Mon-Fri, to 5pm Sat) rents mountain bikes/downhill bikes/e-bikes/kids bikes for Sfr40/60/49/18 per day in summer, plus snowshoes/cross-country skis for Sfr19/30. Enquire about their winter snowshoeing tours (around Sfr50).

Lift queues are rare in Lenzerheide with skiing on 155km of slopes, mostly geared towards beginners and intermediates, as well as some glorious off-piste and back-country skiing. Snowboarders hit the rails, boxes and kickers at the snowpark. A one-day ski pass costs Sfr65 for adults and Sfr21 for children. Cross-country skiers can glissade along 52km of tracks. Off-piste and family-oriented activities include 80km of winter walking trails and a 3km toboggan run.

🛏 Sleeping & Eating

Pop into the tourist office for a list of holiday apartments and chalets.

Hotel Kurhaus   BOUTIQUE HOTEL **$$**
(☑081 384 11 34; www.kurhaus-lenzerheide.ch; Voa Principala 40, Lenzerheide; s Sfr90-100, d Sfr120-230, apt Sfr340-380; ℙ) Historic meets modern at this young-at-heart hotel. The pick of the rooms sport razor-sharp decor, with monochrome hues, funky log tables and mountain-facing balconies. Downstairs you'll find a rustic-chic restaurant (mains Sfr25 to Sfr40) and a cinema-turned-nightclub.

Camping St Cassian   CAMPGROUND **$**
(☑081 384 24 72; www.st-cassian.ch, in German; Lenz; sites per adult/child/tent/car Sfr8/4.50/7/2.50; ⊙year-round; 🛜📶) Popular with cyclists, this tree-shaded campsite is 3km south of town. Expect pin-drop peace, mountain vistas and first-rate facilities, including barbecue areas and a restaurant.

Bauernhof Tgantieni   FARMSTAY **$**
(☑081 384 24 30; Maiensäss; per adult/child Sfr25/15, ⊙Jun-Sep; 📶) High on a hill above Lenzerheide, this rural idyll is ideal for those willing to swap creature comforts for a night in the straw. Brave an icy wash at the spring before a hearty breakfast of homemade bread and preserves. Tots love the resident cats, rabbits and goats. Bring your own sleeping bag.

Seerestaurant Forellenstube   SEAFOOD **$$**
(☑081 384 11 41; Am Heidsee; mains Sfr16-49; ⊙lunch & dinner Mon-Sun) Hailed for the freshness of its trout, this lakefront restaurant is worth the 2km toddle north of Lenzerheide. Go for the fish or specialities such as homemade venison sausage. Gracing the wall is the head of a *Wolpertinger*, a fictional critter said to roam Alpine forests.

ℹ Information

The **Lenzerheide tourist office** (☑081 385 11 20; www.lenzerheide.ch; Voa Principala; ⊙8.30am-6pm Mon-Sat, 9.30am-1pm Sun Jun-Aug & mid-Dec–early Apr, closed lunchtimes & Sun rest of year) is on the main road.

ℹ Getting There & Away

Either resort is easily reached by an hourly bus from Chur (Sfr10.40, 40 minutes). They're on the route from Chur to St Moritz (Sfr28; two hours) spanning the Julier Pass. In the high summer and winter seasons, a free bus operates between Lenzerheide and Valbella.

Arosa

POP 2300 / ELEV 1800M

Framed by the peaks of Weisshorn, Hörnli and moraine-streaked Schiesshorn, Arosa is a great Alpine all-rounder: perfect for downhill and cross-country skiers in winter, hikers and downhill bikers in summer, and families year-round with heaps of activities to amuse kids.

Although only 30km southeast of Chur, getting here is nothing short of spectacular. The road zigzags up from Chur in a series of 365 hairpin bends so challenging that Arosa cannot be reached by postal buses. The scenic train ride from Chur makes an excellent alternative.

✦ Activities

Winter Sports

Arosa attracts beginner and intermediate skiers with 70km of red and blue runs, rising as high as Weisshorn at 2653m. Big air fans should check out the half-pipe and fun park. Contact the ski school (☑081 378 75 00; www.sssa.ch; Seeblickstrasse; ☉8.30am-5.30pm) for lessons. Ski passes cost Sfr61/20 for an adult/child for one day and Sfr310/105 for one week.

Cross-country skiing is equally superb, with 30km of prepared *Loipen* (tracks) stretching from Maran's gentle forest trails to challenging routes at La Isla and Ochsenalp. A cross-country day/week pass costs Sfr7/25. Langlauf- und Skiwanderschule Geeser (☑081 377 22 15; www.geeser-arosa.ch;

☉9am-noon & 1-6pm) offers equipment rental and instruction, with cross-country and snowshoe taster sessions starting at Sfr55. You can also book guided snowshoe hikes (Sfr50 to Sfr70).

There's plenty to amuse families and nonskiers in winter. Prätschli is the start of a floodlit 1km toboggan run through twinkling woodlands. Otherwise, you can stomp through the snow on 40km of prepared winter walking trails, twirl across an open-air ice rink, or rock up for a game of curling.

Summer Activities

Arosa's backyard has 200km of maintained hiking trails, including the 18km, five- to seven-hour trek to Parpaner Rothorn. From the Hörnli Express gondola station, this hike climbs up through fragrant meadows, past the aquamarine lakes of Schwellisee and Älplisee, to the rust-red peak of Parpaner Rothorn, then down the other side to Lenzerheide. Scenic alternatives include the 3½-hour uphill trudge to Weisshorn and the easy forest rambles shadowing the Plessur to Litziütti (one hour) and Langwies (two hours). Kids love to spot red squirrels on the Eichhörnchenweg. Contact Capriola (☑079 778 07 58; www.capriola.ch; adult/child Sfr45/30) to take in the Alpine scenery with a nimble-footed goat in tow.

Mountain bikers are in their element with 700km of trails to explore. For knuckle-whitening thrills, hire a downhill bike at Obersee (☑081 377 23 77; ☉10am-5pm) to race from Mittelstation to Litziütti or from Hörnli to Arosa; both tracks involve descents of more than 500m.

WORTH A TRIP

PARC ELA

Dropping south of Lenzerheide towards Tiefencastel, you enter the wilderness of Switzerland's biggest nature park, Parc Ela (www.parc-ela.ch, in German). Spanning 600 sq km and encompassing 21 communities in the Albula-Bergün and Savognin-Bivio areas, the park is three and a half times the size of the Swiss National Park. If you have the time and inclination, the spectacular 15-day Veia Parc Ela hike takes you through the park's most enchanting Alpine landscapes.

Driving through the Albulatal (Albula Valley), you'll pass flower-strewn pastures, thick pine and larch forests, lonely moors, bizarre rock formations and tiny hamlets with Italianate churches. Family-friendly Wiesen is a superb base for hikers. Mountains rise abruptly above the valley floor in Filisur to frame the magnificent 65m-high Landwasser viaduct, part of the early 20th-century, Unesco-listed Albulabahn (www.rhb-Unesco.ch).

SUMMER FREEBIES

Stay in Arosa between mid-June and late October and you'll receive the free all-inclusive card giving unlimited access to mountain transport, local buses, boats on Obersee and the lido at Untersee. The card also allows free entry to the ice rink, mini-golf course and rope park. Day trippers can buy the same card for Sfr13 from the train station or tourist office.

✦ Festivals & Events

Look out for horse racing and football on snow in January.

Arosa Classic Car   EVENT
(www.arosaclassiccar.ch) Vintage motors make a mad dash on the winding road from Langwies to Lenzerheide in September.

Arosa Comedy Festival   COMEDY
(www.humorfestival.ch) Attracting the big names of the Swiss–German comedy and cabaret scene, this 11-day festival infuses Arosa with pre-Christmas cheer in December.

🛏 Sleeping

Many hotels and restaurants close in shoulder seasons (mid-April to early June and mid-October to early December). Room rates drop 30% to 40% in summer.

Vetter   HOTEL $$
(☎081 378 80 00; www.arosa-vetter-hotel.ch; Seeblickstrasse; s/d Sfr165/240; 🅿🛜🍴) Looking good following a top-to-toe makeover, Vetter has rustic-chic rooms done out in dark wood and stone. The friendly owners will squeeze in a cot for free if you ask. Breakfast is a treat with local yoghurt, cheese, eggs, bread and homemade jam. The inviting restaurant (mains Sfr20 to Sfr40) dishes up seasonally inspired fare.

Waldhotel   HISTORIC HOTEL $$$
(☎081 378 55 55; www.waldhotel.ch; s/d/ste Sfr235/550/690; 🅿@🛜🍴) You'll pray for the flakes to fall at this forest hideaway, where Nobel Prize–winning German novelist Thomas Mann spent the first weeks of his exile. The luxurious chalet exudes old-world charm with its warm pine-clad rooms and guests arriving by horse-drawn carriage. Soothe tired post-ski muscles in the spa or

sip fine Swiss wines as the pianist plays in the lounge.

Hotel Arlenwald   HOTEL $$
(☎081 377 18 38; www.arlenwaldhotel.ch; Prätschli; s Sfr120-140, d Sfr230-270; 🅿🛜) Direct access to Burestübli is just one of the perks of staying at this hotel. The spacious, light-flooded rooms feature loads of chunky pine, antique family heirlooms and mountain-facing balconies. Venture down to the sauna for dreamy, steamy views of snowcapped peaks.

Hotel Erzhorn   HOTEL $$
(☎081 377 15 26; www.erzhorn.ch; Kirchweg; s Sfr100-120, d Sfr200-265; 🅿) Up near Arosa's 500-year-old Bergkirchli chapel, this timber chalet is in a silent part of town. The Nau family run the place like (Swiss) clockwork and the bright, pine-ceilinged rooms with balconies are kept spotless.

🍴 Eating & Drinking

TOP CHOICE Burestübli   SWISS $$
(☎081 377 18 38; Arlenwald Hotel, Prätschli; mains Sfr25-42; ⊙lunch & dinner Fri-Tue May-Jun, lunch & dinner Fri-Wed Sep-Nov) This woodsy chalet on the forest edge affords magical above-the-treetop views. Come winter, it's beloved by ruddy-faced sledders who huddle around pots of gooey fondue, butter-soft steaks and mugs of glühwein before a floodlit dash through the snow. The marvellously eccentric chef prides himself on using first-rate local produce.

Grischuna   SWISS $$
(☎081 377 17 01; Poststrasse; mains Sfr16.50-38.50; ⊙lunch & dinner, closed mid-Sep–Oct, Mon & Tue in summer) The enormous cowbells hanging in the window of this low-beamed, antique-filled tavern grab your attention. It's a convivial spot for delicacies such as thinly sliced home-smoked salmon and fresh game in season.

Sennerei Maran   DAIRY $
(www.sennerei-maran.ch; ⊙9am-6pm Mon-Sun Jun-Oct, 10am-4.30pm Tue-Sun Dec-Apr) Fill your picnic basket with award-winning cheese from this dairy.

Hörnlihütte   BAR
(☎081 377 15 04; snacks & light meals Sfr8.50-20; ⊙9am-5pm) This top-of-the-mountain hut at 2513m is a scenic spot for a bowl of goulash or macaroni.

Los Café BAR
(www.losbar.ch; Haus Madrisa; ⊙4pm-late Mon-Fri, 2pm-late Sat & Sun) Slope-side imbibing aside, this is where the party is in winter. Expect a laid-back crowd, DJs, table football and shots aplenty.

❶ Information

The train station has money-exchange counters, luggage storage and scooter rental.

From Oberseeplatz, head uphill along Poststrasse towards Innerarosa. Within five minutes you'll reach the **tourist office** (🗷081 378 70 20; www.arosa.ch; Poststrasse; ⊙8am-6pm Mon-Fri, 9am-1pm & 2-4pm Sat, 9am-noon Sun).

❶ Getting There & Away

The only way to reach Arosa is from Chur: take the hourly narrow-gauge train that leaves from in front of the train station (Sfr14.20, one hour). It's a winding journey chugging past mountains, pine trees, streams and bridges. The train crosses the oldest steel-and-concrete rail bridge ever built. At 62m high, it is a dizzying engineering feat, completed in 1914.

Buses in the resort are free. Drivers should note a traffic ban from midnight to 6am.

Surselva Region

The mainly Romansch-speaking Surselva area west of Chur stretches out along the lonely N19 highway snaking west towards the canton of Uri and, not far beyond, to Valais. Beyond the twinkling cheer of Flims, Laax and Falera, the pickings are slim along this road, although a few points along the Vorderrhein River are worth a stop. More compelling are a couple of wild valleys extending south of the road, which itself trails out in Alpine wilderness as it rises to the wind-chilled Oberalp Pass (2044m) that separates Graubünden from Uri.

ⓘ **GRAUBÜNDENPASS**

With the graubündenPASS (Sfr127/157) valid for seven/14 days from May to October, you get three/five days of unlimited free travel on all Rhätische Bahn (RhB) trains, the SBB line between Chur and Bad Ragaz, the Matterhorn Gotthard Railway and cantonal postal buses. The pass also offers half-price on many cable cars.

FLIMS, LAAX & FALERA

They say that if the snow ain't falling elsewhere, you'll surely find some around Flims, Laax and Falera. This high-altitude trio forms the Weisse Arena (White Arena) ski area, with 220km of slopes catering for all levels. Host of the Burton European Open in January, Laax is a mecca for party-loving snowboarders seeking big air. Both Flims and Laax have witnessed a design explosion in recent years, with architects eschewing cutesy Alpine kitsch in favour of contemporary cool.

◉ Sights

St Remigiuskirche CHURCH
This Romanesque church in Falera is perched on a hill that has been a site of worship since prehistoric times, as attested by the line-up of modest menhirs leading up to it. Inside the shingle-roofed church is a striking mid-17th-century fresco depicting the Last Supper. From the cemetery you can see deep into the Vorderrhein Valley.

Caumasee LAKE
Ringed by thick woods, this exquisitely turquoise lake is a 15-minute hike or five-minute stroll and then take by lift south of Flims Waldhaus. It's an attractive spot for a cool summer swim. You can hire a row boat and eat at a restaurant terrace overlooking the lake.

✦ Activities

WINTER ACTIVITIES

Ask clued-up snowboarders to rattle off their top Swiss resorts and Laax will invariably make the grade. The riders' mecca boasts both Europe's smallest and largest half-pipe, excellent freestyle parks and many off-piste opportunities. Skiers are equally content to bash the pistes in the interlinked resorts, with 220km of varied slopes (most above 2000m) to suit all but the most hard-core black-run freaks. Slaloming downhill, you'll probably spy the unfortunately named Crap da Flem (*crap* means 'peak' in Romansch). The season starts in late October on the 3018m Vorab glacier and mid-December elsewhere. A one-day ski pass includes ski buses and costs Sfr68/45.50 for an adult/child. There are 60km of cross-country skiing trails.

SUMMER ACTIVITIES

In summer, the hiking network spans 250km. The *Naturlehrpfad* circuit at the summit of Cassons is brilliant for spotting wild Alpine

LOCAL KNOWLEDGE

GIAN SIMMEN, OLYMPIC HALF-PIPE CHAMPION

Snowboard Faves

For freeriding and freestyle, Laax, Davos, Meiringen and Andermatt. Davos really looks after their parks and half-pipes, and the Riders Palace in Laax has a great off-snow program with DJs and concerts. Arosa is an alternative if you don't want to ride with the pros, as it's relaxed and attitude free. I know almost every rock here...

Top Tips

Have fun and don't give up. Respect your own limits but don't be afraid to fall with freestyle. If you're prepared to hike, you will always find good snow. Get up early in the morning and walk.

flowers and critters. Even more dramatic is the 3½-hour trek through the glacier-gouged, 400m-deep **Ruinaulta** (Rhine Gorge), hailed the 'Swiss Grand Canyon'. Beginning in Trin, 7km east of Flims, the trail shadows the swiftly flowing Vorder-rhein River and shimmies past limestone cliffs that have been eroded into a veritable forest of pinnacles and columns.

For more of a challenge, traverse soaring rock faces and get an eagle's-eye view of the valley on the **Pinut** *via ferrata*. It costs around Sfr25 to hire the gear from sports shops or the tourist office in Flims.

Swissraft   RAFTING
(☎081 911 52 50; www.swissraft.ch) Taking you through the Rhine Gorge, the turbulent 17km stretch of the Vorderrhein between Ilanz and Reichenau is white-water-rafting heaven. This company organises half-/full day rafting trips for Sfr109/160, as well as canoeing (Sfr90) and hydrospeeding (Sfr120). The meeting spot is Ilanz train station.

🛏 Sleeping

Ask the tourist office for a list of good-value holiday houses and apartments. Most places close from mid-April to June and late September to mid-November.

TOP CHOICE Posta Veglia   HISTORIC HOTEL **$$**
(☎081 921 44 66; www.postaveglia.ch; Via Principala 54, Laax; s/d/ste Sfr150/250/330; P🐕)

Today this 19th-century post office delivers discreet service and rustic flavour. The seven country-cottage-style rooms and suites are filled with beams, antiques and mod cons like DVD players. The wood-panelled restaurant (mains Sfr28 to Sfr42) is feted for creative dishes like speck-wrapped chicken with tangy apricot-balsamic sauce.

Fidazerhof   HOTEL **$$**
(☎081 920 90 10; www.fidazerhof.ch; Flims-Fidaz; s/d Sfr150/250; @) This dark-wood chalet is a relaxing escape, with its expansive Alpine views, sunny rooms sporting hardwood floors and a spa where Ayurveda treatments invite a post-ski unwind. Slow food is the word in the restaurant (mains Sfr24 to Sfr43), which prepares wonderful regional and vegetarian food. Snuggle by the fireplace in winter.

Riders Palace   HOSTEL **$$**
(☎081 927 97 00; www.riderspalace.ch; Laax Murschetg; dm Sfr30-60; d Sfr180-280; 🐕) Sleep? Dream on. This design-focused boutique hostel draws a party-mad crowd of young riders to its strikingly lit, bare concrete spaces. Choose between basic five-bed dorms, slick rooms with Philippe Starck tubs, and hi-tech suites complete with PlayStation and Dolby surround sound. It's 200m from the Laax lifts.

Arena Flims   GUESTHOUSE **$$**
(☎081 911 24 00; Via Prau da Monis 2, Flims; d Sfr110-190, tr Sfr165, q Sfr180; P🐕) At the base station in Flims, this funky li'l shack lures snowboarders with its designer digs, DJs and gigs. Breakfast costs Sfr15 extra.

Capricorn   HOSTEL **$**
(www.caprilounge.ch; Via Cons, Laax; dm Sfr25, d Sfr90-108, tr Sfr126, q Sfr144; P@🐕) You won't find anything cheaper than this friendly chalet-style hostel scattered with art and retro furnishings.

🍴 Eating

Many of the top-end hotels in Flims and Laax have first-rate restaurants.

Cavigilli   SWISS **$$**
(☎081 911 01 25; www.cavigilli.ch; Via Arviul 1, Flims Dorf; mains Sfr30-50; ⊙lunch & dinner Tue-Sun) Flims' oldest house, dating to 1453, comprises a Gothic parlour and an elegant beamed dining room. The accent is on market-fresh produce in dishes like beef with chanterelles and brook trout with saffron risotto.

MUST-TRY BÜNDNER SPECIALITIES

Pizokel Stubby wheat and egg noodles, seasoned with parsley and often served with speck, cheese and onions.

Bündnerfleisch Seasoned and air-dried beef or game.

Capuns A hearty dish consisting of egg pasta and sausage or *Bündnerfleisch*, which is wrapped in chard, flavoured with herbs and cooked in milky water.

Maluns Potatoes soaked for 24 hours, then grated and slowly roasted in butter and flour. Apple mousse and Alpine cheese add flavour.

Nusstorte Caramelised nut tart usually made with walnuts.

Bündner Gerstensuppe Creamy barley soup with smoked pork, beef, speck, leeks, celery, cabbage, carrots and potatoes.

Clavau Vegl　　　　　　　　SWISS **$$**
(☑081 911 36 44; Via Nova 29, Flims Dorf; mains Sfr19-30; ☺8.30am-9pm Tue-Sat) All pine and giant cowbells, this one-time stable has kept its down-on-the-farm feel. Join locals for well-prepared regional grub such as *Capuns* and *Pizokel*.

La Vacca　　　　　　　　FUSION **$$$**
(☑081 927 99 62; Plaun Station, Laax-Murschetg lifts; mains Sfr40-70; ☺lunch & dinner late Dec–mid-Apr) *Rawhide* meets the Alps at this funky tepee, where cowhide-draped chairs surround a roaring open fire. Forget stringy fondue, the menu here is as exciting as the design – think melt-in-your-mouth bison steaks paired with full-bodied Argentine wines.

🍷 Drinking

Riders Palace　　　　　　　　BAR
(☑081 927 97 00; www.riderspalace.ch; Laax Murschetg; ☺7pm-4am) The favourite hangout of freestyle dudes, this too-cool bar in the lobby of the eponymous hostel rocks to gigs and DJs spinning beats into the blurry-eyed hours.

Crap Bar　　　　　　　　BAR
(☑081 927 99 45; Laax-Murschetg lifts; ☺4pm-2am) Crap by name but not by nature, this après-ski hot spot is shaped from 24 tonnes

of granite. It's the place to slam shots, check your email and shimmy in your snow boots after a day pounding powder.

ℹ Information

There are tourist offices in all three, but the **main tourist office** (☑081 927 77 77; summer information www.flims.com, winter information www.laax.com; Via Nova, Flims; ☺8am-6pm Mon-Fri, 8am-noon Sat mid-Jun–mid-Aug, 8am-5pm Mon-Sat mid-Dec–mid-Apr) is in Flims.

ℹ Getting There & Away

Postal buses run to Flims and the other villages in the White Arena area hourly from Chur (Sfr13.20 to Flims Dorf, 35 minutes), which lies 20km to the east. A free local shuttle bus connects the three villages.

ILANZ

A bustling town with a pleasant-enough Old Town, Ilanz is, for most visitors, a transport hub. The main N19 road ribbons westward, passing through quaint towns in the predominantly German-speaking Obersaxen area before reaching the Romansch monastery village of Disentis/Mustér. Ilanz is also the departure point for two enchanting southern valleys.

VALSERTAL

Shadowing the course of the babbling Glogn (Glenner) stream south, the luxuriantly green Valsertal (Vals Valley) is full of sylvan beauty, sleepy hamlets and thundering waterfalls. The delightful drive passes Uors and St Martin before arriving at Vals (1252m). About 2km short of the village, you emerge into verdant Alpine pastures, liberally scattered with chalets and shepherds' huts.

Vals, home to Valser mineral water, stretches 2km along its glittering stream. The secret of this chocolate-box village and its soothing waters is out since Basel-born architect Peter Zumthor worked architectural magic to transform Therme Vals' thermal baths into a temple of cutting-edge cool.

⊙ Sights & Activities

There is some modest downhill skiing in the heights above Vals in winter.

Therme Vals　　　　　　　　SPA
(☑081 926 89 61; www.therme-vals.ch; Vals; adult/child Sfr40/26, treatments Sfr55-255; ☺11am-8pm mid-Jun–early Apr) Using 60,000 slabs of local quartzite, Peter Zumthor created one of the country's most enchanting thermal

spas. Aside from heated indoor and outdoor pools, this grey-stone labyrinth hides all sorts of watery nooks and crannies, cleverly lit and full of cavernous atmosphere. You can drift away in the bath-warm Feuerbad (42°C) and perfumed Blütenbad, sweat it out in the steam room and cool down in the teeth-chattering Eisbad.

Zervreilasee HIKING
Less well known than the spa is an exhilarating 8km trip south to this turquoise lake, overshadowed by the frosted 3402m peak of Rheinwaldhorn. Access is usually only possible from June to October. From above the lake various hiking options present themselves.

Val Lumnezia VALLEY
Running parallel to the Valsertal from Ilanz, and then gradually branching away to the southwest, is the Val Lumnezia, as broad and sunlit green as the Valsertal is deep and narrow. The road runs high along the west flank of the valley. Where it dips out of sight of the valley, you arrive in Vrin, a cheerful huddle of rural houses gathered around a brightly frescoed church.

🛏 Sleeping
There are dozens of private rooms and holiday homes in the valley; expect to pay between Sfr40 and Sfr50 per person. Visit www.vals.ch for details.

Hotel Therme DESIGN HOTEL $$$
(☑081 926 80 80; www.therme-vals.ch; Vals; s Sfr155-265, d Sfr270-450; P@) In this 1960s colossus, Peter Zumthor has revamped many of the rooms; the newest sport stucco lustro, parquet floors and satin sheets. Some of the hotel's annexes have not been given the Zumthor treatment and are cheaper and, frankly, ugly. Peter Jörimann emphasises market-fresh cuisine in gourmet restaurant Red.

Gasthaus Edelweiss GUESTHOUSE $
(☑081 935 11 33; www.edelweiss-vals.ch; Dorfsplatz, Vals; s Sfr54-80, d Sfr108-160) Right on the village square, this century-old guesthouse has humble timber-lined rooms. The restaurant bakes its own delicious bread and does a great *Capuns*.

Hotel Glenner HOTEL $$
(☑081 935 11 15; www.glenner.ch; in German; Vals; d Sfr170-190) Ablaze with red geraniums in summer, this dark-wood chalet shelters cosy,

if slightly old-fashioned, rooms with pine trappings and squeaky-clean bathrooms.

ℹ Getting There & Away
Postal buses run more or less hourly to Vrin (Sfr13.20, 49 minutes) and Vals (Sfr12.20, 42 minutes) from Ilanz (itself reached by regular train from Chur, Sfr14.80, 40 minutes).

DISENTIS/MUSTÉR & VAL MEDEL
Rising like a vision above Disentis/Mustér is a baubly Benedictine monastery with a lavishly stuccoed baroque church attached. A monastery has stood here since the 8th century, but the present immense complex dates from the 18th century. Left of the church entrance is a door that leads you down a corridor to the **Klostermuseum** (adult/child Sfr7/3; ⊙2-5pm Tue, Thu & Sat Jun-Oct, 2-5pm Wed Christmas-Easter), crammed with memorabilia on the history of the monastery. Head left upstairs to the **Marienkirche**, a chapel with Romanesque origins which is filled with ex-voto images from people in need of (or giving thanks for) some miraculous intervention from the Virgin Mary.

Festooned with geraniums in summer, central **Hotel Alpsu** (☑081 947 51 17; s Sfr69-90, d Sfr120-150; P) has individually decorated rooms. In one you find a four-poster, in another exposed beams and a bubble bath opposite the bed. The restaurant does fine renditions of *Capuns* and *Pizokel*.

South of Disentis, the **Val Medel** starts in dramatic style with the **Medelser-Schlucht** (Medel Gorge). You pass through several villages, of which **Platta** is noteworthy for its shingle-roofed Romanesque church. About 20km on, by the petrol-blue **Lai da Sontga Maria** lake and surrounded by 3000m peaks, the road hits the wiggly **Lukmanier Pass** (Passo di Lucomagno, 1914m) and crosses into Ticino.

Disentis/Mustér is where hourly Matterhorn-Gotthard trains from Brig (Sfr47, 3¼ hours) via Andermatt (Sfr19.40, one hour) terminate, and local RhB trains heading to Chur (Sfr27, 1¼ hours) start. Five buses a day rumble over the Lukmanier Pass, four of them heading on to Biasca in Ticino. There is an hourly train from Disentis/Mustér to the Oberalp Pass (Sfr10.40, 35 minutes).

South of Chur
The main route south of Chur leads through a remote wilderness of castle-topped crags, waterfalls and one of Switzerland's most

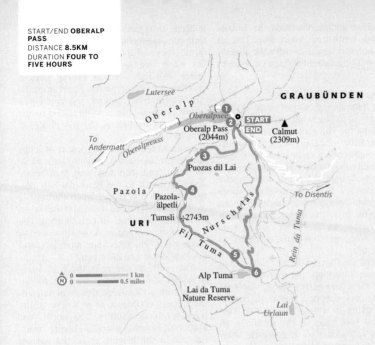

START/END **OBERALP PASS**
DISTANCE **8.5KM**
DURATION **FOUR TO FIVE HOURS**

Walking Tour
Lai da Tuma Circuit

❯ This high-level route takes you through an Alpine nature reserve and along the crest of the Pazolastock Range to the source of the mighty Rhine, Lai da Tuma. The SAW 1:50,000 walking map *Disentis/Mustér* (Sfr21.50) is recommended.

Flanked by granite peaks, the ❶ **Oberalpsee** at the Oberalp Pass (2044m) is the trailhead. From the train station, walk 200m up to the ❷ **Restaurant Alpsu**. Take the dirt road opposite, then cut right over the open slopes. The path climbs alongside a grassy and rocky spur and through highland moors in the tiny upper valley of ❸ **Puozas**. Negotiate a series of tight switchbacks uphill through scree-strewn slopes.

Pass makeshift stone bunkers, coming to a signpost on the exposed ridgetop at 2571m after one to 1½ hours. Andermatt is now visible to the west in the valley of the Reuss, and, behind, the 3500m summits of the Winterberg Massif and Galenstock rise up on the Uri–Valais cantonal border.

The white-red-white marked route continues up the ridge past two rustic military buildings just under the 2739m ❹ **Pazolastock** (Piz Nurschalas).The trail now traverses the exposed crest of the craggy range with just enough rockhopping to make the going not too strenuous for the sure-footed.

At point 2743 follow the Fil Tuma southeastward, and sidle steadily down along the grassy, rock-strewn right-hand side of the ridge to arrive at the ❺ **Badushütte**, a cosy hut for a snack at 2505m, a further one to 1½ hours on. From here the path descends quickly over boulders to a signposted trail leading down to the shore of ❻ **Lai da Tuma** (2343m), 15 to 20 minutes from the hut. This dazzling blue-green lake lies in a cirque formed by the grinding action of an extinct hanging glacier. The Vorderrhein, the true source of the Rhine, rises here.

Continue northward, winding your way down the initially rocky hillside, then past cow-grazed pastures and waterfalls. Follow the often-boggy banks gently up to arrive back at the Oberalp Pass, one to 1½ hours from the Lai da Tuma.

breathtaking gorges, Via Mala. An important north–south trade route since Roman times, the road heads on into the forlorn Italian-speaking Valle Mesolcina en route to Ticino.

VIA MALA & AVERS VALLEY

The A13 freeway and railway south of Chur first veer west to Reichenau before swinging south along the Hinterrhein River between the Domleschg mountain range to the east and the Heinzenberg to the west. A string of villages and ruined robber-knight castles dot the way to Thusis, a bustling town whose main draw lies in the far-reaching views from ruined Obertagstein castle about an hour's walk from the centre. Trains from Chur en route for St Moritz call in here, before heading east toward the ski resort via Tiefencastel.

South of Thusis, take the N13 rather than the freeway to explore the narrow, breathtakingly sheer and narrow gorge Via Mala (Evil Rd), once part of a pack-mule trail to Italy. Starting in Thusis, the 11.5km Veia Traversina hike takes in the ravine in all its giddy splendour; see the website www .viamala.ch for route descriptions in German. The deep chasm opens out just before Zillis, famed for its St Martinskirche (adult/child Sfr4/2; ⊙9am-6pm), whose wooden Romanesque ceiling bears 153 extraordinarily vivid panels depicting the lives of Christ and St Martin.

To really get out into the wild, head south another 8km past Andeer (known for its thermal baths) for the junction with the road into the remote Avers Valley. This lonely trail wriggles 24km south through thick forests, a stark Alpine valley and tiny hamlets to reach Juf (2126m), claiming to be Europe's highest permanently inhabited village. With a population of just 30, it's more likely you'll meet resident marmots and cud-chewing cows than locals.

Postal buses trundle between Thusis and Bellinzona in Ticino (Sfr40, two to 2½ hours), stopping at Zillis, Andeer, Splügen and towns along the Valle Mesolcina. Buses from Andeer run to Juf (Sfr15.20, 52 minutes).

SPLÜGEN & VALLE MESOLCINA

From the Avers turn-off, the A13 and N13 branch west into the pine-brushed Rheinwald (Rhine Forest), leading to the 1460m-high town of Splügen. The Via Mala website (www.viamala.ch, in German) covers Splügen, the Avers area, Andeer and Zillis.

Splügen intrigues with its mix of dark timber, slate-roofed Walser (Valais-style) farmhouses and mansions of trading families made wealthy by 19th-century commerce with Italy over the nearby Splügen and San Bernardino passes. Apart from the riverside camping ground, you could stay in one of the simple, pine-furnished rooms at Haus Teuriblick (✆081 664 16 56; s/d Sfr75/130; ℗).

South of Splügen, a dizzying road loops 9km to the like-named pass into Italy, while the main roads continue west 8km before dropping south to the Passo del San Bernardino (take the tunnel when the pass is closed) and the rugged Valle Mesolcina, an Italian-infused corner of Graubünden. The main towns are Mesocco, where towering castle ruins will grab your attention, and low-key Soazza and Roveredo.

Just north of Roveredo, the wild, barely visited Val Calanca opens up to the north, with a 19km road that terminates in the hamlet of Rossa, from where a dirt track continues another 5km north past Valbella. Several peaceful hiking trails roll out in the heights above the narrow valley. From Roveredo, it is about 10km to Bellinzona, the capital of Ticino.

Buses run roughly every 1½ hours up the Val Calanca to Rossa from Bellinzona (Sfr17.20, 1½ hours) via Rovoredo (change at Grono).

Bündner Herrschaft

The A13 freeway blasts northward from Chur, through the wine-growing region called Fünf Dörfer (Five Villages), of which bucolic Zizers is probably the prettiest. Follow the country lane out of industrial Landquart for Malans, which takes you into the Bündner Herrschaft. This is the canton's premier wine region, dominated by the Blauburgunder (Pinot noir) grape variety that yields some memorable reds. This is also, rather unforgettably, Heidiland.

MALANS & JENINS

Through vineyards and woods you arrive in Malans, dominated by the private castle of the Salis dynasty, a name in local wine and historic rivals to the Planta clan, whose town houses line the village square. A few kilometres north is Jenins, scenically planted between the vines and mountains. Stop off for a glass of the local Pinot noir and lunch on the vine-facing terrace at **Weinstube Alter Torkel** (☏081 302 36 75; www.torkel.ch, in German; Jeninserstrasse 3; mains Sfr30-40; ⊙10am-11pm Mon-Sun). The rustic wine cellar churns out terrific local fare from crispy roast pork to white-wine risotto.

Some trains from Chur to Malans (Sfr7.20, 22 to 32 minutes) require a change in Landquart. To push on to Jenins (from Sfr10, 42 minutes from Chur) get a connecting postal bus from Landquart, Malans or Maienfeld.

MAIENFELD & HEIDIDORF

The most impressive of these wine villages is **Maienfeld**, another 2km through lush woods and vineyards. Dominated by a colourfully frescoed **Rathaus** (town hall) and haughty church, it's worth hanging out for the local cuisine. Make for **Schloss Brandis** (☏081 302 24 23; www.schlossbrandis .ch, in German; mains Sfr30-50; ⊙lunch & dinner Mon-Sun), a lofty 15th-century tower housing one of the canton's best restaurants. Pull up a chair in the beamed, lantern-lit dining room, in the garden or in the vaulted cellar for Maienfeld riesling soup and meatier specialities (including excellent game in autumn). For wine tasting, head to the convivial **Vinothek von Salis** (Kruseckgasse 3; ⊙2-6pm Mon-Fri, 9.30am-4pm Sat).

Each year the four Bündner Herrschaft towns (Maienfeld, Malans, Jenins and Fläsch) take turns to celebrate the **Herbstfest** in late September. This autumnal wine fest brings much drinking, eating and merrymaking to the normally quiet streets.

OK, we've held out till now – Maienfeld is where to start your Heidiland experience. Johanna Spyri (1827–1901) had the idea of basing the story of Heidi in the countryside around Maienfeld, and the locals had the worse idea of identifying one local village as Heidi's. It is now called – oh dear! – **Heididorf**, a 20-minute signposted walk from Maienfeld across idyllic country. In peak periods you might be able to get the Heidi Express bus, which will pass by the Heidihof Hotel. Apart from the **Heidihaus** (www.heidi -swiss.ch; adult/child Sfr7/3; ⊙10am-5pm mid-Mar–mid-Nov), where of course she never lived because she never existed, you could visit the Heidishop to buy Heidi colouring-in books, Heidi videos or just plain Heidikitsch. For little-girl-of-the-Alps overkill, you could skip along the Heidiweg into the surrounding hills (Heidialp). When you're done, you might be in need of some Heidiwein for your Heidiheadache…or perhaps just hit the A13

road and Heiditail it out of here north into Liechtenstein.

Maienfeld is on the train line between Chur (Sfr7.80, 15 minutes) and Bad Ragaz (Sfr3.90, 12 minutes).

BAD RAGAZ
POP 530 / ELEV 502M

The perfect cure for a bad case of Heidiness could be the graceful little spa town of Bad Ragaz, a couple of kilometres west of Maienfeld, which opened in 1840 and has attracted the bath-loving likes of Douglas Fairbanks and Mary Pickford. The fabled waters are said to boost the immune system and improve circulation.

Bad Ragaz' ultra-sleek **Tamina Therme** (☏081 303 27 40; www.taminatherme.ch; Hans-Albrecht-Strasse; day ticket adult/child Sfr34/21; ⊙8am-10pm Mon-Sun, to 11pm Fri), a couple of kilometres south of town, has several pools for wallowing in the 34°C thermal waters, as well as massage jets, whirlpools, saunas and an assortment of treatments and massages.

The forest-cloaked slopes of **Pizol** (www .pizol.com, in German), rising up above Bad Ragaz, attract beginner and intermediate skiers with 40km of runs in winter. A day pass will set you back Sfr53/26.50 for an adult/child. Those same slopes buzz with hikers in summer. One of the region's top day hikes, the **Fünf Seen Wanderung** (Five Lake Walk) begins at the 2227m Pizolhütte. The five-hour walk takes in a crest of limestone peaks, glaciers and five jewel-coloured lakes. The views of the Swiss and Austrian Alps are incredible.

It costs a small fortune to stay at the lavish **Grand Resort** (www.resortragaz .ch), but there are other options if you fancy staying overnight. **Hotel Schloss Ragaz** (☏081 303 77 78; www.hotelschloss ragaz.ch; s/d Sfr130/270) is a petite, turreted castle with spacious, quiet quarters framed by manicured gardens. The spa soothes away stress with back-to-nature treatments like hay-flower wraps and the hotel has city/e-bikes that can be hired for Sfr15/45 per day. Alternatively, opt for the humble yet comfy **HotelKrone** (☏081 303 84 44; www.kroneragaz.ch; Kronenplatz 10; s Sfr70-80, d Sfr150-160).

Bad Ragaz is on the Chur–Zürich train line. Trains from Chur via Maienfeld run hourly (Sfr8.40, 15 minutes).

KLOSTERS & DAVOS

Following the N28 road east from Landquart, you enter the broad Prättigau Valley, which stretches east to Klosters. Several valley roads spike off the highway before Klosters, and the one leading to **St Antönien** is the most attractive. This high Alpine country is punctuated by villages and burned-wood Walser houses raised by this rural folk since migrating here from eastern Valais from the 13th century onward.

Klosters

POP 3900 / ELEV 1194M

No matter whether you come in summer to hike in the flower-speckled mountains or in winter when the log chalets are veiled in snow and icicle-hung – Klosters is postcard stuff. Indeed, the village has attracted a host of slaloming celebrities and royals with its chocolate-box looks and paparazzi-free slopes. This is where a 14-year-old Prince Charles learned to ski, and where Harry and William whizzed down the slopes as tots.

Activities

Winter Activities

Davos and Klosters share 320km of ski runs, covered by the Regional Pass (adult/child/youth Sfr69/28/48 per day), as well as some glorious off-piste terrain. **Parsenn** beckons confidence-building novices, while experts can tackle black runs like panoramic Schlappin and Gotschnawang. **Madrisa** is a great all-rounder, with long, sunny runs, mostly above the treeline for intermediates, a kids' club, tubing and skidoo park, and a fun park with kickers and rails. For a back-to-nature experience, 35km of **cross-country** trails loop through the frozen plains and forest.

Toboggan Run SNOW SPORTS
(Madrisa; day ticket adult/child Sfr35/14-25; 8.15am-4pm Dec-Apr) Kid-friendly winter activities include this bumpy downhill dash from Madrisa to Saaseralp.

Horse-Drawn Sleigh SNOW SPORTS
(081 422 18 73; www.pferdekutschen.ch, in German) When the flakes are falling, nothing beats a horse-drawn sleigh ride. Expect to pay around Sfr80 per hour.

Summer Activities

Hikers hit the trail on one of the region's 700km of well-maintained footpaths, which range from gentle family strolls to high-altitude, multiday treks. Would-be climbers can tackle the rope bridges and climbing trees at Madrisa.

Mountain and downhill biking are equally popular and you can hire wheels from **Bertram's Bike Shop** (Bahnhofstrasse 16). Flyer e-bikes cost Sfr30/49 per half-/full-day. See www.davosklosters.ch for inspiration, GPS downloads and maps.

Gotschna Freeride MOUNTAIN BIKING
(Jul-Oct) This breathtakingly steep 5.7km trail from Gotschnaboden to Klosters is freeride heaven. Warm up at the skill centre before tackling the banks, jumps and tables.

R&M Adventure ADVENTURE SPORTS
(079 384 29 36; www.ramadventure.ch; Landstrasse 171) Tailor your own adventure with this reputable company offering whitewater rafting (Sfr150) and canyoning (Sfr150).

Klosters Lido SWIMMING
(Doggilochstrasse 51; adult/child Sfr6/4; 9am-7pm May-Sep) Enjoy views of the Silvretta Alps as you splash at this heated outdoor pool. There's a kids' play area, volleyball court and a climbing wall suspended above the diving pool.

Madrisa Land AMUSEMENT PARK
(Madrisa; www.madrisa-land.ch, in German; admission Sfr10; 10am-4.45pm Jul-Oct) This new kiddie wonderland on Madrisa has a fairy-tale-themed adventure playground with a flying fox (Sfr5), petting zoo, pony riding (Sfr5), and daily goat milking at 4pm.

Sleeping & Eating

Pick up a list of private rooms and apartments from the tourist office. Prices are 30% to 50% cheaper in summer.

TOP CHOICE Gasthaus Bargis GUESTHOUSE $$
(081 422 55 77; www.bargis.ch, in German; Kantonsstrasse 8; apt Sfr100-190) Erika is your kindly host at this quaint dark-wood chalet on the road into Klosters Dorf, run by the Ambühl family since the 18th century. The sunny, immaculate apartments brim with homely touches from ornamental ducks to open fireplaces. The pine-clad restaurant (mains Sfr24 to Sfr32.50, open from Wednesday to Sunday) is a cosy spot for Bündner specialities like creamy Klosterser hay soup and veal cordon bleu prepared with beer.

When the sun's out, eat on the mountain-facing terrace.

Hotel Chesa Grischuna HISTORIC HOTEL $$$
(☏081 422 22 22; www.chesagrischuna.ch; Bahnhofstrasse 12; s/d/ste Sfr259/439/549) An archetypal vision of a Swiss chalet, this family-run pad has toasty pine rooms with antique flourishes and ornately carved ceilings. The lantern-lit restaurant (mains Sfr42 to Sfr60) is an Alpine charmer, too. Dirndl-clad waitresses bring fresh, seasonal dishes from local trout to roast beef to the table.

Soldanella HOSTEL $
(☏081 422 13 16; www.youthhostel.ch/klosters; Talstrasse 73; dm Sfr53.50; @🛜) Even the HI hostel in Klosters has Alpine appeal, spanning two mountain chalets. Dorms are clean and bright, there's a sun-drenched terrace, games room and kids' play corner. It's a 12-minute amble from the station.

Steinbock HOTEL $$
(☏081 422 45 45; www.steinbock-klosters.ch; Landstrasse 194; d Sfr265-365; P🛜) The Steinbock has a real up-in-the-mountains feel with its expansive mountain views, rooms clad in honeyed pine and trio of restaurants dishing up heart-warming Swiss fare. Up the budget and you'll even get your own open fire. All guests can warm up in the whirlpool, sauna and steam room.

R&M Adventure Hostel HOSTEL $
(☏081 422 12 29; www.ramadventure.ch; Landstrasse 171; r per adult Sfr70, child Sfr45-55; P@🛜♿) Bang in the heart of Klosters, R&M has colourful digs, a lounge where you can prepare tea and snacks, and a TV and playroom in the attic. Children's beds are available on request and breakfast costs Sfr10 extra.

ⓘ Information

In the centre of the village is the **tourist office** (☏081 410 20 20; www.klosters.ch; Alte Bahnhofstrasse 6; ⏰8.30am-6pm Mon-Fri, 9am-6pm Sat, 9am-1pm Sun). The post office is opposite the station.

ⓘ Getting There & Away

Klosters is split into two sections. Klosters Platz is the main resort, grouped around the train station. Two kilometres to the left of the station is smaller Klosters Dorf and the Madrisa cable car.

See Davos, as Klosters is on the same train route between Landquart and Filisur. Klosters and Davos are linked by free buses for those with Guest Cards or ski passes.

ⓘ SUMMER SAVER

Stay overnight in Davos or Klosters in summer and you'll receive the Davos-Klosters Inclusive guest card, which entitles you to free use of buses and cable cars, limited travel on the Rhaetian Railway, plus free entry to Schatzalp botanical gardens and Davos' artificial ice rink. The card also gives discounts on activities from guided hikes to introductory climbing sessions. See www.klosters.ch for details.

Davos
POP 11,300 / ELEV 1560M

Unlike its little sister Klosters, Davos is more cool than quaint. But what the resort lacks in Alpine prettiness, it makes up for with seductive skiing, including monster runs descending up to 2000m, and après-ski parties. It is also the annual meeting point for the crème de la crème of world capitalism, the World Economic Forum. Global chat fests aside, Davos inspired Sir Arthur Conan Doyle (of Sherlock Holmes fame) to don skis and Thomas Mann to pen *The Magic Mountain*.

Davos comprises two contiguous areas, each with a train station: Davos Platz and the older Davos Dorf.

◉ Sights

Kirchner Museum ART MUSEUM
(Ernst-Ludwig-Kirchner-Platz; adult/child Sfr12/5; ⏰10am-6pm Tue-Sun) This giant cube of a museum showcases the world's largest Ernst Ludwig Kirchner (1880–1938) collection. The German expressionist painted extraordinary scenes of the area. When the Nazis classified Kirchner a 'degenerate artist' and emptied galleries of his works, he was overcome with despair and took his own life in 1938.

Wintersportmuseum MUSEUM
(Promenade 43; adult/child Sfr5/3; ⏰4.30-6.30pm Tue & Thu Dec-Mar & Jul-Oct) This ski-obsessed museum races you back to an age when skis were wooden planks and snowshoes improvised tennis rackets.

🏃 Activities
Winter Sports

Naturally blessed with awesome scenery and great powder, Davos has carved out a name for itself as a first-class skiing

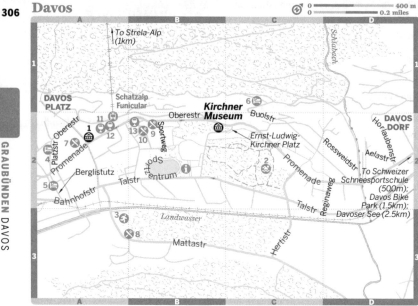

destination, with varied runs in five different areas. The vast **Parsenn** area reaches as high as Weissfluhjoch (2844m), from where you can ski to Küblis, more than 2000m lower and 12km away. Alternatively, take the demanding run to Wolfgang (1629m) or the scenic slopes to Klosters.

Across the valley, **Jakobshorn** is a favourite playground for snowboarders and freestylers with its half-pipe, terrain park and excellent off-piste opportunities. See p304 for ski-pass prices.

Davos is a cross-country hot spot, with 75km of well-groomed trails, including classic and skating options, plus a floodlit track for starlit swishing. It is also laced with toboggan runs, such as the 2.5km floodlit track from Schatzalp to Davos Platz; hire your sled at base station Schatzalp.

Schweizer Schneesportschule   SKIING
(☎081 416 24 54; www.ssd.ch; Promenade 157)
One of the best ski and snowboard schools in the country.

Summer Activities

Together, Davos and Klosters provide 700km of marked hiking paths and 600km of mountain bike tracks, including some challenging descents and single-track trails; see www.bike-davos.ch for routes, maps and rental outlets.

Summer water sports include windsurfing and sailing on the Davoser See (Davos Lake).

FREE Davos Bike Park   MOUNTAIN BIKING
(Flüelastrasse; ⊙dawn-dusk Jul-Oct) Test your skills on the tables, curves and jumps. Dirt bikes can be hired for Sfr20 per hour.

Luftchraft – Flugschule   PARAGLIDING
(☑079 623 19 70; www.luftchraft.ch, in German; Mattastrasse 9) Daredevils eager to leap off Jakobshorn or Gotschnagrat can book tandem flights for Sfr175 at this reputable school.

eau-là-là   SWIMMING
(☑081 413 64 63; www.eau-la-la.ch; Promenade 90; pool adult/child Sfr9/5, day spa Sfr26; ⊙10am-10pm Mon-Sat, 10am-6pm Sun) If you prefer horizontal sightseeing to vertical drops, try this leisure centre, with heated outdoor pools, splash areas for the kids and a spa with mountain views.

✯✯ Festivals & Events

Classical music resounds at the Davos Festival (www.davosfestival.ch) in August. It's preceded by a week-long jazz festival. Swiss craziness peaks at Sertig Schwinget (www.schwingerverband-davos.ch, in German) in August, with *Schwingen* (Alpine wrestling) champs doing battle in the sawdust. Davos hosts the FIS Cross-Country World Cup (www.davosnordic.ch) in December.

🛏 Sleeping

Room rates plunge by up to 30% in the summer season.

Hotel Alpenhof   HOTEL $$
(☑081 415 20 60; www.alpenhof-davos.ch; Hofstrasse 22; s/d Sfr148/276; 🐾) You'll feel right at home in the Alpenhof's light-filled rooms with chunky pine furnishings, downy duvets and DVD players. The restaurant places the emphasis on fresh, regional fare and has a kids' menu. Family reductions are available. The hotel is 1.5km south of the centre; buses 428 and 432 to Crestannes stop close by.

Waldhotel Bellevue   HISTORIC HOTEL $$$
(☑081 415 15 15; www.waldhotel-bellevue.ch; Buolstrasse 3; s Sfr205-275, d Sfr390-460; 🅿🐾) The Magic Mountain in Thomas Mann's eponymous 1924 novel, this sanatorium turned hotel has recently been given a stylish facelift. Even standard rooms come with sunny balconies and luxuries like fruit, mineral water and bathrobes. When you tire of mountain views from your balcony, head down to the spa's saltwater pools and saunas. The restaurant matches Grisons cuisine with wines drawn from the award-winning cellar.

Davoser Hüsli   B&B $
(☑081 417 67 77; Berglistutz 2; dm/s/d Sfr45/50/100) A cheap 'n' cheerful choice in Davos Platz, this cute log chalet offers a mix of cosy, low-ceilinged dorms and rooms with shared bathrooms. Claustrophobics may find them a trifle stifling, however. You'll find wi-fi and breakfast in the hotel next door.

DON'T MISS

UNIQUE SLEEPS

Whether you fancy sleeping in the snow, straw or treetops, here are our three favourite unique sleeps in Davos-Klosters.

Iglu Dorf (☑041 612 27 28; www.iglu-dorf.com; Parsenn; per person Sfr149-189; ⊙late Dec–mid-Apr; 🏂) Live out your Eskimo fantasies with a night at this igloo village at 2620m. After mulled wine, fondue and a bubble in the whirlpool, you'll barely notice the subzero temperatures.

Baum Hotel (☑081 410 21 70; www.madrisa-land.ch, in German; tree house q Sfr350, straw/tepee Sfr65 per person; ⊙Jul-late Oct; 🏂) Snooze in a cosy family-sized tree house or in a tepee complete with totem pole at Madrisa Land.

Hotel Post Glaris (☑081 413 64 64; www.postglaris.ch, in German; Landwasserstrasse 66; Sfr25 per adult, child Sfr1 per yr) Sleep soundly on a bed of straw at this rustic farmhouse in peaceful Davos Glaris. Kids love the resident farm animals.

ArtHausHotel Davos　　HOTEL **$$**
(☎081 410 05 10; www.arthaushotel.ch; Platz-strasse 5; s/d Sfr150/260; P⊛) Sprinkled liberally with owner Diego do Clava-detscher's abstract acrylics, this self-defined art hotel shelters modern and fairly spacious rooms (minuscule bathrooms aside).

✕ Eating

TOP CHOICE Kaffee Klatsch　　CAFE **$**
(Promenade 72; light meals & snacks Sfr9-22; ☺7.30am-9.30pm Mon-Sun) Warm brick and wood, rustling newspapers and mellow music create a relaxed feel in this arty cafe. Try the delicious filled focaccia, or stop by for cake with a speciality coffee like vanilla bean or Heidi latte (made with roasted organic oats). The adjacent craft shop sells kitsch-free Swiss gifts. Shorter hours in low season.

Hänggi's　　ITALIAN **$$**
(☎081 416 20 20; Mattastrasse 11; pizza Sfr16-26, mains Sfr33-51; ☺lunch & dinner) Wood-fired pizza, crisp and delicious, is what this cosy beamed restaurant is known for. Or go for well-executed Italian-inspired dishes such as basil risotto with fresh tomatoes, market-fresh fish and tangy homemade sorbet.

Bistro Gentiana　　SWISS **$$**
(☎081 413 56 49; Promenade 53; mains Sfr25-42; ☺5-10.30pm Thu-Tue summer, 11am-2pm & 5pm-midnight Mon-Sun winter) This art deco bistro specialises in snails (Schnecken) and rich cheese fondues. A dish of six juicy snails ovencooked in mushroom heads costs Sfr29.80.

Strela-Alp　　SWISS **$**
(www.strela-alp.ch; mains Sfr15-30; ☺9am-5pm Sun-Thu, 9am-11pm Fri & Sat) Expansive mountain views, a sunny terrace and Swiss grub like rösti and fondue await at this rustic haunt near Schatzalp funicular top station.

Schneider's　　CAFE **$**
(Promenade 68; pastries Sfr3-6; ☺7am-6.30pm) Crumbly pastries, beer-filled truffles and Bündner Nüsstorte (nut tart) lure the sweet toothed to this patisserie.

🍸 Drinking

Mountain's Akt　　BAR
(Promenade 64; ☺2pm-4am Tue-Sat; ⊛) DJs spin house and electro at the weekend at this funky bar. There's a great selection of beers from Kilkenny to Leffe. The summer beer garden becomes a snow bar in winter.

Jatzhütte　　BAR
(Jakobshorn) Perched at 2530m, this is Davos' wackiest après-ski joint. Those who dare to partially bare can soak in a 39°C whirlpool framed by icy peaks. Prefer to keep your thermals on? Grab a flame-grilled burger, try the sex coffee (the mind boggles!) or take your ski boots grooving inside.

Ex Bar　　BAR
(☎081 413 56 45; Promenade 63; ☺5pm-6am Mon-Sun Dec-Apr, shorter hours rest of year) Europop tunes, free salty popcorn and a huge toy reindeer hanging over the door sum up this crowded party den.

Cabanna Club　　CLUB
(Promenade 63; ☺8pm-3am Dec-Apr) Techno dominates the decks of this ever-popular club in Hotel Europe.

ℹ Information

The most central branch of the **tourist office** (☎081 415 21 21; www.davos.ch; Bahnhofstrasse 8; ☺8.30am-6.30pm Mon-Fri, 1-5pm Sat, 9am-1pm Sun) is in Davos Dorf. Hours are reduced in low season (spring and autumn).

ℹ Getting There & Away

For trains to Chur (Sfr27, 1½ hours) or Zürich (Sfr52, 2½ hours), you will change at Landquart. For St Moritz (Sfr27, 1½ hours), take the train at Davos Platz and change at Filisur. For the hourly service to Scuol (Sfr28, 1¼ hours) in the Unterengadin, take the train from Davos Dorf and change at Klosters.

The Guest Card allows free travel on local buses and trains, as does the general ski pass (and the Swiss Pass).

THE ENGADINE

The almost-3000km-long Inn River (En in Romansch) springs up from the snowy Graubünden Alps around the Maloja Pass and gives its name to the Engadine. The valley is carved into two: the Oberengadin (Upper Engadine), from Maloja to Zernez; and the Unterengadin (Lower Engadine), stretching from Zernez to Martina, by the Austrian border.

Oberengadin is dominated by the ritzy ski resort of St Moritz, while Unterengadin, home to the country's only national park, is characterised by quaint villages with sgraffito-decorated houses and pristine countryside.

SWISS NATIONAL PARK

The Engadine's pride and joy is the Swiss National Park (www.nationalpark.ch), easily accessed from villages such as Scuol, Zernez and S-chanf. Created in 1914 and spanning 172 sq km, Switzerland's only national park is a nature-gone-wild swathe of dolomitic peaks, shimmering glaciers, larch woodlands, pastures, waterfalls and high moors strung with topaz-blue lakes. It is a remote and totally enchanting place to step off the beaten track for a few days. Bear in mind that the park goes into hibernation in winter.

Still largely untouched, the park is a glimpse of the Alps before the dawn of tourism. Some 80km of well-marked hiking trails lead through the park, where, with a little luck and a decent pair of binoculars, ibex, chamois, marmots and golden eagles can be sighted. The National Park Centre (p311) in Zernez should be your first port of call for information on activities and accommodation. It sells an excellent 1:50,000 park map (Sfr20), which covers 21 different walks through the park.

You can easily head off on your own, but you might get more out of one of the informative guided hikes run by the National Park Centre from late June to mid-October. These include wildlife-spotting treks to the Val Trupchun and high-alpine hikes to the Offenpass and Lakes of Macun. Most are in German but many guides speak a little English. Expect to pay around Sfr25 to Sfr35 per person. You should book ahead by calling ☑081 851 41 41.

Entry to the park and its car parks is free. Conservation is paramount here, so stick to footpaths and respect regulations prohibiting camping, littering, lighting fires, cycling, picking flowers and disturbing the animals.

Chalandamarz, a spring and youth festival, is celebrated in the Engadine on 1 March. During Schlitteda in St Moritz, Pontresina and Silvaplana in January, lads on flamboyant horse-drawn sleds whisk girls (to their delight or dismay) on rides through the snow.

Unterengadin

The thickly wooded Unterengadin (Lower Engadine) in eastern Switzerland juts like a wolf's snout into neighbouring Austria and Italy. From Davos, the N28 highway climbs up to the barren Flüela Pass (2383m) in a series of loops before dropping over the other side, opening up majestic vistas of Alpine crags, valleys and silvery mountain streams.

The road descends to Susch, close to the exit point of Sagliains for the car train through the Vereina Tunnel from Selfranga (just outside Klosters), the only way to make the trip when snow blocks the pass. Trains run every 30 to 60 minutes during the day and cost Sfr29 to Sfr41 per car, depending on the season.

From Susch you can head 6km south to Zernez and then east into the Swiss National Park and Val Müstair, or further southwest to the Oberengadin. Or you can follow the Inn River on its gradual eastern progress to Austria.

GUARDA & AROUND
POP 180 / ELEV 1653M

With its twisting cobbled streets and hobbit-like houses in candy shades, Guarda, 6km east of Susch, has storybook appeal. Guarda is 30 minutes' uphill trudge from its valley-floor train station, or take the hourly postal bus (Sfr3). A trail leads 8km north to the foothills of 3312m Piz Buin (of sunscreen fame), dominating the glaciated Silvretta range on the Swiss–Austrian border.

Guarda has plenty of lodgings in its traditional houses, including family-run, flower-bedecked Hotel Piz Buin (☑081 861 30 00; www.pizbuin.ch; s Sfr75-90, d Sfr140-200), where many of the cosy rooms are clad in Swiss stone pine. Take breakfast on the terrace to the backbeat of cowbells before a soak in the outdoor hot tub overlooking the mountains.

A couple of wooded kilometres east lies the hamlet of Bos-cha, but by car you can't get any further. To continue, return to the low road and follow the signs up to Ardez, a tiny village with a ruined medieval tower, well-preserved oriels and 17th-century Chesa Claglüna, decorated with elaborate sgraffito. Another 8km brings you to Ftan, where forested slopes rise gently to brooding pinnacles. From here, the narrow road slithers down to Scuol.

SCUOL

POP 2340 / ELEV 1250M

Surrounded by rippling peaks and dense forests, Scuol is ideal for remote Alpine hikes in summer, crowd-free cruising in winter and relaxation in its thermal baths year-round. It's a joy to stroll the Old Town (Lower Scuol), an attractive jumble of frescoed chalets, cobbled squares and fountains that spout mineral water tapped from one of 20 springs in the region.

◎ Sights & Activities

There's skiing on 80km of runs and fun for boarders at the snow park at Motta Naluns. A one-day pass costs Sfr55/28 for adults/children.

In summer the same slopes attract hikers and downhill bikers. At the cable car station you can hire scooters (Sfr18), mountain bikes (Sfr35), downhill bikes (Sfr42) and e-bikes (Sfr38) to whiz through meadows and forests.

Schloss Tarasp   CASTLE
(www.schloss-tarasp.ch; tour adult/child Sfr10/5; ⊙guided visits 2.30pm & 3.30pm Jun–mid-Oct, plus 11am & 4.30pm mid-Jul–Aug) Perched on a clifftop, this turreted castle is definite fairy-tale material. Guided tours of the almost 1000-year-old castle lead through wood-panelled, chandelier-lit chambers, a ruby red banqueting hall and a humble Romanesque chapel with some highly atmospheric frescoes.

Engadin Bad Scuol   SPA
(☑081 861 20 00; www.engadinbadscuol.ch; Stradun; adult/child Sfr25/16; ⊙8am-9.45pm Mon-Sun) Saunas, massage jets, waterfalls and whirlpools pummel you into relaxation at these thermal baths. Linger for a starlit soak in the snail-shaped outdoor pool by night. For full-on pampering, book a 2¼-hour Roman-Irish bath (Sfr66), combining different baths and massages, all done naked.

Engadin Adventure   ADVENTURE SPORTS
(☑081 861 14 19; www.engadin-adventure.ch) Tailors outdoor adventures that include half-day rafting trips (Sfr95) and knuckle-whitening single-track bike tours from Motta Naluns (Sfr69).

⌂ Sleeping & Eating

Scuol has a campsite, a youth hostel and several attractive hotels.

Hotel Engiadina   HISTORIC HOTEL $$
(☑081 864 14 21; www.engiadina-scuol.ch, in German; Rablüzza 152; d Sfr194-254; P) Each of the light-filled rooms is different at the Engiadina –some whitewashed, some vaulted, some with intricate timber ceilings. Best of all is the award-winning restaurant (mains Sfr25 to Sfr54), serving specialities like regional game and homemade peppermint *Pizokel* with Engadine mountain cheese.

Hotel Conrad   HOTEL $$
(☑081 864 17 17; www.conrad-scuol.ch; Rablüzza 158; d Sfr170-206, tr Sfr255-285, q Sfr340-380; ⊛) Nothing is too much trouble for Claudio and Claire Gianotti at this frescoed chalet, tucked down a cobbled lane in the Old Town. The bright, airy rooms feature plenty of pine and comfy beds.

⊕ Information

For info on outdoor activities in the region, nip into the **tourist office** (☑081 861 22 22; www .scuol.ch; Stradun; ⊙8am-6.30pm Mon-Fri, 9am-12.30pm & 1-5.30pm Sat, 9am-noon Sun, reduced hours between seasons) in the town centre.

⊕ Getting There & Away

The train from St Moritz (Sfr26, 1½ hours), with a change at Samedan, terminates at Scuol-Tarasp station. There are direct trains from Klosters (Sfr22, 45 minutes). From Scuol, the train to Guarda (Sfr7.20) takes 17 minutes. Postal buses from the station operate year-round to Tarasp (Sfr4, 15 minutes), Samnaun (Sfr20.20, 1¼ hours) and Austria (as far as Landeck).

SAMNAUN

POP 820 / ELEV 1377M

Sidling up to Austria in Switzerland's remote northeast corner is the duty-free town of Samnaun. Sights are few, but this makes a relaxed base for striking out into the surrounding wilderness. Part of the Silvretta Arena, Samnaun is great for cross-border skiing, with 235km of groomed pistes, some reached by the Twinliner, the world's first double-decker cable car. As in over-the-mountain Ischgl, snowboarders are in their element, especially at the Idjoch fun park. Hiking trails thread high into the Silvretta Alps in summer. Stay overnight and you'll receive an all-inclusive card entitling you to free use of the cable cars, buses and spa.

The central **tourist office** (☑081 868 58 58; www.samnaun.ch; Dorfstrasse 4; ⊙9am-6.30pm Mon-Fri, 9am-noon Sat, 1-5.30pm Sun) can provide information on activities and help arrange accommodation.

Postal buses run along the valley between Zernez and Müstair (Sfr20.20, one hour).

DON'T MISS

YOU BETTER WATCH OUT

For most of the year Samnaun is but a sleepy little town. Yet on the last weekend in November, it steals Lapland's reigns by staging **ClauWau** (www.clauwau.ch), aka the Santa Claus World Championships. Some 100 pseudo-Father Christmases gather to compete for the title of world's best Santa. The men in red prove their X-mas factor in disciplines like chimney climbing, gingerbread decorating, horse-drawn sleigh races and snow sculpting. It's an event full of Yuletide cheer and ho-ho-ho-ing overkill.

Snug against the forest and ski slopes, chalet-style **Hotel Aurora** (☑081 868 51 31; www.aurora-samnaun.ch; Waldweg 3; d Sfr180-196; P@) has pleasantly bright rooms with hardwood floors and balconies, and a tiny spa.

MÜSTAIR
POP 770 / ELEV 1375M

Squirreled away in a remote corner of Switzerland, just before the Italian border, Müstair is one of Europe's early Christian treasures and a Unesco World Heritage Site. When Charlemagne supposedly founded a monastery and a church here in the 8th century, this was a strategically placed spot below the Ofen Pass, separating northern Europe from Italy and the heart of Christendom.

For information on lodgings along the Val Müstair, check with the village **tourist office** (☑081 858 50 00; www.val-muestair.ch; ⊙9am-6pm Mon-Fri, 1.30-6pm Sat & Sun).

Vibrant Carolingian (9th century) and Romanesque (12th century) frescos smother the interior of the church of Benedictine **Kloster St Johann** (St John's Convent; www.muestair.ch; admission free; ⊙7am-8pm May-Oct & 7am-5pm Nov-Apr). Beneath Carolingian representations of Christ in Glory in the apses are Romanesque stories depicting the grisly ends of St Peter (crucified), St Paul (decapitated) and St Steven (stoned). Above all reign images of Christ in Heavenly Majesty. Next door, the **museum** (adult/child Sfr12/6; ⊙9am-noon & 1.30-5pm Mon-Sat, 1.30-5pm Sun) takes you through part of the monastery complex, with Carolingian art and other relics.

ZERNEZ
POP 1100 / ELEV 1474M

One of the main gateways to the Swiss National Park, Zernez is an attractive cluster of stone chalets, outlined by the profile of its baroque church and the stout medieval tower of its castle, Schloss Wildenberg.

The village is home to the hands-on **Swiss National Park Centre** (☑081 851 41 41; www.nationalpark.ch; adult/child Sfr7/3; ⊙8.30am-6pm Jun-Oct, 9am-noon & 2-5pm Nov-May), where an audioguide gives you the low-down on conservation, wildlife and environmental change. The tourist office here can provide details on hikes in the park, including the three-hour trudge from S-chanf to Alp Trupchun (which is particularly popular in autumn, when you might spy rutting deer) and the Naturlehrpfad circuit near Il Fuorn, where bearded vultures can often be sighted.

🛏 Sleeping & Eating

Hotel Bär & Post   HOTEL $$
(☑081 851 55 00; www.baer-post.ch; Zernez; dm Sfr19, s Sfr87-115, d Sfr140-220) Welcoming all-comers since 1905, these central digs have inviting rooms with lots of stone pine and downy duvets, plus basic bunk rooms. There's also a sauna and a rustic restaurant (mains Sfr15 to Sfr43), dishing up good steaks and pasta.

Il Fuorn   GUESTHOUSE $$
(☑081 856 12 26; www.ilfuorn.ch; Il Fuorn; s/d/tr/q Sfr95/150/195/220; ⊙mid-Jun–Oct) Bang in the heart of the national park, this guesthouse shelters light, comfy rooms with pine furnishings. Fresh trout and game are big on the restaurant menu.

Chasa Veglia   GUESTHOUSE $$
(☑081 284 48 68, www.chasa-veglia.ch; Runatsch; s Sfr85-90, d Sfr160-180) Step through the heavy arched door and back a few centuries at this lovingly restored 300-year-old house. Warm stone and hunting trophies are in keeping with the history of the place, as are the rooms done out in pine.

❶ Getting There & Away

Trains run regularly from Zernez to St Moritz (Sfr18, 50 minutes), stopping at S-chanf, Zuoz and Celerina. For the latter and St Moritz, change at Samedan.

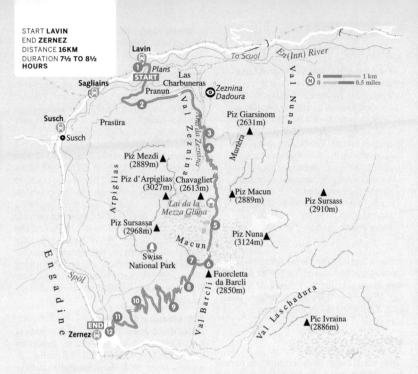

START **LAVIN**
END **ZERNEZ**
DISTANCE **16KM**
DURATION **7½ TO 8½ HOURS**

Walking Tour
Lakes of Macun

This highly rewarding day walk leads from the main valley of the Engadine into the lakeland of the Macun Basin. The tourist office's 1:50,000 *Wanderkarte Scuol* (Sfr16) is a decent map. Hourly trains operate between Zernez and Lavin (Sfr5.80, 15 minutes).

From the village of ① **Lavin**, cross the Inn River on a wooden bridge. Head along a gravelled lane, then left on a track twisting up eastward through forest to ② **Plan Surücha** (1577m). The trail veers gradually southward to cross the Aua da Zeznina. The 2889m Piz Macun and 2850m Fuorcletta da Barcli slide into view as you approach ③ **Alp Zeznina Dadaint** (1958m) around two hours from Lavin. Scenes from Heidi were shot at this idyllic Alpine spot.

Make your way into the ④ **Val Zeznina**, negotiating steep switchbacks through rhododendron-flecked meadows. The gradient eases as you rise to a rustic shelter built against cliffs beside a tarn. Cross the streamlet and continue along its rocky western banks to enter the national park. The upper valley opens into the basin of ⑤ **Macun**, 1½

to two hours from Alp Zeznina Dadaint. Like a natural amphitheatre, the cirque is ringed by craggy, 3000m peaks and sprinkled with almost two dozen Alpine lakes and tarns.

Cross the stream and follow the white-red-white markings southward up sparsely vegetated ridges of glacial debris. Ascend steep slopes of loose rock to ⑥ **Fuorcletta da Barcli**, a gap in the range at 2850m. From here traverse west along an exposed ridgetop to reach a minor peak at 2945m, one to 1½ hours from Macun. The ⑦ **lookout** commands top-of-the-world views.

Trace a prominent spur running southwest directly from the summit, then drop away rightward out of the national park. The route descends through rows of avalanche grids on the open slopes of ⑧ **Munt Baselgia** to meet an Alpine track at ⑨ **Plan Sech** (2268m). Make a long serpentine descent into the coniferous forest via ⑩ **La Rosta** and ⑪ **God Baselgia**. The final stretch leads out onto grassy fields just above the town, then down to arrive in ⑫ **Zernez** after 2½ to three hours.

Oberengadin

Just as the Unterengadin is loaded with rural charm, the Oberengadin (Upper Engadine) is charged with skiing adrenalin. St Moritz, possibly the slickest resort of the lot in Switzerland, is joined by a string of other piste-pounding hotspots along the Oberengadin Valley and nearby Pontresina.

ZUOZ

POP 1300 / ELEV 1750M

Zuoz, 13km southwest of Zernez, is a quintessential Engadine town, with colourful sgraffito houses, flower boxes bursting with geraniums and Augusto Giacometti stained-glass windows illuminating the church chancel. Though skiing is fairly limited, Zuoz is unquestionably one of the Oberengadin's prettiest towns and makes a fantastic base for hiking or cycling in the Swiss National Park.

Overlooking the central plaza is Hotel Crusch Alva (☑081 854 13 19; www.hotelcrusch alva.ch; Via Maistra 26; s/d Sfr150/220; ☺closed Nov & May). The 12 rooms in this beautiful 500-year-old Engadine house are full of timber-flavoured rustic charm. Savour fondue or fish in the little *Stüva* (parlour) on the 1st floor.

Design trailblazer Castell (☑081 851 52 53; www.hotelcastell.ch; Via Castell 300; d/ste Sfr340/505; Ⓟ☎⛟) gets rave reviews for its rural-meets-minimalist interiors. Some of Europe's leading architects have pooled their creativity to transform this turn-of-the-century hotel, which now boasts art-slung spaces, chic and colourful rooms and a restaurant serving seasonally inspired cuisine. Unwind with a steam or a soapy massage in the hammam. The hotel has family appeal, too, with its kindergarten, children's meal times and own ice rink.

There are trains at least hourly between Zuoz and St Moritz (Sfr9.80, 30 minutes).

CELERINA

Hugging the banks of the Inn River, sunny Celerina is a 45-minute amble northeast of St Moritz and shares the same ski slopes. It's often mentioned in the same breath as its 1.6km Olympic bob run (☑081 830 02 00; www.olympia-bobrun.ch), which is the world's oldest – dating to 1904 – and made from natural ice. A hair-raising 135km/h 'taxi ride' trip costs a cool Sfr250, but the buzz is priceless. Equally heart-stopping is the head-first 1km Cresta Run (www

.cresta-run.com), created by British tourists in 1885, which starts near the Schiefer Turm in St Moritz. A set of five rides including tuition costs Sfr600 (and Sfr50 a ride thereafter).

The tourist office (☑081 830 00 11; www .celerina.ch; cnr Via Maistra & Via da la Staziun; ☺8.30am-6pm Mon-Fri, 9am-noon & 2-6pm Sat, plus 4-6pm Sun high season) is in the village centre.

Hotel Cresta Run (☑081 833 09 19; www .hotel-cresta-run.ch; Via Maistra; d/tr/q Sfr180/ 225/280; Ⓟ) is on a minor road linking Celerina and St Moritz, about 500m south of Celerina's town centre. It's a simple family hotel, with its own pizzeria, located by the finish of the Cresta bob run.

Celerina is easily reached from St Moritz by train (Sfr3, five minutes).

St Moritz

POP 5200 / ELEV 1856M

Switzerland's original winter wonderland and the cradle of Alpine tourism, St Moritz (San Murezzan in Romansch) has been luring royals, celebrities and moneyed wannabes since 1864. With its shimmering aquamarine lake, emerald forests and aloof mountains, the town looks a million dollars.

Yet despite the string of big-name designer boutiques on Via Serlas and celebs bashing the pistes (Kate Moss and George Clooney included), this resort isn't all show. The real riches lie outdoors with superb carving on Corviglia, hairy black runs on Diavolezza and miles of hiking trails when the snow melts.

◉ Sights

Segantini Museum ART MUSEUM
(www.segantini-museum.ch; Via Somplaz 30; adult/ child Sfr10/3; ☺10am-noon & 2-6pm Tue-Sun, closed May & Nov) Housed in an eye-catching stone building topped by a cupola, this museum shows the paintings of Giovanni Segantini (1858–99). The Italian artist beautifully captured the dramatic light and ambience of the Alps on canvas.

Engadiner Museum MUSEUM
(www.engadiner-museum.ch; Via dal Bagn 39; adult/child Sfr8/3; ☺10am-noon & 2-5pm Sun-Fri, closed May & Nov) For a peek at the archetypal dwellings and humble interiors of the Engadine Valley, visit this museum showing traditional stoves and archaeological finds.

St Moritz

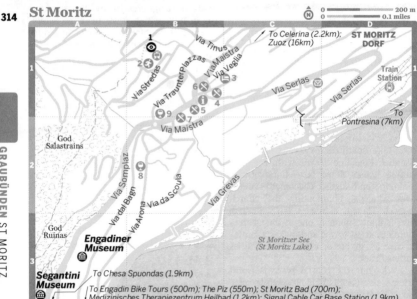

St Moritz

🏃 Activities

Winter Activities

With 350km of slopes, ultramodern lifts and spirit-soaring views, skiing in St Moritz is second to none, especially for confident intermediates. For groomed slopes with big mountain vistas, head to **Corviglia** (2486m), accessible by funicular from Dorf. From Bad a cable car goes to **Signal** (shorter queues), giving access to the slopes of Piz Nair. There's varied skiing at **Corvatsch** (3303m), above nearby Silvaplana, including spectacular glacier descents and the gentle black run Hahnensee. Silhouetted by glaciated four-thousanders, **Diavolezza** (2978m)

is a must-ski for freeriders and fans of jaw-dropping descents. A general ski pass that covers all the slopes, including Silvaplana, Sils-Maria, Celerina, Zuoz, Pontresina and Diavolezza, costs Sfr410/137 for adults/children for seven days in high season. Visit the website www.engadin .stmoritz.ch for the low-down on skiing facilities and services.

Skiing or snowboarding group tuition (adult/child Sfr85/55 per day) can be arranged at the **Schweizer Skischule** (☎081 830 01 01; www.skischool.ch; Via Stredas 14; ☺8am-noon & 2-6pm Mon-Sat, 8-9am & 4-6pm Sun).

If cross-country skiing is more your scene, you can glide across sunny plains and through snowy woods on 180km of groomed trails. A day/week pass costs Sfr8/25.

Summer Activities

In summer, get out and stride one of the region's excellent hiking trails, such as the Corvatsch *Wasserweg* (water trail) linking six mountain lakes. Soaring above St Moritz, **Piz Nair** (3057m) commands views of the jewel-coloured lakes that necklace the valley below. For head-spinning views of the Pers glacier and the Bernina Alps, tackle the vertiginous, 2½-hour **Piz Trovat** *via ferrata* at Diavolezza; equipment rental is available at the base station. The tourist office has a map providing more suggestions (in English) for walking in Oberengadin.

🏞️ **Clean Energy Tour**   HIKING
(www.clean-energy.ch, in German) Beginning at Piz Nair, this eco-friendly 2½-hour hike presents different kinds of renewable energy in natural settings. You'll hike down from Chantarella along the flower-speckled Heidi Blumenweg, then Schellenursliweg past Lord Norman Foster's eco-sound, wood-tiled **Chesa Futura**.

Medizinisches Therapiezentrum Heilbad   SPA
(☎081 833 30 62; www.heilbad-stmoritz.ch; Plazza Paracelsus 2; admission to mineral baths Sfr35; ⏰8am-7pm Mon-Fri, 8am-12.30pm Sat) After exerting yourself on the slopes, rest in a mineral bath or with an Alpine herb pack here.

⭐ Festivals & Events

St Moritz hosts the notoriously gruelling **Engadine Ski Marathon** (www.engadin-ski marathon.ch) in early March, where cross-country skiers skate 42km from Maloja to S-chanf. The frozen lake is the centre of attention again in late January for the **Cartier Polo World Cup on Snow** (www .polostmoritz.com) and in early February for the **WhiteTurf** (www.whiteturf.ch) winter horse races.

🛏️ Sleeping

Many hotels throw in free mountain transport when you stay more than two nights in summer, when you can expect rates to drop up to 30%. St Moritz virtually shuts down in the shoulder seasons.

The Piz   B&B $$
(☎081 832 11 11; Via dal Bagn 6; www.piz-stmoritz .ch, in German; s/d/apt Sfr120/210/500; 📶) Splashes of crimson, hardwood floors and clean lines define this contemporary B&B in St Moritz Bad. Fitted with rain showers and flat-screen TVs, the rooms are sleek and comfy, though street noise may disturb light sleepers.

Chesa Spuondas   FAMILY HOTEL $$
(☎081 833 65 88; www.chesaspuondas.ch; r incl half board Sfr202-282; 🅿️@) This family hotel nestles amid lush meadows at the foot of forest and mountains. Rooms are in keeping with the Jugendstil villa, with high ceilings, parquet floors and the odd antique. Kids are the centre of attention here, with dedicated meal times, activities, play areas and the children's ski school a 10-minute walk away. Bus 1 from St Moritz stops nearby.

Hotel Eden   HOTEL $$
(☎081 830 81 00; www.edenstmoritz.ch; Via Veglia 12; s Sfr159-186, d Sfr266-314; 🅿️📶) Right in the heart of town, the Eden centres on an attractive central atrium and antique-strewn lounge where a fire crackles in winter. The old-style, pine-panelled rooms are cosy and those on the top floor afford terrific lake and mountain views.

DON'T MISS

ON YOUR BIKE

The St Moritz region is exhilarating biking terrain, criss-crossed by 400km of trails. One of the finest routes is the five-hour **Suvretta Loop** at Corviglia, taking in forests and meadows en route to the Suvretta Pass (2615m), before making a spectacular descent to Bever. You can rent bikes, e-bikes and children's bikes for Sfr29/50/24 per day from **Engadin Bikes** (Via dal Bagn 1; ⏰8.30am-12.30pm & 1.30-6.30pm Mon-Fri, to 5.30pm Sat).

Single-track fans can book guided rides with **Engadin Bike Tours** (☎081 837 53 56 www.engadinbiketours.ch), which leave at 9.30am daily (except on Tuesdays) from Celerina base station. Among the most scenic are the Suvretta Loop and the Via Engiadina (both Sfr50). The latter affords tremendous views of the lakes in the valley on a round circuit to Maloja via Sils and back.

Jugendherberge St Moritz HOSTEL $
(☎081 836 61 11; Via Surpunt 60; www.youthhostel
.ch/st.moritz; dm/d Sfr59/146; ᴘ🛇) On the edge
of the forest, this hostel has clean, quiet four-
bed dorms and doubles. There's a kiosk, children's toy room, bike hire and laundrette. Bus
9 stops in front of the hostel in high season.

✕ Eating

ᵀᴼᴾ
CHOICE Chesa Veglia ITALIAN $$$
(☎081 837 28 00; Via Veglia 2; pizza Sfr22-36,
mains Sfr40-70, ☺Mon-Sun Dec-Mar & Jul-Sep)
This slate-roofed, chalk-white chalet is St
Moritz' oldest restaurant, dating from 1658.
The softly lit interior is all warm pine and
creaking wood floors, while the terrace
affords lake and mountain views. The wood-
oven pizzas are a good pick, as are regional
specialities like *Bündner Gerstensuppe*
(creamy barley soup) and venison medallions
with *Spätzli* (egg noodles).

Mathis Brasserie SWISS $$
(☎081 833 63 55; www.mathisfood.ch; Corviglia;
mains Sfr22.50-36.50; ☺Mon-Sun) Swiss celebrity chef Reto Mathis has seriously upped
the ante in slopeside dining. Spectacularly
perched at 2486m, this panoramic brasserie
is the most casual of his culinary ventures.
Enjoy wide-screen mountain views over
fresh pasta, rösti or polenta with venison
sausage. See the website for details on
cookery courses.

⯐Hatecke CAFE $
(Via Maistra 16; snacks & mains Sfr15-25; ☺9am-
6.30pm Mon-Fri, 9am-6pm Sat) Organic, locally sourced *Bündnerfleisch* and melt-in-
your-mouth venison ham are carved into
wafer-thin slices on a century-old slicing
machine in this speciality shop. Take a seat
on a sheepskin stool in the cafe next door to
lunch on delicious Engadine beef carpaccio
or *Bündnerfleisch* with truffle oil.

Posthaus FUSION $$
(☎081 838 00 00; www.posthaus.ch; Via dal Vout
3; lunch Sfr11.50-16.50, mains Sfr35-60; ☺7.30am-
10.30pm Mon-Sun) Chunky tree-trunk tables
and stag antlers festoon this new rustic-chic
lounge bar and restaurant. It's a laid-back,
architecturally striking place for a succulent
Argentine beef steak, lunchtime bowl of
pasta, or cocktails by candlelight.

Hanselmann CAFE $
(Via Maistra 8; pastries & cakes Sfr3-6; ☺7.30am-
7pm Mon-Sun) You can't miss the lavishly fres-
coed facade of St Moritz' celebrated bakery
and tea room, famous for its caramel-rich,
walnut-studded Engadine nut tart.

☕ Drinking

Around 20 bars and clubs pulsate in winter.
DJs, slinky lounge bars and relaxed cafes
attract post-slope partygoers to Plazza dal
Mulin.

Bobby's Pub PUB
(Via dal Bagn 50a; ☺9.30am-1.30am) This
friendly English-style watering hole serves
30 different brews and attracts young
snowboarders in season. It's among the
few places open year-round.

Roo Bar BAR
(Via Trauter Plazzas 7; ☺2-10pm Dec-Apr) Snow
bums fill the terrace of this après-ski joint
at Hauser's Hotel. Hip hop, techno and hot
chocolate laced with rum fuel the party.

ℹ Information

Uphill from the lakeside train station on Via
Serlas is the post office and five minutes further
on is the **tourist office** (☎081 837 33 33; www
.stmoritz.ch; Via Maistra 12; ☺9am-6.30pm
Mon-Fri, 9am-12.30pm & 1.30-6.30pm Sat,
4-6pm Sun, shorter hours rest of year).
Audioguide city tours are available for Sfr10.

ℹ Getting There & Away

St Moritz Bad is about 2km southwest of the
main town, St Moritz Dorf. Local buses and
postal buses shuttle between the two.

The **Glacier Express** (www.glacierexpress
.ch) runs St Moritz to Zermatt (adult/child
Sfr136/68) via the 2033m Oberalp Pass. The
majestic route takes 7½ hours to cover the
290km and crosses 291 bridges. Seat
reservation costs an additional Sfr33 in summer
and Sfr13 in winter.

Regular trains, as many as one every 30
minutes, run from Zürich to St Moritz (Sfr70, 3½
hours) with one change (at Landquart or Chur).

Postal buses run frequently in high season
from St Moritz southwest to Maloja (Sfr10.40,
40 minutes) with stops at Silvaplana (Sfr4.20, 20
minutes) and Sils-Maria (Sfr7.20, 30 minutes).

Silvaplana

With two startlingly turquoise, wind-buffeted
lakes framed by densely forested slopes,
Silvaplana (Silvaplauna in Romansch),
7.5km southwest of St Moritz, is a kitesurfing
and windsurfing mecca. Slip into a wetsuit

at **Sportzentrum Mulets** (☎081 828 97 67; www.kitesailing.ch; Silvaplana; intro/2-day/5-day course Sfr190/300/750; ☺10am-6pm), offering instruction and equipment rental. Four-hour introductory lessons take place on Thursdays from June to September.

A virtual ode to surfing, **Julier Palace** (☎081 828 96 44; www.julierpalace.com; Via Maistra 6, Silvaplana; r per person Sfr90-150; @) has a party vibe, chill-out lounge and free internet. The retro-style rooms stretch from bare-bones noisy ones with futons to larger deluxe pads with snazzy paint jobs. The restaurant rolls out decent pizza and pasta dishes.

Sils-Maria

Another 4km brings you to Sils-Maria (Segl in Romansch), a chocolate-box village of pastel-painted, slate-roofed chalets set against a dramatic backdrop of rugged, glacier-capped mountains. A cable car ascends to Furtschellas (2312m), where there is a network of hiking trails and ski slopes.

Sils might be a sleepy lakeside village now, but the rumble of existential philosophy once reverberated around these peaks, courtesy of Friedrich Nietzsche who spent his summers here from 1881 to 1888 writing texts concerning the travails of modern man, including *Thus Spake Zarathustra*. Housed in a geranium-bedecked chalet, the **Nietzsche Haus** (☎081 826 53 69; www.nietzschehaus.ch; adult/child Sfr8/free; ☺3-6pm Tue-Sun) was the summer retreat of the legendary German philosopher. The little museum contains a collection of photos, memorabilia and letters.

If you want to overnight in Sils, a terrific choice is family-run **Pensiun Privata** (☎081 832 62 00; www.pensiunprivata.ch; s Sfr170-210, d Sfr280-420; ☎), a dreamy country-style hotel with huge pine-clad rooms, antique-style furniture and forest views from the herb and flower garden. For five-star grandeur, try the palatial **Hotel Waldhaus** (☎081 838 51 00; www.waldhaus-sils.ch; s/d with half-board Sfr455/890; P☎⊞⊞), set on a rise amid the woods. Along with modern comforts (pool, Turkish baths, tennis courts), the owners have retained the opulence of the 1908 building. It's a great family choice with its connecting rooms, childcare, and activities and menus geared towards kids.

Hole-in-the-wall **Bar Gaia** (snacks Sfr9.50-17.50; ☺11am-9pm Mon-Sun) serves delicious organic snacks in colourful, art-strewn surrounds. The savoury crêpes (try them with local mountain cheese), salads and homemade ice cream are terrific. Otherwise, head across to **Chesa Marchetta** (cakes Sfr5-6; ☺3.30-11pm Mon-Sun), where you can sample delicious Engadine nut tart under the beams. The little shop at the front sells preserves made with home-grown fruit.

Maloja

The road from Sils follows the north shore of its lake to the pretty one-street village of **Maloja** and, shortly after, the **Maloja Pass**, which separates the Engadine from the Val Bregaglia. The artist Giovanni Segantini lived in the village from 1894. His **studio** (atelier; adult/child Sfr3/1.50; ☺3-5pm Wed & Sun) can be visited. Paintings are also on display

VAL FEX

Silence blankets the remote Val Fex, a car-free valley tucked away in the Upper Engadine. Life here is that bit closer to nature, with high pastures flecked with wildflowers in summer and streaked gold with larch forests in autumn, and a shimmering glacier crowning a host of rocky peaks. Nietzsche, Thomas Mann and Marc Chagall were among the greats who found the space and peace here to think and dream.

Reaching the valley is an experience in itself, whether you hike (around 2½ hours from Sils-Maria) or arrive by horse-drawn carriage. For the latter, head to Hotel Maria, where carriages depart for Val Fex at 9.50am, 10.45am, noon, 2.10pm and 3.10pm. The scenic journey costs Sfr10/20 one way/return to Fex-Platta, Sfr15/25 to Fex-Cresta and Sfr20/30 to Hotel Fex.

If you fancy staying overnight, check into the grand 19th-century **Hotel Fex** (☎081 832 60 00; www.hotelfex.ch; d incl half-board Sfr310), a mountain retreat with snug pine-clad rooms and sensational views.

in the **Belvedere Tower** (admission free; ☺9am-5pm Mon-Sun). There are a handful of places to stay and eat.

BERNINA PASS ROAD

Bare, brooding mountains and glaciers that sweep down to farmland give the landscape around the Bernina Pass (2323m; Passo del Bernina in Italian) austere grandeur. The road twists spectacularly from Celerina southeast to Tirano in Italy, linking Val Bernina and Val Poschiavo. There is some great hiking in these heights, shown in detail on walking maps available from Pontresina tourist office.

From St Moritz, as many as 10 trains run via Pontresina (Sfr5, 10 minutes) direct to Tirano (Sfr33, 2½ hours) in northern Italy. This stretch of track, known as the **Bernina Line** (www.rhb-Unesco.ch), was added to the Unesco World Heritage list in 2008 along with the Albula Pass (p295). Constructed in 1910, it is one of the world's steepest narrow-gauge railways, negotiating the highest rail crossing in Europe and taking in spectacular glaciers, gorges and rock pinnacles.

Pontresina & Around

POP 2000 / ELEV 1800M

At the mouth of the Val Bernina and licked by the ice-white tongue of Morteratsch Glacier, Pontresina is a low-key alternative to St Moritz. Check out the pentagonal Moorish tower and the Santa Maria Chapel, with frescos dating from the 13th and 15th centuries.

Pontresina's own mountain, **Piz Languard** (3262m), is well suited to families and novice skiers. Use the resort as a base to explore slopes further down the valley at **Piz Lagalb** (2959m) and **Diavolezza** (2973m), with its phenomenal 10km glacier descent. In summer, it's worth taking the cable cars to either for views. The walk from Diavolezza to Morteratsch affords

MOVING ON?

For tips, recommendations and reviews, head to http://shop.lonelyplanet.com to purchase a downloadable PDF of the Italy or Austria chapters from Lonely Planet's *Western Europe* guide.

striking glacier close-ups. For ski pass prices, see p314.

Pontresina's dramatic cliffs and glaciated summits create a backdrop for other vigorous pursuits too. **GoVertical** (☏081 834 57 58; www.govertical.ch; Chesa Curtinatsch) covers the entire adventure spectrum from rock climbing and canyoning in summer to freeriding and snowshoeing in winter. Call ahead for times and prices. The **Bergsteigerschule Pontresina** (☏081 842 82 82 Via Maistra 163) is the go-to place for high-alpine tours, climbs and guided hikes to Diavolezza's crevassed Pers glacier (Sfr60).

🛏 Sleeping

Hotel Albris HOTEL $$
(☏081 838 80 40; www.albris.ch; Via Maistra; s/d Sfr160/290; 🅿@) On Pontresina's main drag, Albris has supremely cosy rooms done out in Swiss stone pine, and a feng shui-inspired spa with a mountain-facing relaxation room. Cots are available free of charge. The restaurant is famous for its market-fresh fish and the bakery for its Engadine nut tart.

Pension Hauser GUESTHOUSE $$
(☏081 842 63 26; www.hotelpension-hauser.ch; Cruscheda 165; s/d 85/170; 🅿) Quiet and welcoming, this century-old Engadine house has pine-clad rooms that overlook Pontresina's rooftops. You'll find solid home cooking and possibly accordion-playing locals in the restaurant.

❶ Information

From the train station, west of the village, cross the two rivers, Rosegg and Bernina, for the centre and the **tourist office** (☏081 838 83 00; www.pontresina.ch; Rondo Bldg, Via Maistra; ☺8.30am-6pm Mon-Fri, 8.30am-noon & 3-6pm Sat & 3-6pm Sun, closed Sun mid-Oct–mid-Dec).

Val Poschiavo

Once over the **Bernina Pass** (2328m), you drop into the sunny Italian-speaking Val Poschiavo. A fine lookout is Alp Grüm (2091m), reached on foot (2½ hours) from Ospizio Bernina restaurant at the pass. The hike takes you through wildflower-cloaked pastures and affords crisp views of turquoise Lago Bianco and the Palü Glacier.

Fourteen kilometres south of the pass lies **Poschiavo**, 15km from the border with Italy. At its heart is Plazza da Cumün, framed by pastel-hued townhouses and pavement cafes. Right on the square, **Hotel Albrici** (☏081 844 01 73; www.hotelalbrici.ch; Plazza da Cumün; s Sfr85-120, Sfr150-180; P) is a 17th-century lodging whose spacious rooms have polished-timber floors, antique furniture and plenty of charm. Sit on the restaurant terrace to munch crisp wood-fired pizza.

You could pop down from St Moritz one day for a change of speed. Just past the glittering **Lago di Poschiavo**, the town of **Brusio** is known for its distinctive circular train viaduct. Another 5km and you reach **Tirano**, just over the Italian border.

For hiking tips and details on the valley's accommodation, visit www.valposchiavo.ch.

Val Bregaglia

From the Maloja Pass (1815m), the road corkscrews down into the Val Bregaglia (Bergell in German), a wildly beautiful valley of horn-shaped granite peaks, chestnut forests and stone villages crowned by Italianate churches. The road then splits, with one arm leading north and back into Switzerland via the Splügen Pass, and the other going south to Lago di Como and on to Milan. The postal bus from St Moritz to Lugano branches off from the Milan road to circle the western shore of the lake.

As you proceed down the valley, the villages reveal an increasing Italian influence. **Stampa** was the home of the artist Alberto Giacometti (1901–66), and is the location of the valley's **tourist office** (☏081 822 15 55; www.bregaglia.ch; ☉9-11.30am & 2-5.30pm Mon-Fri). Look out for the medieval ruins of **Castelmur** castle nearby.

Soglio (1090m), a hamlet near the Italian border, faces the smooth-sided Pizzo Badile (3308m) on a south-facing ledge, reached from the valley floor by a narrow road. The village, a warren of lanes and stone houses, lies at the end of a steep, thickly wooded trail off the main road and is the starting point for hiking trails, most notably the historic 11km **La Panoramica** route to Casaccia down in the valley.

There are several modest guesthouses in Soglio alongside the dazzling white four-storey **Palazzo Salis** (☏081 822 12 08; www .palazzosalis.ch; Soglio; s Sfr100, d Sfr200-300; ☉early Mar-late Nov), a truly regal resting place with portraits gracing the walls, coats of armour and ornate furniture. Built in 1630, it has rooms with stucco or wooden ceilings and centuries-old antique furniture. Its vaulted restaurant (mains Sfr20 to Sfr35) has an open fire and there are mature gardens shaded by giant sequoias.

Buses from St Moritz to Castasegna travel along Val Bregaglia. Alight at the post office at Promontogno and take the bus to Soglio from there (Sfr3.40, six to 10 departures daily, 12 minutes).

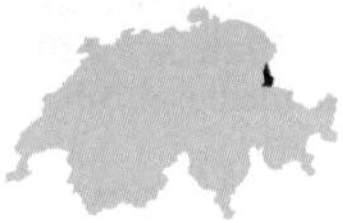

Liechtenstein

POP 36,281 / AREA 160 SQ KM / LANGUAGE GERMAN

Best Places to Eat

» Torkel (p324)

» Hotel Schatzmann (p325)

» Adler Vaduz (p324)

Best Places to Stay

» Parkhotel Sonnenhof (p323)

» Hotel Gorfion (p326)

» Gasthof Löwen (p324)

Why Go?

If Liechtenstein didn't exist, someone would have invented it. A tiny mountain principality governed by an iron-willed monarch in the heart of 21st-century Europe, it certainly has novelty value. Only 25km long by 12km wide (at its broadest point) – just larger than Manhattan – Liechtenstein doesn't have an international airport, and access from Switzerland is by local bus. However, the country is a rich banking state and, we are told, the world's largest exporter of false teeth.

Most blaze through Liechtenstein en route to Switzerland, stopping only for snapshots of the castle and a souvenir passport stamp. That's a shame, as the country has an overwhelming amount of natural beauty for its size. Strike out into the Alpine wilderness beyond Vaduz and, suddenly, this landlocked sliver of a micro-nation no longer seems *quite* so small.

When to Go

Slow travel is the word at cycle-happy Slow Up Liechtenstein in May. The country strums to Guitar Days in July and celebrates National Day with fireworks on 15 August. Come in summer for high-alpine hiking and cycling along the Rhine. Downhill and cross-country skiers glide along Malbun's twinkling slopes in winter. Wildflowers bring a burst of spring colour, while golden autumn days are a fine time to sample new wine and game in Liechtenstein's top restaurants.

0 ____ 5 km
0 ____ 3 miles

To St Gallen (40km)
To Bregenz (32km);
Lake Constance (32km)

Feldkirch
Sennwald○ ○Hinterschellenberg
Ruggell○ Schellenberg
  ○Tisis
Haag○ ○Mauren
N16 ○Eschen ○Schaanwald
Bendern○ ○Nendeln AUSTRIA
A13 Planken○
Rhine Three Sisters
  (Drei Schwestern)
Buchs○ ○Schaan ▲(2052m)
  ⑤Fürstensteig
  ⑥①
Vaduz○ ○Gaflei
⑦
Sevelen○ ○Silum
  ④Triesenberg
  Steg
  ③
  ○Triesen Malbun
Trübbach○ ▲Camping
  Mittagspitze
  ○Balzers
○Sargans
A3 Grauspitz
  (2599m)
SWITZERLAND

Liechtenstein Highlights

❶ Hike up to perkily turreted **Schloss Vaduz** (p322) for postcard views of the Alps and Vaduz

❷ Pedal along the sprightly Rhine and over to Switzerland and Austria on the **Drei Länder Tour** (p325)

❸ Strap on walking boots or skis and head to the slopes of family-focused **Malbun** (p325)

❹ Delve into the deeply rural world of the Walser community in **Triesenberg** (p324)

❺ Play among the peaks on the vertiginous **Fürstensteig** (p325), Liechtenstein's flagship walk

❻ Eat like a king (or at the very least a prince) at **Torkel** (p324) above the royal vineyards

❼ Ponder the idiosyncrasies of this curious little land at **Liechtensteinisches Landesmuseum** (p322)

History

Austrian prince Johann Adam Von Liechtenstein purchased the counties of Schellenberg (1699) and Vaduz (1712) from impoverished German nobles and gave them his name. Long a principality under the Holy Roman Empire, Liechtenstein gained independence in 1866. In 1923, it formed a customs union with Switzerland.

Even then, none of the ruling Liechtensteins had bothered to leave their Viennese palace to see their acquisitions. It wasn't until 1938, in the wake of the Anschluss (Nazi Germany's takeover of Austria) that Prince Franz Josef II became the first monarch to live in the principality, when he and his much-loved wife, Gina, began transforming a poor rural nation into today's rich banking state. Their son, Prince Hans Adam II, ascended the throne on the prince's death in 1989.

The Liechtenstein clan lost considerable territories and possessions (including various castles and palaces) in Poland and the then Czechoslovakia after WWII, when the authorities of those countries seized them. The family has been trying, unsuccessfully, to recover these possessions in international courts ever since.

The country's use of the Swiss franc encourages people to see it as a mere extension of its neighbour, but Liechtenstein has very different foreign policies, having joined the UN and the European Economic Area (EEA) relatively early, in 1990 and 1995 respectively.

Known as a tax haven, the principality banned customers from banking money anonymously in 2000. However, it remains under pressure (mainly from the European Union) to introduce more reforms.

In 2003, Hans Adam won sweeping powers to dismiss the elected government, appoint judges and reject proposed laws. The following year, he handed the day-to-day running of the country to his son Alois.

ⓘ Information

For general information on the country, have a look at www.liechtenstein.li. For more tourism-related information, check out www.tourismus.li. Liechtenstein's international phone prefix is 📞423.

Prices are comparable with those found in Switzerland. Shops usually open 8am till noon and 1.30pm to 6.30pm Monday to Friday, and 8am to 4pm Saturday, although souvenir shops also open on high-season Sundays. Banks open from 8am till noon and 1.30pm to 4.30pm, Monday to Friday. Swiss currency is used.

Devoutly Catholic, Liechtenstein takes off all the main religious feast days, plus Labour Day (1 May) and National Day (August 15), totalling a healthy 22 public holidays annually.

The official language is German, although most speak an Alemannic dialect. The Austrian 'Grüss Gott' is as common as the Swiss 'Grüezi'. English is widely spoken.

ⓘ Getting There & Away

The nearest airports are Friedrichshafen (Germany) and Zürich, with train connections to the Swiss border towns of Buchs and Sargans. From each of these towns there are frequent buses to Vaduz (Sfr3.40/5.80 from Buchs/ Sargans, Swiss Pass valid). Buses run every 30 minutes from the Austrian border town of Feldkirch; you sometimes have to change at Schaan to reach Vaduz.

A few Buchs-Feldkirch trains stop at Schaan (bus tickets are valid).

By road, the A16 from Switzerland passes through Liechtenstein via Schaan and ends at Feldkirch. The N13 follows the Rhine along the border; minor roads cross into Liechtenstein at each freeway exit.

ⓘ Getting Around

Buses traverse the country. Single fares (buy tickets on the bus) are Sfr2.40/3.40/4.60 for one/two/three zones, while a weekly bus pass costs Sfr15/18/21. The latter is available from post offices and tourist offices. Swiss travel passes are valid on all main routes. Timetables are posted at stops.

For bicycle hire, try the Swiss train stations in Buchs or Sargans, the tourist office in Vaduz, or **Sigi's Velo Shop** (☑384 27 50; www.sigis

---

THE INSIDE READ

Liechtenstein sounds quite wacky but it is really like a small village where everyone knows everyone else's business. Liechtensteiners are warm-hearted folk who know what's important in life, as you soon realise reading Charlie Connelly's amusing *Stamping Grounds: Liechtenstein's Quest for the World Cup,* possibly the longest and most engrossing read ever about Liechtenstein.

In fact, the more you read about Fürstentum Liechtenstein (FL) the easier it is to see it as the model for Ruritania – the mythical kingdom conjured up in fiction as diverse as The *Prisoner of Zenda* and Evelyn Waugh's *Vile Bodies.*

-veloshop.li; Balzers; per day from Sfr35; ⊙8.30am-noon & 1.30-6pm Mon, Wed-Fri, 8.30am-noon Tue & Sat). For a taxi, try calling ☑233 35 35 or ☑231 20 41.

Vaduz

POP 5450 / ELEV 455M

A tiny capital for a tiny country, Vaduz is a postage-stamp-sized city with a postcard-perfect backdrop. Crouching at the foot of forested mountains, hugging the banks of the Rhine and crowned by a turreted castle, its location is visually stunning.

The centre itself is curiously modern and sterile, with its mix of tax-free luxury-goods stores and cube-shaped concrete buildings. Yet just a few minutes' walk brings you to traces of the quaint village that existed just 50 years ago and quiet vineyards where the Alps seem that bit closer.

⊙ Sights & Activities

Schloss Vaduz   CASTLE
Vaduz Castle looms over the capital from the hill above and, although closed to the public, is worth the climb for the vistas. Trails climb the hill from the end of Egertastrasse. For a rare peek inside the castle grounds, arrive on 15 August, Liechtenstein's National Day, when there are magnificent fireworks and the prince invites all 36,281 Liechtensteiners over to his place for a glass of wine or beer.

**Liechtensteinisches
Landesmuseum**   MUSEUM
(www.landesmuseum.li in German; Städtle 43; adult/child Sfr8/free, combined with Kunstmuseum Sfr15/free; ⊙10am-5pm Tue-Sun, to 8pm Wed) In the centre, the well-designed museum provides a surprisingly interesting romp through the principality's history, from medieval witch-trials and burnings to the manufacture of false teeth.

Kunstmuseum Liechtenstein   GALLERY
(www.kunstmuseum.li; Städtle 32; adult/free Sfr12/8, combined with Landesmuseum Sfr15/free; ⊙10am-5pm Tue-Sun, to 8pm Thu) This black concrete and basalt cuboid hosts temporary exhibitions, revolving around the gallery's collection of contemporary art, which includes Ernst Ludwig Kirchner and Joseph Beuys originals. The prince's collection of old masters was relocated to the Liechtenstein Museum in Vienna. The cafe-sushi bar revives art-weary eyes.

Vaduz

LIECHTENSTEIN VADUZ

Hofkellerei WINERY
(www.hofkellerei.li; Feldstrasse 4; ⊘8am-noon &
1.30-6pm Mon-Fri, 9am-1pm Sat) A short walk
leads through the vineyards to the prince's
wine cellar. It is possible to sample the wines
here only in a large group and if you have
booked ahead.

Citytrain GUIDED TOUR
(🗗777 34 90; www.citytrain.li; adult/child Sfr10.50/
5; ⊘1pm & 4.30pm Mon-Sun late Apr-Sep) This
touristy train does a 35-minute loop of
Vaduz.

🛏 Sleeping & Eating

Visit www.tourismus.li for details on B&Bs
and holiday apartments. Cafes, pizzerias and
nondescript restaurants vie for your franc
along Städtle.

Parkhotel Sonnenhof BOUTIQUE HOTEL $$$
(🗗239 02 02; www.sonnenhof.li; Mareestrasse
29; s Sfr300-395, d Sfr410-650; P🕸🌐🏊) Wow,
what a view! The Sonnenhof's landscaped
gardens command a breathtaking vista of
the Alps and Rhine Valley. This romantic
boutique hotel piles on the luxury with its
oriental-style pool and spa, plush rooms and
polished service. The Michelin-starred res-
taurant (mains Sfr47 to Sfr59) emphasises
seasonal cuisine: from goose liver praline
with cherries and elderflower to saddle of
venison with chanterelles.

FREE Postmuseum MUSEUM
(Städtle 37; ⊘10am-noon & 1-5pm Mon-Sun) Liech-
tenstein once made a packet producing sou-
venir stamps for enthusiasts, but that market
has been hit by the rise of email. Here you'll
find all national stamps issued since 1912.

Mitteldorf NEIGHBOURHOOD
To see how Vaduz once looked, amble
northeast to Mitteldorf. This and the sur-
rounding streets form a charming quarter
of traditional houses and rose-strewn gar-
dens. Particularly eye-catching is the late-
medieval, step-gabled Rote Haus perched
above the vineyards.

Planetenweg WALKING
Kids can have fun spotting Jupiter, Mars
and Pluto on the so-called 'Planet Trail',
which starts at the car park by the Rhein-
park stadium. The path shadows the Rhine
and maps out the solar system on a scale
of 1:1 billion.

Gasthof Löwen   HISTORIC HOTEL $$
(✆238 11 41; www.hotel-loewen.li; Herrengasse 35; s/d Sfr199/299; P🐾) Historic and creakily elegant, this six-century-old guest house has eight spacious rooms with antique furniture and modern bathrooms. There's a cosy bar, fine-dining restaurant and a rear outdoor terrace overlooking grapevines for quaffing home-grown white and red wines.

Landgasthof Au   GUESTHOUSE $
(✆232 11 17; www.gasthof-au.li, in German; Austrasse 2; s/d/tr Sfr100/150/200, s/d without bathroom Sfr70/120; P🚗) This simple family-run place is a couple of bus stops or 10-minute walk south of Vaduz town centre. The light, pine-furnished rooms are kept spotless, and a couple of the bigger doubles have a terrace. The garden restaurant (mains Sfr20 to Sfr35, Monday to Friday) serves everything from schnitzel with potato salad to vegetarian dishes and kids' favourites.

Landhaus am Giessen   GUESTHOUSE $$
(✆235 00 35; www.giessen.li; Zollstrasse 16; s Sfr110-130, d Sfr160-180; P🐾🏊) Virtually around the corner from the Landgasthof Au, this is a fairly modern affair with comfortable and good-sized, if comparatively charmless, rooms. They have a sauna and offer massages.

TOP
CHOICE **Torkel**   FUSION $$$
(✆232 44 10; www.torkel.li, in German; Hintergasse 9; mains Sfr42-58; ⏰lunch & dinner Mon-Fri, dinner Sat) Just above the prince's vineyards sits His Majesty's ivy-clad restaurant. The garden terrace enjoys a wonderful perspective of the castle above, while the ancient, wood-lined interior is fantastically cosy in winter. Food puts a modern spin on local fare: think pike-perch curry and courgette soup with samosa ravioli. The set lunch menu (Sfr69.50) gives a good overview.

Adler Vaduz   SWISS $$
(✆232 21 31; Herrenstrasse 2; dishes Sfr19.50-48; ⏰lunch & dinner Mon-Fri) Creaking wood floors and lilac walls create a rustic-chic backdrop for Swiss classics at the Adler. Dishes like *Zürcher Geschnetzeltes* (sliced veal in a creamy mushroom sauce) go nicely with Vaduz Pinot noir wines.

ℹ️ Information

The **Liechtenstein Center** (✆239 63 00; www.tourismus.li; Städtle; ⏰9am-5pm) offers brochures, souvenir passport stamps (Sfr3) and multi-video screens with scenes from all over the country. Philatelie Liechtenstein will interest stamp collectors. The **post office** (Äulestrasse 38) is nearby.

Around Vaduz

Away from the tiny capital, Liechtenstein's big draw is its magnificent Alpine scenery, best savoured in slow motion on foot or by bicycle. Serene mountain villages like Triesen, Balzers and Schaan are great for slipping away from the crowds and tiptoeing back to nature for a few days.

⦿ Sights

Walsermuseum   MUSEUM
(Jonaboda 2, Triesenberg; adult/child Sfr2/1; ⏰7.45-11.45am & 1.30-5.45pm Mon-Fri, 7.45-11am & 2-5pm Sat) Triesenberg's star attraction is this museum, telling the intriguing story of the Walsers and containing some curious carvings out of twisted tree trunks and branches. The Walsers were a German-speaking 'tribe' from the Valais (Wallis in German) that emigrated across Europe in the 13th century and settled in many places, including Liechtenstein, where they still speak their own dialect. Ask at the museum about visiting the nearby Walserhaus (Hag 19), a 400-year-old house furnished in 19th century fashion. Bus 21 runs from Vaduz to Triesenberg.

Hinterschellenberg   VILLAGE
Hinterschellenberg briefly entered the stream of world history when about 500 Russian soldiers who had fought on the German side in WWII crossed the border in search of asylum in 1945. They remained for about two-and-a-half years, after which most made for Argentina. Liechtenstein was the only country not to cede to the Soviet Union's demands that such soldiers (considered traitors) be extradited to the USSR – which generally meant death. A memorial about 100m from the Austrian border marks the event. Take bus 11 from Vaduz to Mauren and then bus 33.

Burg Gutenberg   CASTLE
Balzers' most visible icon is this now state-owned, hilltop 13th-century castle, which only opens for concerts. It cuts a striking figure on the horizon and boasts nice strolls in the vicinity. The area was settled as early as the Neolithic period and Roman elements have been found in the castle foundations.

Much of the original castle's stonework was used to rebuild the village below after fire in 1795. The castle was restored in the early 20th century. Bus 12 shuttles between Vaduz and Balzers.

🏃 Activities

Some 400km of hiking trails criss-cross the principality. For some ideas, check out www.wanderwege.llv.li (in German).

The country's most famous trail is the **Fürstensteig**, a rite of passage for nearly every Liechtensteiner. You must be fit and not suffer from vertigo, as in places the path is narrow, reinforced with rope handholds and/or falls away to a sheer drop. The hike (up to four hours) begins at the **Berggasthaus Gaflei** (bus 22 from Triesenberg). Travel light and wear good shoes.

A steep two-hour climb from **Planken** (bus 26 from Schaan Post) brings you to the panoramic **Gafadurahütte** (☑787 14 28; www.gafadurahuette.li; dm adult/child Sfr13/8; ☺mid-May–mid-Oct) at 1428m. From here, over the **Drei Schwestern (Three Sisters)** mountain, you can meet up with the Fürstensteig.

🛏 Sleeping & Eating

Hotel Schatzmann   HOTEL $
(☑399 12 12; www.schatzmann.li; Landstrasse 80, Triesen; s/d Sfr130/165, half-board Sfr55; P⚡🛜) The rooms at this hotel are fairly standard, but the Michelin-starred restaurant is

DON'T MISS

TWO WHEELS, THREE COUNTRIES

Liechtenstein may be little, but its location on the border to Austria and Switzerland makes it easy to pedal across borders by bike in a day. One of the most scenic and memorable rides is the 59km **Drei Länder Tour** (Three Countries Tour), which leads from Vaduz to the medieval town of Feldkirch in Austria. The route heads on to Illspitz and along the Rhine to Buchs in Switzerland, dominated by its 13th-century castle, Schloss Werdenberg, before heading back to Vaduz.

Maps and e-bikes (Sfr50/35 per half-/full day) are available at the tourist office in Vaduz.

anything but. Gourmets come from afar for cooking that places the accent on seasonal ingredients, from chanterelles to venison, asparagus to truffles, matched with first-rate wines drawn from the cellar.

Camping Mittagspitze   CAMPGROUND $
(☑392 36 77; www.campingtriesen.li; camping per adult/child/car/tent Sfr9/4/5/6, dm Sfr22; 🏊) This well-equipped campground in a leafy spot is excellent for families, with a playground and pool as well as a restaurant, TV lounge and kiosk. It's south of Triesen on the road to Balzers.

Hotel Garni Säga   HOTEL $$
(☑392 43 77; www.saega.li; Alte Landstrasse 17, Triesen; s Sfr89-115, d Sfr170; P) This modern family-run pension, next door to the campground, has pleasant, sunny rooms.

SYHA Hostel   HOSTEL $
(☑232 50 22; www.youthhostel.ch/schaan; Untere Rütigasse 6, Schaan; dm/s/d Sfr33.50/58/85/150; ☺mid-Mar–Oct; 🛜🛏) This hostel caters particularly to cyclists and families. Halfway between Schaan and Vaduz, it's within easy walking distance of either.

Malbun

POP 50 / ELEV 1600M

At the end of the road from Vaduz, the 1600m-high resort of Malbun feels – in the nicest possible sense – like the edge of the earth.

It's not really as remote as it seems and in high season Malbun is mobbed. However, generally it's perfect for unwinding, especially with the family. The skiing is inexpensive, if not too extensive (23km of pistes), while the hiking is relaxing and beautiful. The place is dead out of season.

🏃 Activities

Skiing is aimed at beginners, with a few intermediate and cross-country runs thrown in. Indeed, older British royals like Prince Charles learnt to ski here. A general ski pass (including the Sareis chairlift) for a day/week costs Sfr49/226 for adults and Sfr29/127 for children. One day's equipment rental from **Malbun Sport** (Im Malbun 34; ☺8am-6pm Mon-Fri, plus Sat & Sun high season) costs Sfr58 including skis, boots and poles.

Two kilometres before Malbun is the Väluna Valley, the main **cross-country skiing** area, with 15km of classic and

IT'S LIECHTENSTEIN TRIVIA TIME!

» Liechtenstein is the only country in the world named after the people who purchased it.

» In its last military engagement in 1866, none of its 80 soldiers was killed. In fact, 81 returned, including a new Italian 'friend'. The army was disbanded soon afterwards.

» Low business taxes means around 75,000 firms, many of them so-called 'letter box companies', with nominal head offices, are registered here – about twice the number of the principality's inhabitants.

» Liechtenstein is Europe's fourth-smallest nation (only the Vatican, Monaco and San Marino are smaller).

skating track, including a 3km stretch that is illuminated at night. The trails start at Steg.

Some hiking trails, including to **Sassfürkle**, stay open during the winter. During the summer, other treks include the **Furstin-Gina Path**, with views over Austria, Switzerland and Liechtenstein. This walk starts at the top of the Sareis chairlift (Sfr9.10/14.20 single/return in summer) and returns to Malbun.

🛏 Sleeping & Eating

Hotel Gorfion   HOTEL **$$**
(☑264 43 23; per adult incl half-board Sfr165, child Sfr50-90; P @ 🛜 🏊 🐕) Tots in tow? This

is your place. Kids are kept amused with a playground, petting zoo and activities. Parents, meanwhile, can enjoy a lie-in with the (like it!) sleep-in service and relax in the whirlpool. Kids' mealtimes are supervised and the hotel will let you borrow buggies, backpacks, highchairs – you name it.

Alpenhotel Malbun   GUESTHOUSE **$**
(☑263 11 81; www.alpenhotel.li; d with/without bathroom Sfr160/120; P 🏊) Rooms in the sienna-coloured main chalet are cute if cramped, with traditional painted doors and plenty of timber and shared bathrooms. En suite rooms in the nearby annexe are larger and comfier but straight from the 1970s. Enjoy the kitschy Alpine decor and hearty food in the hotel restaurant.

Bergrestaurant Sareiserjoch   SWISS **$$**
(☑263 46 86; mains Sfr20-35; ⊙lunch & dinner Jun-Oct & Dec-Apr) For gob-smacking mountain views while eating, it is hard to beat this woodsy hut, at the end of the Sareis chairlift. *Käsknöpfli* (cheese-filled dumplings) and rösti are on the menu. Thursday in winter is Raclette night.

ℹ Information

The **tourist office** (☑239 63 00; www.malbun .li; ⊙9am-noon & 1-4.30pm Mon-Sat Jun-Oct & mid-Dec–mid-Apr) is on the main street, not far from Hotel Walserhof.

ℹ Getting There & Around

Bus 21 travels more or less hourly from Vaduz to Malbun between 7.03am and 8.33pm every day (Sfr3.40, Swiss Pass valid, 38 minutes), returning between 8.20am and 7.20pm.

Understand Switzerland

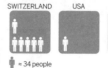

visitors per sq km

SWITZERLAND   USA   UK

≈ 34 people

Switzerland Today

Victim of its own Success: Franc Matters

Peaceful and prosperous, safe and sound, a magnet for the rich and a safe haven for wealth: this privileged land of quality living and global finance, of outdoor magnificence and Alpine aesthetic found itself the victim of its own success in 2011. The Swiss franc, long recognised as one of the world's most stable currencies, had become so overvalued it was threatening the traditionally robust Swiss economy. So strong was the franc that Swiss exports were falling along with the number of incoming tourists as price-conscious visitors from abroad suddenly realised just how much a cup of coffee in Switzerland was going to cost them. Even the Swiss were abandoning their local shops and hopping across the border into the cheaper France, Germany and Italy to do their weekly shop. So the Swiss National Bank, in an unprecedented move, made the value of the Swiss franc tumble in an instant (by 9% in 15 minutes!) by pegging it at 1.20 to the euro. An entire nation waited with bated breathe to see if the contrived depreciation would pay off. Critics were not convinced.

» Highest point: Dufourspitze (4634m)

» Internet domain: ch

» Annual chocolate consumption (per person): 11.3kg

» Non-Swiss nationals (of total population): 20.7%

To the Polls: Parliamentary Elections

Federal elections, held every four years, saw 49% of the Swiss electorate turn out to cast their vote in the 2011 nationwide ballot. The incumbent Swiss People's Party (SVP; UDC or Union Démocratique du Centre in French) lost the greatest share of votes – a disappointment for the right-wing party who'd hoped to beat the record 29% of votes it had set four years previously. The country's other main political party, left-wing rivals the Social Democrat Party, likewise saw a drop in support, as Swiss punters hedged their bets with smaller, relatively new parties like the Liberal Greens and Conservative Democrats.

Top Films

Home (2008) By a motorway, by Geneva director Ursula Meier
The Kite Runner (2007) Film adaption of Khaled Hosseini's novel by Oscar-winning Swiss-German director Marc Forster
The Pledge (2001) Love-it-or-loathe-it adaption of Friedrich Dürrenmatt's *Das Versprechen*

Journey of Hope (1991) Oscar-winning tale of a Kurdish family seeking a better life in Switzerland
Breathless (1960) New wave classic by Swiss avant-garde film-maker Jean-Luc Godard

Top Books

Swiss Watching (Diccon Bewes) Amusing, astute portrait
The Alpine Set in Switzerland (Lindsay Greatwood) Charlie Chaplin, Graham Greene et al
The Swiss Cookbook (Betty Bossi) Culinary culture by canton/region

belief systems
(% of population)

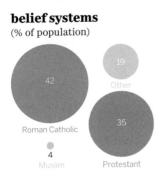

42 — Roman Catholic

19 — Other

35 — Protestant

4 — Muslim

if Switzerland was 100 people

64 would speak German   7 would speak Italian
20 would speak French   1 would speak Romansch
8 would speak another language

Mad about their Land: Go Green

Given the overwhelming beauty of their country, it's natural that the Swiss are mad about their land. 'Go green' is the dominant vibe and 'sustainable technology' the buzzword for the man on the street and pioneering scientists striving to go around the world Jules Verne-style in solar-powered boats and planes (see p339). As recently as September 2011, the Swiss parliament banned the construction of new nuclear power plants and called for a nuclear phase-out (in favour of hydroelectric power) by 2034. Currently, five nuclear power plants generate 40% of Switzerland's energy needs.

Reinventing the Alps is the hot topic at higher altitudes. World-class architects are respectfully weaving futuristic apartments clad in larch-wood tiles (Sir Norman Foster in St Moritz) and spiralling hotel towers of ecological dimensions (Herzog & de Meuron in Davos) into Switzerland's quintessential Heidi-postcard landscape with great success. But how to be green and how to burn clean energy are not the most pressing matters. Rather, it is what must be done to keep ski resorts sustainable as the globe warms; experts say we can forget sure-thing snow below 1500m by 2050.

» Population: 7.63 million

» Area: 41,277 sq km

» GDP: US$523.8 billion

» GDP per capita: US$42,600

» GDP growth: 2.6%

» Inflation: 0.7%

» Unemployment: 3.9%

Dining Timing

» Lunch is from noon and dinner as early as 6.30pm.

» Dining hours are generous in cities; many places serve non-stop from 11am to 11pm.

» Restaurants close one or two days a week (often Monday).

Street Food

» Hot chestnuts (autumn and winter)

» Freshly baked *brezel* (pretzel) studded in rock salt or seeds (pumpkin, sunflower)

» *Bratwurst* (sausage) in a bread bun, wildly popular in St Gallen

Swiss Fizz

» Tap water is fine to drink and there are bottled local mineral waters galore.

» Apple juice is always bubbly.

» Rivella is a German-Swiss fizzy drink made with lactose; it comes in three varieties.

History

Switzerland is unique and nowhere is this more startlingly explicit than in its history. Commonly regarded as *Sonderfall Schweiz* (literally 'special case Switzerland'), this small landlocked country in Europe is an exception to the nation-state norm. It is a rare and refined breed, a privileged and neutral country born out of its 1874 constitution and tried-and-tested by two world wars (during which Switzerland remained firmly neutral). Despite the overwhelming presence of global institutions (like the UN, World Health Organization and International Red Cross in Geneva) and moves towards greater international cooperation (such as finally ditching border controls for Schengen countries at the end of 2008), modern-day Switzerland remains idiosyncratic, insular, parochial and unique. Few countries promote 'direct democracy' through referenda and practise 'armed neutrality' with a trained militia that will never find itself face to face with an enemy.

Regardless of whether or not the patriotic William Tell existed or was responsible for even half the deeds attributed to him, the 14th-century crossbow maker from the Uri canton is a key figure in Swiss identity. A national legend, the man who helped drive out Switzerland's foreign rulers by shooting an apple off his son's head has perfectly embodied the country's rather singular approach to independence throughout the ages.

Clans & Castles: Swiss Roots

Modern Swiss history might start in 1291 but that is not to say that the thousands of years leading up to Switzerland's birth are not significant – this was the period that gave Switzerland the best of its fairy-tale châteaux and *schlösser* (castles).

The earliest inhabitants were Celtic tribes, including the Helvetii of the Jura and the Mittelland Plain, and the Rhaetians near Graubünden. Their homelands were first invaded by the Romans, who had gained a

Best Swiss History Museums

» Bundesbrief-museum, Schwyz

» Schweizerisches Landesmuseum, Zürich

» Historisches Museum Bern, Bern

» Château de Prangins, Nyon

» Château de Chillon, Montreux

TIMELINE

58 BC
Julius Caesar establishes the Celtic tribe, Helvetii, between the Alps and the Jura to watch over the Rhine frontier and keep Germanic tribes out of Roman territory.

AD 1032
Clans in western Switzerland, together with the kingdom of Burgundy, are swallowed up by the Holy Roman Empire but left with a large degree of autonomy.

1273
Habsburg ruler Rudolph I becomes Holy Roman Emperor and so takes control of much Swiss territory. As the Habsburgs increase tax pressure, resistance grows.

foothold under Julius Caesar by 58 BC and established Aventicum (now Avenches) as the capital of Helvetia (Roman Switzerland). Switzerland's largest Roman ruins are at Augusta Raurica. By AD 400, Germanic Alemanni tribes arrived to drive out the Romans.

The Alemanni groups settled in eastern Switzerland and were later joined by another Germanic tribe, the Burgundians, in the western part of the country. The latter adopted Christianity and the Latin language, laying the seeds for the division between French- and German-speaking Switzerland. The Franks conquered both tribes in the 6th century, but the two areas were torn apart again when Charlemagne's empire was partitioned in 870.

When it was reunited under the pan-European Holy Roman Empire in 1032, Switzerland was initially left to its own devices. Local nobles wielded the most influence: the Zähringen family, who founded Fribourg, Bern and Murten, and built a fairy-tale castle with soaring towers and red turrets in Thun in the Bernese Oberland, and the Savoy clan, who established a ring of castles around Lake Geneva, most notably Château de Morges and magnificent Château de Chillon, right on the water's edge near Montreux.

When the Habsburg ruler Rudolph I became Holy Roman Emperor in 1273, he sent in heavy-handed bailiffs to collect more taxes and tighten the administrative screws. Swiss resentment grew quickly.

Confoederatio Helvetica: Modern Switzerland

Rudolph died in 1291, prompting local leaders to make an immediate grab for independence. On 1 August that year, the forest communities of Uri, Schwyz and Nidwalden – so the tale goes – gathered on Rütli Meadow in the Schwyz canton in central Switzerland to sign an alliance vowing not to recognise any external judge or law. Historians believe this to be a slightly distorted version, but, whatever the scenario, a pact does exist, preserved in the town of Schwyz. Displayed at the Bundesbriefmuseum in Schwyz, the pact is seen as the founding act of the Swiss Confederation whose Latin name, Confoederatio Helvetica, survives in the 'CH' abbreviation for Switzerland (used, for example, on car number plates and in internet addresses).

In 1315, Duke Leopold I of Austria dispatched a powerful army to quash the growing Swiss nationalism. Instead, however, the Swiss inflicted an epic defeat on his troops at Morgarten, which prompted other communities to join the Swiss union. The next 200 years of Swiss history was a time of successive military wins, land grabs and new memberships. The following cantons came on board: Lucerne (1332),

Best Castles

» Château de Chillon, Montreux
» Château de Morges, Morges
» Schloss Thun, Thun
» Medieval castles, Bellinzona
» Burg Hohenklingen, Stein am Rhein
» Wasserschloss Hallwyl, Aargau Canton

1291	1315	1476	1499
Modern Switzerland officially 'begins' with the independence pact at Rütli Meadow. Many historians consider the event, and the accompanying William Tell legend, to have actually taken place in 1307.	Swiss irregular troops win a surprise victory over Habsburg Austrian forces at the Battle of Morgarten. It was the first of several Swiss victories over imperial invaders.	Charles the Bold, Duke of Burgundy, is crushed at the Battle of Murten, one of three defeats at the hands of the Swiss Confederates and the French.	The Swiss Confederation wins virtual independence from the Habsburg-led Holy Roman Empire after imperial forces are defeated in a series of battles along the Rhine and on Swiss territory.

Zürich (1351), Glarus and Zug (1352), Bern (1353), Fribourg and Solothurn (1481), Basel and Schaffhausen (1501), and Appenzell (1513). In the middle of all this, the Swiss Confederation gained independence from Holy Roman Emperor Maximilian I after a victory at Dornach in 1499.

Protestant Swiss first openly disobeyed the Catholic Church during 1522's 'affair of the sausages', when a printer and several priests in Zürich were caught gobbling *Würste* on Ash Wednesday when they should have been fasting.

No More Stinging Defeats: Swiss Neutrality

Swiss neutrality was essentially born out of the stinging defeat the rampaging Swiss, having made it as far as Milan, suffered against a combined French and Venetian force at Marignano, 16km southeast of Milan, in 1515. After the bloody battle, the Swiss gave up their expansionist dream, withdrew from the international scene and declared neutrality for the first time. For centuries since, the country's warrior spirit has been channelled solely into mercenary activity – a tradition still echoed in the Swiss Guard that protects today's pope at the Vatican.

When the religious Thirty Years War (1618–48) broke out in Europe, Switzerland's neutrality and diversity combined to give it some protection. The Protestant Reformation led by preachers Huldrych Zwingli and Jean Calvin made some inroads in Zürich and Geneva, while Central Switzerland (Zentralschweiz) remained Catholic. Such was the internal division that the Swiss, unable to agree even among themselves which side to take in the Thirty Years War, stuck to neutrality.

The French invaded Switzerland in 1798 and established the brief Helvetic Republic, but they were no more welcome than the Austrians before them and internal fighting prompted Napoleon (then in power in France) to restore the former Confederation of Cantons in 1803 – the cantons of Aargau, St Gallen, Graubünden, Ticino, Thurgau and Vaud joined the Confederation at this time.

Swiss neutrality as we know it today was formally established by the Congress of Vienna peace treaty in 1815 that, following Napoleon's defeat by the British and Prussians at Waterloo, formally guaranteed Switzerland's independence and neutrality for the first time. (The same treaty also added the cantons of Valais, Geneva and Neuchâtel to the Swiss bow.)

Switzerland is the country that has been neutral for the second longest time (after Sweden, neutral since ending its involvement in the Napoleonic Wars in 1814).

Despite some citizens' pro-German sympathies, Switzerland's only involvement in WWI lay in organising Red Cross units. After the war, Switzerland joined the League of Nations, but on a strictly financial and economic basis (which included providing its headquarters in Geneva) – no military involvement.

WWII likewise saw Switzerland remain neutral, the country being largely unscathed bar some accidental bombings on Schaffhausen when Allied pilots mistook the town in northeastern Switzerland for Germany, twice dropping bombs on its outskirts in April 1944. Indeed, the most momentous event of WWII for the Swiss was when Henri Guisan,

1515	1519	1590–1600	1847
After Swiss forces take Milan and Pavia in Italy in 1512, the Swiss are defeated at Marignano by a French-Venetian army. Chastised, the Swiss withdraw and declare neutrality.	Protestant Huldrych Zwingli preaches 'pray and work' in Zürich, promoting marriage for clerics and a new common liturgy to replace the Mass. In 1523, the city adopts his reform proposals.	Some 300 women in Vaud are captured, tortured and burned alive on charges of witchcraft, even as Protestants in other Swiss cantons strive to end witch-hunts.	'Hare shoot' civil war between Protestants and Catholics lasts just 26 days, leaving 86 dead and 500 wounded, and paving the way for the 1848 federal constitution.

general of the civilian army, invited all top military personnel to Rütli Meadow (site of the 1291 Oath of Allegiance) to show the world how determined the Swiss were to defend their own soil.

Give Cantons a Voice: The Constitution

In 1847, civil war broke out. The Protestant army, led by General Dufour, quickly crushed the Sonderbund (Special League) of Catholic cantons, including Lucerne. The war only lasted 26 days, prompting the German chancellor Otto von Bismarck to subsequently dismiss it as 'a hare shoot'. But for the peace-loving Swiss, the disruption and disorder were sufficient to ensure they rapidly consolidated the victory by Dufour's forces with the creation of a new federal constitution. Bern was named the capital.

The 1848 constitution, largely still in place today, was a compromise between advocates of central control and conservative forces wanting to retain cantonal authority. The cantons eventually relinquished their right to print money, run postal services and levy customs duties, giving these to the federal government. However, they retained legislative and executive control over local matters. Furthermore, the new Federal Assembly was established in a way that gave cantons a voice. The lower national chamber, the *Nationalrat,* has 200 members, allocated from the

> Visit www .parliament.ch and www.admin. ch for insight into Switzerland's unusual political system, with its 'direct democracy', 'magic formula' and part-time politicians.

THE MAGIC FORMULA: SWISS GOVERNMENT

The make-up of Switzerland's Federal Council, the executive government, is determined not by who wins the most parliamentary seats (ie the winning party rules), but by the 'magic formula' – a cosy power-sharing agreement made between the four main parties in 1959.

» The Federal Council consists of seven ministers.

» The four largest parties in parliament are guaranteed seats in the Federal Council in accordance with their shares of the popular vote.

» The president is drawn on a rotating basis from the seven federal ministers, so there's a new head of state each year.

» Many federal laws must first be approved by public referendum; several are held every year.

Until 2003, the 'magic formula' decreed that the Socialists (left wing), Radical Party (conservative) and Christian Democrats (centre right) had two council members each, with one going to the right-wing Swiss People's Party (SVP). This was upset in 2003 when the SVP made hefty gains in national elections and took over the Christian Democrats' second seat.

1863
After witnessing slaughter and countless untended wounded at the Battle of Solferino in 1859 in northern Italy, businessman and pacifist Henri Dunant co-founds the International Red Cross in Geneva.

GLENN BEANLAND/LONELY PLANET IMAGES ©

1918
With a sixth of the population living below the poverty line and 20,000 dead of a flu epidemic, workers strike; the 48-hour week is among the long-term results.

» The Red Cross emblem inverts the Swiss flag

26 cantons in proportion to population size. The upper states chamber, the *Ständerat,* comprises 46 members, two per canton.

Opposition to political corruption sparked a movement for greater democracy. The constitution was revised in 1874 so that many federal laws had to be approved by national referendum – a phenomenon for which Switzerland remains famous today. A petition with 50,000 signatures can challenge a proposed law; 100,000 signatures can force a public vote on any new issue.

Famously Secret: Swiss Banking

Banking confidentiality, dating back to the Middle Ages, was enshrined in Swiss law in 1934 when numbered (rather than named) bank accounts were introduced. The Swiss banking industry has thrived ever since, thanks mainly to the enviable stability that guaranteed neutrality brings. When the Bank for International Settlements (BIS, the organisation that facilitates cooperation between central banks) chose Basel as base in 1930 it was for one good reason – Switzerland was a neutral player.

In the late 1990s a series of scandals erupted, forcing Switzerland to start reforming its famously secretive banking industry, born when a clutch of commercial banks were created in the mid-19th century. In 1995, after pressure from Jewish groups, Swiss banks announced that they had discovered millions of dollars lying in dormant pre-1945 accounts and belonging to Holocaust victims and survivors. Three years later, amid allegations they'd been sitting on the money without seriously trying to trace its owners, Switzerland's two largest banks, UBS and Crédit Suisse, agreed to pay US$1.25 billion in compensation to Holocaust survivors and their families.

Switzerland has long been a favourite spot for the wealthy to deposit their fortunes in private banks. Almost one-third of the world's US$7 trillion offshore deposits are said to be in Switzerland – hence the immense pressure on Switzerland in 2009 from the US, Britain, Germany and other high-tax countries to change its 1934 banking law protecting depositors accused of tax evasion by their home countries. The Swiss conceded, prompting critics to triumphantly ring the death knell for Swiss banking secrecy. This followed hot on the heels of the Swiss decision in 2004 to tax accounts held in Switzerland by EU citizens – again in reaction to external pressure.

When Switzerland finally joined the UN in 2002, officials mistakenly ordered a rectangular Swiss flag to fly outside the organisation's New York headquarters. Swiss functionaries strenuously objected, insisting the UN run up the proper square flag pretty damn quick.

Forever Neutral: A Nation Apart

Since the end of WWII, Switzerland has enjoyed an uninterrupted period of economic, social and political stability – thanks, in predictable Swiss fashion, to the neutrality which saw it forge ahead from an already powerful commercial, financial and industrial base while the rest

1940	1979	1990	2001
General Guisan's army warn offs WWII invaders; 430,000 troops are placed on borders but most are put in Alpine fortresses to carry out partisan war in case of German invasion.	Five years after a first vote in favour in 1974, Jura (majority French-speaking Catholics), absorbed by Bern in 1815, leaves Bern (German-speaking Protestants) to become an independent canton.	The internet is 'born' at Geneva's CERN research centre, where Tim Berners-Lee develops HTML, the language used to prepare pages for the World Wide Web and link text to graphics.	National airline Swissair collapses, a gun massacre in Zug parliament kills 14 politicians, 21 people perish in a canyoning accident and 11 die in a fire in the St Gotthard Tunnel.

of Europe was still picking up and rebuilding the broken pieces from the war. Zürich developed as an international banking and insurance centre, and the World Health Organization and a stash of other international bodies set up headquarters in Geneva. To preserve its much-vaunted neutrality, however, Switzerland opted to remain outside the UN (although Geneva has hosted its second-largest seat after the main New York headquarters from the outset) and, more recently, the European Union.

A hefty swing to the conservative right in the 2003 parliamentary elections served to further enhance Switzerland's standing as a nation staunchly apart. In 2006, the anti-EU, anti-immigration Swiss People's Party (SVP) called for the toughening up of immigration and political asylum laws; the policies were passed with an overwhelming majority at national referendum. Then there was the rumpus over its bid to ban building new minarets for Muslim calls to prayer – an idea that aroused much anger internationally, but was approved by the constitution after 57.7% of voters said yes to the ban in a national referendum. During the campaign, the SVP published anti-immigrant posters featuring three white sheep kicking one black sheep off the striking white cross of the Swiss flag.

In spite of the SVP's tough conservative line, there have been concrete signs that Switzerland is opening up to the wider world. The country became the 190th member of the UN in 2002 (a referendum on the issue had last been defeated in 1986) and three years later it voted to join Europe's passport-free travel zone, Schengen (finally completing the process at the end of 2008). In another referendum the same year, the Swiss narrowly voted in favour of legalising civil unions for same-sex couples (but not marriage), one more defeat for the SVP.

Yet few expect Switzerland to even consider joining either the EU or the Euro single-currency zone any time soon (if ever). Traditionally, the western, French-speaking cantons have long desired both, while the German-speaking cantons (and Ticino) have generally been opposed.

Even in a new, fiscally transparent world, neutral Switzerland remains an exceedingly attractive place to stash away wealth. Every Swiss canton sets its own tax rates, encouraging individuals and businesses to 'play' the canton market; Zug entices tycoons with Switzerland's lowest income and corporate tax rates and breaks.

HISTORY FOREVER NEUTRAL: A NATION APART

2008	**2009**	**2010**	**2011**
The world financial crisis affects Switzerland's two biggest banks, UBS and Crédit Suisse. The government bails out UBS with a US$60 billion package, while Crédit Suisse seeks funds elsewhere.	The first experiments in the world's largest particle accelerator are successfully conducted with the Large Hadron Collider at CERN, the European Centre for Nuclear Research in Geneva.	*Solar Impulse*, the solar plane of Lausanne adventurer Bertrand Piccard, successfully completes the world's first day and all-night solar-powered flight – the first step to flying around the world on solar power.	A soaring, over-valued Swiss franc prompts the Swiss National Bank to peg it to the euro. In federal elections the Swiss elect a new parliament for a four-year term.

The Swiss Way of Life

One-stop shop for books in English about Swiss culture, attitudes and cultural diversity: Basel-based Bergli Publications (www.bergli.ch).

Chocolate, cheese, cuckoo clocks, precision watches, banking secrecy, bircher muesli, Heidi, William Tell, yodelling and the Alps: a swath of stereotypes envelope Switzerland and the Swiss, like every other nation. This perfectly well-behaved country is hard-working, super organised, efficient, orderly, obedient (have you ever seen a Swiss pedestrian cross the road when the little man is red?), overly cautious and ruthlessly efficient – a mother-in-law's dream.

Or maybe not...

Sonderfall Schweiz: The Swiss Halo

The Swiss see themselves as different, and they are. Take their country's overwhelming cultural diversity, eloquently expressed in four languages and attitudes; German-, French- and Italian-speaking Swiss all display similar characteristics to German, French and Italian people respectively, creating an instant line-up of reassuringly varied, diverse and oftentimes surprising psyches. Then, of course, there are those in Graubünden who speak Romansch with its many dialects that no one outside the valley concerned understands. One cookie-cutter shape definitely does not fit *Sonderfall Schweiz* (literally 'special case Switzerland') and its dramatically different inhabitants.

Quite the contrary: from centuries-old Alpine traditions, positively wild in nature, such as wrestling and stone throwing, to new-millennium Googlers in Zürich who shimmy into work each morning down a fire pole, to Geneva jewellers who make exclusive watches from moon dust, to fashionable 30-somethings who strut savvy in recycled truck tarps and Cambodian fish sacks, the Swiss know how to innovate.

Not just that: they have the determination to complement their creativity, keenly demonstrated by both their restless quest to test their limits in the sports arena and the extraordinarily tough, independent spirit with which Swiss farmers resolutely work the land to mete out a sustainable lifestyle. That *Sonderfall Schweiz* halo might not shine quite as brightly as it did a few decades back, but it definitely still glints.

Assisted suicide is legal in Switzerland and international debate surrounds the role of Dignitas (www.dignitas.ch) who offer medical help to the terminally or chronically ill foreign nationals who travel to the country.

Healthy, Wealthy & Wise: Quality Lifestyle

'They are', wrote the *Guardian* in 2004, 'probably the most fortunate people on the planet. Healthy, wealthy and, thanks to an outstanding education system, wise. They enjoy a life most of us can only dream about. For ease of reference we commonly refer to them as the Swiss.' This deadpan doffing of the cap from a nation that usually scorns 'dull' Switzerland was prompted by yet another report listing Zürich, Geneva and Bern among the planet's best cities to live. Those ratings change

Given their comfortable and privileged lifestyle it's hardly surprising that the Swiss have the greatest life expectancy in Europe: women live to an average 83.7 years, men to 77.9.

'The Swiss are most armed and most free', wrote Machiavelli. Yet more than 400 years after their last major military excursion, even the Swiss are losing enthusiasm for 'armed neutrality'.

While Switzerland is the only Western nation to retain conscription, the country's armed defences are diminishing. At the height of the Cold War, the country had more than 600,000 soldiers and 'universal militia' of reservists with a gun at home, comprising almost the entire male population. Today, every able-bodied Swiss man must still undergo military training and serve 260 days' military service between the ages of 20 and 36. But community service is now an option and the number of soldiers that can be mobilised within 48 hours has been reduced to 220,000.

For many years, Switzerland maintained bunkers with food stockpiles to house just about the entire population underground in the event of attack. As a result of army cost-cutting measures, thousands have been decommissioned – and, in true Swiss spirit, recycled as innovative tourist sights. These include the once top-secret bunkers disguised as farmhouses at Faulensee in the Bernese Oberland and the world's first zero-star bunker hotel (www.null-stern-hotel.ch) in Teufen in northeastern Switzerland. Exactly one year after it opened, the latter – a groundbreaking, eco-luxury hotel – was turned into a museum instead to allow the 'Null Stern' brand to concentrate on opening hotels in more urban parts of Switzerland.

little: Zürich was ranked second, Geneva third in Mercer Consultancy's 2010 quality-of-life report.

Yet the Swiss don't necessarily enjoy a particularly different lifestyle from other Westerners; they just enjoy it more. They can rely on their little nation, one of the world's 10 richest in terms of GDP per capita, to deliver excellent health services, efficient public transport and all-round security. Spend a little time among them and you realise their sportiness, attention to diet and concern for the environment is symptomatic of another condition: they simply want to extract as much as possible from life.

Swiss lifestyle is not all sipping Sfr10,000 champagne cocktails from carved ice glasses in Verbier or hobnobbing on the ski slopes during weekend visits to the chalets many Swiss own or rent for the season. Rural regions – particularly Appenzellerland, Valais and the Jura – are not about money-driven glam, but traditional culture that talks as people don folk costumes during festivals and mark the seasons with time-honoured Alpine rituals. Fathers teach their sons the fine art of alpenhorn playing like their fathers did when they were young, while younger siblings learn how to wave the Swiss flag. The autumnal grape harvest is celebrated with ancient feasts and in spring shepherds decorate their cattle with flowers and bells to herd them in procession to mountain pastures, where they spend a long and glorious summer.

A Sporting Backbone: Alpine Tourism

Those mountain pastures where shepherds hang out in summer crafting milk from their cows into fragrant *fromage d'alpage* (mountain cheese) have an awful lot to answer for: if Switzerland did not have 4000m-plus peaks at every turn, its very persona, culture and vibe would be mightily different.

The geography of Switzerland is what gives the country its sporting backbone and makes the country and its people so outrageously outdoor-orientated. It is also how small Switzerland put itself on the map as a big tourist destination. In the 19th century during the golden age of Alpinism, it was the Swiss Alpine peaks that proved so alluring to

The Swiss are conservative with money and their currency. Since the Swiss franc went into circulation in the 1850s, it has rarely been tampered with; the 2005 decision to drop the five-cent coin because it cost six cents to mint was a minor earthquake in a country where change is viewed warily.

British climbers. Alfred Wills made the first ascent of the Wetterhorn (3692m) above Grindelwald in 1854, which was followed by a rash of ascents up other Swiss peaks, including Edward Whymper's famous Matterhorn expedition in 1865. This flurry of pioneering activity in the Swiss Alps prompted the world's first mountaineering club, the Alpine Club, to be founded in London in 1857, followed by the Swiss Alpine Club six years later.

With the construction of the first mountain hut on Tödi (3614m) the same year and the emergence of St Moritz and its intoxicating 'champagne climate' a year later as the hip place to winter among British aristocracy, winter alpine tourism was born. Hotels, railways and cable cars followed, and by the time St Moritz hosted the second Winter Olympics in 1928, small Switzerland was the winter-wonderland-action buzzword on everyone's lips. Not surprisingly, one year on, the first ski school in Switzerland opened its doors in the same Upper Engadine resort.

Reinventing the Wheel: Wacky Sports

No nation has better reinvented the sporting wheel than the Swiss. Take Hornussen, a game of medieval origin played between two 16- to 18-strong teams. One launches a 78g *Hornuss* (ball) over a field; the other tries to stop it hitting the ground with a *Schindel*, a 4kg implement resembling a road sign. To add to the game's bizarre quality, the *Hornuss* is launched by whipping it around a steel ramp with a flexible rod, in a motion that's a cross between shot putting and fly-fishing. The *Schindel* can be used as a bat to stop the 85m-per-second ball or simply tossed into the air at it.

Verging on the vicious, *Schwingen* is a Swiss version of sumo wrestling, battled out between everyone from 10-year-old girls to fat-bellied farmers and brawny farmhands. Two people, each wearing short hessian shorts, face off across a circle of sawdust. They lean towards each other, grabbing their opponent by the back of the shorts. Through a complicated combination of prescribed grips (including crotch grips), jerks, feints and other manoeuvres, each tries to wrestle their opponent onto his or her back. Go to any mountain fair or Alpine festival and there is sure to be a *Schwingen* surrounded by a very large cheering crowd.

Other eclectic pursuits include *Steinstossen* (stone throwing); cricket, polo and horse racing on ice; trotti-biking where rural hipsters race down hills on an off-road version of the '90s urban microscooter; and *Waffenlaufen* (weapon running) where macho men don camouflage, military garb, rucksack and rifle, and run up and down mountains. No thank you.

E=mc², WWW & LSD: The Scientific Swiss

If only to prove just how creative and innovative they are, the Swiss gave the world Einstein, the World Wide Web and lysergic acid diethylamide (LSD). Indeed, the Swiss have more registered patents and Nobel Prize winners (mostly in scientific disciplines) per capita than any other nationality.

It was while he was working in Bern (between 1903 and 1905) that Albert Einstein developed his special theory of relativity. German-born, Einstein studied in Aarau and later in Zürich, where he trained to be a physics and maths teacher. He was granted Swiss citizenship in 1901 and, unable to find a suitable teaching post, wound up working as a lowly low-paid clerk in Bern patent office. He gained his doctorate in 1905 and subsequently became a professor in Zürich, remaining in Switzerland until 1914, when he moved to Berlin. Bern's Einstein Haus museum tells the full story.

The internet meanwhile was born in Geneva at the European Organisation for Nuclear Research, better known as CERN, on Christmas Day

---

Alpine History Museums

» Matterhorn Museum, Zermatt

» Swiss Alpine Museum, Bern

» Engadiner Museum, St Moritz

» Rätisches Museum, Chur

» Freilichtmuseum Ballenberg, near Brienz

» Saaser Museum, Saas Fee

No region sports wackier fests than French-speaking Valais where cow fighting is a mighty serious business – watch it in the Val d'Hérens. *Chüefladefäscht* (cow-dung smashing) sees fired-up Swiss farmers in Riederalp wielding golf clubs and pitch forks in Alpine pastures polka-dotted with cow pats.

In typical green-thinking Swiss fashion, the Swiss are playing around with solar power – and setting new ground-breaking records in sustainable technology on the way. In July 2010, *Solar Impulse,* an ultra-light aeroplane, took off from an airstrip in the canton of Vaud and stayed airborne all day and all night – with no fuel. A first for solar-powered flight, the plane flew at a steady 50km/h to maximise the solar power it had garnered at a sunny height of 8700m earlier in the day.

The ground-breaking flight put Lausanne adventurers, explorers and scientists André Borschberg and Bertrand Piccard one step closer to their ambitious mission of flying *Solar Impulse* around the world in five stages over a course of 20 to 25 days in 2013. Follow the team's progress at www.solarimpulse.com.

The Swiss are not restricting their solar mobility innovations to the air. On water, *PlanetSolar,* the world's largest solar-powered boat, set sail in 2010 from Monaco on a world tour covering 50,000km. The catamaran, flying the Swiss flag, is energised by 536 sq m of photovoltaic panels on deck and has a four-person Swiss-French-German crew at its helm, headed by Swiss expedition leader and project founder, Raphaël Domjan. Follow the boat at www.planetsolar.org and read the fascinating log book via Twitter at @PlanetSolarTeam ('... to celebrate the beginning of our crossing of the Indian Ocean, we prepared a raclette – probably the first raclette from the solar energy!').

1990. The genius behind the global information-sharing tool was Oxford graduate Tim Berners-Lee, a software consultant for CERN who started out creating a program for the research centre to help its hundreds of scientists share their experiments, data and discoveries. Two years on it had become a dramatically larger and more powerful beast than anyone could imagine. Equally as dramatic, large and powerful is CERN's Large Hadron Collider where Geneva scientists play God with Big Bang experiments. A guided tour of the world's biggest physics experiment quietly conducted in a Geneva suburb is phenomenal.

Other great Swiss science trips: the ground-breaking glacial research carried out by courageous 19th-century scientists on the extraordinary 23km-long Aletsch Glacier in the Upper Valais and a chemist in Basel called Albert Hofmann inadvertently embarking on the world's first acid trip in 1943.

Forever Innovating: Architecture

Switzerland's contribution to modern architecture is pivotal thanks to Le Corbusier (1887–1965), born in the small Jura town of La Chaux-de-Fonds. Known for his radical economy of design, formalism and functionalism, Le Corbusier spent most of his working life in France but graced his country of birth with his first and last creations.

Swiss architects continue to innovate. Basel-based partners Jacques Herzog and Pierre de Meuron are the most well known. Strings in their bow include London's Tate Modern gallery and the main stadium for the 2008 Beijing Olympics. In Switzerland you can admire their work at an art gallery in Basel and, sometime within the next decade, in Davos in the shape of a 105m-tall pencil twisting above the mythical Schatzalp hotel (work is expected to start in 2012).

The other big home-grown architect is Ticino-born Mario Botta, who basks in the international limelight as creator of San Francisco's Museum of Modern Art. Closer to home, his Chiesa di San Giovanni Battista in Mogno in Ticino's Valle Maggia, and cathedral-style Tschuggen Bergoase spa hotel in Arosa, Graubünden, are soul-soothing creations, while his futuristic remake of Leuk's Romanesque *schloss* (castle) in the Upper

Science Trips

» CERN, Geneva

» Technorama, Winterthur

» Eiswelt, Bettmeralp

» Einstein Haus, Bern

» Maison d'Ailleurs, Yverdon-les-Bains

Switzerland has always attracted celebrities. Famous non-Swiss residents and former residents include Charlie Chaplin, Yehudi Menuhin, Audrey Hepburn, Richard Burton, Peter Ustinov, Roger Moore, Tina Turner, Phil Collins, the Aga Khan, Michael Schumacher, *Wallpaper* magazine founder Tyler Brûlé, Formula One star Lewis Hamilton and Queen lead singer Freddie Mercury. Native Swiss who've made their mark on the world stage:

Ursula Andress (b 1936) Actress and '60s sex symbol, most famous for her bikini-clad appearance in the James Bond flick *Dr No*.

Sepp (Joseph) Blatter (b 1936) Outspoken president of Zürich-based FIFA, world football's governing body, who famously said of women's football that the shorts should be tighter. He was re-elected for a fourth term in 2011.

Alain de Botton (b 1969) Zürich-born pop philosopher and globally best-selling author of *The Art of Travel*.

Louis Chevrolet (1878–1941) Founder of the Chevrolet Manufacturing Company in 1911, producer of archetypal 'American' automobiles.

Roger Federer (b 1981) Swiss tennis ace and world number one for a record 237 consecutive weeks and 285 weeks overall; currently ranked number three in the world.

Martina Hingis (b 1980) Czech-born Swiss tennis player ranked world number one for 209 weeks before retiring from the game in 2006.

Elisabeth Kübler-Ross (1926–2004) Psychiatrist whose *On Death and Dying* articulated the famous five stages of grief: denial, anger, bargaining, depression and acceptance.

Erich von Däniken (b 1935) Controversial expounder of far-fetched early-history theories in the 1970s bestseller *Chariots of the Gods?*

Valais is nothing short of wacky. His latest creation is Rigi Kaltbad mineral baths and spa (2012) with designer views of Lake Lucerne from its fabulous Mt Rigi perch in Central Switzerland.

Then there is the award-winning Therme Vals by Basel-born Peter Zumthor (b 1943), Davos' Kirchner Museum by Zürich's Annette Gigon and Mike Guyer (www.gigon-guyer.ch) and a clutch of design hotels in Zermatt by resident avant-garde architect Heinz Julen (www.heinz-julen .com).

In true Swiss fashion – forever creative and forever dutiful to their mountains – contemporary Swiss architects don't confine their work to urban Switzerland. Increasingly their focus is on the mountain hut and how it can be modernised in keeping with nature, ecology and the environment. Stunning examples are the Tschierva Hütte (2753m) in the Engadine Valley, Chetzeron, a concrete 1960s cable-car-station-turned-hip-piste-hangout on the slopes in Crans-Montana, and, most significantly of all, the visionary Monte Rosa Hütte (2883m) on Monte Rosa.

**Archi-
tectural
Pilgrim-
ages**

» La Maison Blanche, La Chaux-de-Fonds

» Villa Le Lac, Corseaux

» Schaulager, Basel

» Le Corbusier Pavilion & Heidi Weber Museum, Zürich

» Therme Vals, Vals

» Freilichtmuseum Ballenberg, near Brienz

Heidi & Co: Literature

Thanks to a 1930s Shirley Temple film, Johanna Spyri's *Heidi* is the most famous Swiss novel. The story of an orphan living with her grandfather in the Swiss Alps who is ripped away to the city is unashamedly sentimental and utterly atypical for Swiss literature, which is otherwise quite serious and gloomy.

Take German-born, naturalised Swiss Hermann Hesse (1877–1962). A Nobel Prize winner, he fused Eastern mysticism and Jungian psychology to advance the theory that Western civilisation is doomed unless humankind gets in touch with its own essential humanity – as in *Siddharta* (1922) and *Steppenwolf* (1927). Later novels such as *Narzissus und Goldmund* (1930) and the cult *The Glass Bead Game* (1943) explore the tension between individual freedom and social controls.

Similarly, the most recognised work by Zürich-born Max Frisch (1911–91), *Ich bin nicht Stiller* (1954, I'm Not Stiller/I'm Not Relaxed) is a dark, Kafkaesque tale of mistaken identity. More accessible is Friedrich Dürrenmatt (1921–90), who created a rich wealth of detective fiction.

Green Henry (1854), by Gottfried Keller (1819–1900), is a massive tome revolving around a Zürich student's reminiscences and is considered one of the masterpieces of Germanic literature.

Pastoral to Political: Music

Yodelling and alpenhorns are the traditional forms of Swiss 'music'. Yodelling began in the Alps as a means of communication between peaks, but became separated into two disciplines: *Juchzin* consists of short yells with different meanings, such as 'it's dinner time' or 'we're coming', while *Naturjodel* sees one or more voices sing a melody without lyrics. Yodelling is fast becoming the trendy thing to do in urban circles thanks in part to Swiss folk singers like Nadja Räss who yodel with great success.

'Dr Schacher Seppli', a traditional song reyodelled by Switzerland's best-known yodeller, farmer and cheesemaker, Rudolf Rymann (1933–2008), is an iconic iPod download. The other big sound is Sonalp (www .sonalp.com), a nine-person band from the Gruyères/Château d'Œx region, whose vibrant ethno-folk mix of yodelling, cow bells, musical saw, classical violin and didgeridoo is contagious.

If folk ballads are more your cup of tea, the fragile voice of Bern-born singer Sophie Hunger (www.sophiehunger.com) who flips between English, German and Swiss German, will instantly win you over. Her second and third albums, *Monday's Ghost* (2008) and *1983* (2010) were huge internationally.

The alpenhorn, a pastoral instrument used to herd cattle in the mountains, is a wind instrument, 2m to 4m long with a curved base and a cup-shaped mouthpiece; the shorter the horn the harder it is to play. Catch a symphony of a hundred-odd alpenhorn players blowing in unison on the 'stage' – usually alfresco and invariably lakeside between mountain peaks – and you'll be won over forever. Key dates include September's Alphorn In Concert festival (www.alphorninconcert.ch, in German) in Oesingen near Solothurn and July's International Alphorn Festival (www.nendaz.ch), emotively held on the Alpine shores of Lac de Tracouet in Nendaz, 13km south of Sion in the Valais; hike or ride the cable car up for a complete Alpine experience.

James Joyce spent much of WWI in Zürich, where he wrote *Ulysses*. Listen to weekly readings of excerpts from *Ulysses* and *Finnegan's Wake* at the James Joyce Foundation.

COMPLETELY DADA

Antibourgeois, rebellious, nihilistic and deliberately nonsensical, the Dada art movement grew out of revulsion to WWI and the mechanisation of modern life. Its proponents paved the way for nearly every form of contemporary art by using collage, extracting influences from indigenous art, applying abstract notions to writing, film and performance and taking manufactured objects and redefining them as art.

Zürich was the movement's birthplace. Hugo Ball, Tristan Tzara and Emmy Jenning's creation of the Cabaret Voltaire in February 1916 kicked off a series of raucous cabaret and performance-art events in a bar at Spiegelgasse 1. The name Dada was allegedly randomly chosen by stabbing a knife through a French/German dictionary.

By 1923 the movement was dead, but its spirit lives on in the works of true Dadaists like George Grosz, Hans Arp and Max Ernst and those infected with its ideas like Marcel Duchamp (whose somewhat damaged urinal-as-art piece conveys the idea succinctly) and photographer Man Ray. See Dadaist works in Zürich's Kunsthaus and Museum für Gestaltung.

THE SWISS FLAG

No national flag better lends itself to design than Switzerland's.

Swiss Army Recycling Collection (www.swissbags.de) Created by a Valais shoemaker and saddler, this hip line makes bags from the rough wool blankets used by the Swiss Army until the 1960s when they switched to sleeping bags. Handles are recycled gun straps or soldiers' belts and the icing on the cake is the bold white cross emblazoned across the front.

Sigg (www.sigg.ch) Known the world over, Switzerland's simple signature water bottle, emblazoned with a white cross and stopped with a black hockey-puck shaped lid, is the essential companion on any mountain hike. It was born out of a kitchenware manufacturing company founded in Biel in 1908.

Victorinox (www.victorinox.com) Take the Swiss flag, remodel it as a pocket knife and you have the Original Swiss Army knife, aka Victorinox. Recent models, complete with USB key, metal saw and hard wire cutter, quite put those made in the 1880s to shame.

Alprausch (www.alprausch.ch) The last word in street- and snow-garb thanks, in no small part, to the gargantuan street cred of its hip Zürich creator, champion snowboarder Andy Tanner. But what is that emblazoned on his latest ski-jacket design (deemed so cool Victoria Beckham was snapped wearing an Alprausch jacket in St Moritz a few years back) or knitted hat? Why, a white cross on a red square...

Then there is Stress, Switzerland's hottest hip-hop artist known for, at times, his political and controversial lyrics.

Painting, Sculpture & Design

Dada aside, there have been few Swiss art movements. The painter who most concerned himself with Swiss themes was Ferdinand Hodler (1853–1918), who depicted folk heroes, like William Tell, and events from history, such as the first grassroots Swiss vote. Unlike many fellow Swiss artists Hodler remained resident in Switzerland.

Abstract artist and colour specialist Paul Klee (1879–1940) spent most of his life in Germany, including with the Bauhaus school, but the largest showcase of his work is in Bern at the striking and fascinating Zentrum Paul Klee. Likewise, sculptor Alberto Giacometti (1901–66) worked in Paris, but many of his trademark stick figures have made it back to Zürich's Kunsthaus. Quirky sculptures by Paris-based Jean Tinguely (1925–91) are clustered around Basel and Fribourg.

Then there is Gianni Motti (b 1958), an Italian artist considered Swiss – he lives and works in Geneva – notorious for his 'artistic' stunts, such as selling bars of soap made from Silvio Berlusconi's liposuctioned fat for US$18,000 a piece. Delightful.

The Swiss excel in graphic design. The 'new graphics' of Josef Müller-Brockmann (1914–96) and Max Bill (1908–94) are still extremely well regarded, as is the branding work by Karl Gerstner (b 1930) for IBM and the Búro Destruct (www.burodestruct.net) studio's typefaces, a feature of many music album covers.

Product design and installation art are Switzerland's other fortes. It gave the world Europe's largest urban lounge in St Gallen in north-eastern Switzerland, courtesy of Pipilotti Rist (b 1962) and Cow Parade, processions of life-size, painted fibreglass cows trotting around the globe. The first 800-head herd had their outing in Zürich in 1998 and stray animals in different garbs continue to lurk around the country.

Of course, there's also the flag.

Climb to the top of the first skyscraper in Zürich's trendy Kreis 5 district, aka a pile of containers inside the Freitag factory shop. Pioneers in Swiss design, the Freitag brothers turn truck tarps into chic, water-resistant bags for every occasion.

The Swiss Table

This land of Heidi is the land of hearty. And there is far more to Swiss cuisine than chocolate, cheese and Swiss-German rösti. The very best of Swiss dining in this essentially rural country is as much about experience as culinary extraordinaire. Autumnal game and air-dried meats on a farm with cud-chewing cows and magnificent views; fondue in a forest followed by a star-lit toboggan race between trees; a sweet-wafer cornet outrageously filled with thick rich cream in a mountain chalet, 4000m peaks as eye candy: these are the culinary moments you remember best, that you crave more of.

If alpine tradition gives Swiss food its soul and staying power, geography gives it its unexpected edge. The chic city crowd feasts on pasta, dumplings, strudel and urban tapas; the Swiss kitchen is extraordinarily rich and varied thanks to a trio of powerful neighbouring cuisines. Cooks in French-speaking cantons take cues from France, Ticino kitchens turn to Italy and a fair chunk looks to Germany and Austria for culinary clues. The result: a novel cuisine rooted firmly in the land and seasons, with ever-fabulous desserts.

Beer flows famously freely in German-speaking Switzerland, but it is lovers of wine whose taste buds get the biggest kick – see p348 to find out why.

For details about the price ranges used in this guide see p356.

For a really Swiss hike, pack in your knapsack a bar of Toblerone chocolate, a bottle of fizzy Rivella and a packet of herbal Ricola sweets. End with a warming mug of Ovomaltine.

Not Only Holes: Cheese

First things first: not all Swiss cheese has holes. Emmental, the hard cheese from the Emme Valley east of Bern, does – as does the not dissimilar Tilsiter from the same valley. But, contrary to common perception, most of Switzerland's 450 different types of cheese (*käse* in German, *fromage* in French, *formaggio* in Italian) are hole-less. Take the well-known hard cheese Gruyère made in the town of Gruyères near Fribourg, the overwhelmingly stinky Appenzeller used in a rash of tasty, equally strong-smelling dishes in the same-name town in northeastern Switzerland, or Sbrinz, Switzerland's oldest hard cheese and transalpine

---

HOT BOX

It's hot, it's soft and it's packed in a box. Vacherin Mont d'Or, an Appellation d'Origine Contrôllée–protected cheese, is the only Swiss cheese to be eaten with a spoon – hot. Only eaten between September and March, the Jurassien speciality derives its unique nutty taste from the spruce bark in which it's wrapped.

Connoisseurs dig a small hole in the centre of the soft-crusted cheese, fill it with finely chopped onions and garlic, pour white wine on top, wrap it in aluminium foil and bake it for 45 minutes to create a *boîte chaude* (hot box) – into which bread and other tasty titbits can be dunked to create an alternative fondue.

ancestor to Italian parmesan, ripened for 24 months to create its distinct taste – eat it straight and thinly sliced like carpaccio or grated on top of springtime asparagus.

Another distinctive Swiss cheese with not a hole in sight is hard, nutty-flavoured Tête de Moine (literally 'monks's head') from the Jura that comes in a small round and is cut with a flourish in a flowery curl using a special handled cutting device known as a *girolle* (great present to take back home – supermarkets sell them).

As unique is L'Etivaz which, in the finest of timeless alpine traditions, is only made up high on lush summer pastures in the Alpes Vaudoises (Vaud Alps). As cows graze outside, shepherds inside their century-old *chalets d'alpage* (mountain huts) heat up the morning's milk in a traditional copper cauldron over a wood fire. Strictly seasonal, the Appellation d'Origine Contrôllée (AOC) cheese can only be made from May to early October using milk from cows which have grazed on mountains between 1000m and 2000m high.

This is by no means the only cheese to be made at altitude using traditional methods; when travelling around the Valais, Bernese Alps, Ticino and other predominantly rural mountain areas in summer, look for signs pointing to isolated farmsteads where *fromage d'alpage* (mountain cheese, *hobelkäse* in German, *fromaggio d'Alpe* in Italian) is made and sold.

On the Swiss–Italian border, Zincarlìn is a raw-milk, cup-shaped cheese unusually made from unbroken curds.

A Feast of a Meal: Fondue & Raclette

It is hard to leave Switzerland without dipping into a fondue (from the French verb *fondre,* meaning 'to melt'). The main French contribution to the Swiss table, a pot of gooey melted cheese is placed in the centre of the table and kept on a slow burn while diners dip in cubes of crusty bread using slender two-pronged fondue forks. If you lose your chunk in the cheese, you buy the next round of drinks or, should you be in Geneva, get thrown in the lake. Traditionally a winter dish, the Swiss only eat it as long as there's snow around – unlike tourists who tuck in year-round.

The classic fondue mix in Switzerland is equal amounts of Emmental and Gruyère cheese, grated and melted with white wine and a shot of kirsch (cherry-flavoured liquor), then thickened slightly with potato or corn flour. It is served with a basket of bread cubes and most people order a side platter of cold meats and tiny gherkins to accompany it. *Fondue moitié moitié* (literally 'half half fondue') mixes Gruyère with Vacherin Fribourgeois, and *fondue savoyarde* sees equal proportions of Comté, Beaufort and Emmental thrown into the pot. Common variants involve adding ingredients such as mushrooms or tomato.

Switzerland's other signature alpine cheese dish, another fabulous feast of a meal in itself, is raclette. Unlike fondue, raclette – both the name of the dish and the cheese at its gooey heart – is eaten year-round. A half-crescent slab of the cheese is screwed onto a specially designed 'rack oven' that melts the top flat side. As it melts, cheese is scraped onto

Best Fondues

» Tour de Gourze, Lavaux – over lake & vineyard view

» Café du Midi, Martigny – with beer or goat's cheese

» Le Namasté, Verbier – ski, eat, sledge

» La Ferme des Moulins, Sembrancher – aboard a horse & cart

» Café Tivoli, Châtel-St-Denis – Fribourgeois fondue temple

LA RELIGEUSE

Whatever the mix, everyone loves *la croûte* or, as it is more poetically known, *la religieuse* – the delicious, crispy cheese crust left on the bottom of the fondue pot or on the side of the raclette cheese as its salted skin sizzles. Vie with your neighbour for a scraping or cross your fingers and hope that your host deems you the honoured guest who gets the lion's share.

plates for immediate consumption with boiled potatoes, cold meats and pickled onions or gherkins.

When buying your own tangy round wheel of raclette (or, indeed, discussing the topic with a born-and-bred Valaisian), be aware of the difference between *raclette Suisse* (Swiss raclette), made industrially with pasteurised milk anywhere in Switzerland, and Raclette du Valais, produced in the Valais using *lait cru* (raw milk) since the 16th century. In 2007 Raclette du Valais – never more or less than 29cm to 31cm in diameter, 4.8kg to 5.2kg in weight – gained its own AOC, much to the horror of cheese-makers in other cantons who vehemently argued, to no avail, that raclette (from the French verb *racler,* meaning 'to scrape') refers to the dish, not the cheese, and thus shouldn't be restricted to one region.

Butter-soft Steak & Autumnal Game: Meat

For a quintessential Swiss lunch, nothing beats an al fresco platter of air-dried beef, a truly sweet and exquisitely tender delicacy from Graubünden that is smoked, thinly sliced and served as *Bündnerfleisch.* Eat it neat or in *Capuns,* a rich mix of *Spätzli* dough, air-dried beef, ham and herbs cooked, cut into tiny morsels, wrapped with spinach and mixed with yet more *Spätzli* (a Germanic cross between a pasta and dumpling). The same wafer-thin slices of *viande séchée* (air-dried beef) are a staple in the Val d'Hérens, a delightfully remote valley in the Valais where fertile pastures are mowed by silky black Hérens cattle and local gourmets feast on butter-soft Hérens beef served in every imaginable way. Au Vieux Mazot in Evolène and Au Cheval Blanc in Sion are two Swiss-simple but superb insider addresses to sample this succulent local beef any way you like it.

Travel east and *Würste* (sausages) become the local lunch feast, typically served with German-speaking Switzerland's star dish: rösti (a shredded, oven-crisped potato bake), perhaps topped with a fried egg. (If only to prove they're different, Swiss French cook it in oil while Swiss Germans throw a lump of butter or lard in the frying pan.) As common and cheap as chips it might be these days, but be aware that the nasty vacuum-sealed packs of rösti sold in supermarkets cannot even be compared to the real McCoy homemade dish cooked up in authentic mountain restaurants. Baked to a perfect crisp, often in a wood-fuelled oven, the shredded potato is mixed with seasonal mushrooms and bacon bits to create a perfect lunch, paired with nothing more than a simple green salad. This is Swiss Alpine heaven.

Veal is highly rated and is tasty thinly sliced and smothered in a cream sauce as *geschnetzeltes Kalbsfleisch* in Zürich. Horse meat is also eaten. Two unusual Swiss salami to look out, sufficiently rare to be on Slow Food's list of endangered world food products (www.slowfoodfoundation.com), are *sac* (made from pork, liver, lard and spices aged for 12 months) and *fidighèla* (packed in veal intestine when straight, pork intestine if curved and aged for two to three weeks). In the canton of Vaud pork goes into *taillé* (pork-speckled savoury bread).

For true, blue-blooded meat lovers there is no better season to let tastebuds rip in this heavily forested country than autumn, when restaurants up and down the country cook up *Wildspezialitäten/specialités de gibier (*or *chasse)/cacciagione* (fresh game). Venison and wild boar are wildly popular.

Around the Lake: Fish

Fish is the speciality in lakeside towns. Perch (*perche,* in French) and whitefish fillets *(féra)* are common, but don't be fooled into thinking the *filets de perche* chalked on the blackboard in practically every Lake

Drinking water while dipping into a fondue is said to coagulate the warm cheese in your stomach and bring on unpleasant gut ache – not necessarily true, but why risk it? Opt instead for a local white wine like Fendant from the Valais – the perfect partner to cheesy fondue and raclette.

Geneva restaurant are from the lake; the vast majority cooked around its shores, Geneva included, come frozen from Eastern Europe.

Festive Fun: Kill the Pig!

Traditionally it was not with a pig, but with onions, that medieval townsfolk in German-speaking Bern celebrated Martinmas (St Martin's Day). Today's Zibelemärit (Onion Fair), the 4th Sunday in November, is an extraordinary extravaganza of onion-themed produce.

Autumn, with its fresh game, abundance of wild mushrooms, chestnuts and grape harvests, is exquisitely gourmet in Switzerland, and as the days shorten this season only gets better. Fattened over summer, the family pig – traditionally slaughtered on the feast of St Martin (11 November) marking the end of agricultural work in the fields and the start of winter – is ready for the butcher. On farms and in villages for centuries, the slaughter would be followed by the salting of meat and sausage-making. Work done, folk would then pass over to feasting to celebrate the day's toil. The main dish for the feast: pork.

In the French-speaking Jura, in particular, the feasting tradition around Fête de la St-Martin lives on with particular energy and enthusiasm in Porrentruy. Local bars and restaurants organise feasts for several weekends on the trot in October and November. A typical pork feast consists of gorging on seven copious courses, kicking off perhaps with *gelée de ménage,* a pork gelatine dish. *Boudin, purée de pommes et racines rouges* (black pudding, apple compote and red vegetables) and piles of sausages accompanied by rösti and *atriaux* (a dish based on pork fat, sausage and liver, all roasted in sizzling fat) follows. Next up is the main course, with *rôti, côtines et doucette* (roast pork, ribs and a green salad). A liquor-soaked sorbet might follow to aid digestion, followed by a serving of *choucroute* (boiled cabbage enlivened by, yum, bacon bits). Finally, a traditional dessert, such as *striflate en sauce de vanille* (strings of deep-fried pastries in vanilla sauce), is served.

Pork dishes to look out for year-round include *Rippli* (a bubbling pot of pork rib meat cooked up with bacon, potatoes and beans) in and around Bern, and in the canton of Vaud, *papet vaudois* (a potato, leek, cabbage and sausage stew) and *taillé aux greubons* (a crispy savoury pastry, soft and dotted inside with pork-lard cubes). In the Engadine, sausage is baked with onions and potato to make *pian di pigna.*

Ever Fabulous Desserts: Fruit, Sweets & Chocolate

Sensible Swiss: they don't simply eat the plump Valais apricots, plums, pears and sweet black cherries that fill their orchards with a profusion of pretty white blossoms in April and May. As their 19th-century cookbook

HARVEST SUPPERS

Nothing prompts a party more than a harvest and every village and region has their own way of partying in thanks.

In the Valais' French-speaking vineyards, grapes are harvested as *châtaignes* (chestnuts) tumble from chestnuts trees – prompting family and friends to gather for La Brisolée, a copious feast, unchanged for centuries and far more than 'just a meal'. It comprises hot roasted chestnuts, five local cheeses – *d'alpage* (high-pasture), *de laiterie* (dairy), tomme (semi-hard made from raw milk), *sérac* (whey) and Tête de Moine – ham, air-dried beef, *lard sec* (air-dried bacon face), buttered rye bread, grapes and apples. All this is washed down with *vin nouveau* (the first wine of the year) and *le moût* (must, wine that is still fermenting).

Around Fribourg, the centuries-old harvest festival, Le Bénichon, is another marathon affair with much eating, drinking and merriment. The traditional meal starts with *cuchaule,* a saffron-scented bread served with *moutarde de Bénichon* (a thick mustard condiment made of cooked wine must, spices, sugar and flour).

SWISS CHOCOLATE

In the early centuries after Christ's death, as the Roman Empire headed towards slow collapse on a diet of rough wine and olives, the Mayans in Central America were pounding cocoa beans, consuming the result and even using the beans as a system of payment.

A millennium later, the Spanish conquistador Hernando Cortez brought the first load of cocoa to Europe in 1528. He could not have anticipated the subsequent demand for his cargo. The Spaniards, and soon other Europeans, developed an insatiable thirst for the sweetened beverage produced from it. The solid stuff came later.

Swiss chocolate (www.chocolat.ch) built its reputation in the 19th century, thanks to pioneering spirits such as François-Louis Cailler (1796–1852), Philippe Suchard (1797–1884), Henri Nestlé (1814–90), Jean Tobler (1830–1905), Daniel Peter (1836–1919) and Rodolphe Lindt (1855–1909). Cailler established the first Swiss chocolate factory in 1819 near Vevey. Daniel Peter added milk in 1875 and Lindt invented conching, a rotary aeration process that gives chocolate its melt-in-the-mouth quality.

If you like chocolate, see p18.

clearly spells out, the Swiss also dry, preserve and distil their abundance of fruit to create fiery liqueurs, winter compotes and thick-as-honey syrups for baking or spreading on bread.

Berudge eau de vie is from made Berudge plums grown on the slopes of Mont Vully in the Fribourg canton, and cherries from around Basel go into thick *Chriesimues* syrup and sweet cherry kirsch – the ingredient that gives Zug's to-die-for *Zuger Kirschtorte* (cherry cake made from pastry, biscuit, almond paste and butter cream, all infused with cherry liqueur) its extra special kick. (The real McCoy Swiss version of kirsch is feared for as fruit farmers replace ancient cherry varieties with less-aromatic modern equivalents.) Apple or pear juice is simmered for 24 hours to make Fribourgois *vin cuit* (a dense, semi-hard concentrate used in tarts and other fruity desserts) and Vaudois *raisinée; Buttemoscht* is a less common rose-hip equivalent.

The Botzi pear cultivated around Gruyères is deemed precious enough to have its own AOC. Bite into it as nature intended or try it with local *crème de Gruyères*, the thickest cream ever, traditionally eaten by the spoonful with sugary-sweet meringues – quite simply to die for, darling. *Cuisses de dame* (lady's thighs) are sugary deep-fried thigh-shaped pastries, found in French-speaking cantons next to amandines (almond tarts). Apart from the ubiquitous *Apfelstrudel* (apple pie), typically served with runny vanilla sauce, German cantons cook up *Vermicelles,* a chestnut-cream creation resembling something like spaghetti.

Then, of course, there is chocolate...

Müsli (muesli) was invented in Switzerland at the end of the 19th century. The most common form of this very healthy breakfast is *Birchermüsli*, sometimes served with less-than-slimming dollops of cream.

Swiss Wine

Savouring local wine in Switzerland is an exquisite, increasingly rare gastronomic joy in this globalised world: Switzerland exports little of its wine; meaning that most of its quality reds, whites and rosé vintages, including dozens by small vignerons, can only be tasted and enjoyed in situ.

The bulk of Swiss wine production takes place in the French-speaking part of the country where vineyards pirouette on the shore of Lake Geneva, from where they stagger sharply up hillsides in tightly-packed terraces knitted together by ancient dry-stone walls. Festivals piggyback on the agricultural cycle. Winemakers around Lausanne kick off the viticultural party with their May-time Millésime, but the real cause for celebration is in late September and October when the grapes are harvested and the *vin nouveau* (new wine) tasted. Nowhere is this respected more fiercely than in and around Sion, gourmet capital of the Valais, where the harvest is marked with La Brisolée (p346).

The annual Vinea wine fair (www.vinea.ch), held for three days each year in early September in Sierre, Valais, is a brilliant one-stop opportunity to meet winegrowers from all over Switzerland and taste their wine.

When ordering wine in a wine bar or restaurant, use the uniquely Swiss approach of *déci* (100ml) multiples – or order a bottle.

Lake Geneva & Vaud

A generous smattering of small family vignerons open their doors for *dégustation* (tasting) on the fringes of Geneva – the canton's annual *Caves Ouvertes* (Open Cellars) day held one weekend in late May is a fabulous opportunity to discover the wines of cellars and *domaines viticoles* (estates) otherwise closed to visitors.

But most of Lake Geneva's winemaking estates languish further east, either side of Lausanne in the canton of Vaud. Whites from the pea-green terraced vineyards of the Lavaux wine region between Lausanne and Montreux are so outstanding that the area has been designated a Unesco World Heritage Site. Lavaux's two grands crus are Calamin and Dézaley.

The generic Vaud red is the Salvagnin, divided into several labels and generally combining Pinot noir and Gamay grapes. A home-grown offshoot is the Gamaret or Garanoir, created in the 1970s to produce a throaty red that ages particularly well.

Straddling Vaud is the small Chablais winemaking area, best known for its Yvorne whites.

Valais

Drenched in an extra bonanza of sunshine and light from above the southern Alps, much of the land north of the Rhône River in western Valais is planted with vines – and this is where some of Switzerland's best wines are produced. Unique to the Valais are the *bisses* (p156; narrow irrigation channels) that traverse the vineyards.

Digital Viticulture

» www.swisswine.ch

» www.lesvinsdegeneve.ch

» www.vins-vaudois.ch

» www.lesvinsduvalais.ch

» www.ovpt.ch

» www.ticinowine.ch

Best Wine Tasting

» Domaine du Daley, Lutry

» Lavaux Vinorama, Rivaz

» Musée de la Vigne, Aigle

» Le Cube, Bisse de Clavaux

» Château de Villa, Sierre

» Vinethek Viniterra Bielersee, Twann

Locally produced fruit brandies are often served with or in coffee. Kirsch is made from the juice of compressed cherry pits. Appenzeller Alpenbitter (Alpine Bitters) is a liquor made from the essences of 67 different flowers and roots. Damassine, which you are more likely to find in the French cantons, is made of small prunes and makes a good postprandial digestive. A pear-based drop is the popular Williamine, and Pflümli is a typical plum-based schnapps in the German cantons.

After a century on the index of banned beverages, absinthe – aka the green fairy – is legal in Switzerland again, to the joy of the valley in Neuchâtel Canton where the wormwood drink was first distilled in the 18th century. For more on this aniseed-based rocket fuel with a typical alcohol reading approaching Richter-scale proportions of 56% or more, see p93.

SWISS WINE

Dryish white Fendant, the perfect accompaniment to fondue and Raclette, and best served crisp cold, is the region's best-known wine, accounting for two-thirds of Valais wine production. Johannisberg is another excellent white and comes from the Sylvaner grape; while Petite Arvine and Amigne are sweet whites.

Dôle, made from Pinot noir and Gamay grapes, is the principal red blend and is as full bodied as an opera singer with its firm fruit flavour. Reds from Salgesch are generally outstanding and increasingly use innovative blends to create exciting wines like Maîtresse de Salquenen, an assemblage of 13 grape varieties.

Wine tasting and exploring opportunities in the Valais are naturally rife. Year-round, the region's many gentle walking trails through vines make a perfect introduction: top trails include the Chemin du Vignoble (www.cheminduvignoble.ch) from Martigny (Lower Valais) to Leuk (Upper Valais), which passes the world's highest drystone walls ensnaring green vines near Sion; the Sierre-Salgesch Sentier Viticole (6km) linking a twinset of wine museums and host to September's fabulous Marché des Cépages (p160); and the 2½-hour trail from Visp up to Europe's highest vineyards (1150m) in Visperterminen.

Enticing wine-and-food pairings, wine-tasting courses and vineyard walks are among the many viticultural discoveries waiting to be explored at www.campagnon.ch and www.vins-vaudois.com

Lacs de Neuchâtel & Bienne

Further north the fruity rosé Œil-de-Perdrix, literally 'Partridge's Eye') kicks in along the scenic shores of Lake Neuchâtel: taste and drink it along the Route du Vignoble, a wine itinerary that trails the 30km of steeply terraced water-facing vineyards between Lac de Neuchâtel and the western shore of Lac de Bienne (Bieler See) in Mittelland.

For stunning scenery sufficiently magnificent to rival Unesco-protected Lavaux and sublime vineyard trails and tasting, the enchanting winegrowing hamlet of Ligerz on Lake Biel's northern shore is the address to savour this magnificent wine-growing area.

Ticino

The favourite liquid for lunch in Switzerland's Italianate climes is merlot, which accounts for almost 90% of Ticino's wine production. Some white merlots are also produced, as well as wines made from a handful of other grape varieties. The main winemaking areas are between Bellinzona and Ascona, around Biasca and between Lugano and Mendrisio (lovely September wine festival).

Swiss German Wines

Less known than their French Swiss counterparts and produced in substantially smaller quantities, Swiss German vintages are nonetheless

Best Vineyard Sleeps

» Auberge de Dully, La Côte

» Auberge du Raisin, Cully

» Hôtel Masson, Montreux

» Hotel Arkanum, Salgesch

» Hotel Kreuz Ligerz, Ligerz

» Eulenhof, Mur, Around Murten

SWISS WINE

worth tasting. About 75% are reds, predominantly Pinot noir (Blauburgunder) – taste and enjoy in wine taverns and tasting rooms in
Bündner Herrschaft, Graubünden's premier wine region north of Chur.

Gewürztraminer is a dry white variety. The main white though is
Müller-Thurgau (a crisp mix of riesling and Sylvaner), produced in the
wine-growing town of Spiez on Lake Thun in the Bernese Oberland.
The best time to taste is at the nearby Läset-Sunntig wine festival in
late September.

Survival
Guide

Directory A–Z

Accommodation

Switzerland sports accommodation in every price range and the reviews in this guidebook run from budget to midrange and top end, arranged by author preference. Prices listed are for high season and include breakfast (unless otherwise noted). They are categorised according to the following guidelines:

Budget ($) Includes campsites, dormitories, farmstays, hostels and simple hotels, many of which offer rooms with shared bathroom facilities. These generally cost up to Sfr150 for a double, but this can differ slightly, depending on city or countryside addresses.

Midrange ($$) With all the comforts of a private bathroom, TV, telephone and more. Prices go up to approximately Sfr350 for a double, again depending on where you're staying.

Top end ($$$) Where you can wallow in pure unadulterated, time-honoured Swiss luxury; starts at Sfr350 for a double.

Rates in cities and most towns stay constant throughout the year bar the Christmas and New Year periods, when rates rise. In mountain resorts prices are seasonal: low season (mid-September to mid-December and mid-April to mid-June) is the cheapest time to visit, mid-season (January to mid-February and mid-June to early July and September) begins to get pricy, and high season (July to August, Christmas, and mid-February to Easter) is the busy period. Seasonal differences are less marked at budget hotels.

Tourist offices have accommodation listings and most will make a hotel reservation for you, for as little as Sfr5 or no commission. A handy resource for tracking down accomodation is www.myswitzerland.com.

B&Bs

Some of Switzerland's most charming accommodation comes in the form of bed and breakfast – a room in a private home (anything from a castle to a farm), which includes breakfast, often made from homemade produce. Some hosts will also, if you order in advance, cook up an evening meal served for an additional Sfr20 to Sfr30 per person, often with wine.

Tourist offices have lists of B&Bs in their areas – urban rarities but plentiful in the countryside areas – and 800-odd can be tracked through **BnB** (www.bnb.ch), which also publishes an annual guide (Sfr28). In rural areas, private houses frequently offer inexpensive 'room(s) vacant' (*Zimmer frei* in German, *chambres libres* in French, *camere libere* in Italian), with or without breakfast.

Camping

Camp sites brandish one to five stars depending on their amenities and convenience of location. They are often scenically situated in an out-of-the-way place by a river or lake, so having your own transport is useful. Telephone ahead, as camps might be full in the high season, and at the start or end of the season camps may close if demand is low or the weather poor. Charges per night are from around Sfr8 per person plus Sfr6 to Sfr12 for a tent, and from an additional Sfr4 for a car.

Wild camping (*wildes camping* in German, *camping sauvage* in French) is not strictly allowed and should be discreet, but it's viable in the wide-open

---

BOOK YOUR STAY ONLINE

For more accommodation reviews by Lonely Planet authors, check out hotels.lonelyplanet.com/Switzerland. You'll find independent reviews, as well as recommendations on the best places to stay. Best of all, you can book online.

mountain spaces and is fairly common in places like Ticino. A fine is theoretically possible.

The following organisations offer useful information:

Camping NET (www.camping.ch)

Schweizerischer Camping und Caravanning Verband (Swiss Camping & Caravanning Federation, SCCV; ☑062 777 40 08; www.sccv.ch, in German & French)

Touring Club der Schweiz (Swiss Touring Club, TCS; www.tcs.ch, in German, French & Italian) Has an English-language *Camping Holidays in Switzerland* brochure downloadable from its website if you go to the Reisen & Freizeit/Voyages & Loisirs/Viaggi & Svaghi section and hit 'Camping'.

Verband Schweizer Campings (Swiss Camping Association; ☑031 852 06 26; www.swisscamps.ch)

Dorms

Dormitory accommodation (*Touristenlager* or *Massenlager* in German, *dortoir* in French) has been well established for years in ski and other resorts. Mattresses are often crammed side by side in massive bunks, but there are usually no curfews and the doors aren't usually locked during the day. Take care when studying accommodation lists, as dormitories may only take groups.

Hostels

Swiss youth hostels (*Jugendherberge* in German, *auberge de jeunesse* in French, *alloggio per giovani* in Italian) range from older, institutional affairs to modern establishments bordering on designer accommodation. Most charge from Sfr31 for a dorm bed (single and double rooms are available in many for a higher price), including breakfast and sheets, and are run by Switzerland's Hostelling International (HI)–affiliated,

national hostelling organisation **Schweizer Jugendherbergen** (Swiss Youth Hostel Association, SYHA; ☑044 360 14 14; www.youthhostel.ch). Non-HI members who want to stay in one of its 54 hostels can become a member straight away (Sfr33 for adults or Sfr22 for persons under 18 years of age) or pay a nightly 'guest fee' of Sfr6 on top of the bed price.

Hostels do get full; telephone reservations are not accepted but bookings can be made via the website. During busy times a three-day maximum stay may apply.

Then there are backpacker hostels, which tend to be more flexible in their regulations, reception times and opening hours, and are usually free of school or youth groups. Membership is not required; 31 such hostels are loosely affiliated under **Swiss Backpackers** (☑033 823 46 46; www.swissbackpackers.ch). Eighty Alpine chalets and rural farmhouses offer hostel-style accommodation under the

green umbrella group **Naturfreundehaus** (Friends of Nature; www.nfhouse.org, in German & French).

Hotels & Pensions

The standard at the lower end of the market can vary. **Swiss Budget Hotels** (☑084 880 55 08; www.rooms.ch) has a downloadable hotel guide of good-quality cheaper hotels and regular special offers.

The cheapest rooms have a sink, but share the toilet and shower in the corridor, costing around Sfr60 for a single and Sfr90 for a double in a small town, and around Sfr80 for a single and Sfr120 for a double in cities or mountain resorts. Pop in a private shower and the nightly rate rises by at least Sfr20.

A *Frühstückspension* or *Hotel-Garni* serves only breakfast. Small pensions with a restaurant often have a 'rest day' when check-in may not be possible except by prior arrangement (telephone ahead).

PRACTICALITIES

» **Newspapers** For German-language readers, there's Zürich's *Neue Zürcher Zeitung* (www.nzz.ch) and *Tages Anzeiger* (www.tagesanzeiger.ch); Geneva's *Le Temps* (www.letemps.ch) and *La Tribune de Genève* (www.tdg.ch) are available in Suisse Romande; Lugano-based *Corriere del Ticino* (www.cdt.ch, in Italian) is in Italian. Free tabloid *20 Minuten* (www.20min.ch) is available in German and French.

» **TV & Radio** Largely broken down along linguistic lines: German-language SF-DRS operates three TV and numerous radio stations; French and Italian TV operators are TSR and RTSI, respectively, with RSR and RSI their radio equivalents; and TvR and Radio Rumantsch (RR; www.rtr.ch) are Switzerland's Romansch TV and radio stations. WRS (FM 101.7; www.worldradio.ch) is a Geneva-based English-language station broadcasting music and news countrywide.

» **Websites** Swissinfo (www.swissinfo.org) is a national news website available in several languages, including English.

» **Weights & Measures** The metric system is used. Like other continental Europeans, the Swiss indicate decimals with commas and thousands with full points.

The **Steinbock Label** (www.steinbock-label.ch, in German) hotels are recognised as eco-hotels and labelled with one to five *Steinböcke* (ibexes) to reflect their sustainability.

Rental Accommodation

Self-caterers can opt for a chalet or apartment, both of which need booking in advance; for peak periods, reserve six to 12 months ahead. A minimum stay of one week (usually Saturday to Saturday) is common.

Useful online resources for bargain-basement deals, particularly out of high season or for last-minute bookings, include **REKA** (Schweizer Reisekasse; ☎031 329 66 33; www.reka.ch), **Interhome** (☎043 810 91 91; www.interhome.ch) and **Switzerland Tourism** (www.myswitzerland.com).

KIP WITH THE COWS

A unique way to experience life on a Swiss farm is Switzerland's **Aventure sur la paille/Schlaf im Stroh** (☎041 678 12 86; www.schlaf-im-stroh.ch) – the ultimate roll in the hay.

When the cows are out to pasture in summer, Swiss farmers charge travellers Sfr20 to Sfr30 per adult and Sfr10 to Sfr20 per child under 15 to sleep on straw in their hay barns or lofts (listen to the jangle of cow bells!). Farmers provide cotton undersheets (to avoid straw pricks) and woolly blankets for extra warmth, but guests need their own sleeping bags and – strongly advisable – pocket torch. Nightly rates include a farmhouse breakfast, and a morning shower and evening meal are usually available for an extra Sfr2 and Sfr20 to Sfr30, respectively. Advance reservations are necessary in summer. A list of the 170-odd farms across Switzerland offering this accommodation is available online.

Should you prefer a room in the farmhouse rather than above the cows, try **Swiss Holiday Farms** (☎031 329 66 99; www.bauernhof-ferien.ch), an association of 210 farms countrywide that open their doors to both overnight B&B guests and self-caterers keen to rent a renovated barn or farmhouse cottage for a week or longer, or **Rural Tourism** (☎021 619 44 37; www.tourisme-rural.ch), which allows you to search its countryside-property listings by Alpine or vineyard location, chalet, farmhouse, hut, hay barn and so on.

Business Hours

The reviews in this guidebook won't list hours unless they differ from the hours listed here. Hours are given for high season (April through October) and tend to decrease in low season.

Banks 8.30am to 4.30pm Monday to Friday, usually with late opening hours one day a week.

Offices 8am to noon, 2pm to 5pm Monday to Friday

Restaurants Noon to 2pm, 6pm to 10pm

Shops 9am to 7pm Monday to Friday (sometimes with a one- to two-hour break for lunch at noon in small towns), 9am to 6pm Saturday. In cities, there's often shopping until 9pm on Thursday or Friday. Sunday sees some souvenir shops and supermarkets at some train stations open.

Children

Orderly, clean and not overly commercial, Switzerland is a dream for family travel and promotes itself heavily as such: the meaty Swiss tourist board *Families* brochure (order or download it online at www.myswitzerland.com) is jam-packed with ideas, as is its website, which lists kid-friendly accommodation, family offers and so on.

Family train travel is good-value. Kids under six years travel for free with **Swiss Railways** (www.rail.ch) and those aged six to 16 years revel in free unlimited rail travel with its annual Junior Card (Sfr30) or – should it be grandparents travelling with the kids – the grandchild travel card (Sfr30). Switzerland's mountain of scenic journeys by train and boat (p363) enchant children of all ages. Upon arrival at point B, dozens of segments of the perfectly signposted hiking, biking, rollerblading and canoeing trails designed strictly for non-motorised traffic by **Switzerland Mobility** are flagged as suitable for younger children.

Staying in a B&B (p352) is family fabulous: little kids can sweetly slumber upstairs while weary parents wine and dine in peace downstairs (don't forget your baby monitor!). Pick a B&B on a farm or kip on straw in the hay barn for adventurous kids to have the time of their life.

Those with kids aged six to 12 years should buy Dianne Dicks' *Ticking Along with Swiss Kids*, part children's book about Switzerland, part guide for parents on what to see, where to eat and what to do. Also check out Lonely Planet's *Travel with Children*.

Customs Regulations

Visitors may import 200 cigarettes, 50 cigars or 250g of pipe tobacco. The allowance

Climate

Geneva

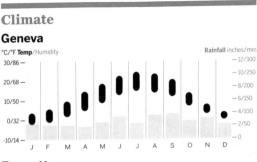

Zermatt

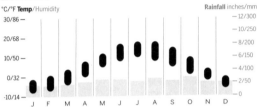

Zürich

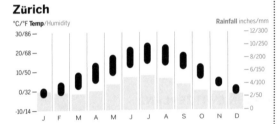

for alcoholic beverages is 1L for beverages containing more than 15% alcohol by volume, and 2L for beverages containing less than 15%. Alcohol and tobacco may only be brought in by people aged 17 or over.

Gifts up to the value of Sfr100 may also be imported, as well as food provisions for one day.

Discount Cards

Senior Cards

Senior citizens are not entitled to discounts on Swiss railways, but there are various discounts available on museum admission, ski passes and some cable cars, so it's worth asking.

The discounts often start for those as young as 62 (proof of age necessary), although sometimes a higher limit is observed. The abbreviation for senior citizens is AHV in German and AVS in French.

Student & Youth Cards

An International Student Identity Card (ISIC) yields discounts on admission prices, air and international train tickets, and even some ski passes. If you're under 26 but not a student, apply for the IYTC (International Youth Travel Card). Travel agency **STA Travel** (www.statravel .ch, in German & French) issues ISIC (Sfr 20) and both cards should be issued by student

unions and by youth-oriented travel agencies in your home country.

Swiss Museum Pass

Regular or long-term visitors to Switzerland may want to buy the **Swiss Museum Pass** (www.museumspass .ch; adult/family Sfr144/255), which covers entry to the permanent collection (only) of 450 museums.

Visitors' Cards

In many resorts and cities there's a visitors' card (Gästekarte), which provides various benefits such as reduced prices for museums, swimming pools or cable cars. Cards are issued by your accommodation.

Electricity

The electricity current is 220V, 50Hz, Swiss sockets are recessed, three-holed, hexagonally shaped and incompatible with many plugs from abroad. They usually, however, take the standard European two-pronged plug.

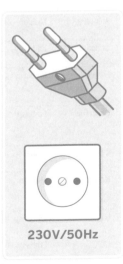

230V/50Hz

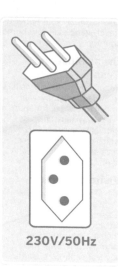

230V/50Hz

Embassies & Consulates

For a list of Swiss embassies abroad and embassies in Switzerland, go to www.eda.admin.ch. Embassies are in Bern but cities such as Zürich and Geneva have several consulates.

Food

This guide includes options for all tastes and budgets, reviewed in order of preference and categorised as follows:

Budget ($) Mains less than Sfr25

Midrange ($$) Mains between Sfr25 and Sfr45

Top End ($$$) Mains from Sfr45

Gay & Lesbian Travellers

Attitudes to homosexuality are progressive. Same-sex partnerships are recognised (although gay couples are not permitted to adopt children or have fertility treatment). The age of consent for gay sex is the same as for heterosexuals, 16 years.

Major cities have gay and lesbian bars, and pride marches are held in Geneva (early July) and Zürich (mid-July). **Cruiser magazine** (☑044 388 41 54; www.cruiser.ch, in German) has extensive listings of organisations, places and events and a searchable online agenda.

The following are some other useful websites:

www.gay.ch (in German)

www.lesbian.ch (in German)

www.myswitzerland.com Information on gay-friendly accommodation and events if you type 'Gay & Lesbian' into the search function.

www.pinkcross.ch (in German and French)

Health

An embassy, consulate or hotel can usually recommend a local doctor or clinic. The quality of

EMBASSIES & MISSIONS IN SWITZERLAND

COUNTRY	TYPE	TELEPHONE	WEBSITE	ADDRESS
Australia	Mission	☑022 799 91 00	www.australia.ch	Chemin des Fins 2, Geneva
Canada	Embassy	☑031 357 32 00	www.canada-ambassade.ch	Kirchenfeldstrasse 88, Bern
France	Embassy	☑031 359 21 11	www.ambafrance-ch.org, in German & French	Schosshalden-strasse 46, Bern
Germany	Embassy	☑031 359 41 11	www.bern.diplo.de, in German & French	Willadingweg 83, Bern
Italy	Embassy	☑031 350 07 77	www.ambitalia.ch	Elfenstrasse 14, Bern
New Zealand	Mission	☑022 929 03 50	www.nzembassy.com/switzerland	Chemin des Fins 2, Grand-Saconnex, Geneva
UK	Embassy	☑031 359 77 00	www.ukinswitzerland.fco.gov.uk	Thunstrasse 50, Bern
USA	Embassy	☑031 357 70 11	http://bern.usembassy.gov	Sulgeneckstrasse 19, Bern

health care in Switzerland is generally very high.

Altitude Sickness

This disorder can occur above 3000m, but very few treks or ski runs in the Swiss Alps reach such heights – Mont Blanc is one exception – so altitude sickness is unlikely. Headache, vomiting, dizziness, extreme faintness, and difficulty in breathing and sleeping are signs to heed. Treat mild symptoms with rest and simple painkillers. If mild symptoms persist or get worse, descend to a lower altitude and seek medical advice.

Ticks

These small creatures can be found throughout Switzerland up to an altitude of 1200m, and typically live in underbrush at the forest edge or beside walking tracks.

You should always check your whole body if you've been walking through a potentially tick-infested area. If a tick is found attached, press down around the tick's head with tweezers, grab the head and gently pull upwards. Avoid pulling the rear of the body as this may squeeze the tick's gut contents through the attached mouth-parts into the skin, increasing the risk of infection and disease. Smearing chemicals on the tick is not recommended.

LYME DISEASE

This is an infection transmitted by ticks that may be acquired in Europe. The illness usually begins with a spreading rash at the site of the tick bite and is accompanied by fever, headache, extreme fatigue, aching joints and muscles, and mild neck stiffness. If untreated, these symptoms usually resolve over several weeks, but over subsequent weeks or months, disorders of the nervous system, heart and joints may develop. Treatment works best early in the illness. Seek medical help.

TICK-BORNE ENCEPHALITIS

This disease is a cerebral inflammation carried by a virus. Tick-borne encephalitis can occur in most forest and rural areas of Switzerland. If you have been bitten, even having removed the tick, you should keep an eye out for symptoms, including blotches around the bite, which is sometimes pale in the middle. Headache, stiffness and other flu-like symptoms, as well as extreme tiredness, appearing a week or two after the bite, can progress to more serious problems. Medical help must be sought. A vaccination is available.

Hypothermia

Hypothermia occurs when the body loses heat faster than it can produce it and the core temperature of the body falls. It is surprisingly easy to progress from very cold to dangerously cold due to a combination of wind, wet clothing, fatigue and hunger, even if the air temperature is above freezing. It is best to dress in layers of good insulating materials and to wear a hat and a strong, waterproof outer layer when hiking or skiing. A 'space' blanket for emergencies is essential. Carry basic supplies, including food containing simple sugars and fluid to drink.

Symptoms of hypothermia are exhaustion, numb skin (particularly toes and fingers), shivering, slurred speech, irrational or violent behaviour, lethargy, stumbling, dizzy spells, muscle cramps and violent bursts of energy.

To treat mild hypothermia, get the person out of the wind and/or rain, remove their clothing if wet and replace it with dry, warm clothing. Give them hot liquids – not alcohol – and high-kilojoule, easily digestible food. Do not rub victims; allow them to slowly warm themselves. This should be enough to treat the early stages of hypothermia. The early recognition and treatment of mild hypothermia is the only way to prevent severe hypothermia, which is a critical condition.

Insurance

Free health treatment in Switzerland is very limited; health care generally is very expensive.

If you're skiing, snowboarding or trekking, check whether your policy covers helicopter rescue and emergency repatriation. Mountain rescue is shockingly expensive and most normal policies don't cover many outdoor activities; you'll need to pay a premium for winter-sports cover and further premiums for adventure sports like bungee jumping and skydiving.

Worldwide travel insurance is available at www.lonelyplanet.com /travel_services. You can buy, extend and claim online anytime – even if you're already on the road.

Internet Access

Public wireless access points can be found at major airports, at 35-odd Swiss train stations and airports, and in business seats of 1st-class train carriages on routes such as Basel–Zürich–Chur, Geneva–Bern–Zürich–St Gallen, Basel–Bern–Interlaken–Lucerne–Zurich Airport, Geneva–Lausanne–Bern–Lucerne and Bern–Biel-Bienne.

Many hotels have wi-fi (often free), and it's available at lots of cafes and public spaces. Most hotspots, like those provided by **Swisscom** (☎080 080 08 00; www .swisscom-mobile.ch), levy a charge – usually around Sfr5 for 30 minutes access over seven days to Sfr125 for 150 hours access over 31 days, payable by credit card or prepaid card sold at Swisscom's 1350 hot spots; locate them with its online hot-spot locator.

Internet cafes can be found in larger towns and cities, but are practically non-existent in small towns and remote areas. Prices range from Sfr5 to Sfr15 per hour.

Legal Matters

Swiss police have wide-ranging powers of detention, allowing them to hold a person without charges or a trial. If approached by them, you will be required to show your passport, so always carry it.

There are some minor legal variations between the 26 cantons: busking (playing music in the streets) is allowed in some places but not in others. If in doubt, ask.

Maps

Hallwag, Kümmerly + Frey (www.swisstravelcenter.ch; Grubenstrasse 109, CH-3322 Schönbühl) has a vast range of road atlases, city maps and hiking maps, which can be bought online. Swiss Hiking Federation maps and maps produced by the Bundesamt for Topographie (sometimes down to 1:15,000 scale) are also found in most travel bookshops.

The 48-page *Swiss Travel System* brochure, free from Switzerland Tourism and major train stations, has a clear A3 map of bus and train routes. Tourist offices also have free maps and brochures.

DRUGS

In the cities, police tend not to do much about drug possession, but if they do decide to enforce the law you face a fine of several hundred francs. Possession of over about 30g of cannabis, or any amount of a harder drug, may mean being looked upon as a dealer, and you'll possibly be liable for a larger fine, jail or deportation.

Money

A guide to costs and exchange rates can be found on p14.

ATMs

Automated teller machines (ATMs) – called *Bancomats* in banks and *Postomats* in post offices – are common and accessible 24 hours. They accept most international bank or credit cards and they have multilingual instructions. Your bank or credit-card company will usually charge a 1% to 2.5% fee, and there may also be a small charge at the ATM end.

Cash

Swiss francs are divided into 100 centimes (*Rappen* in German-speaking Switzerland). There are notes for 10, 20, 50, 100, 200 and 1000 francs, and coins for 5, 10, 20 and 50 centimes, as well as for one, two and five francs.

Businesses throughout Switzerland, including most hotels and some restaurants and souvenir shops, will accept payment in euros. Change will be given in Swiss francs at the rate of exchange calculated on the day.

Credit Cards

The use of credit cards is less widespread than in the UK or USA and not all shops, hotels or restaurants accept them. EuroCard/MasterCard and Visa are the most popular.

Moneychangers

Change money at banks, airports and nearly every train station until late into the evening. Banks tend to charge about 5% commission; some money-exchange bureaus don't charge commission at all. Exchange rates are *slightly* better for travellers cheques than for cash.

See p354 for bank opening hours and p15 for exchange rates.

Tipping

» Tipping is not necessary, given that hotels, restaurants, bars and even some taxis are legally required to include a 15% service charge in bills.

» You can round up the bill after a meal for good service, as locals do.

» Hotel and railway porters expect a franc or two per bag.

» Bargaining is non-existent.

Post

Post office hours vary, but they're usually open from at least 8am to noon and 2pm to 5pm Monday to Friday, and from 8.30am to noon on Saturday. Larger post offices stay open over lunch. Many post offices have an ATM (*Postomat*).

Within Switzerland, deliveries are by A-Post (delivered next working day) or B-Post (three working days). International priority (*prioritaire*) deliveries to Europe take two to four days, and to elsewhere roughly seven days. Economy (*economique*) service to Europe takes four to eight days and seven to 12 days to other destinations. An 'Urgent' service is also available for same-day or next-day international deliveries.

For prices and locations, visit www.post.ch.

Public Holidays

New Year's Day 1 January
Good Friday March/April
Easter Sunday & Monday March/April
Ascension Day 40th day after Easter
Whit Sunday & Monday 7th week after Easter
National Day 1 August
Christmas Day 25 December
St Stephen's Day 26 December

Some cantons observe their own special holidays and religious days, eg 2 January, Labour Day (1 May), Corpus Christi, Assumption (15 August) and All Saints' Day (1 November).

Safe Travel

» Street crime is relatively uncommon. However, watch your belongings; pickpockets thrive in city crowds.
» The Swiss police aren't very visible, but have a reputation for performing random street searches of questionable necessity on people of non-European background or appearance.
» Cities such as Zürich, Basel and Bern have a heroin problem, but you generally have to be way off the main thoroughfares to notice it.

Telephone

National telecom provider **Swisscom** (☑080 080 08 00, from abroad +41 62 286 12 12; www.swisscom.ch) operates one of the world's densest networks of public phone booths – 8100 of them. The minimum charge for a call is Sfr0.50, with billing in blocks of Sfr0.10, and phones take coins (Swiss francs or euros) and 'taxcards' (phonecards), sold in values of Sfr5, Sfr10 and Sfr20 at post offices, newsagencies and so on. Some 4000 booths also accept major credit cards and can be used to send SMS worldwide.

The Swiss phone book is searchable online at http://tel.local.ch/en. Dial ☑1812 (connection charge Sfr.0.80 plus Sfr0.10 a minute) to speak to an automated machine, or the pricier ☑1811 (connection charge Sfr1.70 for two queries, Sfr1.40 for the first minute and Sfr0.22 per minute thereafter) to speak to a real person; the latter can also find international telephone numbers for you. Calls from mobiles for these services cost more.

Mobile Phones

Most phones on European GSM networks work perfectly in Switzerland; check with your provider about costs.

Prepaid local SIM cards are available from the three network operators: **Orange** (www.orange.ch; from Sfr10 with Sfr10 credit), **Sunrise** (www.sunrise.ch; from Sfr10 with Sfr10 credit) and **Swisscom Mobile** (www.swisscom-mobile.ch; from Sfr19.95 with Sfr20 credit). Buy these via the nationwide **Mobile Zone** (www.mobilezone.ch, in German, French & Italian) chain of shops. Prepaid cards must be officially registered, so bring your passport.

Phone Codes

» The country code for Switzerland is ☑41. When calling Switzerland from abroad drop the initial zero from the number; hence to call Bern, dial ☑41 31 (preceded by the overseas access code of the country you're dialling from).

WARNING: DIAL ALL NUMBERS

Area codes do not exist in Switzerland. Although the numbers for a particular city or town share the same three-digit prefix (for example Bern 031, Geneva 022), numbers always must be dialled in full, even when calling from next door.

» The international access code from Switzerland is ☑00. To call Britain (country code ☑44), start by dialling ☑00 44
» Telephone numbers with the code 0800 are toll-free; those with 0848 are charged at the local rate. Numbers beginning with 156 or 157 are charged at the premium rate.
» Mobile phone numbers start with the code 076, 078 or 079.

Phonecards

Save money on the normal international tariff by buying a prepaid Swisscom card worth Sfr10, Sfr20, Sfr50 or Sfr100.

Time

The Swiss use the 24-hour clock when writing times. Swiss time is GMT/UTC plus one hour. Daylight-saving time comes into effect at midnight on the last Saturday in March, when the clocks are moved forward one hour, making Switzerland two hours ahead of GMT/UTC; clocks go back again on the last Saturday in October.

Note that in German *halb* is used to indicate the half-hour before the hour, hence *halb acht* (half eight) means 7.30, not 8.30.

The following table shows time difference between

Switzerland and in major cities around the world; times do not take daylight saving into account.

CITY	LOCAL TIME
Auckland	11pm
Bern	noon
London	11am
New York	6am
San Francisco	3am
Sydney	9pm
Tokyo	8pm
Toronto	6am

Toilets

» Public toilets are, as a rule, clean and in reasonable supply.

» Urinals are often free, and many cubicles are too, but some of the latter may have a charge of Sfr0.50.

» The spotless Mr Clean range of facilities in big train stations is more expensive – Sfr2 to pee.

Tourist Information

Make the Swiss tourist board, **Switzerland Tourism** (www.myswitzerland.com), your first port of call. For detailed information, contact local tourist offices, listed under Information in the town and city sections of this guide. Information and maps are free and somebody invariably speaks English; many book hotel rooms, tours and excursions for you. In German-speaking Switzerland tourist offices are called *Verkehrsbüro*, or *Kurverein* in some resorts. In French they are called *office du tourisme* and in Italian *ufficio turistico*.

Travellers with Disabilities

Switzerland ranks among the world's most easily navigable countries for travellers with physical disabilities. Most train stations have a mobile lift for boarding trains, and many hotels have disabled access (although budget pensions tend not to have lifts).

The following organisations may be helpful:

Switzerland Tourism (www.myswitzerland.com). Website and tourist offices can offer travel tips for people with physical disabilities.

Mobility International Schweiz (☎062 212 67 40; www.mis-ch.ch, in German; Amthausquai 21, CH-4600 Olten) A helpful resource.

Visas

For up-to-date details on visa requirements, go to the **Swiss Federal Office for Migration** (www.bfm.admin.ch) and click 'Services'.

Visas are not required if you hold a passport from the UK, Ireland, the USA, Canada, Australia or New Zealand, whether visiting as a tourist or on business. Citizens of the EU, Norwegians and Icelanders may also enter Switzerland without a visa. A maximum 90-day stay in a 180-day period applies, but passports are rarely stamped.

Other people wishing to come to Switzerland have to apply for a **Schengen Visa**, named after the agreements that abolished passport controls between 15 European countries: Austria, Belgium, Denmark, Finland, France, Germany, Greece, Iceland, Italy, Luxembourg, the Netherlands, Norway, Portugal, Spain and Sweden.

It allows unlimited travel throughout the entire zone for a 90-day period. Apply to the consulate of the country you are entering first, or your main destination.

In Switzerland, carry your passport at all times. Swiss citizens are required to always carry ID, so you will also need to be able to identify yourself at any time.

Women Travellers

Minor sexual harassment (catcalls etc) is much less common than in some neighbouring countries, such as Italy and France. Common sense is the best guide to dealing with potentially dangerous situations such as hitching or walking alone at night.

Work

Nationals of the EU-25, plus Norwegians and Icelanders, may work in Switzerland for up to 90 days a year without a permit. Other foreigners and EU citizens on longer assignments will need a permit. For details visit the **Swiss Federal Office for Migration** (www.bfm.admin.ch) online.

Language skills are crucial for work in service industries and usually necessary for work in ski resorts and chalets. *Working in Ski Resorts: Europe & North America* by Victoria Pybus provides detailed information about how to organise winter work. Two good websites for contacts and tips are **Season Workers** (www.seasonworkers.com) and **Natives Guides** (www.natives.co.uk).

In October, work is available in vineyards in Vaud and Valais. Conditions are usually better than in other countries.

Transport

GETTING THERE & AWAY

Flights, tours and rail tickets can be booked online at www.lonelyplanet.com /bookings.

Entering the Country

Formalities are minimal when entering Switzerland by air, rail or road. In December 2008 Switzerland implemented the Schengen Agreement, so those arriving from the EU don't need to show a passport.

Arriving from a non-EU country, you have to show your passport or EU identity card, and visa if you need one, and clear customs.

Air

Airports & Airlines

The main airports are **Zürich Airport** (www.zurich-airport. com), **Geneva Airport** (www .gva.ch) and increasingly France-based **EuroAirport** (www.euroairport.com), which serves Basel (as well as Mulhouse in France and Freiburg, Germany). **Bern-Belp** (www.flughafen bern.ch) and **Lugano Airport** (www.lugano-airport .ch) are secondary airports, but growing.

Swiss International Air Lines (☑0848 700 700; www.swiss.ch), the national carrier, is commonly known as Swiss Air.

Budget Airlines

Air Berlin (www.airberlin .com) Links EuroAirport (Basel), Geneva and Zürich with dozens of destinations throughout Europe.

Darwin Airline (www.fly baboo.com) Swiss carrier linking Geneva and Lugano with destinations in Spain, France, Italy and Greece.

Bmibaby (www.bmibaby .com) Flights to Geneva from Belfast, Birmingham and East Midlands.

easyJet (www.easyjet.com) UK budget carrier flying into Geneva and EuroAirport (Basel) from dozens of European and UK destinations, and with flights between Zürich and the UK.

Flybe (www.flybe.com) Links Geneva with 10 destinations across the UK, and Bern-Belp with Southampton.

Germanwings (www.german wings.com) German budget carrier flying from Zürich to European and UK destinations via Cologne-Bonn.

Helvetic (www.helvetic.com) Swiss budget carrier hubbed in Zürich, with flights from there and Bern to southern Italy, Germany, Wales and Scotland.

Jet2.com (www.jet2.com) Links Geneva with Belfast, Glasgow, Leeds Bradford and Manchester.

CLIMATE CHANGE & TRAVEL

Every form of transport that relies on carbon-based fuel generates CO_2, the main cause of human-induced climate change. Modern travel is dependent on aeroplanes, which might use less fuel per kilometre per person than most cars but travel much greater distances. The altitude at which aircraft emit gases (including CO_2) and particles also contributes to their climate change impact. Many websites offer 'carbon calculators' that allow people to estimate the carbon emissions generated by their journey and, for those who wish to do so, to offset the impact of the greenhouse gases emitted with contributions to portfolios of climate-friendly initiatives throughout the world. Lonely Planet offsets the carbon footprint of all staff and author travel.

FLY-RAIL BAGGAGE SERVICE

Travellers bound for Geneva and Zürich airports can send their luggage directly on to any one of 50-odd Swiss train stations, without waiting for their bags at the airport. Upon departure, they can also check their luggage in at any of these train stations up to 24 hours before their flight and collect it upon arrival at their destination airport. The charge is Sfr20/US$15 per item of luggage; the maximum weight per item is 32kg and bulky stuff like bicycles and surfboards are no go. Similar luggage forwarding is likewise possible within Switzerland; see www.sbb.ch

Land

Bus

Eurolines (www.eurolines .com), via local operator **Alsa+Eggman** (www.alsa -eggmann.ch), operates services to Austria, Belgium, Bosnia and Herzegovina, Bulgaria, Croatia, Czech Republic, England, France, Germany, Hungary, Kosovo, Macedonia, Moldavia, the Netherlands, Poland, Portugal, Romania, Serbia, Slovakia and Spain from seven Swiss cities.

Car & Motorcycle

There are fast, well-maintained freeways to Switzerland through all bordering countries. The Alps present a natural barrier to entering Switzerland, so main roads generally head through tunnels. Smaller roads are more scenically interesting, but special care is needed when negotiating mountain passes.

An EU driving licence is acceptable throughout Europe for up to a year, otherwise obtain an International Driving Permit (IDP). Third-party motor insurance is a minimum requirement; get proof of this in the form of a Green Card issued by your insurers. Also ask for a 'European Accident Statement' form. Taking out a European breakdown assistance policy is a good investment.

A warning triangle, to be displayed in the event of a breakdown, is compulsory. Recommended accessories include a first-aid kit, a spare bulb kit and a fire extinguisher.

Train

Eco-friendly Switzerland makes rail travel a joy. Contact www.raileurope.co .uk, www.raileurope.com or your local European rail operator.

From the UK, the **Eurostar** (www.eurostar.com) scoots from London (St Pancras International) to Paris (Gare du Nord) hourly, then onwards by French TGV from Paris (Gare de Lyon) to Geneva, Lausanne, Bern, Basel, Biel-Bienne and Zug, Zürich and more; passengers aged under 26 and over 60 get slight discounts.

Zürich is Switzerland's busiest international terminus, with trains to Munich and Vienna, from where there are extensive onward connections to cities in Eastern Europe.

Most connections from Germany pass through Zürich or Basel. Nearly all connections from Italy pass through Milan before branching off to Zürich, Lucerne, Bern or Lausanne.

Sea & River

Switzerland can be reached by steamer from several lakes, but it's a slightly more unusual option. From Germany, arrive via Lake Constance and from France via Lake Geneva. You can also cruise down the Rhine to Basel.

GETTING AROUND

Switzerland's fully integrated public transport system is among the world's most efficient. However, travel within Switzerland is expensive and visitors planning to use public transport on inter-city routes should consider investing in a Swiss travel pass (p366).

Timetables often refer to *Werktags* (work days), which means Monday to Saturday, unless there is the qualification '*ausser Samstag*' (except Saturday).

Air

Switzerland's compact size and excellent rail transport render internal flights almost unnecessary. **Swiss International Air Lines** (www.swiss.com) serves the major hubs of EuroAirport (Basel), Geneva and Zürich airports, with return fares fluctuating wildly. Swiss no-frills carrier **Darwin Airlines** (www.flybaboo.com) flies between Geneva and Lugano.

Bicycle

Hire

Rent a Bike (☑041 925 11 70; www.rent-a-bike.ch, in German & French; ☉daily) offers bike hire at 100-odd train stations. Prices start from Sfr25 for a half-day and Sfr33 for a full day (returned to the same station) or Sfr40 per day (returned to a different station); Swiss travel pass-holders and under 16s pay less. In summer, reserve at least a day or two ahead.

There's free bike rental in Bern, Geneva, Zug and Zürich.

Transport

Bikes can be taken on slower trains (for the price of a regular adult 2nd-class ticket), and sometimes even on InterCity (IC) or EuroCity (EC) trains, when there's room in the luggage carriage (one-/six-day bike ticket Sfr18/72, one-day ticket with Swiss Travel Pass Sfr12). Between 21 March and 31 October, you must book (Sfr5) to take your bike on ICN (inter-city tilting) trains.

Trains that don't permit accompanied bikes are marked with a crossed-out pictogram in the timetable. Sending a standard bike unaccompanied costs Sfr16. Taking your bike as hand luggage in a transport bag is free.

Boat

All the larger lakes are serviced by steamers operated by Swiss Federal Railways (SBB/CFF/FFS), or allied private companies for which national travel passes are valid. These include Geneva, Constance, Lucerne, Lugano, Neuchâtel, Biel, Murten, Thun, Brienz and Zug, but not Lago Maggiore.

SCENIC JOURNEYS

Swiss trains, buses and boats are more than a means of getting from A to B. Stunning views invariably make the journey itself the destination. Switzerland boasts the following routes among its classic sightseeing journeys. Bear in mind that you can choose just one leg of the trip, and that scheduled services ply the same routes for standard fares. In addition to these journeys, almost any train in the Jungfrau region provides beautiful views.

Panorama Trains

The first three trains on this list have panoramic coaches with extended-height windows:

Glacier Express (☑027 927 77 00; www.glacierexpress.ch; 2nd/1st class Sfr136/226, obligatory seat reservation summer/winter Sfr33/13; ⏱7½hr, daily) Spectacular journey between Zermatt and St Moritz, Chur or Davos. The Brig-Zermatt Alpine leg makes for pretty powerful viewing, as does the area between Disentis/Mustér and Brig.

Golden Pass Route (☑021 989 81 90; www.goldenpass.ch; one-way 2nd/1st class Sfr70/116) Travels between Lucerne and Montreux. The journey is in three legs, and you must change trains twice. Regular trains, without panoramic windows, work the whole route hourly.

Bernina Express (☑081 288 65 65; www.rhb.ch; one-way 2nd/1st class Sfr58/96, obligatory seat reservation summer/winter Sfr12/9; ⏱2½hr, daily) Cuts 145km through Engadine from Chur to Tirano. May and October, you can opt to continue onwards from Tirano to Lugano by bus.

Chocolate train (www.mob.ch) Return trip in a belle époque Pullman car from Montreux to the chocolate factory at Broc.

Mont Blanc/St Bernard Expresses (www.tmrsa.ch) From Martigny to Chamonix, France, or over the St Bernard Pass.

Voralpen Express (www.voralpen-express.ch, in German) Lake Constance to Lake Lucerne, through St Gallen, Rapperswil and Romanshorn.

Rail/Boat

The **Wilhelm Tell Express** (☑041 367 67 67; www.williamtellexpress.ch; adult standard/premium Sfr169/209, Swiss Pass free, standard/premium supplement Sfr39/79; ⏱May-Oct) starts with a wonderful 2½-hour cruise across Lake Lucerne to Flüelen, from where a train winds its way through ravines and past mountains to Locarno.

Postal Bus

The **Palm Express** (☑058 386 31 66; www.palmexpress.ch; ticket Sfr70, obligatory Alpine Ticket Sfr15) travels between St Moritz and Lugano, travelling through Engadine and the mountains via the Maloja Pass before skirting the Mediterranean-style Lago di Lugano and Lago di Como (in Italy).

Another half a dozen scenic Alpine routes can be found at www.postbus.ch.

	Basel	Bellinzona	Bern	Biel-Bienne	Brig	Chur	Fribourg	Geneva	Interlaken	Lausanne	Lucerne	Lugano	Neuchâtel	St Gallen	St Moritz	Schaffhausen	Sion
Bellinzona	241																
Bern	97	253															
Biel-Bienne	93	247	41														
Brig	190	161	91	129													
Chur	228	115	242	237	174												
Fribourg	132	285	34	71	179	274											
Geneva	267	420	171	209	214	409	138										
Interlaken	153	195	57	92	73	209	92	230									
Lausanne	203	359	107	146	151	346	72	62	167								
Lucerne	103	140	115	107	149	140	147	280	71	218							
Lugano	267	28	279	273	187	141	331	446	221	383	166						
Neuchâtel	141	294	46	31	141	283	43	123	104	73	156	320					
St Gallen	191	217	204	197	288	102	236	371	225	307	138	243	244				
St Moritz	313	150	327	321	241	85	359	494	294	430	225	176	368	178			
Schaffhausen	161	246	173	167	259	182	205	340	228	276	108	272	214	80	266		
Sion	252	214	160	195	53	399	128	161	86	98	271	240	166	356	294	329	
Zürich	113	195	125	119	208	118	157	292	177	229	57	221	166	81	203	51	281

Rail passes are not valid for cruises offered by smaller boat companies.

Bus

Yellow **Post Buses** (www .postbus.ch) supplement the rail network, following postal routes and linking towns to the less accessible mountain regions. They are regular, and departures tie in with train arrivals, invariably from next to train stations. Travel is one class only and fares are comparable to train fares.

For those schlepping home late from a club or rushing to make a red-eye flight, there are several night buses at weekends. Check with local transport providers for details.

Bus Passes

Swiss national travel passes are valid on postal buses, but a few tourist-oriented Alpine routes levy a surcharge.

Details are in the relevant chapters.

Reservations

Tickets are purchased from the driver, though on some scenic routes over the Alps (eg the Lugano–St Moritz run) advance reservations are necessary. See www .postbus.ch for details.

Car & Motorcycle

Public transport is excellent in city centres, and parking cars an inconvenience.

Automobile Associations

The **Swiss Touring Club** (TCS; ☎022 417 22 20; www .tcs.ch, in German, French & Italian) and **Swiss Automobile Club** (Automobil -Club der Schweiz, ACS; www .acs.ch, in German, French & Italian) provide details on driving in Switzerland.

The larger TCS operates the national **24-hour emergency breakdown service** (☎0800 140 140), free for members of the Swiss motoring clubs and their affiliates.

Car Sharing

Mobility (☎0848 824 812; www.mobility.ch) has some 2600 cars at 1300 points throughout Switzerland and you can use the cars from one hour to up to 16 days, although one-way travel is not permitted. You reserve a car by internet or phone, collect it at the reserved time and drive off. Daytime rates start at Sfr2.80 per hour, with distance costing from Sfr0.52 per kilometre.

Fuel

Unleaded (*bleifrei, sans plomb, senza piombo*) petrol is standard, found at green pumps, and diesel is also widely available. Expect to pay around Sfr1.75 per litre for unleaded and Sfr1.85 for diesel.

Hire

It's cheaper to book car hire ahead from your own country. If you're flying into Geneva Airport, it's cheaper to rent a car on the French side. The minimum rental age is usually 25, but falls to 20 at some local firms; you always need a credit card. Rental cars are equipped with winter tyres in winter.

The following are some of the main rental companies:

Avis (☑084 881 18 18; www.avis.ch)

Europcar (☑084 880 80 99; www.europcar.ch)

Hertz (☑084 882 20 20; www.hertz.ch)

Holiday Autos Australia (☑1300 554 507, www.holidayautos.com.au); Switzerland (☑056 675 75 85; www.holidayautos.ch, in German & French); UK (☑0871 472 5229; www.holidayautos.co.uk); USA (☑866 392 9288; www.holidayautos.com)

Sixt (☑084 888 44 44; www.sixt.ch, in German & French)

Road Conditions

Swiss roads are well built, well signposted and well maintained. Phone ☑163 for up-to-the-hour traffic conditions (recorded information in French, German, Italian and English).

Most major Alpine passes are negotiable year-round, depending on the weather. However, you will often have to use a tunnel instead of the Great St Bernard, St Gotthard and San Bernardino passes. Passes that are open only June to October are Albula, Furka, Grimsel, Klausen, Oberalp, Susten and Umbrail. Other passes are Lukmanier (open May to November), Nufenen (June to September), and Splügen (May to October).

Take your car on trains through these tunnels and passes, open year-round:

Lötschberg Tunnel (☑0900 553 333; www.bls.ch) From Kandersteg to Goppenstein (car and passengers Monday to Thursday/Friday to Sunday Sfr22/27, 15 minutes) or Iselle in Italy (car and passengers Sfr91, book in advance).

Furka Pass (☑027 927 70 00; www.mgbahn.ch) From Oberwald to Realp.

Vereina Tunnel (☑081 288 65 65; www.rhb.ch) Alternative to the Flüela Pass, which is closed in winter; from Selfranga outside Klosters to Sagliains in the Engadine (car and passengers low/mid-/high season Sfr29/36/41).

Road Signs

Signs you may not have seen before include these:

» Criss-crossed white tyre on a blue circular background, which means that snow chains are compulsory.

» Yellow bugle on a square blue background, which means that you should obey isntructions given by postal bus drivers.

Road Rules

» The minimum driving age for cars and motorcycles is 18 and for mopeds, 14.

» The Swiss drive on the right-hand side of the road.

» Give priority to traffic approaching from the right. On mountain roads, the ascending vehicle has priority, unless a postal bus is involved, as it always has right of way.

» The speed limit is 50km/h in towns, 80km/h on main roads outside towns, 100km/h on single-lane freeways and 120km/h on dual-lane freeways.

» Car occupants must wear a seatbelt at all times and vehicles must carry a breakdown-warning triangle.

» Dipped headlights must be turned on in all tunnels and are recommended for

motorcyclists during the day.

» Headlights must be used in rain or poor visibility.

» Motorcyclists and their passengers must wear crash helmets.

» The blood alcohol content (BAC) limit is 0.05%.

» If you're involved in a car accident, the police must be called if anyone receives more than superficial injuries.

» Proof of ownership of a private vehicle should always be carried.

Road Tolls

There's an annual one-off charge of Sfr40 to use Swiss freeways and semi-freeways, identified by green signs. The charge is payable at the border (in cash, including euros), at petrol stations and from Swiss tourist offices abroad. The sticker (*vignette* in French and German, *contrassegno* in Italian) you receive upon paying the tax can also be bought at post offices and petrol stations. It must be displayed on the windscreen and is valid for one calendar year. If you're caught without it, you'll be fined Sfr100. A separate *vignette* is required for trailers and caravans. Motorcyclists are also charged the Sfr40. For more details, see www.vignette.ch.

On the Swiss–Italian border you'll need to pay an additional toll if using the Great St Bernard Tunnel between Aosta, Italy and Valais (car and passengers one-way/return Sfr30/48, motorcycles Sfr17.70/23.90).

Urban Parking

Street parking in city centres (assuming traffic isn't banned, as it often is) is controlled by parking meters during working hours (8am to 7pm Monday to Saturday). Parking costs around Sfr2 per hour, with maximum time limits from 30 minutes to two hours. Central streets

SWISS TRAVEL PASSES

The following national travel passes generally offer better savings than Eurail or Inter Rail passes on extensive travel within Switzerland. Before arriving in Switzerland passes can be purchased in the UK from the **Switzerland Travel Centre** (☎0207 420 49 34; www.stc.co.uk; 30 Bedford St, London WC2E 9ED) or online from its hugely informative website. In Switzerland larger train-station offices sell travel passes.

Find comprehensive information on all of them at http://traintickets.myswitzerland .com.

Swiss Pass The Swiss Pass entitles the holder to unlimited travel on almost every train, boat and bus service in the country, and on trams and buses in 41 towns, plus free entry to 400-odd museums. Reductions of 50% apply on funiculars, cable cars and private railways. Different passes are available, valid between four days and one month.

Swiss Flexi Pass This pass allows you to nominate a certain number of days (anywhere from three to six) during a month when you can enjoy unlimited travel.

Half-Fare Card Almost every Swiss owns one of these. As the name suggests, you pay only half the fare on trains with this card, plus you get some discounts on local-network buses, trams and cable cars. An adult one-year Half-Fare Card costs a local Sfr165 (photo necessary).

Family Card A free Family Card gets free travel (on trains, buses and boats – even on some cable cars) for those aged six to 15 years when travelling with at least one of their parents. Children within that age bracket and travelling with an adult who is not a relative get 50% off.

Regional Passes Network passes valid only within a particular region are available in several parts of the country. Such passes are available from train stations in the region.

outside these metered areas are usually marked as blue zones, allowing a 1½-hour stay during working hours. Either way, you need to display a parking disc in your window indicating the time you first parked. Discs are free from tourist offices, car-rental companies and police stations.

Local Transport
Public Transport

All local city transport is linked via the same ticketing system, so you can change lines on one ticket. Buy tickets before boarding, from dispensers at stops. Single tickets may give a time limit (eg one hour) for travel within a particular zone, and you can only break the journey within that time. Multistrip tickets may be available at a discount (validate them in the on-board machine at the outset of the journey) and

one-day passes are even better value.

Inspectors regularly check for people travelling without tickets. On-the-spot fines are Sfr100.

Taxi

Metered taxis can be found outside train stations or can be called.

Mountain Transport

The Swiss have many words to describe mountain transport: funicular (*Standseilbahn* in German, *funiculaire* in French, *funicolare* in Italian), cable car (*Luftseilbahn, téléphérique, funivia*), gondola (*Gondelbahn, télécabine, telecabinoia*) and chair lift (*Sesselbahn, télésiège, seggiovia*). All are subject to regular safety inspections.

Always check what time the last cable car goes down the mountain, as this can

be as early as 4pm in some resorts.

Train

The Swiss rail network combines state-run and private operations. The **Swiss Federal Railway** (www.rail.ch, www.sbb.ch/en) is abbreviated to SBB in German, CFF in French and FFS in Italian.

All major train stations are connected to each other by hourly departures, at least between 6am and midnight, and most long-distance trains have a dining car.

Classes

Second-class compartments are perfectly acceptable, but are often close to full, especially when the army is on the move. First-class carriages are even more comfortable, spacious and have fewer passengers. Power points for laptops let you work aboard and some seats are in wi-fi hotspots –

look for the insignia on the carriage.

Costs

Ordinary fares are relatively expensive, about Sfr38 per 100km; best buy a rail pass. Return fares are only cheaper than two singles for longer trips. Special deals are sometimes available in the low season.

All fares quoted in this guide are for second-class travel unless otherwise stated; first-class fares average 50% to 65% higher.

Information

All stations can provide advice in English and free timetable booklets. Timetables are also available online and can be personalised and downloaded onto your mobile. Train schedules are revised every December; double-check fares and frequencies quoted here.

For information see www .sbb.ch or call **train information & reservations**

(☎0900 300 300); calls cost Sfr1.19 per minute.

Luggage

Most stations have 24-hour lockers (Sfr6 for a small locker and Sfr9 for a large locker), usually accessible 6am to midnight.

Nearly all stations allow ticket-holders to send their luggage ahead (Sfr20 per item up to 25kg). You dispatch your bag before 9am and collect it at your destination station after 6pm the same day – useful if you're stopping off en route at other places.

Reservations & Tickets

Seat reservations (Sfr5) are advisable for longer journeys, particularly in high season.

Some smaller, rural rail routes, marked in the timetable with a yellow eye pictogram, have a 'self-control' ticketing system. On these routes, buy a ticket before boarding or

risk a fine. Ticket inspectors appear frequently.

One-way and return train tickets for journeys up to 115km are valid for one day. One-way tickets over 116km are also valid for one day while return tickets over 116km are valid for 10 days and allow you to break your journey.

Train Passes

European rail passes (www .raileurope.co.uk, www.rail europe.com), including Eurail and Inter Rail passes, are valid on Swiss national railways. However, you cannot use them on postal buses, city transport, cable cars or private train lines (eg the Zermatt route and the Jungfraubahn routes at the heart of the Bernese Oberland). So, while they're practical if you're covering several countries in one journey, they're less useful than Swiss travel passes for exploring scenic Switzerland.

WANT MORE?

For in-depth language information and handy phrases, check out Lonely Planet's *French, German* and *Italian* phrasebooks. You'll find them at **shop .lonelyplanet.com**, or you can buy Lonely Planet's iPhone phrasebooks at the Apple App Store.

Language

Switzerland *(Schweiz/Suisse/Svizzera)* has three official federal languages: German (the native language of about 64% of the population), French (19%) and Italian (8%). A fourth language, Romansch, is spoken by less than 1% of the population, mainly in the canton of Graubünden. Since 1996 it has enjoyed status as a semi-official federal language, with guarantees for its preservation and promotion.

If you read the coloured pronunciation guides in this chapter as if they were English, you shouldn't have problems being understood. The stressed syllables are indicated with italics. Masculine, feminine, informal and polite forms are indicated with (m), (f), (inf) and (pol) where needed.

FRENCH

Nasal vowels (pronounced 'through the nose') are indicated with o or u followed by an almost inaudible nasal m, n or ng. Note also that air is pronounced as in 'fair', eu as the 'u' in 'nurse', ew as ee with rounded lips, r is a throaty sound, and zh is pronounced as the 's' in 'pleasure'. Syllables in French words are, for the most part, equally stressed.

Basics

Hello.	*Bonjour.*	bon·zhoor
Goodbye.	*Au revoir.*	o·rer·vwa
Excuse me.	*Excusez-moi.*	ek·skew·zay·mwa
Sorry.	*Pardon.*	par·don
Please.	*S'il vous plaît.*	seel voo play
Thank you.	*Merci.*	mair·see
Yes./No.	*Oui./Non.*	wee/non

What's your name?
Comment vous appelez-vous? — ko·mon voo·za·play voo

My name is ...
Je m'appelle ... — zher ma·pel ...

Do you speak English?
Parlez-vous anglais? — par·lay·voo ong·glay

I don't understand.
Je ne comprends pas. — zher ner kom·pron pa

Accommodation

campsite	*camping*	kom·peeng
guesthouse	*pension*	pon·syon
hotel	*hôtel*	o·tel
youth hostel	*auberge de jeunesse*	o·berzh der zher·nes

Do you have a ... room?	*Avez-vous une chambre ...?*	a·vey·voo ewn shom·bre ...
single	*à un lit*	a un lee
double	*avec un grand lit*	a·vek un gron lee

How much is it per night/person?
Quel est le prix par nuit/personne? — kel ey le pree par nwee/pair·son

Eating & Drinking

What would you recommend?
Qu'est-ce que vous conseillez? — kes·ker voo kon·say·yay

Do you have vegetarian food?
Vous faites les repas voo fet ley re·pa
végétariens? vey·zhey·ta·ryun

I'll have ...
Je prends ... zhe pron ...

Cheers!
Santé! son·tay

I'd like the ..., *Je voudrais ...,* zhe voo·drey ...
please. *s'il vous plaît.* seel voo pley
  bill *l'addition* la·dee·syon
  menu *la carte* la kart

beer *bière* bee·yair
coffee *café* ka·fay
tea *thé* tay
water *eau* o
wine *vin* vun

Emergencies

Help!
Au secours! o skoor

Leave me alone!
Fichez-moi la paix! fee·shay·mwa la pay

Call a doctor.
Appelez un médecin. a·play un mayd·sun

Call the police.
Appelez la police. a·play la po·lees

I'm lost.
Je suis perdu/ zhe swee pair·dew
perdue. (m/f)

I'm ill.
Je suis malade. zher swee ma·lad

Where are the toilets?
Où sont les toilettes? oo son ley twa·let

Shopping & Services

I'd like to buy ...
Je voudrais acheter ... zher voo·dray ash·tay ...

How much is it?
C'est combien? say kom·byun

It's too expensive.
C'est trop cher. say tro shair

<table>
<tr><td colspan="2">**Signs – French**</td></tr>
<tr><td>**Entrée**</td><td>Entrance</td></tr>
<tr><td>**Sortie**</td><td>Exit</td></tr>
<tr><td>**Ouvert**</td><td>Open</td></tr>
<tr><td>**Fermé**</td><td>Closed</td></tr>
<tr><td>**Interdit**</td><td>Prohibited</td></tr>
<tr><td>**Toilettes**</td><td>Toilets</td></tr>
</table>

<table>
<tr><td colspan="3">**Numbers – French**</td></tr>
<tr><td>1</td><td>*un*</td><td>un</td></tr>
<tr><td>2</td><td>*deux*</td><td>der</td></tr>
<tr><td>3</td><td>*trois*</td><td>trwa</td></tr>
<tr><td>4</td><td>*quatre*</td><td>ka·trer</td></tr>
<tr><td>5</td><td>*cinq*</td><td>sungk</td></tr>
<tr><td>6</td><td>*six*</td><td>sees</td></tr>
<tr><td>7</td><td>*sept*</td><td>set</td></tr>
<tr><td>8</td><td>*huit*</td><td>weet</td></tr>
<tr><td>9</td><td>*neuf*</td><td>nerf</td></tr>
<tr><td>10</td><td>*dix*</td><td>dees</td></tr>
</table>

market *marché* mar·shay
post office *bureau de* bew·ro der
poste post
tourist office *office de* o·fees der
tourisme too·rees·mer

Transport & Directions

Where's ...?
Où est ...? oo ay ...

What's the address?
Quelle est l'adresse? kel ay la·dres

Can you show me (on the map)?
Pouvez-vous m'indiquer poo·vay·voo mun·dee·kay
(sur la carte)? (sewr la kart)

One ... ticket, *Un billet ...,* um bee·yey ...
please. *s'il vous plaît.* seel voo pley
  one-way *simple* sum·ple
  return *aller et retour* a·ley ey re·toor

boat *bateau* ba·to
bus *bus* bews
plane *avion* a·vyon
train *train* trun

GERMAN
Vowels in German can be short or long. Note that air is pronounced as in 'fair', aw as in 'saw', eu as the 'u' in 'nurse', ew as ee with rounded lips, ow as in 'now', kh as in Scottish *loch* (pronounced at the back of the throat), r is also a throaty sound, and zh is pronounced as the 's' in 'pleasure'.

Basics

Hello. *Grüezi.* grew·e·tsi
Goodbye. *Auf* owf
Wiedersehen. vee·der·zey·en

Excuse me.	Entschuldigung.	ent·shul·di·gung
Sorry.	Entschuldigung.	ent·shul·di·gung
Please.	Bitte.	bi·te
Thank you.	Danke.	dang·ke
Yes./No.	Ja./Nein.	yaa/nain

What's your name?
Wie ist Ihr Name? — vee ist eer *naa*·me

My name is ...
Mein Name ist ... — main *naa*·me ist ...

Do you speak English?
Sprechen Sie Englisch? — *shpre*·khen zee *eng*·lish

I don't understand.
Ich verstehe nicht. — ikh fer·*shtey*·e nikht

Accommodation

campsite	Campingplatz	kem·ping·plats
guesthouse	Pension	paang·zyawn
hotel	Hotel	ho·tel
youth hostel	Jugend-herberge	yoo·gent·her·ber·ge

Do you have a ... room?	Haben Sie ein ...?	haa·ben zee ain ...
single	Einzelzimmer	ain·tsel·tsi·mer
double	Doppelzimmer mit einem Doppelbett	do·pel·tsi·mer mit ai·nem do·pel·bet

How much is it per night/person?
Wie viel kostet es pro Nacht/Person? — vee feel *kos*·tet es praw nakht/per·*zawn*

Eating & Drinking

What would you recommend?
Was empfehlen Sie? — vas emp·*fey*·len zee

Do you have vegetarian food?
Haben Sie vegetarisches Essen? — haa·ben zee ve·ge·*taa*·ri·shes e·sen

I'll have ...
Ich hätte gern ... — ikh *he*·te gern ...

Cheers!
Prost! — prawst

Signs – German
Eingang	Entrance
Ausgang	Exit
Offen	Open
Geschlossen	Closed
Verboten	Prohibited
Toiletten	Toilets

I'd like the ..., please.	Bitte bringen Sie die ...	bi·te bring·en zee dee ...
bill	Rechnung	rekh·nung
menu	Speisekarte	shpai·ze·kar·te

beer	Bier	beer
coffee	Kaffee	ka·fey
tea	Tee	tey
water	Wasser	va·ser
wine	Wein	vain

Emergencies

Help!	Hilfe!	hil·fe
Go away!	Gehen Sie weg!	gey·en zee vek
Call ...!	Rufen Sie ...!	roo·fen zee ...
a doctor	einen Arzt	ai·nen artst
the police	die Polizei	dee po·li·tsai

I'm lost.
Ich habe mich verirrt. — ikh haa·be mikh fer·irt

I'm ill.
Ich bin krank. — ikh bin krangk

Where are the toilets?
Wo ist die Toilette? — vo ist dee to·a·le·te

Shopping & Services

I'm looking for ...
Ich suche nach ... — ikh zoo·khe nakh ...

How much is it?
Wie viel kostet das? — vee feel kos·tet das

That's too expensive.
Das ist zu teuer. — das ist tsoo toy·er

market	Markt	markt
post office	Postamt	post·amt
tourist office	Fremden-verkehrs-büro	frem·den·fer·kairs·bew·raw

Transport & Directions

Where's ...?
Wo ist ...? — vaw ist ...

What's the address?
Wie ist die Adresse? — vee ist dee a·dre·se

Can you show me (on the map)?
Können Sie es mir (auf der Karte) zeigen? — keu·nen zee es meer (owf dair kar·te) tsai·gen

Numbers – German

1	*eins*	ains
2	*zwei*	tsvai
3	*zdrei*	drai
4	*vier*	feer
5	*fünf*	fewnf
6	*sechs*	zeks
7	*sieben*	zee·ben
8	*acht*	akht
9	*neun*	noyn
10	*zehn*	tseyn

One ... ticket, please.	*Einen ..., bitte.*	ai·nen ... bi·te
one-way	*einfache Fahrkarte*	ain·fa·khe faar·kar·te
return	*Rückfahr- karte*	rewk·faar· kar·te

boat	*Boot*	bawt
bus	*Bus*	bus
plane	*Flugzeug*	flook·tsoyk
train	*Zug*	tsook

ITALIAN

Italian vowels are generally shorter than in English. The consonants sometimes have a more emphatic pronunciation – if the word is written with a double consonant, use the stronger form. Note that ow is pronounced as in 'how', dz as the 'ds' in 'lads', and r is rolled and stronger than in English.

Basics

Hello.	*Buongiorno.*	bwon·jor·no
Goodbye.	*Arrivederci.*	a·ree·ve·der·chee
Excuse me.	*Mi scusi.* (pol)	mee skoo·zee
	Scusami. (inf)	skoo·za·mee
Sorry.	*Mi dispiace.*	mee dees·pya·che
Please.	*Per favore.*	per fa·vo·re
Thank you.	*Grazie.*	gra·tsye
Yes./No.	*Sì./No.*	see/no

What's your name?
Come si chiama? (pol)   ko·me see kya·ma
Come ti chiami? (inf)   ko·me tee kya·mee

My name is ...
Mi chiamo ...   mee kya·mo ...

Do you speak English?
Parla inglese?   par·la een·gle·ze

I don't understand.
Non capisco.   non ka·pee·sko

Accommodation

campsite	*campeggio*	kam·pe·jo
guesthouse	*pensione*	pen·syo·ne
hotel	*albergo*	al·ber·go
youth hostel	*ostello della gioventù*	os·te·lo de·la jo·ven·too

Do you have a ... room?	*Avete una camera ...?*	a·ve·te oo·na ka·me·ra ...
single	*singola*	seen·go·la
double	*doppia con letto matri- moniale*	do·pya kon le·to ma·tree· mo·nya·le

How much is it per ...?	*Quanto costa per ...?*	kwan·to kos·ta per ...
night	*una notte*	oo·na no·te
person	*persona*	per·so·na

Eating & Drinking

What would you recommend?
Cosa mi consiglia?   ko·za mee kon·see·lya

Do you have vegetarian food?
Avete piatti vegetariani?   a·ve·te pya·tee ve·je·ta·rya·nee

I'll have ...
Prendo ...   pren·do ...

Cheers!
Salute!   sa·loo·te

I'd like the ..., please.	*Vorrei ..., per favore.*	vo·ray ... per fa·vo·re
bill	*il conto*	eel kon·to
menu	*il menù*	eel me·noo

beer	*birra*	bee·ra
coffee	*caffè*	ka·fe
tea	*tè*	te
water	*acqua*	a·kwa
wine	*vino*	vee·no

Signs – Italian

Entrata	Entrance
Uscita	Exit
Aperto	Open
Chiuso	Closed
Proibito	Prohibited
Gabinetti	Toilets

Numbers – Italian

1	uno	oo·no
2	due	doo·e
3	tre	tre
4	quattro	kwa·tro
5	cinque	cheen·kwe
6	sei	say
7	sette	se·te
8	otto	o·to
9	nove	no·ve
10	dieci	dye·chee

Emergencies

Help!	Aiuto!	ai·yoo·to
Go away!	Vai via!	vai vee·a
Call ...!	Chiami ...!	kya·mee ...
a doctor	un medico	oon me·dee·ko
the police	la polizia	la po·lee·tsee·a

I'm lost.
Mi sono perso/a. (m/f)   mee so·no per·so/a
I'm ill.
Mi sento male.   mee sen·to ma·le
Where are the toilets?
Dove sono i   do·ve so·no ee
gabinetti?   ga·bee·ne·tee

Shopping & Services

I'm looking for ...
Sto cercando ...   sto cher·kan·do ...
How much is it?
Quant'è?   kwan·te
That's too expensive.
È troppo caro.   e tro·po ka·ro

market	mercato	mer·ka·to
post office	ufficio postale	oo·fee·cho pos·ta·le
tourist office	ufficio del turismo	oo·fee·cho del too·reez·mo

Transport & Directions

Where's ... ?
Dov'è ... ?   do·ve ...
What's the address?
Qual'è l'indirizzo?   kwa·le leen·dee·ree·tso
Can you show me (on the map)?
Può mostrarmi   pwo mos·trar·mee
(sulla pianta)?   (soo·la pyan·ta)

One ... ticket, please.	Un biglietto ..., per favore.	oon bee·lye·to ... per fa·vo·re
one-way	di sola andata	dee so·la an·da·ta
return	di andata e ritorno	dee an·da·ta e ree·tor·no

boat	nave	na·ve
bus	autobus	ow·to·boos
plane	aereo	a·e·re·o
train	treno	tre·no

ROMANSCH

Derived from Latin and part of the Rhaeto-Romanic language family, Romansch dialects tend to be restricted to their own particular mountain valley. Usage is gradually declining with German taking over as the lingua franca in the Romansch areas. The main street in villages is usually called Via Maistra.

Hello.	Allegra.
Goodbye.	Adieu./Abunansvair.
Please.	Anzi.
Thank you.	Grazia.

bed	letg
closed	serrà
cross-country skiing	passlung
left	sanester
right	dretg
room	chombra
tourist office	societad da traffic

bread	paun
cheese	chaschiel
fish	pesch
ham	schambun
milk	latg
wine	vin

1	in
2	dus
3	trais
4	quatter
5	tschinch
6	ses
7	set
8	och
9	nouv
10	diesch

GLOSSARY

The language of origin of non-English terms is noted in brackets: French (F), High German (G), Italian (I), Romansch (R) and Swiss German (S).

abbaye – (F/G) abbey
AOC – (F) Appellation d'Origine Contrôlée; food and wine products that have met stringent government regulations governing where, how and under what conditions the ingredients and final product are produced
albergo – (I) hotel
Altstadt – (G) old town
auberge – (F) inn, guest house
auberge de jeunesse – (F) youth hostel

Bach – (G) stream; often in compound nouns such as Milibach
Bad – (G) spa, bath
Bahnhof – (G) train station
belvédère/belvedere – (F/I) 'beautiful view'; scenic high point
Berg – (G) mountain
Berggasthaus, Berghaus – (G) mountain inn
billetterie – (F) box office
bisse – (F) mountain aqueduct in the Valais
boulangerie – (F) bakery
Brücke – (G) bridge
Burg – (G) castle, also *Schloss*

cabane/capanna – (F/I) mountain hut offering basic accommodation
cairn – piles of stones, often used to mark a route or path junction
cantons – the self-governing regions within the Swiss Confederation
castello – (I) castle
cave – (F) wine or cheese cellar
château – (F) castle

chiesa – (I) church
cirque – a rounded high precipice formed by the action of ice in the high-Alpine zone
col/passo – (F/I) a mountain pass

dégustation – (F) the fine art of tasting wine or cheese
domaine – (F) wine-producing estate
dortoir – (F/I) dormitory

église – (F) church

föhn – warm southerly wind

gare – (F) train station
gare routière – (F) bus station
Garni – (G) B&B
Gasthaus – (G) guest house
Gletscher – (G/I) glacier
Grat – (G) ridge
grotto – (I) rustic Ticino-style restaurant

Hauptbahnhof – (G) central train station
haute route/Höhenweg – (F/G) literally 'high route', a high-level mountain route; also the classic Chamonix to Zermatt skiing and walking route through the Valais
Hütte – (G) hut, usually used in compounds, eg Zwinglihütte

Kathedrale – (G) cathedral
Kirche – (G) church
Kunstmuseum – (G) fine-arts museum

lac/lago/lai – (F/I/R) lake
lido – (I) beach
locanda – (I) inn serving food, small hotel

Markt – (G) market, covered market
menu – (F) meal at a fixed price with two or more courses

murata – (I) city walls

Oberland – (G) a term used to describe the regional 'uplands' of various cantons, eg Bernese Oberland
ostello della gioventù – (I) youth hostel
osteria – (I) cheap restaurant, snack bar

pizzo – (I) peak, summit
place/platz/piazza – (F/G/I) square
plat du jour – (F) dish of the day
pont – (F) bridge
postal bus – regional public bus network run by Swiss Post

Röstigraben – French-German linguistic divide

SAC – Swiss Alpine Club; Schweizer Alpen-Club
SAW – Swiss Hiking Federation; Schweizer Wanderwege
SBB/CFF/FSS – (G/F/I) Swiss Federal Railways
Scheidegg – (S) watershed
Schloss – (G) palace, castle
See – (G) lake
Stadt – (G) city or town

Tal – (G) valley; often in compound place names, eg Mattertal
tarn – tiny Alpine lake
trattoria – (I) traditional, inexpensive, often family-run restaurant

val – (I/R) valley
valle/vallée – (I/F) valley
vieille ville – (F) old town
ville – (F) city or town
Voralpen – (G) Pre-Alps

Wald – (G) forest
Weg – (G) way, path

behind the scenes

SEND US YOUR FEEDBACK

We love to hear from travellers – your comments keep us on our toes and help make our books better. Our well-travelled team reads every word on what you loved or loathed about this book. Although we cannot reply individually to postal submissions, we always guarantee that your feedback goes straight to the appropriate authors, in time for the next edition. Each person who sends us information is thanked in the next edition – and the most useful submissions are rewarded with a free book.

Visit **lonelyplanet.com/contact** to submit your updates and suggestions or to ask for help. Our award-winning website also features inspirational travel stories, news and discussions.

Note: We may edit, reproduce and incorporate your comments in Lonely Planet products such as guidebooks, websites and digital products, so let us know if you don't want your comments reproduced or your name acknowledged. For a copy of our privacy policy visit lonelyplanet.com/privacy.

OUR READERS

Many thanks to the travellers who used the last edition and wrote to us with helpful hints, useful advice and interesting anecdotes:

Nathan, Garry Aslanyan, Joerg Bachthaler, Guy Badman, Nadav Bergfreund, Michael Duxfield, Stefanei Graf, Paul Grant, Jim Harris, Sabrina Hartley, Avery Henderson, Eric Jolly, Anton Krivtsun, Maria Liechti, Mike Long, Eriane Mobaek, Sandra Mortal, Pallab Mukherjee, Philip Newton, Rudolf Niemoeller, Kathryn Pigdon, Michael Radtke, Silvie Schmutz, Sue Selkrig, Vic Sofras, Arthur Spencer, Sebastian Springer, Sabine Stern, Marisa Thoma, Rosemary Thomas, Dan Toller, Matthias Uhlmann, Janee Young

AUTHOR THANKS

Nicola Williams

As always, friends ensured I knew about the next best place to eat, sleep, drink, ski in *Suisse Romande*. *Un grand merci* in Geneva to Ciara Browne, Fon Mathuros Chantanayingyong, Georgie Pilcher, Lucy Jay Kennedy and Anna Sims; Nicolas Ortiz for sterling Verbier tips; Laurent Haug, Aude Gauthier, Thierry Weber and co-author Sally O'Brien for the Lausanne low-down; and Valaisian father–daughter duo extraordinaire Jean-Pierre de Kalbermatten and Sabine Van Vliet. My chunk is dedicated to Matthias and our own trilingual tribe, Niko, Mischa and Kaya.

Kerry Christiani

I'd like to thank all the super-efficient Swiss tourism professionals I met on the road, especially those in the Jungfrau Region, Chur, Interlaken, Schaffhausen and Lugano. *Merci vielmals* to Gian Simmen for his snowboarding insight and to Stephan Siegrist for his invaluable climbing tips. At Lonely Planet, thanks go to Joe Bindloss and my expert co-authors. Last but not least, special thanks to my husband and travel companion, Andy, for his support and skilful driving up those dizzying mountain passes.

Sally O'Brien

Without the support and encouragement of my husband, Denis Balibouse, who kept the home fires burning, and the babysitting skills par excellence of my parents-in-law, Ellen and Guy Balibouse, I would not have been able to do this wonderfully fun job – thanks for all your help and for giving Bas so many cuddles in my absence. Thanks also to my fellow authors, Nicola and Kerry, for such terrific blueprints to work from, and Joe Bindloss, Sasha Baskett and Amanda Sierp for in-house guidance.

Damien Simonis

Particular thanks go to Thierry Délèze in Zürich. An accomplished interloping Romand journalist, he is also an inveterate hedonist and mine of local information. A big thank you also goes to Ellinor von Kauffungen and Marcel Naegler for their help in Winterthur. Finally, a big fat spassibo for Sarah, who cheerfully pottered about with me on the Germanic side.

ACKNOWLEDGMENTS

Climate map data adapted from Peel MC, Finlayson BL & McMahon TA (2007) 'Updated World Map of the Köppen-Geiger Climate Classification', *Hydrology and Earth System Sciences*, 11, 163344.

Cover photograph: the Engadine, HP Huber/ 4 Corners. Many of the images in this guide are available for licensing from Lonely Planet Images: www.lonelyplanetimages.com.

THIS BOOK

This 7th edition of Lonely Planet's Switzerland guidebook was researched and written by Nicola Williams, Kerry Christiani, Sally O'Brien and Damien Simonis. Nicola, Damien and Kerry also wrote the previous edition. This guidebook was commissioned in Lonely Planet's London office, and produced by the following:

Commissioning Editor Joe Bindloss

Coordinating Editors Elin Berglund, Kate Taylor

Coordinating Cartographer Peter Shields

Coordinating Layout Designer Paul Queripel

Managing Editors Anna Metcalfe, Kirsten Rawlings

Managing Cartographers Corey Hutchison, Amanda Sierp

Managing Layout Designer Jane Hart

Assisting Editors Kathryn Glendenning, Michala Green, Emma Sanster, Ceinwen Sinclair, Helen Yeates

Assisting Cartographers Ildiko Bogdanovits, Valeska Cañas, Eve Kelly

Cover Research Kylie McLaughlin

Internal Image Research Rebecca Skinner

Colour Designer Tim Newton

Indexer Amanda Jones

Language Content Annelies Mertens, Branislava Vladisavljevic

Thanks to Bruce Evans, Ryan Evans, Yvonne Kirk, Susan Paterson, Trent Paton, Martine Power, Gerard Walker

index

000 Map pages
000 Photo pages

how to use this book

These symbols will help you find the listings you want:

◉	Sights	☞	Tours	♥	Drinking
🏖	Beaches	🎊	Festivals & Events	☆	Entertainment
🏃	Activities	🛏	Sleeping	🛍	Shopping
🍴	Courses	✕	Eating	❶	Information/Transport

These symbols give you the vital information for each listing:

♩	Telephone Numbers	📶	Wi-Fi Access	🚌	Bus
⊙	Opening Hours	≋	Swimming Pool	🚢	Ferry
Ⓟ	Parking	✔	Vegetarian Selection	Ⓜ	Metro
⊖	Nonsmoking	📋	English-Language Menu	Ⓢ	Subway
✳	Air-Conditioning	🧒	Family-Friendly	🚋	Tram
@	Internet Access	🐾	Pet-Friendly	🚆	Train

Reviews are organised by author preference.

Look out for these icons:

TOP CHOICE	Our author's recommendation
FREE	No payment required
🍃	A green or sustainable option

Our authors have nominated these places as demonstrating a strong commitment to sustainability – for example by supporting local communities and producers, operating in an environmentally friendly way, or supporting conservation projects.

Map Legend

Sights
- ◉ Beach
- ◬ Buddhist
- ◬ Castle
- ◉ Christian
- ◉ Hindu
- ◉ Islamic
- ◉ Jewish
- ◉ Monument
- ⊕ Museum/Gallery
- ◉ Ruin
- ◉ Winery/Vineyard
- ◉ Zoo
- ◉ Other Sight

Activities, Courses & Tours
- ◯ Diving/Snorkelling
- ◯ Canoeing/Kayaking
- ◯ Skiing
- ◯ Surfing
- ◯ Swimming/Pool
- ◯ Walking
- ◯ Windsurfing
- ◯ Other Activity/Course/Tour

Sleeping
- ⊜ Sleeping
- ⊜ Camping

Eating
- ✕ Eating

Drinking
- ◯ Drinking
- ⊖ Cafe

Entertainment
- ⊗ Entertainment

Shopping
- ⊕ Shopping

Information
- ⊕ Post Office
- ❶ Tourist Information

Transport
- ◯ Airport
- ⊗ Border Crossing
- ⊜ Bus
- +⊕+ Cable Car/Funicular
- -⊕- Cycling
- -⊖- Ferry
- Ⓜ Metro
- ⊗ Monorail
- Ⓟ Parking
- Ⓢ S-Bahn
- Ⓢ Taxi
- +⊕+ Train/Railway
- ⊗ Tram
- ⊙ Tube Station
- Ⓤ U-Bahn
- • Other Transport

Routes
- Tollway
- Freeway
- Primary
- Secondary
- Tertiary
- Lane
- Unsealed Road
- Plaza/Mall
- Steps
-)≡ ⊏ Tunnel
- Pedestrian Overpass
- Walking Tour
- Walking Tour Detour
- Path

Boundaries
- International
- State/Province
- Disputed
- Regional/Suburb
- Marine Park
- Cliff
- Wall

Population
- ◉ Capital (National)
- ◉ Capital (State/Province)
- ◉ City/Large Town
- ◦ Town/Village

Geographic
- ◉ Hut/Shelter
- ◔ Lighthouse
- ◉ Lookout
- ▲ Mountain/Volcano
- ◉ Oasis
- ◉ Park
-)(Pass
- ◉ Picnic Area
- ◉ Waterfall

Hydrography
- River/Creek
- Intermittent River
- Swamp/Mangrove
- Reef
- Canal
- Water
- Dry/Salt/Intermittent Lake
- Glacier

Areas
- Beach/Desert
- + + + Cemetery (Christian)
- × × × Cemetery (Other)
- Park/Forest
- Sportsground
- Sight (Building)
- Top Sight (Building)

OUR STORY

A beat-up old car, a few dollars in the pocket and a sense of adventure. In 1972 that's all Tony and Maureen Wheeler needed for the trip of a lifetime – across Europe and Asia overland to Australia. It took several months, and at the end – broke but inspired – they sat at their kitchen table writing and stapling together their first travel guide, *Across Asia on the Cheap*. Within a week they'd sold 1500 copies. Lonely Planet was born.

Today, Lonely Planet has offices in Melbourne, London and Oakland, with more than 600 staff and writers. We share Tony's belief that 'a great guidebook should do three things: inform, educate and amuse'.

OUR WRITERS

Nicola Williams

Coordinating Author, Geneva, Lake Geneva & Vaud, Valais **Ever since Nicola moved to a village on the southern side of Lake Geneva, she has never been able to shake off that uncanny feeling that she is on holiday – a garden tumbling down the hillside towards that same glittering lake and Switzerland's mysterious Jura mountains beyond is her wake-up call. Nicola has lived and worked in France since 1997 and when not flitting to Geneva, skiing or dipping into the Swiss countryside (or fondue), she can be found at her desk writing. She has worked on numerous titles for Lonely Planet. She blogs at tripalong.wordpress.com and tweets as @Tripalong.**

Read more about Nicola at:
lonelyplanet.com/members/nicolawilliams

Kerry Christiani

Bernese Oberland, Ticino, Northeastern Switzerland, Graubünden, Liechtenstein **Post-grad stints on a vegetable farm near Bern and snowbound winters in Arosa and Wengen sparked Kerry's passion for this boundlessly beautiful country. Since then, she has returned to Switzerland as often as possible to hike in the Alps, sail on Lake Constance and dig out the craziest Alpine events. Kerry's wanderlust has taken her to six continents, inspiring numerous articles and some 20 guidebooks, including Lonely Planet's guides to Germany, Austria, Sardinia and France.**

Read more about Kerry at:
lonelyplanet.com/members/kerrychristiani

Sally O'Brien

Fribourg, Neuchâtel & Jura, Mitteland, Central Switzerland **A Lonely Planet writer for over 10 years, Sally has called Vaud Canton home for the last five years. In the course of her research for this guidebook, she visited 11 of the confederation's 26 cantons and, most importantly, ate a whole lot of cheese.**

Damien Simonis

Basel & Aargau, Zürich **Having spent years shuttling back and forth between Switzerland and elsewhere – often to update this tome – fate finally took Damien to gentle Geneva, where he is now ensconced. That does not preclude the occasional foray across the Röstigraben, which is always a treat!**

Read more about Damien at:
lonelyplanet.com/members/damiensimonis

Published by Lonely Planet Publications Pty Ltd
ABN 36 005 607 983
7th edition – June 2012
ISBN 978 1 74179 584 4
© Lonely Planet 2012   Photographs © as indicated 2012
10 9 8 7 6 5 4 3 2 1
Printed in China

Although the authors and Lonely Planet have taken all reasonable care in preparing this book, we make no warranty about the accuracy or completeness of its content and, to the maximum extent permitted, disclaim all liability arising from its use.

All rights reserved. No part of this publication may be copied, stored in a retrieval system, or transmitted in any form by any means, electronic, mechanical, recording or otherwise, except brief extracts for the purpose of review, and no part of this publication may be sold or hired, without the written permission of the publisher. Lonely Planet and the Lonely Planet logo are trademarks of Lonely Planet and are registered in the US Patent and Trademark Office and in other countries. Lonely Planet does not allow its name or logo to be appropriated by commercial establishments, such as retailers, restaurants or hotels. Please let us know of any misuses: lonelyplanet.com/ip.